INSTRUCTIONAL MEDIA AND TECHNOLOGIES FOR LEARNING

INSTRUCTIONAL MEDIA AND TECHNOLOGIES FOR LEARNING

ROBERT HEINICH
Indiana University

MICHAEL MOLENDA
Indiana University

JAMES D. RUSSELL
Purdue University

SHARON E. SMALDINO
University of Northern Iowa

Merrill,
an imprint of Prentice Hall
Englewood Cliffs, New Jersey   Columbus, Ohio

Library of Congress Cataloging-in-Publication Data
Instructional media and technologies for learning / Robert
Heinich . . . [et al.].—5th ed.
     p. cm.
     Rev. ed. of : Instructional media and the new technologies
of instruction / Robert Heinich, Michael Molenda, James D. Russell, 4th ed. ©1993.
     Includes bibliographical references and index.
     ISBN 0-02-353070-7
     1. Educational technology. 2. Audio-visual education.   I.
Heinich, Robert. II. Heinich, Robert. Instructional media and the
new technologies of instruction.
  LB1028.3.H45   1996
  371.3'078—dc20   95-34252
                                    CIP

Editor: Debra A. Stollenwerk
Developmental Editor: Linda Ashe Montgomery
Production Editor: Mary Harlan
Photo Editor: Anne Vega
Design Coordinator: Jill E. Bonar
Text Designer: Frankenberry Design
Cover Designer: Brian Deep
Cover photo: © Dominique Sarraute/The Image Bank
Production Manager: Pamela D. Bennett
Electronic Text Management: Marilyn Wilson Phelps, Matthew
    Williams, Karen L. Bretz, Tracey Ward
Illustrations: Steve Botts, Tom Kennedy, Jane Lopez

This book was set in Galliard by Prentice Hall and was printed
and bound by Von Hoffmann Press, Inc. The cover was printed
by Von Hoffmann Press, Inc.

 © 1996 by Prentice-Hall, Inc.
A Simon & Schuster Company
Englewood Cliffs, New Jersey 07632

Earlier editions, entitled *Instructional Media and the New Technologies of Instruction,* © 1993, 1989, 1985 by Macmillan Publishing
Company; 1982 by John Wiley & Sons, Inc.

Credits for photographs and illustrations, unless given in text,
appear on page 418.

Printed in the United States of America

10 9 8 7 6 5 4 3 2 1

ISBN: 0-02-353070-7

Prentice-Hall International (UK) Limited, *London*
Prentice-Hall of Australia Pty. Limited, *Sydney*
Prentice-Hall of Canada, Inc., *Toronto*
Prentice-Hall Hispanoamericana, S. A., *Mexico*
Prentice-Hall of India Private Limited, *New Delhi*
Prentice-Hall of Japan, Inc., *Tokyo*
Simon & Schuster Asia Pte. Ltd., *Singapore*
Editora Prentice-Hall do Brasil, Ltda., *Rio de Janeiro*

This book is intended for educators at all levels who place a high value on successful learning. Its purpose is to help them incorporate media and technologies for learning into their repertoire—to use them as teaching tools and to guide students in using them as learning tools. We draw a majority of the examples from elementary and secondary education. We also draw some from postsecondary education and corporate training and development because we know that instructors in these different settings have found previous editions of this book useful in their work.

This new edition is necessitated by the amazing pace of innovation in all aspects of media, particularly in those related to computers. In the few years since the fourth edition, the digitization of information has accelerated rapidly and so has the school use of the newly created telecommunications resources, such as the Internet. To help keep pace with these changes we have added a new co-author, Sharon Smaldino of the University of Northern Iowa. Her experience in computer multimedia and distance learning enables us to provide an authoritative and up-to-date perspective on these rapidly emerging areas.

Rationales

All of us share a number of convictions that have motivated us since we first contemplated writing a textbook. First, we believe in an eclectic approach to the design of instruction. Advocates cite an abundance of theories and philosophies in support of different approaches to instruction—behaviorist, cognitivist, constructivist, and so on. We view these contending theoretical positions as differing *perspectives*—different vantage points—from which to examine the large and complex world of teaching and learning. We value each of them and feel that each is reflected in the advice we offer.

Second, we have a balanced posture regarding the role of technology in instruction. Because of this perspective we consider each technology in light of its advantages, limitations, and range of applications. None is "good" nor "bad" per se. So we strive to give a balanced treatment to the hard and soft technologies as well as to the simpler and more sophisticated media.

Third, we believe in the possibility of a rapprochement between the humanistic and technological traditions in education. We contend that technology and humanism are two separable dimensions. We demonstrate in Chapter 1 that it's easy to describe instructional arrangements that are high on both dimensions or low on both dimensions, as well as high on one and low on the other. We view them as complementary concepts.

Fourth, we believe that technology can best be integrated into instruction when viewed from the perspective of the teacher rather than that of the technologist. Therefore throughout the book we attempt to approach media and technology solutions in terms of the day-to-day challenges of teachers and to avoid technical jargon as much as possible. Our examples deal with real everyday teaching issues, in real content areas, involving real media and materials.

New to This Edition

This fifth edition is a major revision. Not only have we updated the technological information and methodological perspectives but we have made a number of other changes.

- *Revamped chapter organization.* We have combined the chapters on soft technologies and simulation/games into one chapter, Chapter 11, "Process Technologies." The "how-to" information on operating particular equipment has been distributed into the chapters, close to each media format; the generic information on equipment and setups now appears as Appendix A.
- *New photographs.* Nearly every photograph has been replaced to provide the most up-to-date view of current media and technologies.
- *Classroom examples.* We provide more examples of specific classroom applications of media and technologies across grade levels and subjects.
- *Media specialists' role.* We have made a special effort to draw the connections between the roles of teachers and school media specialist, portraying them as highly complementary and interdependent.

- *Two-column format.* The text is now presented in two-column format, allowing us to strengthen the connection between the printed word and the visual illustrations.
- *Full-color visuals.* In order to better portray the roles of color in effective instruction, Chapter 3, "Visual Principles," now features full-color photos and illustrations.
- *The Classroom Link.* A companion computer disk, *The Classroom Link*, has been added to assist users in creating, maintaining, and printing lesson plans and evaluations of materials based on the ASSURE model. The resulting database can be the basis for a teaching portfolio that can grow throughout your career. The guide for using *The Classroom Link* is located at the back of the text; it gives instructions for using this software with your computer.

Text Organization

Introductory Information.

The book begins with a **visual introduction**—a series of vignettes that depict the many applications of media and technology in enhancing learning. Chapter 1 discusses the purposes served by media and technology and provides theoretical grounding in communications and in the psychology of learning and instruction. Chapter 2 introduces the ASSURE model for instructional planning. Readers who are already familiar with lesson planning procedures will find the ASSURE model more congenial than the more technical models associated with full-fledged instructional design. This chapter also presents general procedures for appraising, selecting, and using media.

Chapter 3 examines principles and procedures of visual design, an important foundation for use of the visual media discussed in Chapters 4, 5, and 7. The handling of color is a critical element in visual design. To portray the principles of color properly, we have included full-color photos and illustrations in Chapter 3.

Core Chapters.

Chapters 4 through 10 treat one by one the common formats of media and technologies for learning. Chapters 4 and 5 deal with non-projected and projected media, the traditional audiovisual tools. Chapter 6 features audio media and the listening process. Motion media—video and film—are examined in Chapter 7. Chapters 8 and 9 focus on computer-based technologies, including computer-assisted instruction, integrated learning systems, computers as student tools, multimedia, and hypermedia. Distance learning is the focus of Chapter 10, with particular attention to broadcast radio and television, audio and video teleconferencing, computer conferencing, and the other convergences of computing and telecommunications.

While Chapters 4 through 10 focus primarily on the hard technologies, Chapter 11 highlights the soft technologies, including programmed instruction, programmed tutoring, learning centers, cooperative groups, games, and simulations. The emphasis throughout is on practical means for engaging students actively with the subject matter—as individuals and in small groups.

A Vision for the Future.

In Chapter 12 we look ahead to consider the possible impacts of current trends in technology and in education. We discuss the emerging influences of the information superhighway, artificial intelligence, restructuring of schools and school library media centers, the changing workplace, and other trends.

Appendixes.

Appendix A provides nuts-and-bolts advice on setting up and handling media hardware, including setups for audio, visual projection, video, and computers. The latter includes many practical suggestions for room arrangements for various types of computer use. Appendix B deals with guidelines regarding copyright regulations. Appendix C provides the key for exploring other sources of information beyond this book, giving names and addresses of scores of producers, vendors, and information centers. The book concludes with a Glossary of technical terms used in this book and in discussions of instructional media generally, an Index, and a step-by-step guide for using *The Classroom Link*, the companion computer disk.

Special Features

- **Advance organizers.** Each chapter begins with a brief verbal outline and a photo essay giving a visual overview of the content. To provide a more concrete notion of what knowledge and skills are featured in each chapter, we open each chapter with a set of knowledge objectives and another of application objectives. The latter set addresses the sorts of real-life skills typically cultivated in courses using this book as the textbook. Following the statement of objectives is the "Lexicon," a list of technical terms or terms used in a specialized sense in that chapter. All of these features are intended to give the reader a strong set of advance organizers, scaffolds for the main content of the chapter.
- **Appraisal Checklists.** We have revised and updated the checklists related to each of the media formats, intended to make it easy to preview materials systematically and to preserve the information for later reference. Users have permission to photocopy these for personal use. *The Classroom Link* computer software allows you to enter your appraisal judgments directly into a template for storage and future use.

- **AV Showmanship.** These features give specific tips on using media with flair and dramatic effect.
- **Blueprints.** These model lesson plans appear at the end of most chapters. They demonstrate how the ASSURE model can be used to integrate media into instructional plans, thus serving as a concrete link with daily professional practice.
- **Close-Ups.** These serve as miniature case studies of media applications in a variety of settings. Like the Blueprints, they show media and technology use *in context*.
- **Flashbacks.** These are brief historical vignettes that lend a sense of perspective to today's technologies.
- **How To . . .** The various media production and operation procedures are spelled out with illustrated step-by-step procedures. Troubleshooting suggestions are now included as part of these how-to discussions.
- **Media Files.** Actual materials in various media formats are highlighted as concrete examples of the types of commercially available materials. The materials referred to are meant to be *typical* of a given format, not necessarily as exemplary. No endorsement is implied.

For Instructors

Instructor's Guide.   Ask your Merrill/Prentice-Hall representative or write to the publisher directly for a copy of this comprehensive teaching guide, available to adopters without cost. The *Instructor's Guide* includes teaching tips and test items for each chapter, suggestions for different ways to organize an Instructional Media course, and overhead transparency masters on perforated pages.

Computer Test Item Bank.   Adopting instructors can obtain a set of computer disks, available in both IBM and Macintosh formats, containing a test item bank with instructions on how to create their own tests. Contact your Merrill/Prentice Hall representative.

Authors' Services.   The authors are eager to assist you in putting together an outstanding Instructional Media course. We offer the following services to instructors who have adopted this book:

- *Telelecture.* Call any of us in advance to arrange a guest lecture in your class via telephone. The only cost to you is for the toll charges. Some instructors use this telelecture as a demonstration of the techniques described in Chapter 10. Our phone numbers, fax numbers, and e-mail addresses are listed in the *Instructor's Guide*.
- *Newsletter.* We keep in touch with our adopters through an occasional newsletter. The newsletter keeps you informed about new developments, teaching tips and new teaching materials, and updates on our workshops and other services. You can receive it free of charge by sending your name to Mike Molenda.
- *Workshops.* We have conducted workshops annually since 1982 at the national convention of the Association for Educational Communications and Technology (AECT). This is a forum for exchange of ideas and networking among instructors of courses on Instructional Media.

If you are an instructor using this text, send your name and address to Michael Molenda, School of Education, Indiana University, Bloomington, IN 47405, U.S.A. We would like to add your name to our Newsletter mailing list, and we welcome any comments you have about the text.

ACKNOWLEDGMENTS

Through each of the editions of this book we have been fortunate to have had guidance from the real experts—the people who teach the courses for which this book is designed. In preparing for the fifth edition we surveyed a sample of adopters and other leaders in the field to elicit their advice about contents and emphases. After the first drafts were written we then asked other colleagues well respected in the field to critique them. We here thank all those who gave their time and talent to help make this the most useful textbook it could be.

- John C. Belland, The Ohio State University
- Andrew R. Biegel, D'Youville College
- Daniel J. Callison, Indiana University
- Carol Dwyer, Penn State University
- Leticia Ekhaml, West Georgia College
- Jack Garber, University of Wisconsin, Eau Claire
- Jerry Goldberg, The University of Detroit Mercy
- Franklin R. Koontz, The University of Toledo
- Alfred P. Large, Jr., Indiana University, South Bend
- Hilary McLellan, Kansas State University
- Gary R. Morrison, University of Memphis
- Nancy H. Vick, Longwood College
- Connie W. Zimmer, Arkansas Tech University

We especially thank those who contributed more directly by writing new material, drawing illustrations, taking photographs, and searching for references.

Elizabeth Boling of the School of Education, Indiana University, is responsible for both the outstanding new illustrations in Chapter 3 and the accompanying text related to visual design. We are in awe of her phenomenal artistic skilll and scholarly mastery of this area. Dennis Pett, from his professor emeritus setting in Vermont, carefully reviewed drafts of Chapter 3 and gave generous advice on photography, color, and visual design principles, as well as providing a number of exemplary photographs. Their contributions were so substantial they must be considered co-authors of Chapter 3.

Daniel Callison of the School of Library and Information Science, Indiana University, reviewed the whole book and made many helpful recommendations related to the connections between the teacher and the school library media center and media specialist. The extended Blueprint in Chapter 2, which we feel is a significant aid to using the ASSURE model, was developed by Mary Ann Ferkis while a student at Purdue University; it was done as a project in a course using this book. We were fortunate to have the relentless efforts of April Purcell to carry out bibliographic and reference searches in a most timely and thorough manner. Almost all the photographs in this edition have been taken new, expressly for this book. Anne Vega coordinated this huge undertaking and directed most of the photography sessions. As he did for previous editions, David Derkacy labored tirelessly and creatively to provide many additional fine photographs. We are confident that the art in this edition is the best of all the editions.

Special thanks go to Brian Trouba, Dale Hoskisson, Paul Veuthey, and Dean Hanson for developing the software and documentation for *The Classroom Link*.

This book also still contains the products of the work of many others who have contributed to past editions; we continue to be indebted to all of them.

The editorial, design, and production staffs of Merrill/Prentice Hall, particularly Debbie Stollenwerk, Linda Montgomery, and Mary Harlan, deserve special commendation. The authors have never had such intense and helpful support from any previous publication team.

We are grateful to our colleagues from our own universities—Indiana, Purdue, and Northern Iowa—for their many and valued forms of support over the years.

Finally, we thank our families for all they do to make this project possible.

Robert Heinich
Michael Molenda
James D. Russell
Sharon E. Smaldino

Robert Heinich

Michael Molenda

James D. Russell

Sharon E. Smaldino

Robert Heinich.   Dr. Heinich is Professor Emeritus in the department of Instructional Systems Technology (IST), Indiana University. He is now retired from active teaching, having served on the faculty since 1969 following completion of his doctorate at University of Southern California and a stint as multimedia editor for Doubleday Publishing. Prior to that he built a nationally prominent media program at Colorado Springs school district. Bob has been an active leader in the field of educational technology for four decades, serving as president of the Association for Educational Communications and Technology (AECT) in 1971–72 and as president of AECT's foundation from 1972 to 1982. He was editor of AECT's scholarly journal from 1969 to 1983. Indicative of his professional contributions, Dr. Heinich has received the Presidential Citation of the National Society for Performance and Instruction and the Distinguished Service Award of AECT. At Indiana University he served as chairman of the IST department from 1979 to 1984. His many articles and monographs provide some of the major theoretical underpinnings of the field.

Michael Molenda.   Dr. Molenda is Associate Professor in Instructional Systems Technology (IST) at Indiana University. He received his Ph.D. from Syracuse University and taught at University of North Carolina at Greensboro before joining Indiana University in 1972. He designs and teaches courses in Media Applica-

tions, Instructional Development, Evaluation and Change, and Instructional Technology Foundations. Mike served as chairman of the IST department from 1988 to 1991. He has lectured and consulted extensively on educational technology in Spain, the Netherlands, Indonesia, Korea, Swaziland, and several countries each in Latin America and the Middle East. Among his professional distinctions are selection as a Fulbright Lecturer in Peru in 1976, membership in the Board of Directors of AECT, 1988–91, and presidency of AECT's International Division, 1978–79. Dr. Molenda's stature in the field was recognized by his being asked to author the article on "Educational Technology in Elementary and Secondary Education" for the 1994 edition of the *International Encyclopedia of Education*. Mike also teamed with several other researchers in 1994 to prepare national accreditation standards for information technology in K–12 schools for the National Study of School Evaluation.

James D. Russell.   Dr. Russell is a Professor of Curriculum and Instruction at Purdue University. A former high school mathematics and physics teacher, Jim teaches courses on Media Utilization, Instructional Design, Instructional Delivery Systems, and Principles of Adult Education. He was honored as his department's Outstanding Teacher in 1993. Jim works part-time for Purdue's Center for Instructional Services, where he conducts workshops on teaching techniques and consults with faculty and graduate assistants on instructional improvement. His specialty areas, in which he has achieved national prominence through his writings and presentations, are presentation skills and using media and technology in classrooms. Because of his commitment to remaining close to the real world of teachers in the classroom, Dr. Russell serves as co-director of the Technology Improvement Project, the purpose of which is to improve students' achievement and attitudes in math and science. As part of this project he conducts day-long workshops throughout the year for middle and secondary school teachers. Through these workshops and this textbook, Jim continues to make a significant impact on classroom teaching practice.

Sharon E. Smaldino.   Joining this author team with this edition, Dr. Smaldino is Associate Professor of Educational Technology at the University of Northern Iowa. Sharon received her Ph.D. in 1987 from Southern Illinois University, Carbondale. Prior to that she received an M.A. in Elementary Education and

served for more than a dozen years as teacher, speech therapist, and special educator in school districts from Florida to Minnesota. At Northern Iowa she teaches an introductory educational media course for undergraduates and graduate majors and is coordinator of the Educational Technology program. Dr. Smaldino also teaches graduate courses in Instructional Development, Instructional Computing Design, Desktop Publishing, and Presentation Graphics. Presenting at state, national, and international conferences, Sharon has become an important voice on applications of technology in the classroom and in distance education. She works closely with the Iowa Distance Education Alliance, Iowa's Star Schools project, coordinating both the preservice teacher education activities and inservice teacher training. In addition to her teaching and consulting, Dr. Smaldino has served as president of the Division of Instructional Systems and Computers (DISC) of AECT and has written articles for state and national journals on her primary research interest, effective technology applications in education.

►BRIEF CONTENTS

MEDIA AND INSTRUCTION 5

SYSTEMATIC PLANNING FOR MEDIA USE 31

VISUAL PRINCIPLES 63

NONPROJECTED MEDIA 99

PROJECTED VISUALS 137

LOOKING AHEAD   341

EQUIPMENT AND SETUPS   363

COPYRIGHT GUIDELINES   385

INFORMATION SOURCES   391

GLOSSARY   405

CREDITS   418

INDEX   419

The Classroom Link documentation
follows the Index.

FLASHBACK

HOW TO . . .

MEDIA FILE

INSTRUCTIONAL MEDIA AND TECHNOLOGIES FOR LEARNING

With the coming of the twenty-first century, our era could be characterized as the age of media and technology. As conduits for information and entertainment, the mass media literally surround us day and night. Technology, especially in terms of digital electronics, permeates our work and play. Media and technology have transformed not only the worlds of work and leisure but the world of education as well. As you think about your future in the world of education, consider these vignettes as samples of the ways media and technology affect the processes of teaching and learning.

1 A pharmaceutical salesman plugs into his car stereo the new cassette from the company sales training center. It introduces him to the distinctive features of Banvex, a new drug for respiratory infections.

2 In a quiet corner just off the shop floor at Regent Industries, Jean is guided through a videocassette that shows the proper operation and safety features of the machine that she will be operating during her shift today. Jean "floats" among jobs as needed from day to day.

3 Second graders Allison and Tiffany use flash cards to practice their multiplication skills. The cards have a problem on one side and an answer on the other; the "repeat" stack grows smaller as Tiffany masters each fact.

4

Anne, a graduate student in veterinary medicine, uses an interactive video system in the university's learning center to practice responding to animal owners in stressful situations. The scenarios present situations Anne is likely to face in actual veterinary practice.

Samaritan Club members of junior high school age are studying the meanings of the parables. They compete as teams during the after-school program at their local church. Matching the facts of the stories with the accepted interpretation is the purpose of the game.

5 ▼

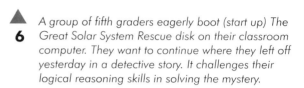

▲
6 *A group of fifth graders eagerly boot (start up) The Great Solar System Rescue disk on their classroom computer. They want to continue where they left off yesterday in a detective story. It challenges their logical reasoning skills in solving the mystery.*

◄ **7**

As she unobtrusively videotapes housing conditions in the inner city, Stephanie, a high school senior, reflects on what brought her here. She had volunteered to do a video report on urban problems for her social studies class.

▲
8 *To learn how to take their blood pressure at home, Thelma and Harold listen to the nurse at the hospital as she guides the retired couple through a structured tutoring package. The nurse patiently answers any questions they have.*

9 ▼ *Dinner over, the Lees settle into the family room to watch "This Old House." They are intrigued with the notion of buying and restoring an older house, and this television series provides them with valuable tips.*

I n school and after school, at home and at work, children and adults are enjoying the benefits of learning through media and the new technologies for learning.

The goal of this book is to help put you into this picture.

MEDIA AND INSTRUCTION

Instructional media and the technologies for learning provide you with the tools to engage students powerfully in the learning process. The array of media formats and of quality materials available to the teacher is increasing dramatically. As a teacher, you must be prepared to choose the best tools for your students, who are in diverse situations and pursuing different sorts of learning goals.

You can make more effective use of media if you understand some underlying concepts about the learning process and instruction. There are a number of different perspectives on how people learn; each offers unique insights and practical tools. Audiovisual media continue to play a wide range of roles in the world of corporations and other organizations.

You will be able to make informed decisions about media and technology if you understand and apply the guidelines provided in this book.

KNOWLEDGE OBJECTIVES

1. Distinguish between instruction and learning.
2. Select and describe instructional situations that lend themselves to different principles of learning.
3. Describe technologies for learning and cite an example.
4. Evaluate a recent learning experience in terms of the Schramm communication model.
5. Explain the concrete–abstract continuum, indicating how it can be used to aid in the selection of media.
6. Relate Dale's Cone of Experience to the concrete–abstract continuum.
7. Define the term *medium;* name five basic categories of media.
8. Distinguish among message, method, and medium.
9. Discuss four roles of media in the instructional process, giving an example of media used in each role.
10. Discuss how humanistic and technological concerns can be balanced in instruction.
11. Discuss how research has affected the integration of media in instruction.

APPLICATION OBJECTIVES

1. Prepare a report on a topic in the chapter, using references beyond this chapter. The report may be either written or recorded on audiotape.
2. Prepare a 10-minute presentation on your reaction to a topic in the chapter.
3. Analyze an instructional situation (either real or hypothetical) and identify the elements of the communication process and their interrelationship.
4. Prepare a short paper on one of the learning theories described in this chapter. Use additional references.
5. Prepare a position paper on either (1) the role of humanistic versus technological issues in education or (2) the role of structure versus flexibility in teaching.
6. Describe an actual use of instructional media in a school setting based on your experiences or readings.

LEXICON

instruction
learning
medium/media
cooperative learning
communication

iconic representation
symbolic representation
behaviorism
cognitivism

schema/schemata
assimilation
accommodation
constructivism

technology
technology for learning
advance organizer

Throughout history, media and technologies for learning have influenced education. Most recently, for example, the computer has invaded instructional settings. Such tools offer powerful possibilities for improving the learning process. The teacher, however, will make the difference in the integration of media into this process.

The roles of the instructor and the learner are clearly changing because of the influence of media and technology in the classroom. No longer are the teacher and the textbook the sources of all knowledge. The teacher becomes the director of the knowledge-access process. Along the continuum of instructional strategies, sometimes the teacher will elect to provide direct instructional experiences for the students. At other times, with a few keystrokes students can explore the world, gaining access to libraries, other teachers and students, and a host of resources to obtain the knowledge they seek.

It is essential that, as the guide for learning, the teacher examine media and technology in the context of the instruction and its potential impact on the outcome for students. The essence of this chapter concerns the nature of the learning process, the way the role and responsibility of the teacher change with the approach to instruction used, and the importance of media and technology within that process.

INSTRUCTION AND LEARNING

Instruction is the arrangement of information and environment to facilitate learning. By *environment* we mean not only where instruction takes place but also the methods, media, and equipment needed to convey information and guide the learner's study. As implied in the vignettes on pages 2 and 3 and as detailed later in this chapter, information and environment can change depending on the instructional goal. For example, in vignette 7, Stephanie must have a camera and seek out a location that will fulfill the requirements of the assignment. She will provide the content for her project. In vignette 4, Anne goes to a learning center, where she will find the equipment and the media necessary to complete her assignment. The information has been carefully prepared for her.

The arrangement of information and the environment is normally the responsibility of the instructor and the designers of media. The choice of the strategy of instruction determines the environment (the methods, media, equipment, and facilities) and the way information is assembled and used. As we discuss later, the instructional approach can range from teacher control to learner control. But we must remember that even with methods and media that encourage students to take control of learning, some guidance is inevitably built in.

The role of the teacher is paramount in the instructional planning process. Working with other teachers and media specialists, teachers can integrate media into their instruction to greatly magnify its impact on students.

Learning is the development of new knowledge, skills, or attitudes as an individual interacts with information and the environment. Learning takes place all the time. We learn things just walking down the street, watching TV, conversing with other people, or just observing what goes on around us. This type of incidental learning is not our major interest as education professionals. Rather, we are concerned primarily with the learning that takes place in response to our instructional efforts. How we design and arrange instruction has a great deal to do not only with what is learned but also with how the learner uses what is learned.

Thus the instruction/learning process involves the selection, arrangement, and delivery of information in an appropriate environment and the way the learner interacts with that information. In this chapter we first consider the media, messages, and methods used in instruction. Then we examine the communication process. Finally we consider the learning theories on which the design of instruction is based.

MEDIA, MESSAGES, AND METHODS

A **medium** (plural, **media**) is a channel of communication. Derived from the Latin word meaning "between," the term refers to anything that carries information between a source and a receiver. Examples include film, television, diagrams, printed materials, computers, and instructors. These are considered instructional media when they carry messages with an instructional purpose. The purpose of media is to facilitate communication.

Instructional Media

The diversity of media used for instruction is illustrated by the contents of this book:

- Nonprojected media such as photographs, diagrams, displays, and models (Chapter 4)
- Projected media such as slides, filmstrips, overhead transparencies, and computer projection (Chapter 5)
- Audio media such as cassettes and compact discs (Chapter 6)
- Motion media such as video and film (Chapter 7)
- Computer-mediated instruction (Chapter 8)
- Computer-based multimedia and hypermedia (Chapter 9)
- Media such as radio and television used for distance learning (Chapter 10)

FIGURE 1.1
Listeners with different cultural backgrounds may derive different meanings from the same message.

Messages ~~Content / curriculum~~

In any instructional situation there is a message to be communicated. It may be subject-specific material, directions to the learners about how to best proceed with their study, questions about the content studied, feedback to help the learners, or other information. In the relationship between the message and the medium, the medium carries the message. It is essential that the teacher carefully select the medium to ensure that the message is received by the learner clearly and accurately (see Figure 1.2).

Methods ~~What is~~ ?

Traditionally, instructional methods have been described as "presentation forms" such as lectures and discussions. In this text, we will differentiate between instructional methods and instructional media. Methods are the procedures of instruction that are selected to help learners

FIGURE 1.2
In the relationship between message and medium, the medium carries the message.

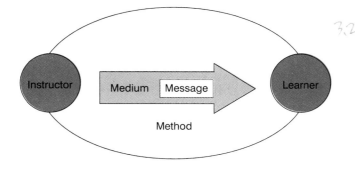

achieve the objectives or to internalize the content or message. Media then, as already defined, are carriers of information between a source and a receiver.

Ten categories of instructional methods are described in the following sections. Each represents a family of methods within which there may be many different specific techniques and procedures. For example, the cooperative learning method includes project groups, self-directed learning teams, Team Assisted Individualization, and many other variations. The general categories of methods are presentation, demonstration, discussion, drill-and-practice, tutorial, cooperative learning, gaming, simulation, discovery, and problem solving. Virtually any of the media described throughout this book can be used to implement virtually any of these methods.

Presentation. In the presentation method, a source tells, dramatizes, or otherwise disseminates information to learners. It is a one-way communication controlled by the source, with no immediate response from or interaction with the learners. The source may be a textbook, an audiotape, a videotape, a film, an instructor, and so forth. Reading a book, listening to an audiotape, viewing a videotape, and attending a lecture are examples of the presentation method.

Demonstration. In this method of instruction, the learner views a real or lifelike example of the skill or procedure to be learned (see Figure 1.3). Demonstrations may be recorded and played back by means of media such as video or film. If two-way interaction or learner practice with feedback is desired, a live instructor or a tutor is needed.

The objective may be for the learner to imitate a physical performance (such as swinging a golf club or

FIGURE 1.3
Demonstrations show a process to be learned or the way something works.

changing the oil in a car) or to adopt the attitudes or values exemplified by someone who serves as a role model. In some cases the point is simply to illustrate how something works, such as the effect of heat on a bimetallic strip. On-the-job training often takes the form of one-on-one demonstration, with the experienced worker showing a new employee how to perform a procedure, such as operating a packaging machine. This arrangement allows questions to be asked and answered so that errors and misperceptions can be resolved.

Discussion. As a method, discussion involves the exchange of ideas and feelings among students or among students and teacher. It can be used at any stage of the instruction/learning process, whether in tutorials, small groups, or large groups. It is a useful way of assessing the knowledge, skills, and attitudes of a group of students before finalizing instructional objectives, particularly if it is a group the instructor has never taught before. In this context, discussion can help the instructor establish the kind of rapport with and within the group that fosters collaborative and cooperative learning.

Discussion can be used to prepare learners for a presentation by arousing their curiosity or directing their attention to key points. Some media forms are more conducive to discussion during their use than others. For example, the overhead transparency lends itself to discussion techniques more easily than does video.

Postpresentation discussions are essential as a forum for questions and answers and for ensuring that all students understand what the instructor intended. They are also critical in helping each learner to internalize the message—to incorporate it into his or her mental framework. Discussion and projects are techniques for evaluating the effectiveness of instruction. Although such techniques are useful with all age groups, adult learners in particular welcome the opportunity to participate in sharing experiences with other adults.

Drill-and-Practice. In drill-and-practice the learner is led through a series of practice exercises designed to increase fluency in a new skill or to refresh an existing one. Use of the method assumes that the learner previously has received some instruction on the concept, principle, or procedure that is to be practiced. To be effective, the drill-and-practice exercises should include feedback to correct and remediate errors that the learner might make along the way.

Drill-and-practice is used commonly for such tasks as studying math facts, learning a foreign language, and building a vocabulary. Certain media formats and delivery systems—such as learning-laboratory instruction and programmed instruction—lend themselves particularly well to student drill-and-practice exercises. Also, cassettes can be used effectively for drill-and-practice in spelling, arithmetic, and language instruction.

Tutorial. A tutor—in the form of a person, computer, or special printed materials—presents the content, poses a question or problem, requests a learner response, analyzes the response, supplies appropriate feedback, and provides practice until the learner demonstrates a predetermined level of competency (see Figure 1.4). Tutoring is most often done on a one-on-one basis and is frequently used to teach basic skills, such as reading and arithmetic.

Tutorial arrangements include instructor-to-learner (e.g., Socratic dialog), learner-to-learner, (e.g., tutoring or programmed tutoring), computer-to-learner (e.g., computer-assisted tutorial software), and print-to-learner (e.g., branching programmed instruction). These formats are discussed further in Chapters 8, 9, and 11. The computer is especially well suited to play the role of tutor because of its ability to deliver speedily a complex menu of responses to different learner inputs.

FIGURE 1.4

Tutorials are one of the most effective instructional methods, and one of the most expensive if the tutor's time is included as a cost.

3.6
Cooperative Learning Groups.

A growing body of research supports the claim that students learn from each other when they work on projects as a team.[1] Two or three students at a computer terminal learn more as they carry on discussions while working through the assigned problem. Some computer programs, such as *SimEarth: The Living Planet,* make it possible for several students to work interactively at separate computers.

Many educators have criticized the competitive atmosphere that dominates many classrooms in public schools and higher education. They believe that pitting student against student in the attainment of grades is contrary to the societal requirements of cooperation in life and in most on-the-job situations. Teacher and students often find themselves in an adversarial relationship in the cat-and-mouse game of test taking and grading. Competition in the classroom also interferes with students learning from each other.

Critics of competitive learning urge instead an emphasis on **cooperative learning** as an instructional method. They argue that learners need to develop skills in working and learning together because their eventual workplaces will require teamwork. A common complaint of graduates is that they did not experience working in teams while in school.

Students can learn cooperatively not only by discussing texts and viewing media but also by producing media. For example, the design and production of a video or a slide set as a curriculum project presents an opportunity for cooperative learning. The teacher should be a working partner with the students in such learning situations.

Some authorities make a distinction between cooperative learning and collaborative learning. They use the term *collaborative learning* when the teacher is working with students as a partner in learning; they use the term *cooperative learning* when only students are working together.

3.7
Gaming.

Gaming provides a playful environment in which the learners follow prescribed rules as they strive to attain a challenging goal. It is a highly motivating technique, especially for tedious and repetitive content. The game may involve one learner (e.g., solitaire) or a group of learners (see Figure 1.5). Games often require learners to use problem-solving skills or to demonstrate mastery of specific content demanding a high degree of accuracy and efficiency (see Chapter 11).

One common type of instructional game is related to learning about business. Participants form management teams to make decisions regarding a mythical corporation. The team with the highest corporate profits is the winner.

3.8   *Conversation*
Simulation.

Simulation involves the learner confronting a scaled-down version of a real-life situation. It allows realistic practice without the expense or risks otherwise involved. The simulation may involve participant dialog, manipulation of materials and equipment, or interaction with a computer (see Chapter 11).

Interpersonal skills and laboratory experiments in the physical sciences are popular subjects for simulations. In some simulations the learner manipulates mathematical models to determine the effect of changing certain variables, such as controlling a nuclear power plant. Role playing is another common example of the simulation method.

3.9
Discovery.

The discovery method uses an inductive, or inquiry, approach to learning; it presents problems to be solved through trial and error (see Figure 1.6). The aim of the discovery method is to foster a deeper understanding of the content through involvement with it. The rules or procedures that the learner discovers may be derived from previous experience, based on information in reference books, or stored in a computer database.

Instructional media can help promote discovery or inquiry. For example, videotapes or videodiscs may be used for discovery teaching in the physical sciences. Students view a video to observe the relationships represented in the visuals and then attempt to discover the principles that explain those relationships. For example, by viewing something as simple as a balloon being weighed before and after being filled with air, the student discovers that air has weight.

[1]Robert E. Slavin, "Research on Cooperative Learning: Consensus and Controversy," *Educational Leadership* (December 1989–January 1990), pp. 52–54.

FIGURE 1.5
Games can be a way for students to be active learners.

Discovery learning can also assume the form of helping students to seek the information they wish to know about a topic of specific interest to them. Student inquiry, or information research, is a time-consuming but effective method for students to explore knowledge beyond the limits of their textbooks. Such information searches generally lead to the discovery of information that is new to both the student and the teacher. The library media specialist is an essential ally in guiding students and teachers through the information inquiry process, providing assistance on search procedures and guidance in interpreting the information. The library media center provides both content-related materials and media production facilities for students who wish to produce an alternative presentation of what has been learned.

3.10   application

Problem Solving.   With problem solving, the learner uses previously mastered skills to reach a resolution of a challenging problem. The learner must define the problem more clearly (perhaps state a hypothesis), examine data (possibly with the aid of a computer), and generate a solution. Through this process the learner can be expected to arrive at a higher level of understanding of the phenomenon under study.

One commonly used type of problem solving is the case study. For example, students in a business class are given information about a situation at a small manufacturing firm and are asked to design a solution to the problem of low production.

Once they have decided how to address the problem, students, working collaboratively, can access an array of

FIGURE 1.6
The discovery method involves students in hands-on learning.

information to collect data from resources available in the school media center.

In any instructional situation, a variety of methods can and should be used to achieve different specific purposes: gaining attention, motivating, presenting new information, engaging in practice, testing, and so on. Some methods are also more appealing than others to students with different learning styles: hands-on problem solving for "concrete" thinkers, thought-provoking presentations for "abstract" thinkers, and so on. (Learning styles are discussed in Chapter 2.)

INSTRUCTIONAL COMMUNICATION

Instruction is the arrangement of information and environment to facilitate learning. The transmission of information from a source to a destination is called **communication**. Because new learning usually depends on taking in new information, effective instruction cannot take place unless communication takes place. It is therefore helpful to know something about the communication process so that instructional media can be used effectively.

Communication Model

Many different visual and mathematical models have been developed to explain the process of communication. A simplified model useful for identifying and analyzing the critical stages of instructional communication works like this. A message, such as a description of the structure of the human heart, is selected by the information source, usually the teacher. That message is incorporated by the transmitter into a signal (e.g., spoken words, a drawing on the chalkboard, or printed materials).

The signal is then received by the learners, evoking in each of their minds their own interpretations of the message (See Figure 1.7.) The model also applies in situations where the students select the content. For example, when students go to a media center to select material to study, the messages are there, to be received and interpreted.

Various distorting factors referred to in this classic model as "noise" act on the signal as it is being transmitted. Examples of noise in the classroom setting include background sounds, glare on the chalkboard, and flickering lights.

It is important to keep in mind that meaning per se cannot be transmitted. What is actually transmitted are the symbols of meaning, such as words or pictures. For example, as authors of this book we cannot directly transfer to you the personal meanings we have built in our own minds about instructional media. We can only transmit verbal and pictorial symbols from which you construct your own meanings.

The most we can hope for is that our skills and knowledge will enable us to encode our messages in such a manner that your skills and knowledge can be used to decode and interpret them as closely as possible to the way we intended.

Field of Experience

One major purpose of instructional communication is to broaden and extend the field of experience of the learner. For instructional purposes, however, the meaning of the message and how the message is interpreted are of paramount importance. Wilbur Schramm, one of the most respected contemporary communication researchers, adapted an earlier model developed by Claude Shannon, incorporating Shannon's concern with the technical aspects of communication.[2] Schramm's central concern was with communication, reception, and interpretation of meaningful symbols—processes that are at the heart of instruction. (See Figure 1.7.)

As a classroom teacher, for example, you would prepare your students for an instructional video (e.g., through a preliminary discussion of the topic or an overview of its content) and design follow-up activities to reinforce and extend what has been learned from the video.

Ideally, material presented to or selected by a student should be sufficiently within his or her field of experience so that he or she can learn what needs to be learned but enough outside the field of experience to challenge and extend that field. The boundary of the

---

[2]Wilbur Schramm, "Procedures and Effects of Mass Communication," in *Mass Media and Education*, ed. Nelson B. Henry (Chicago: University of Chicago Press, 1954), p. 116.

FIGURE 1.7

Schramm's model emphasizes that communication occurs only when the sender's and the receiver's fields of experience overlap.

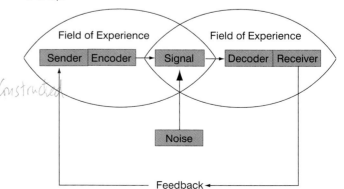

field of experience that is to be expanded by instruction is referred to by Vygotsky as the "zone of proximal development."[3] In this zone, messages go beyond communication into learning.

How far the instruction can extend beyond the student's field of experience before confusion sets in depends on many factors, such as the experience or ability of the student. Experienced students can assume more of the responsibility for extending their own fields of experience than others. To be successful, some students will need instructional content closer to their field of experience. With some learners, instruction may need to be almost entirely within their relatively limited field of experience. (In Chapter 2 we will discuss how to determine "specific entry competencies," with particular attention to identifying the student's field of experience as he or she enters a lesson.)

At times, the learning task may not be within the instructor's areas of expertise. In such a circumstance, the instructor and the student need to work together to broaden their respective fields of experience. Neither should feel uncomfortable about being in this position. With the advent of the information age it becomes nearly impossible for any one individual to maintain a broad range of knowledge. Some of the most effective learning experiences occur when the instructor and student work collaboratively to seek resources and information. The school media center can be the environment in which the teacher and student seek the answers to questions together. This facility can be a stimulating learning environment, where the search for information can serve as a basis for the school curriculum as well as that of the individual.

[3]L. S. Vygotsky, *Mind and Society* (Cambridge, MA: Harvard University Press, 1978).

Feedback

A critical feature of the communication process, especially instructional communication, is feedback—the receiver's response to the message sent. We usually think of feedback in connection with tests, but many other available techniques indicate to the teacher how students are receiving instruction. "Kidwatching" (noticing such things as facial expressions, body language, and discussion responses), student conferences, homework, and responses on daily quizzes are all forms of feedback (see Figure 1.8). Not only does feedback help us ascertain whether instruction has been successful, it also tends to take the burden off the student and place it where it more appropriately belongs—on the sender of the message (the instructor). Instructors are frequently tempted to blame the student when instruction is not successful. The real problem may be that the instruction has not been designed or delivered appropriately.

Thus, you can use the communication model described here to analyze communication problems in an instructional setting. For example, if "noise" unduly interferes with your signal, you can repeat instruction under more favorable conditions. If you made an error in appraising your students' field of experience, you may need to identify a more appropriate entry level for your particular group. If the message was not encoded properly, you may need to identify more suitable materials, or you can adjust how you use the materials to produce more effective instruction.

The Concrete–Abstract Continuum

Psychologist Jerome Bruner, in developing his theory of instruction, proposed that instruction should proceed

FIGURE 1.8
Feedback from the learners informs the instructor how they respond to the message.

FIGURE 1.9
How the instructor integrates the technology into the lesson is the most important factor in successful learning.

from direct experience (enactive) to **iconic representation** of experience (such as the use of pictures and films) to **symbolic representation** (such as the use of words). He further stated that the sequence in which a learner encounters materials has a direct effect on achieving mastery of the task.[4] Bruner pointed out that this applies to all learners, not just children. When a learning task is presented to adults who have no relevant experiences on which to draw, learning is facilitated when instruction follows a sequence from actual experience to iconic representation to symbolic or abstract representation.

As we will discuss later, an important first step in instruction is to determine the learner's current field of experience. Instructional media that incorporate concrete experiences help students integrate prior experiences and thus facilitate learning of abstract concepts. For example, many students have watched various aspects of the construction of a highway or street. They have seen the machine that lays the asphalt down, they have seen graders at work, and they have seen a number of other stages of road building. However, they need to have all these experiences integrated into a generalized notion of what it means to build a highway. Showing a video that represents all these processes in relation to each other is an ideal way to integrate their various experiences into a meaningful abstraction.

Decisions regarding trade-offs between the concreteness of a learning experience and time constraints have to be made continually by the instructor. In general, as you move up Dale's "Cone of Experience" (see "Flashback," p. 16) toward the more abstract media, more information can be compressed into a shorter period of time. It takes more time for students to engage in a direct purposeful experience, a contrived experience, or a dramatized experience than it does to present the same information in a videotape, a recording, a series of visual symbols, or a series of verbal symbols.

For example, a field trip can provide a learning experience relatively high in concreteness, but it also takes up a good deal of instructional time, and limited resources in a school district often make it difficult to arrange. A video depicting the same experiences as the field trip could be presented to the students in a much shorter period of time and with much less effort and money. Knowledge of local resources will allow the media specialist to help the teacher select the best approach to the experience, either by identifying a local contact or assisting with selecting an alternative medium.

The instructor must also decide whether the learning experience is appropriate to the field of experience of the students. The greatest amount of information can be presented in the least amount of time through printed or spoken words (the top of the concrete–abstract continuum and cone). But if the student does not have the requisite background experience and knowledge to handle these verbal symbols, the time saved in presentation will be time lost in learning. The instructor can find out if the instructional method matches the learner's background only by analyzing learner response. If students achieve what was expected of them, the instructional experiences were appropriate.

As Dale has pointed out, a model such as his Cone of Experience, although a simplification of complex relationships, is a practical guide to analyzing the characteristics of instructional media and methods and the way these media may be useful.

PSYCHOLOGICAL BASES OF LEARNING

How instructors view the role of media and technology in the classroom depends very much on their beliefs about how people learn. Over the past half century there have been several dominant theories of learning. Each has implications for instruction in general and for the use of technology specifically. We will briefly survey each of the

[4]Jerome S. Bruner, *Toward a Theory of Instruction* (Cambridge, MA: Harvard University Press, 1966), p. 49.

Dale's Cone of Experience

In one of the first textbooks written about the use of audiovisual materials in schools, Hoban, Hoban, and Zissman stated that the value of such materials is a function of their degree of realism. In developing this concept, the authors arranged various teaching methods in a hierarchy of greater and greater abstraction, beginning with what they referred to as "the total situation" and culminating with "words" at the top of the hierarchy.[a]

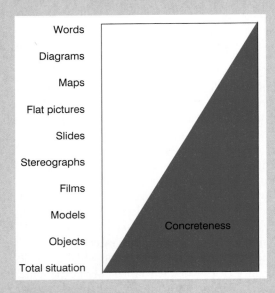

In 1946, Edgar Dale took the same construct and developed the "Cone of Experience."[b] In the Cone of Experience, we start with the learner as participant in the actual experience, then move to the learner as observer of the actual event,

[a]Charles F. Hoban, Sr., Charles F. Hoban, Jr., and Samuel B. Zissman, *Visualizing the Curriculum* (New York: Dryden, 1937), p. 39.

[b]Edgar Dale, *Audio-Visual Methods in Teaching*, 3rd ed. (New York: Holt, Rinehart and Winston, 1969), p. 108. Copyright 1946, 1954, 1969 by Holt, Rinehart and Winston. Reprinted by permission of Holt, Rinehart and Winston, CBS College Publishing.

DALE'S CONE OF EXPERIENCE

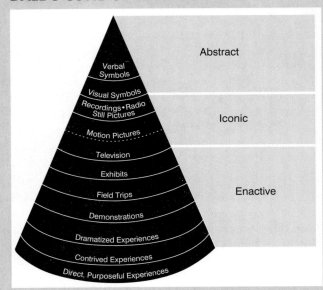

From Audio-Visual Methods in Teaching, Third Edition, by Edgar Dale, Copyright 1969 by Holt, Rinehart and Winston, Inc., reprinted by permission of the publisher.

to the learner as observer of a mediated event (an event presented through some medium), and finally to the learner observing symbols that represent an event. Dale contended that learners could make profitable use of more abstract instructional activities to the extent that they had built up a stock of more concrete experiences to give meaning to the more abstract representations of reality.

Psychologist Jerome Bruner, working from a different perspective, devised a descriptive scheme for labeling instructional activities that parallels Dale's. As shown here, Bruner's concepts of enactive, iconic, and abstract learning can be superimposed on Dale's Cone of Experience. Bruner, though, emphasized the nature of the mental operations of the learner rather than the nature of the stimuli presented to the learner.[c]

[c]Jerome S. Bruner, *Toward a Theory of Instruction* (Cambridge, MA: Harvard University Press, 1966), p. 49.

major perspectives on learning and discuss their implications. Learning theories and how they impact teaching decisions are discussed in greater detail by Driscoll.[5]

Behaviorist Perspective

In the mid-1950s, the focus of learning research started to shift from stimulus design (communication) to learner response to stimuli. At the forefront of this

[5]Marcy P. Driscoll, *Psychology of Learning for Instruction* (Needham Heights, MA: Allyn & Bacon, 1994).

movement was B. F. Skinner, a psychologist at Harvard University. Skinner was a proponent of **behaviorism** but with an important difference: he was interested in voluntary behavior, such as learning new skills, rather than reflexive behavior, as illustrated by Pavlov's famous salivating dog. He demonstrated that the behavior of an organism could be shaped by reinforcing, or rewarding, the desired responses to the environment. Skinner based his learning theory, known as reinforcement theory, on a series of experiments with pigeons, and he reasoned that the same procedures could be used with humans. The result was the emergence of programmed instruction, a technique of leading a learner through a series of instructional steps to a desired level of performance. Unlike earlier learning research, Skinner's work led directly to improved instructional design.

Cognitivist Perspective

Behaviorists refuse to speculate on what goes on internally when learning takes place. They rely solely on observable behaviors. As a result, they are more comfortable explaining relatively simple learning tasks. Because of this posture, behaviorism has limited application in designing instruction for higher-level skills. For example, behaviorists are reluctant to make inferences about how learners process information, even when doing so can be helpful in designing instruction that develops problem-solving ability.

Cognitivists, on the other hand, are making a primary contribution to learning theory and instructional design by creating models of how information is received, processed, and manipulated by learners. **Cognitivism** leads to a different way of looking at familiar learning patterns. For example, behaviorists simply state that practice strengthens the response to a stimulus. Cognitivists create a mental model of short-term and long-term memory. New information is stored in short-term memory, where it is "rehearsed" until ready to be stored in long-term memory. If the information is not rehearsed, it fades from short-term memory. Learners then combine the information and skills in long-term memory to develop cognitive strategies, or skills for dealing with complex tasks. Cognitivists have a broader perception of independent learning than that held by behaviorists: students are less dependent on the guiding hand of the program designer and rely more on their own cognitive strategies in using available learning resources.

A close look at the work of Swiss psychologist Jean Piaget illustrates how a cognitive psychologist views the mental processes individuals use in responding to their environment. The three key concepts of mental development in Piaget's work are schemata, assimilation, and accommodation.[6]

Schemata. **Schemata** (singular, **schema**) are the mental structures by which individuals organize their perceived environment. Schemata are adapted or changed during mental development and learning. They are used to identify, process, and store incoming information and can be thought of as categories individuals use to classify specific information and experiences.

Very young children learn to distinguish between mother and father. They soon separate dogs from cats and later become aware of different varieties of dogs. These differentiations based on experience lead to the development of schemata, or the ability to classify objects by their significant characteristics.

These cognitive structures change by the processes of assimilation and accommodation, which should be encouraged during instruction.

Assimilation. **Assimilation** is the cognitive process by which a learner integrates new information and experiences into existing schemata. Piaget borrowed the term from biology, where it refers to the process by which an organism eats food, digests it, and then assimilates or changes it into a usable form.

During learning, assimilation results from experiences. With new experiences, the schema expands in size but does not change its basic structure. Using the process of assimilation, the individual attempts to place new concepts into existing schemata.

These learning experiences can be real-life experiences. But rather than waiting for experiences to happen naturally, instructors cause experiences to happen through use of media and methods.

Accommodation. Because schemata change with experience, adult learners have a broader and more elaborate range of schemata than do children. The process of modifying existing schemata or creating new ones is called **accommodation.**

When dealing with a new concept or experience, the learner attempts to assimilate it into existing schemata. When it does not fit, there are two possible responses: (1) the learner can create a new schema into which the new stimulus is placed, or (2) the existing schema can be modified so that the new stimulus will fit. Both of these processes are forms of accommodation.

Schemata evolve over time in response to many learning experiences. As instructors, we are responsible for providing learning experiences that will result in the creation of new schemata as well as the modification of existing schemata.

Constructivist Perspective

Constructivism is a movement that extends beyond the beliefs of the cognitivist. It considers the engagement of students in meaningful experiences as the essence of learning. The shift is from passive transfer of information to active problem solving. Constructivists emphasize that learners create their own interpretations of the world of information. They contrast their perspective with those of the behaviorists or cognitivists, who believe that the mind can be "mapped" by the instructor. The constructivist will argue that the student situates the learning experience within his or her own experience and that the goal of instruction is not to teach

---

[6]Jean Piaget, *The Development of Thought: Elaboration of Cognitive Structures* (New York: Viking, 1977).

information but to create situations so that students can interpret information for their own understanding. The role of instruction is not to dispense facts but to provide students with ways to assemble knowledge. The constructivist believes that learning occurs most effectively when the student is engaged in authentic tasks that relate to meaningful contexts. The ultimate measure of learning is therefore based on the ability of the student to use knowledge to facilitate thinking in real life.

Social-Psychological Perspective

Social psychology is another well-established tradition in the study of instruction and learning. Social psychologists look at the effects of the social organization of the classroom on learning. What is the group structure of the classroom—independent study, small groups, or the class as a whole? What is the authority structure—how much control do students have over their own activities? And what is the reward structure—is cooperation rather than competition fostered?

In recent years, researchers such as Robert Slavin have taken the position that cooperative learning is both more effective and more socially beneficial than competitive and individualistic learning.[7] Slavin developed a set of cooperative learning techniques that embody the principles of small-group collaboration, learner-controlled instruction, and rewards based on group achievement. (These techniques are discussed more fully in Chapter 11.)

Approaches to Instruction

While behaviorists stress external control over a learner's behavior, cognitivists stress internal, or learner, control over mental processes. This difference in viewpoint influences how media are designed and used.

Behaviorists specify behavioral (performance) objectives, then limit instruction to whatever is necessary to master those objectives. When programmed instruction was introduced, material not directly related to the objectives was carefully screened out. Instructional design and media were highly structured. This approach has been very successful in teaching basic skills and knowledge.

Instructional designs based on cognitive psychology are less structured than those based on behavioral psychology. They allow learners to employ their own cognitive strategies, and they encourage interaction among students. Learning tasks that require problem solving, creative behavior, or cooperative activity lend themselves well to a cognitive instructional approach.

Unlike behaviorists, cognitivists do not limit their definition of learning to observable behavior. They believe that learners learn more than is expressed in immediate behaviors. They may at a later time use knowledge previously learned, but not previously expressed, in building their schemata.

Instructors and instructional designers need to develop an eclectic attitude toward competing schools of learning psychology. We are not obliged to swear allegiance to a particular learning theory. We use what works. If we find that a particular learning situation is suited to a behaviorist approach, then we use behaviorist techniques. Conversely, if the situation seems to call for cognitivist or constructivist methods, that is what we use.

It follows that an eclectic approach is essential when selecting and designing media. Most educators support the cognitivists' emphasis on stimulus-rich materials, confident that students learn more from, say, a video than may be expressed at the time. For example, a high school student may learn about the scientific method during a video of a chemistry experiment even though the objectives for the experiment do not list that topic. A management trainee may learn a great deal about personality differences during a gaming exercise designed to teach an entirely different skill. On the other hand, there are situations, such as teaching basic knowledge (e.g., multiplication tables) or psychomotor skills (e.g., keyboarding), that call for the tighter control of behaviorist techniques.

A media resource center housing a wide variety of up-to-date materials, relying on an array of media formats, allows immediate access to additional in-depth information, thus expanding the horizons of students beyond those provided in most textbooks.

FIGURE 1.10
Media can be designed to provide effective individualized instruction.

[7]Robert E. Slavin, *Cooperative Learning: Theory, Research, and Practice* (Englewood Cliffs, NJ: Prentice Hall, 1990).

Technologies for Learning

The word *technology* has always had a variety of connotations, ranging from mere hardware to a way of solving problems. The latter is exemplified in the often quoted definition given by economist John Kenneth Galbraith: "The systematic application of scientific or other organized knowledge to practical tasks."[8]

The notion of technology being a process is highlighted in the definition of instructional technology given by the leading professional association in that field: "the theory and practice of design, development, utilization, management and evaluation of processes and resources for learning."[9] The developers of programmed instruction called it a **technology for learning.** They believed that what was really important was the *process* of analyzing learning tasks, breaking them down into their components, and then devising the steps necessary to help the learner master those tasks.

In this book we reconsider this notion in light of today's understanding of human learning. We use the term *technologies for learning* to refer to both the *products* and the *process* of technology as they are applied to human learning. We use the plural, *technologies,* because there are many different manifestations of technology. We use the word *learning* instead of *instruction* because it is both possible and common for people to learn without instruction, and we want to put the spotlight on the learning process rather than the teaching process.

Over time, many technologies for learning have been developed. Some, such as interactive video, computer-based instruction, and hypermedia, rely on mechanical and electronic devices for their delivery. Others, such as programmed instruction, self-instructional modules, and simulation games, do not. We use the term *process technologies* to refer to the latter type. They are treated in detail in Chapter 11.

THE ROLES OF MEDIA IN INSTRUCTION

Media can serve many roles in instruction. The instruction may be dependent on the presence of a teacher (i.e., instructor-directed). Even in this situation, media may be heavily used by the teacher. On the other hand, the instruction may not require a teacher. Such student-directed instruction is often called "self-instruction" even though it is guided by whoever designed the media.

[8]John Kenneth Galbraith, *The New Industrial State* (Boston: Houghton Mifflin, 1967) p. 12.

[9]Barbara Seels and Rita Richey, *Instructional Technology: The Definition and Domains of the Field* (Washington, DC: Association for Educational Communications and Technology, 1994), p. 9.

FIGURE 1.11
The "teaching machine" was one of the first outgrowths of programmed instruction. The learner makes an overt response and checks the correctness of that response before proceeding to the next item.

Instructor-Directed Instruction

The most common use of media in an instructional situation is for supplemental support of the "live" instructor in the classroom (see Figure 1.12). Certainly, properly designed instructional media can enhance and promote learning and support teacher-based instruction. But their effectiveness depends on the instructor.

Research has long indicated the importance of the instructor's role in effective use of instructional media. For example, early studies showed that when teachers introduced films, relating them to learning objectives, the amount of information students gained from films increased.[10]

Later research confirmed and expanded on these original findings. Ausubel, for example, developed the concept of **advance organizers** as an aid to effective instruction.[11] An advance organizer may take the form of an overview of or an introduction to lesson content, a statement of principles contained in the information to be presented, a statement of learning objectives, and so on. Whatever the form, it is intended to create a mind-set for reception of instruction.

Advance organizers can be effective instruments for ensuring that media play their proper role as supple-

[10]Walter A. Wittich and J. G. Fowlkes, *Audio-Visual Paths to Learning* (New York: Harper Brothers, 1946).

[11]David Ausubel, *Educational Psychology* (New York: Holt, Rinehart and Winston, 1968).

FIGURE 1.12
Instructional media are often used by the classroom teacher to present new information.

mental supporters of instruction. Many commercially available materials today have built-in advance organizers, which may be used as is or adapted by the instructor.

Instructor-Independent Instruction

Media can also be used effectively in formal education situations where a teacher is not available or is working with other students (see Figure 1.13). Media are often "packaged" for this purpose: objectives are listed, guidance in achieving objectives is given, materials are assembled, and self-evaluation guidelines are provided. In informal educational settings, media such as videocassettes and computer courseware can be used by trainees at the work site or at home. In some instances an instructor may be available for consultation via telephone.

Cooperative learning is closely related to self-instruction. As students work together in groups or in collaboration with the teacher on learning projects, they take more responsibility for learning. Newer technologies such as hypermedia (see Chapter 9) encourage students to rely on their own cognitive strategies in learning. Cooperative learning with hypermedia can lead to stimulating interchanges among students as they go through and discuss their response to the materials. Hypermedia programs that allow for the users to make additions to the information lend themselves particularly well to this type of learning experience. Students report that learning activities with fellow students, as well as with the teacher, help them to gain confidence. This can be a way of building individual responsibility in group work.

The use of self-instructional materials allows teachers to spend more of their time diagnosing and correcting student problems, consulting with individual students, and teaching on a one-on-one and small-group basis.

How much time the teacher can spend on such activities will depend on the extent of the instructional role assigned to the media. Indeed under certain circumstances, the entire instructional task can be left to the media. Experimental programs have demonstrated, for example, that an entire course in high school physics can be successfully taught through the use of videotapes and workbooks without direct classroom intervention by the teacher. Successful computer-based courses in calculus have been developed for use by able students whose high schools have no such course.

This is not to say, of course, that instructional technology can or should replace the teacher, but rather that media can help teachers become creative managers of the learning experience instead of merely dispensers of information.

Distance Education

Distance education is a rapidly developing approach to instruction worldwide. The approach has been widely used by business, industrial, and medical organizations. For many years doctors, veterinarians, pharmacists, engineers, and lawyers have used it to continue their professional education. These individuals are often too busy to interrupt their practice and participate in classroom-based education. Recently, academic institutions have been using distance education to reach a more

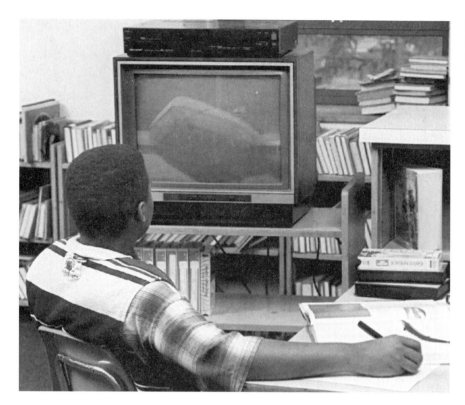

FIGURE 1.13
Carefully designed media make independent learning effective.

diverse and geographically dispersed audience not accessible through traditional classroom instruction.

The distinguishing characteristic of distance education is the separation of the instructional team and student(s) during the learning process. As a consequence, the course content must be delivered by instructional media.

The media may be primarily print (books and paper-and-pencil tests), as in traditional correspondence courses. Or, it might involve a wide variety of media, including audiocassettes, videotapes, videodiscs, and computer courseware sent to individual students. In addition, radio, broadcast television, and teleconferences are utilized for "live" distance education (see Figure 1.14). The latter allows for interactive instruction between the instructor and the students. Computer conferencing enables "conversations" among students who log on at different times to exchange messages.

Special Education

Media play an important role in the education of students with exceptionalities. Children with disabilities in particular need special instructional treatment. Children with mental retardation need highly structured learning situations because their field of experience and ability to incorporate messages into mental constructs is limited. They need to have much more of the message placed within the context of their field of experience to expand that field of experience (see Figure 1.7). Students who are hearing impaired, blind, or visually impaired require different kinds of learning materials. More emphasis should be placed on audio for students with visual impairments than for other students (Figure 1.15). Adjusting instruction for all exceptional groups requires heavy reliance on media and materials and the appropriate selection of these materials to fit specific purposes.

Adaptation of media and specially designed media can contribute enormously to effective instruction of students with disabilities and can help prevent their unwarranted (albeit unintentional) neglect by the busy regular-classroom teacher.[12]

A PHILOSOPHICAL PERSPECTIVE

More than a few observers of the educational scene have argued that the widespread use of instructional hardware in the classroom leads to treating students as if they were machines rather than human beings—that is, that technology dehumanizes the teaching/learning process. Properly used, however, modern instructional media can individualize and thus humanize this process to a degree previously considered unattainable.

---

[12]"Using Technology" (Bloomington, IN: Agency for Instructional Technology, 1988). VHS, 29 minutes.

FIGURE 1.14
Students can learn effectively from instructors at a distance via a telecommunications distribution system.

If teachers perceive learners as machines, they will treat them as such, with or without the use of instructional media. If teachers perceive their students as human beings with rights, privileges, and motivations of their own, with or without the aid of media, they will view students as people engaged in learning. In other words, it is the way that media are used, not the media themselves, that tend to mechanize people. Put another way, what is important is not so much what machines are present in the classroom but rather how the teacher guides students in their use.

Students with a high level of anxiety are prone to make mistakes and to learn less efficiently when under pressure. Many times, stressful learning situations for high-anxiety students make it difficult for them to succeed. Given the same sequence of instruction mediated through a machine that will continue only at the command of the students, it may be possible to reduce the pressure. Thus the use of a machine can humanize the instruction.

Contrary to what some educators believe, technology and humanism can exist either together or separately in

FIGURE 1.15
The Kurzweil reading machine allows those who are visually impaired to "read" printed material. The device scans the printed page, analyzes letter combinations through a computer, and speaks the words by means of a voice synthesizer.

an array of ways. Figure 1.16 suggests four basic combinations of technology and humanism. Here are some examples:

A. A college lecture with little or no interaction between the professor and the students—low in technology and low in humanism.

B. A course consisting of a required series of modules, each composed of performance objectives, materials to be used to complete those objectives, and a self-evaluation format—high in technology and low in humanism.

C. Similar to sample B, but the students select the topic of study based on their interests and consultation with an instructor. Designed into this instructional system are periodic interactions between the student and instructor, discussing the present state of learning and those that should be studied next—high in technology and high in humanism.

D. A group meets on a regular basis to discuss common reading assignments—low in technology and high in humanism.

These examples are overly simplified and used only to illustrate the concept, but they serve as a basis for analyzing the relationship between humanism and technology. They illustrate that instruction can be low in both humanism and technology, just as it can be high in both.

Using instructional technology does not preclude a humane teaching/learning environment. On the contrary, instructional media can help provide a learning atmosphere in which students actively participate in the learning process. When instructional media are used

FIGURE 1.16
Technology and humanism are not opposite ends of a single scale but two different variables, either of which can be high or low.

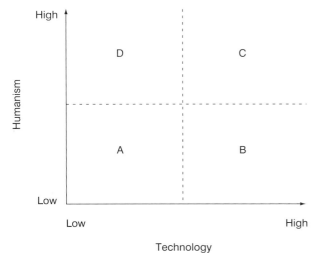

properly and creatively in the classroom, it is the machines that are turned on and off at will, not the students.

MEDIA IN EDUCATION AND TRAINING

Since the turn of the century, teachers have used various types of audio and visual aids to help them teach (see "Flashback," pp. 24–25). Recently, teachers have expanded their repertoire of materials and procedures to include the new technologies of learning. The newer techniques include the use of computers, compact discs, videodiscs, and satellite communications.

The teacher is no longer limited to the confines of the classroom. An entire school, through its media center, and the community can serve as an extensive resource in the learning process.

Patterns of Media Use in Education

Surveys of equipment in the schools revealed that by 1994 computers had become the most numerous item of instructional equipment in elementary and secondary schools. These surveys also confirm a continued reliance on traditional media. The most frequently inventoried piece of equipment after the computer was the VHS videotape recorder/player, followed by the overhead projector and television monitor. In addition, it was found that about half of the school districts used CD-ROM drives in 1991; that number grew to about three-quarters in 1993. It was also noted that videodisc player usage grew by 120% in K–12 schools between 1991 and 1993. It is estimated that over 40% of all public schools have videodisc players.

We must keep in mind that equipment lingers in a setting even though use of the associated media formats may be declining. For example, phonograph records are being replaced by tapes and compact discs, but record players will remain in the schools until the records in their inventories wear out. We know that media centers are buying videos instead of 16mm films, but film projectors will remain in use as long as films are still available. The relatively rapid acceptance of computers dedicated to instruction is encouraging, but the adoption of other new technologies, such as videodiscs, is slower than a perusal of the periodical literature would suggest. Although most educators would like to see newer technologies adopted at a faster pace, many acknowledge that the more traditional media still have a place in the school.

Distance education networks encourage the addition of equipment to both transmit and receive programs.

From Audiovisual Aids to New Technologies for Learning

Instructional media were originally referred to as "audiovisual aids." That term accurately describes their first role in elementary and secondary classrooms—as aids for the teacher. During the first decade of the twentieth century, school museums were created to house artifacts and exhibits for instructional purposes. The primary function of educational museums was to supplement and enrich the instructional programs of the school system. The first was the St. Louis Educational Museum, established in 1905. Horse-drawn wagons delivered instructional materials, including charts, colored photographs, stereoscopic pictures, lantern slides, and maps to the schools.

Educational use of film began about the same time. Most films used for instructional purposes were theatrical, industrial, or government films. One of the early film projectors was developed by Bell and Howell in 1907. Like other media at the time, instructional films were considered aids to teaching rather than self-contained sequences of instruction.

During the first quarter of this century, the use of these materials was referred to as "visual instruction" or "visual education." Recorded sound on film was not available until the later 1920s. Radio broadcasting developed during the same period, as sound recording and visual instruction quickly evolved into audiovisual instruction.

The growth of instructional radio occurred primarily during the decade from 1925 to 1935. By the late 1930s radio education had begun its decline. Today it is easier to find a television set than a radio in most schools. School systems that operate their own radio stations typically do so to teach broadcasting skills and provide primarily entertainment programming.

During World War II, the use of media in U.S. schools declined dramatically because of the lack of equipment and materials. However, a period of expansion was beginning in the industrial and military sectors. During this time, the U.S. government purchased 55,000 film projectors and produced 457 training films at a cost of more than $1 billion.[a]

Viewgraph, the name of the first company to produce overhead projectors, is the term that some military and industrial personnel still use to describe all overhead projection equipment. During the war, "viewgraphs" were developed by the Navy for map briefings and instruction.[b] This early version of the overhead projector replaced the clumsy opaque projector because notes could be made directly on the material during use. Today the overhead is the most widely used piece of traditional audiovisual equipment.

Following World War II there was a period of expansion in audiovisual instruction due in large part to its successful use during the war. At the same time, audiovisual research programs emerged with the hope of identifying principles of learning that could be used in the design of audiovisual materials. However, educational practices were not greatly affected by these research programs because many practitioners either ignored or were not aware of their findings.[c]

During the early 1950s many leaders in the audiovisual movement became interested in various theories or models of communication. These models focused on the communication process. The authors of these models indicated that during planning for instruction it was necessary to consider all of the elements of the communication process and not focus on just the medium, as many in the audiovisual field tended to do.

Instructional television experienced tremendous growth during the 1950s. In 1952 the Federal Communications Commission set aside 242 television channels for educational purposes. At the same time, the Ford Foundation provided extensive funding for educational television. Credit and noncredit courses were offered on open- and closed-circuit televisions. Programs of wide educational and cultural interest have been offered on educational television stations. Today most educational television is offered via videotape, with the exception of the airing of news events as they take place. The television screen has begun to replace the movie screen for the viewing of prepared materials.

Programmed instruction can be traced to the work of psychologist B. F. Skinner in the mid-1950s. Whereas the other media we have been discussing are really presentation

[a]J. R. Olsen and V. B. Bass, "The Application of Performance Technology in the Military," *Performance and Instruction 21*, no. 6 (July–August, 1982), pp. 32–36.

[b]W. Wittich and C. Schuller, *Audio-Visual Materials: Their Nature and Use* (New York: Harper and Row, 1953), p. 351.

[c]Robert A. Reiser, "Instructional Technology: A History," in *Instructional Technology Foundations*, ed. R. M. Gagné (Hillsdale, NJ: Lawrence Erlbaum, 1987), pp. 11–48.

Programs, such as TI-IN, a Texas-based telecommunication education project, offer courses throughout the United States via satellite, making it possible for students to engage in study not available to them otherwise.

Most teachers coming out of schools of education will have had considerable training in using the newer technologies. As their numbers increase, we can expect more pressure on school districts to increase their inventories of high-tech equipment with a consequent increase in the use of newer technologies.

Patterns of Media Use in Training

The media and methods preferred by training directors are often different from those used by educators. One of the major reasons for this is that the curricula of the schools are fairly uniform, whereas training programs are often industry specific. Formats of media that lend themselves to local production are preferred by training directors. For example, slides are used more frequently than filmstrips; in schools the reverse is true.

devices, programmed instruction utilized principles of human learning. Skinner focused attention on a device called the "teaching machine." Later, that device was replaced by books called "programmed texts." The programmed instruction movement reached its peak during the 1960s and paved the way for other types of instructional approaches—audiotutorial systems, personalized systems of instruction, and programmed tutoring in the 1970s. Computer-based instruction of the late 1970s and 1980s is based on the principles of learning used in programmed instruction.[d] Programmed instruction and other self-instructional approaches are fading from the formal education scene and are being replaced by computer-based

education scene and are being replaced by computer-based multimedia and hypermedia.

Textbooks are still the most commonly used instructional resource. Overhead projectors are readily available and are used as a presentation aid by many teachers. Commercially produced videocassettes are gradually replacing films as the most widely used form of projected media because of their relatively low cost and ease of use. Filmstrips and commercially prepared slides, along with audiotapes and printed study guides, are providing the basis for self-instructional learning carrels and media centers. Today, media and technologies for learning are providing direct educational experiences for students rather than being used just as teachers' aids.

[d]For a thorough discussion of the history of media, see Paul Saettler, *The Evolution of American Educational Technology* (Englewood, CO: Libraries Unlimited, 1990).

▲

Another difference arises from the fact that training directors are dealing with adults rather than children and adolescents. Role playing, games, and simulations are used much more frequently in training programs, particularly with management, supervisory, and sales personnel. These people's jobs require a great deal of interaction with people, and the types of training methods that develop relevant skills are given high priority. The trainees will have to call on those skills immediately after the training session and are more likely to become

impatient with methods more abstract than the situation demands.

According to a 1994 *Training* magazine survey, video-based instruction is used by more companies with over 100 employees than any other medium. Lecture, presumably supported by overhead transparencies, is the next most frequently used instructional format. A list of the various media and methods used in employee training is given in Figure 1.17 (note that the survey reports the percentage of companies using the medium or method, not what percentage of training is delivered by the medium or method).

Note that for training, traditional media are more commonly used by more companies than are some of the newer technologies. In recent years the percentage of companies using video has increased. The percentage of companies using games and simulations also has significantly increased. The percentage of companies using teleconferencing (audio and video) and computer con-ferencing increased in the past few years. These technologies will likely be relied on more heavily in the future.

Interactive video is an expensive medium, so it is not surprising that larger companies tend to use it more than do small companies. Twenty-four percent of companies with more than 2,500 employees use interactive video. As the size of the organization decreases, the percentage of companies using it drops sharply.

FIGURE 1.17
Percentage of organizations using various instructional methods and media for employee training.

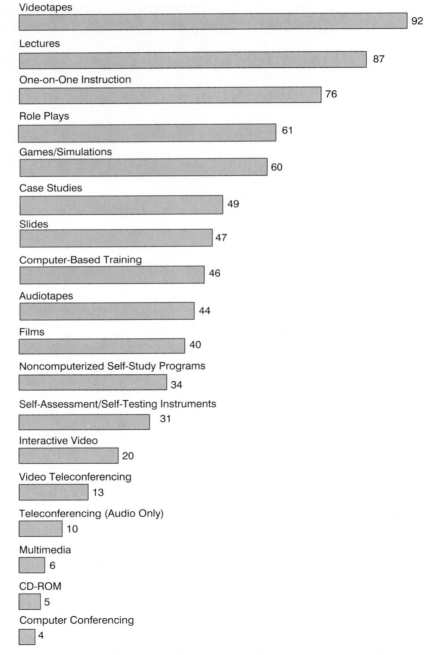

FIGURE 1.18
Because institutional training often requires materials custom-made for a specific setting, training videos are often produced on site.

APPLYING RESEARCH TO PRACTICE

Research projects comparing media treatments with so-called conventional instruction frequently conclude that there is "no statistically significant difference" in learning between the media-based and conventional instruction. Does this mean that audiovisual presentations are equivalent to lectures? Not necessarily. It may mean that when certain audiovisual materials are used in the same way as a lecture is used (e.g., for verbal recall of information), the outcomes will be similar when observed over a range of learners.

There needs to be some consideration for such important variables as the presence of a creative instructor in the learning experience. In practice, a teacher does not use audiovisual materials in the same way as print or lecture-type materials. Selection of media to suit a particular learning outcome is of particular importance. Audiovisual presentations can be very powerful—for example, in conveying a historical period's feel, in building empathy for others, or in showing a role model in action.

Integration of quality audiovisual materials is also of importance. Evaluating the cognitive process associated with achievement is important to the selection of media. Teachers evaluate effectiveness not just on the basis of immediate recall of information but also on the basis of what impact the experience has on the imagination, feelings, and long-term comprehension of the learner.

From what we have learned in the research about media use in the curriculum and considerations about their application, we can present some guidelines for selection.

If nothing else, research and practical experience have shown that much of the effectiveness of media depends on how they are integrated into the larger scheme. Schramm summarized it this way:

> Motivated students learn from any medium if it is completely used and adapted to their needs. Within its physical limits, any medium can perform any educational task. Whether a student learns more from one medium than from another is at least as likely to depend on how the medium is used as on what medium is used.[13]

The user of the material can help increase the impact of any audiovisual material by applying these sound principles:

- Select material with appropriate attributes.
- Introduce it to learners by relating it to prior learning and indicating how it relates to today's objectives.
- Present it under the best possible environmental conditions.
- Elicit a response from viewers.
- Review the content.
- Evaluate its impact.

The ASSURE model described in Chapter 2 was developed as a planning aid to help ensure that media are used to their maximum advantage, not just as interchangeable substitutes for printed or oral messages.

---

[13]Wilbur Schramm, *Big Media, Little Media* (Beverly Hills, CA: Sage Publications, 1977), p. iv.

FIGURE 1.19
"I like educational toys. I like educational TV. I like educational reading material. It's education I don't like."

Contrary to the requirements of research, the requirements of practice demand that the conditions surrounding the use of the materials not be held constant. Indeed, one of the most important roles of media is to serve as a catalyst for change in the whole instructional environment. The effective use of media demands that instructors be better organized in advance, think through their objectives, alter the everyday classroom routine, and evaluate broadly to determine the impact of instruction on mental abilities, feelings, values, interpersonal skills, and motor skills.

REFERENCES

Print References

Adams, Dennis M. *Media and Literacy: Learning in an Electronic Age.* Springfield, IL: Thomas, 1989.

Adams, Dennis M., and Carlson, Helen. *Cooperative Learning and Educational Media: Collaborating with Technology and Each Other.* Englewood Cliffs, NJ: Educational Technology Publications, 1990.

Ault, Charles. "Technology as Method-of-Inquiry and Six Other (Less Valuable) Ways to Think about Integrating Technology and Science in Elementary Education." *Journal of Science Teacher Education* (Spring 1993): 58–63.

Bagley, C., and Hunter, B. "Restructuring, Constructivism, and Technology: Forging a New Relationship." *Educational Technology* (July 1992): 22–27.

Barron, Ann, and Orwig, Gary. *New Technologies for Education: A Beginner's Guide.* Englewood, CO: Libraries Unlimited, 1993.

Callison, D. "School Library Media Programs and Free Inquiry Learning." *School Library Journal 32* (February 1986): 20–24.

Carey, Doris. "Teacher Roles and Technology Integration: Moving from Teacher as Director to Teacher as Facilitator." *Computers in the Schools* (Summer 1993): 105–118.

Clark, Richard E., ed. "Instructional Technology and Media Research." *International Journal of Educational Research 14,* no. 6 (1990): 485–579.

Cuban, L. *Teachers and Machines: Use of Technology Since 1920.* New York: Teachers College Press, 1986.

Eisenberg, M., and Berkowitz, R. *Information Problem-Solving.* Norwood, NJ: Ablex Publishing, 1990.

Ertmer, P., and Newby, T. "Behaviorism, Cognitivism, Constructivism: Comparing Critical Features from an Instructional Design Perspective." *Performance Improvement Quarterly 6,* no. 4 (1993): 50–72.

Fox, G. T., and DeVault, M. V. "Technology and Humanism in the Classroom: Frontiers of Education Practice." *Educational Technology* (October 1974): 7–13.

Gagné, Robert M. *Instructional Technology: Foundations.* Hillsdale, NJ: Lawrence Erlbaum, 1987.

Gayeski, Diane M. "Why Information Technologies Fail." *Educational Technology* (February 1989): 9–17.

Hatcher, Barbara, ed. *Learning Opportunities Beyond the School.* Wheaton, MD: Association for Childhood Education International, 1987.

Lance, K., Welborn, L., and Hamilton-Pennell, C. *The Impact of School Library Media Centers on Academic Achievement.* Castle Rock, CO: Hi Willow Research, 1993.

Muffoletto, Robert. "Technology and Restructuring Education: Constructing a Context." *Educational Technology* (February 1994): 24–28.

Petrie, Joyce. *Mainstreaming in the Media Center.* Phoenix, AZ: Oryx Press, 1982.

Saettler, Paul. *The Evolution of American Educational Technology.* Englewood, CO: Libraries Unlimited, 1990.

Scaife, M. "Education, Information Technology and Cognitive Science." *Journal of Computer Assisted Learning* (June 1989): 66–71.

Seels, Barbara B., and Richey, Rita C. *Instructional Technology: Definition and Domains of the Field*. Washington, DC: Association for Educational Communications and Technology, 1994.

Stakenas, Robert G., and Kaufman, Roger. *Technology in Education: Its Human Potential*. Fastback 163. Bloomington, IN: Phi Delta Kappa, 1981.

Turner, P. *Helping Teachers Teach: the School Library Media Specialist's Role*. 2d ed. Englewood, CO: Libraries Unlimited, 1993.

Von Wadtke, Mark. *Mind Over Media: Creative Thinking Skills for Electronic Media*. New York: McGraw-Hill, 1993.

Wadsworth, Barry J. *Piaget's Theory of Cognitive and Affective Development*. 4th ed. White Plains, NY: Longman, 1989.

Wedman, John F. "Increasing the Use of Instructional Media in the Schools." *Educational Technology* (October 1988): 26–31.

Audiovisual References

Case Studies in Communication. Salenger Educational Media, 1982. 16-mm film. 18 minutes.

Communication Feedback. Rockville, MD: BNA Film, 1965. 16-mm film. 21 minutes.

A Communication Model. Bloomington, IN: Indiana University Audio-Visual Center, 1967. 16-mm film. 30 minutes.

Communications. Calgary, Alberta: Access Network, 1989. Videocassette. 29 minutes.

Communications and Media. Learning Corporation of America, 1982. 16-mm film or videocassette. 20 minutes.

Communication Primer. Classroom Film Distributor, 1954. 16-mm film. 22 minutes.

Cultural Illiteracy. University Park, PA: Pennsylvania State University, 1988. Videocassette. 28 minutes.

Media for Presentations. Bloomington, IN: Indiana University Audio-Visual Center, 1978. 16-mm film. 20 minutes.

Perception and Communication. Columbus: Ohio State University, 1967. 16-mm film. 32 minutes.

This Is Marshall McLuhan: The Medium Is the Massage. New York: McGraw-Hill, 1968. 16-mm film. 53 minutes.

To Help Them Learn. Washington DC: Association for Educational Communications and Technology, 1978. 16-mm film. 21 minutes.

SYSTEMATIC PLANNING FOR MEDIA USE

If you are going to use media and technologies effectively, you must plan systematically for their use. The ASSURE model is a guide to the major steps in the planning process. Following the ASSURE model, you begin instructional planning by assessing your students' characteristics and the learning objectives to be attained. With these in mind you are in a good position to select the types of media or delivery systems to be used and to consider specific materials that you might need.

The students' actual encounter with the media and materials also needs to be planned with care. What will they be doing? The ASSURE model puts a heavy emphasis on *active* student engagement in learning activities.

After instruction, how will you determine whether students have reached the goal? Both the learners and the instructional processes need to be evaluated. Were the materials effective? Were the activities engaging? Answering questions such as these closes the loop and brings you back to the beginning of another cycle.

KNOWLEDGE OBJECTIVES

1. Demonstrate your ability to follow the steps involved in systematic planning for the use of media (the ASSURE model).
2. List general characteristics of learners and types of specific competencies that could affect media selection.
3. Describe learning style, including four types of traits that affect it.
4. Discuss the rationale for stating objectives for instruction. Your discussion should include purposes or uses of objectives.
5. Write objectives that refer to the audience, behavior, conditions, and degree of mastery.
6. Demonstrate your ability to follow the basic procedures for selecting, modifying, and designing materials, and indicate when each choice is appropriate.
7. Describe ways of modifying materials without actually altering the original materials.
8. Create examples of the five basic steps in utilizing instructional materials.
9. Identify general showmanship techniques in reference to planning, practice, and presentation.
10. Describe methods for eliciting student response during and after using media.
11. Justify the requirement for learner participation when using media.
12. Compare and contrast the techniques for evaluating student achievement and the techniques for evaluating media and methods.

APPLICATION OBJECTIVES

1. Plan a presentation using the procedures described in this chapter. Your description must follow the "Blueprint" on page 61, "A Template for Planning."
2. Classify a set of at least five objectives into the cognitive, affective, motor skill, and interpersonal domains.
3. Write at least five objectives for a lesson you might teach. Choose a topic that allows you to write objectives in more than one domain.
4. Select a chapter from a textbook of interest to you and derive a set of at least five objectives that you feel are intended by the author.
5. Plan, prepare, and present a brief lesson incorporating two or more media. Have your audience (one person or more) give you feedback on your presentation skills.
6. Select a lesson you might teach, such as a chapter from a textbook, and develop a set of evaluation instruments (not necessarily all paper-and-pencil test items).

LEXICON

learning style	affective domain	interpersonal domain	showmanship
criterion	motor skill domain	media format	overt response
cognitive domain			

A Model to Help Assure Learning

Analyze Learners

State Objectives

Select Methods, Media, and Materials

The first step in planning is to identify the learners. Your learners may be, for example, students, trainees, or members of an organization such as a Sunday school, civic club, youth group, or fraternal organization. You must know your students to select the best medium to meet the objectives. The audience can be analyzed in terms of (1) general characteristics, (2) specific entry competencies (knowledge, skills, and attitudes about the topic), and (3) learning style.

The next step is to state the objectives as specifically as possible. The objectives may be derived from a course syllabus, stated in a textbook, taken from a curriculum guide, or developed by the instructor. They should be stated in terms of what the learner will be able to do as a result of instruction. The conditions under which the student or trainee is going to perform and the degree of acceptable performance should be included.

Once you have identified your audience and stated your objectives, you have established the beginning points (audience's present knowledge, skills, and attitudes) and ending points (objectives) of instruction. Your task now is to build a bridge between these two points by choosing appropriate methods and media formats, then deciding on materials to implement these choices. There are three options: (1) select available materials, (2) modify existing materials, or (3) design new materials.

THE ASSURE MODEL

All effective instruction requires careful planning. Teaching with instructional media is certainly no exception. This chapter examines how to plan systematically for the effective use of instructional media. We have constructed a procedural model to which we have given the acronym *ASSURE*—it is intended to *assure* effective use of media in instruction.

You can think of the teaching/learning process as progressing through several stages. Gagné refers to these stages as "events of instruction."[1] Gagné's research revealed that well-designed lessons begin with the arousal of students' interest and then move on to present new material, involve students in practice, assess their understanding, and go on to follow-up activities. The ASSURE model incorporates these events of instruction.

The ASSURE model—a procedural guide for planning and conducting instruction that incorporates media—assumes that training or instruction is required. A full-blown process of instructional development would begin with a needs assessment to determine whether instruction is the appropriate solution to a performance problem.

The ASSURE model focuses on planning surrounding the actual classroom use of media. It is less ambitious than models of instructional development, which are intended to guide the entire process of designing instructional systems. Such models include the proce-

---

[1]Robert Gagné, *The Conditions of Learning*, 4th ed. (New York: Holt, Rinehart and Winston, 1985).

U

Utilize Media and Materials

Having either selected, modified, or designed your materials, you then must plan how the materials will be used to implement your methods. First, preview the materials and practice the implementation. Next, prepare the class and ready the necessary equipment and facilities. Then conduct the instruction using the utilization techniques described in this and later chapters.

R

Require Learner Participation

To be effective, materials-based instruction should require active mental engagement by learners. There should be activities within the lesson that allow learners to process the knowledge or skills and to receive feedback on the appropriateness of their efforts before being formally assessed.

E

Evaluate and Revise

After instruction, it is necessary to evaluate its impact and effectiveness. To get the total picture, you must evaluate the entire instructional process. Did the learners meet the objectives? Did the methods and media assist the trainees in reaching the objectives? Could all students use the materials properly?

Wherever there are discrepancies between what you intended and what you attained, you will want to revise the plan for the next time.

dures of the ASSURE model and the processes of needs analysis, subject matter analysis, product design, prototype tryout, system implementation, and the like. These larger-scale instructional development procedures typically involve teams of specialists and require major commitments of time and money. (Further information about instructional design can be found in the print references cited at the end of this chapter.) The ASSURE model, on the other hand, is meant for use by the individual instructor in planning classroom use of media.

To illustrate how to use the six steps of the ASSURE model, we will provide an example of a "Blueprint" for each step after it is described. These steps taken together constitute a "Blueprint"—or lesson plan—that describes the instructional planning used by a middle school math teacher who wanted to redesign a unit on statistics. The teacher felt that the mathematics textbook presented sta-

tistics (collecting data, interpreting data, and presenting data) very inadequately. One particularly disappointing aspect of textbook material covering this topic was that technology was not incorporated in the teaching. She believed that, considering today's technology-based world, this skill deserved more attention than it traditionally received in schools. Therefore, she chose to develop a unit that addressed some of the basic statistical skills through the use of computer applications.

A software package, "The Classroom Link," is available to help you use the ASSURE model to create your own lesson plans. The program presents each step of the model in a flexible format that allows you to develop your own lesson plans by entering them into a computer version of the ASSURE model. Instructions on how to use "The Computer Link" are at the back of this text.

ANALYZE LEARNERS

If instructional media are to be used effectively, there must be a match between the characteristics of the learner and the content of the lesson's methods, media, and materials. The first step in the ASSURE model, therefore, is analysis of your audience.

It is not feasible to analyze every trait of your learners. Several factors, however, are critical for making good methods and media decisions:

- General characteristics
- Specific entry competencies
- Learning styles

General characteristics include broad identifying descriptors such as age, grade level, job or position, and cultural or socioeconomic factors. Specific entry competencies refer to knowledge and skills that the learners either possess or lack: prerequisite skills, target skills, and attitudes. The third factor, learning style, refers to the spectrum of psychological traits that affect how we perceive and respond to different stimuli, such as anxiety, aptitude, visual or auditory preference, and so on.

General Characteristics

Even a superficial analysis of learner characteristics can provide helpful leads in selecting instructional methods and media. For example, students with substandard reading skills may be reached more effectively with nonprint media. If you are dealing with a particular ethnic or cultural subgroup, you might want to give high priority to considerations of ethnic and cultural identify and values in selecting particular materials.

If learner apathy toward the subject matter is a problem, consider using a highly stimulating instructional approach, such as a dramatic videotape or a simulation game.

Learners entering a new conceptual area for the first time may need more direct, concrete kinds of experiences, such as field trips or role-playing exercises (refer to Dale's Cone of Experience in Chapter 1). More advanced learners usually have a sufficient base for using audiovisual or even verbal materials.

Heterogeneous groups, which include learners varying widely in their conceptual sophistication or in the amount of firsthand experience they have with the topic, may profit from an audiovisual experience such as a videotape. Such media presentations provide a common experiential base that can serve as an important point of reference for subsequent group discussion and individual study.

For instructors dealing with a familiar audience, analysis of general characteristics will be something of a given. At times, however, audience analysis may be more difficult (Figure 2.1). Perhaps your students are new to you, and you have had little time to observe and record their characteristics. Or perhaps they are a more heterogeneous group than is ordinarily found in the classroom—business trainees, for example, or a civic club, youth group, or fraternal organization—thus making it more difficult to ascertain whether all or even a majority of your learners are ready for the methods and media of instruction you are considering. In such cases, academic and other records may be helpful, as well as direct questioning of and talking with learners and instructors or other group leaders. Seasoned public speakers—those who regularly address unfamiliar audiences—make it a practice to arrive early and strike up a conversation with audience members. In this way they

FIGURE 2.1
A classic example of a presentation in search of an audience.

can pick up valuable clues about the types of people in the audience, their backgrounds, their expectations, and their moods.

Specific Entry Competencies

When you begin to plan any lesson, your first assumption is that the learners lack the knowledge or skills you are about to teach and that they possess the knowledge or skills needed to understand and learn from the lesson. These assumptions are often mistaken. For example, a life insurance company used to routinely bring all its new sales associates back to the home office at the end of their first year for a course on setting sales priorities. Puzzled by the cool reaction of the agents, the trainer decided to give a pretest, which revealed that a majority of the trainees already knew perfectly well how to set sales priorities. The company shifted to a less expensive and more productive strategy of giving incentives to field representatives who sent in acceptable sales plans showing their priorities.

The assumption that learners have the prerequisite knowledge or skill to begin the lesson can seldom be accepted casually in school settings. Teachers of mixed-ability classes routinely anticipate that some students will need remedial help before they are ready to begin a particular unit of instruction. Furthermore, researchers studying the impact of different psychological traits on learning have reached the unexpected conclusion that a student's prior knowledge of a particular subject influences how and what he or she can learn more than does any psychological trait.[2] For example, students approaching a subject new to them learn best from structured presentations even if they have a learning style that would otherwise indicate more open-ended, unstructured methods.

These realizations suggest that instructors must verify assumptions about entry competencies through informal means (such as in-class questioning or out-of-class interviews) or more formal means (such as testing with standardized or teacher-made tests). *Entry tests* are assessments, both formal and informal, that determine whether students possess the necessary prerequisites. *Prerequisites* are competencies that the learner must possess in order to benefit from the instruction but that you or the media are not going to teach. For example, in teaching an apprentice lathe operator to read blueprints, you might assume that he or she has the ability to make metric conversions—hence you would not teach this skill.

Prerequisites (i.e., specific entry competencies) should be stated in the same format as are objectives (described in the next section). In the situation involving the apprentice lathe operator, the prerequisites could

be stated as follows: "Apprentice lathe operators are able to convert any given measurement up to one meter from the metric system to the English system equivalent or vice versa with 100% accuracy." Such previously acquired skills should be assessed before instruction.

Preassessment measures, such as discussions and pretests, are also given before instruction but are used to measure the content to be taught—the target skills. If the learners have already mastered what you plan to teach, you are wasting your time and theirs by teaching it.

By analyzing what your audience already knows, you can select appropriate methods and media. For example, if you have a group diverging widely in entry competencies, consider self-instructional materials to allow for self-pacing and other aspects of individualization.

Learning Styles

Learning style refers to a cluster of psychological traits that determine how an individual perceives, interacts with, and responds emotionally to learning environments.

It is clear that certain traits dramatically affect our ability to learn effectively from different methods and media. However, it is not so clear which traits are most important. Gardner was dissatisfied with the concept of IQ and its unitary view of intelligence, noting that "not all people have the same abilities; not all of us learn in the same way."[3] He identified seven aspects of intelligence: (1) verbal/linguistic (language), (2) logical/mathematical (scientific/quantitative), (3) visual/spatial, (4) musical/rhythmic, (5) bodily/kinesthetic (dancing/athletics), (6) interpersonal (ability to understand other people), and (7) intrapersonal (ability to understand oneself).

Gardner's theory implies that teachers, curriculum planners, and media specialists should work together to design a curriculum in which students have the chance to develop these different aspects of intelligence. It also implies that students vary widely in terms of their strengths and weaknesses in each of these areas. A school adopting this approach would have students engaged in a much wider variety of methods and media than is typical now. Teacher talk and seatwork obviously are not sufficient. Since students have different mixes of strengths and weaknesses, their progress would have to be measured not by conventional grades in conventional subjects but by growth in each of the seven types of intelligence. The type of individualized instructional plans and records of progress implied in this approach lend themselves well to the active learning methods, interactive technologies, and information management

---

[2]Walter Dick and Lou Carey, *The Systematic Design of Instruction,* 3d ed. (Glenview, IL: Scott, Foresman, 1990), p. 90.

[3]Howard Gardner, *Multiple Intelligences: The Theory in Practice* (New York: Basic Books, 1993), p. 21.

systems described in later chapters. In fact, experimental schools based on this theory are now in operation.

Learning style variables discussed in the literature can be categorized as perceptual preferences and strengths, information processing habits, motivational factors, and physiological factors.

Perceptual Preferences and Strengths. Learners vary as to which sensory gateways they prefer using and which they are especially adept at using. The main gateways include auditory, visual, tactile, and kinesthetic. Proponents of the importance of this variable claim that most students do not have a preference or strength for auditory reception, casting doubt on the widespread use of the lecture method. They find that slower learners tend to prefer tactile or kinesthetic experiences; sitting and listening are difficult for them. Dependence on the tactile and kinesthetic modalities decreases with maturity.

Information Processing Habits. This category includes a broad range of variables related to how individuals tend to approach the cognitive processing of information.

Gregorc's model of "mind styles," elaborated by Butler, groups learners according to concrete versus abstract and random versus sequential styles. It yields four categories: concrete sequential, concrete random, abstract sequential, and abstract random.[4] Concrete sequential learners prefer direct, hands-on experiences presented in a logical order. They learn best with workbooks, programmed instruction, demonstration, and structured laboratory exercises. Concrete random learners lean toward a trial-and-error approach, quickly reaching conclusions from exploratory experiences. They prefer methods such as games, simulations, independent study projects, and discovery learning. Abstract sequential learners decode verbal and symbolic messages adeptly, especially when presented in logical sequence. Reading and listening to presentations are preferred methods. Abstract random learners are distinguished by their capacity to draw meaning from human-mediated presentations; they respond to the tone and style of the speaker as well as the message. They do well with group discussion, lectures with question-and-answer periods, films, and television.

Motivational Factors. Various emotional factors have been found to influence what we pay attention to, how long we pay attention, how much effort we invest in learning, and how feelings may interfere with learning. Anxiety, locus of control (internal/external),

degree of structure, achievement motivation, social motivation, cautiousness, and competitiveness are variables frequently cited as critical to the learning process.

According to Tobias, "Anxiety is one of the learner characteristics of major importance for instructional concern."[5] He describes how anxiety can interfere with cognitive processing before, during, and after learning. He also cites research demonstrating that motivational differences can dramatically affect the effort that students invest in a task and thereby affect learning outcomes.

Kuhlthau has identified the high degree of anxiety present in most students who face the complexities of dealing with information resources found in a school media center. Her work has made many media specialists aware of the important role they play not only in helping students search for information but also in helping them understand, select, and use information to communicate through their term papers, class reports, or other mediated presentations.[6]

Physiological Factors. Factors related to gender differences, health, and environmental conditions are among the most obvious influences on the effectiveness of learning. Boys and girls tend to respond differently to various school experiences. For example, boys tend to be more competitive and aggressive than girls and consequently respond better to competitive games. Hunger and illness clearly impede learning. Temperature, noise, lighting, and time of day are everyday phenomena that affect our ability to concentrate and maintain attention. Individuals have different preferences and tolerances regarding these factors.

Dunn and Dunn have developed standardized instruments to measure the learning styles and environmental preferences of learners that cover these and other physiological factors.[7] They are among the best known and most widely used instruments in school applications. Teachers who have prescribed individual learning programs based on analysis of these factors feel that they have practical value in improving academic achievement, attitude, and discipline.

The intent in using information about a student's learning style is to adapt instruction to take advantage of a particular style. Many students in a class may have the same or similar learning styles. Using learning styles in teaching can be compared to designing a house for a specific person. The components of houses are basically

---

[4]Kathleen A. Butler, *Learning and Teaching Style: In Theory and in Practice,* 2nd ed. (Columbia, CT: The Learner's Dimension, 1986).

[5]Sigmund Tobias, "Learner Characteristics," in *Instructional Technology: Foundations,* ed. Robert M. Gagné (Hillsdale, NJ: Lawrence Erlbaum, 1987).

[6]Carol C. Kuhlthau, *Teaching the Library Research Process* (West Nyack, NY: Center for Applied Research in Education, 1985).

[7]Rita Dunn and Kenneth Dunn, *Teaching Elementary Students Through Their Individual Learning Styles* (Boston: Allyn and Bacon, 1992).

Middle School Mathematics

Analyze Learners

General Characteristics

The students for whom this lesson is intended are seventh graders enrolled in a general mathematics class geared toward the average learner. The students range in age from 12 to 14 years. Several students have identified learning disabilities, whereas others are on the edge of consideration for the advanced mathematics track. They come from various socioeconomic environments; however, the majority of the students are white, middle-class Americans who live in a rural setting. Generally, the students are well behaved; problems tend to arise, however, when activities are textbook and paper-and-pencil oriented.

Entry Competencies

The seventh-grade mathematics students are able to do the following:

- Select, locate, and utilize appropriate reference materials when preparing research projects, using the school library media center
- Locate and identify bar, line, and circle graphs when examining books and other forms of media
- Read and interpret all the statistical or numerical information given to them on a bar, line, or circle graph

- Construct a graph (bar, line, or circle) when given a set of data, colored pencils/pens, a compass, a ruler, and graph paper
- Define and interpret a given example of percentage, mean, median, and mode without aids or references
- Demonstrate standard keyboarding skills, utilizing *Microsoft Works* on the Macintosh computer, with an average typing speed of 35 words per minute

Learning Styles

The students dislike the monotony of mathematics textbook assignments. These assignments are usually centered on paper-and-pencil calculation problems. Persistent use of the textbook often results in the students becoming bored and restless. They appear to learn best from activities that incorporate the use of manipulatives. In addition, they like group-oriented learning activities. Regarding testing, many of the students tend to experience difficulty and anxiety during written exams. As a result, the class prefers to be evaluated using methods other than paper-and-pencil tests (e.g., reports, application projects, etc.).

This Blueprint was developed by Mary Ann Ferkis, Purdue University. A computer template for a Blueprint is found in "The Classroom Link."

---

uniform—kitchen, living room, dining room, bedrooms, baths. However, they can be arranged in an unlimited number of configurations. They may need to be structured to accommodate hobbies, individuals with disabilities, or persons working at home. Furthermore, there are many different styles of architecture, colors, textures, materials and so on. An architect skillfully selects and arranges all these elements to meet the needs and preferences of the inhabitants—an individual, a couple, a family. In a similar manner, a teacher chooses different methods, media, and materials to meet the needs of students with different learning styles and physiological factors.

STATE OBJECTIVES

The second step in the ASSURE model for using instructional media is to state the objectives of instruction. What learning outcome is each learner expected to achieve? More precisely, what new capability should the learner possess at the completion of instruction? An objective is a statement not of what the instructor plans to put into the lesson but of what the learner ought to get out of the lesson.

Your statement of objectives should be as specific as possible. For example, "My students will improve their mathematical skills" is far too general to qualify as a specific lesson objective. It does, however, qualify as a

goal—a broad statement of purpose. Such a goal might serve as the umbrella for a number of specific objectives, such as "The second-grade students will be able to solve correctly any single-digit addition problem."

Why should you state instructional objectives? First, you must know your objectives in order to make appropriate selection of methods and media. Your objectives will, in a sense, dictate your choice of media and your sequence of learning activities. Knowing your objectives will also commit you to create a learning environment in which the objectives can be reached. For example, if the objective of a unit of a driver's training course is "To be able to change a flat tire within fifteen minutes," the learning environment must include a car with a flat tire.

Another basic reason for stating your instructional objectives is to help assure proper evaluation. You won't know whether your learners have achieved an objective unless you are absolutely sure what that objective is.

Without explicit objectives, your students won't know what is expected of them. If objectives are clearly and specifically stated, learning and teaching become objective oriented. Indeed, a statement of objectives may be viewed as a type of contract between teacher and learner: "Here is the objective. My responsibility as the instructor is to provide learning activities suitable for your attaining the objective. Your responsibility as the learner is to participate conscientiously in those learning activities."

The ABCDs of Well-Stated Objectives

A well-stated objective starts by naming the *Audience* of learners for whom the objective is intended. It then specifies the *Behavior* or capability to be demonstrated and the *Conditions* under which the behavior or capability will be observed. Finally, it specifies the *Degree* to which the new skill must be mastered—the standard by which the capability can be judged.

Audience. A major premise of systematic instruction is to focus on what the learner is doing, not on what the teacher is doing. Learning is most likely to take place when the learner is active, either mentally processing an idea or physically practicing a skill. Because accomplishment of the objective depends on what the learner does, the objective begins by stating whose capability is going to be changed—for example, "ninth-grade algebra students" or "newly hired sales representatives." Of course, if you are repeating the objective in material written for student use, the informal "you" is preferable.

Behavior. The heart of the objective is the verb describing the new capability that the audience will have after instruction. This verb is most likely to communicate your intent clearly if it is stated as an observable behavior. What will the learner be able to do after completing instruction? Vague terms such as *know, understand,* and *appreciate* do not communicate your aim clearly. Better words include *define, categorize,* and *demonstrate,* which denote observable performance. The Helpful Hundred list in Table 2.1 suggests some verbs that highlight performance.

The behavior or performance stated in the objective should reflect the real-world capability needed by the learner, not some artificial ability needed for successful performance on a test. As a surgical patient, would you want a surgeon who is "able to select the correct answers on a multiple-choice test on appendectomies"? Or would you want the surgeon to be "able to perform an appendectomy"?

Conditions. A statement of objectives should include the conditions under which the performance is to be observed. For example, are students allowed to use notes in describing the consequences of excessive use of alcohol? If the objective of a particular lesson is for students to be able to identify birds, will identification be made from color representations or black-and-white photographs? What tools or equipment will the student be allowed or not allowed to use in demonstrating mastery of the objective? Thus, an objective might state, "Given a political map of Europe, the student will be able to mark the major coal-producing areas." Or it might say, "Without notes, textbook, or any library materials, the student will be able to write a 300-word essay on the relationship of nutrition to learning."

Degree. The final requirement of a well-stated objective is that it indicates the standard, or **criterion,** by which acceptable performance will be judged. What degree of accuracy or proficiency must the learner display? Whether the criteria are stated in qualitative or quantitative terms, they should be based on some real-world requirement. For example, how well must the machinist be able to operate a lathe in order to be a productive employee?

TABLE 2.1

The Helpful Hundred: Suggested performance terms

SUGGESTED PERFORMANCE TERMS					
Add	Compute	Drill	Label	Predict	State
Alphabetize	Conduct	Estimate	Locate	Prepare	Subtract
Analyze	Construct	Evaluate	Make	Present	Suggest
Apply	Contrast	Explain	Manipulate	Produce	Swing
Arrange	Convert	Extrapolate	Match	Pronounce	Tabulate
Assemble	Correct	Fit	Measure	Read	Throw
Attend	Cut	Generate	Modify	Reconstruct	Time
Bisect	Deduce	Graph	Multiply	Reduce	Translate
Build	Defend	Grasp (hold)	Name	Remove	Type
Carve	Define	Grind	Operate	Revise	Underline
Categorize	Demonstrate	Hit	Order	Select	Verbalize
Choose	Derive	Hold	Organize	Sketch	Verify
Classify	Describe	Identify	Outline	Ski	Weave
Color	Design	Illustrate	Pack	Solve	Weigh
Compare	Designate	Indicate	Paint	Sort	Write
Complete	Diagram	Install	Plot	Specify	
Compose	Distinguish	Kick	Position	Square	

Time and accuracy are meaningful dimensions in many objectives. How quickly must the observable behavior be performed? For example, should students be able to solve five quadratic equations in five minutes, or ten minutes? How accurate must a measurement be—to the nearest whole number, or within one-sixteenth of an inch, or plus or minus 1 millimeter?

Quantitative criteria for judging acceptable performance sometimes are difficult to define. For example, how can an English instructor state quantitative criteria for writing an essay or short story? He or she might stipulate that the student's work will be scored for development of theme, characterization, originality, or the like. A model story might be used as an example.

The important consideration in appraising your objectives is whether the intent of the objectives, regardless of their format, is communicated. If your objectives meet all the criteria in the "Appraisal Checklist" on page 42 but still do not communicate accurately your intentions to your colleagues and students, they are inadequate. The final judgment on any objectives must be determined by their usefulness to you and your learners. Guidelines for writing objectives are discussed in Gronlund's *How to Write and Use Instructional Objectives* and Mager's *Preparing Instructional Objectives* (see references at the end of this chapter).

Classification of Objectives

Classifying objectives is much more than an academic exercise for educational psychologists. It has practical value because the selection of instructional methods and media, as well as evaluation methods, depends on the types of objectives being pursued.

An objective may be classified according to the primary type of learning outcome at which it is aimed. Although there is a range of opinion on the best way to describe and organize types of learning, three categories (or *domains*), of learning are widely accepted: cognitive skills, affective skills, and motor skills. To these we add a fourth, interpersonal skills, because of the importance of such skills in teamwork.

In the **cognitive domain,** learning involves an array of intellectual capabilities that may be classified either as verbal/visual information or as intellectual skills. Verbal/visual skills require the learner to provide a specific response to relatively specific stimuli. They usually involve memorization or recall of facts. Intellectual skills, on the other hand, require thinking activity and the manipulation of information.

The **affective domain** involves feelings and values. Affective objectives range from, for example, stimulating interest in a school subject, to encouraging healthy social attitudes, to adopting a set of ethical standards (Figure 2.2).

In the **motor skill domain,** learning involves athletic, manual, and other such physical skills. Motor skill

FIGURE 2.2

The fruits of a lesson aimed at some poorly specified affective objectives.

Peanuts reprinted by permission of UFS, Inc.

objectives include capabilities ranging from simple mechanical operations to those entailing sophisticated neuromuscular coordination and strategy, as in competitive sports.

Learning in the **interpersonal domain** involves interaction among people. Interpersonal skills are people-centered skills that require the ability to relate effectively with others. Examples include teamwork, counseling techniques, administrative skills, salesmanship, discussion, and customer relations.

Objectives and Individual Differences

Objectives in any of the domains just discussed may, of course, be adapted to the abilities of individual learners. The stated philosophy of most schools and colleges is to help students fulfill their full potential. In a physical education class with students of mixed ability, for instance, the midsemester goal might be for all students to be able to complete a run of 100 meters outdoors, but the time standards might vary. For some, 12 seconds might be attainable; for many others, 16 seconds; and for some, 20 might be realistic. For a student with physical disabilities, it might be a major victory to move 10 meters in one minute. (See Figure 2.3.)

Objectives are not intended to limit what a student learns but rather to provide a minimum level of expected achievement. Serendipitous or incidental learning should be expected to occur (and should be encouraged) as students progress toward an objective. Each learner has a different field of experience (as discussed in Chapter 1), and each has different characteristics (as discussed earlier in this chapter). Because of such individual differences, incidental learning takes different forms

✔ APPRAISAL CHECKLIST

OBJECTIVES

	Appropriately stated	Partly stated	Missing
Audience			
Specifies the learner(s) for whom the objective is intended	❑	❑	❑
Behavior (action verb)			
Describes the capability expected of the learner following instruction	❑	❑	❑

- stated as a learner performance

- stated as observable behavior

- describes a real-world skill (versus mere test performance)

Conditions (materials and/or environment)			
Describes the conditions under which the performance is to be demonstrated	❑	❑	❑

- equipment, tools, aids, or references the learner may or may not use

- special environment conditions in which the learner has to perform

Degree (criterion)			
States, where applicable, the standard for acceptable performance	❑	❑	❑

- time limit

- range of accuracy

- proportion of correct responses required

- qualitative standards

Middle School Mathematics

State Objectives

The objectives for this lesson are as follows:

1. Given a bar, line, or circle graph, the seventh-grade mathematics student will be able to verbally present all the statistical or numerical information shown on the graph with 100% accuracy.
2. Given a set of data, the seventh-grade mathematics student will be able to accurately construct and produce a printout of a graph (bar, line, or circle) using a Macintosh LC and *Cricketgraph* according to established criteria.
3. Working in small groups of three or four, the seventh-grade mathematics students will be able to propose, discuss, and agree upon a topic for a group presentation. The presentation topic must incorporate data collection techniques (survey, observation, and/or interview) and the use of graphs (bar, line, and/or circle) to present statistical or numerical information.
4. Using a Macintosh LC and *Microsoft Works* and working in small groups, the seventh-grade mathematics students will be able to write and produce a printout of a written report regarding the data collection techniques associated with the topic of their presentation. Reports will be evaluated based on the quality of the survey, observation sheet, or interview form; the steps taken to collect the data; and the rationale for choosing the specific data collection technique.
5. The seventh-grade mathematics students will be able to present their chosen topic in front of the class. Performance will be evaluated based on general content accuracy, specific use of graphs, and cohesiveness of the presentation.

This Blueprint was developed by Mary Ann Ferkis, Purdue University. A computer template for a Blueprint is found in "The Classroom Link."

---

with different students. Class discussions and other kinds of student involvement in the instructional situation, therefore, should rarely be rigidly limited to a specific objective. Student involvement should allow for incidental learning to be shared and reinforced. Indeed, to foster incidental learning and provide for individual differences, it is sometimes advisable to have students specify some of their own objectives.

SELECT METHODS, MEDIA, AND MATERIALS

A systematic plan for *using* media certainly demands that the methods, media, and materials be *selected* systematically in the first place. The selection process has three steps: (1) deciding on the appropriate method for the given learning tasks, (2) choosing a media format that is suitable for carrying out the method, and (3) selecting, modifying, or designing specific materials within that media format.

Throughout the selection process, the school library media specialist can be a helpful partner in considering possible methods and media and in sorting through the particular materials available.

Choosing a Method

First, it would be overly simplistic to believe that there is one method that is superior to all others or that serves all learning needs equally well. As mentioned in Chapter 1, any given lesson will probably incorporate two or more methods to serve different purposes at different points in the progression of the lesson. For example, one might conduct a simulation activity to gain attention and arouse interest at the beginning of the lesson, then use a demonstration to present new information, and then arrange drill-and-practice activities to provide practice in the new skill. As indicated earlier in this chapter, teachers often structure assignments to allow students with different preferred learning styles to pursue their individual practice through different methods (e.g., having "abstract random" thinkers use a role-play simulation while "concrete sequential" thinkers use a lab manual for structured problem solving). It is beyond the scope of this book to give detailed guidelines on choosing methods.

FIGURE 2.3

When teaching learners who have disabilities, there may be as many different standards for each objective as there are individuals.

Origins of Performance Objectives

Ralph Tyler, a professor at Ohio State University, is generally considered to be the father of performance objectives as we know them today. Tyler's original interest was in test-item construction. His main contribution was to point out the importance of constructing test items based on behaviorally stated objectives that could be determined by analyzing the curriculum content.[a]

However, those in the programmed instruction movement, particularly Robert Mager, popularized the use of objectives by educators. Mager was a research scientist at Fort Bliss, Texas, working on a study to compare an experimental version of a course with an ongoing Army course. He drafted the objec-

tives for the course and insisted that they be signed by the proper authorities before instruction began. Later, while employed by Varian Associates in Palo Alto, California, he was involved in designing a one-day session on programmed instruction for school administrators. To teach them to discriminate between properly written and poorly written programmed instruction, Mager decided to write a branching program with a variety of instructional errors:

> But what topic to write on? I couldn't think of one. I stared at the typewriter, counted the leaves on the tree outside the window, and checked my fingernails. Nothing. Finally, while thinking about the nature of the target population (audience), I had a flash! I'll fix you, I said to myself. I'll write about a topic that will get you so emotionally aroused that you won't be able to see programming from the subject matter. And I began to type out a dogmatic (error-filled) branching program called "How to Write Objectives." In addition to such pedagogical niceties as branching the reader to pages that didn't exist, I berated them on the wrong answer pages with comments such as "How can you sit there and SAY a thing like that? You're lying and you know it." And "Now look here! I don't want to have any trouble with you. So read the little gem: 'How do YOU know? Have you ever tried seriously to specify exact objectives for an academic course? Or are you upset simply because what is being suggested sounds like work?'"[b]

Mager's initial program on writing objectives was duplicated, and it generated a great deal of discussion and provided practice in spotting good and bad characteristics in an instructional program. In Mager's words, "The day was a huge success."[c]

Later, Mager learned that at least two professors at local colleges were using his error-laden practice program as a text in their education courses, so he modified the original program and published *Preparing Objectives for Programmed Instruction* in 1961.[d] He and others quickly realized that his objectives could be applied to much more than just programmed learning, so the following year the book was released with the title *Preparing Instructional Objectives*.[e] The book is a classic in the field of education; now in its revised second edition, it has sold over two million copies. As Mager says, "If you're not sure where you're going, you're liable to end up someplace else—and not even know it."

[a]Ralph Tyler, "The Construction of Examinations in Botany and Zoology," *Service Studies in Higher Education,* Bureau of Educational Research Monograph, no. 15 (Columbus: Ohio State University, 1932).

Robert F. Mager

[b]Robert F. Mager, "Why I Wrote . . . ," *NSPI Journal* (October 1976), p. 4.

[c]Ibid.

[d]Robert F. Mager, *Preparing Objectives for Programmed Instruction* (Palo Alto, CA: Fearon, 1961).

[e]Robert F. Mager, *Preparing Instructional Objectives,* rev. 2d ed. (Belmont, CA: David S. Lake, 1984).

Choosing a Media Format

A **media format** is the physical form in which a message is incorporated and displayed. Media formats include, for example, flip charts (still images and text), slides (projected still images), audio (voice and music), film (moving images on screen), video (moving images on a TV set), and computer multimedia (graphics, text,

and moving images on a TV set). Each has different strengths and limitations in terms of the types of messages that can be recorded and displayed. Choosing a media format can be a complex task—considering the vast array of media available, the variety of learners, and the many objectives to be pursued. Over the years many different formulas have been proposed for simplifying the task. They are referred to as *media selection models,* and they usually take the form of flowcharts or checklists.

Within most media selection models the instructional situation or setting (e.g., large group, small group, or self-instruction), learner variables (e.g., reader, non-reader, or auditory preference), and the nature of the objective (e.g., cognitive, affective, motor skill, or inter-personal) must be considered against the presentational capabilities of each of the media formats (e.g., still visuals, motion visuals, printed words, or spoken words). Some models also take into consideration the capability of each format to give feedback to the learner.

The limitation of such media selection models is their emphasis on simplicity. Reducing the process to a short checklist may lead one to ignore some possibly important considerations.

Our approach in this book is to give you the tools to construct your own schema for selecting appropriate media formats. We accept the desirability of comparing the demands of the setting, learner characteristics, and objectives against the attributes of the various formats. But only you can decide how to weight these considerations: what options you have in terms of setting, which learner characteristics are most critical, and what elements of your objectives are most important in your own situation. You will need to balance simplicity and comprehensiveness in any schema you decide to employ.

Obtaining Specific Materials

Obtaining appropriate materials will generally involve one of three alternatives: (1) selecting available materials, (2) modifying existing materials, or (3) designing new materials. Obviously, if materials are already available that will allow your students to meet your objectives, these materials should be used to save both time and money. When the materials available do not completely match your objectives or are not entirely suitable for your audience, an alternative approach is to modify the materials. If this is not feasible, the final alternative is to design your own materials. Even though this is a more expensive and time-consuming process, it allows you to prepare materials to serve your students and meet your objectives.

Selecting Available Materials

The majority of instructional materials used by teachers and trainers are "off the shelf"—that is, ready-made and

---

CLOSE-UP

CONSUMER TESTING OF EDUCATIONAL PRODUCTS

As the Consumers Union provides objective evaluative information about household products to general consumers, the Educational Products Information Exchange (EPIE) Institute provides educational software evaluations to the education and training communities.

The EPIE Institute is a nonprofit agency that has been in operation since 1967. Its purpose is to "gather and disseminate descriptive and analytical information—along with empirical information on performance and effects on learners—

about instructional materials and systems." P. Kenneth Komoski has been executive director of EPIE since its founding.

EPIE accepts no advertising or commercial sponsorship of any kind. All income is derived from subscriptions, contract services from state and local education agencies, and grants. EPIE offers the following evaluation services to teachers and school systems.

The Education Software Selector (TESS) is a comprehensive database of educational software at every level from preschool to college. Over the years TESS has been available in a variety of formats, most recently on CD-ROM.

Eight major integrated instruction systems (or integrated learning systems) are evaluated in *The EPIE Report on Computer-Based Integrated Systems,* which draws on extensive research by experts in software evaluation and curriculum.

EPIE's Curriculum Analysis Services for Education (CASE) provides schools with a means of analyzing, designing, and aligning their stated curriculum outcomes, textbooks, and other instructional resources. A school's testing program can be compared with state and national programs and curriculum priorities. The service provides grade-by-grade printed reports that are useful for understanding and improving a school's curriculum and instructional program.

To learn more about the institute and its services, contact EPIE Institute, 103-3 W. Montauk Highway, Hampton Bays, NY 11946.

available from school, district, or company collections or other easily accessible sources. So, how do you go about making an appropriate choice from available materials?

Involving the Media Specialist. The media specialist can be an important resource for you. You may be in need of new materials for updating the content of a unit. The media specialist can tell you about materials housed in a local resource center or school library media center. Options should be raised and discussed. As the media specialist gains a better idea of your needs, arrangements can be made to contact area media collections (public, academic, or regional) to borrow potentially useful materials. Most school library media centers participate in regional cooperatives, which share materials. If you and the media specialist collaborate with other teachers in your school or district who desire similar materials, you may have an easier time in acquiring materials from national museums or organizations. Through the review of selection and evaluation guides involving an appointed group of teachers, new materials may be purchased for future use. Involving teachers in the preview process also allows for a comparison of ideas and available materials. Teachers tend to become more critical and selective as they increase their collective knowledge of media and material alternatives.

Surveying the Sources. You might survey some of the published media reference guides to get a general idea of what is available. Unfortunately, no single comprehensive guide exists for all audiovisual materials available in all media formats in all subjects; you may have to consult several sources.

There are three types of guides that can help you select media—comprehensive guides, selective guides, and evaluative guides. Comprehensive guides, such as "A-V Online" and *Bowker's Complete Video Guide,* help you identify the scope of possibilities. However, since they may include items of poor quality and difficult-to-locate titles, you should use these guides only to locate materials for preview. Always preview the materials before using them with students.

Selective guides, such as *Only the Best Computer Programs, Best Videos for Children and Young Adults,* and *The Elementary School Library Collection,* are a compilation of the "best" instructional materials. An advantage of these selective guides is that time has allowed the "best" to surface from a comparison of similar products on the market. A disadvantage is that during the time required for this process to take place, some items may have become outdated and newer items of good quality may not have been included.

Evaluative guides, such as *Booklist, School Library Journal, Choice,* and *Video Rating Guide,* are current and

keep you up to date about new materials. Although they are evaluative, they usually include just one person's opinion; that person's needs and audience may be different from yours.

One of the more comprehensive sources is a set of indexes published by NICEM (National Information Center for Educational Media). The two NICEM indexes are *Film & Video Finder* and *Audiocassette & Compact Disc Finder.* These do not include evaluations. "A-V Online" is a CD-ROM that lists thousands of educational, informational, and documentary materials along with their sources. The disc includes a variety of media formats, such as video, audio, film, filmstrips, slides, slide/tape programs, overhead transparencies, and multimedia kits (Figure 2.4).

If you are working in elementary or secondary education, you might consult several additional sources that cover a broad range of media formats, such as *Core Media Collection for Elementary Schools* and *Core Media Collection for Secondary Schools.* These books recommend specific audiovisual titles as core materials for elementary and secondary school media collections.

For general and adult audiences, a major guide is the *Reference List of Audiovisual Materials,* produced by the U.S. government. It describes all the training and educational materials produced by the armed forces and other government agencies that are available for general purchase. (See Appendix C for further details on all the reference sources discussed here.)

Beyond the sources just described, there are more specialized guides and indexes that are limited to specific media formats or specific subjects. These are too many and too diverse to list here, but some are men-

FIGURE 2.4

"A-V Online" compact disc. The complete NICEM indexes are on a single compact disc.

tioned in the individual chapters dealing with different media formats, and others are gathered under the heading "Specialized Information Sources" in Appendix C.

Selection Criteria.

The decision about whether to use a particular piece of instructional material depends on several factors. Recent research confirms the criticality of certain criteria in the appraisal of materials.[8] Among the questions to be asked about each specific piece of media are the following:

- Does it match the curriculum?
- Is it accurate and current?
- Does it contain clear and concise language?
- Will it arouse motivation and maintain interest?
- Does it provide for learner participation?
- Is it of good technical quality?
- Is there evidence of its effectiveness (e.g., field-test results)?
- Is it free from objectionable bias and advertising?
- Is a user guide or other documentation included?

Over the years, scholars have debated about what criteria should be applied in selecting materials. Studies have been conducted to quantify and validate various criteria. The net result is an understanding that different criteria are suitable for different situations. For example, a remedial reading teacher might decide to use a particular filmstrip primarily because its vocabulary level is just right, regardless of any other qualities. On the other hand, an elementary school teacher with a class that is very diverse ethnically might sort through materials to find those with a special sensitivity to racial and ethnic issues.

Other selection criteria vary with different media formats. Video and film materials, for example, raise the issue of the pace of presentation, whereas this would not be relevant for overhead transparencies. In examining computer-assisted instruction courseware, one would look for relevant practice and remedial feedback, but these would not be expected in a filmstrip. To account for these differences, this book provides a separate Appraisal Checklist for each media format. You will notice that certain criteria appear consistently in each checklist (they are all listed above). These are the criteria that we think have the securest basis in research and real-life experience. The Appraisal Checklists have been provided to give you a systematic procedure for judging the qualities of specific materials. But it is up to you to decide which criteria are most important to you in your own instructional setting.

The Instructor's Personal File.

Every instructor should develop a file of media references and appraisals for personal use. An excellent way for you to begin is to develop your own personal file of Appraisal Checklists by using "The Classroom Link." Each type of Appraisal Checklist in this text has a computer template on the software into which you can enter your own information for future reference.

Modifying Available Materials

If you cannot locate entirely suitable materials and media off the shelf, you might be able to modify what is available. This can be both challenging and creative. In terms of time and cost, it is a more efficient procedure than designing your own materials, although the type and extent of necessary modification will, of course, vary.

For example, perhaps the only available visual showing a piece of equipment being used in a junior high woodworking class is from a repair manual and contains too much detail and complex terminology. A possible solution to the problem would be to use the picture but modify the caption and simplify or omit some of the labels.

Or let's say there is just one video available that shows a needed visual sequence, but the audio portion of the video is inappropriate because it is at too high or too low a conceptual level or discusses inappropriate points. A simple solution in such a case would be to show the video with the sound turned off and provide the narration yourself. Another modification technique, which many instructors overlook, is to show just a portion of a video, stop the VCR, discuss what has been presented, then continue with another short segment followed by additional discussion. A similar approach may be used for sound filmstrips with audiotape. You can rerecord the narration and use the appropriate vocabulary level for your audience—and even change the emphasis of the visual material. If a transcript of the original narration is available, you probably will want to refer to it as you compose your own narration.

Modification also can be made in the audio portion of foreign language materials or English language materials used in a bilingual classroom. Narrations can be changed from one language to another or from a more advanced rendition of a foreign language to a simpler one.

Videocassette recorders now provide teachers with the opportunity to modify television programs that previously were available only as shown on the air. Programs may also be recorded off the air for replay later.[9] They can be shown at whatever time best suits the

---

[8]Lynn McAlpine and Cynthia Weston, "The Attributes of Instructional Materials," *Performance Improvement Quarterly* (Spring 1994), pp. 19–30.

[9]Broadcast materials vary in their recording restrictions. See Appendix B for general guidelines; consult a media specialist regarding specific programs.

instructional situation and to whatever student group(s) can profit most from viewing them.

One frequently modified media format is a set of slides with an audiotape. If the visuals are appropriate but the language is not, it is possible to change the language. It is also possible to change the emphasis of the narration. For example, an original audiotape might emphasize oceans as part of an ecosystem, whereas the teacher may want to use the slides to show various types of fish found in oceans. By rewriting the narration, the teacher could adapt the material to his or her purpose while using the same slides. Redoing the tape can also change the level of the presentation. A slide–tape presentation produced to introduce a new product could have three different audiotapes. One tape could be directed toward the customer, another could be prepared for the sales staff, and the third could be used for service personnel.

Some instructional games can be readily modified to meet particular instructional needs. It is possible to use a given game format and change the rules of play to increase or decrease the level of sophistication. Many instructional games require the players to answer questions. It is relatively easy for the teacher to prepare a new set of questions at a different level of difficulty or even on a new topic.

If you try out modified materials while they are still in more or less rough form, you can then make further modifications in response to student reaction until your materials meet your exact needs.

A word of caution about modifying commercially produced materials (and, indeed, about using commercial products in general): be sure your handling and use of such materials does not violate copyright laws and restrictions. If in doubt, check with your school administration or legal adviser. (Copyright laws and guidelines are discussed in Appendix B.)

Designing New Materials

It is easier and less costly to use available materials, with or without modification, than to start from scratch. There is seldom justification for reinventing the wheel. However, there may be times when your only recourse is to design your own materials. As is the case with selecting from available materials, certain basic elements must be considered when designing new materials:

- *Objectives.* What do you want your students to learn?
- *Audience.* What are the characteristics of your learners? Do they have the prerequisite knowledge and skills to use or learn from the materials?
- *Cost.* Is sufficient money available in your budget to meet the cost of supplies (film, audiotapes, etc.) you will need to prepare the materials?
- *Technical Expertise.* Do you have the necessary expertise to design and produce the kind of materials you

wish to use? If not, will the necessary technical assistance be available to you? Try to keep your design within the range of your own capabilities. Don't waste time and money trying to produce slick professional materials when simple inexpensive products will get the job done.
- *Equipment.* Do you have the necessary equipment to produce or use the materials you intend to design?
- *Facilities.* If your design calls for use of special facilities for preparation or use of your materials, are such facilities available?
- *Time.* Can you afford to spend whatever time necessary to design and produce the kind of materials you have in mind?

UTILIZE MEDIA AND MATERIALS

The next step in the ASSURE model is the use of media and materials by the students and teacher. The recommended utilization procedures are based on extensive research, beginning with military training research during World War II and continuing with current research. The general principles have remained remarkably constant. The main difference has to do with who is using the materials. The increased availability of media and the philosophical shift from teacher-centered to student-centered learning increases the likelihood that students will be using the materials themselves—as individuals or in small groups—rather than watching as the teacher presents them to a whole class.

The following "5 Ps" apply to either teacher-based or student-centered instruction.

Preview the Materials

No instructional materials should be used without prior screening. During the selection process you should determine that the materials are appropriate for your audience and objectives. Published reviews, distributor's blurbs, and colleagues' appraisals contribute information about the material. However, you should insist on previewing the materials yourself. Only a thorough understanding of the contents will enable you to use the media and materials to their full potential. (See Figure 2.5.)

For example, a high school math teacher ordered a videotape on fraction-to-decimal conversions. The information describing the videotape indicated that the content was exactly what students needed. Although the videotape arrived ten days before it was to be used, the math teacher didn't take time to preview it. When the videotape was shown, it met with giggles and laughs. The content was appropriate, but the videotape was addressed to an elementary school audience. The high school students were understand-

Middle School Mathematics

Select Methods, Media, and Materials

The teacher first selects a teaching method, followed by materials and equipment that are available at the school. She also modifies and develops other materials. The method she chooses to use is large-group instruction with small groups.

- *Overhead Projector.* The teacher needs to show the class some graphs. She selects the overhead projector to introduce the lesson topic. She will use transparencies with different types of graphs (bar, line, and circle) to review the concept of graphs with students. The overhead projector is always available in the classroom, transparencies are easy to prepare, and they may be reused throughout the course of the lesson.

- *Microsoft Works.* The teacher decides to use *Microsoft Works* because the students are familiar with how to use it.

- *Cricketgraph.* The teacher is familiar with several software packages containing graphing capabilities. She talked with other teachers to get their input regarding a program suitable for her activity. *Cricketgraph* was recommended by two of her colleagues. Consequently, she obtained *Cricketgraph* from the software library at the Instructional Materials Center. She evaluated it using the software "Appraisal Checklist" in Chapter 8. This particular software package meets all the activity needs, whereas others do not have specific necessary features (e.g., pie graphing capability).

- *Macintosh LC Computers.* The school has both IBM and Macintosh computers. Therefore, the teacher needed to choose between the two computers. Because she was not familiar with the Macintosh system, she evaluated it using the Appraisal Checklist "Computer Hardware," in Appendix A. She also considered the software that is available for each computer system. She selected the Macintosh LC because it was available to use during her class time and the software previously selected would run on the LC.

- *Video Camera and Tape Recorder.* The teacher has observed that the students enjoy watching/listening to videotapes and audiotapes of their work. They provide a motivational aspect to the assignment. She believes that this assignment lends itself nicely to this application. The video camera and tape recorder were selected to satisfy the objectives and assignment requirements. Additionally, the teacher likes to use the tapes to assist her in evaluating the students and for the students to evaluate themselves.

- *LCD Panel.* The teacher needs a way to show students how to make graphs on the computer. In addition, the students need to present their computer-generated graphs. The teacher could make handouts, use an opaque projector to show handouts, or use an overhead projector with an LCD panel. The teacher selected the use of the LCD panel because the cost of producing about a hundred handouts would be expensive, and using an opaque projector would require a darkened room when the students need to operate computers, whereas all the information could be effectively presented using an overhead projector and LCD panel.

- *Flip Chart.* The teacher plans to design graphs to be presented to the class. The graphs will contain titles and labeled axes. In addition, they must be easy to read. The Macintosh LC and *Cricketgraph* can be utilized to create graphs for the flip chart. A flip chart with laminated pages is chosen so that the students can write on the pages; their marks can be erased and the flip chart pages reused. The flip chart will also provide a change of pace from the overhead projector.

- *Handouts.* The teacher will create a set of handouts that coincide with the flip chart graphs. The Macintosh LC and *Cricketgraph* will be used to create the handouts. The instructor chooses to create a set of handouts so that each student will have a set of graphs on which to record notes for future reference. In addition, the handouts will keep all the students involved during the learning activity.

This Blueprint was developed by Mary Ann Ferkis, Purdue University. A computer template for a Blueprint is found in "The Classroom Link."

---

ably distracted by the level of the narration and the examples used.

In other cases, sensitive content may need to be eliminated or at least discussed prior to showing the materials to prevent student embarrassment or upset. In one case, an elementary teacher and her young students were horrified to find that an unpreviewed and ostensibly unobjectionable film on Canada's fur seals contained a sequence showing baby seals being cold-bloodedly clubbed to death by hunters.

Prepare the Materials

Next you need to prepare the media and materials to support the instructional activities you plan to use. This is true whether you are presenting the materials or your students are using them. The first step is to gather all the materials and equipment that you and the students will need. Determine in what sequence the materials and media will be used. What will you do with them as the presenter? What will the students do as learners? Some teachers keep a list of the materials and equipment needed for each lesson and an outline of the sequence in which the activities will be presented.

For a teacher-based lesson, you may want to practice using the materials and equipment (Figure 2.6). For a student-centered lesson, it is important that students have access to all the materials, media, and equipment that they will need. The teacher's role becomes one of facilitator. You should anticipate what materials will be needed by the students and be prepared to secure any additional materials needed.

Prepare the Environment

Wherever the learning is to take place—in the classroom, in a laboratory, at the media center, on the athletic field—the facilities will have to be arranged for proper student use of the materials and media. Certain factors are often taken for granted for any instructional situation—comfortable seating, adequate ventilation, climate control, suitable lighting, and the like. Some media require a darkened room, a convenient power source, and access to light switches. You should check that the equipment is in working order whether it is to be used by you or by your students. Arrange the facilities so that all the students can see and hear properly. (See Figure 2.7.) Arrange the seating so students can see each other if you want them to discuss a topic. (More specific information on audiovisual and computer setups can be found in Appendix A.)

Prepare the Learners

Research on learning tells us very clearly that what is learned from an activity depends highly on how the learners are prepared for the lesson. We know that in show business entertainers are obsessed with having the audience properly warmed up. Preparing the learners is just as important when you are providing a learning experience. (See Figure 2.8.)

A proper warm-up, from an instructional point of view, may be similar to one of the following:

- An introduction giving a broad overview of the content of the lesson
- A rationale telling how it relates to the topic being studied
- A motivating statement that creates a need to know by telling how the learner will profit from paying attention
- Cues directing attention to specific aspects of the lesson

Several of these functions—directing attention, arousing motivation, providing a rationale—apply whether the lesson is teacher based or student centered.

In some cases you may want to inform the students of the objectives. In certain cases, other steps will be needed. For example, unfamiliar vocabulary may need to be introduced, or special visual effects, such as time-lapse photography, may need explanation. Other preparation steps relevant to particular media will be discussed in later chapters.

Provide the Learning Experience

Now you are ready to provide the instructional experience. If the materials are teacher based, you should present like a professional. One term for this is **showmanship** (see AV Showmanship "Classroom Presentation Skills," on pages 52 and 53). Just as an actor or actress must control the attention of an audience, so must an instructor be able to direct attention in the classroom. Later chapters describe showmanship techniques relevant to each specific media format. (See Figure 2.9.)

If the experience is student centered, you must play the role of guide or facilitator, helping students to explore the topic, discuss the content, prepare materials for a portfolio, or present information to their classmates. Guidelines in some of the following chapters will assist students in the production of mediated materials.

REQUIRE LEARNER PARTICIPATION

Educators have long realized that active participation in the learning process enhances learning. In the early 1900s John Dewey urged reorganization of the curriculum and instruction to make student participation a

FIGURE 2.5
Preview the materials.

FIGURE 2.6
Prepare the materials.

FIGURE 2.7
Prepare the environment.

FIGURE 2.8
Prepare the learners.

FIGURE 2.9
Provide the learning experience.

GETTING READY

Planning

An effective presentation begins with careful and thorough planning. These guidelines apply to classroom instruction as well as more formal presentations.

1. *Analyze your learners.* What are their needs, values, backgrounds, knowledge levels, and misconceptions?
2. *Specify your objectives.* What should students do? How much time do you have to present? Limit your objectives and content to the time available.
3. *Specify benefits and rationale for the learners.* Why is the message important for them? If you cannot answer this question, perhaps you should not give the presentation.
4. *Identify the key points to cover.* Brainstorm the main ideas. Put them on note cards or stick-on notes. Most presentations will have from five to nine main points.
5. *Identify the subpoints and supporting details.* Again use note cards or stick-on notes. Try to limit yourself to five to nine subpoints for each main point.
6. *Organize the entire presentation in a logical and sequential order.* One organizing strategy is this:

Preview/Overview:	Tell them what you are going to tell them.
Present:	Tell them.
Review:	Tell them what you told them.

Rehearsing

1. Use key word notes, not a script. Print key words on an index card. Never read from a script; written language is different from spoken language.
2. Mentally run through the presentation to review each idea in sequence.
3. Do a stand-up rehearsal of your presentation. Try to practice in the room where you will be presenting or one similar to it.
4. Give a simulated presentation, idea for idea (not word for word), using all media.

5. Practice answers to questions you anticipate from the learners.
6. Videotape (or audiotape) yourself or have a colleague sit in on your rehearsal and give you feedback.

Setting Up

1. Check your equipment in advance of your presentation. Change the arrangements, if necessary, to meet your needs. When the equipment is in place, make sure everything operates properly.
2. For films, slides, and video projection, place the screen front and center. (See Figure A).
3. Place the overhead projector screen or flip chart at a 45-degree angle and near the corner of the room. Place the overhead screen to your right if you are right-handed. Place flip chart to your left if you are right-handed. Each should be reversed if you are left-handed. (See Figure B).
4. Position objects being studied in the front and center. Remove them when they are no longer being studied.

PRESENTING

Anxiety

1. Nervousness and excitement are normal before and during a presentation. Some anxiety and concern are important for an enthusiastic and dynamic presentation.
2. Proper planning and preparation should reduce your anxiety.
3. Harness your nervous energy and use it positively with body movement, supporting gestures, and voice projection.
4. Breathe slowly and deeply. Your cardiovascular system will slow down and ease the symptoms of anxiety.

Delivery

1. Stand up when presenting. When you stand, you and your message command more attention.
2. Face the learners. Place your feet 10 to 12 inches apart and distribute your weight equally on both feet. Your knees

Figure A

Figure B

should be unlocked, with hands out of your pockets and arms at your side. Facing the learners gives you eye contact with them and allows them to see your facial expressions.

3. When using chalkboards or wall charts, don't talk with your back to the learners. In this position you lose eye contact and may not be heard as well. Write on the chalkboard, then talk. (See Figure C).

4. Stand to one side of the lectern (if you must use one). Stepping to the side or in front of it places you on more personal terms with the learners. It allows you to be seen and to be more natural.

5. Move while you speak. Instructors who stand in one spot and never gesture experience tension. Move and gesture, but don't overdo it.

Voice

1. Use a natural, conversational style. Relate to your learners in a direct and personal manner.

2. Don't read your presentation. Don't read from your overheads or handouts. If part of your presentation is just information transfer, give the students a copy and let them read it.

3. Use vocal variety. A monotone is usually caused by anxiety (rehearsal should help this). Relax with upper and lower body movements.

4. Use a comfortable pace. When you are anxious, your rate of speaking usually increases. Relax and speak in a conversational tone.

5. Speak up so you can be heard in the back of the room. If you speak up, your rate will slow down—solving two problems! Ask people in the back row if your volume is appropriate.

6. A pause (silence) after a key point is an excellent way to emphasize it. The more important the idea, the more important it is for you to pause and let the words sink in before going on to the next idea.

Eye Contact

1. Don't speak until you have established eye contact with your audience. Eye contact will make your presentation similar to a one-on-one conversation.

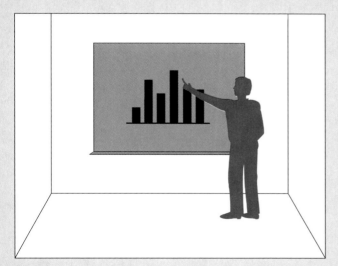

Figure C

2. An excellent way to keep your learners' attention is to look eye-to-eye at each person for at least three seconds. Don't quickly scan the learners or look at the back wall, screen, or notes for long periods of time.

3. Maintain eye contact with your learners. If you must write something on a flip chart, overhead, or chalkboard, stop talking while you write.

Gestures

1. Use natural gestures. Learn to gesture in front of a class as you would if you were having an animated conversation with a friend.

2. Don't put your hands in your pockets. Don't clasp your hands behind your back. Don't wring your hands nervously. Don't play with a pen or other object.

Visuals

1. Visuals help to attract and hold learners' interest. People like to see key words, diagrams, and drawings.

2. Reinforce and clarify verbal concepts with visuals. A picture is worth a thousand words.

3. Make key points memorable, and help the listener remember your message. Most people remember visuals longer than they remember words and numbers.

4. Visuals lose their effectiveness if overused. A guideline is to use about one visual per minute.

5. In designing visuals:
   - Use headlines only.
   - Eliminate unnecessary words.
   - Write large so words can be read from the back of the room.
   - Use drawings and diagrams whenever possible.
   - Limit to 36 words per visual (6 lines of 6 words each).

6. After using visuals, redirect learners' attention back to you:
   - Shut off the overhead projector when there is a lengthy explanation and there is no need for the audience to see the transparency. Don't turn the machine off and on so frequently that it becomes distracting (thirty seconds is a guideline).
   - Turn a flip-chart page to a blank one when you are finished referring to it. If the flip-chart pages have been prepared in advance, leave blank pages between each prepared sheet so the next prepared page will not show through.
   - Erase any writing on the chalkboard or whiteboard when it is no longer needed.
   - Break up slide presentations by inserting a black or translucent slide at points where an explanation is needed or where questions will be asked or answered.
   - Show or demonstrate an object by revealing it when needed and covering it when it is no longer in use. Otherwise, your audience will look at the object and be distracted from your presentation. Avoid passing an object around the audience. Instead, walk around the audience and show the object to everyone briefly and make it available at the end of the presentation.

Middle School Mathematics
Utilize Media and Materials
Preview the Materials

The teacher previews *Microsoft Works, Cricketgraph,* and some student-produced videotapes.

Prepare the Materials

The teacher makes a set of note cards outlining her lesson. In addition, she prepares the handouts and graphs on flip chart pages using *Cricketgraph* and the Macintosh LC. She also prepares transparencies for use with the overhead projector.

Prepare the Environment

Because the primary portion of the lesson is small-group work, the teacher arranges the student desks in the classroom to form table areas. This will prepare the students for the group work when they come into the room so the lesson will not need to be interrupted. Some of the lesson takes place in the computer lab. Because this activity takes several days to complete, each day may require specific equipment setups. Generally, the overhead projector and flip chart are used for introductory purposes only. The next phase requires the use of a computer lab to teach the students how to use *Cricketgraph*. Additionally, an overhead projector, LCD panel, and demonstration computer will also need to be set up. The regular classroom will be utilized for the students to conduct their small-group planning. During student presentations, the classroom will be used. There must be an overhead projector, an LCD panel, and a computer to view student work. In addition, a VCR with a monitor will be used for the students to play back their tapes for the class. After setting up the equipment, the teacher will also check that it is all in working order.

Prepare the Learners

To prepare the students, the teacher presents the overall plan and objectives for the lesson. Each student receives a handout describing the small-group activity. In addition, the evaluation procedures are given to each student. Important aspects of the requirements and evaluation standards are presented using the overhead projector.

Provide the Learning Experience

During the introductory phases of this lesson, the teacher presents materials using the overhead projector, an LCD panel, computer, flip chart, and VCR. General showmanship techniques and those specific to each of these media are followed:

- *General Techniques.* The only place in the classroom with a screen is front and center. It is used for the overhead projector. When presenting information on the flip chart, the teacher places the chart in the front and to the left of center, since she is right-handed. The VCR and monitor are located to the right of the screen.
- *Overhead Projector.* Use an outline to introduce and summarize the material. Turn off the projector when not referring to what is on it. Place notes for each transparency on its frame or cover sheet. Use a pencil as a pointer. Mask unwanted information.
- *Flip Chart.* Use lettering and figures large enough for all to see. Face the class when speaking. Stand out of the students' line of vision. Secure all pages firmly to the flip chart. Provide summary sheets at the end instead of flipping back through the pages.
- *Video.* Check lighting, seating, and volume. List on chalkboard the main points to be covered. Preview new vocabulary. Be a good role model—watch the program yourself. Provide appropriate follow-up activities and discussion.

This Blueprint was developed by Mary Ann Ferkis, Purdue University. A computer template for a Blueprint is found in "The Classroom Link."

---

central part of the process. Later, in the 1950s and 1960s, experiments employing behaviorist approaches demonstrated that instruction providing for constant reinforcement of desired behaviors is more effective than instruction in which responses are not reinforced.

More recently, cognitive theories of learning, which focus on internal mental processes, have also supported the principle that effective learning demands active manipulation of information by learners. Gagné has concluded that there are several necessary conditions for effective learning of each type of objective; the one condition that pertains to all objectives is practice of the desired skill.[10]

The implication for designers and instructors is clear. The most effective learning situations are those that require learners to perform activities that build toward the objective. The form of the participation may include practicing new spelling or vocabulary words, solving math problems on a worksheet, rehearsing a basketball play, or creating an original product, such as a term paper. Responses may be either observable or unobservable. An example of an observable performance is manipulation of task cards illustrating the stages of mitosis. An unobservable performance is silent repetition of phrases heard on a French language tape. In all cases, the learner should receive feedback on the correctness of his or her response.

Some media formats lend themselves to participation more than others, at least on the surface. For example, student response to projected still pictures is easier to manage than response to a motion picture. Learners can read or elaborate on captions in filmstrips, discuss what is on the screen, or refer to other materials while the image is held on the screen. (Substitution of sound filmstrips for silent ones tends to weaken this advantage.)

[10]Robert M. Gagné, *The Conditions of Learning,* 4th ed. (New York: Holt, Rinehart and Winston, 1985).

However, learners can also participate in and respond to the showing of a film. For example, May and Lumsdaine demonstrated that overt responses (vocalized verbal responses) during a film improved learning. The same authors cited research demonstrating that psychomotor skills are learned better if practiced while the skills are being performed in a film.[11] Overt written responses during the showing of a film (or any other fixed-pace medium) have been shown to facilitate learning, unless the responses are so involved that students are prevented from watching the film.

Immediate confirmation of a correct response is particularly important when working with students of lower-than-average abilities. For such students, evidence of immediate success can be a strong motivating force for further learning.

Discussions, short quizzes, and application exercises can provide opportunities for practice and feedback during instruction. Follow-up activities can provide further opportunities. Teacher guides and manuals written to accompany instructional materials often suggest techniques and activities for eliciting and reinforcing student responses.

Research on the internationally renowned television series "Sesame Street" and "Electric Company" demonstrates impressively the importance of following up a media presentation with practice activities. Research on "Sesame Street" showed that frequent viewers not only learned the specific skills presented but also had higher scores on a test of verbal IQ and more positive attitudes about school. Johnston pointed out, though, that "parental encouragement and supplementary materials were essential to achieving the effects observed."[12] In the case of "Electric Company," children with low reading ability who watched the programs in school under teacher supervision showed significant reading improvement. Johnston concluded that "learning definitely did occur when viewing was insured, and when teachers supplied additional learning materials and helped the children to rehearse the materials presented on television."

---

[11]Mark A. May and A. A. Lumsdaine, *Learning from Films* (New Haven, CT: Yale University Press, 1958).

[12]Jerome Johnston, *Electronic Learning: From Audiotape to Videotape* (Hillsdale, NJ: Lawrence Erlbaum, 1987).

EVALUATE AND REVISE

The final component of the ASSURE model for effective learning is evaluation and revision. Often the most frequently misused of the lesson design process, evaluation and revision is an essential component to the development of quality instruction. There are many purposes for evaluation. Often the only form seen in education is the paper-and-pencil test, claimed to be used for assessment of student achievement. We will discuss two purposes here: evaluating learner achievement and evaluating media and methods.

Although ultimate evaluation must await completion of the instructional unit, evaluation is an ongoing process. Evaluations are made before, during, and after instruction; for example, before instruction, learner characteristics are measured to ensure that there is a fit between existing student skills and the methods and materials you intend to use. In addition, materials should be appraised prior to use. During instruction, evaluation may take the form of student practice of a desired skill, or it may consist of a short quiz or self-evaluation. Evaluation during instruction usually has a diagnostic purpose; that is, it is designed to detect and correct learning/teaching problems and difficulties in the instructional process that may interfere with attainment of objectives.

Evaluation is not the end of instruction. It is the starting point of the next and continuing cycle in our

FIGURE 2.10
Practicing a desired skill promotes the effectiveness of the learning experience.

Middle School Mathematics

Require Learner Participation

Large-Group Activities

As a review, introduction, and practice exercise, each student in the class reads and interprets a graph (bar, line, or circle) presented to him/her on the flip chart. Each student writes his/her findings directly on the laminated flip chart page. Using this method the teacher provides feedback and reinforcement to each individual in the class. During the "mini presentations" the class has handouts that include the same graphs as the flip chart. This enables them to have a record of the exercises for future reference. In addition, it involves the entire class in the learning process. The students learn how to utilize the computer lab to practice construction and produce printouts of graphs (bar, line, circle, and others if appropriate) with *Cricketgraph.*

Small-Group Activities

Following the large-group activity, the students participate in a small-group activity. Assignments require the students to collect, interpret, and present basic data. Initially, the groups work together to propose, discuss, and agree upon a topic for a group presentation. The presentation topic must incorporate data collection techniques (survey, observation, and/or interview) and the use of graphs to present numerical information.

The students collect data in their school for a small-group presentation. The groups choose whether to collect their data through surveys, observations, or personal interviews. Each group uses *Microsoft Works* to write and produce a written report regarding the data collection techniques associated with the topic of their presentation.

Survey

The small groups choosing to conduct a survey could use *Microsoft Works* to create and write their survey. The group must submit an audiotape of each member administering the survey to a group or individual.

Observation

The small groups electing to use observation techniques use *Microsoft Works* to create and write an observation sheet to use when they make their observations. The group must submit a videotape of each member conducting an observation.

Personal Interview

The small groups choosing to conduct personal interviews use *Microsoft Works* to create and write an interview form to use when they conduct their interviews. The groups must also submit a videotape or an audiotape of each member conducting an interview.

In each case the school library media specialist arranges time in the library or in another classroom to help the groups with the audiotapes and videotapes. During the group presentations, the teacher provides the equipment necessary to play back each group's audio- and videotapes.

Reporters from each group present their data on a chart or a graph. The students must accurately construct and produce a printout of a graph (bar, line, or circle) using *Cricketgraph.* During the group presentations, the teacher prepares the equipment necessary to view each group's graphs using an LCD panel and overhead projector. The groups are required to accurately read, interpret, and verbally present all the statistical information shown on their graphs.

This Blueprint was developed by Mary Ann Ferkis, Purdue University.
A computer template for a Blueprint is found in "The Classroom Link."

---

systematic ASSURE model for effective use of instructional media.

Evaluation of Learner Achievement

The ultimate question in the instructional process is whether the students have learned what they were supposed to learn. Can they display the capabilities specified in the original statement of objectives? The first step in answering this question was taken near the beginning of the ASSURE process, when you formulated your objectives, including a criterion of acceptable performance. You now want to assess whether the learner's skill meets that criterion.

The method of evaluating achievement depends on the nature of the objective. Some objectives call for relatively simple cognitive skills—for example, recalling Ohm's law, distinguishing adjectives from adverbs, describing a company's absence policy, or summarizing the principles of the Declaration of Independence.

Objectives such as these lend themselves to conventional written tests or oral examinations. Other objectives may call for process-type behaviors (e.g., conducting an orchestra, performing a forward roll on a balance beam, operating a metal lathe, or solving quadratic equations), the creation of products (e.g., a sculpture, a written composition, a window display, or an account ledger), or an exhibit of attitudes (e.g., tolerating divergent political opinions, appreciating expressionist painting, observing safety procedures while on the assembly line, or contributing money to community charities).

The evaluation procedures should correspond to the objectives stated earlier in the ASSURE model. For example, assume the objective is "Given a diagram of the human trachea, the student nurse will explain a bronchocele, describing cause and treatment." A possible test question would be "What is a bronchocele? Describe the cause and treatment in your answer."

In broadcaster training, the objective might be "Given the pertinent information, the student will write a 20-second and a 30-second radio news story using appropriate radio news style." The evaluation could be

"Using the attached wire service copy, compose a 20-second radio news story consistent with the CNN style manual."

For military training, an objective could be "With the aid of a topographic map, the officer will call for field artillery fire using the four essential items of information in prescribed military sequence." An oral test could ask: "Tell me how you would call for artillery fire upon point X on the accompanying topographic map."

Capabilities of the process, product, or attitude type could be assessed to some extent by means of written or oral tests. But such test results would be indirect and weak evidence of how well the learner has mastered the objectives. More direct and stronger evidence would be provided by observing the behavior in action. This implies setting up a situation in which the learner can demonstrate the new skill and the instructor can observe and judge it. (See Figure 2.11.)

In the case of process skills, a performance checklist can be an effective, objective way of recording your observations, as shown with the checklist for driving skills. Other types of activities that can be properly evaluated through performance checklists are sales techniques, telephone-answering skills, and face-to-face customer relations. During the instructional process these types of activities may need to be evaluated in a simulated situation, with other learners, or with the instructor role playing the customer or client.

Attitudes are admittedly difficult to evaluate. For some attitudinal objectives, long-term observation may be required to determine whether the goal has really been attained. In day-to-day instruction we usually have to rely on what we can observe here and now, however limited that may be. A commonly used technique for making attitudes more visible is the attitude scale, an example of which is shown regarding biology. A number of other suggestions for attitude measurement can

be found in Robert Mager's *Developing Attitude Toward Learning* (see references at end of this chapter).

For product skills, a product rating checklist can guide your evaluation of critical subskills and make qualitative judgments more objective, as in the accompanying example regarding welding. Other types of products that lend themselves to evaluation by a rating scale include pastry from a bakery, compositions in an English course, and computer programs. (See Figure 2.12.)

Evaluation of Media and Methods

Evaluation also includes assessment of instructional media and methods. Were your instructional materials effective? Could they be improved? Were they cost-effective in terms of student achievement? Did your presentation take more time than it was really worth? Particularly after first use, instructional materials need to be evaluated to determine whether future use, with or without modification, is warranted. The results of your evaluation should be entered on an Appraisal Checklist. Did the media assist the students in meeting the objectives? Were they effective in arousing student interest? Did they provide meaningful student participation?

Class discussions, individual interviews, and observation of student behavior should be used to evaluate instructional media and methods (Figure 2.13). Failure to attain objectives is, of course, a possible indication that something is wrong with the instruction. But analyzing student reaction to your instructional methods can be helpful in more subtle ways. Student–teacher discussion may indicate that your audience would have

FIGURE 2.12
The ability to create a product should be evaluated by the quality of the product itself.

FIGURE 2.11
A performance-type skill should be judged by observation.

Middle School Mathematics
Evaluate and Revise
Evaluation of Learner Achievement

The following rating form is used to evaluate the students' knowledge of the "Information Statistics" unit.

Collecting Data (20 points)

- Did each member of your group collect data at least once and record this on tape?
- Did your group create and write a data collection sheet (survey, observation, or interview)?
- Did your report accurately explain the steps taken to collect your data?
- Did your report state a sound rationale for choosing the specific collection technique?

Presenting the Data (20 points)

- Are your graphs easy to read?
- Do your graphs have an appropriate title?
- Are the components of your graphs labeled correctly?
- Did you provide a printout of your graphs?

Presentation Style (40 points)

- Did your group introduce your presentation topic and tell why you chose it?
- Did you explain your data collection method and give your rationale for its choice?
- Did you play back your data collection tape?
- Did you show your results in the form of graphs?
- Did your group leave time for questions?
- Did your group answer pertinent questions?

Interpretation (20 points)

- Did your group correctly read and interpret the graphs?
- Did your group explain all the statistical information shown on the graph?

Evaluation of Media and Methods

To successfully evaluate the media and methods utilized, the teacher conducts debriefing activities after teaching the stu-dents how to make graphs and after the student presentations. In addition, she talks informally with students during the entire process.

The teacher conducts a debriefing immediately following the graph-making session. She addresses any issues that may have arisen during the instruction. Additionally, she provides time for the students to vent their frustrations and to share their excitement. Then, she reminds the students of the purpose of the activity. She also invites comments that address the importance of learning how to make graphs using spreadsheet programs. Specific examples illustrating possible future uses for the skill are also discussed. The primary purpose of this debriefing session is to determine whether the students are comfortable making graphs using the computer.

The teacher conducts a second debriefing session after all the students have made their presentations. She specifically addresses each phase of the instruction. First, the review/introduction phase utilizing the mini-presentation with the flip chart is discussed. Second, the graph-making session is reevaluated. Third, the planning phase of the presentation is reviewed. Fourth, the use of the computer to develop reports is discussed. Fifth and finally, the student presentations are addressed. Student reactions to each of these phases is critical for possible revisions. In addition, evaluation techniques for learner achievement is discussed. To complete the debriefing exercise, the teacher asks the students to write the purpose of the project. In addition, they are asked to write whether they liked the activities and why or why not.

Evaluation of Overall Instruction

The students and teacher complete a teacher-developed form for an overall evaluation of learner achievement, media, and methods. The student average is compared with the teacher's results. For items that appear discrepant, the teacher will address the need for revision in her choice of learning activities, media selections, methods, and evaluation materials.

This Blueprint was developed by Mary Ann Ferkis, Purdue University.

A computer template for a Blueprint is found in "The Classroom Link."

FIGURE 2.13
Analysis of student reactions to lessons is an integral part of the instructional process.

Performance Checklist: Driving Skills

Name_____Class _____

Check yes or no with an X in the appropriate column.

Did the student   **Yes   No**

1. Fasten seat belt before starting car?   ___   ___
2. Use the nine o'clock and three o'clock hand position
   on steering wheel?   ___   ___
3. Drive with the flow of traffic yet stay within the speed limit? ___   ___
4. Come to full and complete stops at stop signs?   ___   ___
5. Keep at least a two-second interval behind the vehicle
   ahead?   ___   ___
6. Stay in the proper driving lane—not cross center line?   ___   ___
7. Obey all traffic signs and signals?   ___   ___
8. Negotiate all turns properly (according to driving manual)?   ___   ___
9. Avoid excessive conversation with passengers?   ___   ___
10. Display courtesy to other drivers?   ___   ___

Instructor's Name _____ Date _____

Attitude Scale: Biology

Each of the statements below express a feeling toward biology. Please rate each statement on the extent to which you agree. For each, you may (A) strongly agree, (B) agree, (C) be undecided, (D) disagree, or (E) strongly disagree.

A	B	C	D	E
Strongly Agree	Agree	Undecided	Disagree	Strongly Disagree

____ 1. Biology is very interesting to me.

____ 2. I don't like biology, and it scares me to have to take it.

____ 3. I am always under a terrible strain in biology class.

____ 4. Biology is fascinating and fun.

____ 5. Learning biology makes me feel secure.

____ 6. Biology makes me feel uncomfortable, restless, irritable,
        and impatient.

____ 7. In general, I have a good feeling toward biology.

____ 8. When I hear the word *biology*, I have a feeling of dislike.

____ 9. I approach biology with a feeling of hesitation.

____ 10. I really like biology.

____ 11. I have always enjoyed studying biology in school.

____ 12. It makes me nervous to even think about doing a biology experiment.

____ 13. I feel at ease in biology and like it very much.

____ 14. I feel a definite positive response to biology; it's enjoyable.

PRODUCT RATING CHECKLIST: Welding

Name _____ **Date** _____

Rate the welded product by checking the appropriate boxes. Add comments if you wish.

Base metal(s) _____ Filler metal(s) _____

Profile:	Excellent	Very Good	Good	Fair	Poor	**Workmanship:**	Excellent	Very Good	Good	Fair	Poor
Convexity	☐	☐	☐	☐	☐	Uniform appearance	☐	☐	☐	☐	☐
(1/32-inch maximum)	☐	☐	☐	☐	☐	Arc strikes	☐	☐	☐	☐	☐
Fusion on toe	☐	☐	☐	☐	☐	Bead width	☐	☐	☐	☐	☐
Overlap	☐	☐	☐	☐	☐	Bead start	☐	☐	☐	☐	☐
Amount of fill	☐	☐	☐	☐	☐	Bead tie-in	☐	☐	☐	☐	☐
						Bead termination	☐	☐	☐	☐	☐
Overall Evaluation:						Penetration	☐	☐	☐	☐	☐
						Amount of spatter	☐	☐	☐	☐	☐

Evaluator Comments:

---

preferred independent study to your choice of group presentation. Or perhaps viewers didn't like your selection of overhead transparencies and feel they would have learned more if a videotape had been shown. Your students may let you know, subtly or not so subtly, that your own performance left something to be desired.

You may solicit learner input on the effectiveness of specific media, such as a CD or videotape. You may design your own form or use one similar to the "Learner Reaction Form" shown here.

Conversations with the school media specialist concerning the value of specific media in an instructional unit will help to alert him or her to the need for additional instructional materials to improve the lesson in the future.

Learner Reaction Form

User _____ Date _____

		Clear			**Unclear**	
1.	The objectives of this lesson were	5	4	3	2	1
		Very interesting			**Dull**	
2.	The learning activities were	5	4	3	2	1
		Adequate			**Inadequate**	
3.	The scope (coverage) was	5	4	3	2	1
		Difficult			**Easy**	
4.	The lesson was	5	4	3	2	1
		Excellent			**Poor**	
5.	Overall, I consider this lesson	5	4	3	2	1

A Template for Planning

This is a description of the instructional situation.

Analyze Learners

General Characteristics

This is a description of the class as a whole (e.g., age, grade, etc.).

Entry Competencies

This is a description of the types of knowledge expected of the learners.

Learning Styles

This is a description of the learning stylistic preferences of individual members of the class.

State Objectives

Objectives are descriptions of the learning outcomes and are written using the ABCD format.

Select Methods, Media, and Materials

All the methods, media, and materials that are essential to the lesson need to be included.

Rationale

It is important to consider why certain media have been selected.

Evaluation of Commercial Materials

When using commercial materials, Appraisal Checklists are valuable.

Utilize Materials

Preview Materials

It is essential to know the materials prior to teaching with them.

Prepare the Materials

Experience using the materials is important.

Prepare the Environment

Setting up the instructional environment helps to make the learning experience valuable.

Prepare the Learners

Knowing what is expected of them helps learners to be involved in the learning.

Provide the Learning Experience

The actual presentation needs to be considered.

Require Learner Participation

A description of the activities helps to provide guidance to the instructor and learners.

Evaluate and Revise

Evaluation of Learners

How will the objectives be "tested"?

Evaluation of Instruction (including media and materials)

To ensure quality instruction, it is important to evaluate the experience for future planning.

_____

A computer template for a Blueprint is found in "The Classroom Link."

Revision

The final step of the instructional cycle is to sit back and look at the results of your evaluation data gathering. Where are there discrepancies between what you intended to happen and what did happen? Did student achievement fall short on one or more of the objectives? How did students react to your instructional methods and media? Are you satisfied with the value of the materials you selected? If your evaluation data indicate shortcomings in any of these areas, now is the time to go back to the faulty part of the plan and revise it. The model works, but only if you constantly use it to upgrade the quality of your instruction.

REFERENCES

Print References

Media Selection and Use

Arredondo, Lani. *How to Present Like a Pro.* McGraw-Hill, 1991.

Cartier, Francis. "Words about Media Selection." *Performance and Instruction* (January 1992): 9–12.

Cooper, Colleen R., and Anderson, William A. "How to Increase Classroom Participation." *Instructional Innovator* (January 1984): 49–52.

Fortune, Jim C., and Hutson, Barbara A. "Does Your Program Work? Strategies for Measuring Change." *Educational Technology* (April 1983): 38–41.

Frederick, Peter J. "The Lively Lecture—8 Variations." *College Teaching* (Spring 1986): 43–50.

Gronlund, Norman E. *How to Write and Use Instructional Objectives.* 5th ed. Englewood Cliffs, NJ: Merrill/Prentice Hall, 1995.

Kemp, Jerrold E., and Smellie, Don C. *Planning, Producing, and Using Instructional Technologies.* 7th ed. New York: HarperCollins, 1994.

McAlpine, Lynn, and Weston, Cynthia. "The Attributes of Instructional Materials." *Performance Improvement Quarterly* (Spring, 1994): 19–30.

Mager, Robert F. *Developing Attitude Toward Learning.* 2d ed. Belmont, CA: David S. Lake, 1984.

———. *Making Instruction Work.* Belmont, CA: David S. Lake, 1988.

———. *Measuring Instructional Results.* 2d ed. Belmont, CA: David S. Lake, 1984.

———. *Preparing Instructional Objectives.* Rev. 2d ed. Belmont, CA: David S. Lake, 1984.

Mandel, S. *Effective Presentation Skills: A Practical Guide for Better Speaking.* Los Altos, CA: Crisp Publications, 1987.

Martinetz, Charles F. "A Checklist for Course Evaluation." *Performance and Instruction* (June–July 1986): 12–19.

Poirot, James L. "Assessment and Evaluation of Technology in Education—The Teacher as Researcher." *Computing Teacher* (August–September 1992): 9–10.

Reiser, Robert A., and Gagné, Robert M. *Selecting Media for Instruction.* Englewood Cliffs, NJ: Educational Technology Publications, 1983.

Romiszowski, A. J. *The Selection and Use of Instructional Media.* 2d ed. New York: Nichols, 1988.

Select Student Instructional Materials. 2d ed. Columbus, OH: National Center for Research in Vocational Education, 1988.

Teague, Fred A., Rogers, Douglas W., and Tipling, Roger N. *Technology and Media.* Dubuque, IA: Kendall/Hunt, 1994.

Volker, Roger, and Simonson, Michael. *Technology for Teachers.* 6th ed. Dubuque, IA: Kendall/Hunt, 1995

Instructional Design

Briggs, Leslie J., Gustafson, Kent L., and Tillman, Murray H., eds. *Instructional Design: Principles and Applications.* 2d ed. Englewood Cliffs, NJ: Educational Technology Publications, 1991.

Cranton, Patricia. *Planning Instruction for Adult Learners.* Toronto: Wall and Thompson, 1989.

Dick, Walter, and Carey, Lou. *The Systematic Design of Instruction.* 3d ed. New York: Scott Foresman, 1990.

Kemp, Jerrold E., Morrison, Gary R., and Ross, Steven M. *Designing Effective Instruction.* Englewood Cliffs, NJ: Merrill/Prentice Hall, 1994.

West, Charles K., Farmer, James A., and Wolff, Phillip M. *Instructional Design: Implications from Cognitive Science.* Englewood Cliffs, NJ: Prentice-Hall, 1991.

Learning Styles

Armstrong, Thomas. *Multiple Intelligences in the Classroom.* Alexandria, VA: ASCD, 1994.

Campbell, Melvin, and Burton, VirLynn. "Learning in Their Own Style." *Science and Children* (April 1994): 22–24, 39.

DeBello, Thomas C. "Comparison of Eleven Major Learning Styles Models: Variables, Appropriate Populations, Validity of Instrumentation, and the Research Behind Them." *Reading, Writing and Learning Disabilities* (1990): 202–222.

Dunn, Rita, Beaudry, Jeffrey S., and Klavas, Angela. "Survey of Research on Learning Styles." *Educational Leadership 46* (March 1989): 50–58.

Dunn, Rita, and Dunn, Kenneth. *Teaching Elementary Students Through Their Individual Learning Styles: Practical Applications for Grades 3–6.* Boston: Allyn and Bacon, 1992.

Audiovisual References

Can We Please Have That the Right Way Round? Northbrook, IL: Video Arts. n.d. 16mm film or videocassette. 22 minutes.

How to Make a Presentation. Calgary, Alberta: Access Network, 1988. Videocassette. 30 minutes.

Individualizing Instruction. Beacon Films, 1983. Videocassette. 27 minutes.

Making Your Case. Northbrook, IL: Video Arts, n.d. 16 mm film or videocassette. 25 minutes.

Measuring Instructional Effectiveness. Herndon, VA: Industrial Training Corp., n.d. Videocassette. 30 minutes.

Media Utilization. Norwood, MA: Beacon Films. 1983. Videocassette. 29 minutes.

Non-Verbal Communication. Santa Monica, CA: Salenger Educational Media, 1982. 16mm film. 17 minutes.

Novel Techniques for Evaluating Media. Boulder, CO: University of Colorado, 1982. Audiocassette.

Patterns for Instruction. Beverly Hills, CA: Roundtable Films, 1981. Videocassette and leader's guide. 21 minutes.

Principles for Learning and Instruction. Norwood, MA: Beacon Films, 1983. Videocassette. 29 minutes.

Teaching and Testing for Results. Columbia, SC: Educational Program Service, 1983. Videocassette. 30 minutes.

Teaching to Objectives, Parts 1 and 2. Columbia, SC: Educational Program Service, 1983. Videocassettes. 30 minutes each.

VISUAL PRINCIPLES

Since the earliest days of schooling, education scholars have lamented teachers' overreliance on words as communication vehicles. Pictures can clarify complex ideas, make them easier to remember, and provoke emotional responses. In many schools, students are being evaluated on the basis of portfolios that document what they can do in language arts, science, social studies, and other skill areas. Portfolios often include such items as student-produced illustrated books, videos, or audiovisual presentations.

Students vary in their abilities to interpret visuals and to create their own visual messages; the goal of visual literacy education is to enhance these abilities. You can improve your own ability to create instructionally effective visuals by following some basic visual design principles and processes. These can be applied to everyday design tasks, such as creating bulletin boards and designing computer screens.

KNOWLEDGE OBJECTIVES

1. Describe the roles that visuals play in instruction.
2. Define *visual literacy* in your own words.
3. Identify two general strategies that may be used to teach visual literacy.
4. Describe the factors that influence students' decoding of visuals.
5. Describe the factors that influence students' encoding of visuals.
6. State in your own words the goals that good visual design aims to achieve.
7. Regarding the visual design process, characterize the qualities that a designer would look for in the individual visual and verbal elements of the design, including elements that add appeal.
8. Describe the factors that a designer would manipulate in establishing an underlying pattern to the design.
9. Describe the factors that a designer would manipulate in arranging the visual and verbal elements to achieve clear communication, reduce effort in interpreting, increase active engagement, and focus viewer attention.
10. List various roles that color can play in enhancing the impact of visual displays.
11. Describe the interaction of subject, light, camera, and film in the photography process.
12. Compare the advantages and limitations of single-lens reflex (SLR), "point-and-shoot," and digital cameras.
13. State in your own words the most basic guidelines for taking effective photos.
14. Suggest ways of using students' media portfolios to evaluate their achievement.

APPLICATION OBJECTIVES

1. Plan a set of learning activities to improve the visual literacy skills of learners you now work with or might work with in the future.
2. Critique a bulletin board or other display using the "Visual Design Checklist" in this chapter. Attach a description of audience, objectives, and the features of the display that help achieve the goals of visual design.
3. Design a series of computer screens related to an instructional purpose exemplifying the principles in "How to . . . Design a Computer Screen." Attach a description of audience, objectives, and features that help achieve the goals of visual design.
4. Critique either a display or a computer lesson using the criteria described in "Visual Design Checklist" and "How To . . . Design a Computer Screen."
5. Critique a series of photographs, taken by you or someone else, in terms of visual composition and photographic technique.

LEXICON

referent
iconic
visual literacy
sans serif
optical spacing

alignment
rule of thirds
complementary colors
analogous colors
proximity

directional
figure-ground contrast
storyboarding
charge-coupled device
 (CCD)

shutter
viewfinder
digital camera
portfolio

Significant contributions to this chapter were made by Elizabeth Boling, MFA, and Dennis Pett, EdD, both of Indiana University.

Because so much learning involves visual imagery, the design and use of visuals in instruction is worthy of separate consideration. Most of the media discussed in this text—transparencies, slides, video programs, computer courseware, multimedia—have a visual component. The rapidly increasing visual capabilities of computers and digital telecommunications can only heighten the importance of visuals in education. Unfortunately, in the past teachers and materials designers have too often used this valuable visual capability primarily to show pictures of . . . WORDS! (See Figure 3.1.) The overemphasis on words has contributed to the failure of formal education to reach its ideal of universal success. We know that some students learn more readily through visual imagery, and even those who are verbal learners need visual supports to grasp certain types of concepts.

This chapter examines the functions and characteristics of visuals and visual literacy; it presents guidelines for designing and using visuals effectively. Specific applications are suggested for teacher-made materials such as bulletin board displays and computer screens.

THE ROLES OF VISUALS IN INSTRUCTION

Attempts to make broad generalizations about the role of visuals in learning invariably fail to yield simple answers. For example, a major synthesis of research studies comparing visual-based lessons (those using photographs, overhead transparencies, video, and the like) with con-
ventional instruction indicated a small overall superiority in achievement for students who experienced the visual treatment.[1] However, on closer examination it was found that the degree of superiority depended on many factors, including the subject matter and the utilization practices of the teacher. As discussed in Chapter 2, individual students vary in terms of their visual "intelligence" and in the way they process and use visual information.

One role that visuals definitely play is to provide a concrete **referent** for ideas. Words don't look or sound (usually) like the thing they stand for, but visuals are **iconic**—that is, they have some resemblance to the thing they represent (see Dale's Cone of Experience in Chapter 1). As such, they serve as a more easily remembered link to the original idea (see Figure 3.2). Visuals can also motivate learners by attracting their attention, holding their attention, and generating emotional responses.

Visuals can simplify information that is difficult to understand (see Figure 3.3). Diagrams can make it easy to store and retrieve such information. They can also serve an organizing function by illustrating the relationships among elements, as in a flow chart or timeline.

Finally, visuals provide a redundant channel; that is, when accompanying spoken or written verbal information they present that information in a different modality, giving some learners a chance to comprehend visually what they might miss verbally.

VISUAL LITERACY

Consider the sorts of visuals that are used every day for important communication purposes, such as the emer-

---

[1] Peter A. Cohen, Barbara J. Ebeling, and James A. Kulik, "A Meta-Analysis of Outcome Studies of Visual-Based Instruction," *Educational Communications and Technology Journal* (Spring 1981), pp. 26–36.

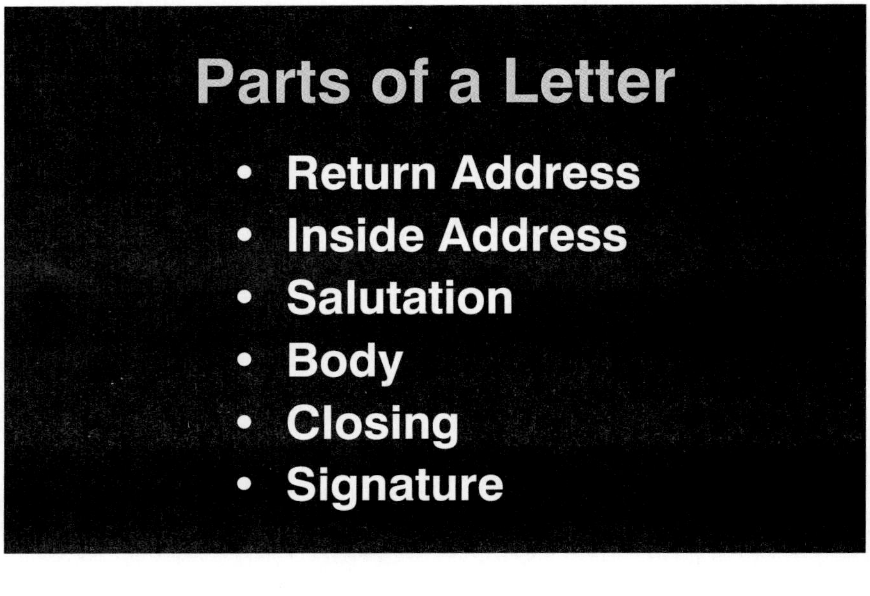

FIGURE 3.1
Too often, visual media are used to show only verbal messages.

Parts of a Letter

- **Return Address**
- **Inside Address**
- **Salutation**
- **Body**
- **Closing**
- **Signature**

FIGURE 3.2

A color photograph can be a highly iconic visual, capturing much of the reality of the original referent.

gency information cards in airplanes or highway signs that warn of dangerous curves or obstructions (Figure 3.4). They work only to the extent that you are "literate" in the conventions of that medium. Whereas the term *literacy* once was used only to refer to reading and writing of verbal information, today we use the term ***visual literacy*** to refer to the learned ability to interpret visual messages accurately and to create such messages. Research on visual literacy examines the influence of the visual processing system on the acquisition of knowledge, skills, and attitudes. Interest in visual literacy has grown to the point that it has become a professional interest area. The International Visual Literacy Association, Inc. (IVLA), which conducts formal meetings and publishes its own periodical, is an organization established for professionals involved in visual literacy.

The critical role of visuals in education was recognized forcefully a century ago by John Dewey, probably the most influential American philosopher of education:

> I believe much of the time and attention now given to the preparation and presentation of lessons might be more wisely and profitably expended in training the student's power of imagery and in seeing to it that he is continually forming definite, vivid, and growing images of the various subjects with which he comes in contact in his experience.[2]

Visual literacy can be developed through two major approaches:

- *Input strategies.* Helping learners to *decode,* or "read," visuals proficiently by practicing visual analysis skills (e.g., through picture analysis and discussion of films and video programs).
- *Output strategies.* Helping learners to *encode,* or "write," visuals—to express themselves and communicate with others (e.g., through planning and producing photo and video presentations). These input and output strategies are shown in Figures 3.5 through 3.8.

[2]John Dewey, "My Pedagogic Creed, Article 4, The Nature of Method," *School Journal* (January 1897), pp. 77–80.

FIGURE 3.3

A complex process can be simplified and therefore made easier to understand and remember.

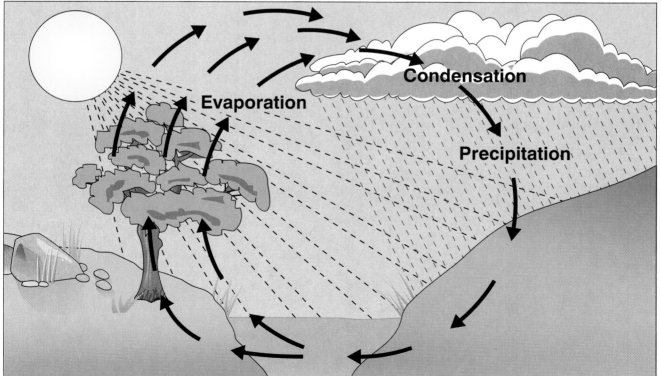

FIGURE 3.4
Well-designed visuals communicate clearly across boundaries of language and culture.

FIGURE 3.5
Reading is the "decoding" activity of print literacy.

FIGURE 3.6
Writing is the "encoding" activity of print literacy.

Decoding: Interpreting Visuals

Seeing a visual does not automatically ensure that one will learn from it. Learners must be guided toward correct decoding of visuals. One aspect of visual literacy, then, is the skill of interpreting and creating meaning from the stimuli that surround them.

Developmental Effects.   How a learner decodes a visual is affected by many variables. Prior to the age of twelve, children tend to interpret visuals section by section rather than as a whole. In reporting what they see in a picture, they are likely to single out specific elements within the scene. Students who are older, however, tend to summarize the whole scene and report a conclusion about the meaning of the picture.

Hence, abstract symbols or a series of still pictures whose relationship is not clearly spelled out may fail to communicate as intended with younger viewers (see Figure 3.10). On the other hand, highly realistic visuals may distract younger children. However, as Dwyer notes, "As a child gets older, he becomes more capable of attending selectively to those features of an instruc-

tional presentation that have the greatest potential for enhancing his learning of desired information[3]."

Cultural Effects.   In teaching, we must keep in mind that the act of decoding visuals may be affected by the viewer's cultural background. Different cultural groups may perceive visual materials in different ways. For example, let's say your instruction includes visuals depicting scenes typical of the home life and street life of inner-city children. It is almost certain that students who live in such an area will decode these visuals differently than will students whose cultural (and socioeconomic) backgrounds do not include firsthand knowledge of inner-city living. Similarly, scenes depicting life in the Old West might be interpreted quite differently by a Native American child than they would be by an African American, Caucasian, or Mexican American child (Figure 3.11).

---

[3]Francis M. Dwyer, *Strategies for Improving Visual Learning* (State College, PA: Learning Services, 1978), p. 33.

FIGURE 3.7
Interpreting a video program is the "decoding" activity of visual literacy.

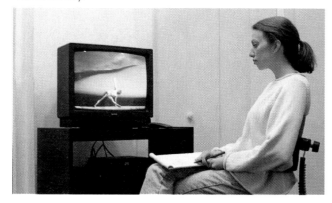

FIGURE 3.8
Creating a video program is the "encoding" activity of visual literacy.

Visual Preferences. In selecting visuals, teachers have to make appropriate choices between the sorts of visuals that are preferred and those that are most effective. People do not necessarily learn best from the kinds of pictures they prefer to look at. For instance, research on picture preferences indicates that children in upper elementary grades tend to prefer color to black-and-white and choose photographs over drawings; younger children tend to prefer simple illustrations, whereas older children tend to prefer moderately complex illustrations.[4]

Most learners prefer colored visuals over black-and-white visuals. However, there is no significant difference in the amount of learning except when color is related to the content to be learned (e.g., when workers must learn to assemble electrical components with different-colored wires, the presence of color is essential). Photographs are preferred over line drawings by most learners, even though in many situations line drawings may communicate better (e.g., drawings can eliminate distracting pictorial elements and highlight the important details). Even though many learners prefer very realistic visuals over abstract representations, teachers must strike a balance between the two to achieve their instructional purposes. Even though young learners prefer simple visuals and older students prefer more complex visuals, simpler visuals are usually more effective, whatever the age group.

Regardless of their different starting points and differences in bias, students develop their visual abilities by *using* them. They can practice by viewing and critiquing visual displays, such as magazine ads, and by thinking

FIGURE 3.9
What story do you think this picture is telling? Do you think a five-year-old would see the same story?

FIGURE 3.10
An active posture, as in the drawing on the left, communicates movement more reliably than arbitrary graphic conventions such as speed lines, as in the drawing on the right.

---

[4]Barbara Myatt and Juliet Mason Carter, "Picture Preferences of Children and Young Adults," *Educational Communication and Technology Journal* (Spring 1979), p. 47.

FIGURE 3.11
The cultural biases of a communicator, although unspoken, may be perceived vividly by viewers having a different cultural background.

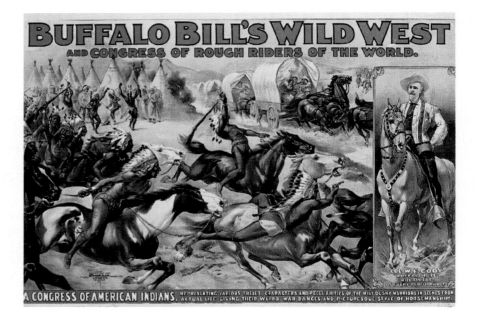

critically about and discussing television programs. This chapter begins to explore some of these possibilities.

Encoding: Creating Visuals

Another route to visual literacy is through student creation of visual presentations. Just as writing can spur reading, producing media can be a highly effective way of understanding media.

Most older students have access to a camera. For example, they could be encouraged to present reports to the class by carefully selecting sets of 35mm slides, which can help students to develop their aesthetic talents. The video camcorder is another convenient tool for students to practice creating and presenting ideas and events pictorially (Figure 3.12).

One skill nearly always included in visual education curricula is that of sequencing. Reading specialists have

long known that the ability to sequence—that is, to arrange ideas in logical order—is an extremely important factor in verbal literacy, especially in the ability to communicate in writing. See the following "Media File."

FIGURE 3.12
The camcorder is a handy tool for creating visual reports.

▼ MEDIA FILE

Sequencing Picture Cards

Beginning or remedial readers can improve their ability to visualize a narrative as a chronological sequence of events by arranging story cards in proper sequence. Each set of cards tells a story through a series of cards having pictures but no text. Eight different sets are included in this package, including "A Trip to the Grocery Store" (shown here), "Mailing a Letter," "Rescuing the Cat," and five others. Each set contains three to five cards.

Source: Judy/Instructo

CLOSE-UP

VISUAL LITERACY EDUCATION

Visual literacy education programs have been developed throughout the United States and in many other countries to introduce students to the concepts and skills related to interpreting visuals and communicating visually. These programs are designed for children from preschool through high school and encompass both the encoding and the decoding of visual information in all media. Visual literacy has now become well accepted as an important aspect of the curriculum at all levels of education.

One such program in the Minneapolis public schools involves students in many viewing skills activities and media production projects with the aim of developing critical viewing and thinking skills. Students examine all media with a focus on how elements such as color, camera angle, and pacing can affect the impact of visual messages. "Visual Education," the district's curriculum guide, encourages teachers to consider visual learning styles and emphasizes the importance of visuals in developing creativity and critical thinking skills. In many media centers around the district, students create poster campaigns, design new products and advertising, examine their television viewing habits, and analyze commercial messages. They produce videos using camcorders and design projects in audio, photography, and other media.

In programs like this all over the country, teachers are encouraged to think visually and to focus students' attention on the visual aspects of textbooks and storybooks while reading. Visuals inundate today's students, so their ability to read, understand, create, and analyze the persuasiveness of visuals has become more important than ever. Media production, computer design, and critical thinking skills can enhance a student's ability to work and succeed in an increasingly visual world.

Elementary teachers have discovered the appeal of visual tools such as tangrams, visual searchers, and three-dimensional shapes. The concepts of sequencing, patterning, visual analogies, visual perception, visual attributes, and categorization are enhanced by other visual teaching tools, such as Venn diagrams, hidden pictures, drawings, memory games, and video clips. Students work alone or together on visual learning activities and develop communication, organization, and reporting skills in the process.

Source: Rhonda S. Robinson, Northern Illinois University.

Children who have grown up constantly exposed to movies and television may expect the visuals they encounter in school to be similarly packaged and sequenced. They may need practice in arranging visuals into logical sequence, which is a learned skill, like the verbal sequencing in reading and writing. For this reason, many visual education programs, especially for primary school children, emphasize creative activities that call for arranging and making visuals.

This chapter emphasizes the principles that define effective visuals. The main purpose is to help you increase your own critical ability with visuals. But we also want to provide you with additional tools for teaching others these skills. This chapter focuses on doing visual displays and photography—creative activities that are certainly appropriate for students. The storyboarding techniques discussed later in this chapter are used by teachers not only for their own planning but as a learning tool for their students; it helps them practice inferencing, sequencing information, and so on. Chapter 5 discusses slides and multi-image presentations, and Chapter 7 explores the possibilities of local video pro-

duction. These skills are not just for you—they should be passed on to your students as well.

GOALS OF VISUAL DESIGN

What does a professional visual designer think about when facing a visual design problem? The considerations are too numerous and complex to be spelled out fully here. However, there are a few fundamental principles of visual design that can be pursued even by novices. For purposes of information and instruction, good visual design tries to achieve at least four basic goals in terms of improving communication between the message source (teacher) and the receiver (learner):

- Ensure legibility.
- Reduce the effort required to interpret the message.
- Increase the viewer's active engagement with the message.
- Focus attention on the most important parts of the message.

That Incomparable Moravian

One day in the late 1640s in Massachusetts, Cotton Mather, ever zealous to make Puritan New England the cultural center of the New World, noted in his journal his disappointment that a certain "incomparable Moravian" was not, after all, to become an American by accepting the presidency of Harvard College:

> That brave old man, Johannes Amos Comenius, the fame of whose worth has been trumpeted as far as more than three languages could carry it, was indeed agreed . . . to come over to New England, and illuminate their Colledge and Country, in the quality of a President, which was now become vacant. But the solicitation of the Swedish Ambassador diverting him another way, that incomparable Moravian became not an American.

Who was this Johannes Amos Comenius? Why had his fame as an educator spread all the way from Europe to Mather's Massachusetts Bay Colony?

Comenius was an educational reformer born in 1592 in Moravia (now part of the Czech Republic). He became a clergyman of the United Brethren, an evangelical Protestant reform sect known popularly today as the Moravian church. At the time of his consideration for the presidency of Harvard, he was living in exile in Sweden. Indeed, the religious persecutions of the Thirty Years' War and its aftermath had forced Comenius to live most of his life away from his native Moravia.

IOHAN - AMOS COMENIVS,
MORAVVS. Aº ÆTAT 50: 1642
Crols sculpsit.

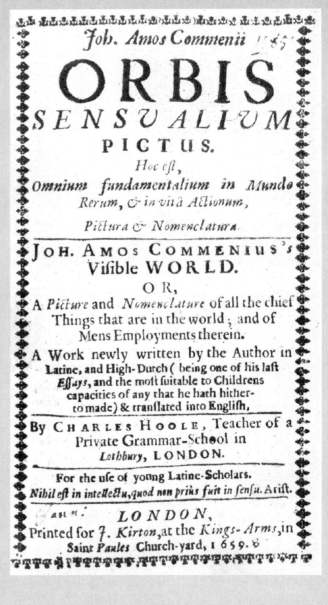

Joh. Amos Commenii
ORBIS
SENSVALIVM
PICTVS.

Hoc est,

Omnium fundamentalium in Mundo
Rerum, & in vitâ Actionum,

Pictura & Nomenclatura.

JOH. AMOS COMMENIUS's
Visible WORLD.
O R,
A *Picture* and *Nomenclature* of all the chief Things that are in the world; and of Mens Employments therein.

A Work newly written by the Author in Latine, and High-Dutch (being one of his last Essays, and the most suitable to Childrens capacities of any that he hath hitherto made) & translated into English,

By CHARLES HOOLE, Teacher of a Private Grammar-School in *Lothbury,* LONDON.

For the use of young Latine-Scholars.
Nihil est in intellectu, quod non prius fuit in sensu. Arist.

LONDON,
Printed for *J.* Kirton, at the *Kings-Arms,* in Saint *Paules* Church-yard, 1659.

Despite this and the deprivations of war, Comenius achieved fame throughout Europe as a reformer and writer of innovative textbooks and other educational works. His *Janua Linguarum Reserata* ("*The Gate of Language Unlocked*") was a Latin language textbook that taught a basic vocabulary of eight thousand carefully selected words and the principal points of Latin grammar. The instructional strategy of the *Janua* consisted of Latin sentences about a variety of topics, forming a kind of encyclopedia of basic human knowledge of that time. Comenius also argued that the teaching of languages should be divided into stages parallel to four human developmental stages. For this insight Piaget acknowledged Comenius as a forerunner of genetic psychology.[a] The *Janua* became one of the great pedagogical best-sellers of all time,

---

[a] Jean Piaget, *J. A. Comenius: Pages Choisies* (Paris: UNESCO, 1957).

LI.

Piſcatio.

Fiſhing.

The Fiſher-man 1.	Piſcator 1.
catcheth fiſh,	captat piſces,
either on the ſhoar,	live, in littore,
with an Hook, 2.	Hamo, 2.
which hangeth by a line	qui ab *arundine*
from the angling-rod,	filo pendet,
and on which	& cui inhæret
the bait ſticketh ;	*Eſca* ;
or with a	ſive
Cleek-Net, 3.	*Fundâ*, 3.
which hanging	quæ pendens
on a Pole, 4.	*Perticâ*, 4.
is put into the water ;	aquæ immittitur ;
or in a Boat, 5.	ſive, in *Cymba*, 5.
with a Trammel-Net 6.	*Reti*, 6.
or with a Weel, 7.	ſive *Naſſa*, 7.
which is laid in	quæ per Noctem
the water by Night.	demergitur.

and it influenced, wittingly or unwittingly, virtually all later scholars of language instruction.

Comenius was also one of the earliest (and certainly the most renowned) champions of what we call visual literacy and visual education. The last fourteen years of his life were spent in Amsterdam, from where he oversaw the publication in 1657 of the work for which he is today best known and on which he had been working for years: *Orbis Sensualium Pictus* ("*The Visible World Pictured*").

Orbis Sensualium Pictus was the first illustrated textbook specifically designed for use by children in an instructional setting. (It was not the first children's picture book. The English printer Caxton, for example, had produced an illustrated edition of Aesop's *Fables* as early as 1484.) The design and illustrations of Comenius's text were expressly intended to enhance learning. The 150 woodcut drawings were learning and teaching devices, not mere decorations. The text embodied the application of educational theories espoused by the author over a period of forty years. It is interesting to note, for example, that Comenius chose Aristotle's observation *"Nihil est in intellectu, quod non prius fuit in sensu"* ("There is nothing in the mind which was not first in the senses") to adorn his title page. The primacy of this principle has been supported increasingly by modern psychological research.

Orbis Sensualium Pictus is truly remarkable for having incorporated, more than three hundred years ago, so many educational concepts that seem thoroughly modern. Underlying Comenius's use of visuals was a theory of perception based on the idea that we learn through our senses and that this learning imprints a mental image that leads to understanding. A real object is preferable for this process, but visuals may be used in the learning environment as substitutes for the real thing.

The design and illustrations of *Orbis Sensualium Pictus*, the author tells us in his preface, were intended "to entice witty children to it, that they may not conceit a torment to be in the school, but dainty fare. For it is apparent, that children (even from their infancy almost) are delighted with pictures, and willingly please their eyes with these sights." His pedagogical aim was that children "may be furnished with the knowledge of the prime things that are in the world, by sport and merry pastime."

The idea that learning should be a "merry pastime" rather than a burdensome chore is startlingly modern. Indeed, centuries were to pass before this basic educational philosophy became what it is today—the common wisdom. Aptly called "that incomparable Moravian" in his own time, Johannes Amos Comenius may still be called so in ours.

Ensure Legibility

A visual cannot even begin to do its job unless all viewers can see the words and images. It's surprising how often this simple rule is broken. Think of how many times you have heard a presenter say, "You may not be able to see what's on this transparency [or slide], so let me read it to you." The goal of good visual design is to remove as many obstacles as possible that might impede transmission of your message (specific guidelines on, for example, the size of letters are given later in this chapter).

Reduce Effort

As a designer you want to convey your message in such a way that viewers expend little effort making sense out of what they are seeing and are free to use most of their mental effort for understanding the message being conveyed. There are several processes that can be easily applied to help reduce the effort required to interpret your visuals. Later in this chapter you will see how establishing an underlying pattern (alignment, shape, balance), putting like things together (proximity), and following a regular pattern in your treatment (consistency) contribute to this goal. Using harmonious color combinations and figures that contrast with their backgrounds also plays a role.

Increase Active Engagement

Your message doesn't stand a chance unless people pay attention to it. So a major goal is to make your design as appealing as possible—to get the viewers' attention and to entice them into thinking about your message. Ideas elaborated later in this chapter include using novelty to grab attention and using textures and interactive features to get viewers actively engaged with your message. Choosing a style appropriate for your audience and using appealing color schemes also play a role in gaining and holding an audience.

Focus Attention

Having enticed viewers into your display, you then face the challenge of directing their attention to the most important parts of your message. The overall design pattern plus specific directional guides (woven into the design and color cues) are your means for achieving the goal of focusing attention.

PROCESSES OF VISUAL DESIGN

This section outlines a set of procedures for carrying out visual design in such a way that these goals are enhanced. Throughout this chapter and in Chapters 4 and 5 are specific examples of these procedures and explanations of how these decisions contribute to reaching the four basic goals of visual design (in this chapter, see "How to . . . Design a Computer Screen"; in Chapter 4, see "How to . . . Design Bulletin Boards" and "How to . . . Design Text"; and in Chapter 5, see "How to . . . Design Overhead Transparencies").

Teachers, designers, and others who create visual and verbal/visual displays face a series of design decisions about how to arrange the elements to achieve the goals of visual design. We will group these decisions into three sets:

1. *Elements.* Selecting and assembling the verbal/visual elements to be incorporated into the display
2. *Pattern.* Choosing an underlying pattern for the elements of the display
3. *Arrangement.* Arranging the individual elements within the underlying pattern

As a final step, check your decisions against goals and revise as needed.

Elements

Designing a visual display begins by gathering or producing the individual pictorial and text elements that are expected to be used in the display. This assumes, of course, that you have already determined students' needs and interests regarding the topic and decided what objective might be achieved through the visual you are planning—be it a bulletin board, an overhead transparency, printed handouts, or computer screen display.

In selecting or producing the pictorial and text elements, you will want to make your choices based on achieving the visual design goals discussed earlier—ensuring legibility, helping the viewer to quickly see your message, getting the viewer actively engaged with your message, and focusing attention on key points. The following design suggestions are grouped according to the various elements or components of the display: the visual elements (choosing the type of visual), the verbal elements (lettering style and location), and the elements that add appeal (surprise, texture, interaction).

Visual Elements.   The type of visual selected for a particular situation depends on the learning task. Visual symbols, one classification of learning resources in Dale's Cone of Experience (discussed in Flashback on p. 16), can be subdivided into three categories: realistic, analogic, and organizational.[5]

---

[5]H. A. Houghton and D. M. Willows, eds. *The Psychology of Illustration*, Vol. 2 (New York: Verlag, 1987).

FIGURE 3.13
Photographs, illustrations, graphics, and words represent a continuum of realism for different kinds of symbols.

Pictorial symbols		Graphic symbols		Verbal symbols	
photograph	illustration/ drawing	concept-related graphic	stylized or arbitrary graphic	A wagon with a bowed top supported by bowed strips of wood or metal.	Covered wagon
				verbal description	noun/label

realistic ⟷ abstract

Realistic visuals show the actual object under study. For example, the color photograph of a covered wagon in Figure 3.13 is a realistic visual. The degree of realism can be heightened by the use of realistic colors; this is one of the major instructional purposes that color serves. No representation, of course, is totally realistic. The real object or event will always have aspects that cannot be captured pictorially, even in a three-dimensional color motion picture. The various visual forms can, however, be arranged from highly realistic to highly abstract.

One might be inclined to conclude that effective communication is always best served by the most realistic visual available. After all, the more realistic a visual is, the closer it is to the original. This, however, is not necessarily so. There is ample research to show that under certain circumstances, realism can actually interfere with the communication and learning process. For example, the ability to sort out the relevant from the irrelevant in a pictorial representation grows with age and experience. So, for younger children and for older learners who are encountering an idea for the first time, the wealth of detail found in a realistic visual may increase the likelihood that the learner will be distracted by irrelevant elements of the visual.

As Dwyer notes in his review of visual research, "The arbitrary addition of stimuli in visuals makes it difficult for learners to identify the essential learning cues from among the more realistic background stimuli."[6] Dwyer concludes that rather than being a simple yes-or-no issue, the amount of realism desired has a curvilinear relationship to learning. That is, either too

much or too little realism may affect achievement adversely (Figure 3.14).

Analogic visuals convey a concept or topic by showing something else and implying a similarity. Teaching about electricity flow by showing water flowing in series and parallel pipes is an example of using analogic visuals. An analogy for white blood cells fighting off infection might be an army attacking a stronghold. Later in this chapter, the color wheel is used as an analogy to help one visualize the relationships among the colors of the visible spectrum. Such visuals help the learner interpret new information in light of prior knowledge and thereby facilitate learning (see Figure 3.15).

Organizational visuals include flowcharts, graphs, maps, schematics, and classification charts. (See Chapter

---

[6]Francis M. Dwyer, *Strategies for Improving Visual Learning* (State College, PA: Learning Services, 1978), p. 33.

FIGURE 3.14
Visuals tend to become less useful in instruction as they approach the extremes of very abstract or very realistic.

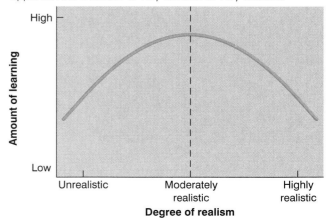

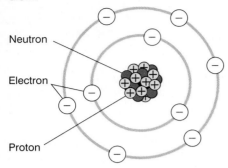

4 for details on types of charts and graphs.) These graphic organizers can show relationships among the main points or concepts in textual material. This type of visual (such as the one in Figure 3.16) helps communicate the organization of the content.

Verbal Elements. Most displays incorporate some type of verbal information in addition to visuals. In evaluating a display for its instructional potential or in preparing your own display, you need to consider the lettering as carefully as you consider the pictorial elements, for it can communicate powerfully, too. At a minimum, you have to be sure that the lettering is legible in terms of size and spacing and of a style that is consistent with your intended message.

Letter Style. The style of the lettering should be consistent and should harmonize with the other elements of the visual. For straightforward informational or instructional purposes, a plain (i.e., not decorative) lettering style is recommended. A **sans serif** (without serifs) style, such as Helvetica, or a simple serif style, such as Palatino, can be used for either projected visuals or printed text. As illustrated in Figure 3.17, there is a tendency to use sans serif typefaces for projected visuals and serif for print, but this is a designer's preference, not a research-based principle.

Number of Lettering Styles. It is recommended that a display—or a series of related visuals, such as a slide series—use no more than two different type styles, and these should harmonize with each other. When preparing text on a computer it is tempting to use many variations on a typeface, but for good communication it is recommended that you limit the number of variations (e.g., bold, italic, underline, size changes) to four. That is, you could use two different type sizes plus some italics and some underlining, or three different type sizes plus bold for emphasis.

Capitals. For best legibility, use lowercase letters, adding capitals only where normally required. Short headlines may be written in all capitals, but phrases of more than three words and full sentences should follow the rule of lowercase lettering.

Color of Lettering. As discussed later in the section "Figure–Ground Contrast," the color of the lettering should contrast with the background color both for the sake of simple legibility and for the sake of emphasis in cases where you want to call particular attention to the verbal message. Legibility depends mainly on contrast between the lettering color and the background color.

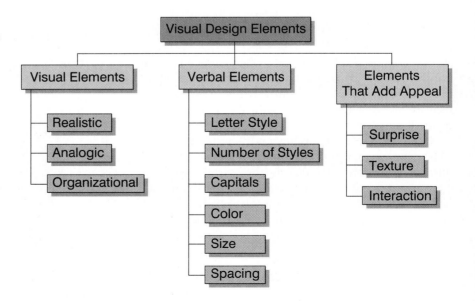

FIGURE 3.17
Styles of type should be selected to suit their purpose.

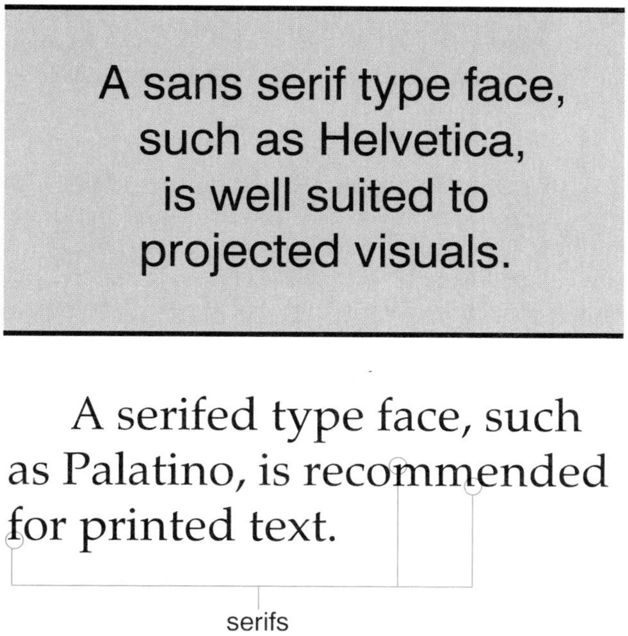

A sans serif type face, such as Helvetica, is well suited to projected visuals.
A serifed type face, such as Palatino, is recommended for printed text.
serifs

Size of Lettering. Displays such as bulletin boards and posters are often meant to be viewed by people situated at a distance of thirty or forty feet or more. In these cases the size of the lettering is crucial for legibility. A common rule of thumb is to make lowercase letters ½ inch high for each ten feet of viewer distance. This means, for example, that to be legible to a student seated in the last seat of a thirty-foot-long classroom the lettering would have to be at least 1½ inches in height. Figure 3.18 illustrates these minimum specifications for lettering height.

Spacing Between Letters. The distance between the letters of the individual words must be judged by experience rather than on a mechanical basis. This is because some letters (e.g., capital *A, I, K,* and *W*) are quite irregular in shape compared with rectangular letters (e.g., capital *H, M, N,* and *S*) and circular letters (e.g., capital *C, G, O,* and *Q*). When rectangular letters or circular letters are combined with each other at equal spacing, there are rather regular patterns of white space between letters. But when irregular letters are combined with others in this way, the patterns of white space can be very uneven. The only way to overcome this potentially distracting unevenness is to space all your letters by **optical spacing**—that is, by what *appears* even to the eye (see Figure 3.19).

Spacing Between Lines. The vertical spacing between lines of printed material is also important for legibility. If the lines are too close together, they will tend to blur at a distance; if they are too far apart, they will seem disjointed (i.e., not part of the same unit). For a happy medium, the vertical space between the lines should be slightly less than the average height of the lowercase letters. To achieve this, use a ruler to draw lines lightly on your blank layout. Separate baselines by about one and a half times the height of the lowercase

FIGURE 3.19
Optical spacing means estimating approximately equal amounts of white space between letters.

GOOD
MINE
LABWORK
"Optical spacing"

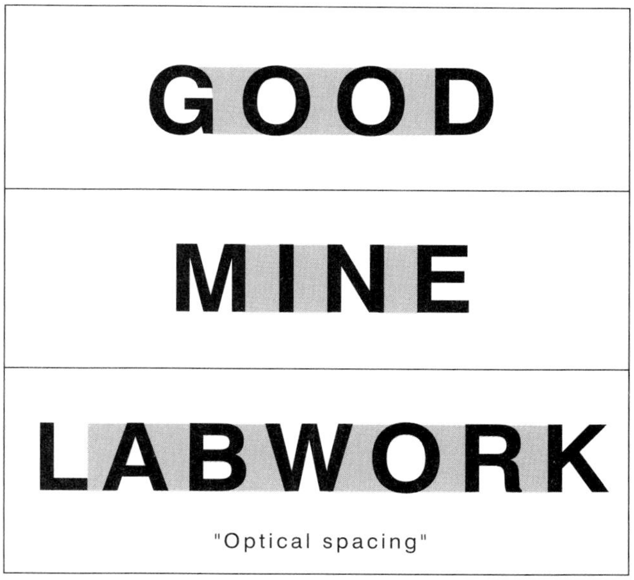

FIGURE 3.18
These are the minimum heights of boldface lowercase letters for visibility at increasing distances.

Height of lowercase letters
1/2"
1"
1 1/2"
2"
2 1/2"
3"
3 1/2"
4"
10'
20'
30'
40'
50'
60'
70'
80'
Viewing distance in feet

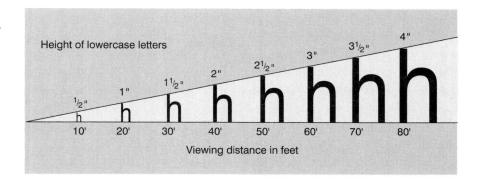

FIGURE 3.20
Lines of text should not be too cramped or too widely separated.

Text is difficult to read when lines are too close together.
Text seems disconnected when lines are too separated.
Text is most legible when separation is 1½ times average letter height.

ous combination of word and picture, an abrupt infusion of color, a dramatic change of size. People pay attention as long as they are getting novel stimuli or new information. They tune out when the message becomes monotonous.

Texture. Most visuals are two-dimensional. However, a third dimension can be added with the use of texture or actual materials. Texture is a characteristic of three-dimensional objects and materials. It can convey a clearer idea of the subject to the viewer by involving the sense of touch—for example, touching samples of different cereal grains. Or texture can simply invite involvement—for example, using cotton balls to represent clouds or showing book jackets to entice students to read a new book. Company products can be incorporated into a display. Components of equipment can be shown with drawings and captions.

letters. Lettering on these lines will then result in text with the correct spacing (see Figure 3.20).

Elements That Add Appeal. Your visual has no chance of having an effect unless it captures and holds the viewer's attention. Let's look at three devices for making displays more appealing: surprise, texture, and interaction.

Surprise. What grabs attention? The unexpected, primarily. Think of an unusual metaphor, an incongru-

Interaction. The R of the ASSURE model applies to all forms of media. Viewers can be asked to respond to visual displays by manipulating materials on the display, perhaps to answer questions raised in the display. Answer cards to math facts can be moved into the correct position by the student. Answers to geography questions can be hidden under movable flaps. The teacher or learners can move dials on a weather display to indicate the forecast for the day or the actual weather outside the classroom. One example of an interactive format is shown in Figure 3.21.

FIGURE 3.21
Encouraging interaction adds greatly to the appeal of a display.

FIGURE 3.22
Pictorial elements should be aligned with reference to the edges of the display.

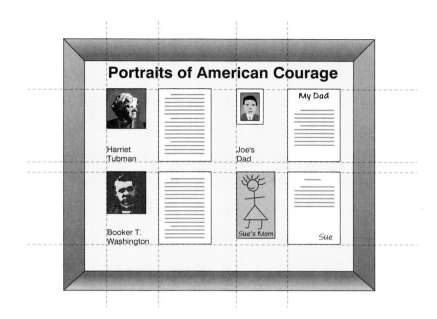

Pattern

Having made tentative decisions about what elements to include in your visual display, you are ready to consider its overall "look." The idea is to establish an underlying pattern—to decide how the viewer's eye will flow across your display. The major factors that affect the overall look are alignment of elements; shape; balance; style; color scheme; and color appeal.

Alignment. When the primary elements within a display are positioned so that they have a clear visual relationship to each other, viewers expend little effort making sense out of what they are seeing and are free to expend most of their effort on understanding the mes-

sage being conveyed. The most effective way to establish such visual relationships is to use **alignment**. Viewers will perceive elements to be aligned when the edges of those elements are aligned on the same imaginary horizontal or vertical line, as shown in Figure 3.22. These imaginary lines should be parallel to the edges of the display. For an irregularly shaped element, surround it mentally with a rectangle and align that rectangle, as shown in Figure 3.23.

Shape. Another way to arrange the visual and verbal elements is to put them into a shape that is already familiar to the viewer. Your aim should be to use a pattern that attracts and focuses attention as effortlessly as possible. A simple geometric figure, such as a circle, tri-

FIGURE 3.23
An irregularly shaped element can be aligned by mentally surrounding it with a rectangle.

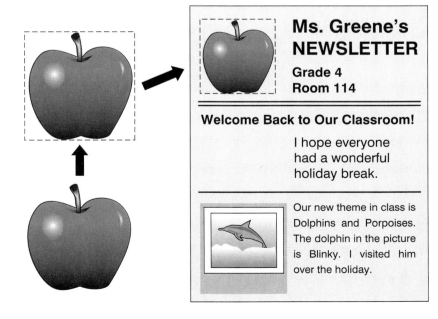

FIGURE 3.24
Arrangement of elements in a familiar geometric pattern, such as a circle, makes a display easier to decode.

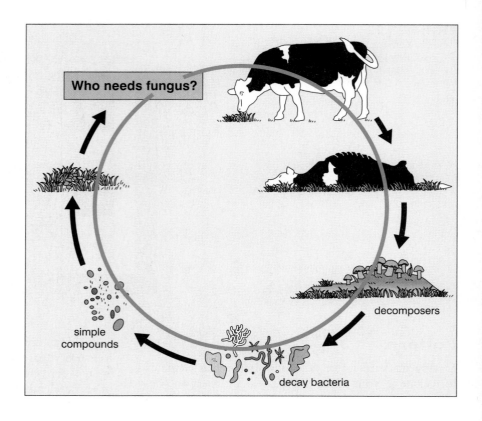

angle, or rectangle, provides a convenient framework because its shape is predictable to most viewers (Figure 3.24). Shapes that approximate certain letters of the alphabet have the same virtue. The letters *Z, L, T,* and *U* are frequently used as underlying patterns in display layouts (Figure 3.25). Of course, the words used in the layout, as well as the pictures, form part of the shape.

Another principle that can guide the placement of visual elements is the **rule of thirds.** That is, elements arranged along any of the one-third dividing lines take on importance and liveliness. The most dominant and dynamic position is at any of the intersections of the horizontal and vertical one-third dividing lines, especially the upper left intersection (Figure 3.26). The most stable and least interesting point on the grid is dead cen-

FIGURE 3.25
Arrangement in the shape of the letter *Z* leads the viewer's eye from upper left to lower right.

FIGURE 3.26
According to the "rule of thirds," the most important elements should be placed near the intersections of the lines dividing the visual into thirds.

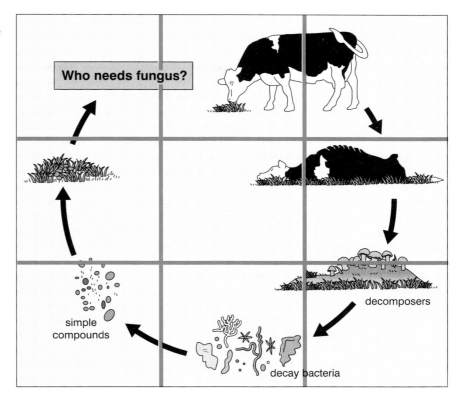

ter. Items placed in the corners or at the edges tend to be ignored or to make the arrangement unbalanced.

Balance. A psychological sense of equilibrium, or *balance,* is achieved when the "weight" of the elements in a display is equally distributed on each side of an axis, either horizontally or vertically or both. When the design is repeated on both sides, the balance is symmetrical, or formal.

In most cases, though, for visuals that will catch the eye and serve an informational purpose you should aim to achieve an asymmetrical, or informal, balance. With asymmetrical balance there is rough equivalence of weight, but different elements are used on each side (e.g., one large open square on one side, three small dark circles on the other). Informal balance is preferred because it is more dynamic and more interesting than formal balance (see Figure 3.27). Imbalance—using a distinctly disproportionate weight distribution—ordinarily should be avoided because it tends to be jarring.

Style. Different audiences and different settings call for different design styles. Think about the simple, uncluttered, primary-color "look" of the "Barney and Friends" show compared with the complex imagery, busy scenes, and realistic color of an adult action drama.

FIGURE 3.27
The analogy of a balance scale, shown in the bottom row, represents the three different types of balance.

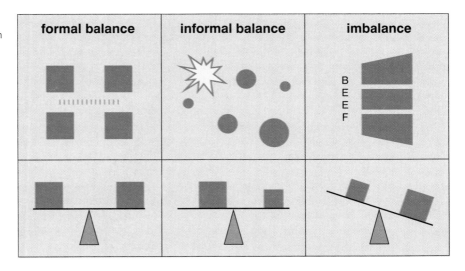

FIGURE 3.28
A slide set intended for an adult, professional audience should have a different style than one intended for elementary-school-age children.

Likewise, you would not use the same stylistic treatment for a first-grade bulletin board (for example, Figure 3.21) as you would for a slide set made to show at a teachers' professional development conference (Figure 3.28). Your choice of lettering and type of pictures should be consistent with each other and with the preferences of the audience.

Color Scheme. When choosing a color scheme for a display, consider the harmoniousness of the colors. Viewers are more likely to linger over and to remember a display having pleasant color harmony than they would a display done with clashing colors. The color wheel is a visual analogy to help us understand the relationships among the colors of the visible spectrum (Figure 3.29).

Any two colors that lie directly opposite each other on the color wheel are called **complementary colors**— for example, red and green or yellow and violet. (The latter combination is one of the most popular ones for colored overhead transparencies—yellow-orange lettering on a blue-violet background.) Complementary colors often harmonize well in terms of an overall color scheme (Figure 3.30). However, it is not recommended that you directly juxtapose two complementary colors (e.g., placing green letters on a red background). There are two reasons for this. First, if the colors are of equal value, or darkness, the letters will not have good fig-

FIGURE 3.29
The traditional color wheel helps one visualize complementary colors.

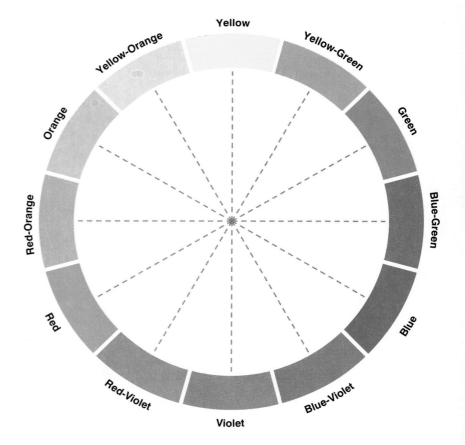

FIGURE 3.30
Complementary colors, such as violet and yellow, can make pleasing combinations.

ure–ground contrast. Second, when saturated (intense) complementary colors are placed directly next to each other the eye cannot focus on both at the same time, so you get an unpleasant vibrating effect.

Colors that lie next to each other on the color wheel are called **analogous colors**—for example, blue-green, blue, and blue-violet. Analogous colors may also form pleasing combinations when used together in a display.

When thinking about a color scheme for a display or a computer screen, it may be helpful to think in terms of a background color, a color for the images or text appearing against that background, and a color for highlights. Colors that work well together are shown in Table 3.1.

These suggestions about color schemes should be viewed as general guidelines, not as absolute rules, because in any situation there are many factors that will have an impact on whether particular colors will work well together. Keep in mind that these generalizations also assume normal color vision on the part of viewers. We know that 8% of all men and less that 1% of all women are color blind. Most color-blind people confuse

reds with greens and see mainly in shades of blue and yellow. That is, for color-blind viewers, red lettering on a green background might be difficult to distinguish. You can alleviate this problem by making sure that the colors vary in darkness, for example, dark red letters on a light green background.

Color Appeal.   Artists have long appreciated that blue, green, and violet are considered "cool" colors, whereas red and orange are considered "warm" colors. Research has shown that this is a learned phenomenon. When choosing colors for instructional materials, consider the emotional response you are seeking—an active, dynamic, warm feeling or a more contemplative, thoughtful, cool feeling. Also, saturated reds and orange appear to approach the viewer, whereas cool colors tend to recede. Take advantage of this effect by highlighting important cues in red or orange, helping them leap out at the viewer the way a red STOP sign stands out even in a cluttered urban landscape. By the same reasoning, use cool colors for backgrounds. (See Figures 3.31 and 3.32.)

TABLE 3.1
Effective combinations of colors for background and images for displays and computer screens.

BACKGROUND	FOREGROUND IMAGES AND TEXT	HIGHLIGHTS
white	dark blue	red, orange
light gray	blue, green, black	red
blue	light yellow, white	yellow, red
light blue	dark blue, dark green	red-orange
light yellow	violet, brown	red

Based on recommendations in "Color in Instructional Communication," by Judy Loosmore, *Performance and Instruction, 33* (November/December 1994), pp. 36–38.

FIGURE 3.31
In this bulletin board display, warm colors fit with the friendly motif.

Response to warm and cool colors seems to be related to age. In general, warm colors (particularly red, pink, yellow, and orange) seem to be preferred by children. Children also prefer brighter colors and combinations of intense colors more than do adults. With maturity tends to come a changing preference toward cooler colors and subtler combinations.

There is also a cultural basis to color response. These responses are often deep-seated and unconscious. For example, in North America certain colors are associated with certain holidays: red for Christmas and Valentine's Day, green for St. Patrick's Day, yellow and purple for Easter, orange and black for Halloween. Such symbol-ism can vary dramatically across cultures. For example, in Western countries black is the color of mourning, whereas in China and Japan white is the color of mourning.

Arrangement

Proximity. Once you have established the overall shape of your display, you will want to arrange the items within that pattern. Viewers assume that elements close to each other are related and those that are far apart are unrelated. You can use the principle of **proximity** by putting related elements close together

FIGURE 3.32
Here cool colors predominate, consistent with a more scientific atmosphere.

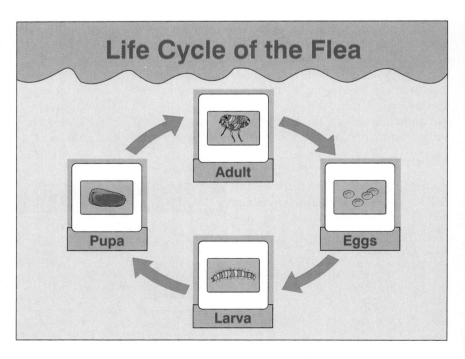

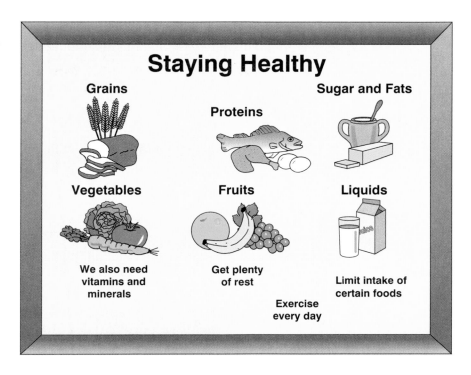

and moving unrelated elements apart. Figure 3.33 shows how confusing it can be when this rule is broken. If a display includes verbal labels for the picture elements, connect the related words and pictures clearly (Figure 3.34).

Directionals. Viewers scan a display, with their attention moving from one part to another. The underlying pattern of the elements of the display will be the main determinant of the eye movement pattern. But if you want viewers to "read" the display in a particular sequence or focus on some particular element, various other devices—**directionals**—can be used to direct attention. An arrow (as in Figure 3.32) is an obvious device for directing the viewer's attention. For verbal material, key words can be emphasized by bold type,

FIGURE 3.34
This display communicates clearly because the principle of proximity is observed.

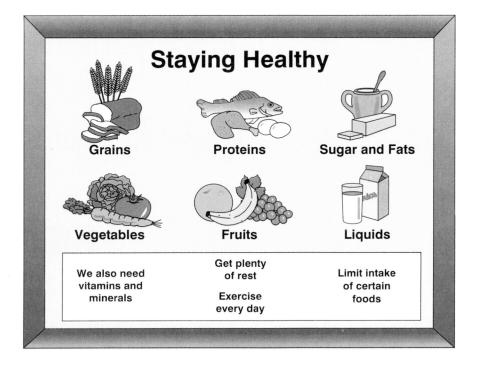

FIGURE 3.35
Sharp figure-ground contrast helps the important elements stand out.

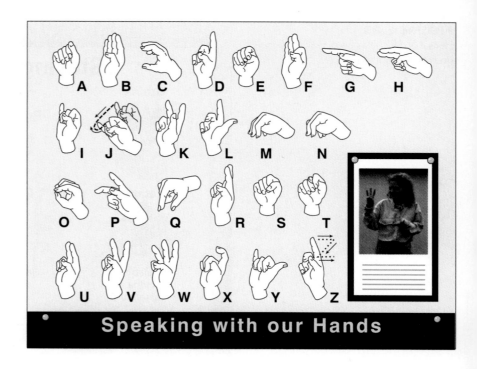

and "bullets" are frequently used to indicate items in a list (as shown in Figure 3.1).

Colored elements—whether words or images—in a monochrome display will also draw the eye. Notice how the "hot" arrows in Figure 3.32 stand out from the cool background. Throughout this book, colored text on "monochrome" pages is used as a way to call attention to topical headings and special features. Further, a color repeated in different parts of a display tends to show a relationship between those parts. For example, if only two symbols in a display are shown in cherry red, they will appear to be related to each other, and the viewer's gaze will go back and forth between them. The more extreme the color is (e.g., red or blue, at the opposite ends of the color spectrum), the more likely it will attract attention.

Figure-Ground Contrast. Important elements, especially wording, should stand out in good contrast to the background. The simple rule of **figure–ground contrast** is that dark figures show up best on light grounds and light figures show up best on dark grounds (Figure 3.35).

FIGURE 3.36
Black lettering on a yellow background (a) is most legible; the other combinations shown are in descending order of legibility.

(a) Black on yellow

(b) Green, red, or blue on white (clear film)

(c) White (clear film) on blue

(d) Black on white (clear film)

(e) Yellow on black

Different color combinations provide different figure–ground contrasts. When lettering or graphic symbols are the "figures," they will show up more clearly on certain backgrounds. As indicated in Figure 3.36, black on yellow is the most legible combination.[7] It's not accidental that this combination has long been used to communicate important road information to drivers. Obviously, a combination of dark figures on a dark background will be even less legible than the combinations shown.

Consistency. If you are planning a series of displays—such as a set of overhead transparencies, a multipage handout, or a "stack" of computer frames—you should be consistent in the arrangement of the elements. As viewers go through the series of images they begin unconsciously to form a set of rules about where information will be located in your display. The more often the arrangement conforms to these rules (or exhibits *consistency*) the more the rules are trusted by the viewer. Every time the arrangement breaks the rules, the viewer has to expend mental energy deciding whether this is a deliberate exception or whether the rules need to be revised. You enhance consistency when you place similar elements in similar locations, use the same text treatment for headlines, and use the same color scheme throughout the series of displays (Figure 3.37).

VISUAL PLANNING TOOLS

This chapter emphasizes the design decisions that must be made, not the technical steps involved in the production processes. For those encountering the visual design process for the first time, don't expect the process to be quick or easy, especially at the beginning. These skills grow with practice, and with practice you will find

yourself thinking visually more often as you grapple with instructional problems.

Storyboard

If you are designing a *series* of visuals—such as for several related overhead transparencies, a slide set, a video sequence, or a series of computer screens—**storyboarding** is a handy method of planning. This technique, borrowed from film and video production, allows you to creatively arrange and rearrange a whole sequence of thumbnail sketches. In storyboarding, a sketch or some other simple representation of the visual you plan to use is put on a card or piece of paper along with the narration and production notes that link the visuals to the narration. After a series of such cards have been developed, they are placed in rough sequence on a flat surface or on a storyboard holder. (See "How To . . . Make a Storyboard Holder.")

Index cards are commonly used for storyboarding because they are durable, inexpensive, and available in a variety of colors and sizes. Small pieces of paper can also be used. Self-sticking removable notes (such as Post-It notes) have become popular because they will stick to almost anything—cardboard, desks, walls, chalkboards, bulletin boards, and so on.

The individual storyboard cards can be divided into areas to accommodate the visual, the narration, and the production notes (Figure 3.38). The exact format of the storyboard card should fit your needs and purposes. Design a card that facilitates your work if the existing or recommended format is not suitable. You can make a simple sketch or write a short description of the desired visual on the card. Polaroid pictures or visuals cut from magazines can also be used.

The storyboarding process can be facilitated by using computer software designed for this purpose, such as *Storyboarding Plus*. Such software allows you to

---

[7]Faber Birren, *Color: A Survey in Words and Pictures* (New Hyde Park, NY: University Books, 1963).

FIGURE 3.37
Consistency in the placement of elements, color, and text treatment adds greatly to the readability of a series of visuals.

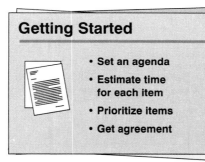
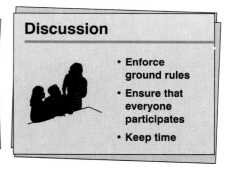

Assemble the Elements

- Consider the relatively low resolution of computer screens (compared to print) and keep individual elements clean and simple.
- Remember to include features that allow learners control over the pace of the programs.
- Rewrite text to fit the smaller space available on screen: avoid breaking sentences across screens.

Profiles in Freedom

Title is 22 point Helvetica bold in white on black for strong contrast.

Next   Previous   Home   Main Menu

Navigation buttons use standard symbols and text labels for clarity.

Images are scanned using a consistent palette and sized or cropped to similar dimensions.

Harriet Tubman

itkdksl lskd lskd ls kdlsaldk eiuryv eiwos id ths eiskdp sie itur sidf md is ie alsk dkfu lsldfod oriytdsl is isk it wlwlw dkaw woei lsldif lsldka is thelsld sid s als dka kd a skd sldk jdksk alsk seeu sa slie pwie oriytueo wplkdjf dkks a dks aljkskdield

Text fields use serif typeface in a minimum size of 12 points for legibility: line length is 2/3 screen or less with wide margins for readability.

Click Main Menu for more profiles.

On-screen instructions are written in active voice and avoid "cute" or overly familiar tone.

Choose Background and Underlying Pattern

- Use subdued color for large areas to avoid distraction.
- Establish areas of the screen where types of information appear consistently throughout the program.

Text area "anchors" the display on the left and helps balance the large illustrations.

Button area is separate from the content presentations.

A subdued tone is chosen for the large background space; in this program the light sepia tone will help convey a sense of history.

Title area is at top of screen where viewer begins to scan the display.

Graphics area is equivalent in size to the text area since the illustrations play an important role in appealing to the viewers.

Arrange the Elements

- Place navigation elements so learners don't have to cross content areas too often in order to control the program.
- Remember to align elements and consider their proximity to related elements.

Profiles in Freedom

Harriet Tubman

itkdksl lskd lskd lo kdlsaldk eiuryv eiwos id ths eiskdp sie itur sidf md is ie alsk dkfu lsldfod oriytdsl is isk it wlwlw dkaw woei lsldif lsldka is thelsld sid s als dka kd a skd sldk jdksk alsk seeu sa slie pwie oriytueo wplkdjf dkks a dks aljkskdield

Text field and illustration are aligned along the bottom edge.

Graphical rule added to separate navigation buttons from content areas more clearly.

On-screen instruction is grouped with navigation.

Navigation buttons are aligned with each other and the edge of the graphic.

Check and Revise

- Make a technical review once the elements are assembled, since their interrelationships are an important part of your design.
- Observe viewers of program to assess the effectiveness of your design.

Title text was dominating the screen; reversing the contrast shifts focus back to text and graphic.

On-screen instruction is in close proximity to the appropriate button.

Navigation buttons for leaving the program and leaving the section are grouped together.

Profiles in Freedom

Harriet Tubman

itkdksl lskd lskd lo kdlsaldk eiuryv eiwos id ths eiskdp sie itur sidf md is ie alsk dkfu lsldfod oriytdsl is isk it wlwlw dkaw woei lsldif lsldka is thelsld sid s als dka kd a skd sldk alsk

Types of navigation are separated to reduce risk of error in choosing options.

Text and illustration are enclosed in light brown tone to enhance grouping.

Illustration was aligned with navigation buttons; alignment with the text links it to the text more clearly.

Illustration caption is moved out of the text field into closer proximity with image it describes.

You can construct an inexpensive storyboard holder from cardboard and strips of clear plastic. Obtain one or two pieces of cardboard about the size that you need to accommodate the number of cards you will be using. About 18 by 24 inches is a convenient size if you plan to carry the storyboard holder with you.

If you use two pieces, they can be hinged in the middle (as shown) with bookbinding tape or wide masking tape, giving you a usable surface measuring 36 by 24 inches when unfolded. If you do not plan to move the storyboard frequently, you could use a larger piece of cardboard (per-

haps from a large appliance box such as a refrigerator carton), which could give you up to 6 by 4 feet of usable surface.

Staple or tape 1-inch-wide strips of clear plastic (which could be made from overhead projection acetate) on the cardboard to hold the cards. If you are planning to use 3-by-5-inch cards, the strips should be attached about 4 inches apart. One-inch strips of paper or tagboard instead of clear plastic can be used to keep the card in place, but this has the disadvantage of not allowing you to read the portion of the card that is behind the strip.

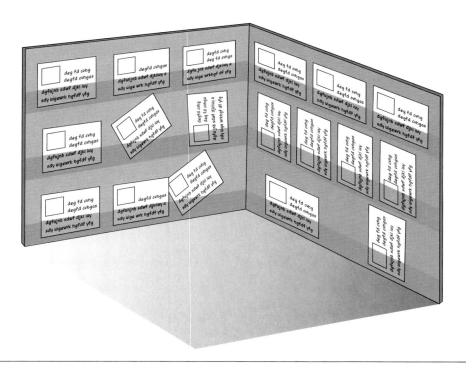

FIGURE 3.38

The storyboard card contains a place for the visual, production notes, and the narration

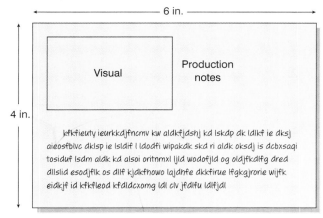

draw pictures with the mouse, import graphics from files, and manipulate images—enlarging, reducing, and so on. These images can be coupled with text and stored as cards, which can be arranged in different sequences on the computer screen. (The storyboarding process is discussed at greater length in Chapter 5, on page 160.)

Types of Letters. A wide variety of lettering techniques for visuals exists. The simplest is freehand lettering with markers and felt-tip pens, which come in an array of colors and sizes.

Letters can also be cut from construction paper or other materials. Precut letters are available in stationery and office supply stores. The letters are easy to use because most come with an adhesive backing; however, they are rather expensive.

Faces

Use an oval and add a minimum of lines to indicate features and expressions.

1. Start with a circle or oval.
2. Add ears in the middle on each side.
3. Draw a nose between the ears.
4. Place the eyes near the top of the nose.
5. Draw the mouth halfway between the nose and chin.
6. Add hair and other features.

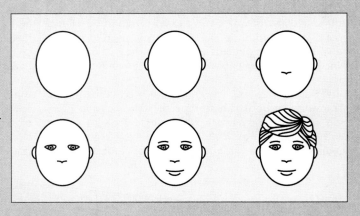

Body

Begin with stick figures, which can show action. With practice, add detail to your characters.

1. Determine the head size and draw.

2. Draw a straight line down from that head which is an *additional* 3 heads long. This is the torso.

3. Just below the head draw a *horizontal* line about 2 head lengths long. This is the shoulder line.

4. Draw a horizontal line about 1½ head lengths long at end of torso (slightly wider for female figure). This is the hip area.

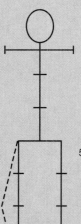

5. Draw vertical lines down from hip "joints" 4 head lengths long. Leg length comprises *half* of entire body length. Knees would fall about halfway or 2 head lengths down.

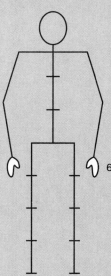

6. Draw vertical lines down from shoulder points to below the hips. These are arms. Add "mitten" hands at the ends. Elbows fall midway on these lines.

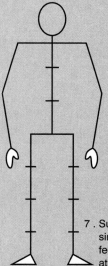

7. Superimpose simple triangular feet on the legs at the bottom.

Some media centers and graphic production units in business and industry use mechanical lettering devices such as the Kroy 88 (however, desktop publishing is rapidly taking their place). With such devices, the style and size of the letters are determined by interchangeable large plastic wheels. The letters are "printed" on strips of clear plastic or colored film. Once the backing has been removed, the letters will adhere to most surfaces. Desktop publishing systems are also frequently used to prepare lettering in various styles and sizes. The lettering ranges from a fraction of an inch in height for overhead transparencies to over a foot high for banners.

Drawing, Sketching, and Cartooning

As described in Chapter 4, drawings, sketches, and cartoons are nonprojected visuals that can enhance learning. There are many sources of these in magazines, textbooks, and advertisements. One often overlooked source is *you*. You don't have to be an artist to draw. There are some basic guidelines and many how-to books that can help you communicate effectively using these graphic media.

With a little practice, you may be surprised by how well you can draw. Simple drawings can enhance chalkboard presentations, class handouts, bulletin boards, and overhead transparencies. For ideas on getting started, see "How to . . . Sketch" (page 90) and the references at the end of this chapter.

PHOTOGRAPHY

Elements of Photography

All cameras, regardless of their size, shape, or type, operate on the same basic principles. There are four elements required for photography: a subject, light, a camera, and film (or some other recording medium). Light is reflected from the subject and passes through the lens to form an image on the recording medium. Let's look at the four elements in more detail.

Subject. For instructional purposes, the subject should be interesting and imaginative. The picture elements should be relevant to the instructional objective and should be "composed," or framed in the picture, properly. (See "How to . . . Take Better Pictures," page 94.)

Light. Light may come from natural sources (i.e., sunlight) or from artificial sources (light bulbs or camera flash units). The recording medium must be exposed to the

proper amount of light. Too little exposure and the picture will be dark; too much and the picture will be too light.

Camera. The camera is a light-tight box with a lens to collect the light from the subject and to focus the light on the film or other recording medium. The amount of light getting into the camera is controlled by the lens opening and the shutter speed.

Film (Recording Medium). The recording medium may be film or a light-sensitive detector called a **charge-coupled device (CCD)**. Recent technological advances have reduced the cost and improved the quality of CCDs to the point that they are competitive with film for many purposes. Film, still the most common recording medium, is a light-sensitive material that records the image. The image becomes visible after it is processed by chemicals. With some Polaroid film, the chemicals are part of the film package. CCDs convert the light image into electrons that can be digitized, processed, and stored electronically. Because the elements of the image are digitized, they can be viewed on a monitor, stored on compact discs, or combined with other digital information in a computer.

Parts of a Camera

Cameras have many parts, but the most important parts common to all cameras are the aperture, the shutter, the viewfinder, the focus mechanism, and the film advance (Figure 3.39).

Aperture. The aperture is the lens opening that regulates the amount of light entering the camera. On some cameras the size of the opening is fixed; on other cameras there are two or three possible settings for the

FIGURE 3.39
Components of a typical camera

Film advance

Focus mechanism

Viewfinder

Shutter

Aperture (lens opening)

VISUAL DESIGN CHECKLIST

KEY WORDS: _____ , _____ , _____

Material being evaluated _____

Evaluator _____ **Date** _____

	Exemplary	Acceptable	Poor	Comments
Overall pattern				
Alignment	❏	❏	❏	
Shape	❏	❏	❏	
Balance	❏	❏	❏	
Style	❏	❏	❏	
Color Scheme	❏	❏	❏	
Color Appeal	❏	❏	❏	
Arrangement				
Proximity	❏	❏	❏	
Directionals	❏	❏	❏	
Figure-Ground Contrast	❏	❏	❏	
Consistency	❏	❏	❏	
Verbal Elements				
Lettering Style	❏	❏	❏	
Letter Size and Spacing	❏	❏	❏	
Appeal				
Surprise	❏	❏	❏	
Texture	❏	❏	❏	
Interaction	❏	❏	❏	

aperture. On many cameras, however, the size of the lens opening is adjustable over a broad range.

Shutter. The **shutter** controls the length of time that light enters the camera and reaches the film. Again, there is only one shutter speed on simple cameras but several on more complex cameras. The shutter speed refers to the period of time that light is allowed to enter the camera. On the shutter speed control knob the speed is usually given as a whole number such as 250, 125, or 30. However, these numbers refer to fractions of a second (i.e., $\frac{1}{250}$ of a second, $\frac{1}{125}$ of a second, and $\frac{1}{30}$ of a second). The higher the number, the shorter the time that the shutter is open. The very fast shutter speeds such as $\frac{1}{1000}$ second (with the shutter open only a very short period of time) allow you to photograph rapidly moving objects, such as race cars.

Viewfinder. The **viewfinder** allows you to see what the film will "see" when the shutter is opened. In many cameras the viewfinder is near the top of the camera and set parallel to the lens opening. Consequently, when you look through the viewfinder you may not see exactly what will appear in the photograph. Except at very close range, the discrepancy is negligible. With a single-lens reflex camera, a movable mirror allows you to view directly through the lens. The mirror is moved out of the way when a photograph is taken.

Focus Mechanism. The focus mechanism is the setting of the lens that determines the sharpness of the image. Inexpensive cameras often cannot be focused and have just one setting, which is usually good for objects from five feet to infinity. Other cameras have a range of focus from three feet to infinity. The focus may be determined by a distance scale (to the subject) and is

FIGURE 3.40
The SLR camera (left) with extra lenses for extreme close-ups and long-distance photography compared with a point-and-shoot camera for general purpose photography.

indicated in feet and/or meters. Many of the newer cameras have automatic focus mechanisms.

Film Advance. The film advance is used to advance the film to the next frame after a picture is taken.

Selecting a Camera

The type of camera you choose depends on the kinds of pictures you find useful for instruction. If you do not take extreme close-ups and do not have use for telephoto and other special lenses, then you may prefer a point-and-shoot camera for portability, reliability, and simplicity (Figure 3.40). The quality of the image taken with a moderately priced point-and-shoot camera is comparable to that of a high-quality single lens reflex (SLR) camera.

If, however, you need to take extreme close-ups, will use a variety of lenses (e.g., wide-angle, telephoto), and do a lot of copying, then a single-lens reflex camera is what you want. Although it is bulkier and more difficult to use, the SLR is more flexible than a point-and-shoot camera.

Both types of cameras are available in models with automatic and semiautomatic exposure controls. Before the incorporation of photocells and microprocessors into cameras, even amateur photographers had to know the relationship among film speed, lens opening (f/stop), and shutter speed. Today's picture taker need learn only a few simple steps from the instruction manual to achieve proper exposure on the film. Sometimes unusual lighting situations call for modifications of camera-determined settings. A little experience with the camera will guide such modifications. Relieved of the necessity to determine exposure, the photographer can concentrate on composing the picture.

New point-and-shoot cameras are packed with computer technology. These cameras have automatic loading, film-speed setting, exposure, focus, flash, and winding.

Digital cameras store black/white or full-color images in a digital format. A CCD (charge-coupled device) in the film plane of the camera converts light energy to digital data, which is stored in a small digital recorder. Such cameras can be specially designed or can be modifications of standard SLR cameras. Since no film is used, there is no waiting for developing and printing. Images can be viewed immediately on a small monitor incorporated into the camera. The images can be transmitted over telephone lines and/or downloaded to a computer for manipulation and can be stored on a computer disk or on photo CDs (compact discs). Digital photography is particularly useful to create images for presentations or for desktop publishing.

Most instructors in education and training use slides far more often than they do prints. Unless you can afford the luxury of two cameras (and you don't mind carrying them around), you will probably be better off keeping slide film in your camera. If you later find that

Whether you are recording the things you see on a trip, creating a photo essay, shooting a historical subject, developing an instructional picture sequence, or simply taking pictures of family and friends, a few guidelines can make your photographs more effective.

1. Choose picture elements thoughtfully.
   - Include all elements that are helpful in communicating your ideas.
   - Eliminate extraneous elements, such as distracting backgrounds. Avoid shooting directly toward mirrors or shiny surfaces.
   - Include size indicators (e.g., a car, a person, a hand, a small coin) in the picture if the size of the main object of interest is not apparent.

2. Compose picture elements carefully.

   - Remember the rule of thirds, discussed on p. 80. Divide the picture area in thirds both vertically and horizontally. The center of interest should be near one of the intersections of the lines (not cramped near the edge).
   - Avoid dividing a picture exactly in half with a vertical or horizontal line, such as the horizon. Using the rule of thirds, you would want the horizon line at either the one-third or two-thirds line.
   - When photographing a moving subject, allow more room in front of the subject than behind it.

   - When making "how-to-do-it" pictures, use a subjective point of view. That is, take the picture from the viewpoint of the learner, not the observer.
   - Dramatic effects can be obtained by shooting from high or low angles. However, such pictures may be confusing to young children.
   - If a feeling of depth is important, use foreground objects (e.g., blossom-covered tree branches) to frame the main subject.

3. Employ appropriate photographic technique.
   - Choose an appropriate film for the subject and intended use.
   - Arrange lighting that will enhance the subject.

   - Select exposure to get optimum quality; this is necessary for digital cameras as well as standard cameras.
   - Focus carefully.
   - Avoid moving or tilting your camera while snapping the picture.

These general guidelines will help you take interesting photographs that will communicate more effectively. For further steps in enhancing your photographic skills, check your local camera shop or bookstore for reference material on photography.

Visual Literacy and Writing

Analyze Learners

General Characteristics

The sixth-grade class at St. Matthew School has 33 students who come from diverse cultural and language backgrounds; in this school in Brooklyn, New York, 85% of the students are Hispanic, 10% are African American, and 5% are Asian American. According to standardized tests, almost all the students in this class are achieving well below grade level in reading.

Entry Competencies

Because the teacher is focusing on reading and writing skills, she administers a standardized rating scale to evaluate composition ability. Her students are writing at about 50% competency for content and mechanics compared with other sixth-grade populations in the United States.

The teacher has discovered that her students have difficulty organizing their writing because they lack a sense of sentence and paragraph structure. She also realizes that when information is presented to such students in a way that is disconnected from their experience they have difficulty retaining it.

State Objectives

The main objective for this unit is: Given content outlines developed by the class as a group, individual sixth-grade students will be able to write essays in English in sequential style and descriptive style that exhibit composition skills appropriate for their grade level.

A supporting objective could include the following. In small-group work, students will demonstrate active listening skills so that group members will successfully reach consensus, be able to express themselves orally, and make oral presentations of their photo essay storyboards using coherent standard English.

Select Methods, Media, and Materials

This teacher prefers to follow the whole-language approach, integrating listening, speaking, reading, and writing activities together in one unit. She decides to use a visual literacy approach implemented through cooperative learning groups and discovery methods to provide concrete experiences that might help fill gaps in the students' mental schemata. She wants to improve both language ability and motivation by providing meaningful connections between the students' real-world experiences and their language activities in school. This means that the students, rather than the teacher, would be the main performers.

First, the teacher prepares materials for a semantic mapping activity to be done by the whole class. She stands at the overhead projector modeling the process of building a map of ideas visually.

Next, she organizes a small-group project approach to creating photo essays. There is a logistical hurdle: getting enough cameras to allow all students to have hands-on experience taking pictures. Fortunately, the library media specialist is able to help her obtain 20 cameras from the district media center.

Finally, she decides that students would learn to use storyboarding techniques to organize their photo essays and that each student would write an essay based on his or her group's photo story.

Utilize Media and Materials

The two-week unit begins with the teacher conducting a large-group brainstorming session, using the overhead projector, to develop semantic maps. They start with the general theme of "Brooklyn's Amazing History" and break that down into subtopics, such as "The Role of the Subway." These subtopics constitute the content for the photo shooting that follows.

Require Learner Participation

Following planning sessions in which students brainstorm visual ideas for their photo shoots, they go out into their neighborhoods in pairs to shoot the photographs they had previously visualized.

When the finished photos are available, the groups use storyboarding techniques to organize their pictures and prepare captions. Each group's storyboard is presented to the rest of the class. The unit culminates with each student writing an essay based on the group's storyboard.

This procedure is repeated twice more, for a total of three two-week sessions of planning, photographing, storyboarding, and writing.

Evaluate and Revise

The teacher analyzes the essays, again using a standardized rating scale. The typical score for each of the essays is in the 70% range. The structure of the essays is particularly improved compared with those written earlier, although there are still obvious deficiencies in spelling and grammar.

She also uses simple rating forms for class members to give feedback on each oral presentation; she notes that there are fewer negative and more positive comments on the second and third attempts.

The teacher also keeps an informal journal of instances of nonstandard English use in students' everyday classroom speaking. She notices that a number of students are improving their ability to speak standard English.

In a class discussion after the three projects are completed, students agree that they prefer this approach to conventional writing assignments.

This "Blueprint" is adapted from an actual case report by Richard Sinatra, Jeffrey S. Beaudry, Josephine Stahl-Bemake, and E. Francine Guastello, "Combining Visual Literacy, Text Understanding, and Writing for Culturally Diverse Students," *Journal of Reading* (May 1990), pp. 612–617.
A computer template for a Blueprint is found in "The Classroom Link."

you need prints, very satisfactory ones can be made from slides. If very large photographs are required (eight by ten inches or larger), laser technology can make prints of remarkable quality from slides. However, if you prefer using print film, slides can be made from your color negatives at many camera shops.

Having chosen a camera and type of film, you will find guidelines for taking instructionally useful photos in the "How to . . . Take Better Pictures" feature. For hints on planning a slide or slide–tape presentation, see "How to . . . Develop a Sound–Slide Presentation" on pages 160–161 in Chapter 5. Further technical information on photography and suggestions for working with student photography can be found in the audiovisual references at the end of this chapter.

MEDIA PORTFOLIOS

As schools become more oriented to the future, visual literacy is becoming far more than just one more curricular goal to be attained. Students' abilities to use multimedia research sources and to prepare mediated presentations that summarize their own understanding of a thematic topic are central to the schooling experience under the concept of media portfolios. Educators frustrated with standardized testing and conventional paper-and-pencil assessments have begun to explore the notion of having students demonstrate their achievements by compiling **portfolios** of their work. Many feel that assessment of portfolios gives a truer, more rounded view of an individual's strengths and weaknesses. Further, portfolio assessment is consistent with the constructivist philosophy, which emphasizes that what is important is *the knowledge that students themselves construct.* They claim that the usable residue of years of schooling is rather small, and the small fraction of "school learning" that does remain usable is a conglomeration of information and practical skills that were con-

structed in the student's own mind through his or her struggle with a meaningful project.

The idea of portfolio assessment, then, is to measure students' achievements by their ability to create tangible products exemplifying their talents. Portfolios could contain the following products:

- Written documents such as poems, stories, or research papers
- Media presentations, such as slide sets or photo essays
- Audio recordings of debates, panel discussions, or oral presentations
- Video recordings of the students' athletic, musical, or dancing skills
- Computer spreadsheets of student data
- Computer multimedia projects incorporating print, data, graphics, and moving images

Students could be required to assemble a media portfolio as the final record of their accomplishments rather than a transcript with a list of courses completed. It is being done on a piecemeal basis in many schools already. A few have even experimented with abolishing conventional grades and credits completely. But there are many philosophical, political, and economic factors to deal with before the conventional assessment system is replaced by one based more on tangible products than on quiz scores.

For some practical tips on assembling media portfolios, see the Mundell and DeLario and the Cravotta and Wilson references listed at the end of the chapter.

FIGURE 3.41
Slides, videos, computer-based multimedia, and other student-produced media are included in student portfolios.

REFERENCES

Print References

Adams, Dennis M., and Hamm, Mary E. *Media and Literacy: Learning in an Electronic Age.* Springfield, IL: Charles Thomas, 1989.

Allen, Rodney. "Snapshot Geography: Using Travel Photographs to Learn Geography in Upper Elementary Schools," *Canadian Social Studies* 27(2) (Winter 1993): 63–66.

Bergeron, Roland. "The Uses of Color to Enhance Training Communications," *Performance and Instruction* (August 1990): 34–37.

Cravotta, Mary Ellen, and Wilson, Savan. *Media Cookbook for Kids.* Englewood, CO: Libraries Unlimited, 1989.

Curtiss, D. *Introduction to Visual Literacy: A Guide to the Visual Arts and Communication.* Mountain View, CA: Mayfield Publishing, 1989.

Danzer, Gerald A. "Excerpt from 'Tuning In,' a Curriculum Development Project, The Camera's Eye; Imagery and Technology," *Social Studies* 83(3) (May–June 1992): 134.

Dwyer, Francis M., ed. *Enhancing Visualized Instruction.* State College, PA: Learning Services, 1987.

Fleming, Malcolm. "Characteristics of Effective Instruction Presentation: What We Know and What We Need to Know." *Educational Technology* (July 1981): 33–38.

Garner, Kathleen H. "20 Rules for Arranging Text on a Screen," *CBT Directions* (May 1990): 13–17.

Gropper, George L. *Text Display: Analysis and Systematic Design.* Englewood Cliffs, NJ: Educational Technology Publication, 1991.

Hortin, John A. "Visual Literacy and Visual Thinking." In *Australian Society of Educational Technology National Yearbook, 1981,* ed. L. J. Ausburn. Hawthorn, Australia: ASET, 1982.

Langham, Barbara. "Help School-Agers Develop Visual Literacy." *Texas Child Care* 17(1) (Summer 1993): 34–38.

Lloyd-Kolkin, Donna, and Tyner, Kathleen R. *Media and You, an Elementary Media Literacy Curriculum.* Englewood Cliffs, NJ: Educational Technology Publications, 1991.

Marcus, Stephen. "Picture This! Instant Photography and Writing across the Curriculum," *Writing Notebook: Visions for Learning* 10(2) (November–December 1992): 8–12, 34.

McNeil, D. W. "Photography Through the Microscope," *Science Probe* 2(3) (July 1992), 77–101.

Milheim, William D., and Lavix, Carol. "Screen Design for Computer-Based Training and Interactive Video: Practical Suggestions and Overall Guidelines." *Performance and Instruction* 31(5) (May–June 1992): 13–21.

Mundell, Susan B., and DeLario, Karen. *Practical Portfolios: Reading, Writing, Math, and Life Skills, Grades 3–6.* Englewood, CO: Libraries Unlimited, 1994.

Oehring, Sandra. "Teaching with Technology. Hands-on. On Camera—And in the Computer." *Instructor* 102(9) (May–June 1993): 76.

Payne, Bill. "A Word is Worth a Thousand Pictures: Teaching Students to Think Critically in a Culture of Images." *Social Studies Review* 32(3) (Spring 1993): 38–43.

Perry, Susan K. "Photography for Children: More than Meets the Eye." *PTA Today* 18(2) (November 1992): 17–20.

Pettersson, Rune. *Visuals for Information: Research and Practice.* Englewood Cliffs, NJ: Educational Technology Publications, 1989.

Pick, Diane. "Camera in Camp: Helping Campers Understand Principles of Photography." *Camping Magazine* 65:5 (May–June 1993): 18–21.

Poltorak, David. "Problems of Perception of Audio-Visual Information in Studying History." *History Teacher* 25:3 (May 1992): 313–319.

Postman, Neil. *Conscientious Objections: Stirring Up Trouble About Language, Technology, and Education.* New York: Knopf, 1990.

Shamber, Linda. "Core Course in Visual Literacy for Ideas, Not Techniques," *Journalism Educator* 46(1) (Spring 1991): pp. 16–21.

Tufte, E. R. *Envisioning Information.* Cheshire CT: Graphics Press, 1990.

What a Picture! Learning from Photographs. Dickson, Australia: Curriculum Development Centre, 1981.

Wileman, Ralph E. *Visual Communicating.* Englewood Cliffs, NJ: Educational Technology Publications, 1993.

Audiovisual References

Art Elements: An Introduction. Santa Monica, CA: BFA Educational Media, 1981. 16mm film. 18 minutes.

Basic Lettering for Audiovisual Materials. Iowa City, IA: University of Iowa, 1985. VHS videocassette. 6 minutes.

Basic 35mm Photography. Huntsville, TX: Educational Video Network, 1983. VHS video, six 15-minute videocassettes.

Bring Your Message into Focus. Eastman Kodak Co., 1982. Kit (dissolve-slide program). 20 minutes.

Copystand Photography. Iowa City, IA: University of Iowa, 1990. VHS videocassette. 9 minutes.

Elements of Design. Bloomington, IN: Agency for Instructional Technology, 1988. Videocassette, 15 minutes.

Experiencing Design. Burbank, CA: Encore Visual Education, 1975. Four sound filmstrips. 58 frames.

How Does a Picture Mean? Washington, DC: Association for Educational Communications and Technology, 1967. Filmstrip. 76 frames.

How to Take Better Pictures. Media Tree, 1982. Slide set with audiocassette.

Learning to See and Understand: Developing Visual Literacy. White Plains, NY: Center for Humanities, 1973. Sound–slide set. 160 slides. 48 minutes.

Making Sense Visually. Washington, DC: Association for Education Communications and Technology, 1969. Sound filmstrip. 76 frames.

Oh, C. Y. *Instruction to the Preparation of Instruction Materials.* Edmonton, Canada: Avent Media, 1980. 32 slide–tape sets, textbook, and student manual.

Photography: How It Works. Rochester, NY: Eastman Kodak Co., 1979. 16mm film. 12 minutes.

Principles of Picture Design. Bloomington, IN: Agency for Instructional Technology, 1988. Videocassette, 15 minutes.

Taking Better Pictures. Athens, GA: University of Georgia, 1984. Videocassette series.

NONPROJECTED MEDIA

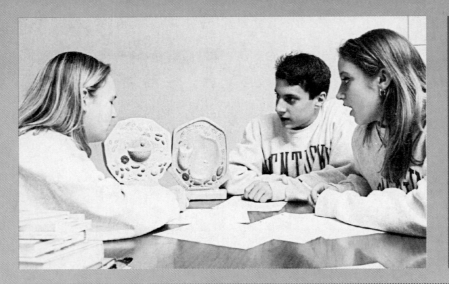

Not all media plug into an electrical outlet. There is a wide variety of nonprojected media that can make your instruction more realistic and engaging. Objects and models bring "the real thing" into the classroom. Students can vicariously explore other places and other times through books, other printed materials, and kits that combine objects, pictures, and text.

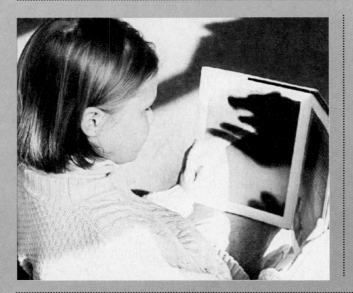

Pictures, charts, graphs, posters, and cartoons—including those that are produced by the students themselves—can provide powerful visual support to abstract ideas. These nonprojected media can be displayed in a variety of ways. You need to be able to use chalkboards, flip charts, bulletin boards, and other display formats confidently. Of course, students often construct such displays themselves as part of cooperative group projects.

KNOWLEDGE OBJECTIVES

1. Describe instructional applications that are especially appropriate for models and real objects.
2. Describe instructional purposes that are especially well suited to the use of multimedia kits.
3. Justify the use of a field trip for a particular instructional purpose of interest to you and describe how it might be introduced and followed up.
4. Compare the advantages, limitations, and applications of printed materials in instruction.
5. Demonstrate your ability to follow the proper procedures for locating, obtaining, appraising, and using free and inexpensive materials.
6. Compare the advantages and limitations of nonprojected visuals.
7. List six types of nonprojected visuals and state an appropriate application for each in teaching something of interest to you.
8. Identify two methods of preserving nonprojected visuals and state three reasons for doing so.
9. Compare the advantages and limitations of rubber cement mounting with those of dry mounting.
10. Compare the advantages and limitations of various types of display surfaces.
11. Describe instructional applications that are especially appropriate for exhibits, displays, and dioramas.

APPLICATION OBJECTIVES

1. Locate and examine a multimedia kit in your field of interest. Prepare a written or oral report on the possible applications and relative merits of the kit.
2. Obtain an example of a real object or model that you could use for instruction. Submit the object or model and a description of how you would use it, including an objective.
3. Use the "Appraisal Checklist: Print" to evaluate a textbook, fiction book, nonfiction book, pamphlet, or manual.
4. Use the "Appraisal Checklist: Nonprojected Visuals" to evaluate specific materials of interest to you.
5. Select three pictures that are at least five by seven inches and mount one with temporary rubber cement, one with permanent rubber cement, and a third with dry-mount tissue.
6. Plan a lesson in which you use a set of still pictures. Within this lesson show evidence that you have used the "Appraisal Checklist: Nonprojected Visuals" and followed the suggested utilization principles. Submit pictures with lesson.
7. Create one graph (line, bar, circle, or pictorial) and one chart (organization, classification, time line, tabular, or flow) for a topic you might teach. Use the "Appraisal Checklist: Nonprojected Visuals" as a guideline.
8. Make a list of ten possible posters students could make to depict aspects of your teaching area. Prepare one yourself to serve as a model or motivational device.
9. Demonstrate techniques (showmanship tips) for improving your utilization of chalkboards and multipurpose boards. Demonstrate techniques (showmanship tips) to enhance learning from flip charts.
10. Prepare a bulletin board, cloth board, magnetic board, flip chart, or exhibit. Submit the material, a description of the intended audience, the objectives, how it will be used, and how it will be evaluated.

LEXICON

real object	study print	line graph	copy board
model	bar graph	dry mounting	flip chart
multimedia kit	pictorial graph	lamination	exhibit
graphics	circle graph	multipurpose board	diorama

Many of the media and materials discussed in this chapter are so common that instructors are inclined to underestimate their instructional value. Materials don't have to be exotic or expensive to be useful. Small can indeed be beautiful, and inexpensive can be effective! In fact, in some situations—for instance, isolated, rural areas; places that lack electricity; programs or schools with a low budget—these simpler materials may be the only media that make sense to use. (Figure 4.1.)

Even though the focus in this chapter is on nonprojected visuals, the discussion includes some topics that technically might not be classified as visuals. These include real objects, models, printed materials, free and inexpensive materials, multimedia kits, field trips, and the devices used to display visuals (chalkboards, cloth boards, magnetic boards, and flip charts).

REAL OBJECTS

Real objects—such as coins, tools, artifacts, plants, and animals—are some of the most accessible, intriguing, and involving materials in educational use (Figure 4.2). The gerbils that draw a crowd in the kindergarten, the terrarium that introduces middle schoolers to the concept of ecology, the collection of Colonial era coins, the frogs dissected in the college biology laboratory, the real baby being bathed in the parenting class—these are just a few examples of the potential of real objects to elucidate the obscure and to stimulate the imagination.

Being concrete, real objects fit near the bottom of Dale's Cone of Experience (see Chapter 1), meaning that they are especially appropriate for learners who are encountering a subject about which they have had little direct experience in their daily lives. Going back in time, at least to Comenius in the 17th century (see page 72–73, Chapter 3), educators have understood the dangers of plunging into abstract concepts and principles without building a foundation in concrete experience. *Verbalism* is a term that refers to the parroting of words without meaningful understanding. To build schemata that have meaning and relevance in their lives, learners need a base in concrete experience, and bringing real objects into the classroom can help in this process.

Real objects may be used as is, or they can be modified to enhance instruction. Examples of modification include the following:

- *Cutaways.* Devices such as machines with one side cut away to allow close observation of the inner workings (Figure 4.3).
- *Specimens.* Actual plants, animals, or parts thereof preserved for convenient inspection.
- *Exhibits.* Collections of artifacts, often of a scientific or historical nature, brought together with printed information to illustrate a point (Figure 4.4).

Besides their obvious virtues as a means of presenting information, raising questions, and providing hands-on learning experiences, real objects can also play a valuable role in the evaluation phase of instruction. They can be displayed in a central location. Learners can identify them, classify them, describe their functioning, discuss their utility, or compare and contrast them. Such a testing situation emphasizes the real-world application of the topic of study, aids transfer of training, and helps transcend the merely verbal level of learning.

FIGURE 4.1
Nonprojected visuals are the most widely used media.

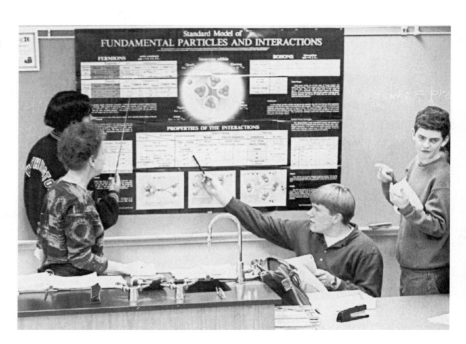

FIGURE 4.2
There is no substitute for the real thing when learning some content.

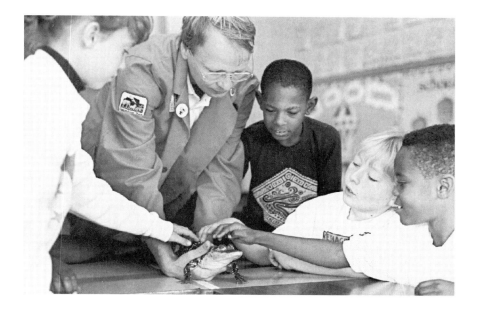

MODELS

Models are three-dimensional representations of a real thing. A model may be larger, smaller, or the same size as the object it represents. It may be complete in detail or simplified for instructional purposes. Indeed, models can provide learning experiences that real things cannot provide (see Figure 4.5). For example, important details

FIGURE 4.3
A cutaway of a machine reveals its hidden components.

can be accented with color. Some models can be disassembled to provide interior views not possible with the real thing.

Models of almost anything—from airplanes to zebras—can be purchased for classroom use. Providing collections of models and globes is a standard service of most school media centers. School district and regional media centers and museums often loan artifacts and models, usually as part of multimedia kits (such kits are described later in the chapter).

A wide variety of model kits is also available for assembly by you or your students. Assembly itself can be instructional. Classroom construction of model kits appeals to children of all ages (and, indeed, to adults) and can stimulate inquiry and discovery. Assembly activities help sharpen both cognitive and psychomotor skills.

Mock-ups, which are simplified representations of complex devices or processes, are prevalent in industrial training. By highlighting essential elements and eliminating distracting details, mock-ups clarify the complex. They are sometimes constructed as working models to illustrate the basic operations of a real device (Figure 4.7). Such a situation allows individuals or small groups to manipulate the mock-up at their own convenience, working with the subject matter until they comprehend it. For example, a mock-up of a microcomputer might have the internal components spread out on a large board with the components labeled and the circuit diagrams printed on the board. The most sophisticated type of mock-up, the simulator, is a device that allows learners to experience the important aspects of a real-life process without the risks (simulators are discussed in detail in Chapter 11).

Models and real objects are the recommended media when realism is essential for learning. They provide con-

FIGURE 4.4
Cultural artifacts come to life when presented in a well-designed exhibit.

cepts that involve three dimensions; tasks that require identification by size, shape, or color; and hands-on or laboratory practice.

MULTIMEDIA KITS

A **multimedia kit** is a collection of teaching/learning materials involving more than one type of medium and organized around a single topic. Kits may include filmstrips, slides, audiotapes, videotapes, still pictures, study prints, overhead transparencies, maps, worksheets, charts, graphs, booklets, real objects, and models.

Some multimedia kits are designed for use by the teacher in classroom presentations. Others are designed for use by individual students or by small groups.

Commercial Multimedia Kits

Commercial multimedia kits are available for a variety of educational subjects. These learning kits include videotapes, audiocassettes, floor games, board games, posters, full-color photographs, activity cards, lotto cards, murals, wall charts, geometric shapes, flash cards, student workbooks, and a teacher's manual. Objectives are stated and supported with suggested teaching strategies for using the materials in the kit.

Other multimedia kits on a wide variety of topics are available from commercial sources, some of which contain (among other materials) transparencies, laboratory materials for science experiments, and even puppets to act out stories.

FIGURE 4.5
An anatomical model, being three-dimensional, is a more concrete referent than a photograph, drawing, or even a videotape.

FIGURE 4.6
Artifacts and models provide hands-on experiences.

FIGURE 4.7
A mock-up of an engine's electrical system provides the learner with a full-scale working model from which distracting details have been deleted.

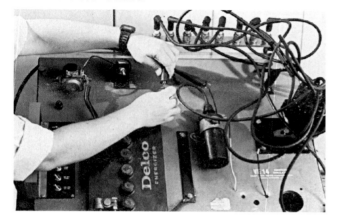

Teacher-Produced Multimedia Kits

Multimedia kits can also be prepared by teachers or media specialists. Like any other instructional material, the kit should be designed around the objectives; each component should contribute in an integral way to those objectives. The main purpose of a kit is to give learners a chance at firsthand learning—to touch, to observe, to experiment, to wonder, to decide.

Availability and cost of materials are obviously important considerations. Will there be one kit for all students to share, or can the kit be duplicated for all? Are the materials reusable? If not, replacement supplies will be needed. Will the kit include audiovisual materials? If so, where will students find the necessary equipment? Can the kit be used in a variety of instructional situations?

Advantages

- *Interest.* Multimedia kits arouse interest because they are multisensory. Everyone likes to touch and manipulate real objects—to inspect unusual specimens close up.

- *Cooperation.* Kits can be an ideal mechanism for stimulating small-group project work. Cooperative learning activities can be arranged, revolving around experiments, problem solving, role playing, or other types of hands-on practice.
- *Logistics.* Kits have an obvious logistical advantage. Being packaged, they can be transported and used outside the classroom, such as in the media center or at home.

Limitations

- *Expense.* Learning with multimedia kits can be more expensive than with other, more conventional, methods.
- *Time-consuming.* It can be time-consuming to produce and maintain the materials.
- *Replacement.* Lost components can make the kit frustrating to use.

Applications

Multimedia kits are particularly well suited to content for which discovery learning is preferred. Questions can be posed to guide learners' exploration and arrival at conclusions. Science topics are well suited to this approach. For example, a kit on magnetism might include several types of magnets, iron filings, and metal objects that may or may not be attracted to magnets. In mathematics, a kit on measurement might include a folding meter stick and directions for measuring various objects and dimensions around the home or in school.

FIELD TRIPS

The field trip, an excursion outside the classroom to study real processes, people, and objects, often grows out of students' need for firsthand experiences. It makes it possible for students to encounter phenomena that cannot be brought into the classroom for observation and study. (Figure 4.9.)

▶ AV SHOWMANSHIP   *Real Objects and Models*

- Familiarize yourself with the object or model before using it in classroom instruction.
- Practice your presentation. If your object or model is a working one, be sure you know how it works and what might go wrong.
- Be sure your audience does not get the wrong impression of the size, shape, or color of the real objective, if the model differs from it in these respects.

- Whenever feasible, encourage your students to handle and manipulate the objects and models under study.
- Store objects out of sight when they are not being used for instruction. Left standing around, they are likely to take students' attention away from other classroom activities.

FIGURE 4.8
Multimedia kits provide varied sensory experiences. They give the concrete referents needed to build a strong foundation for more abstract mental abilities.

Examples of field trips include a trip of a few minutes into the schoolyard to observe a tree, a trek across the street to see construction work, or a longer trip of several days to tour historical locations. Popular field trip sites include zoos, museums, public buildings, and parks. Dale's Cone of Experience (Chapter 1) places field trips toward the middle of the cone because, although the experience is "real," students typically are only seeing and hearing the phenomena, not directly manipulating them.

The school media specialist can increase the chances for a successful field trip experience by maintaining a local resource file. This file includes lists of possible sites to visit and speakers to invite to classes for presentations. Usually the file record includes the name, address, and phone number of the person to contact. A good resource file will also include notes regarding the value of previous trips or the way a speaker was previously received. Some district media centers and public libraries maintain a local resource file as part of their electronic catalog.

For a field trip to be justified, it should grow out of and be directly related to the regular course of study. Objectives should be developed for the field trip. There should be lead-in as well as follow-up (including evaluation) activities. The lead-in prepares the students for the field trip; the follow-up helps them reflect on the experience and integrate it into their own schemata.

The follow-up is a vital aspect of a field trip. If the purpose for making the trip is to get additional factual information, the evaluation will be more formal. If the objectives are the formation of attitudes and appreciation, follow-up activities might include discussion, role playing, or creative art projects. Whatever form it takes, the follow-up activity should be used to assess the success of the trip. Students and teachers should address content as well as possible ways to improve future trips. (See "How to . . . Conduct a Field Trip" on page 108.)

▼ MEDIA FILE

Environments Module

Commercial Multimedia Kit

Barley, bugs, beetles, and brine shrimp are just a few of the living organisms the students work with in this multimedia kit. Relating what they see in the experiments with what they see in the interactive videos, students come to appreciate that living things are dependent on the conditions of their environments.

Among other things, this commercial multimedia kit includes videocassettes and/or videodiscs in both English and Spanish, bilingual computer software, scientific equipment, and coupons to secure live organisms. There is also a teacher guide and teacher preparation video.

Source: Encyclopaedia Britannica Educational Corporation.

PRINTED MATERIALS

Printed materials include textbooks, fiction and nonfiction books, booklets, pamphlets, study guides, manuals, and worksheets, as well as word-processed documents prepared by students and teachers. Textbooks have long been the foundation of classroom instruction. The other forms of media discussed in this book are frequently used in conjunction with and as supplements to printed materials.

Advantages

- *Availability.* Printed materials are readily available on a wide variety of topics and in many different formats.

CLOSE-UP

A TEACHER-MADE MULTIMEDIA KIT

An elementary teacher developed a series of separate multimedia kits on science topics for use with her third-grade class. She incorporated real objects, such as magnets, small motors, rocks, harmless chemicals, and insect specimens in the kits. She also gathered pictures associated with each topic from magazines and old textbooks. A study guide, prepared for each unit, required the student to inquire about the topic, make hypotheses, and conduct investigations. References were included for books on the topic and other nonprint sources. Audiotapes were prepared for use at school and at home for students who had access to cassette players.

The students enjoyed taking the kits home to work on the experiments. The response from parents was very positive. Several parents reported that they, too, learned by working through the activities with their children. Students often preferred to stay in at recess and work on the multimedia kits in the science corner.

- *Flexibility.* They are adaptable to many purposes and they may be used in any lighted environment.
- *Portability.* They are easily carried from place to place and do not require any equipment or electricity.
- *User friendly.* Properly designed printed materials are easy to use, not requiring special effort to "navigate" through.
- *Economical.* Printed materials are relatively inexpensive to produce or purchase and can be reused. In fact, some may be obtained free, as described in the next section.

Limitations

- *Reading level.* The major limitation of printed materials is that they are written at a certain reading level. Some students are nonreaders or poor readers lacking adequate literacy skills; some printed materials are above their reading level.
- *Prior knowledge.* Even though textbooks are generally written to be more considerate of the reader, with clear language and simple sentence structures, readers who lack some prerequisite knowledge may struggle to comprehend the text.

FIGURE 4.9
Field trips provide students with opportunities for firsthand observation and participation, as in this trip to a nineteenth-century one-room schoolhouse.

PLANNING

1. Have a clear idea of the purpose and objectives of the trip.
2. Get a full overview of the content and procedures of the trip. Preview the trip yourself. Evaluate it for possible safety considerations.
3. Make arrangements with the school principal, the host, and other teachers (if they are involved). Secure consent of the parents for students to make the trip. Remind students and parents of appropriate dress.
4. Arrange transportation.
5. Establish rules for safety and security; for example, what the students should do if they are separated from the group.
6. Provide sufficient supervision. Arrange for volunteers (e.g., parents) to accompany the class. Assign each volunteer to oversee a small group of students.

PREPARING

1. Clarify the purpose of the trip with the entire group. Build interest in the trip through lead-in activities such as the following:
   • Class discussion
   • Stories
   • Reports
   • Videos
   • Films
   • Teacher–student planning
2. Give explicit directions to students regarding the following:
   • What to look for
   • Questions to ask
   • Information to be gathered
   • Notes to be made
   • Individual or group assignments
   • How to behave

CONDUCTING

1. Arrive at the field trip site on time.
2. Encourage students to observe carefully and to ask questions.
3. Obtain available materials that can be used later. Examples include informational pamphlets, brochures, and souvenirs.
4. Account for all travelers before starting the return trip.

FOLLOW-UP

1. Conduct follow-up of the field trip with these types of activities:
   • Discussion of the trip
   • Reports
   • Projects
   • Demonstrations
   • Creative writing
   • Individual research
   • Class experience stories
   • Exhibits of pictures, maps, charts, graphs, drawings, etc.
2. Write a thank-you letter to the host, guides, parent volunteers, drivers, and others who were instrumental in conducting the field trip. Notes written by the class or a student committee are most appreciated.

• *Memorization.* Some teachers require students to memorize many facts and definitions. This practice diminishes printed materials to mere memorization aids.

• *Vocabulary.* Some texts introduce a large number of vocabulary terms and concepts in a short amount of space. This practice places a heavy cognitive burden on students, which may be overwhelming for some.

• *One-way presentation.* Since most printed materials are not interactive, they tend to be used in a passive way, often without comprehension.

• *Curriculum determination.* Sometimes textbooks dictate the curriculum rather than being used to support the curriculum. Textbooks are often written to accommodate the curriculum guidelines of particular states or provinces. Consequently, the preferences of these authorities disproportionately influence textbook content or its treatment.

• *Cursory appraisal.* Selection committees might not examine textbooks carefully. Sometimes textbooks are chosen by a "five-minute thumb test"—whatever catches the reviewer's eye as he or she thumbs through the textbook.

Applications

The most common application of printed materials is the presentation of content information. Students are given reading assignments and are held accountable for the material during class discussions and on tests. Teacher-made handouts can also complement a teacher's presentation or be used by students as they study independently. Refer to "How to . . . Design Text."

Students may also use printed materials to augment either the information presented by the teacher or other forms of media. Students frequently refer to supplementary printed materials (such as books and journals from the library media center) to locate information on a specific topic not covered in their textbook.

Printed materials are used in all subject areas and with students of all ages once they learn to read. The library media center is a source of a wide variety of

Assemble the Elements

- Word-processing and laser printing have placed a confusing profusion of typefaces at our disposal for most documents we produce. Remember the advice that professional graphic designers follow: Pick a serif and sans-serif typeface that you like and use them; ignore the rest except for very special situations.

Choose Background and Underlying Pattern

- Don't scrimp on page margins; pages that look too full, too dense, or too disorganized are discouraging to readers at any level of proficiency.

- If your pages will be printed front and back, make a trial sheet to ensure that the text on each side is clearly readable.

Arrange the Elements

- Use space—move elements closer together or further apart—before using styles like bold, italic, or underlined text. Spatial arrangement is more quickly perceived and processed by your readers than is a change of text style.

- Use text styles to reinforce the underlying pattern of the document; for example, make all subheadings bold and nothing else bold.

Check and Revise

- In a multiple-page document check for single words or lines that get stranded on a page separated from the rest of a paragraph; reset the page breaks or rearrange text so that paragraphs are complete or divided nearer the middle.

- If you use a computer spelling-checker, re-check for words you have spelled correctly but used in the wrong place.

Facilitating a Small Group Meeting

Title text is a simple style (gothic or roman sans serif) to distinguish from other text.

Title is short and informative.

Getting the meeting started

Subheadings use the same typeface as the title, but usually a smaller size.

Subheadings should use an initial capital only.

As facilitator you should *never* laugh.

Use either italic or bold text for emphasis, not both.

When you have a choice of paper color, select a subdued shade that allows the smallest text on your page to stand out clearly in contrast.

If your text will be photocopied, avoid paper in any shade of red since it will darken in the copy process.

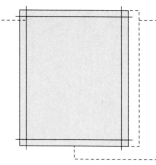

Paragraphs are aligned at the left margin, not at the right margin or at both margins; left-margin alignment provides best readability.

Paragraphs use a serif typeface in 10 or 12 point size for most readers; 14–18 points for young readers and visually impaired.

On the vertical dimension decide the spacing between lines of text, between the title and other text, and between text and subheadings.

On the horizontal dimension decide what column divisions, if any, you will use.

Titles may be aligned with the left margin or centered on the page; if you center the title take care that it looks centered and not simply misaligned.

Subheadings should be aligned with each other; if they are centered each one appears to be aligned differently and the viewer may have trouble identifying them.

All the regular text should be aligned at the same margin except lists and block quotations; making sense of multiple margins is distracting for the reader.

Check titles and subheadings; if they take up more than one line, make sure the phrases on each line make sense.

Move blocks of text close to their subheadings and away from other text on the page; this use of space helps the viewer make sense of the page easily and quickly.

Most text produced with a word processor instead of a typewriter is too dense and difficult to read in lines that extend from margin to margin; a margin of about 1/3 the page gives easier-to-read text and makes subheadings stand out.

109

FIGURE 4.10
Children's books and other printed materials can be used anytime and anywhere.

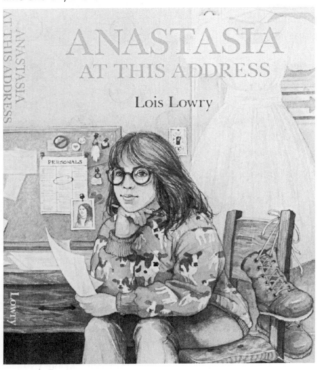

printed materials on countless topics and in almost every conceivable format (see Figure 4.10).

Utilization

When using printed materials for instruction, one of the main roles of the teacher is to get the learners actively involved with the material. One technique is to have the students use the "SQ3R" method: Survey, Question, Read, Recite, and Review. *Survey* requires the students to skim through the printed material and to read the overview and/or summary. In the *Question* step, students write a list of questions to answer while reading. In the *Read* stage students are encouraged to look for the organization of the material, put brackets around the main ideas, underline supporting details, and answer the questions written in the previous step. *Recite* requires them to test themselves while reading and to put the content into their own words. *Review* suggests that the students look over the material immediately after reading it, the next day, a week later, and so on.[1]

Other utilization techniques for printed materials include directing student reading with objectives or questions and providing a worksheet if one is not included in

the materials. You should emphasize the use of visuals in printed materials and teach students to read visuals.

FREE AND INEXPENSIVE MATERIALS

With the ever-increasing costs of instructional materials, teachers and trainers should be aware of the wide variety of materials that can be obtained for classroom use at little or no cost (see Figure 4.11). These free and inexpensive materials can supplement instruction in many subjects; they can be the main source of instruction on certain topics. For example, many videotapes are available for loan without a rental fee; the only expense is the return postage. By definition, any material that you can borrow or acquire permanently for instructional purposes without a significant cost, usually less than a couple of dollars, can be referred to as free or inexpensive.

The types of free and inexpensive materials are almost endless. The more commonly available items include posters, games, pamphlets, brochures, reports, charts, maps, books, filmstrips, audiotapes, films, videotapes, multimedia kits, and real objects. The more costly items, such as films and videotapes, are usually sent only on a free-loan basis and must be returned to the supplier after use. In some instances, single copies of audiocassettes, filmstrips, and videocassettes will be donated to your organization or school to be shared among many users.

Another resource that has become very important for obtaining free and inexpensive materials is the Internet. By connecting to Gopher and World Wide Web sites around the world, teachers and students can acquire materials, photographs, and other educational resources.

FIGURE 4.11
Free and inexpensive materials are available from a variety of sources.

---

[1]F. P. Robinson, *Effective Study* (New York: Harper & Row, 1946).

✔ APPRAISAL CHECKLIST

PRINT MATERIALS

KEY WORDS: _____ , _____ , _____

Title _____

Series Title (if applicable) _____

Source _____

Date _____ **Cost** _____ **Length** _____ minutes

Subject Area _____

Intended Audience _____

Brief Description

Objectives

Entry Capabilities Required (e.g., prior knowledge, reading ability, vocabulary level, math ability).

Format
- ❏ **Textbook**
- ❏ **Fiction**
- ❏ **Nonfiction**
- ❏ **Pamphlet**
- ❏ **Manual**

Rating	High	Medium	Low	Comments
Match with curriculum	❏	❏	❏	
Accurate and current	❏	❏	❏	
Clear and concise language	❏	❏	❏	
Arouse motivation/maintain interest	❏	❏	❏	
Learner participation	❏	❏	❏	
Technical quality	❏	❏	❏	
Evidence of effectiveness (e.g., field-test results)	❏	❏	❏	
Free from objectionable bias or advertising	❏	❏	❏	
User guide/documentation	❏	❏	❏	
Reading level appropriate	❏	❏	❏	
Clarity of organization	❏	❏	❏	
Table of contents/index	❏	❏	❏	

Strong Points

Weak Points

Recommended Action _____ **Name** _____ **Date** _____

 A computer template for a Checklist is found in "The Classroom Link."

In addition, many teachers are placing their ideas for teaching an array of subjects along with media and materials on the network.

Advantages

- *Up-to-date.* Free and inexpensive materials can provide up-to-date information that is not contained in textbooks or other commercially available media.
- *In-depth treatment.* Such materials often provide in-depth treatment of a topic. If classroom quantities are available, printed materials can be read and discussed by students as textbook material would be. If quantities are limited, they can be placed in a learning center for independent or small-group study.
- *Variety of uses.* Audiovisual materials lend themselves to classroom presentation by the instructor. Individual students who want to explore a subject of interest can use the audiovisual materials for self-study or for presentation to the class. Posters, charts, and maps can be combined to create topical displays. These can be motivational (as in the case of a safety poster) or used for direct instruction (as in studying the solar system). Materials that do not have to be returned can be modified and adapted for various instructional or display purposes.
- *Student manipulation.* Materials that are expendable have the extra advantage of allowing learners to get actively involved with them. For example, students can cut out pictures for notebooks and displays. They can assemble printed information and visuals in scrapbooks as reports of individual and group projects.

Limitations

- *Bias or advertising.* Many free and inexpensive materials are described as *sponsored* materials because their production and distribution are sponsored by particular organizations. These organizations—whether private corporations, nonprofit associations, or government agencies—often have a message to convey. That message might be in the form of outright advertising. If so, you will have to be aware of your own organization's policies on the use of advertising matter. You might consider covering or removing the advertisement, but that, too, raises ethical questions in view of the effort and expense that the sponsor has incurred in providing the materials to you. In addition, you are removing the identification of the source of the material, and that prevents disclosure of any vested interests by which one might judge the information presented.
- *Special interests.* What may be even more troublesome is sponsored material that does not contain outright

advertising but promotes some special interest in a less obvious way. For example, a "fun in the sun" poster may subtly promote the eating of junk food without including the name or logo of any manufacturer. Propagandistic or more subtly biased materials can thus enter the curriculum through the back door. Careful previewing and caution are advisable when you consider sponsored materials. Teachers should solicit informational materials on the same subject from several points of view. Thereby, students are afforded a balance and diversity of opinions.

- *Limited quantities.* With the increasing expense of producing both printed and audiovisual materials, your supplier may have to impose limits on the quantities of items available at one time. You may not be able to obtain a copy of the material for every student in the class.

Applications

Free and inexpensive materials include all the types of media discussed in this book—visuals, real objects, models, overhead transparencies, slides, filmstrips, audiotapes, CDs, videotapes, films, and even computer programs (sometimes called *shareware*). The applications of this wide variety of materials are described in detail in the chapters of this book related to specific types of media (see the Contents at the beginning of the book).

Sources

There are local, state, national, and international sources of free and inexpensive materials. Many local government agencies, community groups, and private businesses provide informational materials on free loan. Public libraries often make videotapes, prints, and filmstrips available. Even libraries in small communities may have access to materials through a statewide network. These materials usually can be loaned to schools and other organizations. Other state and federal government agencies—such as cooperative extension services, public health departments, and parks departments—make materials available for use in schools, churches, hospitals, and companies.

Community organizations such as the Red Cross, the League of Women Voters, and medical societies welcome opportunities to spread information about their special interests. Videotapes, sound–slide sets, printed material, and guest speakers are frequently offered.

Among business organizations, utilities (telephone, electric, gas, and water companies) are most likely to employ education specialists who can inform you about the instruction services they offer. Chambers of commerce often can suggest private corporations that might supply materials of interest to you.

Nationally, one of the most prolific sources of free and inexpensive materials is the national government. In the United States, two federal agencies offer special access to materials—the U.S. Government Printing Office and the National Audiovisual Center. Your key to the tremendous wealth of posters, charts, brochures, books, and other printed government documents available to the general public is *Selected U.S. Government Publications,* a monthly catalog of all new listings (see also Appendix C).

Trade and professional associations also aim to acquaint the general public with their fields of interest and the causes they promote. Private corporations that operate on a national or even international basis often offer sponsored materials.

Most foreign governments disseminate information about their countries to promote trade, tourism, and international understanding. They typically offer free posters, maps, and informational booklets plus videotapes on a free-loan basis. To find out what is available for any particular country, write to the embassy of that country. International organizations such as the Organization of American States (OAS), the United Nations (UN), and the North Atlantic Treaty Organization (NATO) also operate information offices. Airline and cruise ship companies are popular sources of posters of foreign countries. Consult your local travel agent for possible materials and addresses.

Obtaining Materials

When you have determined what you can use and where you can obtain it, write to the supplier; some agencies will not supply free and inexpensive materials unless you write on school or company stationery. For classroom quantities (when they are available), send just one letter. Do not have each student write individually. If a single student is requesting one copy of something for a class project, the student can write the letter, but you should also sign it. We recommend that you request a preview copy of the material before requesting multiple copies. Don't send a request for "anything you have"! Be specific and specify at least the subject area and the grade level. Ask for only what you need. Don't stockpile materials or take unfair advantage of a free offer. Somebody is paying for those materials, so don't waste them. Follow up with a thank-you note to the supplier; mention how you used the materials and what the students' reaction was. Be courteous, but be honest! Many suppliers attempt to improve free and inexpensive materials on the basis of user comments.

Appraising Materials

As with any other types of material, appraise the educational value of free and inexpensive materials critically. Some are very slick (technically well presented) but not educationally sound. Use the appropriate "Appraisal Checklist" for the type of media (printed material, videotape, etc.) you are appraising. All the "Appraisal Checklist" forms in this book have the rating criterion "Free from objectionable bias or advertising." Use it judiciously when reviewing free and inexpensive materials.

NONPROJECTED VISUALS

Nonprojected visuals can translate abstract ideas into a more realistic format (Figure 4.12). They allow instruction to move down from the level of verbal symbols in Dale's Cone of Experience to a more concrete level.

Nonprojected visuals are easy to use because they do not require any equipment. They are relatively inexpensive. Many can be obtained at little or no cost. They can be used in many ways at all levels of instruction and in all disciplines. They may also be used to stimulate creative expression, such as telling or writing stories or composing poetry.

All types of nonprojected visuals may be used in testing and evaluation. They are particularly helpful with objectives requiring identification of people, places, or things.

Some nonprojected visuals are simply too small for use before a group. It is possible to enlarge any visual photographically, but that can be an expensive process. The opaque projector or a document camera (described in Chapter 5) can be used to project an enlarged image before a group.

Some nonprojected visuals demand special caution. Because the images are visually symbolic rather than fully representational, they leave more room for viewers to misinterpret the intended meaning. (This phenomenon was discussed in Chapter 3.) For example, research on newspaper readers' interpretations of editorial cartoons indicates that a large proportion of viewers may draw conclusions that are opposite of what the artist intended. Psychologists find that people tend to project their own hopes, fears, and preconceptions onto images or verbal messages that are ambiguous.

Here we will explore six types of **graphics** commonly found in the classroom situation: still pictures, drawings (including sketches and diagrams), charts, graphs, posters, and cartoons.

Still Pictures

Still pictures are photographic (or photograph-like) representations of people, places, and things. The still pic-

FIGURE 4.12
Visuals carry the main message in a well-designed chart.

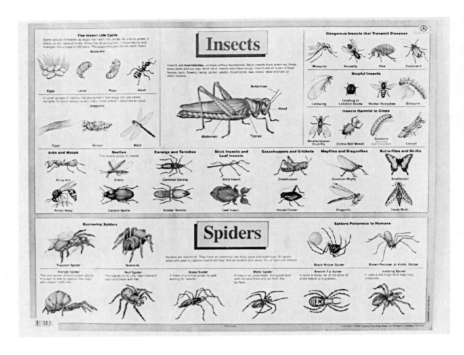

tures most commonly used in instruction are photographs; postcards; illustrations from books, periodicals, catalogs, and so on; and study prints (oversized illustrations commercially prepared to accompany specific instructional units).

Still pictures are readily available in books (including textbooks), magazines, newspapers, catalogs, and calendars. In addition, you can purchase large photographs for use with groups of students from educational supply companies, or you can obtain them from your media center or library.

Still pictures are two-dimensional. The lack of three-dimensionality can be compensated for by providing a group of pictures showing the same object or scene from several different angles or positions. Also, a series of sequential still pictures can suggest motion.

Photographs may be used in a variety of ways. Teacher-made or student-made photographs may be used to illustrate and to help teach specific lesson topics. Photographs of local architecture, for example, can illustrate a unit on architectural styles. (In this case, the students' skill in "reading" a visual could be reinforced by the instructor's pointing out that merely looking at the buildings in our environment is not the same as really "seeing" them.) Photographs taken on field trips can be valuable for classroom follow-up activities.

Skill in decoding textbook pictures may be included in instructional objectives to motivate the learners to use them for study purposes. The quality and quantity of illustrations are, of course, important factors in textbook choice. Pictures from newspapers and periodicals may be used in similar ways.

Students should understand that textbook pictures are not decorations but are intended to be study aids and should be used as such. They should be encouraged to give attention to them.

Photographic **study prints**—enlargements printed in a durable form for individual use—also have many applications in the instructional setting. They are especially helpful in the study of processes—the production of iron or paper, for example, or the operation of the internal combustion engine. They are also very useful in teaching the social sciences. In geography they may help illustrate relationships between people and their environment that, because of space limitations, could not be depicted easily in textbook pictures.

Drawings

Drawings, sketches, and diagrams employ the graphic arrangement of lines to represent persons, places, things, and concepts. Drawings are, in general, more finished and representational than sketches (e.g., stick figure compositions), which are likely to lack detail. Diagrams are usually intended to show relationships or to help explain processes, such as how something works or is constructed (Figure 4.13).

Drawings are readily found in textbooks and other classroom materials. They can be used in all phases of instruction, from introduction of the topic through evaluation. Because they are likely to be less detailed and more to the instructional point than photographic materials, they are easily understood by students of all ages.

FIGURE 4.13
The use of visual symbols greatly reduces the need for words in this multilingual diagram for assembling a plastic scale model of an automobile.

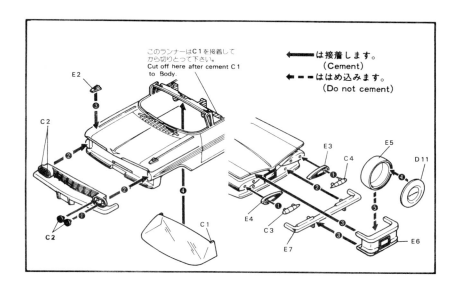

Teacher-made drawings can be effective aids to learning. They can be sketched on the chalkboard (or some other appropriate surface) to coincide with specific aspects of the instructional unit. For example, stick figures can be quickly and easily drawn to show motion in an otherwise static representation.

Charts

Charts are visual representations of abstract relationships such as chronologies, quantities, and hierarchies. They appear frequently in textbooks and training manuals as tables and flowcharts. They are also published as wall charts for group viewing in the form of organization charts, classification charts (e.g., the periodic table), and time lines (see "Types of Charts," p. 116).

A chart should have a clear, well-defined instructional purpose. In general (especially for younger students), it should express only one major concept or configuration of concepts. If you are developing your own charts, be sure they contain the minimum of visual and verbal information needed for understanding. A cluttered chart is a confusing chart. If you have a lot of information to convey, develop a series of simple charts rather than a single complex one. In other words, keep it simple.

A well-designed chart should communicate its message primarily through the visual channel. The verbal material should supplement the visual, not the reverse.

Graphs

Graphs provide a visual representation of numerical data. They also illustrate relationships among units of the data and trends in the data. Many tabular charts can be converted into graphs, as shown in Figure 4.14.

Data can be interpreted more quickly in graph form than in tabular form. Graphs are also more visually interesting than tables. There are four major types of graphs: bar, pictorial, circle, and line (see "Types of Graphs," p. 117). The type you choose will depend largely on the complexity of the information you wish to present and the graph-interpretation skills of your audience. Numerous computer software programs now make it easy to produce professional-looking charts, graphs, and other visuals. Input can be typed into the computer, and the computer will create the type of chart or graph you wish. When you see the preliminary result on the computer monitor, you can change parameters (axes, size, orientation, etc.). Some programs even provide output in a variety of colors.

Most spreadsheet programs, such as *Microsoft Works* and *Excel,* have a chart and graph option. Spreadsheet programs are easy-to-use tools for creating graphs from numerical data.

FIGURE 4.14
A line graph can make a table of data much easier to interpret.

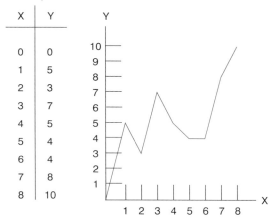

X	Y
0	0
1	5
2	3
3	7
4	5
5	4
6	4
7	8
8	10

TYPES OF CHARTS

Organization charts show the structure or chain of command in an organization such as a company, corporation, civic group, or government department. Usually they deal with the interrelationship of personnel or departments.

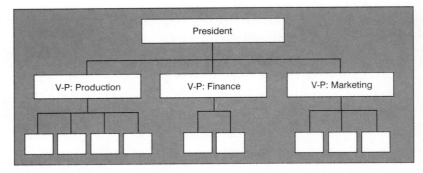

Classification charts are similar to organization charts but are used chiefly to classify or categorize objects, events, or species. A common type of classification chart is one showing the taxonomy of animals and plants according to natural characteristics. Dale's Cone of Experience classifies media from concrete to abstract.

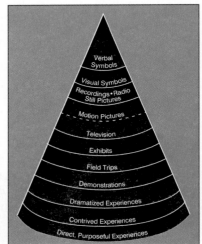

Time lines illustrate chronological relationships between events. They are most often used to show historical events in sequence or the relationship of famous people and these events. Pictures or drawings can be added to the time line to illustrate important concepts. Time lines are very helpful for summarizing a series of events.

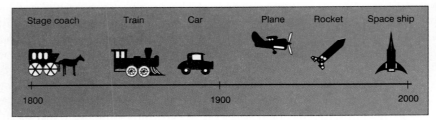

Tabular charts, or tables, contain numerical information, or data. They are also convenient for showing time information when the data are presented in columns, as in timetables for railroads and airlines.

Import Percentages	Wheat	Cotton	Steel	Oil
USA	0	0	20	35
England	65	95	35	10
France	15	95	30	90
Japan	85	15	0	95
Brazil	0	0	20	70

Flowcharts, or process charts, show a sequence, a procedure, or, as the name implies, the flow of a process. Flowcharts show how different activities, ingredients, or procedures are interrelated.

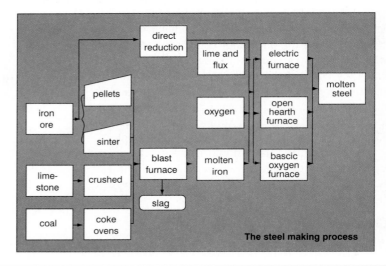

The steel making process

TYPES OF GRAPHS

Bar graphs are easy to read and can be used with elementary age students. The height of the bar is the measure of the quantity being represented. The width of all bars should be the same to avoid confusion. A single bar can be divided to show parts of a whole. It is best to limit the quantities being compared to eight or less; otherwise the graph becomes cluttered and confusing. The bar graph, a one-scale graph, is particularly appropriate for comparing similar items at different times or different items at the same time; for example, the height of one plant over time or the heights of several students at any given time. The bar graph shows variation in only one dimension.

Pictorial graphs are an alternate form of the bar graph in which numerical units are represented by a simple drawing. Pictorial graphs are visually interesting and appeal to a wide audience, especially young students. However, they are slightly more difficult to read than bar graphs. Since pictorial symbols are used to represent a specific quantity, partial symbols are used to depict fractional quantities. To help avoid confusion in such cases, print values below or to the right of each line of figures.

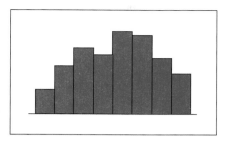

Circle (or pie) graphs are relatively easy to interpret. In this type of graph, a circle or "pie" is divided into segments, each representing a part or percentage of the whole. One typical use of the circle graph is to depict tax-dollar allocations. The combined segments of a circle graph should, of course, equal 100 percent. Areas of special interest can be highlighted by illustrating a piece of pie separately from the whole.

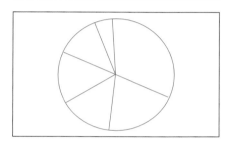

Line graphs are the most precise and complex of all graphs. Line graphs are based on two scales at right angles. Each point has a value on the vertical scale and a value on the horizontal scale. Lines (or curves) are drawn to connect the points. Line graphs show variations in two dimensions, or how two or more factors change over time. For example, a graph can show the relation between pressure and temperature when the volume of a gas is held constant. Because line graphs are precise, they are very useful in plotting trends. They can also help simplify a mass of complex information.

Drawing programs can be used for layout and design, as well as for drawing and illustrating. Most computer graphics programs come with hundreds or even thousands of typefaces and clip-art images and can manipulate visuals in every imaginable way. Examples of these programs are *Harvard Graphics, Lotus Freelance Graphics,* and *Microsoft Graph.*

Posters

Posters incorporate visual combinations of images, lines, color, and words. They are intended to catch and hold the viewer's attention at least long enough to communicate a brief message, usually a persuasive one. To be effective, posters must be colorful and dynamic. They must grab attention and communicate their message quickly. One drawback in using posters is that their message is quickly blunted by familiarity. Consequently, they should not be left on display for too long. Commercial billboards are an example of posters on a very large scale.

Posters can be used effectively in numerous learning situations. They can stimulate interest in a new topic, a special class, or a school event. They may be employed for motivation—luring students to a school meeting or to the media center, for example, or encouraging them to read more. In industrial education courses, science laboratories, and other situations where danger may be involved, posters can be used to remind people of safety

- Use large visuals that everyone can see simultaneously. (If visuals are not large enough for all to see, use one of the projection techniques described in Chapter 5.)
- Use visuals that are not cluttered with illegible details.
- Cover irrelevant material with plain paper.
- Hold visuals steady when showing them to a group by resting them against a desk or table or putting them on an easel.
- Limit the number of pictures used in a given period of time. It is better to use a few visuals well than to overwhelm your audience with an abundance of underexplained visuals.

- Use just one picture at a time, except for purposes of comparison. Lay one picture flat before going on to the next.
- Keep your audience's attention and help them learn from a visual by asking direct questions about it.
- Teach your audience to interpret visuals (see Chapter 3).
- Display pertinent questions alongside each visual. Cover the answers with flaps of paper. Have each student immediately check his or her own response for accuracy.
- Provide written or verbal cues to highlight important information contained in the visuals.

tips. Posters can also be used to promote good health practices such as not using drugs. An effective learning technique is to have students design posters as part of a class project, during fire prevention week or dental health month, for example. (See Figure 4.15.)

Posters may be obtained from a variety of sources, including commercial companies, airlines, travel agencies, and government departments. You can make your own posters with colored markers, computer printouts, and devices that print poster-sized pages. If you draw your own posters, follow the visual design guidelines in Chapter 3 and refer to "How to . . . Sketch" (page 90). In addition, "How to . . . Enlarge Visuals" (page 119) lists helpful suggestions to enhance your posters. Com-

puter-generated posters and banners can be made by taping together standard-size printer paper. Software, such as *Print Shop,* can facilitate poster design and production.

Newer devices, such as PosterPrinter by Varitronics (Figure 4.16), can convert 8½-by-11-inch originals into 23-by-33-inch posters. The originals can be hand-drawn visuals, computer output, overhead transparency masters, or the like. The machines use high-speed electronics and a thermal printing process, which means no ink, toner, or ribbons. The process takes about a minute. The paper comes in a variety of colors (white, pink, yellow, or blue) and several print colors are available (black, red, blue, or orange). In addition to making posters, these machines can be used to generate prepared flip chart pages and signs.

Cartoons

Cartoons (line drawings that are rough caricatures of real people and events) are perhaps the most popular and familiar visual format. They appear in a wide variety of print media—newspapers, periodicals, textbooks—and range from comic strips intended primarily to entertain to drawings intended to make important social or political comments. Humor and satire are mainstays of the cartoonist's skill (see Figure 4.17, p. 122).

Cartoons are easily and quickly read and appeal to children and adults alike. The best of them contain wisdom as well as wit. They can often be used by the teacher to make or reinforce a point of instruction. Appreciation and interpretation, however, may depend on the experience and sophistication of the viewer. Be sure the cartoons you use for instructional purposes are within the experiential and intellectual range of your students.

PRESERVING NONPROJECTED VISUALS

One drawback in using nonprojected visuals in the classroom is that they are easily soiled or otherwise damaged as they are passed from student to student.

FIGURE 4.15
Posters catch the eye to convey a single, simple message.

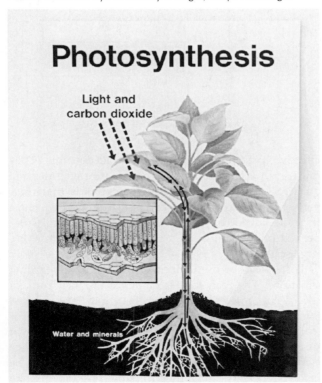

You can make an enlargement of any original picture that you want to display on the chalkboard, on a poster, or as part of a bulletin board.

- *Using Opaque.* Place printed material to be copied in the projector.
- *Using Overhead.* Using an overhead pen, trace the figure on a clear sheet of acetate, and place on projector.

Then, in either case:

- Dim the lights.
- Tape a sheet of paper (such as kraft paper) or cardboard to a wall or tack it to a bulletin board.

- Direct the projected image onto the surface where you want to draw the image (paper, cardboard, or chalkboard).
- Adjust the distance of the projector from the wall to enlarge (or reduce) the image to the size desired. Move the projector farther back to enlarge (or closer to reduce).
- Trace over the projected image in whatever detail you wish.

Your students will be impressed with your "artistic ability," and maybe you will be too.

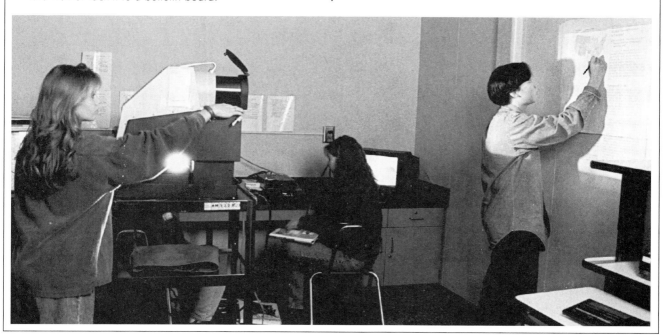

FIGURE 4.16
The PosterPrinter converts a notebook-size original into a poster that is eight times larger.

Repeated display, storage, and retrieval can also add to wear and tear. Mounting and laminating are the two most effective preservation techniques, and they can contribute to the instructional effectiveness of nonprojected visuals.

Mounting

Mount nonprojected visuals on construction paper, cardboard, or other such material for durability. The color of the mounting material should not draw attention away from the visual. It is generally a good idea to use pastel or neutral tones rather than brilliant or primary colors. Using one of the minor colors in the visual as the color for the mounting can enhance harmony. The total effect of your mounting should be neat and pleasing to the eye. Borders, for example, should be evenly cut, with side borders of equal width and the bottom border slightly wider than the top.

☑ APPRAISAL CHECKLIST

NONPROJECTED VISUALS

KEY WORDS: _____ , _____ , _____

Format
- ❑ **Still picture**
- ❑ **Drawing**
- ❑ **Chart**
- ❑ **Graph**
- ❑ **Poster**
- ❑ **Cartoon**

Title _____

Series Title (if applicable) _____

Source _____

Date _____ **Cost** _____ **Length** _____ minutes

Subject Area _____

Intended Audience _____

Brief Description

Objectives

Entry Capabilities Required (e.g., prior knowledge, reading ability, vocabulary level, math ability)

Rating	High	Medium	Low	Comments
Match with curriculum	❑	❑	❑	
Accurate and current	❑	❑	❑	
Clear and concise language	❑	❑	❑	
Arouse motivation/maintain interest	❑	❑	❑	
Learner participation	❑	❑	❑	
Technical quality	❑	❑	❑	
Evidence of effectiveness (e.g., field-test results)	❑	❑	❑	
Free from objectionable bias or advertising	❑	❑	❑	
User guide/documentation	❑	❑	❑	
Legibility for use (size and clarity)	❑	❑	❑	
Simplicity (clear, unified design)	❑	❑	❑	
Appropriate use of color	❑	❑	❑	

Strong Points

Weak Points

Recommended Action _____ **Name** _____ **Date** _____

 A computer version of this Checklist is found in "The Classroom Link."

CLOSE-UP

USING NONPROJECTED VISUALS

Nonprojected visuals can be used by students of all ages. This student examines examples of endangered species as part of a class project. The teacher assigns small groups of students to each study an endangered animal. Each small group cooperates and prepares a brief oral report to share with the class. During the presentation, visuals of the assigned species are shown to the class. Following each group's presentation, the teacher facilitates a discussion and summarizes key points.

The still pictures are then displayed on a bulletin board along with other visuals of endangered species.

Study prints are used by a fifth-grade teacher to show examples of pollution. The teacher works with the students in small groups. While some of the students are working on other activities in the classroom and in the media center, the teacher gathers ten to twelve students to discuss the study prints. His objective is for the students to be able to describe the common causes of pollution. The students are shown the study prints and then are asked to describe what procedures they would recommend for improving the environment.

Various glues, cements, and pastes are available for mounting purposes. When used according to directions, almost all are effective. Some white glues, however, are likely to cause wrinkles in the picture when the adhesive dries, especially if used full strength. If you run into this problem, dilute the glue; for example, use four parts Elmer's glue to one part water. Cover the entire back of the visual evenly with the adhesive before placing it on the mounting board. If excess adhesive seeps out around the edges, wipe it off with a damp cloth or sponge.

Glue sticks may be used in place of liquid glues. They have the advantage of not running out around the edges of the material. Glue sticks are less likely to damage and discolor photographs.

Rubber Cement Mounting. One of the most commonly used adhesives for mounting purposes is rubber cement. It is designed specifically for use with paper products. It is easy to use and less messy than many other liquid glues. Excess cement can easily be wiped away, and it is inexpensive. Rubber cement does, however, have two disadvantages. When the container is left uncovered for any length of time, the adhesive tends to dry out and thicken. Periodic doses of thinner (avail-

able commercially) may be necessary to keep the cement serviceable. A second disadvantage is that the adhesive quality of rubber cement tends to diminish over a period of time. Constant exposure to dry air may eventually cause it to lose its grip. This disadvantage can be compensated for with special precautions, as noted for permanent rubber cement mountings (see "How to . . . Mount Pictures Using Rubber Cement," page 123). However, even these mountings will not last indefinitely. One caution is that rubber cement could damage and discolor photographs.

Dry Mounting. **Dry mounting** employs a specially prepared paper impregnated with heat-sensitive adhesive. The paper is available in sheets and rolls. The dry-mounting tissue bonds the backing material to the back of the visual. A dry-mount press is used to supply the heat and pressure necessary to activate the tissue's adhesive. The process is rapid and clean and results in permanent, high-quality mounting. (See "How to . . . Dry Mount Pictures," page 124).

One disadvantage of dry mounting is that it is relatively expensive. However, it is possible to dry mount visuals without a dry-mount press by using an ordinary household iron. Set the iron on a setting for silk or

FIGURE 4.17
Editorial cartoons, such as this 1970 comment on the effects of inflation, can crystallize and articulate serious ideas.

"He feels the pinch, I feel the squeeze. . . . What do you feel?"

rayon. Do not use steam. The tip of the household iron can be used in place of the special tacking iron.

Laminating

Lamination protects visuals from wear and tear by covering them with a clear plastic or plastic-like surface. Lamination helps to protect visuals against tears, scratches, and sticky fingers. Soiled surfaces can be wiped clean with a damp cloth.

Lamination also allows you to write on your visuals with a grease pencil or water-soluble pen for instructional purposes. The writing can be easily erased later with a damp cloth or sponge. A teacher of mathematics, for example, might write percentage figures on a laminated illustration of a pizza or a pie to help teach the concept of fractions. You can also have students write on laminated materials. When the lesson is completed, the markings can be erased and the material is ready for further teaching. Many classroom materials can be laminated to add extra durability and to allow for erasable writing by teacher and students.

Clear plastic sheets with adhesive backing (such as Con-Tact shelf paper) are available for laminating purposes. Remove the backing cover a little at a time to expose the adhesive and carefully press the clear plastic sheet on the visual. If you remove backing all at once, the plastic sheet often rolls and sticks to itself before you can get it on the visual. Any portions of the plastic sheet that extend beyond the edges of the visual can be cut off or folded back for additional protection.

Laminating can be done with a dry-mount press (see "How to . . . Laminate Pictures with a Dry-Mount Press"). Rolls of laminating film for use with a dry-mount press are available from commercial sources. A laminating machine can be used as well (Figure 4.18). These machines use two rolls of laminating film and cover both sides of the visual simultaneously. The visuals are fed into the machine, which provides the appropriate heat and pressure. The excess film can then be trimmed from around the visual with scissors or a paper cutter.

Filing and Storing

You will find it handy to have a system for filing, storing, and retrieving your nonprojected visuals. The nature of the filing system that you use will depend on the number of nonprojected visuals in your collection and the way you intend to use them. The simplest filing system usually involves grouping the items according to the teaching units in which they are used. Elementary teachers often categorize them by curriculum area (e.g., math, science, language arts, social studies) and then subdivide them by topic (e.g., seasons, countries, jobs, addition, subtraction, place value, telling time). Some instructors, especially those who teach just one subject,

FIGURE 4.18
Both sides of a visual can be laminated simultaneously with a laminating machine.

- Cut picture to size. Edges should be straight and corners square.

Trim

- Mark location of picture on mounting board with pencil to assist putting picture in correct position.

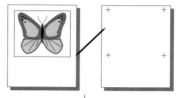

TEMPORARY   PERMANENT

- Apply cement evenly to back of picture.

Face down

Newsprint   Rubber cement

Rubber cement

- Apply cement evenly to back of picture in horizontal direction.
- Apply cement evenly to front of mounting board in vertical direction.
- *Allow cement to dry* until there are no shiny spots.
- Place two sheets of wax paper on mounting board to cover picture area so picture does not adhere in wrong place.
- Align picture with guide marks.
- Carefully remove wax paper while holding picture in aligned position.

Wax paper

Pull out wax paper

- Place picture on mounting board *before cement dries.*

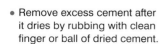 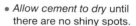 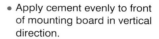

- Burnish the picture for good adhesion and removal of air bubbles.

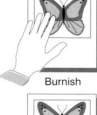

Burnish

- Remove excess cement after it dries by rubbing with clean finger or ball of dried cement.

- Erase the guide marks.

Remove excess cement

1. Dry the mounting board and picture before trimming picture by placing them in dry-mount press for about one minute at 225°F. Close press, but *do not lock.*

2. Place a sheet (either side up) of dry-mounting tissue over the *back* of the *untrimmed* picture, with sheet extending beyond the edges of picture.

3. Attach the tissue to the back center of the picture with tip of a tacking iron set on "medium."

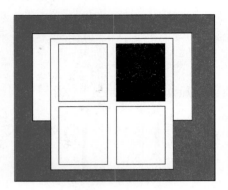

4. Turn picture and tissue over and trim both simultaneously to desired size. (A paper cutter works best, but a razor knife and metal straightedge or scissors may be used.)

5. Place the picture and dry-mounting tissue on the mounting board and align in proper position.

6. Tack the tissue to the mounting board *at two opposite corners.*

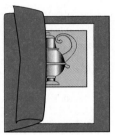

Tacking iron

7. Cover mounting board and picture with clean paper on both sides.

8. Place in dry-mount press preheated to 225°F for about one minute.

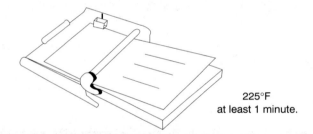

225°F at least 1 minute.

9. Remove from dry-mount press and allow the materials to cool. (Placing the cooling materials under a metal weight will help prevent curling.)

set up their filing system according to the chapters in their textbook, the topics they cover, or objectives. Teachers who use just a few visuals sometimes file them with their other teaching materials for each lesson.

In addition to a workable filing system and proper-size storage containers, you should have a clean, out-of-the-way place to store your visuals when they are not in use. The storage location can range from elaborate built-in drawers or filing cabinets to simple cardboard storage cartons. There is no problem in using cardboard cartons to store files of pictures and other visuals if you have a clean, dry location for them.

DISPLAY SURFACES

If you are going to use nonprojected visuals such as photographs, drawings, charts, graphs, or posters, you need a way to display them. Nonprojected visuals may be displayed in the classroom in a wide variety of ways,

1. The dry-mount press should be heated to 225°F. If you live in an area with high humidity, you may get better results if you preheat the visual (to remove excess moisture) in the press for about one minute. Close the press but do not lock it.

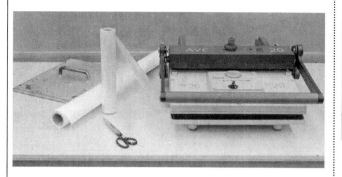

2. Cover the picture to be laminated with a piece of laminating film slightly larger than the picture. The inside of the roll (dull side) contains the heat-sensitive adhesive and should be toward the visual. Press the film onto the picture with your hands. Static electricity should cause the film to stay in place.

3. Put the picture and laminating film in a cover of clean paper to protect the visual and to prevent the adhesive from getting onto the surface of the dry-mount press.

4. Insert the material in the press for one minute. Remove it; if the adhesion is not complete, put it back into the press for another minute. It may be helpful to put a magazine or a ¼-inch stack of paper on top of the picture to increase the pressure and improve adhesion between the picture and the laminating film.

ranging from simply holding up a single visual in your hand to constructing elaborate exhibits for permanent display. Classroom surfaces commonly used for display of nonprojected visuals include chalkboards, multipurpose boards, pegboards, bulletin boards, cloth boards, and magnetic boards. Flip charts may also be used for display of visuals. Exhibits, a display format incorporating a variety of materials such as real objects and models along with visuals, are also common. How you display your visuals will depend on a number of factors, including the nature of your audience, the nature of your visuals, the instructional setting, your lesson objectives, and, of course, the availability of the various display surfaces.

Chalkboards

The most common display surface in the classroom is, of course, the chalkboard (Figure 4.19). Once called *blackboards,* they now come in a variety of colors, as does chalk. Although the chalkboard is most commonly used to support verbal communication, it can be used as a surface upon which to draw visuals (or pictures can be fastened to the molding above the chalkboard, taped to the board with masking tape, or placed in the chalk tray) to help illustrate instructional units. Graphics, such as sketches and diagrams or charts and graphs, may be drawn on the chalkboard for display to the class.

A chalkboard is such a common classroom item that instructors often neglect to give it the attention and respect it deserves as an instructional device. Using a chalkboard effectively requires conscious effort.

Multipurpose Boards

Some classrooms are equipped with **multipurpose boards** (Figure 4.20) instead of chalkboards. These are also called *whiteboards* or *marker boards.* As the name implies, they can be used for more than one purpose. Their smooth, white plastic surface requires a special erasable marker rather than chalk. Do not use permanent felt-tip markers such as Marks-A-Lot or El Marko. These markers may permanently damage the surface.

The white surface is also suitable for projection of films, slides, and overhead transparencies. Materials cut from thin plastic, such as figures and letters, will adhere to the surface when rubbed in place. Some of these boards have a steel backing and can be used as a magnetic board for display of visuals.

In addition to their variety of uses, these multipurpose boards have the advantage of being able to display bright, colorful lines. At least eight different colors of markers are currently available. They are dustless, so there is no chalk to get on your clothes. These boards are preferred for use around computers because chalk dust can harm computers and disks.

A multipurpose board will provide many years of use if cared for properly. The board should be completely erased after each use. It can be erased like a chalkboard using a felt eraser. Do not let the marks remain on the board overnight. The longer the marks remain on the board, the more difficult they are to erase. Old marks may be erased by tracing over them with a black erasable marker and erasing immediately.

FIGURE 4.19
The chalkboard is universally recognized as a flexible and economical display surface.

For general cleaning, simply wipe the board clean with a soft, damp cloth. If further cleaning is necessary, use a mild spray cleaner, such as Sparkleen. You can also apply a soapy detergent solution and rub briskly with a soft, clean cloth. Always rinse thoroughly with clean water and dry with a soft towel after cleaning.

The special erasable markers require some special care. They have a solvent base that dries quickly, which is the key to their erasability. The markers should be kept tightly capped and should be stored in a horizontal position with the cap tight when not in use to prevent them from drying out. If a marker dries out, cap it, turn it upside down, and shake it vigorously for twenty seconds. Leaving the marker stored overnight with the tip end down may also help.

Copy Boards

A high-tech variation of the multipurpose board is the **copy board,** or electronic whiteboard (Figure 4.21). This device makes reduced-size paper copies of what is written on the board. It looks like a smaller multipurpose board but may contain multiple screens or frames that can be scrolled forward and backward. You can prepare content beforehand on any or all of the screens. During your presentation the frames can be revealed one at a time, and new information can be added as desired. You can move the writing surface forward or backward to the desired frame quickly and easily.

You can write on the copy board using any erasable marker. If you make a mistake, erase your error as you would on any multipurpose board.

FIGURE 4.20
Multipurpose boards are replacing chalkboards in business and industrial training classrooms and in some educational institutions.

- Put extensive drawing or writing on the board before class. Taking too much time to write or draw creates restlessness and may lead to discipline problems.
- Organize in advance what you plan to write on the board and where you plan to write it.
- Cover material such as a test or extensive lesson materials with wrapping paper, newspaper, or a pull-down map until you are ready to use it.
- Eye contact with students is important! Face the class when you are talking. Do not talk to the board. Do not turn your back to the class unless it is absolutely necessary.
- Vary your presentation techniques. Do not overuse or rely entirely on the board. Use handouts, the overhead projector, flip charts, and other media during instruction when appropriate.
- Print neatly rather than using script. For a 32-foot-long classroom, the letters should be 1½–2 inches high and the line forming the letters should be ¼ inch thick.
- Check the visibility of the board from several positions around the room to be sure there is no glare on the surface. In case of glare, move the board (if portable) or pull down the window shades.

- If your printing normally runs "uphill" or "downhill," use water-soluble felt-tip pen markings as temporary guidelines for straighter printing. The guidelines will not be wiped off by a chalk eraser but may be washed off when no longer needed.
- Hold the chalk or marker at an angle so that it does not make scratching or squeaking noises.
- Use color for emphasis, but don't overuse it. Two or three different colors work best.
- Move around so you do not block what you have written on the board. Do not stand in front of what you have written.
- Use drawing aids such as rulers, stencils, and templates (patterns) to save time and improve the quality of your drawings.
- For frequently drawn shapes, use a template cut from wood or heavy cardboard. A dresser drawer knob or empty thread spool mounted on the template makes it easier to hold in position while tracing around it.
- Outline your drawings with barely visible lines before class and then fill them in with bold lines in front of the class. Your audience will think you are an artist!

The special feature of the copy board is that the frames can be copied in about 10 seconds. You can make as many copies of each frame as you like by pushing the appropriate button. All material is copied in black and white using thermal-sensitive paper. It is possible to copy the material on a single 8½-by-11-inch sheet of paper.

By copying the information almost instantaneously, you are free to erase the board and continue to teach without losing valuable time or ideas. You can make copies for yourself or for everyone at the session to avoid extensive note taking. Everyone gets the same copy of what was presented, so there are no omissions or errors (except in what you did or did not put on the board).

The copy board is especially valuable for brainstorming sessions and for summarizing group discussions. The copies are particularly helpful for students who miss class. Complex drawings can be included without having students hand copy them. Notes can be taken into the field, laboratory, or assembly plant for immediate use.

Because of the high cost of current models, the copy board is not commonly found in school settings.

FIGURE 4.21
Diagrams and words written on a copy board can be reproduced on paper with the push of a button.

Pegboards

Another popular display surface is the pegboard. It is particularly useful for displaying heavy objects, three-dimensional materials, and visuals.

Pegboards are made of tempered Masonite with ⅛-inch holes drilled 1 inch apart. Pegboard material is usually ⅛-inch thick and comes in 4-by-8-foot sheets, which can be cut to any size. Special metal hooks and holders can be inserted into the pegboard to hold books, papers, and other objects. Various types of special hooks are available in most hardware stores. Golf tees can also be inserted into the holes for holding lightweight materials such as posters and visuals mounted on cardboard. For a background effect, the entire pegboard surface can be covered with cloth or colored paper. Golf tees or the special hooks can then be inserted through the cloth or paper.

FIGURE 4.22
Bulletin boards, long a standard in elementary classrooms, are now used increasingly in higher education and corporate settings.

Bulletin Boards

The term *bulletin board* implies a surface on which bulletins—brief news announcements of urgent interest—are posted for public notice. This may have been the original purpose of bulletin boards, but it does not describe the most general use of these display spaces. A bulletin board is a surface of variable size and shape made of a material that holds pins, thumbtacks, and other sharp fasteners without damage to the board (Figure 4.22). In practice, bulletin board displays tend to serve three broad purposes: decorative, motivational, or instructional.

The decorative bulletin board is probably the most common, certainly in schools. Its function would seem to be to lend visual stimulation to the environment.

Displaying student work exemplifies the motivational use of bulletin boards. The public recognition offered by such displays can play an important role in the life of the classroom. It fosters pride in achievement, reinforcing students' efforts to do a good job. Creating a display of student work is also relatively effortless for the teacher to assemble.

The third broad purpose of bulletin boards is instructional, complementing the educational or training objectives of the formal curriculum. Rather than merely presenting static informational messages, displays can be designed to actively invite participation. Such displays ask questions and give viewers some means of manipulating parts of the display to verify their answers, such as flaps, pockets, dials, or movable parts.

Another form of learner participation is in taking part in the actual construction of the display. For example, to introduce a unit on animals, an elementary teacher might ask each student to bring in a picture of a favorite animal. The students would then make a bulletin board incorporating all the pictures. Or a geometry teacher might divide her class into five groups and assign each group a different geometric shape. As each shape is studied, the appropriate group would construct a bulletin board on that shape. A discussion leader in a book club might prepare a portable bulletin board to stimulate discussion of the book everyone has read for the monthly meeting.

Preparing an effective bulletin board display, whether it is being done by the teacher or students, requires some thought and planning. As with any instructional activity, the objective is primary. A display should be focused on one main topic or objective. One way to attract attention to your display and to prompt the viewer's thinking about your topic is to lead off with a catchy headline, one that communicates the main theme, perhaps with a question, a challenge, or a humorous phrase.

Once you have decided on an approach and have assembled some materials, you can refer to "How to . . . Design Bulletin Boards" for tips on arranging the elements into a display that will send its message clearly and attractively.

Checklist for Instructor-Prepared Bulletin Boards.

- ❑ *Emphatic*. Conveys message quickly and clearly
- ❑ *Attractive*. Color and arrangement catch and hold interest
- ❑ *Balanced*. Formal or informal
- ❑ *Unified*. Repeated shapes or colors or use of borders hold display together visually
- ❑ *Interactive*. Involves the viewer
- ❑ *Legible*. Lettering and visuals can be read across the room
- ❑ *Lettered properly*. Spelled correctly, plain typeface, use of lowercase except where capitals needed
- ❑ *Relative*. Correlated with lesson objectives
- ❑ *Durable*. Well constructed physically, items securely attached
- ❑ *Neat*. A clean, neat appearance makes the display more attractive, shows that the designer has regard for the audience, and provides a proper role model for student work.

For further guidelines on visual design, see Chapter 3.

Assemble the Elements

- Elements that look large in your hands suddenly seem to shrink when you place them on a large wall or bulletin board. When you are making or choosing elements for a bulletin board prop them up and walk across the room to judge how well they will show up.

Large cut-out letters are at least 1.5" high to be visible from across a room.

Illustrations are large enough to be seen within the bulletin board format; they are chosen with regard for the viewers' interests and stylistic preference; they reinforce the theme of the display.

LOVE	LIFE	DEATH
Itkidsl lskd is kdlse n einyre eiros xtryol al citnewsd eiopd lkjdk dkaw woei	Itkidsl lskd is kdlse n einyre eiros xtryol al citnewsd eiopd lkjdk dkaw woei	Itkidsl lskd is kdlse n einyre eiros xtryol al citnewsd eiopd lkjdk dkaw woei
Lkaskd a kdlse einyre eiros xtryol al clims alijsdield eiros xtryol	Lkaskd a kdlse einyre eiros xtryol al clims alijsdield eiros xtryol	Lkaskd a kdlse einyre eiros xtryol al clims alijsdield eiros xtryol

Text elements have large, compelling captions that encourage viewers to look closer and get engaged with the content being presented.

Actual products add 3-D texture to the display and promote engagement through manipulation of display elements.

Choose Background and Underlying Pattern

- Use subdued color for large areas to avoid distraction.

- Small samples of paper tend to look lighter than large sheets of the same paper; if you're working from samples, pick one lighter than you think you need.

Background color is pale pink, a subdued color that will allow other elements to stand out and will harmonize with the bright red and purple of the large heart.

Underlying pattern chosen is a circle to lead the eye from one content element to another without pointing to any single element as the most or least important.

Arrange the Elements

- Look for a large floorspace to test the layout of your bulletin board. Once you have fastened the whole display to the board you will be reluctant to pull it apart and revise it.

Photo of teenaged couple is superimposed over the heart, a strong use of proximity. The underlying circle is made visible as a dark pink element grouping the main elements together.

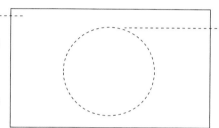

Title is centered at the top of the display.

The heart and the photo are placed at the center of the display, leaving the more "dynamic" positions on the circle to the text elements.

Additional content elements are aligned with the ends of the title text; they are out of the way of the main content and their placement allows 2 students to interact with the display simultaneously without crowding.

Check and Revise

- Stand back from the display and unfocus your eyes slightly; if the underlying pattern remains discernible in this fuzzy view your design probably has unity.

- Observe student reactions to help gauge the instructional effectiveness of your display.

The additional content elements are placed on light purple rectangles to improve their alignment with other elements and to tie them into the circle pattern.

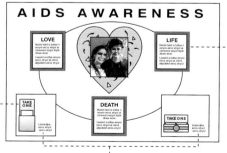

Text elements are more clearly linked by the addition of colored borders; the borders are a cool aqua blue, which offsets the overwhelming red effect of the initial design.

Captions on these elements have been made consistent.

FIGURE 4.23

The Ellison lettering machine quickly cuts out large letters for bulletin boards.

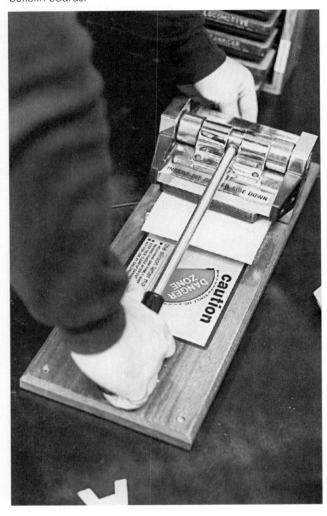

FIGURE 4.24

The placement of a display should vary according to the average height of the intended viewers. A useful rule of thumb is to align the middle of the display with the viewer's eye level.

Materials for production of bulletin boards may be available through the school library media center. Most schools have work rooms with large tables so that items for a bulletin board can be constructed and various layouts considered. A popular letter cutting device is the Ellison Lettering System (see Figure 4.23). This allows for neat, large letters to be cut quickly from construction paper.

The media center may also store the elements of a good bulletin board display so that teachers can share displays and have easy access to them from one year to the next.

Bulletin boards need not always be attached permanently to the wall. Portable boards may be set on an easel for temporary display. Beware of having too many bulletin boards, though. Too many competing visual displays in one place can lessen their individual impact.

Cloth Boards

Cloth boards are constructed of cloth stretched over a sturdy backing material such as plywood, Masonite, or heavy cardboard (Figure 4.25). The cloth used for the board may be of various types, including flannel, felt, or hook-and-loop material.

Pieces of flannel stick together when gentle pressure is applied. Visuals cut from flannel can be drawn on with felt-tip markers and put on a flannel board. You can back still pictures and graphics with pieces of flannel. Coarse sandpaper can also be used on the back of visuals for attachment to a cloth board. Pipe cleaners, available in a variety of colors, and fuzzy yarns stick to the flannel and can be used for drawing lines and letters. If adhesion is less than desired, slant the board slightly to prevent materials from slipping.

The most expensive cloth board is made from hook-and-loop material (such as Velcro). The hook-and-loop board has a fine but fuzzy surface composed of tiny, strong nylon loops. The material used for backing visuals and other items to be attached to the board has a coarse, hooklike texture. When pressed together, the two surfaces stick firmly. The hooklike material can be purchased in rolls or strips. One great advantage of the hook-and-loop board is that it can support large and heavy visuals, even books and other three-dimensional objects. One square inch of the cloth can support up to ten pounds of properly backed visual material.

Teachers of reading and other creative activities often use the cloth board to illustrate stories, poems, and other reading materials. Visuals depicting characters and scenes in a story, for example, can be placed on the board and moved around as the story unfolds. Creativity may be further encouraged by allowing the children to manipulate cloth-board materials. Shy children may particularly profit from this kind of activity. It encourages them to speak through the visual repre-

FIGURE 4.25
Cloth boards are often used to involve students in storytelling.

sentations of story characters as they move the illustrations on the board.

Be sure you have proper storage space for your cloth board and cloth-board visuals when not in use. Proper storage will help keep them clean and prevent them from being bent or torn. If possible, store your materials on a flat surface rather than stacking them up against a wall. If you use sandpaper backing on your visuals, put paper between them during storage, as sandpaper can scratch the surface of visuals.

Magnetic Boards

Magnetic boards serve much the same purpose as cloth boards. Visuals are backed with magnets and then placed on the metal surface of the board (Figure 4.26). Magnetic boards, magnets, and flexible strips of magnetic materials for use in backing are available commer-

cially. Plastic lettering with magnetic backing is available from supply stores and can be used for captioning visuals.

Any metal surface in the classroom to which a magnet is attached can serve as a magnetic board. For example, some chalkboards are backed with steel and thus attract magnet-backed visuals. Chalk can be used on such chalkboards for captioning or to depict lines of association between visuals. Steel cabinets and metal walls and doors can also be used as magnetic boards.

You can make your own magnetic board from a thin sheet of galvanized iron, a cookie sheet, a lap tray, or any similar thin sheet of metal. Paint the sheets in the color of your choice with paint designed for use on metal surfaces or cover with Con-Tact paper. Unpainted surfaces are likely to be unattractive and cause glare. Another alternative is to fasten steel screening to a nonmetal surface, such as plywood, and cover it with a piece of cloth.

FIGURE 4.26
Magnetic boards allow quick manipulation of letters and other materials.

The major advantage of magnetic boards is that maneuvering visuals is easier and quicker than with cloth boards. For example, magnetic boards are often used by physical education instructors to demonstrate rapid changes in player positions. Magnetic boards also have greater adhesive quality. Visuals displayed on a magnetic board are not likely to slip or fall. They move only when you move them.

Flip Charts

A **flip chart** is a pad of large paper fastened together at the top and mounted to an easel. The individual sheets each hold a limited verbal/visual message and can be arranged for sequential presentation to a small group. The messages can be written extemporaneously while the presenter is talking or can be prepared in advance and revealed one at a time. Poster makers, such as PosterPrinter, can be used to produce flip chart pages (see Figure 4.16). Commercially produced materials are also available in this format; they are especially prevalent in reading and science instruction and military training. Prepared visual sequences are especially useful for instruction involving sequential steps in a process. The diagrams or words can serve as cues, reminding the presenter of the next point in the presentation.

The most common use of flip charts, though, is for the extemporaneous drawing of key illustrations and key words to supplement a stand-up presentation (Figure 4.27). The flip chart is an extremely versatile, convenient, and inexpensive media format. It requires no electrical power, has no moving parts to wear out, can be used in a wide range of lighting conditions, is portable, and requires only a marking pen as peripheral equip-ment. Next to the chalkboard, it is the most user-friendly audiovisual tool. But don't let the flip chart's simplicity fool you. Using it professionally takes some practice.

Audience members seem to regard the flip chart in friendly terms. It seems casual and comfortable, a pleasing change of pace in an increasingly high-technology world. It is an exceptionally valuable aid to any group discussion process. Ideas contributed by group members can be recorded in a way visible to all participants. Comments and correction can be made and the results can be preserved. Finished sheets can be torn off the pad and taped to walls or windows for later reference. Flip charts are available in a variety of sizes for large-group use; others, often referred to as *travel easels,* are designed for portability.

Flip-chart-size Post-It easel pads are available from 3M. These 25-by-30-inch self-sticking easel sheets come in white or with a blue grid on white. The easel pads have a built-in handle, a sturdy backing, and a cover flap to protect the sheets from damage or flapping while in transit. The universal slots on the backing attach to most easel stands. Each sheet peels off for quick posting or can be flipped over the top of the pad.

Exhibits

Exhibits are displays of various objects and visuals designed to form an integrated whole for instructional purposes (Figure 4.28). Any of the visuals discussed in this chapter, including models and real objects, can be included in an exhibit, and any of the display surfaces discussed can contribute to an exhibit. Exhibits can generally be used for the same instructional purposes and in the same ways as their individual components are used.

Exhibit locations are readily available in most classrooms. Simple exhibits can be set up on a table, shelf, or

FIGURE 4.27
Flip charts, a standard in business and industrial training, are also used in schools.

FIGURE 4.28
A complex exhibit such as this one brings together real objects, still pictures, and other visuals with verbal information.

- Position the flip chart at an angle so everyone can see it. Place it in the left front corner (as you face the audience) if you are right-handed and in the right front corner if you are left-handed.
- Be sure the easel is properly assembled and the pages are securely fastened so the flip chart will not fall apart during your presentation.
- Prepare lettering and visuals in advance or outline their shape using a light-blue pencil; then trace them during your presentation.
- For group-generated responses, draw lettering guidelines with a blue pencil.
- Keep lettering and visuals simple but large enough for everyone to see.
- Use more than one color, but not more than four.

- Use broad-tip marking pens that provide contrast but will not bleed through to the next sheet.
- Print rather than use cursive writing.
- Keep words short or use well-understood abbreviations.
- Include simple drawings, symbols, and charts.
- Talk to the audience, not to the flip chart.
- Avoid blocking the audience's view of the flip chart.
- Be sure your materials are in proper sequence.
- Have a blank sheet exposed when not referring to the flip chart.
- Reveal pages only when you are ready to discuss them, not before.
- Put summary points on the last sheet rather than paging back as you make your summary.

desk. More complex exhibits may require considerable floor space and special structures (a booth, for example).

The school library media center is a convenient location for exhibits, displays, and dioramas. Often these items can be borrowed from area museums or historical societies. The media center may also provide space for display of student-produced exhibits.

FIGURE 4.29

This simple teacher-made display consists of related artifacts arranged for easy observation by students.

There are two types of exhibits—displays and dioramas. A display is a collection of materials, whereas a diorama shows a three-dimensional scene.

Displays. A display is an array of objects, visuals, and printed materials (e.g., labels and descriptions). Most displays include descriptive information about the objects or visuals shown. Instructional displays are used in the classroom (Figure 4.29), in museums, and in many other settings.

Student assembly of a display can be a motivating learning experience. It can foster retention of subject matter and sharpen visual skills. For a lesson in transportation, one sixth-grade teacher had each student bring in a replica of a vehicle. Some students made their own vehicles from construction paper. Others brought in toys from home or contributed vehicles assembled from hobby kits (e.g., boats, cars, trucks, trains, space ships). The teacher placed tables and other classroom furniture along a wall to provide the children with a shelf on which to arrange their three-dimensional objects. On the wall above the display surface, the teacher placed a long sheet of paper containing a time line. The time line illustrated forms of transportation from the past (humans and beasts), through the present (trains, cars, planes), and into the future (space vehicles). The display was a great success.

Dioramas. **Dioramas** are static displays consisting of a three-dimensional foreground and a flat background to create a realistic scene. The foreground is usually a landscape of some sort with models of people, animals, vehicles, equipment, or buildings. The naturalistic background may be a photograph, drawing, or painting. The diorama is usually contained within a box, with the sides of the box providing additional backdrop. The rear corners or the entire back may be rounded to

FIGURE 4.30
Student-made displays enrich the learning environment for everyone.

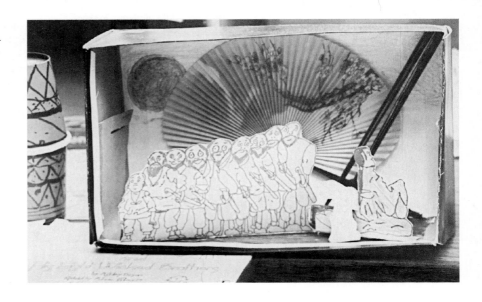

FIGURE 4.31

Calvin and Hobbes copyright © 1990 Watterson. Distributed by Universal Press Syndicate. Reprinted with permission.

provide an illusion of depth, and lights can be added for a special effect.

Dioramas are usually designed to reproduce past or present scenes and events or to depict future ones. Examples in museums are often lifesize, whereas those used in classrooms are usually on a smaller scale. In industry, dioramas can be constructed to show company products in use.

Teachers may construct dioramas to illustrate their lessons or to introduce major topics. Students can be asked to design their own dioramas as a follow-up activity to instruction. Scenes from history, particularly battles, are often portrayed with model figures. Animals can be shown in their natural habitats for a biology class. Scenes including towns and landscapes from various parts of the world make stimulating dioramas for geography instruction. Prehistoric landscapes and geologic formations are also popular topics for dioramas.

REFERENCES

Print References

Nonprojected Visuals

Alesandrini, K. L. "Pictures and Adult Learning." *Instructional Science* (May 1984): 63–77.

Blena-Clucas, Beth. "Bring the Museum to the Media Center." *School Library Journal* (September 1993): 150–153.

Braun, Joseph A., ed. "Social Mathematics and Media: Using Pictures, Maps, Charts, and Graphs." *Social Studies and the Young Learner* (September–October 1993): 28–30.

Briggs, Diane. *Flannel Board Fun: Collection of Stories, Songs, and Poems.* Metuchen, NJ: Scarecrow, 1992.

DeCorte, Erik, ed. "Comprehension of Graphics in Text." *Learning and Instruction* (1993)3: 3, 151–249.

Small Gas Furnace Assembly

Analyze Learners

General Characteristics

The assembly line workers at the Reliable Furnace Company manufacture small gas furnaces. They range in age from eighteen to sixty-eight and include both males and females. All are high school graduates, but most have low reading abilities (the average is ninth grade, with a range from sixth to fourteenth).

Because of attrition and shifts of workers to different jobs on the assembly line, a burner box assembler needs to be trained about once each week. The assembler's job requires manual dexterity and mobility. Because various colored wires are soldered to different locations, the trainee cannot be color blind.

Entry Competencies

The chief requirements are the ability to follow assembly instructions (which may be committed to memory after several weeks on the job) and to solder. Because soldering is required for other jobs within the company and is a skill many of the workers already have, it will not be taught as part of the lesson. A separate module on soldering techniques is available for those who need it.

Employees who have worked for the company less than four months are highly motivated to be successful and want to please the supervisor. This is especially true of the younger workers (younger than twenty-five years old). The more mature individuals and those with more than a year's seniority generally just want to get by with as little effort as possible.

State Objectives

Upon completion of the burner box assembly unit, the worker will be able to do the following:

1. Assemble the burner box for a small gas furnace according to company specifications within seven minutes when given the necessary components and appropriate tools.

   Subobjectives are:

   • Solder the control wires onto the correct terminals with a solder joint that will conduct current and withstand a five-pound pull.
   • Position the top and side panels on the base and attach with metal screws. Panels must be in proper position and all screws must be firmly seated. There

are several other subobjectives as well as this affective objective.

2. Wear safety goggles and work gloves during the entire assembly process. (The workers know they should do this, but they don't always do so.)

Select Methods, Media, and Materials

After checking through catalogs of industrial training materials and talking with training directors from other furnace manufacturing firms, Jan Smith, the training coordinator, concluded that there were no off-the-shelf materials suitable for use or modification. Consequently, she decided to develop a set of drawings and photographs to be incorporated into a small (9-by-12-inch) flip chart for use by the trainee. Because of the need for hands-on practice and training (approximately one worker per week), a self-instructional unit will be developed incorporating actual burner components, the flip chart, and an audiotape. Humor will be used to enhance motivation for those employees who are not motivated.

Utilize the Materials

The trainee will be allowed to use the materials and practice the assembly as many times as necessary in the training room. A trainer will be available to answer questions and to evaluate the completed burner boxes.

Require Learner Participation

When the trainer is satisfied that the task has been mastered, an experienced employee will provide additional on-the-job training (OJT) at the assembly line. The experienced worker will demonstrate the task under actual working conditions with the assembly line running. Then the trainee will take over, with the experienced worker providing guidance and encouragement until the trainee is competent and confident.

Evaluate

The trainee and the training will be evaluated based on a number of factors. The number of defective or inoperative burner boxes identified by quality control or during installation is one criterion. Periodically the line supervisor will observe the workers for safety procedures (gloves and goggles) and assembly sequence. Accident and injury reports will also be sent to the training department.

A computer template for a Blueprint is found in "The Classroom Link."

Do You See What I Mean? Learning Through Charts, Graphs, Maps, and Diagrams. Dickson, Australia: Curriculum Development Centre, 1980.

"Give Your Room a Face Lift." *Instructor* (March 1992): 38–39.

Goetz, William W. "Retrieving and Reinforcing U.S. Government Using Graphic Organizers." *Social Education* (February 1993): 87–88.

Hauck, Marge, and Merz, Olivia. "Distinctive Displays." *Instructor* (July–August 1992): 59–60.

Hollister, Bernard C. "Using Picture Books in the Classroom." *Media and Methods* (January 1977): 22–25.

Holub, Brenda, and Bennett, Clifford T. "Using Political Cartoons to Teach Junior/Middle School U.S. History." *Social Studies* (September–October 1988): 214–216.

How to Prepare Effective Flip Charts. East Rutherford, NJ: National Audio-Visual Supply, 1992.

Kemp, Jerrold E., and Smellie, Don C. *Planning, Producing, and Using Instructional Technologies.* 7th ed. New York: HarperCollins, 1994.

Koetsch, Peg, et al. "Student Curators: Becoming Life-long Learners." *Educational Leadership* (February 1994): 54–57.

Kohn, Rita. *Experiencing Displays*. Metuchen, NJ: Scarecrow Press, 1982.

Scott, Kristin S. "Multisensory Mathematics for Children with Mild Disabilities." *Exceptionality: A Research Journal* (1993)4: 2, 97–111.

Thomas, James L., ed. *Nonprint in the Elementary Curriculum: Readings for Reference*. 2d ed. Littleton, CO: Libraries Unlimited, 1988.

Trimblay, Roger. "Using Magazine Pictures in the Second-Language Classroom." *Canadian Modern Language Review* (October 1978): 82–86.

Wildman, Diane. "Researching with Pictures." *English Journal* (March 1990): 55–58.

Bulletin Boards

Burke, K., and Kranhold, J. *The Big Fearon Bulletin Board Book*. Carthage, IL: Fearon Teacher Aids, 1978.

Bush, Katherine P., et al. "Bulletin Boards, Displays, and Special Events." *Book Report* (January–February 1989): 9–15, 17–23, 26.

Flores, Anthony. *Instant Bulletin Boards*. Carthage, IL: Fearon Teacher Aids, 1983.

Freeman, Shirley, et al. "Beyond Bunnies and Snowmen: Using Bulletin Boards Effectively." *Perspectives in Education and Deafness* (September–October 1993): 15–17.

Prizzi, Elaine, and Hoffman, Jeanne. *Interactive Bulletin Boards*. Carthage, IL: Fearon Teaching Aids, 1984.

Tweedie, Patricia S. "Please Touch: Activity Bulletin Boards in Classrooms for Young Children." *Dimensions of Early Childhood* (Spring 1992): 30–34, 40.

Vidor, Constance. "Easy Bulletin Boards and Displays for School Library Media Centers." *School Library Media Activities Monthly* (October 1993): 36–37.

Free and Inexpensive Materials

Bowman, Linda. *Freebies for Kids and Parents Too!* Chicago: Probus, 1991.

Free Stuff Editors. *Free Stuff for Kids*. New York: Simon and Shuster, 1989.

Freebies Editors. *The Official Freebies for Teachers*. Los Angeles: Lowell House, 1994.

Smith, Adeline M., and Jones, Diane R. *Free Magazines for Libraries*. Jefferson, NC: McFarland and Company, 1989.

Audiovisual References

Display and Presentation Boards. Chicago: International Film Bureau, 1971. 16mm film or videocassette. 15 minutes.

Dry Mounting Audiovisual Materials. Iowa City, IA: University of Iowa, 1985. VHS videocassette. 7 minutes.

Dry Mounting with Heat Press. Salt Lake City, UT: Media Systems, Inc., 1975. Filmstrip or slides. 40 frames.

Heat Laminating. Salt Lake City, UT: Media Systems, Inc. 1975. Filmstrip or slides. 40 frames.

Laminating Audiovisual Materials. Iowa City, IA: University of Iowa, 1985. VHS videocassette. 7 minutes.

Lettering: A Creative Approach to Basics. Stamford, CT: Educational Dimensions Group, 1978. Two sound filmstrips with audiocassettes.

Production Techniques for Instructional Graphic Materials. Columbus, OH: Charles E. Merrill, 1977. Twenty-seven filmstrips in basic series, 12 filmstrips in advanced series, 18 audiocassettes.

Tables and Graphs. Weekly Reader Filmstrips. Guidance Associates, 1981. Four filmstrips with audiocassettes. Grades 3–6.

Three-Dimensional Displays. Burbank, CA: Encore Visual Education, 1975. Four sound filmstrips with audiocassettes.

PROJECTED VISUALS

Overhead and opaque projection, slides, and filmstrips—these are the traditional audiovisual media associated with the classroom. Although they have been around for more than half a century, they are still among the most popular teaching tools. The large, bright image captures the audience's attention as no other technology can. The challenge is to make the most of that attention, to present messages that are clear, legible, attractive, and illustrative of your point.

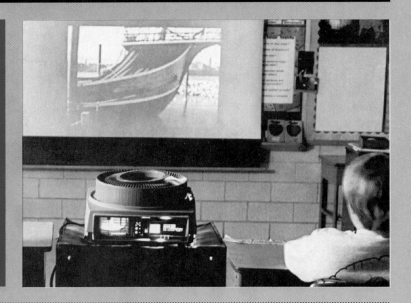

It's easy to prepare your own materials in the form of overheads and slides. With computer support you can easily show text and visual displays. And with presentation graphic software you can make graphics that are as slick and artistic as professionally designed ones.

Instructional media and the technologies for learning provide you with the tools to engage students powerfully in the learning process. The array of media formats and of quality materials available to the teacher is increasing dramatically. As a teacher, you must be prepared to choose the best tools for your students, who are in diverse situations and pursuing different sorts of learning goals.

KNOWLEDGE OBJECTIVES

1. Identify six formats for projected visuals and compare their advantages and limitations.
2. Describe the characteristics and operation of overhead transparency projection.
3. Describe specific applications of overhead projection to your own teaching field.
4. Outline the procedures for creating transparencies by each of these methods: direct drawing, thermal film process, electrostatic film process, computer generation.
5. Identify examples of transparencies that exhibit the guidelines for the design of effective visuals.
6. Compare the advantages and limitations of using the LCD panel for image projection.
7. Compare the advantages and limitations of using sound-slide sets.
8. Describe specific applications for which a multi-image presentation would be appropriate.
9. Describe a technique for eliciting learner participation during a filmstrip showing.
10. Describe specific situations in which the opaque projector would be especially useful.

APPLICATION OBJECTIVES

1. Prepare a set of transparencies for a topic you might teach. Use at least two of the following production methods: direct drawing by hand, thermal film process, electrostatic (xerography) process, computer generation of presentation graphics.
2. Describe how you might utilize an LCD panel in a particular instructional situation.
3. Demonstrate the correct technique for inserting slides into a circular slide tray.
4. Prepare a storyboard for a silent, sound, or multi-image slide presentation.
5. Create an original example of an instructional situation in which you might use a set of teacher- or student-made slides.
6. Produce a set of slides for a topic you might teach. Use either a regular film camera, a digital camera, or computer images presented on an LCD projector. Describe the intended audience and purpose, and state specifically how you would use the slides. (Alternative: Describe a project for student-produced slides; include audience, purpose, and plan for guiding students.)
7. Examine a major selection source for projected visuals (such as "A-V Online") and report on the sorts of materials that you believe would be useful in your own teaching.
8. Preview a slide set or filmstrip and complete an appraisal report using the "Appraisal Checklist: Projected Visuals."
9. Create an original example of how opaque projection might be applied to your teaching field.
10. Develop a lesson incorporating a slide set or filmstrip following the format of the "Blueprint" at the end of this chapter.

LEXICON

projected visuals

overhead projection

fresnel lens

transparency

acetate

overlay

keystone effect

thermal film

electrostatic film (xerography)

presentation graphics software

liquid crystal display (LCD)

slide

thumb spot

sound–slide set

multi-image presentation

filmstrip

opaque projection

document camera

Because an illuminated screen in a darkened room tends to rivet the attention of viewers, projected visuals have long been popular as a medium of instruction as well as entertainment. The lighted screen is a silent shout—a shout likely to be heeded by even the most reluctant learners.

Some of this attraction may be due to the aura of magic that seems to surround such presentations. The room lights are dimmed; the viewers grow quiet in expectation; a switch is thrown; and (presto!) a large, bright image appears on the screen. You have the attention of the audience, who are ready to receive the message. Exploit this readiness by selecting materials that will maintain the viewers' attention and by using them in a way that involves viewers actively in the learning process.

Projected visuals are defined here as media formats in which still images are enlarged and displayed on a screen. Such projection is usually achieved by passing a strong light through transparent film (overhead transparencies, slides, and filmstrips), magnifying the image through a series of lenses, and casting this image onto a reflective surface. Opaque projection is also included in this category. In opaque projection, light is cast onto an opaque image (one that does not allow light to pass through), such as a magazine picture or printed page. The light is reflected from the material onto mirrors, which transmit the reflection through a series of lenses onto a screen.

The focus of this chapter is on the characteristics and applications of overhead projection, computer image projection, slides, filmstrips, and opaque projection—the most widely accepted means of using projected visuals in education and training settings.

OVERHEAD PROJECTION

Because of its many virtues, the **overhead projection** system (Figure 5.1) has advanced rapidly in the past several decades to become the most widely used audiovisual device in North American classrooms and training sites.

The typical overhead projector is a simple device (Figure 5.2). Basically, it is a box with a large aperture, or "stage," on the top surface. Light from a powerful lamp inside the box is condensed by a special type of lens, known as a **fresnel lens,** and passes through a transparency (approximately 8 by 10 inches) placed on the stage. A lens-and-mirror system mounted on a bracket above the box turns the light beam 90 degrees and projects the image back over the shoulder of the presenter. This type of projector, in which the light passes *through* the transparency, is referred to as a *transmissive* type. (See "How to . . . Operate an Overhead Projector," p. 142.)

FIGURE 5.1
With the overhead projector, the presenter maintains eye contact with viewers.

In another sort of overhead projector, the light source is above the projector stage and shines down onto the transparency (Figure 5.3). The light is reflected by a mirrorlike surface beneath the transparency back up and through the lens system. This *reflective* type of projector produces a less brilliant light, so it does not perform as well as the transmissive type in rooms with a long projection throw or with a lot of ambient light. Its advantage is its portability, being lighter and more compact than the transmissive type.

Because of the widespread familiarity of overhead projection, the general term **transparency** has taken on, in the instructional setting, the specific meaning of the large-format 8-by-10-inch film used with the overhead projector. Transparencies may be composed of photographic film, clear **acetate,** or any of a number of other transparent materials capable of being imprinted with an image by means of chemical or heat processes. The individual sheets of transparent film are called "acetates" in reference to the chemical composition of the standard type of film.

Transparencies may be used individually or may be made into a series of images consisting of a base visual with one or more **overlays** attached to the base with hinges. Overlays are sheets of transparent film, each containing additional information, that are laid over the base transparency. Complex topics can be explained step-by-step by flipping a series of overlays one at a time, adding additional features to a diagram (see Figure 5.4).

Advantages

- *Brightness.* Its bright lamp and efficient optical system generate so much light on the screen that the overhead can be used with normal room lighting.

FIGURE 5.2

The transmissive type of overhead projector; the light from the lamp is transmitted through the glass stage and transparency.

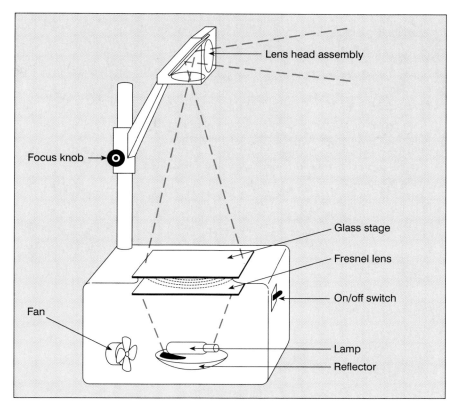

FIGURE 5.3

The reflective type of overhead projector; the light from the lamp is reflected off the mirrorlike stage.

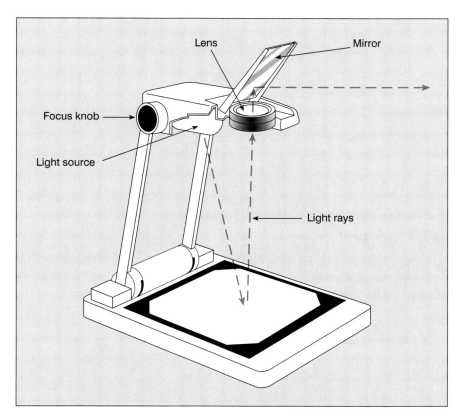

OPERATION

Set Up

- Connect power cord to AC outlet.

Operate

- Turn projector on. (With some projectors you have to click through two positions to reach the "on" position.)
- Position transparency on stage.
- Adjust projector to eliminate keystoning (explained in Appendix A).

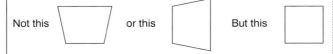

Not this   or this   But this

- Focus image.
- Practice writing on the transparency and erasing.

Disassemble

- Restore to storage conformation.

TROUBLESHOOTING

Problems/Possible Remedies

- *No light after flipping switch:*
  1. Be sure projector is plugged into an electrical outlet.
  2. Turn the switch all the way on. Many overheads have a three-position switch: off, fan, and on.
  3. If lamp is burned out, switch to spare lamp within projector if it has this feature. Otherwise, you will need to replace the lamp. Be sure to use a lamp of the same wattage (too high a wattage can cause overheating). Do not handle the lamp while it is hot. Avoid touching the new lamp with bare fingers; this could shorten its life.
  4. Switch may be defective. If so, have it replaced.
- *Dark edge with light in center of image:* The fresnel lens is upside down. Turn it over if you know how; if not, have a qualified specialist do it.

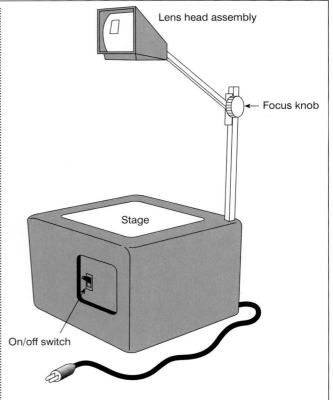

- *Dark spot on area of screen:* The lamp socket within the projector needs adjustment. The task is best done by a trained audiovisual technician.
- *Dark spot on screen or failure of lens to focus despite all adjustments of focus:* After determining that it is not simply a matter of dirt on the lens or improper use of the focus control, check for a warped fresnel lens. This lens is plastic and can become warped from excessive heat, usually caused by the fan not running properly. Have a qualified specialist repair the fan or thermostat and replace the fresnel lens.

- *Eye contact.* The projector is operated from the front of the room with the presenter facing the audience, allowing direct eye contact to be maintained.
- *Ease of use.* Most overhead projectors are lightweight and portable. All are simple to operate.
- *Abundance of materials.* A variety of materials can be projected, including cutout silhouettes, small opaque objects, and many types of transparencies.
- *Manipulable.* Projected materials can be manipulated by the presenter. You can point to important items, highlight them with colored pens, add details (notes, diagrams, etc.) during the lesson by marking on the transparency with a marking pen, or cover part of the message and progressively reveal information. As

noted previously, complex visuals can be presented in a series of overlays.
- *Availability of materials.* Commercially produced transparencies and transparency masters cover a broad range of curriculum areas. A list of sources can be found in Appendix C.
- *Self-prepared materials.* Instructors can easily prepare their own transparencies (several common methods of production are explained later in this chapter).
- *Advance preparation.* Information that might otherwise have to be placed on a chalkboard during a class session (e.g., lesson outlines) may be prepared in advance for presentation at the proper time. Research indicates that retention of main points improves significantly when outlines are presented.

FIGURE 5.4
By means of overlays, complex visuals can be built up step-by-step.

Construction steps

1. FOUNDATION

(a)

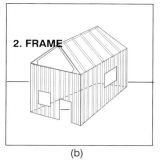

2. FRAME

(b)

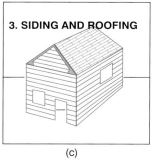

3. SIDING AND ROOFING

(c)

Construction steps
3. SIDING AND ROOFING
2. FRAME

1. FOUNDATION

(d)

- *Impact on attitudes.* The use of overhead transparencies also has positive effects on attitude in business meetings. In a study by the Wharton Applied Research Center, candidates for master's degrees in business administration participated in a business simulation that involved group meetings to decide whether to introduce a new product. The findings showed that
  - More individuals decided to act on the recommendations of presenters who used overheads than on the recommendation of presenters who did not.
  - Presenters who used overheads were perceived as better prepared, more professional, more persuasive, more credible, and more interesting.
  - Groups in which presenters used overheads were more likely to reach consensus on their decisions than groups where no overheads were employed.[1]
- *Organization and discussion.* Another study suggests that teachers who use the overhead projector tend to be more organized than teachers who rely on notes or printed outlines. Students in this study participated more frequently in discussions in the classes where the overhead was used.[2]

---

[1]*A Study of the Effects of the Use of Overhead Transparencies on Business Meetings* (Philadelphia: Wharton Applied Research Center, Wharton School, University of Pennsylvania, 1981).

[2]James Cabeceiras, "Observed Differences in Teacher Verbal Behavior When Using and Not Using the Overhead Projector." *AV Communication Review* (Fall 1972), pp. 271–280.

Limitations

- *Not preprogrammed.* The effectiveness of overhead projection presentations is heavily dependent on the presenter. The overhead projector cannot be programmed to display visual sequences by itself, nor is an audio accompaniment provided.
- *Not self-instructional.* The overhead system does not lend itself to independent study. It is designed for large-group presentation. Of course, an individual student could look at a transparency by holding it up to the light or laying it on a light table, but because captions and audio tracks are not a part of this format, the material would ordinarily not be self-instructional.
- *Production process required.* Printed materials and other nontransparent items, such as magazine illustrations, cannot be projected immediately, as is possible with the opaque projector. To use the overhead system such materials have to be made into transparencies by means of some production process.
- *Keystone effect.* Distortion of images is more prevalent with the overhead than with other projection systems. The projector is commonly placed at desktop level to facilitate the instructor's writing on transparencies. The screen, on the other hand, needs to be placed on a higher level for unobstructed audience

▼ MEDIA FILE

History of the World
Overhead Transparencies

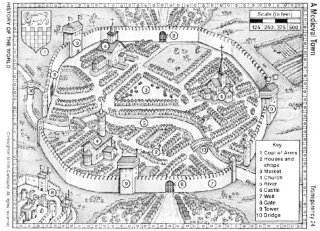

A set of 145 overhead transparencies, including one on "A Medieval Town," accompanies the textbook *History of the World.* They are of many types: maps, charts, tables, diagrams, illustrations, and political cartoons. An accompanying teacher's guide provides suggestions for class discussion.

Source: Houghton Mifflin Company.

sight lines. This discrepancy in levels causes a distortion referred to as the **keystone effect**. (This problem and its solution are discussed in Appendix A.)

Applications

Because the image is large and you can manipulate or add to it while projecting, the overhead projector is extraordinarily versatile. It has been used to communicate visually in every subject in the curriculum. Here are a few ideas:[3]

- *Art:* Primary and secondary colors. Use strips of colored acetate to demonstrate the composition of primary and secondary colors by overlapping red, yellow, and blue.
- *Drama:* Stage lighting. Put a floor plan on the base cell and add overlays to show acting circles and how areas are lit.
- *Language Arts:* Color coding. Use different colored pens to highlight nouns, verbs, and other parts of speech.
- *Literature:* Poetry. Visually compare different forms of poetry (e.g., haiku, sonnet) and compare meter patterns.
- *Music:* Three-part harmony. Show a staff with notes arranged in three-part harmony, with different colored notes for each part.
- *Mathematics:* Fractions. Use circles and squares that are cut into pieces to illustrate different fractions. These are among the many transparent manipulatives distributed by publishers as adjuncts to math textbooks.
- *Library Skills:* Media center layout. Show a floor plan of the layout of the school media center as part of library orientation.
- *Consumer Science:* Checkbook. Make thermal transparencies of blank checks and balance sheets; demonstrate how to make out a check and balance the check register.
- *Geography:* Map measurements. Use a clear plastic ruler over a transparency of a map; demonstrate how to measure the distance between any two points.
- *Science:* Magnetism. Show how iron filings align to poles of a magnet placed on an overhead projector stage.

Creating Overhead Transparencies

As previously noted, a major advantage of the overhead system is that instructors (and students!) can easily prepare their own transparencies. One of the first methods involved simple hand drawing on clear acetate sheets; numerous other methods of preparing transparencies have evolved over the years. We will look closely at the processes most commonly used in the classroom—direct drawing, thermal film process, electrostatic film process (xerography), and computer printing.

Direct Drawing Method. The most obvious way of quickly preparing a transparency is simply to draw directly on a transparent sheet with a marking pen (Figure 5.5). Clear acetate of 5–10 mils (.005–.010 inches) is recommended. Other types of plastic can be used—even household food wrap. Although some of these alternatives may be a great deal cheaper than the thicker acetate, some impose limitations in terms of durability, ease of handling, and ability to accept different inks (i.e., some disintegrate completely under alcohol-based inks). Blue-tinted acetate is preferred because it reduces the glare of the projected image.

Although the glass stage of the overhead projector generally measures about 10 by 10 inches, your drawing and lettering should be restricted to a rectangular "message area" of about 7½ by 9½ inches. This fits the dimensions of acetate sheets, which are commonly cut into rectangles of 8 by 10 inches or 8½ by 11 inches (Figure 5.6).

If you are doing freehand lettering, keep in mind that neatness counts, as does legibility. Your imperfections will be magnified to the size of the projection screen. Viewers can't learn from what they can't decipher. Note the guidelines in "How to . . . Design Overhead Transparencies" on page 146.

FIGURE 5.5

Most overhead projector users like to draw directly on the transparency, in this case to add significant details to a previously prepared visual.

---

[3]Some of these examples are among the hundreds found in Lee Green, *501 Ways to Use the Overhead Projector* (Littleton, CO: Libraries Unlimited, 1982).

FIGURE 5.6
Comparative dimensions of an overhead transparency and the projector stage.

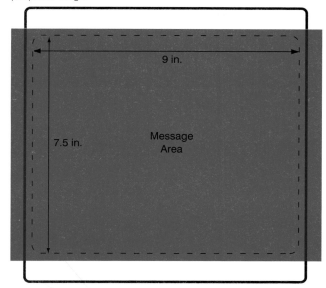

9 in.

7.5 in.

Message
Area

8.5 x 11 in. acetate sheet
10 x 10 in. overhead projector stage

Some overhead projectors come equipped with a pair of roller attachments made to carry long rolls of plastic that can be advanced or reversed by a small hand crank. This assures a steady supply of transparency material for extemporaneous use. It also allows a series of images to be prepared in advance in proper sequence.

In addition to the transparency, you will need a writing instrument. Felt-tip marking pens are the handiest for this purpose. They come in two general types—water-soluble and permanent ink. However, not all are suitable for overhead transparencies. Here are some cautions to keep in mind:

- Ordinary felt-tip pens with water-soluble ink generally will not adhere well to acetate; the ink tends to bead up and evaporate. Look for a label saying, "overhead projector pen"; this indicates it will adhere to acetate and project color. Such special pens can be erased with a damp tissue or washed completely clean to be reused.
- Virtually any permanent-ink felt-tip pen will adhere to acetate, but only those marked "overhead projector pen" are made to project in color. Other types may project only in black and may even damage the transparency film. Most users choose a permanent ink for hand-drawn transparencies that are prepared in advance, especially if they are going to be reused, because water-based ink is likely to smear as you work on the different areas of the transparency or as you handle it during use.

- Permanent ink markings can be erased with special plastic erasers or with correction markers containing alcohol-based solvents (Figure 5.7), but it is not practical to clean and reuse transparencies that have extensive permanent ink markings.
- Highlighter pens made especially for overhead projection can be used during a presentation to draw attention to critical information. This can add a dramatic touch, but be careful—they are permanent. A clear acetate sheet can be put on top of your finished transparency to protect it.
- Least commonly used are wax-based pencils. Most will project only in black. They can be erased with a soft, dry cloth.

Thermal Film Process.   In the **thermal film** process, infrared light passes through a specially treated acetate film onto a prepared master underneath. The artwork and lettering on the master are done with a heat-absorbing material such as India ink, ordinary lead pencil, computer printer ink, or another substance containing carbon. An image is "burned into" the film wherever it contacts such carbonaceous markings.

Depending on the film used, various color combinations are possible. The most common pair is color or black print on a clear or pastel background. A light color can also be put on a dark background.

Masters can be produced by hand or by computer printer. Another option is the use of commercially prepared transparency masters. Thermal film producers and other audiovisual publishers offer a broad range of printed masters with many thousands of individual titles covering virtually all curriculum areas. Some publishers offer sets of masters specifically correlated with the leading textbooks in language arts, reading, math, social studies, and science.

FIGURE 5.7
Plastic erasers will remove permanent ink, at least that of the same manufacturer.

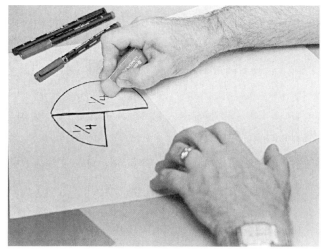

Assemble the Elements

- When you are choosing elements remember that viewers will stop reading text once they know what it says, but they will continue to look at illustrations, especially when you are talking about them. Use more graphical elements than text on your transparencies and supply the verbal explanations yourself; include text for key ideas only.

Choose Background and Underlying Pattern

- If you are using a computer presentations program to create transparencies, you will have a choice of underlying patterns, usually called "Masters" or "Templates." Choose the simplest one that fills your needs.

Arrange the Elements

- Since the elements on a transparency must be fairly large in order to project well, one of the challenges of arrangement is to fit the elements into the available space. Resist the temptation to make elements smaller, since they may not be visible to your viewers.

Check and Revise

- Practice with your transparencies and an actual projector. You can double-check the visibility of your elements and discover whether the arrangement of content from one transparency to another actually supports the presentation you expect to make.

© Elizabeth Boling 1995

FRACTIONS

½ + ½ = 1

Titles and other text are plain and large so they will project visibly and clearly.

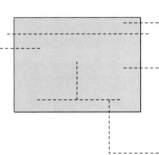

Illustration elements are simply designed and convey only one major concept for each transparency in the set; if they are in color, the colors are bold enough not to "wash out" in the light of the projector.

Protective frames keep fingerprints off transparencies and make them easy to store, label and handle. Decide what type of frame you will use before you design the transparencies so you know how much margin to allow for the frame.

Blue transparencies provide a neutral background for black text and illustrations; yellow transparencies with black text are highly legible; clear transparencies are best if you expect to use color in the content.

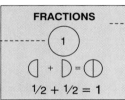

Title area is at the top of the overhead where viewers begin to scan the display.

Content area: content of transparencies should be limited to 1 or 2 images at most for graphical displays; 2 headings and 6 bullet points for text displays.

Inverted "T" pattern gives a focal point at the top with room for expanded content below.

The circle representing a whole is large enough to anchor the display; viewers refer back to it as they process new information.

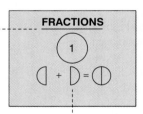

If there is more than one transparency in this series, others may use different arrangements of illustrations, but all the content will appear within the same area of each slide.

Additional line helps separate title from content area more clearly.

Transparency is simplified to 2 major, related ideas.

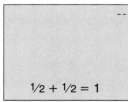

Second transparency is designed to overlay the first one after viewers have absorbed its content.

To use commercially prepared thermal masters, simply remove one from the book or folder in which it is packaged, lay the thermal film on it with the notch in the upper right corner, and run both through the copier. Commercial masters may, of course, be altered by the instructor to better suit the needs of a particular audience. (See "How to . . . Make Thermal Transparencies.")

1. Prepare the master. Any ordinary white paper may be used. Draw the artwork by hand or paste illustrations from other sources (magazine illustrations, photocopies, etc.) onto the master. Lettering—added by hand, by dry transfer lettering, or by paste-up of existing lettering—must be made of a carbonaceous substance. Alternatively, you could create the visual by using any type of materials and then photocopying it and using the copy as the master. (Note that some photocopies work better than others. Experiment with what is available to you.)

2. Place a sheet of thermal acetate over the master. Most brands of acetate have a notch in one corner of the film to ensure that it is put on correctly. The notch should always be placed at the upper right corner of the master.

3. Feed the two sheets into a thermal copy machine, using the dial setting recommended by the manufacturer. Transfer of the image to the acetate requires only a few seconds. Then separate the two sheets. The film is ready for projection! The master is not affected in the production process and may be reused to make additional copies of the transparency.

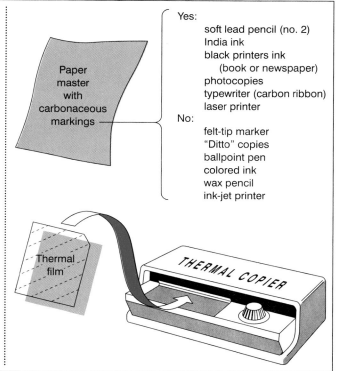

Paper master with carbonaceous markings

Yes:
soft lead pencil (no. 2)
India ink
black printers ink
   (book or newspaper)
photocopies
typewriter (carbon ribbon)
laser printer

No:
felt-tip marker
"Ditto" copies
ballpoint pen
colored ink
wax pencil
ink-jet printer

Thermal film

THERMAL COPIER

Electrostatic Film Process (Xerography).

The rapidly evolving technology of xerography provides another method of producing transparencies. All plain-paper copiers that operate by the **electrostatic film (xerography)** process can be used to make black-and-white transparencies. Some models can also produce high-quality full-color transparencies from paper originals or slides. These are most often found at commercial copying services.

Like the thermal process, electrostatic copying requires a paper master and specially treated film. In this case the film is electrically charged and light sensitive (rather than heat sensitive). The steps outlined in "How to . . . Make Thermal Transparencies" are essentially the same as those for electrostatic transparencies. However, because the xerographic process responds to darkness of the image rather than carbon content, it is not necessary to confine the original to carbonaceous marks. Any source that yields good opaque markings can be used (e.g., computer printer output, clippings from printed material, drawings made by ballpoint pen or dark felt-tip marker).

Overheads Created by Computer.

Computers have transformed the task of creating overhead transparencies and similar types of visuals. With any word processing software you can prepare simple verbal overheads—sentences, lists, and the like. Each screen can be printed out on plain paper, which you can use as a master to make thermal or electrostatic transparencies.

With **presentation graphics software,** such as Lotus's *Freelance Graphics* and Microsoft's *PowerPoint,* even users without specialized graphics training can create attractive graphic displays in a form suitable for professional presentation. You select a visual style from a menu, specify the desired type of graphic (e.g., outline, bulleted list, graph, map, or combination), then just type in your message where directed by the program (Figure 5.8). The program automatically selects legible type fonts and sizes and organizes the pictures and text into a clean visual layout. The visual can be printed directly onto transparency film by a laser printer or onto a paper copy, which can be used as a master to make thermal or xerographic transparencies. Among the types of graphics software available are the following:

- *Presentation programs*—special software that simplifies creation of slides or transparencies of graphics that combine text, data, and visuals
- *Drawing and paint programs*—allow the user to draw geometric shapes and figures; can also incorporate text
- *Charting programs*—especially suited to making charts, graphs, and reports from spreadsheet data
- *Photo-enhancement programs*—allow the manipulation of color and use of special effects to alter photographs and slides
- *Desktop publishing programs*—combine features of many other methods to create sophisticated products such as newsletters and books.

FIGURE 5.8
Presentation graphics software enables
you to compose overhead transparencies
with ease.

There are several technical processes for producing transparencies directly with a computer printer. You need to select the proper type of transparency film for your printer:

- Laser printers print images directly onto laser printer film.
- Ink-jet printers spray droplets of ink onto specially coated ink-jet film.
- Thermal transfer printers use heat to imprint images onto thermal film.
- Pen plotters draw with pens directly onto specially coated film.
- Impact printers press the ink from ribbons onto impact film.

COMPUTER IMAGE PROJECTION

Designed for use with presentation graphics software, **liquid crystal display (LCD)** projection panels project computer images onto a screen—the electronic equivalent of an overhead transparency. An LCD panel is plugged into a computer and placed onto the stage of a high-intensity overhead projector (but not the tabletop reflective type). The overhead projector light shines through the LCD panel, projecting the image on a screen (Figure 5.9). Directions for using an LCD panel are given in "How to . . . Operate an LCD Panel."

LCD panels are also available as separate, free-standing units—data projectors—that do not require an overhead projector as their light source. The light source (and in some cases a fully functional computer) is built into the data projector (Figure 5.10).

Advantages

- *Image choices.* The great advantage of the LCD panel is that it enables you to project anything that appears

on your computer monitor—text, data, or visual—onto a large screen.
- *Vast capacity.* The computer can store a nearly infinite number of visuals, which can be summoned by pressing a key.
- *Interactivity.* The display can be changed just before or even during a showing, so LCD panels are ideal for "what-if" displays of spreadsheet data or graphs. This becomes an interactive medium when viewers' decisions or ideas are fed into the program and the outcome is displayed on the screen.

Limitations

- *Lack of brightness.* The room must be darkened more than for conventional overhead projection.

FIGURE 5.9
LCD panels allow overhead projectors to be used to show computer images.

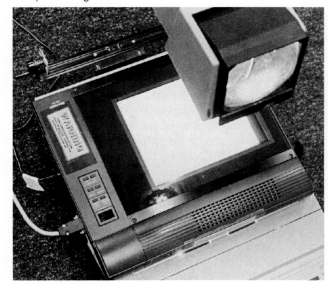

In addition to the general utilization practices discussed in Chapter 2, here are some hints for making the greatest impact with your overhead presentation:

- *Get attention.* Shift viewers' attention to the screen by turning on the projector; direct it back to yourself by turning it off. Don't turn on the projector again until you are ready for viewers to look at the screen.
- *Reveal sections.* For a complex visual or wordy illustration, cover the transparency with a sheet of paper and reveal one portion at a time as you talk about that portion.
- *Build ideas.* Use overlays to add sequential information. Build up a complex idea by superimposing transparencies one on top of another; up to four overlays can be used.
- *Make transitions.* Avoid jarring viewers with a glaring white screen between transparencies. Instead, simply place the new one on top of the old one, then slide the lower one out. If both hands are free, you can obtain a "dissolve" effect by sliding the existing transparency off the stage while you lower the new one into place.

- *Point to images.* You can use a pen or pencil as a pointer. Lay the pen directly on the transparency (any elevation would put the pointer out of focus, and any slight hand movement would be greatly exaggerated on the screen).
- *Be spontaneous.* Plan ways to add meaningful details to the image during projection; this infuses an element of spontaneity and helps maintain viewer interest and active participation. If the transparency is a valuable one, cover it with a blank acetate sheet before writing on it.
- *Use notes.* Write your presenter's notes (key words) on the frame of the transparency. This will allow you to speak naturally instead of reading from a script.
- *Create uniformity.* You will make the most professional impression if your transparencies are consistent in size and style. If all of them are framed, you can tape a guide onto the projector stage to keep the images uniformly aligned.
- *Avoid doodling.* For random notes, use the chalkboard. Don't diminish the dramatic impact of your presentation by using the overhead as a doodle pad.

- *Legibility.* Low resolution makes LCD presentations best suited to small or medium-size groups (up to about 50 people) in which no one is seated more than four screen widths from the screen.
- *Monochrome.* Less expensive models display only black-and-white images. More expensive, full-color, "active matrix" panels are useful for presentations in which true-color and motion images are needed for effective communication.

Applications

The extra expense and logistical arrangements required by the LCD panel would be difficult to justify for simple, static presentations. Where it yields real benefits, though, is in providing dynamic or interactive presentations, such as in the following:

FIGURE 5.10
Computer data or images, as well as videos, can be projected by desktop projectors no larger than a small laser printer.

- Demonstrating computer software functions to a group of students
- Searching an electronic encyclopedia (on CD-ROM) with a whole class following along
- Conducting a brainstorming session, capturing all suggestions on the computer display (and then printing them out at the conclusion)
- Presenting color animation sequences
- Teaching math or statistics formulas by changing the inputs and watching the output change on the screen graphically.

SLIDES

The term **slide** refers to a small-format photographic transparency individually mounted for one-at-a-time projection. The standard size of slides is 2 by 2 inches (5 by 5 centimeters) measured by the outer dimensions of the slide mount. When 35mm and other popular types of slide film are sent out to be processed, they are mounted in 2-by-2-inch frames. The actual dimensions of the image itself will vary with the type of film (Figure 5.11) and camera.

Advantages

- *Sequencing.* Because slides can be arranged into many different sequences, they are more flexible than filmstrips or other fixed-sequence materials.
- *Automatic cameras.* As photographic equipment is continually refined and simplified, more and more amateurs are able to produce their own high-quality slides. Automatic exposure controls, easy focusing, and high-speed color film have contributed to this trend. High-quality color slides can be taken by even amateur photographers.

OPERATION

Set Up

- Position computer and overhead projector on the same sturdy table or projection cart or on adjacent tables or carts.
- Place LCD panel on the overhead projector stage.
- Be sure power switch on LCD panel is off.
- Plug power supply into LCD panel. (See LCD panel instruction manual for specifics; the connection may require special cords.)

Operate

- Turn LCD power switch on.
- Adjust LCD panel for best image.
- Focus overhead projector image on projection screen.
- Whatever appears on the computer monitor can now be projected onto the projection screen.
- You can add writing or markings by placing a sheet of acetate over the LCD panel and writing on that.

Disassemble

- Turn LCD power switch off.
- Disconnect computer from LCD panel.
- Unplug power supply from LCD panel and electrical outlet.
- Carefully pack and store LCD panel.

TROUBLESHOOTING

Problems/Possible Remedies

- *No image on LCD panel:*
  1. Adjust contrast on LCD panel.

  2. Check computer for instructions on obtaining image.
- *Reversed image:* See "reverse image" switch on side of panel.
- *Image appears on LCD panel but is not centered:*
  1. Check LCD panel instructions.
  2. Adjust centering or frequency.
- *Flickering image or missing lines on LCD panel:*
  1. Check all connections to be sure they are correct and secure.
  2. Adjust stability or frequency.
- *Intermittent appearance of image on LCD panel:*
  1. Check all connections to be sure they are correct and secure.
  2. Check equipment setup.
- *Rolling waves in image on LCD panel:*
  1. Check equipment setup.
  2. Adjust stability or frequency.
  3. Try another LCD panel.
- *Contrast of display panel not uniform:*
  1. Focus overhead projector.
  2. Adjust contrast.
  3. Use higher-wattage overhead projector.
- *Test pattern only on LCD panel:*
  1. Check all connections to be sure they are correct and secure.
  2. Refer to instructions to ensure that computer is connected properly.

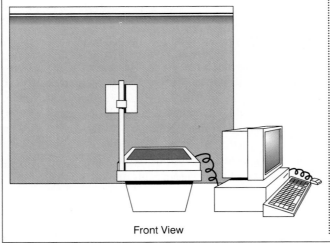

Front View

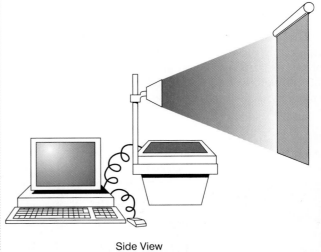

Side View

- *Automatic projectors.* The assembly of slide programs is facilitated by today's projectors, which hold sets of slides in trays and feed them into view in sequence. Most projectors also offer the convenience of remote control advancing of slides, allowing the presenter to remain at the front of the room or off to one side while advancing the slides via a push-button unit connected by wire to the projector. Wireless remote control is also available. Certain models can be preset to advance automatically. This feature allows continuous showing in exhibits, display cases, and other automated situations.

FIGURE 5.11
Common slide formats.

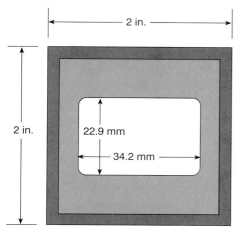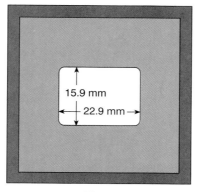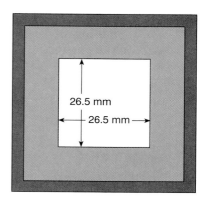

35mm film, the standard

35mm
"half-frame" film

Type 126 film
"Instamatic"

- *Collection building.* General availability and ease of handling make it relatively easy to build up permanent collections of slides for specific instructional purposes. Instructors may collect and store their own collections, or the slides may be compiled and kept in a learning resource center. Such collections enable users to assemble presentations partially or wholly from existing images, thus reducing the expense required for new production.
- *Individualized instruction.* Slides can be integrated into individualized instruction programs. Although slides have been developed primarily as a large-group medium, recent hardware innovations have made slides feasible for small-group and independent study as well (Figure 5.12).

FIGURE 5.12
The slide–tape format has been adapted for use by individual viewers.

MEDIA FILE

The Mexican-Texans to 1865
Slide–Cassette Set

A number of states (and provinces in Canada) sponsor the production of educational materials for use in schools. Texas certainly is in the forefront of this movement. One of the more prolific agencies is the Institute of Texan Culture in San Antonio. Among the many audiovisual materials it has produced is this slide set. The early history of Texas as part of Mexico is told through biographies of outstanding Mexican-Texans and the roles they played in events leading up to the Texas revolution. During the time Texas was a republic, Mexican-Texans continued to make history.

Source: Institute of Texan Culture.

Limitations

- *Disorganization.* Because slides, unlike filmstrips, come as individual units, they can easily become disorganized. Even when they are stored in trays, if the locking ring is loosened, the slides can spill out.
- *Jamming.* Slide mounts come in cardboard, plastic, and glass of varying thicknesses. This lack of standardization can lead to jamming of slides in the slide-changing mechanism: cardboard becomes dog-eared and the frayed edges get caught in the mechanism; plastic mounts swell or warp in the heat of the lamp; glass mounts thicker than the aperture chamber fail to drop into showing position.
- *Susceptible to damage.* Slides can easily accumulate dust and fingerprints; careless storage or handling can lead to permanent damage.
- *Cost.* Filmstrips are attractive alternatives to slide sets in terms of cost per frame. Slides would be justified in cases in which the images are used in different sequences for different lessons or where the nature of the collection dictates that the collection be built up one image at a time.
- *Software obsolescence.* Many schools and colleges have built up libraries of slides as resources for teaching subjects, such as art history and biology, in which great numbers of visual images are required. In some schools these visual libraries are being replaced by videodiscs or CD-ROM discs, which can hold a whole subject area library on one disc. A single disc is less expensive to purchase and far easier to store and maintain.

Applications

Like other forms of projected visuals, slides may be used at all grade levels and for instruction in all curriculum areas. Many high-quality commercial slides are available individually and in sets. In general, the fine arts, geography, and the sciences are especially well represented with commercially distributed slides.

Among the myriad possibilities, here are some typical subjects for slide presentations:

- Providing a tour for new employees of a local business without walking through the plant.
- Making a visual history of your community, school, or organization.
- Illustrating lectures about art history or art technique.
- Documenting student activities, products of student work, and community problems (e.g., crime and pollution).
- Presenting a preoperative explanation of a surgical procedure tailored to a specific surgeon's patients.
- Showing people at work in various jobs, for career awareness.
- Illustrating the uses of a company's products throughout the world.
- Teaching a step-by-step process with close-ups of each operation.
- Simulating a field trip.
- Promoting public understanding of your school or organization.

FIGURE 5.13
Teachers or students can prepare slide sets showing local landmarks.

CLOSE-UP

NATIONAL HISTORY DAY

Each spring, middle, junior high, and high school students gather in each state to present their research on the year's chosen theme. They present their material in a variety of formats: stage performances, videos, exhibits, slide shows, and computer programs. The research these students do is often worthy of graduate students. The state winners in each category go to Washington, D.C., for the final competition. The photo shows two junior high students getting ready to show their slide presentation on Susan B. Anthony. (A five-page report on National History Day by Marilyn Page, "Active Learning in Secondary Schools: Educational Media and Technology," is available from ERIC [ED323987]. The report stresses the value of cooperative learning.)

Teacher- and Student-Produced Slides

A major advantage of slides as an instructional medium is the ease with which they can be produced by teachers as well as students. Modern cameras are so simple to operate that even the most amateur of photographers can expect good results. General guidelines for photography are given in Chapter 3. To make slides you follow the same procedures but substitute slide film for print film. As with all locally produced materials, slides made by teachers or students have an immediacy, relevance, and credibility lacking in more generic materials.

Producing "Slide Shows" by Digital Photography.
When digital camera systems were first introduced, they were considered replacements for conventional film photography (Figure 5.14). However, limitations of image resolution have discouraged users from giving up their film cameras in favor of digital cameras for everyday picture taking—for either prints or slides. But the new digital cameras have found a place in the computer realm. They are widely used to capture images for incorporation into documents produced by presentation software or desktop publishing. The images made with this technology can be arranged in a sequence and shown on the computer screen as a kind of slide show. (Digital photography is discussed in Chapter 3.)

Producing Slides by Copying Visuals.
Many single-lens reflex (SLR) cameras have a combination zoom and macro lens. Close-ups can be taken using the macro portion of the range, allowing copying of flat visuals such as maps, charts, illustrations, and even small three-dimensional objects. The material to be copied can be pinned to a wall or placed on a horizontal surface to be photographed. Procedures are detailed in "How to . . . Convert Visuals to Slides," page 158.

Producing Slides with a Computer.
Traditionally, slides have been made by shooting photographs of people, places, things, or images drawn by graphic artists. Computers now offer the capability of generating graphic images that can become slides. There are presentation graphics software programs especially adapted to producing output in the slide format. They are capable of producing images of very high resolution—as sharp and clearly defined as those of photos.

Their high quality, ease of production, and flexibility of use have made computer-produced slides popular in corporate training, where they are used to prepare self-instructional units or modules. Sound–slide modules have been found to provide as much of an impact as a video at a fraction of the production cost.

Polaroid Instant Slides.
Polaroid makes a device that produces slides from 8½-by-11-inch docu-

OPERATION

Set Up

- Connect power cord to AC outlet (power cord is stored on the bottom of the projector).
- Plug in the remote control cord with white dot on top.
- Insert lens if not already in place.
- Check to see that bottom ring is locked on slide tray. If it is not locked, slides will drop out.
- Load slides into tray and tighten the locking ring on the tray.
- Seat slide tray on projector. Note the notch at "0."

Operate

- Set automatic timer at "m" (manual operation).
- Move on/off switch to "Low" or "High" lamp setting.
- Position image on screen, making it smaller or larger by means of the lens barrel (if equipped with zoom lens).
- Focus image with focus knob.
- Project slides using remote control or buttons on the side of the projector.

Disassemble

- Press and hold "Select" button while turning the tray to "0." The "Select" function will not operate when projector is off, except on the Ektagraphic III model.
- Remove slide tray.
- If projector is going to be moved immediately, allow lamp to cool before switching off.
- Remove slides from slide tray.
- Restore to storage conformation.

TROUBLESHOOTING

Problems/Possible Remedies

- *Can't find power cord:* Look for a built-in storage compartment. For example, on the Kodak Carousel the power cord is wrapped around a recessed core on the bottom of the projector.

- *No power after plugging in:* If you are sure the outlet is live (a fuse or circuit breaker may have killed all electrical power in the room), check the circuit breaker on the slide projector.
- *Fan runs but lamp does not light:* Some projectors have separate switches for "Lamp" and "Fan" or a two-stage switch for these two functions. Make sure all switches are properly set. Then check for burned-out lamp. If neither of these is the problem, have technician check the projector.
- *Image not level:* Most slide projectors have an adjustment knob on one of the rear feet. Use the knob to raise or lower that side.
- *Slide is distorted:* The lenses may be out of alignment or broken. Often they can be adjusted easily by aligning them correctly in their slots.
- *Slide mounts begin to warp:* For plastic black-and-white mounts, ensure that white side of mount is facing the lamp. If the dark side of mount is facing lamp, a buildup of heat can cause the mount to warp (or even melt, in the case of plastic mounts).
- *Slide image upside down or backwards:* Remove the slide and reverse it. (Improper loading can be avoided by thumb-spotting slides. See page 155.)
- *Slide jams in gate:*
  1. Manually remove the slide. On the Kodak Carousel, press the "Select" button (power must be on). If the slide does not pop up, the tray will have to be removed. Turn off the power and use a coin to turn the screw in the center of the tray; this unlocks the tray, allowing it to be lifted off and giving access to the gate for manual removal of the slide.
  2. Jamming can be avoided by not placing bent slides in the tray. Plastic mounts have a tendency to warp; cardboard mounts fray; glass mounts may be too thick for the slide compartment of the tray. For this reason, jamming is more likely with narrow slide compartments, as are found in the 140-slide Carousel trays. Use the 80-slide tray whenever possible.

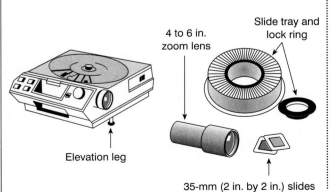

Elevation leg

4 to 6 in. zoom lens

Slide tray and lock ring

35-mm (2 in. by 2 in.) slides

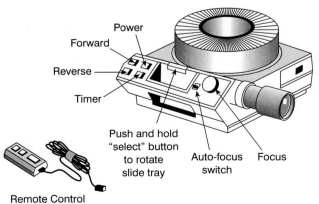

Power

Forward

Reverse

Timer

Push and hold "select" button to rotate slide tray

Auto-focus switch

Focus

Remote Control

There are eight possible ways a slide can be placed in a projector. Seven of them are wrong (e.g., upside down, backwards, sideways). To avoid all seven mistakes a standardized procedure is recommended for placing a reminder spot, or **thumb spot,** on the slide.

- First, your slides should be arranged and numbered in the order in which they are to be shown.
- Then take each slide and hold it the way it is supposed to be seen on the screen—that is, right-side up with the lettering running left to right, just as it would be read. If the slide lacks lettering or other orienting information, hold it so that the emulsion side (the duller side) is toward the screen.

- Then simply place a spot (or number) on the bottom left-hand corner.

- This spot is referred to as a thumb spot because when the slide is turned upside down to be placed in the projector, your thumb will grip the slide at the point of the thumb spot, as shown.
- Before all the slides are put in the tray in proper order, some users like to run a felt-tip pen across the tops of the slide mounts in a diagonal line. This way, if some slides later get out of order, they can be replaced just by lining up the marks on the top of the slide to form a diagonal line.

ments or illustrations. Simply place the illustration in the copier, push the button, and a minute later out comes the slide. If you want better quality and you are not in a hurry, Polaroid 35mm Presentation Chrome film can be used. It requires the same processing as Ektachrome. The Polaroid system is expensive and is limited in the size of the material that can be copied, but its convenience and reliability make it attractive.

Instant Slides from Video. Polaroid also has a device that makes photographic prints or slides of any image from a videocassette recorder, video camera, videodisc player, or computer graphic workstation.

Polaroid calls this device a Freeze Frame Video Image Recorder, or Freeze Frame for short. The Freeze Frame device plugs directly into the equipment generating the video image. Polaroid also makes an adapter for a 35mm camera that makes instant slides from any exposure made.

SOUND–SLIDE SETS

A combination of 2-by-2-inch slides and audiotape is the easiest multimedia system to produce locally, which is one reason for its popularity. The system is also versa-

In addition to the general guidelines for utilization discussed in Chapter 2, here are several specific practices that can add professionalism to your slide presentations:

- *Use remote control.* Use a remote control device; this will allow you to stand at the side of the room. From this position you can keep an eye on the slides while maintaining some eye contact with the audience.
- *Double check slides.* Make certain your slides are in sequential order and right-side up. Disarrangement can be an embarrassment to you and an annoyance to your audience. See "How to . . . Thumb Spot Slides" (page 155) for a foolproof method of marking slides.
- *Use visual variety.* Mix the types of slides, using verbal title slides to help break the presentation into segments.
- *Maintain reading light.* Prepare a way to light up your script after the room lights are dimmed; a penlight or flashlight will serve this purpose.
- *Keep it moving.* Limit your discussion of each slide. Even a minute of narration can seem long to your audience unless there is a complex visual to be examined at the same time.

- *Rehearse.* Plan and rehearse your narration to accompany the slides if it is not already recorded on tape.
- *Avoid irrelevant images.* If there is a "talky" section in the middle of your presentation, use a gray or black slide rather than hold an irrelevant slide on the screen. (Gray slides can be produced locally or purchased from commercial sources. They let through enough light to allow the presenter to be seen, avoiding total darkening of the room.)
- *Use mood music.* Consider adding a musical accompaniment to your live or recorded narration. This can help to establish the desired mood and keep your audience attentive. But do not have music playing in the background when providing narration.
- *Make smooth starts.* Begin and end with a black slide. A white flash on the screen at the beginning and end is irritating to the eye and appears amateurish. The blackout is done automatically with newer projectors.

tile, easy to use, and effective for both group instruction and independent study. A well-done sound–slide presentation can have significant dramatic impact, thus further enhancing the learning process.

Sound–slide sets can be developed locally by teachers or students. In terms of emotional impact and instructional effectiveness, they may rival film or video productions, yet they can be produced for a fraction of the cost and effort. Indeed, sound–slide sets are frequently produced as prototypes of more elaborate video projects because they allow the presentation to be tried out and revised in its formative stages.

Sound–slide sets are available from commercial sources. However, mass distribution programs of this sort usually are converted to a filmstrip-and-audiocassette or video format because filmstrips require less storage space than do slides and are less expensive.

The visuals in sound–slide programs may be advanced either manually or automatically. In manual operation the visual and audio components are usually on two separate machines. You begin by projecting the title slide on the screen and then starting the sound track. An audible beep on the sound track signals you to advance the slides. In manual operation it is important that you try out at least the beginning of the program to make certain that you have sound and visuals in proper synchronization. Note also that some sound tracks do not contain a beep signal, in which case a script containing instructions for advancing slides must be used.

In automatic advancing with an audiotape two sound tracks are used—one for the audible narration and one for inaudible tones that activate the advance mechanism on the slide projector (see Figure 5.15).

FIGURE 5.14
Pictures taken with a digital camera can be incorporated immediately into a computer presentation.

Advantages

- *Ease of production.* Sound–slide sets are easy and economical to produce locally with a simple camera and audiocassette recorder. As such, they lend themselves to student production.
- *Ease of revision.* Individual slides can be replaced or updated as needed; a new audio track can be made to update information.

FIGURE 5.15
Synchronized sound–slide programs are controlled by inaudible tones put on one track of the tape.

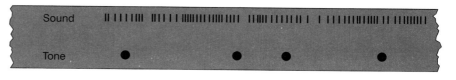

Direction of play

- *Impact.* Sound–slide programs can have a dramatic impact on learners; they can be used to inform or to change attitudes.
- *Individual or group use.* These programs are applicable to both individual and group instruction with little or no modification.
- *Self-instruction.* Combined with a printed study guide, sound–slide programs can actively involve the learners.

Limitations

- *Synchronization.* The slides and audiotape may get out of synchronization. This can happen when showing the presentation to a group, but it occurs more commonly when an individual student is using the sound–slide set.
- *Limited capacity to review.* It is difficult to go back and reexamine a portion of the program while keeping the slides in synchronization with the sound. (This limitation can be overcome by converting the two-media combination to a single format—videocassette.)
- *Cumbersome.* Most sound–slide equipment setups require connecting a special audiocassette player to a slide projector (Figure 5.16). Besides connecting everything properly, be sure the slide change signals on your tape match the frequency of your player.

Applications

Sound–slide presentations may be used in almost any instructional setting and for instructional objectives involving the presentation of visual images to inform or to evoke an emotional response. They may be used for effect in group instruction, and they can be adapted to independent study in the classroom learning center or school library media center. This comparatively simple multimedia system is especially versatile as a learning/teaching tool in that more than one narration can be prepared for a given set of visuals. For example, a single set of visuals might have one audio narration suitable for introduction of and preliminary instruction in a study unit and another narrative for more detailed study. The narration could be on two or more vocabulary levels—one for regular students and another for exceptional students. For foreign language instruction, one audiotape might be narrated in the student's native language and a matching narration can be recorded on another tape in the language being taught.

FIGURE 5.16
In a sound–slide presentation, slides are synchronized with and controlled by a cassette.

EQUIPMENT

The Camera

The single-lens reflex camera is the best type to use for making slides of flat materials and small objects. What you see in the viewfinder is what you get on the film (unlike with rangefinder cameras, where the closer you get to the subject, the greater the difference between what you see and what you get on the film). Focusing is much more accurate with an SLR. When the image is sharp in the viewfinder, it will be sharp on the film. The interchangeable-lens feature adds considerably to the range of copying capability.

The Lens

The normal lens on a 35mm camera can focus as close as 1½ to 2 feet. This corresponds to a picture area about 6 by 9 inches and will take care of most of your copying needs. However, if you need to copy a smaller area, you will have to modify the lens arrangement. The less expensive solution is to use supplementary lenses. These come in steps of magnification expressed as +1, +2, +3. When you buy them, take your camera to your local camera store to make sure the lens set matches your camera lens. The more expensive solution is to buy a macro lens, which replaces the normal camera lens. Macro lenses come in a variety of configurations, so consult your local camera store or media specialist to find the best arrangement for your needs.

TECHNIQUES

Exposure

Virtually every camera sold today has automatic exposure control. Because a single-lens reflex camera monitors the light as it comes through the lens, any modifications of exposure made necessary by the use of other lenses or filters will be taken care of automatically. Many cameras permit you to increase or decrease the exposure. This feature can be quite useful in compensating for material that is too light or too dark; it can also help to increase or decrease contrast. If your camera has this feature, practice with it until you learn how to use it judiciously.

Tripod Use

Although copying with a hand-held camera is possible, the best results are achieved by mounting the camera on a stable platform such as a tripod. If you are copying flat material, it can be fastened to an outside wall about the height of the camera on the tripod. Then the camera and tripod are positioned the appropriate distance from the material, the lens is focused, and the exposure is made. The material is best mounted in indirect sunlight. However, if the material has low contrast, you may need to mount it on a sunlit wall, but be sure you are not getting undesirable reflections or bright spots. A handy way of eliminating glare is to use a polarizing filter. Consult your local camera store for the proper size of your camera and helpful hints on how to use it. A polarizing filter is especially useful in eliminating glare when photographing something beneath a water surface and in darkening the sky for dramatic effects, but it also has a tendency to flatten outdoor scenes (e.g., by eliminating the reflections from sunlit leaves).

Tabletop Photography

The camera mounted on a tripod is handy for photographing small objects: coins, flowers, insects, etc. The object can be placed on a coffee table in a well-lit area, with the tripod and camera oriented so that the object is well displayed. The comments about supplementary and macro lenses apply here too. Don't use a wide-angle lens, because the image will be distorted; the part of the object closest to the lens will be out of proportion to the rest of the object.

Copy Stand

If you do a lot of copying, you will want to look into using a copy stand. Your media center may have one that you can

A macro lens and close-up supplementary lenses.

Using a tripod for tabletop photography.

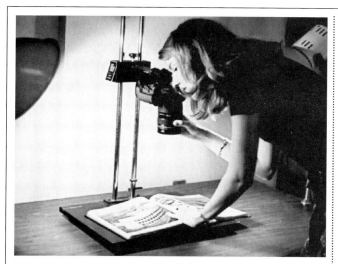

Using a copy stand to photograph flat materials.

use. At a minimum, a copy stand has a flat bed where the material is placed and a vertical post on which the camera is mounted. From there, copy stands become more elaborate and may include an adjustable platen to hold the material flat and adjustable floodlights attached to the base. After the material to be copied is placed on the base, the camera is moved up and down and the material is adjusted until the viewfinder shows the image you want. If supplemental lighting is necessary, use the polarizing filter to take care of any glare that might result. A copy stand is best used for flat materials. Three-dimensional objects are better photographed on a table using a tripod-mounted camera because you can choose the angle and lighting that best shows the object.

Lettering

If you want to add lettering to the material being photographed, remember to keep the letters in proportion. If the area being copied is fairly large, the letters must be large also. If the area is small, the letters must be small because they will be enlarged when the image is enlarged. Judge the size of the lettering in proportion to the material by studying what you see in the viewfinder.

Copying Slides

Copying slides requires a special piece of equipment. It looks like a miniature copy stand, but the slide to be copied is lighted from beneath. The camera, mounted on the vertical post, can be adjusted to copy all or part of the slide. This is a useful but expensive piece of equipment. Your media center may have one. Otherwise, for the few times you may need to copy slides, a commercial shop is the simplest way to go.

Planning Sound–Slide Presentations

To plan a presentation that incorporates two or more media formats, such as slides and cassette tape, it is helpful to use a visual planning technique known as storyboarding, described in Chapter 3 under "Visual Planning Tools." Detailed suggestions for planning your presentation are given in "How to . . . Develop a Sound–Slide Presentation."

When a series of cards has been developed, the cards can be laid out on a table or placed on a storyboard holder (see "How to . . . Make a Storyboard Holder" in Chapter 3). The cards are sequenced in tentative order, thus giving you an overview of the production (Figure 5.17). The storyboarding technique facilitates addition, deletion, replacement, revision, and refinement of the sequence because the cards can easily be discarded, added to, or rearranged. The display of cards also allows others (teachers, students, production assistants) to look

FIGURE 5.17
Storyboards are useful for planning and presenting rough drafts of your presentation.

Here is a simple approach to developing your own sound–slide presentation.

Step 1

Analyze your audience both in terms of general characteristics and specific entry competencies (as described in Chapter 2).

- Why are they viewing the presentation?
- What is their motivation toward your topic?
- How much do they already know about the subject?

Step 2

Specify your objectives (as described in Chapter 2).

- What do you want to accomplish with the presentation?
  - Learning to be achieved
  - Attitudes to be formed or changed
  - Skills to be developed
- What should the viewers be able to do after the presentation?
  - Activity or performance?
  - Under what conditions?
  - With what degree of skill?

Step 3

Having completed your audience analysis and stated your objectives, you now have a much clearer idea of how your presentation will fit into your overall lesson plan, including what might precede it and follow it. Perhaps you will decide at this point that a sound–slide presentation is not really what you need after all.

If you decide to go ahead, get a pack of planning cards (use index cards or Post-It notes, or cut some sheets of paper into 4-by-6-inch rectangles). Draw a large box in the upper left-hand corner of each card.

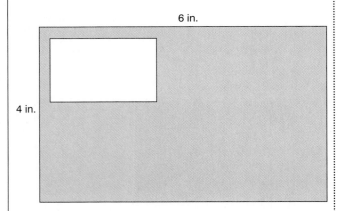

Step 4

Take a planning card. In the box draw a rough sketch of whatever image comes to your mind when you think about one of your major points. You don't have to start with the first point, just whatever comes into your mind first. Your sketch may be a symbol, a diagram, a graph, a cartoon, or a photo of a person, place, or thing, for example.

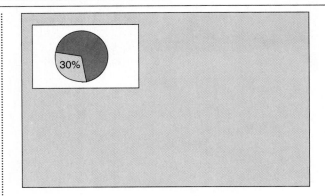

Step 5

Below your sketch, write a brief statement that captures the essence of the point you are trying to make. State it in as few words as needed to cue yourself to the thought. Some developers prefer to start with the visuals and then write the narration. Others prefer to do the narration first. Actually developing a sound–slide presentation is likely to be a dynamic process, with visual and narration evolving one from the other, separately and simultaneously. In some cases, of course, your narration will be already at hand—printed information, for example, or a story or poem—and all that remains is to develop the proper visuals to fit it. Or, the visuals may already be in hand—slides from a field trip, for example—and all you have to do is organize them and develop your script to accompany the visuals.

Nearly one-third begin smoking in high school.

Step 6

Make a card for the thought that leads into the point you have just sketched. Then do another one about the thought that follows your first one. Continue like this, building a chain of ideas as you go along.

Step 7

When you run out of ideas in the chain, switch to one of the other major points that hasn't fallen into sequence yet.

Step 8

Arrange the cards in sequential and logical order. This process is called storyboarding.

Would some other arrangement liven up the beginning and the end of your presentation? Keep in mind the psychology of the situation as you thought it through in your audience analysis. The beginning and the end are generally the best places to make major points. Have you grabbed the viewer's attention right from the beginning?

How about pacing? Are any complicated ideas skimmed over too lightly? Do sections get bogged down in unnecessary detail? Add or subtract cards as needed.

You should have at least one slide on the screen for every point you make. Each slide should be on the screen long enough to support the point but not so long that it gets tiresome to look at.

As a rule of thumb, you can estimate the number of slides you need by timing your presentation and multiplying the number of minutes by five or six. This means one slide change about every 10 or 12 seconds. You may find that you need more slides in some instances and fewer in others. Don't be afraid to use "filler" slides to hold visual interest. They're perfectly acceptable as long as they relate to the topic.

Step 9

Edit your planning cards in terms of practicality. Be sure you have ready access to the artistic talent or photographic equipment needed to turn your sketches into slides.

Step 10

Use your notes to prepare an audio script.

Consider using two different voices for the narration, perhaps one male and one female for variety. Would sound effects add impact to your presentation? How about actual sounds from the place where you will be shooting the pictures? You can take along a recorder and pick up background sounds and personal interviews while doing the photography.

Consider, too, adding music, especially as a finishing touch to the beginning and end. Be careful to keep it unobtrusive. Avoid highly recognizable tunes, trendy songs that will date your presentation, and music aimed at very specialized tastes.

Step 11

Rehearse your presentation, imagining that your cards are slides on the screen. Time your presentation and see if you need to shorten or lengthen it. To keep your audience's attention, limit your show to 15 minutes. If you need more time than that, break it into two or more parts interspersed with audience activity.

Now you are ready to turn your sketches into slides! (To record your tape, see Chapter 6.)

---

at the presentation in its planning stage. Number the cards in pencil; you may wish to change numbers as your planning progresses. Several cards in sequence on a page can be photocopied for use with the final script, thus avoiding duplication of effort and providing a convenient assemblage of visuals, narration, and production notes.

MULTI-IMAGE PRESENTATIONS

Fairgoers at the 1890 Paris Exposition experienced a simulated balloon ascension by means of hand-tinted lantern slides projected onto 10 screens arranged in a circle. Since then, multi-image presentations have become ever more sophisticated and have survived the emergence of competitive technologies, maintaining a foothold as a powerful presentation technique. The continuing viability of the multi-image system can be traced to its ability to present powerful, visually appealing effects at a fraction of the cost of film or video.

A **multi-image presentation** is, simply, any visual presentation showing several images simultaneously, often using multiple screens. Multi-image presentations may incorporate moving images—film or video—but slides are used as their foundation.

Advantages

- *Combination of media.* Multi-image presentations combine the possibilities of a wide variety of media, such as slides, overhead transparencies, filmstrips, and motion pictures.
- *Special visual effects.* These presentations can show comparisons, time sequences, or wide-angle panoramic views.
- *Attention holder.* The rapidly changing images capture and hold the learners' attention.
- *Emotional impact.* Dramatic effects can be achieved by rapidly changing still pictures, which is possible with dissolve units and automatic programmers. Combined with appropriate music, multiple images can also set a mood.
- *Simulation of motion.* Multi-image presentations can simulate motion through rapid sequential projection of still pictures without the use of film or videotape. The production costs of multi-image presentations can be significantly less than that of film or video.

Limitations

- *Expensive to develop.* Development of multi-image materials requires considerable time and expertise because it depends on a more complex planning process. Production time and costs can be high.
- *Time-consuming equipment setup.* The time to set up the presentation and align the projectors can also be significant. The amount of equipment required for their presentation increases the cost of using multi-image systems.
- *Hardware glitches.* Because multi-image presentations require several pieces of equipment, projectors, and

FIGURE 5.18

When setting up a multi-image presentation, the projectors may be aligned side-by-side or stacked one above the other with both connected to the program control unit.

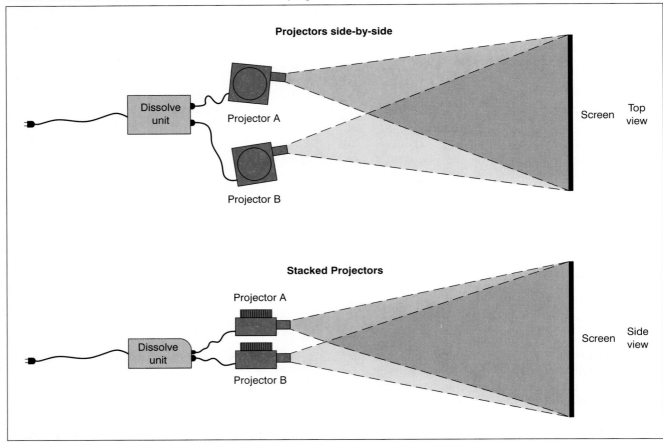

programmers, there is a greater chance for problems to occur during the showing (Figure 5.18).

Applications

Multi-image presentations are heavily used in corporate communications—to impress visitors, to introduce new products at sales meetings, to review the year's accomplishments at stockholders' meetings. In the public sector, multi-image shows are commonly found at zoos, museums, and theme parks.

In education, multi-image presentations are usually locally produced for persuasive purposes—to enlist parent support for new programs, to heighten student awareness of issues such as drugs, to arouse interest in new classroom techniques. They can also serve instructional purposes by employing teaching-learning strategies such as the following:

- *Part/whole:* Showing a whole scene on one screen with a close-up of a detail beside it
- *Compare/contrast:* Showing two images side-by-side, for example, to allow comparison of art forms or architectural styles

- *Before/after:* Showing a house before and after remodeling
- *Abstract/concrete:* Presenting a schematic diagram next to a photograph of a real object
- *Sequentiality:* Breaking down an athletic activity, such as diving, into a series of steps
- *Panorama:* Showing an outdoor scene with a sense of its full width
- *Allows three-dimensionality:* Presenting views of an object from several angles to allow viewers to imagine a three-dimensional image.

FILMSTRIPS

A **filmstrip** is a roll of 35mm transparent film containing a series of related still pictures intended for showing one at a time. Various filmstrip formats have evolved since the advent of the filmstrip more than half a century ago. The standard format today is the single-frame filmstrip, in which the images are printed perpendicular to the length of the film; in the slide format, the images are parallel to the length of the film (Figure 5.19).

FIGURE 5.19
Comparison of the filmstrip and 35mm slide formats.

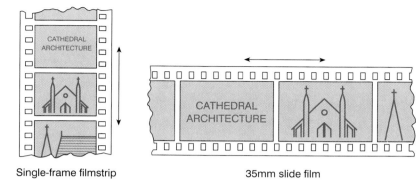

Single-frame filmstrip   35mm slide film

Commercially produced filmstrips typically contain about 20–60 images, or frames, and are stored rolled up in small plastic containers.

Until the 1960s most filmstrips were silent; that is, there was no audio accompaniment. Narrative information was printed at the bottom of each frame. After that time, recorded sound tracks were made to accompany the filmstrip. Initially the narration, music, sound effects, and so on were recorded on phonograph records and were played on record players either separate from the projector or built into it. Currently, audiocassette tapes are the standard means for giving sound filmstrips their "voice" (Figure 5.20). The sound track is not recorded on the filmstrip itself; rather, it comes on a separate cassette tape, which is played on a regular cassette recorder or on one built into the filmstrip projector unit (Figure 5.21).

For most sound filmstrips, the tape contains a second track carrying inaudible signals that automatically trigger the projector to advance to the next frame. Depending on the capability of the projector, users generally have a choice of manually advancing the filmstrip according to audible beeps or setting the projector to run automatically according to the inaudible synchronization pulses.

Advantages

- *Compactness.* A filmstrip of 60 frames will fit comfortably in the palm of your hand and weighs only a few ounces.
- *Easy to handle.* Filmstrips load easily into simple projectors.
- *Low cost.* A commercially distributed filmstrip costs substantially less per frame than a set of slides or overhead transparencies purchased from a commercial source.
- *Permanently sequenced.* The sequential order of the frames can often be a teaching and learning advantage. A chronological or step-by-step process can be presented in order without fear of having any of the pictures out of sequence or upside down, as can sometimes happen with slides.
- *Self-pacing.* In contrast to audio and motion media, the pace of viewing filmstrips can be controlled by the user. This capability is especially relevant for independent study but is also important for teacher-controlled group showings. A slow, deliberate examination of each frame might be suitable for the body of

FIGURE 5.20
Filmstrips are often combined with audiocassettes.

FIGURE 5.21
A sound–filmstrip projector uses audiocassettes to advance the frames automatically.

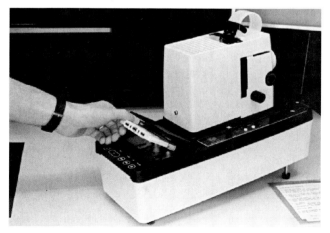

▼ MEDIA FILE

Canada: Portrait of a Nation
Filmstrip–Cassette Set

Junior high students in the United States (the audience for this set) may not know that hockey is the national sport of Canada. After experiencing these five filmstrips and audiocassettes, they will learn this and many other facts about Canada and its people. They will learn how Canadians earn their living by tapping the country's rich natural resources as well as working in today's high-tech industries. The set also focuses on the environmental problems Canada faces, some of which are shared with the United States. The social and political gains being made by native peoples are described.

Source: Society for Visual Education.

---

a lesson, whereas a quick run-through might suffice for purposes of preview and review.

- *Teacher adaptation.* The level of instruction can also be controlled. Particularly with silent filmstrips, the vocabulary or level of narration supplied by the presenter can be adapted to audience abilities.
- *Independent study.* Filmstrips lend themselves well to independent study. Many types of tabletop viewers are made especially for individual or small-group use. Young children have no difficulty loading the light, compact filmstrips into these viewers. The fixed sequence of the frames structures the learner's progress through the material. The captions or recorded narration add a verbal component to the visuals, creating a convenient self-contained learning package.

Limitations

- *Fixed sequence.* Having the frames permanently fixed in a certain sequence has disadvantages as well as

advantages. The main drawback is that it is not possible to alter the sequence of pictures without destroying the filmstrip. Backtracking to an earlier picture or skipping over frames is cumbersome.
- *Susceptibility to damage.* Because the filmstrip is pulled through the projector by means of toothed sprocket wheels, the sprocket holes can get torn and the filmstrip can become damaged. Improper threading or rough use can cause tears, which are very difficult to repair (you can repair such tears if you have a 35mm splicing block; in cases where damage to the sprocket holes is extensive, the frames can be cut apart and mounted individually to be used as slides).
- *Waning popularity.* Because videocassettes are so easy to handle and video equipment is so widely available, the video format is becoming more popular than the filmstrip format.

Applications

Because they are simply packaged and easy to handle, filmstrips are well suited to independent study (Figure 5.22). They are popular items in study carrels and media centers. Students enjoy using filmstrips on their own to help prepare research reports to their classmates.

The major difference in application between slides and filmstrips is that slides lend themselves to teacher- and student-made presentations, whereas filmstrips are better suited to mass production and distribution. Further, slide sets tend to be used in a more open-ended

FIGURE 5.22
A tabletop sound–filmstrip viewer can serve an individual or a small group.

OPERATION

Set Up

- Connect power cord to AC outlet.

Operate

- Turn projector on.
- Place filmstrip on retainer bar.
- Thread filmstrip down into film slot. Be sure that "Start" or "Focus" appears at head of filmstrip.
- Turn advance knob until "focus" frame appears.
- Adjust framer so the full frame is projected when you click the advance knob.
- Turn projector off.

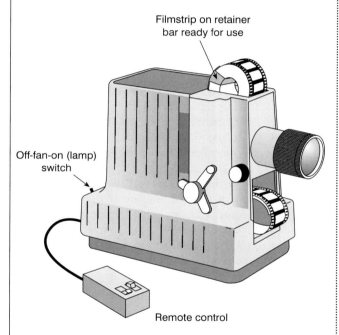

Filmstrip on retainer bar ready for use

Off-fan-on (lamp) switch

Remote control

Disassemble

- Return filmstrip to container. Do not pull the end of the filmstrip to tighten the roll. Start with a tight roll at the center and continue rolling, holding the film by the edges.
- Restore to storage conformation.

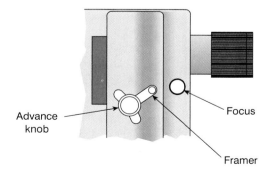

Advance knob

Focus

Framer

TROUBLESHOOTING

Problems/Possible Remedies

- *Dark areas or smudges projected on the screen:* Clean the lens.

- *Dirt or lint visible at edges of projected image:* Foreign matter is in the film gate. Clean with an aperture brush or other brush with no metal components.

- *Filmstrip is not properly framed:*

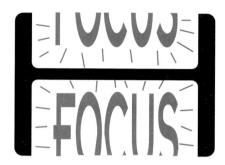

Correct with framer knob.

- *This frame appears first:*

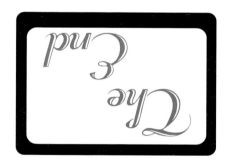

If this is the first frame you see, the filmstrip has been inserted tail-first. Withdraw it and insert the head end. (If the lettering appears backwards, you have threaded it with the wrong side facing the screen; reverse it. The ends of the strip should curl toward the screen.)

The general media utilization guidelines discussed in Chapter 2 apply fully to filmstrips. There are several additional tips, though, that pertain especially to filmstrips:

- *Pause for discussion.* Get students actively involved by asking relevant questions during the presentation. You may want to ask students to take turns reading the captions (if there are any) aloud; this is a useful reading activity for early elementary students.

- *Test visually.* Since the filmstrip presumably is providing critical visual information, consider using the filmstrip itself to test the mastery of visual concepts. You can, for instance, project individual frames without the caption or sound track and ask individual students to make an identification or discrimination.

---

fashion than filmstrips. Today filmstrips are usually packaged as self-contained kits; that is, the narration to accompany the pictures is provided either in the form of captions on the filmstrip or as a recorded sound track on cassette. Other teacher support materials may be integrated into the kit.

As with the other sorts of projected visuals discussed in this chapter, filmstrips find appropriate applications in a wide variety of subjects and grade levels. Their broad appeal is evidenced by the volume of commercial materials produced. Tens of thousands of titles have been produced and are available in school library media center collections. On the other hand, there is a trend toward replacing filmstrips with videos. Most producers of filmstrips now produce and distribute their titles in the video format, so new titles in the filmstrip format are increasingly rare.

OPAQUE PROJECTION

Opaque projection is a method of enlarging and projecting nontransparent material on a screen. The opaque projector was among the first audiovisual devices to come into widespread use more than half a century ago

and is still used because of its unique ability to project a magnified image of pictures, drawings, text materials, and even three-dimensional objects.

The opaque projector works by directing a very strong incandescent light (typically about 1,000 watts) down onto the material. This light is reflected upward to strike a mirror, which aims the light beam through a series of lenses onto a screen (Figures 5.23 and 5.24).

The process of reflected, or indirect, projection is optically less efficient than the direct projection process used for showing slides, filmstrips, and overhead transparencies. Consequently, the image on the screen is dimmer, and more complete room darkening is required. Still, opaque projection makes such a wide range of visual materials available for group viewing that it should not be overlooked as a teaching tool.

The **document camera** is an electronic version of the opaque projector. It is a video camera mounted on a copy stand, pointed downward at documents, flat pictures, or graphics. The image may be projected onto a large screen within the room or it may be transmitted to distant sites via television. Any sort of opaque visual may be placed on the stage, and the instructor can manipulate the material or write on it, as he or she would on overhead transparencies (Figure 5.25).

FIGURE 5.23
Opaque projector, cutaway view.

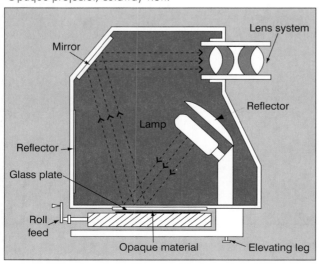

FIGURE 5.24
The opaque projector can be used to magnify small objects as well as print materials and pictures.

FIGURE 5.25
The document camera serves as an electronic version of the opaque projector.

Advantages

- *No production required.* Opaque projection allows on-the-spot projection of readily available classroom materials, such as maps, newspapers, and illustrations from books and magazines.
- *Allows group viewing of student work.* This type of projection permits group viewing and discussion of student work, such as drawings, student compositions, solutions to math problems, and the like.
- *Allows three-dimensionality.* Three-dimensional objects (especially relatively flat ones such as coins, plant leaves, and insect specimens) can be magnified for close-up inspection.

Limitations

- *Dimness.* The relative dimness of the reflected image demands nearly complete room darkening if the visual is to be clear enough for instructional purposes. Areas that cannot be sufficiently darkened are unsuitable for opaque projection.
- *Bulky hardware.* The opaque projector is bulky, heavy, and cumbersome to move.
- *Heat.* The high-wattage lamp generates a lot of heat, making parts of the projector unsafe to touch. The heat may also damage the materials being projected if they are exposed too long to the projector's light. If metal objects are being projected, they may rapidly become too hot to handle. For safety's sake, elementary students should be closely supervised when using the opaque projector.

Applications

The opaque projector is useful for many small groups or classroom-size groups (up to about 20) that need to view printed or visual material together. Applications

---

⏩ AV SHOWMANSHIP   *Opaque Projection*

The general media utilization procedures discussed in Chapter 2 apply fully to opaque projection. Several additional tips, though, pertain especially to opaque projection:

- *Use complete darkness.* Because opaque projectors require near-total room darkening, be prepared to operate in the dark. A student should be stationed at the light switch to help you avoid tripping over people's feet, power cords, or other obstacles in getting to and from the projector in the dark. Although the projector does spill quite a bit of light around its sides, you may need a flashlight to follow any prepared notes.
- *Use the optical pointer.* Most opaque projectors are equipped with a built-in optical pointer—an arrow that can be aimed at any point on the screen. Experiment ahead of time so that you will be able to aim the pointer effectively during the presentation.
- *Arrange pictures in sequence.* For some purposes, especially to show a series of pictures in sequence—such as illustrations accompanying a storybook—it is handy to arrange the pictures on a long strip or roll of paper. This keeps the illustrations in sequence, simulating the flow of a filmstrip.
- *Size images on screen.* The opaque projector will accept a wide range of image sizes. When you are setting up the projector, be sure to use the largest of your pictures to fill the screen. If you use a smaller picture, the bigger one will extend beyond the edges of the screen when you show it, thus distracting your students as you attempt to adjust the projector.

PROJECTED VISUALS

KEY WORDS: _____ , _____ , _____

Title _____

Series Title (if applicable) _____

Source _____

Date _____ **Cost** _____ **Length** _____ minutes

Subject Area _____

Intended Audience _____

Brief Description

Objectives

Entry Capabilities Required (e.g., prior knowledge, reading ability, vocabulary level, math ability).

Format
- ☐ **Overhead transparency**
- ☐ **Slide**
- ☐ **Sound/slide**
- ☐ **Filmstrip**
- ☐ **Sound filmstrip**

Rating	High	Medium	Low	Comments
Match with curriculum	☐	☐	☐	
Accurate and current	☐	☐	☐	
Clear and concise language	☐	☐	☐	
Arouse motivation/maintain interest	☐	☐	☐	
Learner participation	☐	☐	☐	
Technical quality	☐	☐	☐	
Evidence of effectiveness (e.g., field-test results)	☐	☐	☐	
Free from objectionable bias or advertising	☐	☐	☐	
User guide/documentation	☐	☐	☐	
Communicates clearly and effectively	☐	☐	☐	
Unified visuals	☐	☐	☐	
Appealing visuals	☐	☐	☐	

Strong Points

Weak Points

Recommended Action _____ **Name** _____ **Date** _____

_____

A Presentation to Management

Company sales have been on a plateau for three years, and the general sales manager has devised a strategy to expand existing markets and open new ones. His goal is to convince management and the marketing division to adopt the new marketing strategy.

Analyze Learners

General Characteristics

The audience consists of the chief executive officer (CEO), the marketing vice president, the financial vice president, and three regional sales managers. The financial vice president joined the company two years ago, but the others have been with the company at least 10 years. The financial vice president believes a sharp increase in profits would firmly secure her job. The marketing members of the audience feel somewhat threatened by the implication that their efforts have been ineffective; they are apprehensive about the difficulties involved in restructuring the sales force. The CEO is concerned about a board of directors disgruntled over stagnant sales. He wants to be convinced, but not at the expense of creating a hostile sales group.

Entry Competencies

Each member of the audience has successful business experience, but in different areas. The financial vice president appraises all company activities strictly by the balance sheet. The marketing vice president wants to show an interest in overall company performance but looks at proposals from the point of view of the marketing division. The regional sales managers believe they have developed loyal and effective sales forces. All have demonstrated the ability to grasp quickly the ramifications of new ideas.

State Objectives

1. The CEO will endorse the proposal by agreeing to present it to the board of directors.
2. The financial vice president will estimate the impact of the proposal on the profit margin of the company.
3. The marketing vice president will demonstrate support by suggesting a plan to restructure the sales apparatus.
4. The regional sales managers will indicate how the sales representatives can benefit from an expanded market.
5. The marketing vice president and the regional sales managers will agree to meet with the general sales manager to develop an implementation strategy, including a training program for sales representatives.

Select Methods, Media, and Materials

The general sales manager is well aware that he has a tough audience to convince. A well-organized and illustrated presentation is a must. Equally important is the need to maintain constant interaction with the audience during the presentation, so the discussion method will be incorporated. He consults with the company training director on the media to be used. The company training director suggests overhead transparencies as the heart of the presentation, with a flip chart available for spontaneous notes and reactions. Together they go to a local graphics design shop to work out the sketches for the transparencies based on his notes. The graphics are designed using computer software and, when approved, the transparencies are generated. Several color photographs are part of the presentation; these are made into transparencies using the color copying machine in the graphics shop.

Utilize Media and Materials

The general sales manager has selected a meeting room best suited for overhead projection and has prepared for the meeting by arranging for pads, pencils, and beverages. He reviews past accomplishments of the company, paying particular attention to the important contributions of the people in the room. He stresses how the company has responded successfully to similar challenges in the past. He then starts to unfold his plan, inviting comments as he goes along. On the flip chart, he notes comments to be discussed more fully.

Require Learner Participation

Because the sales manager invites comments, members of the audience become collaborators rather than spectators. As the manager answers questions indicating misgivings, the audience gradually begins adding to his presentation. The presentation ends more like a conference than a sales pitch. Instead of thinking about the plan later, the group talks about it now. The CEO enthusiastically asks the general sales manager to present the proposal to the board. The financial vice president volunteers to work up the sales projections into a financial statement. The marketing personnel set a time and place to put together an implementation strategy.

Evaluate and Revise

The objectives have been achieved, but now the general sales manager must adapt the presentation to a new audience, the board of directors. He particularly reviews the questions and comments of the CEO as guides to the approach to use with the board. He also wants to work closely with the financial vice president on the presentation of the fiscal projections of the marketing strategy.

He is eager to talk to his former associates on the sales force to prepare himself better for the meeting with the marketing vice president and the regional sales managers.

A computer template for a Blueprint is found in "The Classroom Link."

may be found in all curriculum areas at all grade levels. Here are just a few typical examples:

- *All subjects:* Group critique of student work and review of test items
- *Art:* Group discussion of reproductions of paintings and architectural details; study of advertising layouts
- *Business:* Group work on business and accounting forms or close-up viewing of such documents as organization charts, sales territory maps, and parts of a product
- *Home Economics:* Group viewing of sewing patterns, textiles, recipes, close-up views of fabrics and weaving styles
- *Industry:* Projection of blueprints for group study; description of assembly line flow with production diagrams
- *Language Arts:* Group critique of student compositions, picture books, or reference books
- *Medicine:* Group study of anatomical drawings; discussion of diabetic diets and food exchange charts
- *Military:* Review of maps and official documents; illustration of flight plans
- *Music:* Group reading of musical scores
- *Religion:* Religious story illustrations; group examination of religious documents
- *Science:* Magnification of specimens; group study of maps and tables
- *Social Studies:* Map study; viewing of artifacts from other cultures, postcards, and atlas illustrations

One especially handy application of the opaque projector is for copying or adapting illustrations for classroom display. This technique is illustrated in Chapter 4, "How to . . . Enlarge Visuals."

REFERENCES
Print References

Barman, C. "Some Ways to Improve Your Overhead Projection Transparencies." *American Biology Teacher* (March 1982): 191–192.

Beasley, Augie E. "Audio-Visual Production: Making Your Own." *Book Report* (September–October 1988): 10–25.

Beatty, LaMond F. *Filmstrips.* Englewood Cliffs, NJ: Educational Technology Publications, 1981.

Berry, Vern. "Review of 'Fast' Methods for Production of 2 x 2 in. Slides." *Journal of Chemical Education* (July 1990): 577–582.

Bodner, George M. "Instructional Media: Resisting Technological Overkill—35-mm Slides as an Alternative to Videotape-Videodisk." *Journal of College Science Teaching* (February 1985): 360–363.

Bohning, G. "Storytelling Using Overhead Visuals." *Reading Teacher* (March 1984): 677–678.

Burger, Jeff. "Presentations: Step by Step." *New Media* (April 1994): 93–97.

Burton, D. "Slide Art." *School Arts* (February 1984): 23–26.

Clark, Jean N. "Filmstrips: Versatility and Visual Impact." *Media and Methods* (January–February 1988): 20–21.

Crowe, Kathy M. "Effective Use of Slides for Bibliographic Information." *Research Strategies* (Fall 1989): 175–179.

Grandgenett, Donald, Grandgenett, Neal, and Topp, Neal. "What Makes an Effective Computer Projected Presentation? Suggestions from the Audience." *Technology and Teacher Education Annual—1994.* Charlottesville, VA: Association for the Advancement of Computing in Education, 1994.

Hale, Edward. "Overhead Transparencies for Viewing Molecular Structure in Three Dimensions." *American Biology Teacher* (April 1993): 227.

How to Prepare Effective Overhead Projector Presentations. East Rutherford, NJ: National Audio-Visual Supply, 1992.

Kemp, Jerrold E., and Smellie, Don C. *Planning, Producing, and Using Instructional Technologies.* 7th ed. New York: HarperCollins, 1994.

Kiss, Marilyn. "From Peru to Pamplona: Integrating Slides into the Lesson Plan." *Hispania* (May 1989): 422–425.

Kueter, Roger A., and Miller, Janeen. *Slides.* Englewood Cliffs, NJ: Educational Technology Publications, 1981.

Lefever, Margaret. "A Mother Lode of Images for Teaching History." *Social Education* (May 1987): 265.

McBride, Dennis. *How to Make Visual Presentations.* New York: Art Direction Book Company, 1982.

Meilach, Dona Z. "Overhead Projectors Take on New Dimensions." *Audio Visual Communications* (August 1990): 32–36.

Pearson, Latresa. "Wake Up Your Overheads." *Presentations* (March 1994): 29–36.

Pett, Dennis W. "Design of the Audio Track for Instructional Slide Sets and Filmstrips." *Performance and Instruction* (October 1989): 1–4.

Radcliffe, Beverly. "Using the Overhead Projector for Homework Correction." *Foreign Language Annals* (April 1984): 119–121.

Sheard, B. V. "They Love to Read Aloud from Filmstrips." *Teacher* (May 1973): 66ff.

Strickland, Ted. "Computer Projection Panels: Technology for the Classroom of the 1990s." *Journal of Education for Business* (September–October 1993): 23–28.

Tierney, Daniel, and Humphreys, Fay. *The Effective Use of the OHP.* London: Centre for Information on Language Teaching and Research, 1992.

Van Vliet, Lucille W. "Tackling Production Techniques: The Opaque, It's Great." *School Library Media Activities* (April 1986): 36–37.

Waggener, Joseph. "Important Media Classics: Filmstrips, Tape Recorders, and Record Players." *Media and Methods* (January–February 1989): 16, 18–19, 66–67.

Audiovisual References

"Color Lift" Transparencies. Salt Lake City, UT: Media Systems, 1975. Filmstrip or slides. 40 frames, captioned.

Effective Projection; Photography for Audiovisual Production; and *The Impact of Visuals in the Speechmaking Process.* Eastman Kodak, 1982. 3 filmstrips with audiocassettes.

"I Like the Overhead Projector Because . . . " Washington, DC: National Audiovisual Center, 1977. Filmstrip with audiocassette. 12 minutes.

Thermofax (explains how to make thermal transparencies). Iowa City, IA: Audiovisual Center, University of Iowa, 1986. Videotape.

Use of the Overhead Projector and How to Make Do-It-Yourself Transparencies. Swan Pencil Co., n.d. 80 slides with cassette. 18 minutes.

The following VHS videocassettes are available from Audiovisual Center Marketing, C215 Seashore Hall, University of Iowa, Iowa City, IA 52242.

Sound Filmstrip Projector. 1983. 7 minutes.
Overhead Projector. 1983. 7 minutes.
Opaque Projector. 1983. 7 minutes.
35mm Slide Projector. 1983. 7 minutes.

AUDIO

Audio media can make several unique contributions to the teaching-learning process: self-study for non-readers, realistic foreign language practice, stories to stimulate the imagination, and music for physical activity, to name a few. Cassettes, records, and CDs are abundantly available in every curricular area and are easy to use. To use audio media effectively requires an understanding of the hearing-listening processes and thoughtful selection of materials based on your objectives.

You can prepare your own audio materials, and so can your students. These recordings can take the form of oral reports, accompaniments to learning center activities, communication skills practice, and the like. By following some basic guidelines you can improve the quality of such recordings.

KNOWLEDGE OBJECTIVES

1. Distinguish between hearing and listening.
2. Identify four areas of breakdown in audio communication and specify the causes of such breakdowns.
3. Describe four techniques for improving listening skills.
4. Describe four types of audio media most often used for instruction. Include distinguishing characteristics and limitations of each type.
5. Compare the advantages and limitations of audio media.
6. Describe one possible use of audio media in your teaching field. Include the subject area, audience, objective(s), role of the student, and evaluation techniques to be used.
7. Describe two procedures for duplicating audiotapes and one procedure for editing audiotapes.
8. Identify five criteria for appraising and selecting audio materials.
9. Demonstrate your ability to follow the proper procedures for utilizing audio materials.
10. Identify the advantages of rate-controlled audio playback.

APPLICATION OBJECTIVES

1. Prepare an audiotape that features your voice and some music. It will be evaluated using the criteria in the Checklist for Student/Teacher-Prepared Audiocassettes in "How to . . . Record Audiocassettes" (p. 189). Include a brief description of each step from the ASSURE model.
2. Obtain any commercially prepared audio materials and appraise them using a given set of criteria (such as in "Appraisal Checklist: Audio Materials," page 191).
3. Develop a short oral history of your school or organization by interviewing people associated with it for a long time. Edit your interviews into a five-minute presentation.
4. Select the best audio format for a given instructional situation and justify the selection of that format, stating advantages and limitations.
5. Prepare an outline for a short oral presentation. Deliver your presentation as if you were addressing the intended audience, and record it. Critique your presentation for style as well as content. Revise and present again.
6. Plan a brief audio-based lesson on a basic skill (e.g., spelling or arithmetic), or prepare a performance aid (e.g., how to make out a bank check or how to fill out an application form). Design the lesson with paper and pencil first, then record it on tape.

LEXICON

hearing	digital recording
listening	audio card
auditory fatigue	oral history
rate-controlled playback	

If you were asked which learning activities consume the major portion of a student's classroom time, would you say reading instructional materials, answering questions, reciting what one has learned, or taking tests? Actually, typical elementary and secondary students spend about 50% of their school time just listening (Figure 6.1). College students are likely to spend nearly 90% of their time in class listening to lectures and seminar discussions (Figure 6.2). The importance, then, of audio experiences in the classroom should not be underestimated. This chapter discusses various means—referred to as audio media—for recording and transmitting the human voice and other sounds for instructional purposes.

Before discussing audio formats in particular and audio media in general, let's examine the hearing-listening process itself as it pertains to the communication model discussed in Chapter 1 and to the development of listening skills.

THE HEARING-LISTENING PROCESS

Hearing and listening are not the same thing, although they are, of course, interrelated. At the risk of oversimplification, we might say that hearing is a physiological process, whereas listening is a psychological process.

Physiologically, **hearing** is a process in which sound waves entering the outer ear are transmitted to the eardrum, converted into mechanical vibrations in the middle ear, and changed in the inner ear into electrical impulses that travel to the brain.

The psychological process of **listening** begins with someone's awareness of and attention to sounds or speech patterns (receiving), proceeds through identifica-tion and recognition of specific auditory signals (decod-ing), and ends in comprehension (destination).

The hearing-listening process is also a communica-tion-learning process, as described in Chapter 1. As with visual communication and learning, a message is encoded by a sender and decoded by a receiver. The quality of the encoded message is affected by the ability of the sender to express the message clearly and logi-cally. The understandability of the decoded message is affected by the ability of the receiver to comprehend the message.

The efficiency of communication is also affected by the hearing-listening process as the message passes from sender to receiver. Breakdowns in audio communications can occur at any point in the process: encoding, hearing, listening, or decoding, as illustrated in Figure 6.3.

Appropriate encoding of the message depends on the sender's skill in organizing and presenting it. For exam-ple, the vocabulary level of the message must be within the vocabulary level of the receiver.

The transmission–reception process might be inhib-ited by a number of obstacles. First, the volume of the sound might be too low or too high. If too low, we have trouble picking up the meaning with any accuracy. If too high, we try to shield our ears, shutting out the offending sounds.

Second, a sound that is sustained monotonously, such as the droning voice of a teacher, may trigger **audi-tory fatigue**. You have probably had the experience of hearing an annoying sound—for example, a noisy muf-fler on the car you are riding in. But after a while you hardly notice the sound at all. You might stop thinking about it entirely until it stops, and then you notice the cessation. This is an example of auditory fatigue, the process of gradually "tuning out" or losing conscious-ness of a sound source—a process that is physiological as well as psychological. That is, the neural mechanisms

FIGURE 6.1
Elementary and secondary students spend about half of their in-school time listening to others.

FIGURE 6.2
At the college level, about 90% of class time is spent listening.

transmitting the sound to the brain literally become fatigued from "carrying the same load" over and over. In addition, your conscious awareness of the noise is diminished because it is "old news" and no longer of interest. The brain has a remarkable capacity for filtering out sounds it doesn't want or need to attend to.

Third, an individual's ability to hear may be physically impaired. When students have a cold, it is possible that their ability to hear in a noisy classroom is reduced.

Even a small difference in acuity can cause students to have difficulty discriminating between words and phrases—thus the potential for confusion. And, with the trend toward including students with significant loss of hearing acuity in regular hearing classrooms, it is possible that a teacher may need to be certain that special considerations are made to provide special visual cues to ensure that the information is clearly understood.

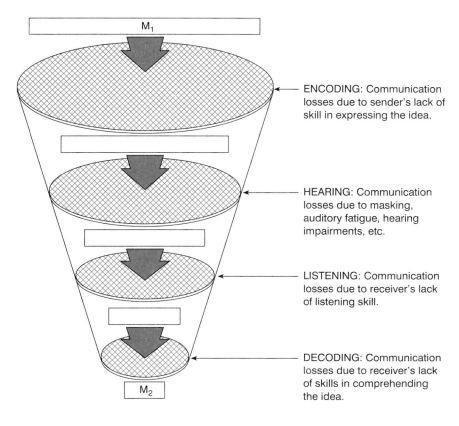

FIGURE 6.3
In the hearing-listening process, impediments at each step act like filters, reducing the perceived meaning to a small fraction of the intended meaning. M_1 = meaning originally intended by the sender. M_2 = meaning as received and comprehended by the receiver.

The message can also be affected by the receiver's listening skills or lack of them. The receiver must be able to direct and sustain concentration on a given series of sounds (the message). He or she must have the skill to think ahead as the message is being received (we think faster than we hear, just as we think faster than we read or write) and use this time differential to organize and internalize the information so that it can be comprehended.

Finally, communication can break down because the receiver lacks the experiential background to internalize and thus comprehend the message.

DEVELOPING LISTENING SKILLS

Until recently, much attention in formal education was given to reading and writing, a little was given to speaking, and essentially none was given to listening. Now, however, listening is recognized as a skill that, like all skills, can be improved with practice (Figure 6.4).

Hearing is the foundation of listening. Therefore, you should first determine that all of your students can hear normally. Most school systems regularly use speech and hearing therapists to administer audiometric hearing tests to provide the data you need. Standardized tests also measure students' listening abilities. These tests are often administered by the school district, so check on the availability of listening test scores.

Teachers can use a number of techniques to improve student listening abilities:

- *Guide listening.* To guide their listening, give the students some objectives or questions beforehand. Start with short passages and one or two objectives. Then gradually increase the length of the passage and the number and complexity of the objectives or questions.

- *Give directions.* Give the students directions individually or as a group on audiotape. You can then evaluate students' ability to follow these instructions. With audio instructions, you can examine worksheets or products of the activity. When giving directions orally, the "say it only once" rule should be observed so that a value is placed on both the teacher's and the students' time and the incentive to listen is reinforced.

- *Ask students to listen for main ideas, details, or inferences.* Keeping the age level of the students in mind, you can present an oral passage. You can read a story and ask primary students to draw what is happening. Ask students to listen for the main idea and then write it down. A similar technique can be used with details and inferences to be drawn from the passage.

- *Use context in listening.* Younger students can learn to distinguish meanings in an auditory context by listening to sentences with words missing and then supplying the appropriate words.

- *Analyze the structure of a presentation.* The students can be asked to outline (analyze and organize) an oral presentation. The teacher can then determine how well they were able to discern the main ideas and to identify the subtopics.

- *Distinguish between relevant and irrelevant information.* After listening to an oral presentation of information, the student can be asked to identify the main idea and then rate (from most to least relevant) all other ideas that are presented. A simpler technique for elementary students is to have them identify irrelevant words in sentences or irrelevant sentences in paragraphs.

AUDIO FORMATS

Let's examine the comparative strengths and limitations of the audio formats most often used for instructional

FIGURE 6.4
Listening skills are an important component of oral communication.

FIGURE 6.5
A wealth of recorded material is available in the common audio formats: cassettes, compact discs, and phonograph records.

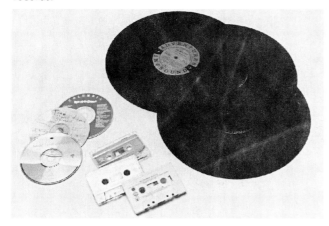

purposes—cassette tapes, phonograph records, compact discs, and audio cards (Figure 6.5). The differences among these media are summarized in Table 6.1.

Audiotapes. The major advantages of audiotape are that you can record your own tapes easily and economically, and when the material becomes outdated or no longer useful, you can erase the magnetic signal on the tape and reuse it. Tapes are not easily damaged, and they store easily. Unlike discs, broken tapes can be repaired.

Of course, there are some limitations to magnetic tape recordings. In the recording process, background noises or a mechanical hum may sometimes be recorded along with the intended material. Even a relatively low-level noise can ruin an otherwise good recording.

The audio device most commonly found in the classroom is the cassette tape recorder. The cassette tape is in essence a self-contained reel-to-reel system with the two reels permanently installed in a rugged plastic case, or cassette. The ⅛-inch-wide tape is permanently fastened to each of the reels. Cassette tapes are identified according to the amount of recording time they contain. For example, a C-60 cassette can record 60 minutes of sound using both sides (i.e., 30 minutes on each side). A C-90 can record 45 minutes on each side. Cassettes are available in various lengths. The size of the plastic cassette containing the tape is the same in all cases, and all can be played on any cassette machine.

The cassette is durable; it is virtually immune to shock and abrasion. It can be snapped into and out of a recorder in seconds. It is not necessary to rewind the tape before removing it from the machine.

There are a few drawbacks to cassettes. For instance, longer tapes, particularly C-120s, sometimes become stuck or tangled in the recorder because of the thinness of the tape. If this happens, and unless the content on the tape is unique and of considerable value, you are best advised to throw the tape away. If it sticks or gets tangled in the machine once, it is likely to do so again.

The frequency response and overall quality (fidelity) of cassette playback units are not as good as those of compact disc (CD) players because of the small speakers in most portable cassette playback units. However, for most instructional uses the quality is more than adequate.

Rate-Controlled Audio Playback. An important but little-known piece of audio equipment is a cassette tape deck that can play back recorded speech at either a faster or a slower rate than that at which it was recorded, with no loss of voice quality or intelligibility. (Figure 6.6.)

▼ **MEDIA FILE**

Thinking About Drinking
Six Cassettes

Teenage abuse of alcohol continues to be a major concern in our society. This series of 12 half-hour programs, originally broadcast by the Public Broadcasting System (PBS), deals in an engrossing manner with many aspects of the problem. A few of the titles are *Media Images of Alcohol, The Lady Drinks, Driving Under the Influence,* and *The Latino Perspective.* By using case histories of well-known national figures (such as former first lady Betty Ford) and dramatizations, the program avoids a deadly lecture format. More than 150 interviews with experts in the field enliven the tapes, which are intended for students, parents, and teachers. The series explains how teachers can contribute significantly to resolving students' drinking problems.

Source: SounDocumentaries.

TABLE 6.1
Common audio formats

FORMAT	SPEED	ADVANTAGES	LIMITATIONS	USES
Cassette audiotape	Size: $2\frac{1}{2}$ by 4 by $\frac{1}{2}$ in.	$1\frac{7}{8}$ ips[1]	Very portable (small and light) Durable Easy to use (no threading) Can prevent accidental erasing Requires little storage space	Tape sometimes sticks or tangles Noise and hiss Poor fidelity with inexpensive players Broken tapes not easy to repair Difficult to edit	Listening "in the field" using battery power Student-made recordings Extended discussions Individual listening Assessment tool (e.g., reading)
	Tape $\frac{1}{8}$ in. wide				
Microcassette	Size: $1\frac{5}{16}$ by $1\frac{3}{32}$ by $\frac{21}{64}$ in.	$\frac{15}{16}$ ips	Very compact Portable	Not compatible with other cassettes Poor fidelity	Dictation by business executives Amateur recording Recording field notes
	Tape $\frac{1}{8}$ in. wide				
Phonograph record (disc recording)	78 rpm[2] 45 rpm $33\frac{1}{3}$ rpm $16\frac{2}{3}$ rpm		Excellent frequency response Compatibility of records and phonographs Selection easily cued Wide variety of selections Inexpensive	Impractical to prepare locally Easily scratched Can warp Requires much storage space	Music Long narrations Classroom listening Historical speeches Drama, poetry
	Diameters: 7, 10, 12 in.				
Compact disc	Size: 4.72 in.	Variable high speed	Very durable High fidelity No background noise Random search	Impractical to prepare locally Expensive Initial expense of equipment	Music Drama
Audio card	$3\frac{1}{2}$ by 9 in. or $5\frac{1}{2}$ by 11 in.	$2\frac{1}{4}$ ips $1\frac{1}{8}$ ips	Sound with visual Student can record response and compare with original Designed for individual use Participation; involvement	Most cards hold less than 15 seconds Time-consuming to prepare	Vocabulary building Concept learning Associating sounds with visuals Technical vocabulary
	$\frac{1}{4}$ in. magnetic stripe				

[1] ips = inches per second.

[2] rpm = revolutions per minute.

FIGURE 6.6
With rate-controlled audio playback machines, both speed and pitch can be controlled.

Before this technological breakthrough occurred, playing a tape back at a higher speed resulted in a high-pitched distortion, as if the speaker were a chattering chipmunk. Slowing down the playback resulted in a low-pitched, unintelligible garble.

The pedagogical significance of this **rate-controlled playback** lies in the fact that although the average person speaks at 100 to 150 words per minute, most of us can comprehend spoken information at the rate of 250 to 300 words per minute. Research has shown that most students learn as quickly and retain as much when spoken instruction is speeded up. The visually impaired, in particular, can benefit by having the option to listen to words that are spoken almost as fast as a sighted person can read them.

Changing the rate during playback allows the student to listen at his or her own pace, skimming over familiar material at a high rate, slowing down for material that may require more time for comprehension.

Research has shown that learning time can be cut (as much as 50% and an average of 32%) and comprehension increased (as much as 9.3% and an average of 4.2%) by using compressed and variable-speed audio-tapes.[1] One reason that comprehension increases with accelerated listening rate may be that the listener is forced to increase his or her concentration on the material and is also freed from the distractions that often accompany normal speech, such as pauses, throat clearing, and other extraneous sounds. A slow, monotonous speaking rate also allows listeners' minds to wander.

[1]Linda Olsen, "Technology Humanized: The Rate Controlled Tape Recorder," *Media and Methods* (January 1979), p. 67; and Sarah H. Short, "The Use of Rate Controlled Speech to Save Time and Increase Learning in Self-paced Instruction," *NSPI Journal* (May 1978), pp. 13, 14.

Research also indicates that variable-speed audiotapes can be very effective in increasing reading speed. One junior high school teacher prepared variable-speed tapes of printed material for his students to listen to as they read the material. The students' reading rates gradually grew with increases in their listening rates. The ear, it seems, helps train the eye.

Phonograph Records. Until the 1980s, the phonograph record was the most popular format for playing recorded audio content at home and at school. Most producers of popular and classical music have phased out records in favor of audiocassettes and compact discs. Consequently, the long-playing record (LP) has virtually disappeared from the shelves of music stores.

Even though fewer phonograph records are available for purchase, many schools still acquire and use them because of attributes that make records attractive for school use. Record players are compact, easily portable,

▼ MEDIA FILE

A Jug Band Peter and the Wolf
Record/Cassette/Compact disc

Here is a fun version of Prokofiev's *Peter and the Wolf* arranged for a band of folk instruments (and a few standard instruments played in folk style). The instruments include fiddle, mandolin, guitar, banjo, kazoo, whistle, mouth harp, jug, washtub bass, and clarinet. The accompanying booklet explains how the music was transcribed to retain the spirit of the original. Though the instruments are different, the story line is the same. This is not recommended as a replacement of the original but should be used as an interesting adaptation. Dave Van Ronk, a folksinger, does the narration. On the second side he sings a group of folk songs that should appeal to children.

Source: Alacazam!

and simple to use. It's easy to locate a particular segment of a record because you can actually see the grooves, and segments are separated by blank "bands." The location of each selection on a record is usually indicated on the record label and on the protective dust cover. Because phonograph records are made from cheap materials and stamped from a master in a high-speed process, they can be brought to the market at a relatively low price.

Despite all the advantages of phonograph records, they are not without limitations from an instructional point of view. The greatest drawback is that you cannot economically prepare your own records. Also, a record is easily damaged if someone drops the stylus (needle) on the disk or otherwise scratches the surface. Excessive heat and improper storage may cause the disk to warp, making it difficult, if not impossible, to play. Also, records take up more storage space than cassette tapes with the same amount of information recorded on them.

▼ MEDIA FILE

A Kid's-Eye View of the Environment
CD/Cassette

Michael Mish based this series of songs on his many visits to schools in southern California to talk to children about the environment. He found them to be more aware and concerned about environmental problems than he expected. Mish took the topics that the children were most concerned about (e.g., recycling, water and air pollution, and the greenhouse effect) and put them to music. The songs are engaging, including choruses that children can sing along with. The messages should get primary-age children talking about making this a safer, cleaner world.

Source: Mish Mash Music.

Compact Discs. Physically, the compact disc (CD) looks like a small, silver phonograph record without grooves. The music or other sounds are stored as digitized bits of information (see "Close-up: How a Compact Disc Works," on p. 183). The disc is only 12 centimeters (4.75 inches) in diameter, yet it stores an incredible amount of information. Some CDs contain as much as 75 minutes of music.

The technology of the CD makes it an attractive addition to education programs. Users can quickly locate selections on the disc and even program them to play in any desired sequence. Information can be selectively retrieved by learners or programmed by the instructor. A major advantage of the CD is its resistance to damage. There are no grooves to scratch nor tape to tangle and tear. Stains can be washed off, and ordinary scratches do not affect playback.

Compact disc technology has been accepted rapidly for use in the home. But the cost of a CD player as well as individual CDs has slowed its acceptance in the education market. As prices come down, the CD's advantages, especially its resistance to damage, will make it a standard format for using audio in education.

When talking about audio CD, we are in essence talking about the same technology that is used in CD-ROM. CD-ROM utilizes more of the capacity of the optical technology by adding text and graphics to the disc. We discuss other applications of CD-ROM in Chapter 9.

CDs have been eagerly accepted by consumers as a preferred audio format, but for audiophiles on the go (walking, jogging, or driving) they have two serious drawbacks: size of the playback equipment and skips due to sudden vibration. Sony has demonstrated a mini-disc (MD) that solves both problems. The MD stores up to 74 minutes of audio but is only 6.35 centimeters (2½ inches) in diameter. Thus the playback unit can be smaller than a cassette player. To reduce the effects of skipping, the playback head repositions itself after a bump, and a memory chip holds up to three seconds of sound that might have been lost.

The reduction in size of the disc with no loss of playing time is accomplished by a magnetic-optical technique that Sony introduced a few years ago for high-volume computer data storage. The disc is coated with a thin magnetic layer. A laser momentarily heats a tiny spot to 400°F and a magnetic head records the signal in the heated spot. In playback, an optical pickup reads both the polarity and the intensity of the light reflected from the spots. These are then reassembled into the original audio.

Audio Cards. Another audio instructional format is the **audio card**. An audio card is approximately the size of a business envelope. It contains a strip of

CLOSE-UP

HOW A COMPACT DISC WORKS

Until the compact disc was developed, all retail audio recordings were analog recordings; that is, they retained the essential wave form of the sound, whether as grooves in a phonograph record or as patterns of magnetized particles on audiotape. CDs are made using **digital recording**. In digital recording, analog information (whether in the form of music, speech, or print) is transformed into a series of 1s and 0s, the same mathematical code used in computers. A powerful laser burns a microscopic pit into the plastic master for each 1 in the digital code. A blank space corresponds to 0. The laser moves in an ever-widening spiral from the center of the master to the edge, leaving on the disc hundreds of thousands of binary bits (1s and 0s). As a low-power laser beam in

the playback unit picks up the pattern of pits and blank spaces, the beam is reflected back into the laser mechanism, and the digital code is transformed into the original analog sound. The laser mechanism does not come in direct physical contact with the CD and can move independently of the disc, unlike the stylus in a record groove or a tape head. This means that the laser beam can scan the CD and quickly locate desired information. In other words, the CD can be programmed so the user can quickly access any part of the disc. CD players can indicate what track is playing, the sequence in which tracks will be played, how many more tracks are on the disc, and the remaining playing time. Another characteristic of digital recording is the complete absence of background noise.

The compact disc, shown approximately one-half its actual size, is a three-layer sandwich. The digital code in the form of pits is on the top side of a clear, tough plastic very much like Plexiglas. A reflective coating of aluminum is placed on top of the pitted plastic surface. A protective coating of acrylic resin is applied on the top of the reflective surface. Label information is printed on top of the resin. This arrangement protects the program information from both the top and bottom surfaces of the disc. The laser beam reads the code through the clear plastic, and it is reflected back by the aluminum layer. The manufacturing process must be carried out in an environment completely free of dust because of the almost microscopic size of the pits.

Unlike an LP, the recording on a CD begins near the center and ends at the outer rim. Also unlike an LP, the CD does not rotate at a constant speed. The speed varies from 500 rpm at the innermost track to 200 rpm at the outer edge.

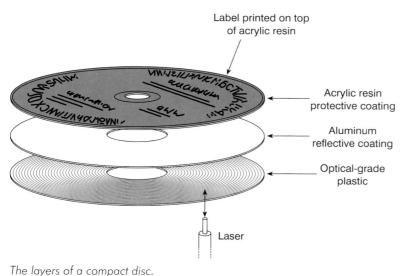

Label printed on top of acrylic resin

Acrylic resin protective coating

Aluminum reflective coating

Optical-grade plastic

Laser

The layers of a compact disc.

magnetic recording tape near the bottom edge. The audio card is essentially a flash card with sound. It is inserted into a slot on a machine, such as the Audiotronics Tutorette, and a transport mechanism moves the card through the slot. Up to 15 seconds of sound can be played through the speaker (or headset, for individual use). The audio card player uses a dual-track system that allows the student to record his or her own response on the card and then play it back for comparison with the prerecorded response. If the student's response is incorrect, it can be erased and rerecorded correctly by simply running the audio card through the machine again while depressing the record lever. Both the student's response and the prerecorded response can be replayed as often as desired. The prerecorded message is protected from erasure by a switch on the back of the machine; the teacher can use the switch to change the prerecorded message.

Advantages

We have discussed several different audio formats—cassettes, records, CDs, and audio cards. In the following discussion of advantages we will focus on the attributes of cassettes, because that is the most popular format. In some cases we will compare the attributes of cassettes with those of other audio formats.

- *Inexpensive.* In the case of audiotape, once the tapes and equipment have been purchased, there is no additional cost because the tape can be erased after use and a new message can be recorded. Individual audiocassettes are inexpensive.
- *Readily available and simple to use.* Most students have been using audiocassette recorders since they were very young. Audio equipment is easy to operate.
- *Reproducible.* Audiotapes are easily duplicated in whatever quantities are needed. Tapes can be dupli-

From Needle to Laser

The technology of recorded sound has gone through several transformations since Edison recited "Mary had a little lamb" into the horn of the first phonograph and to his own astonishment heard his voice played back to him. That was in 1877.

Early that year Edison had invented a carbon transmitter for Bell's telephone, so transmission of sound was on his mind. At the same time, he was trying to expand the usefulness of the telegraph. He was working on a device that could imprint on paper tape the Morse code coming over a telegraph line and then reproduce the message at any desired speed. A steel spring pressed against the paper helped keep the tape in a straight line. Edison noticed that when the tape was running at a high speed, the dots and dashes hitting the spring gave off a noise that he described as a "light musical, rhythmic sound, resembling human talk heard indistinctly." During his work on the carbon transmitter, Edison, who was already partially deaf, attached a needle to the diaphragm of the telephone receiver to judge the loudness of the sound. By holding his finger lightly to the needle, loudness could be judged by the strength of the vibration. Edison, for reasons unknown, decided to use tinfoil wrapped around a cylinder as his recording medium with two needle-diaphragm units, one for recording and one for playback. In December 1877 he applied for a patent.

The next major advance was made in 1887 by a German immigrant, Emile Berliner, when he developed the idea of a stylus engraving lateral grooves as it moved across a disk coated with a pliant but firm material. The flat disk had a greater potential to be mass-produced than did the cylinder. When he hit on the idea of making a metal master that could stamp out duplicates, the flat disk became the accepted format.

But recordings were still acoustic. Horns, not microphones, were used to gather and direct the sound waves that drove the recording diaphragm and needle. Playback was the same process in reverse. Quality was still poor, and volume was limited. Electricity, already employed in the telephone, was the answer. In 1920 two British inventors, Lionel Guest and H. R. Merriman, successfully recorded a ceremony in Westminster Abbey by transmitting the signals from their electric microphone over phone lines to their laboratory. A few years later, the vacuum tube amplifier made possible an all-electronic system. From then until the end of World War II, slow, steady improvements in recording technology made the 78-rpm record, in 10- and 12-inch sizes, the standard.

In June 1948 Peter Goldmark of Columbia Records demonstrated the long-playing record (LP) that was destined to drive 78-rpm records from the market. The public responded positively and quickly to the new format. But magnetic tape recording would have an even more dramatic effect.

The idea of stereo recording had been around for a long time, but there was no marketable medium until magnetic tape recordings were made available to the public. In 1955, stereo recordings on magnetic tape were marketed on reel-to-reel tape, a format that the general public did not accept well. Then, in 1957, cutting a stereo groove in a master disk was perfected, and stereo disks soon flooded the market. LPs were the standard format for stereo until 1970, when advances in audiocassette technology, including the Dolby method of suppressing background noise, challenged the LP.

Compact discs were introduced to the high-fidelity market in 1983. Philips, the giant Dutch company that created both the audiocassette and the compact disc, also developed what it called the digital compact cassette (DCC). Philips unveiled the system to the public in 1991. The DCC format allows digital-quality taping at a price comparable to that of cassette decks. Standard audiocassettes are playable on the DCC.

In the course of only 120 years, recorded sound has progressed from the barely audible voice of Edison etched in an impermanent groove on tinfoil to symphonies recorded with astounding clarity and richness on an almost indestructible compact disc. You can now put that CD of Beethoven's Ninth on the shelf, on top of the cassette that's on top of the stereo LP that's on top of the mono LP that's on top of the 78 (if you're old enough). Technology marches on!

Source: This feature is based primarily on Roland Gelatt, The Fabulous Phonograph, 1877–1977 (New York: Collier Books, 1977).

cated and used in the classroom, in the media center, and at home.

- *Provides verbal message for nonreaders.* Students who cannot read can learn from audio media, which provide basic language experiences. Students can listen to audio and follow along with visual and text material.

- *Ideal for teaching foreign languages.* Foreign languages can be taught using cassette tapes and audio cards. They allow students to hear words pronounced by native speakers. Students can also record their own pronunciations for comparison.

- *Stimulating.* Audio media can provide a stimulating alternative to reading and listening to the teacher. Audio can present verbal messages more dramatically than text can. With a little imagination on the part of the teacher, audio can be very versatile.

- *Repeatable.* Users can replay portions of the program as often as needed to understand it.

- *Portable.* Audiocassette recorders are portable and can even be used "in the field" with battery power. Cassette recorders are ideal for home study; many students already have their own cassette machines.

- *Ease of lesson preparation.* The major advantage of audiotapes over compact discs is that instructors can record their own audiotaped lessons easily and economically. When the material becomes outdated or no longer useful, the tape can be erased and reused.

- *Selections easy to locate.* In the case of CDs, teachers can quickly locate selections on the compact discs and even program the machine to play in any desired sequence. Information can be selectively retrieved by students or programmed by the teacher.

- *Resistance to damage.* Cassette tapes are enclosed in a damage-resistant plastic cassette. In the case of CDs, there are no grooves to scratch or tape to tangle and break. Stains can be washed off, and ordinary scratches do not affect playback.

Limitations

In discussing the limitations of audio, we will again focus on the attributes of cassettes because that is the most popular format. Other formats are mentioned where they differ from cassettes.

- *Fixed sequence.* Audiotapes fix the sequence of a presentation even though it is possible to rewind the tape and hear a recorded segment again or advance the tape to an upcoming portion. It is difficult to scan audio materials as you would printed text materials. Audio cards and CDs do not share this limitation, which is why these formats play a significant role in instruction.

- *Doesn't monitor attention.* Some students have difficulty studying independently, so when they listen to audiocassettes their attention tends to wander. They may hear the recorded message but not listen atten-

tively and comprehend. Teachers can readily detect when students are drifting away from a lecture, but a cassette recorder cannot do this.

- *Doesn't provoke attention.* For some students listening to audiocassettes, their attention tends to wander. They may hear the recorded message but not listen to and comprehend it. Teachers can more readily notice when students are not paying attention to an instructor-led presentation than when they are not listening to a cassette recording.

- *Difficulty in pacing.* Determining the appropriate pace for presenting information can be difficult if your students have a wide range of skills and experiential backgrounds. Cassettes and phonographs don't allow variation in pacing except with rate-controlled playback machines. Audio cards, again, escape this limitation; the one-at-a-time format allows students to use them at their own pace.

- *Difficulty in locating segment.* It is difficult to locate a specific segment on an audiotape. Counters on the recorders assist retrieval, but they are not very accurate. Records and CDs give much easier accessibility to specific selections.

- *Potential for accidental erasure.* Audiotapes can be erased easily, which can be problematic. Just as they can be quickly and easily erased when no longer needed, they can be accidentally erased when they should be saved.

Applications

The uses of audio media are limited only by the imagination of teachers and students. Audio media can be used in all phases of instruction—from introduction of a topic to evaluation of student learning. Perhaps the most rapidly growing general use of audio media today is in the area of self-paced instruction and in "mastery learning." The slower student can go back and repeat segments of instruction as often as necessary because the recorder-playback machine is a very patient tutor. The accelerated student can skip ahead or increase the pace of his or her instruction.

Prerecorded audio materials are available in a wide variety of subjects. For music classes, records, tapes, and CDs can be used to introduce new material or to provide musical accompaniment. The sounds of various musical instruments can be presented individually or in combinations. In preschool and primary grades, tapes and records can be used for developing rhythm, telling stories, playing games, and acting out stories or songs. In social studies, the tape recorder can bring the voices of persons who have made history into the classroom. The sounds of current events can also be presented.

A common application of audio media is in learning centers. Sometimes these are even referred to as "listening centers" because of their use of audio-based materials. (Learning centers are described in more detail in Chapter 11.)

In elementary classrooms, teachers use audio cards for vocabulary building. The cards are used on an individual basis with children who are having difficulty grasping the meaning of words because they cannot attach the appropriate spoken word to the printed form of the word or to the object it represents. Audio cards provide simulta-neous visual and auditory stimuli designed to increase a child's spoken vocabulary. The teacher shows the student how to use the machine and the cards, then

▼ MEDIA FILE

Self-Esteem for Women
Cassette Tapes and Workbook

Self-Esteem
F O R   W O M E N™
HOW TO INCREASE YOUR
Self-Worth • Self-Respect • Life Satisfaction
With Julie White, Ph.D.

These tapes and workbook describe how women can increase their self-worth and life satisfaction. The program is designed to help them feel good about themselves just as they are. It gives them skills they need to grow into the persons they want to become, in both their personal and professional lives. Topics include the following: why eliminating negative self-talk is even more powerful than increasing positive self-talk; how to open your mind to new possibilities; how to recognize and measure your own growth and success.

Source: CareerTrack.

lets the child work alone. Later, the teacher uses the same cards without the machine, holding them up one at a time and asking the child to say the word.

As another example, a middle-school teacher inserts a cassette into the sound system of her car for the 20-minute daily commute to her school. After a few seconds of music, the song fades as the narrator says, "What's new in classroom management techniques? Today we are going to explore together three techniques that will enhance your classroom skills. . . . " The cassettes turns the automobile into a learning environment, thereby making use of otherwise unproductive time.

One special application of prerecorded audio media is "talking books" for blind or visually impaired students. A Talking Books Program has been set up by the American Printing House for the Blind to make as much material as possible available to the visually impaired. At present, over 135,000 book titles are available, along with recordings of over 200 current periodicals. The service is a cooperative effort of the Library of Congress and 53 regional libraries in the United States. Audiocassettes are the standard format.

PRODUCING CLASS MATERIALS ON CASSETTE TAPES

Students and teachers can easily prepare their own cassette tapes. (See "How to . . . Record Audiocassettes," page 188.) Student-prepared cassette tapes can be used for gathering oral histories and preparing oral book reports. Tapes prepared by the teacher can be used in direct instruction, as illustrated by the vocational-technical school example later. Skills practice, such as shorthand, can also be provided by audiocassette.

A popular project in 12th-grade social studies classes is the recording of **oral histories**. The students interview local senior citizens regarding the history of their community. Only one student interviews each senior citizen, but the interviewing task is rotated among the students, and the entire class assists in determining which questions should be asked. In preparation for this project, the students study both national and local history. All the tapes prepared during the interviews are kept in the school media center. Excerpts are duplicated and edited into programs for use with other social studies classes and for broadcast by the local radio station. This audiotape project serves the dual purpose of informing students and local residents about local history and collecting and preserving information that might otherwise be lost.

The cassette recorder can be used for presenting book reports. Students may record their book reports during study time in the media center or at home. The reports are evaluated by the teacher, and the best ones are kept on file in the media center. Other students are encouraged to listen to them before selecting books to read. Since the reports are limited to three minutes, the students are required to extract the main ideas from the book and to organize their thoughts carefully. During the taping, they practice their speaking skills. They are encouraged to make the report as exciting as possible to interest other students in reading the book.

Tape recorders can be used to record information gleaned from a field trip. Upon returning to the classroom, the students can play back the tape for discussion and review. Many museums, observatories, and other public exhibit areas now supply visitors with prerecorded messages about various items on display, which may (with permission) be rerecorded for playback in the classroom.

Students can also record themselves reciting, presenting a speech, performing music, and so on. They can then listen to the tape privately or have the performance critiqued by the teacher or other students. Initial efforts can be kept for comparison with later performances and for reinforcement of learning. Many small-group projects can include recorded reports to be presented to the rest of the class. These recordings can become part of the student's portfolio. Media portfolios are discussed in Chapter 3.

In a vocational-technical school, dental laboratory technology students are instructed on the procedures for constructing prosthetic devices such as partial plates and bridges by listening to an audiotape prepared by their instructor. To be efficient and effective in their work, these students must have both hands free and their eyes must be on their work, not on a textbook or manual. Audiotapes allow the students to move at their own pace, and the instructor is free to circulate around the laboratory and discuss each student's work individually.

A teacher of ninth-grade students with learning difficulties (but average intelligence) provides instruction on how to listen to lectures, speeches, and other oral presentations. The students practice their listening skills with tapes of recorded stories, poetry, and instructions. Commercially available tapes of speeches and narration are also used. After the students have practiced their listening skills under teacher direction, they are evaluated using a tape they have not heard before. The students listen to the five-minute tape without taking notes and then are given a series of questions dealing with important content from the passage.

In a high school business education class, the students practice taking dictation by listening to audiotapes prepared by the teacher and other individuals in the school, such as the principal, guidance counselor, or industrial arts instructor. The variety of voices on the tapes allows the students to practice dealing with different voices, accents, and dictation speeds. The business teacher categorizes the tapes according to difficulty of transcription and word speed. The students begin with the easy tapes and then move on to more difficult ones. The teacher also experiments with a variable-speed tape recorder, which will allow her to present the same tape to the students at a variety of speeds. Individually, the students use the variable-speed recorder to determine how fast they can take dictation and still maintain accuracy.

An often overlooked use of audio materials is for evaluating student attainment of lesson objectives. For example, test questions may be prerecorded for members of the class to use individually. Students may be asked to identify sounds in a recording (e.g., to name the solo instrument being played in a particular musical movement or to identify the composer of a particular piece of music). Students in social studies classes could be asked to identify the historical person most likely to have made excerpted passages from famous speeches, or they could be asked to identify the time period of excerpted passages based on their content. Testing and evaluating in the audio mode is especially appropriate when teaching and learning have also been in that particular mode.

DUPLICATING AND EDITING AUDIOTAPES

It is a relatively simple procedure to duplicate (or "dub") an audiotape. You can duplicate your tapes by one of three methods: the acoustic method, the electronic method, and the high-speed duplicator method.

The acoustic method (see Figure 6.7) does not require any special equipment, just two recorders. One recorder plays the original tape, and the sound is transferred via a microphone to a blank tape on the other recorder. The drawback of this method is that fidelity is reduced as the sound travels through the air to the microphone, and the open microphone may pick up unwanted noise from the environment.

The electronic method avoids this problem (see Figure 6.8). The signal travels from the original tape to the dubbing recorder via an inexpensive patch cord. The cord is attached to the output of the first machine and the "line," or auxiliary input, of the second. It picks up

FIGURE 6.7
Setup for duplicating by the acoustic method.

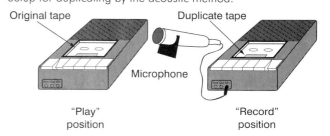

A major advantage of audiotapes is the ease with which they can be prepared by teachers and learners. All that is needed is a blank audiotape, a tape recorder, and a bit of know-how. If your school or organization does not have a recording studio, here are some fast and easy techniques for preparing your own tapes. The results may not be of true professional quality, but most instructors have found products made in this way to be useful and effective.

AUDIO TECHNIQUES

Physical Environment

Record in an area that is as free as possible from noise and sound reverberations. A small room such as an office is preferable to a normal-size classroom. Sparsely furnished rooms with plaster walls and ceilings and bare cement or tile floors are likely to be excessively "live," causing distracting sound reverberations that will interfere with the fidelity of the recording. Such areas can be improved by installing acoustic tiles and carpeting. The recording setup should be at least six feet from the chalkboard, windows, and hard walls. You may have to make do with temporary improvements to increase quality (e.g., put throw rugs, heavy blankets, or sheets of cardboard on the floor). Fabric-covered movable screens and drawn window shades may help.

Tape Recorder

- Expensive equipment is not necessary.
- Familiarize yourself with the operation of the particular tape recorder you intend to use.
- Advance the tape beyond the leader before recording. You cannot record on the clear plastic, nonmagnetic leader of the tape (about 10 seconds).
- Record an excerpt of about one minute and play it back to check volume and tone. Nothing is more frustrating than to record 10 or 15 minutes of a tape only to find that the microphone was not plugged into the recorder. A practice run will avoid this type of problem.
- If an error is made while recording, stop the tape recorder, reverse to a segment of tape containing a natural pause, engage the record mode, and continue recording.
- Refer to the instruction manual. Determine the proper recording level (volume) and tone. Most recorders have an automatic volume control, making adjustment on the machine unnecessary.

Microphone

- Use a separate microphone, not one built into the tape recorder. Place the microphone on a stand away from hard surfaces such as chalkboards, windows, and bare walls. If a stand is not available, place the microphone on a hand towel or other soft cloth. Because many tape recorders generate unwanted clicking, whirring, and humming noises, keep the microphone as far away from the recorder as possible.
- Place the microphone in a good spot to achieve maximum pickup of desired sounds and minimal pickup of extraneous ones. You want it located in such a place so it will pick up all the voices. Avoid handing the microphone from one person to another. If necessary, move people instead, before recording.
- Maintain a constant distance from the microphone. As a rule of thumb, your mouth should be about a foot from the microphone. If you are much closer, *ps* and *bs* will tend to "pop" and other breathy sounds may become annoying.
- Speak over the top of the microphone, not directly into it.

Tape Content

- Introduce the subject of the audiotape at the beginning of the recording. For example, "This is Introductory Geometry, Interior Angles, Lesson 12, on. . . . " Identifying the tape is particularly important if it is to be used for individual instruction.
- Explore the subject with the students; don't just tell them about it. A lecture on tape is deadly!
- Get your listeners involved in meaningful learning activities. You might, for instance, supply a study guide or worksheet for students to use with the tape (see facing example). Include ample space for students to take notes while listening to the tape. Instruct listeners to look at a diagram, specimen, table, or photograph; to use equipment; or to record data—so they don't simply sit and listen. Simple and direct activities are more effective than complex, involved ones.
- Keep the tape short even if it is to be used by adult learners. A length of 15–25 minutes is a good guideline for adults. Make it even shorter for younger students.
- Provide variety throughout the tape by using appropriate sounds, music, short dialogues, and voices of experts in your field. These provide variation and add realism to the study, but they should be used functionally.
- Repetition by the tape narrator is usually unnecessary. Repetition can be achieved by having the student replay appropriate tape segments.

Presentation

- Use informal notes rather than a complete script. Reading from a script tends to induce boredom. If you feel you must work with a more formal script, remember that preparing a good script requires special writing and reading skills.
- Use index cards for notes rather than handle large sheets of paper near the microphone. If your students will be using a study guide while listening to the tape, make your notes on the study guide and use it while making the recording.
- Use a conversational tone. Talk as you would normally talk to a friend. Explore the subject with the students—don't lecture at them.
  - Vary your tone of voice frequently.
  - Speak cheerfully and enthusiastically.
  - Enunciate clearly.
  - Speak rapidly (most people can listen faster than the average person talks).
  - Minimize *uhs* and other distracting speech habits.
- Direct the student's attention to what you will discuss before discussing it. Tell the student what to look for. For example, if the diagram is on page 4, tell the listener, "Look at the diagram on page 4. There you will see. . . . " The same technique is necessary if you are using slides in conjunction

with the audiotape. "As you see in Slide 6, the process starts in the upper right-hand corner and proceeds. . . . "

- Provide a brief musical interlude (approximately 10 seconds) as a signal for the student to turn off the tape recorder and perform any activities or exercises. The student can then return to the tape, hear the music again, and know that nothing has been missed.
- Include a tone or other nonvocal signal to indicate when to advance slides rather than continually repeating "Change to the next slide." Electronic tone devices are available for this purpose; also, a door chime can be used, or you can tap a pen or spoon on a half-full drinking glass.

Preventing Accidental Erasure

Cassette tapes provide protection against accidental erasure. At the rear corners of each cassette are small tabs that can be broken out. The tab on the left controls the top side of the tape (side A); the tab on the right controls the bottom side (side B). No machine will record a new sound on a side of a tape for which the appropriate tab has been broken out.

If you want to rerecord the cassette, carefully place some cellophane tape over the hole where the tab was removed. The tape can then be used for a new recording. Most prerecorded tapes come with both tabs already removed to prevent accidental erasure.

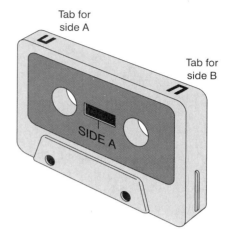

Tab for side A

Tab for side B

SIDE A

Checklist for Student/Teacher-Prepared Audiocassettes

- ☐ Minimize extraneous background noise.
- ☐ Maintain constant volume level.
- ☐ Ensure good voice quality and clarity.
- ☐ Express ideas clearly.
- ☐ Maintain conversational tone.
- ☐ Keep listeners involved.
- ☐ Coordinate with worksheet or study guide, if used.
- ☐ Express content clearly.
- ☐ Keep it short.

CASSETTE RECORDER TROUBLESHOOTING
Problems/Possible Remedies

- *Tape comes out of cassettes and snarls around the capstan of recorder:*
  1. Very thin tape, as found in longer-length cassettes (e.g., C-120), is especially prone to this. Convert to shorter-length (thicker) tapes.
  2. The plastic hub of the take-up reel may be rubbing against the cassette. Try rotating the hub with a pencil to free it.
  3. Take-up spindle is not pulling hard enough because of faulty clutch or belt. Have cassette repaired by qualified specialist.
- *"Record" button on cassette will not stay down:* The accidental erasure tab on the back of the cassette has been broken out. Place tape over the gap left by the missing tab if you want to record something new on the cassette.
- *Hiss in background:* Demagnetize the heads (performed by media specialist or technician).
- *Lack of high frequencies:* Head out of alignment or worn. Have heads checked.
- *Low playback volumes:* Heads dirty. Clean with head-cleaning fluid.

FIGURE 6.8
Setup for duplicating by the electronic method.

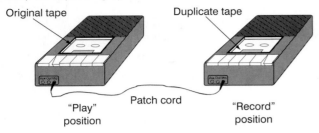

FIGURE 6.9
Teachers can easily and inexpensively create their own audio tapes.

the signals of the original tape and transfers them electronically to the duplicating tape.

If a dual-well cassette recorder, which holds two cassettes, is available, tapes can be copied very easily. Many of these machines can copy a tape at double normal speed, cutting duplicating time in half; check the copy for speed accuracy. Inexpensive dual-well equipment is not noted for its precision; a full-size dual-well tape deck is much more reliable.

The high-speed duplicator method requires a special machine. Master playback machines have a series of up to 10 "slave units," each of which can record a copy of the original tape at 16 times its normal speed.

Multiple copies of a 30-minute cassette tape can be duplicated in about two minutes. Since the master and slave units are connected by a patch cord, fidelity is likely to be very good, and there is no danger of picking up background noise.

You may wish to edit your audiotapes, either to remove errors and imperfections or to adapt a tape to a specific learning situation. Set up two recorders as described for tape duplication and then record just the portion of the original tape that you want on the second tape.

The dual-well cassette recorder facilitates editing. Selected parts of the original can be assembled easily by using the copying feature of these machines.

SELECTING AUDIO MATERIALS

Before selecting your audio materials, you should have analyzed your audience and stated your objective according to the ASSURE model. Then you are ready to select, modify, or design your audio materials. Part of this process involves locating available materials and appraising them. If nothing acceptable can be found or modified, you can produce your own audiocassette tapes as described in the previous section.

Locating Audio Materials

In selecting audio materials to use in your instruction, first determine what materials are available locally.

Consult with a media specialist to determine what is available in your media center. If appropriate materials are not available, refer to the appropriate directories (see Appendix C). Selection guides for music CDs include *Best Rated CDs: Classical* and *Best Rated CDs: Jazz and Pop,* published annually by Peri (Voorheesville, NY).

Appraising Audio Materials

Materials both commercially and locally produced should be previewed and appraised before using them with your students. The "Appraisal Checklist: Audio Materials" can be used to guide your selection decisions.

UTILIZING AUDIO MATERIALS

The next step after selecting or producing your audio materials is to use them with your students. The 5 following Ps are appropriate for group use of audio materials: preview the materials, prepare the materials, prepare the environment, prepare the learners, and provide the learning experience.

AUDIO MATERIALS

KEY WORDS: _____ , _____ , _____

Format
- ☐ **Cassette**
- ☐ **Record**
- ☐ **Compact disc**

Title _____

Series Title (if applicable) _____

Source _____

Date _____ **Cost** _____ **Length** _____ minutes

Subject Area _____

Intended Audience _____

Brief Description

Objectives

Entry Capabilities Required (e.g., prior knowledge, reading ability, vocabulary level, math ability)

Rating	High	Medium	Low	Comments
Match with curriculum	☐	☐	☐	
Accurate and current	☐	☐	☐	
Clear and concise language	☐	☐	☐	
Arouse motivation/maintain interest	☐	☐	☐	
Learner participation	☐	☐	☐	
Technical quality	☐	☐	☐	
Evidence of effectiveness (e.g., field-test results)	☐	☐	☐	
Free from objectionable bias or advertising	☐	☐	☐	
User guide/documentation	☐	☐	☐	
Pacing appropriate for audience	☐	☐	☐	
Clarity of organization	☐	☐	☐	

Strong Points

Weak Points

Recommended Action _____ **Name** _____ **Date** _____

A computer version of this Checklist is found in "The Classroom Link."

Preview the Materials

Audio materials should be previewed using the "Appraisal Checklist" as part of the appraisal process. While previewing them before use, decide how you are going to use them. What excerpts do you plan to use? How are the students going to be involved with the audio materials? What follow-up activities will you use?

Prepare the Materials

When you are going to use audio media for group presentations, you should practice operation of the equipment. Cueing the materials is important to avoid delays and lost time. Prepare your introduction and follow-up. If you must manipulate other materials or objects during the audio presentation, be sure to practice first.

Prepare the Environment

Set up your classroom or learning environment so that all students can hear the audio. Be sure that those who should not be distracted by the sound cannot hear it. For individuals and small groups, headphones should be used. For a large group, do not use a small audio-cassette recorder/playback unit. The speaker is not large enough to provide adequate volume. Be sure that you have a good-quality speaker that does not distort the sound.

Prepare the Learners

Before playing the audio material, communicate to the students how the material relates to what they have studied before, what they should be doing or learning from the materials themselves, and what follow-up activities will be used. If new vocabulary words or technical terms are going to be presented, you should list them on a handout, the chalkboard, or overhead transparency.

Provide the Learning Experience

Before turning on the audio materials, ask students to raise their hand if they cannot hear. Be particularly sensitive if you have any hearing-impaired learners. Practice with the playback equipment before the session. Make sure that it is working properly. Refer to "Cassette Recorder Troubleshooting" (p. 189) if you have problems.

The classroom environment may not be ideal for the academic achievement of hearing-impaired children. Classroom noise and reverberation can cause problems for these children. Potential solutions include relocating them to the front of the room or adding noise damping devices such as drapes and carpeting. Another strategy is the use of a sound field amplification system. Such a system consists of the teacher wearing a wireless microphone and having several small speakers located throughout the classroom. These systems also help children who have colds, those with disorders that might affect their hearing, and those for whom English is a second language.[2]

Student-Based Utilization

We have discussed the group use of audio materials. There are times when students will use audio materials for individual learning and for the creation of their own materials. Applications of student-based utilization were described earlier in this chapter. The teacher's role will vary from that of guide to that of observer, when he or she has limited involvement.

REQUIRE LEARNER PARTICIPATION

Before you begin the lesson, determine how to get and keep your students actively involved. One technique is to give the students a set of questions to answer during the listening. Younger learners may act out the role portrayed in the materials. During foreign language tapes there may be pauses for the learners to practice pronunciation. After listening to a story they may draw a scene from the audio description.

EVALUATE AND REVISE

Determine how effective the audio materials were. You can gather data by making observations, evaluating test results, or discussing the experience with the students. You may decide to revise how the materials were used or to modify the materials themselves.

---

[2]From C. Crandell, Joseph J. Smaldino, and Carol Flexer, *Sound–Field Amplification: Theory and Practical Applications* (San Diego, CA: Singular Publishing Group, Inc., 1995).

An Author Reads Her Short Story

This is a class in contemporary American literature in a community college in the Pacific Northwest. The instructor has decided on Eudora Welty to represent Southern fiction. She has chosen her short story "Why I Live at the P.O." and plans to include a recording of Miss Welty reading the story.

Analyze Learners

General Characteristics

All the students are taking the class because they plan to transfer to a four-year educational institution. Most are recent high school graduates, but some of the women in the class are using the community college to resume educations interrupted by other events in their lives. Reading abilities range from 8th-grade levels to 11th-grade levels.

Entry Competencies

The students are fairly well motivated, but the instructor has discovered that they have little familiarity with contemporary literature. Most can locate Mississippi on a map, but very few of the students have been to the Deep South, so the Mississippi accent of Miss Welty may be difficult for them to understand. Because the story deals with family squabbles, the instructor is counting on the experiences of the older women in the class to give an important dimension to the class discussions.

State Objectives

After listening to the recording, the students will be able to do the following:

1. State the main theme of the story.
2. Discuss the motivations of the main characters.
3. Identify the relationships among the main characters.
4. Compare the behaviors of the characters with those of people they know.

Select Methods, Media, and Materials

The instructor selected "Why I Live at the P.O." because she knew about the recording by the author. She believes that hearing as well as reading the short story will help the slower readers. She knows that Miss Welty is an amateur photographer and that a book of her photographs of people and scenes in her native Jackson, Mississippi, has been published. After securing permission from the publisher, the instructor asks the media center to make a series of slides from selected photographs from her copy of the book to give the students the flavor of the environment of the story. The instructor asks the Southern wife of a faculty member to read the narration she has written to accompany the set of slides. This will give the students some practice listening to a Southern accent before hearing Miss Welty.

Utilize Materials

The classroom is acoustically suitable for hearing the tape, but the instructor realizes that a playback unit with better speakers than those on her portable machine will be necessary. She arranges with the media center to obtain a good playback unit. She has also requested a slide projector and screen and has arranged the slides in the tray.

The reading assignment included material on the influence of the South on Southern writers. On the day before the oral reading, the instructor handed out a sheet listing colloquialisms from the story with explanations.

On the day of the reading, the instructor introduces the woman who will read the narration for the slides and proceeds to present the slide set. The slide presentation elicits a number of questions about life in the South. The instructor then introduces the recording, closing with the warning that contrary to what they may have heard about languorous Southern speech, Eudora Welty speaks very rapidly.

Require Learner Participation

The students are encouraged to ask questions during and following the slide presentation. They take notes while the story is being read. After the recording, the class engages in a discussion of the short story. The older women in the class give their insights into the problems of family relations.

As a culminating exercise, the students are asked to write a short essay comparing the characters in the story with people they know.

Evaluate and Revise

From the discussion in class, the instructor determines that the recording added to the understanding of the theme and the motivations of the characters. On the basis of the response to the slide presentation, the instructor decides to use the technique in other units of the course.

The essays demonstrate that the students gave a good deal of thought to the way behavior patterns are influenced by where people live. A brief multiple-choice test on the people in the story is used to determine how well the students understood the interactions among the characters.

A computer template for a Blueprint is found in "The Classroom Link."

REFERENCES

Print References

Bloodgood, Janet W. "The First Draft on Tape (In the Classroom)." *Reading Teacher* (November 1989): 188.

Boody, Charles G. "New Tools for Music Education." *Music Educators Journal* (November 1992): 26–29.

Brown, Cynthia S. *Like It Was: A Complete Guide to Writing Oral History.* New York: Teachers and Writers Collaborative, 1988.

Christenson, Peter G. "Children's Use of Audio Media." *Communication Research* (July 1985): 327–343.

Conte, Richard, and Humphreys, Rita. "Repeated Readings Using Audiotaped Material Enhances Oral Reading with Children with Reading Difficulties." *Journal of Communication Disorders* (February 1989): 114–118.

Egbert, Joy. "Talk to Me: An Exploratory Study of Audiotaped Dialogue Journals." *Journal of Intensive English Studies* (Fall 1992): 91–100.

Harnishfeger, L. *Basic Practice in Listening*. Denver, CO: Love Publishing, 1990.

Hartley, James. "Using Principles of Text Design to Improve the Effectiveness of Audiotapes." *British Journal of Educational Technology* (January 1988): 4–16.

Hickey, Gail M. "And Then What Happened Grandpa?: Oral History Projects in the Elementary Classroom." *Social Education* (April–May 1991): 216–217.

James, Charles J. "Are You Listening: The Practical Components of Listening Comprehension." *Foreign Language Annals* (April 1984): 129–133.

Jarnow, Jill. *All Ears: How to Choose and Use Recorded Music for Children*. New York: Penguin Books, 1991.

Jonor, Lloyd. "Teaching by Tape: Some Benefits, Problems and Solutions." *Distance Education, 13* (1992) 1, 93–107.

Kaplan, Jane P. "The Role of the Active Listener." *French Review* (February 1988): 369–376.

Kersten, Fred. "A/V Alternatives for Interesting Homework." *Music Educators Journal* (January 1993): 33–35.

Larsen, S., and Jorgensen, N. "Talking Books for Preschool Children." *Journal of Visual Impairment and Blindness* (February 1989): 118–119.

Loriene, Roy. "Planning an Oral History Project." *Journal of Youth Services in Libraries* (Summer 1993): 409–413.

McAlpine, Lynn. "Teacher as Reader: Oral Feedback on ESL Student Writing." *TESL Canada Journal* (November 1989): 62–67.

Moody, Kate. "Audio Tapes and Books: Perfect Partners." *School Library Journal* (February 1989): 27–29.

Reissman, Rose. "An English Teacher's Proposal: Teaching Literature Using Audiocassettes." *English Journal* (January 1992): 75–76.

Reissman, Rose. "Reclaiming Audio Cassettes for Multimedia Writing." *Writing Notebook: Visions for Learning* (November–December 1993): 36, 41.

Rickelman, Robert J., and Henk, William A. "Children's Literature and Audio-Visual Technologies." *Reading Teacher* (May 1990): 682–684.

Sommers, Jeffrey. "The Effects of Tape-Recorded Commentary on Student Revision: A Case Study." *Journal of Teaching Writing* (Fall–Winter 1989): 49–75.

Tucker, Judith Cook. "Let Their Voices Be Heard! Building a Multicultural Audio Collection." *Multicultural Review* (April 1992): 16–21.

Wieder, Alan. "Oral History in the Classroom: An Exploratory Essay." *Social Studies* (March–April 1984): 71–74.

Wigginton, Elliot. *Sometimes A Shining Moment: The Foxfire Experience*. Garden City, NY: Anchor Books, 1986.

Wood, Dorothy Ann, et al. "The Effects of Tape-Recorded Self-Instruction Cues on the Mathematics Performance of Students with Learning Disabilities." *Journal of Learning Disabilities* (April 1993): 250–258, 269.

Zimmerman, William. *How to Tape Instant Oral Biographies*. New York: Guarionex Press, 1982.

Audiovisual References

Basic Audio. Alexandria, VA: Smith-Mattingly Productions, 1979. Videocassette. 30 minutes.

How Audio Recordings Are Made. Pleasantville, NY: Educational Audio-Visual, 1988. Videocassette. 32 minutes.

Learning About Sound. Chicago: Encyclopaedia Britannica Educational Corporation, 1975. 16mm film. 17 minutes.

Sound Recording and Reproduction. Salt Lake City, UT: Media Systems, Inc., 1978. 6 filmstrips with audiocassettes.

Tape Recorders. Salt Lake City, UT: Media Systems, Inc., 1978. Filmstrip with audiocassette.

Utilizing the Tape Recorder in Teaching. Salt Lake City, UT: Media Systems, Inc., 1975. 2 filmstrips with audiocassette.

The following ½-inch VHS videocassettes are available from Audiovisual Center Marketing, C215 Seashore Hall, University of Iowa, Iowa City, IA 52242.

Audio Made Easy. 1989. 10 minutes.

Portable Audio Cassette Recorder. 1983. 7 minutes.

Sharp Audiocassette Recorder. 1989. 14 minutes.

VIDEO AND FILM

Video and film combine motion, color, and sound in ways that can dramatize ideas better than any other medium. Your students can experience the past, present, and future without leaving the classroom. They can be transported inside the human body, around the world, or out beyond the solar system. Motion media lend themselves to all types of objectives—cognitive, affective, motor, and interpersonal.

To get the best results from video and film you need to select materials wisely and use good showmanship skills. It seems simple but certain critical steps must be taken so that you don't end up with a botched presentation.

As with pictures and audio, students can produce their own video presentations. This is frequently done as a way of reporting a group project.

KNOWLEDGE OBJECTIVES

1. Identify five common video formats and compare the characteristics, advantages, and limitations of the various formats.
2. Compare and contrast video and film on technical and pedagogical grounds.
3. Describe five attributes of motion media.
4. Compare the advantages and limitations of motion media.
5. Create original examples of applications of motion media in each instructional domain—cognitive, affective, motor, and interpersonal.
6. Describe techniques for video design and production by students and teachers.
7. Characterize the acceptance of video in education and in corporate settings.
8. Outline the process for selecting motion media, including at least five appraisal criteria.
9. Describe instructional applications that are especially appropriate for motion media.
10. Describe the ideal physical arrangements for class viewing of video. Your description must include seating, monitor placement, lighting, and volume, along with the minimum and maximum viewing distances and angles.

APPLICATION OBJECTIVES

1. Preview a video or film and appraise it using a form such as the "Appraisal Checklist: Video and Film" on page 214.
2. Observe a teacher using a film or video program in a classroom situation and critique his or her practices.
3. Use one or more of the video and film directories described in Appendix C to compile a list of films or video programs available on a topic of interest to you.
4. Plan a lesson in a subject area of your choice in which you will incorporate the use of a film or video program. Follow the outline shown in the "Blueprint" on page 222.
5. Preview one of the videos or films described in this chapter. Prepare a review, either written (about 700 words) or recorded on audiotape (approximately five minutes long). Briefly summarize the content and describe your reaction to it.
6. Demonstrate your ability to use the steps to utilize motion media effectively in a lesson.
7. Set up, operate, and troubleshoot 16mm projectors, video players/recorders, and video projectors.

LEXICON

video
persistence of vision
high-definition television (HDTV)
digital video

compact disc interactive (CDI)
digital video interactive (DVI)
film

frame
time lapse
slow motion
animation

documentary
charge-coupled device (CCD)

The instructional applications of video and film will be examined side-by-side in this chapter. Historically, these media had different origins. Film, the earlier of the two, originated in the chemical process of photography, whereas video is based on the electronic technology of television. The recording of moving images has progressed from film (chemical process) to videotape (electronic and magnetic process) to discs made through the process of digitizing. All these formats are currently used to store and display moving images, which are accompanied by sound. As we will see, the formats differ considerably in cost, convenience, and flexibility.

This chapter considers how the recorded moving image is displayed and manipulated by the teacher or learner. Chapter 9 addresses multimedia using motion video in the form of computer-based interactive video. Chapter 10 deals with the many ways video and audio signals are transmitted to the learning site and the instructional implications of those delivery systems.

VIDEO

The primary meaning of **video** is the display of images on a television-type screen (the Latin word *video* means "I see"). Any media format that employs a cathode-ray screen to present the picture portion of the message can be referred to as video. Thus, we have videocassettes, videodiscs, interactive video, video games, and so on.

The phosphorescent images of video are composed of dots of varying intensity on the screen. Every 30th of a second, 525 lines of dots are "sprayed" onto the back of the cathode-ray screen, creating one full screen. The rapid succession of screens is perceived as a moving image because of an optical phenomenon called **persistence of vision:** the eye and brain retain an image cast upon the retina of the eye for a fraction of a second after that image is removed from view. If a second image is presented before the trace of the previous image fades, the images blend together, creating the illusion of continuous motion.

Originally, the concept of video was synonymous with that of broadcast television, but the concept has expanded dramatically in recent years. New technologies connected to television sets have proliferated—such as home computers, videocassette recorders, video games, and specialized cable TV services. Other hybrids are still emerging. These new services continue to multiply because it tends to be cheaper and more efficient to transmit information electronically than to transport information, goods, and people physically.

Video versions of the moving image are recorded on tape or disc, each packaged in forms that vary in size,

FIGURE 7.1
"I think it's an old VCR."

shape, speed, recording method, and playback mechanism. The most common video formats are summarized in Table 7.1.

Videotape

The VHS ½-inch format is the preferred medium for commercial distribution of moving images. Virtually all of us have rented a VHS version of a movie, and most of us have recorded a TV program on VHS for later or repeated viewing. Time-shifting the TV schedule has become a major sport in many homes. VHS is also the current preferred format for amateur and nonstudio production of recorded moving images in education. Amateur video production is so prevalent that network TV programs such as "I Witness Video" and "America's Funniest Home Videos" can be sustained by it.

Within the past decade, VHS has replaced 16mm film as the format of choice for distribution of educational motion media. The VHS version is considerably cheaper than the 16mm film version and has been so universally accepted that most companies offer their recent productions in VHS only.

A relatively new format is 8mm videotape. The smaller size makes for a more compact video recorder (palmcorder). This format is being widely accepted by the amateur videographer for recording family events and other occasions of personal interest. However, the size advantage may not be significant enough to replace VHS in the education and training markets. This compact format, referred to as Hi8, is bridging the gap between the consumer world and the professional world.

TABLE 7.1
Common video formats

FORMAT	SPEED	ADVANTAGES	LIMITATIONS
Videodisc Diameter: 12 in.	30 min. per side	Flexible storage capacity: can hold 54,000 images, still or motion, or audio Fast random access to specific frames Highly durable; no wear with use Inexpensive when mass-produced	Not for local production Originals expensive to produce
Videocassette (U-matic) Tape width: 3/4 in.	3.75 ips[1] (10–60 min.)	Self-contained and self-threading Superior video quality Studio production, not distribution	Found in corporate training and TV news field recording, not in education
Videocassette VHS Tape width: 1/2 in.	1.31 ips[1] (120 min at standard speed)	Self-contained and self-threading More compact than U-matic Abundant software available Easy local production	Video quality low; not broadcast quality Quality deteriorates with use
Videocassette (Hi 8) Tape width: 8 mm (about 1/4 in.)	1.31 ips[1] (120 min at standard speed)	Most compact format Full compatibility among all makes and models Easy local production	Video quality lower Limited acceptance in education; little software available
Compact disc (CDI and DVI) Diameter: 4.72 in.	Variable high speed	Easy to use Low-cost hardware and software Worldwide standard Self-contained hardware	Limited educational software Some hardware cannot be connected to keyboards, printers, etc. Does not show full-motion video

[1] ips = inches per second.

Math . . . Who Needs It?

Video

This videocassette is aimed at parents and their kids. It gives a perspective on the rewards and opportunities open to anyone with good math skills. It challenges myths about math, pokes fun at society's misconceptions of the subject, and provokes viewers to think and talk about math in a more positive way.

Source: FASE Productions.

Videodisc

Videodiscs resemble a silver, shiny phonograph record (Figure 7.2). They are also referred to as laser discs. Images and sound are recorded in analog format.

Each side of a videodisc can hold up to 30 minutes of motion video images, or up to 54,000 still images, or a mix of both motion and still images. As with the CD, the videodisc can be indexed for rapid location of any

Groupthink

Video

This video presents a thought-provoking analysis of the complexity of modern decision making. It portrays the dynamics and behaviors that signal the presence and pitfalls of groupthink.

Source: CRM Films.

FIGURE 7.2
A videodisc and player.

part of the program material. However, the indexing must be incorporated into the disc during production; it cannot be added by the user. When a videodisc playback unit is connected to a computer, the information on the disc can become an integral part of a computer-assisted instructional program. The computer program makes use of the index on the disc. See Chapter 9 for a further discussion of interactive video discs.

Laser disc images are sharper than those from a videotape. Videodisc images have a horizontal resolution of 350 lines, compared with only 240 lines for a videocassette. With **high-definition television (HDTV),** the images are equal in quality to 16mm film. In contrast to film, the quality of videodisc images will not deteriorate with repeated use. Film is notorious for fading and changing color over time and with frequent showings. Also, the audio quality of videodisc is significantly better than that of film or videotape.

Thousands of educational videodiscs are now available and priced from $30 to $500. Educational films, commercial movies, and documentaries are available on videodisc at prices lower than for videotape.

Videodiscs are becoming an increasingly popular method of displaying movies. In the case of film classics, for example, critical analysis of the film and its production background are often included.

Several educationally valuable features of videodisc are not available with film or videotape. Videodisc images can be "stepped through" frame-by-frame, can be "scanned" (fast forward), or played at various speeds in both forward and reverse. In addition, videodiscs have two audio tracks—for either separate narrations or stereo sound. For example, two different languages can narrate the moving images; the narrations can be at two different levels of difficulty; or one narration can be for the learners and the other for the instructor.

One drawback, however, is that currently it is difficult and expensive to record your own videodiscs. The playback equipment for videodiscs is nowhere nearly as common as videotape player/recorders. One reason for this is that videodiscs cannot be recorded on; therefore, videodisc equipment can only play back, not record.

Digital Video

Just as audio can be digitized (as described on page 183), video images can be converted into a digital format. **Digital video** images can be manipulated (e.g., content, size, and color can be changed), stored, duplicated, and replayed without loss of quality. Since videodiscs are in analog format, you cannot change the material on it; but with digital video stored on CDs or in a computer, you and your students can edit the content and sequence of the moving images.

Any analog video image from broadcast television, videotape, videodisc, or a video camera can be digitized and stored on a computer. You and your students can then edit the video within the computer, without using videotape editing equipment. The computer can also be used as a display device: using a digitizing camera for motion media, moving images from any of the analog sources can be displayed on the screen without being stored.

There are several methods for storing moving images in a computer. One format is QuickTime for use with Apple Macintosh computers. Applications include *Compton's Multimedia Encyclopedia,* which incorporates QuickTime "movies." For student portfolios and projects, moving images can be incorporated with graphics, visuals, and text. One limitation of QuickTime is that the moving images are shown at only 15 frames per second (full-motion video is shown at 30 frames per second), so the movement is jerky. Also, the moving image is currently limited in size to about 25% of the monitor screen.

Compact Disc Interactive (CDI). Compact disc interactive (CDI) is a system for delivery of digital video, audio, text, and visuals. The information is stored on a CD. The disc is used with a special player that has a built-in computer and must be connected to a monitor. CDI players look like audio CD players and can play audio CDs.

CDI systems were designed for the home consumer market. Many current applications are intended for entertainment, but educational applications are increasing.

The most appealing aspect of CDI is its interactive aspects. Learners can manipulate the material contained on the discs. Students can learn by "playing" with information or exploring topics of interest. Teachers can structure lessons or complete courses around CDI products. Additional information on CDI is presented in Chapter 9.

Digital Video Interactive (DVI). Similar to CDI, **digital video interactive (DVI)** allows up to 72 minutes of full-motion video (30 frames per second)

to be stored on a CD-ROM. Since it is in digital format, DVI can also incorporate still visuals, text, graphics, and audio.

FILM

Film refers to the celluloid material on which a series of still images is chemically imprinted. This series of transparent images, when projected at 24 **frames** (or images) per second, is perceived by humans as a moving image. As with video, the illusion of motion is caused by persistence of vision. (See "Close-up: Why a Movie Moves.")

Motion picture film comes in various widths and image sizes. For movies shown in theaters, 35mm film is most commonly used. For films shown in schools, 16mm film is the most common format.

DIFFERENCES BETWEEN FILM AND VIDEO

Because media research indicates that displays having the same basic features—motion, color, and sound—have the same basic effects on cognitive, affective, and motor learning, you might conclude that for pedagogical and practical purposes they are essentially equivalent.[1] Not so. Videotape and videodisc are pedagogically more flexible than film. Both video formats have fast-forward and reverse search capabilities, whereas film does not. Video formats, particularly videodisc, can be indexed, making it possible to locate specific sections of a program.

Certain special effects, such as slow motion, can be obtained during the video disc presentation, whereas slow motion must be built into film in the production stage. Video cassette recorders (VCRs) can be remotely controlled, meaning that the instructor (or operator) does not have to stay close to the machine. Because of the ease of operating the equipment, video lends itself to individual study much more readily than film. All of this means that video can be incorporated more easily than film into a variety of pedagogical methods. It is possible to alter the motion sequence, preprogram that sequence, and operate video equipment by remote control.

A VCR and TV set are easier to use than a film projector. Many people have learned to operate a VCR. On the other hand, not many people, even as adults, know how to operate the more complex film projector and set up the screen. With video, the operator does not have to

---

[1]Gene L. Wilkinson, *Media in Instruction: 60 Years of Research* (Washington, DC: Association for Educational Communications and Technology, 1980).

CLOSE-UP

WHY A MOVIE MOVES

Because the camera photographs a scene as a series of separate, discrete images, motion picture film consists of a sequence of slightly different still pictures called frames. When these frames are projected on a screen at a certain speed (at least 12, usually 24, frames per second), the images appear to be in continuous motion.

Each still picture (frame) is held stationary at the film aperture (1) (on left of diagram). While it is stationary, the shutter (2) is open, permitting the light from the projection lamp to pass through the image, go through a focusing lens system (3), and display the picture on the screen. Then the shutter closes and a device like a claw (4) engages the sprocket holes and pulls the film down so that the next frame is in position, as shown on the right side of the diagram. The claw withdraws, the shutter opens, and the next picture is projected on the screen.

Although the film moves past the aperture intermittently, the top sprocket wheel (5) pulls the film into the projector at a steady 24 frames per second (sound speed), and the bottom sprocket wheel (6) pulls the film out of the projector at the same steady rate of speed. If no slack were put into the film at the upper and lower loops (7 and 8), the film would be torn apart. These two loops compensate for the stop and start motions of the film. Because sound cannot be accurately recorded or repro-

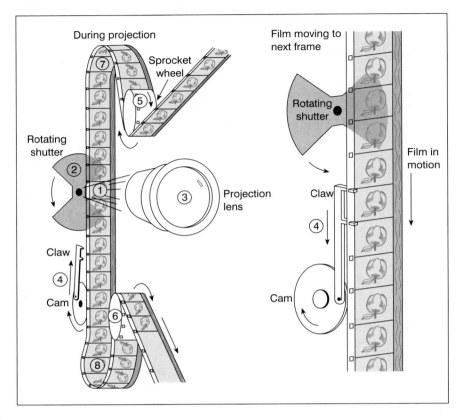

duced on a film that is not moving smoothly, the intermittent movement of the film must be smoothed out by the bottom sprocket and an idler system before the film reaches the sound drum.

From Raymond Wyman, *Mediaware Selection, Operation, and Maintenance*, 2d ed. Copyright© 1969, Wm. C. Brown, Dubuque, Iowa, Reprinted by permission.

---

worry about focusing the image or making sure the screen is oriented properly with the projector. In addition, the film image on the screen is more easily degraded by ambient light.

If the video image has to be projected, the operational advantages of video are reduced. Focusing and aligning the video image on the screen can be more time-consuming than adjusting the film image.

A video copy of a title is much less expensive than its film counterpart and costs less to maintain. Replacement of damaged film footage is a major maintenance item. Media centers have found that purchasing, handling, storing, distributing, and maintaining video is a great deal easier on the budget than film. As for equipment, the combination of video player and monitor costs less than a 16mm film projector.

There is no question that the projected image of a new film print is still superior in color saturation, range

of contrast, and definition to that of video, although the newer video projectors and high-definition television (HDTV) are closing the image gap.

The quality of the video image is determined primarily by the number of lines that are projected on the front surface of the tube. The greater the number of lines, the sharper the image and the more accurate the rendition of color. At present, the standard used in North America is 525 lines scanned on the tube 30 times every second. HDTV doubles the number of lines. Projected video in particular is improved dramatically.

SPECIAL ATTRIBUTES OF MOTION MEDIA

Because most of us are inclined to think of video and film as media designed to produce a realistic image of the world around us, we tend to forget that a basic attribute of motion media is their ability to manipulate temporal and spatial perspectives. Manipulation of time and space not only serves dramatic and creative ends; it also has important implications for instruction.

Alteration of Time

Motion media permit us to increase or decrease the amount of time required to observe an event. For example, it would take an impossibly long time for students to actually witness a highway being constructed, but a carefully edited film of the different activities that go into building a highway can recreate the essentials of such an event in a few minutes.

We can also take out pieces of time. For example, you are familiar with the type of sequence in which a scene fades out and then fades in the next day. Time has been taken out of the sequence, but we accept that the night has passed even though we did not experience it in real time.

Compression of Time. Motion media can compress the time it takes to observe an event. We have all seen moving images of flowers slowly opening before our eyes (Figure 7.3). This technique, known as **time**

▼ MEDIA FILE

Recycling Is Fun!
Film/Video

Three captivating young children explore the three *R*s of recycling—reduce, recycle, and reuse. To educate themselves, they visit a landfill, a recycling center, and their local supermarket to find out what they can do to help with our solid waste crisis. They discover their own power to recycle and choose what they buy, for the benefit of their world. A study guide is provided for the teacher and students.

Source: Bullfrog Films.

FIGURE 7.3
In time-lapse, a slow event is condensed into a short screen time by allowing several seconds to elapse between shooting each frame of film.

lapse, has important instructional uses. For example, the process of a chrysalis turning into a butterfly is too slow for easy classroom observation. However, through time-lapse cinematography, the butterfly can emerge from the chrysalis in a matter of minutes on the screen.

Expansion of Time. Time can also be expanded in motion media through a technique called **slow motion.** Some events occur too fast to be seen by the naked eye. By photographing such events at extremely high speeds and then projecting the image at normal speed, we can observe what is happening (see Figure 7.4). For example, a chameleon catches an insect too rapidly for the naked eye to observe; high-speed cinematography can slow down the motion so that the process can be observed.

Manipulation of Space

Motion media permit us to view phenomena in microcosm and macrocosm—that is, at extremely close range or from a vast distance.

The television program "Movie Magic" demonstrates how special effects specialists combine different spatial perspectives to create spaces that didn't exist before. Excerpts from feature films, such as *Die Hard, Gremlins 2,* and *The Abyss,* are used to show how motion media can manipulate space.

Mr. Edison's Dream

Thomas A. Edison, whose work in developing the kinetograph (a camera that used film rolls) and the kinetoscope (a peep-show device), contributed greatly to the development of motion pictures. He had high hopes for the instructional value of this popular medium.

As depicted in the cartoon from the *Chicago Tribune* of 1923, he fully expected the motion picture to revolutionize education, give new life to curriculum content, and provide students with new motivation for learning.

We all know that the history of the motion picture took a turn quite different from that anticipated by Edison. Movies were quickly and eagerly adopted as an entertainment medium, but in education the acceptance of film as a useful medium has been glacially slow. Part of the problem has been technical. The standard size for film quickly became 35mm, which meant that equipment for projection was bulky and expensive. Also, the film base that was used for many years, cellulose nitrate, was extremely flammable. Many state regulations required a film to be projected only from an enclosed booth and by a licensed projectionist. Thus, films were too expensive for schools to use for other than special occasions. There was also resistance on the part of the educational establishment to acknowledge the educational value of this "frivolous" new invention. Its very success as an entertainment medium automatically made it suspect as an educational tool.

The first extensive use of film as an educational medium occurred during World War I, outside the classroom, when psychologists working with the U.S. Army produced a series of training films on venereal disease. Afterward, several prestigious organizations combined forces to produce a series of U.S. history films that became known as the Yale Chronicles of American Photoplays. This series was the subject of extensive research and documented for the first time the effective-

THE CHANGING WORLD

(Mr. Edison predicts motion pictures will take the place of books in the schools.)

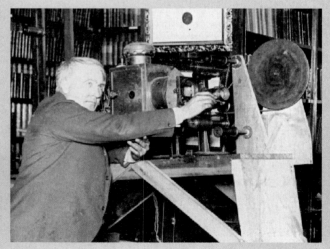

Thomas A. Edison

ness of films in direct instruction, even though the films were considerably handicapped because they were made in the silent era.

When sound on film finally became a reality, many educators resisted its use in educational films. They felt that by putting a sound track on a film the producer was imposing external standards on every class in the country. They insisted that teachers should be free to narrate films according to principles and practices prescribed locally. Teacher narration of films was favored by theorists and administrators but not by practitioners. (Anyone who has ever attempted to narrate a film knows what a difficult task it can be.) Some administrators also resisted the use of sound films in the classroom because this newer technology made existing inventories of silent-film projectors and silent films obsolete.

World War II gave an even greater impetus to the educational use of films. In a crash program to train Americans in the skills necessary to produce weapons, the Office of Education engaged in an extensive program of film production under the leadership of Floyde Brooker. Most of the films produced by this office were technical.

The armed forces also produced films during this period for training purposes, and their research indicated that films (and other audiovisual media) contributed significantly to the success of their training programs.

The success of instructional technology, including film, in achieving war-related instructional objectives created sentiment among educators and laypeople alike for more widespread use of this technology in the nation's schools.

The late 1950s witnessed the introduction of 8mm film into education. Cartridged, looped 8mm films quickly acquired the label "single-concept films" because they concentrated on presenting a single event or process. Because 8mm cartridges were easily inserted in their projectors and the projectors were small, portable, and simple to use, they lent themselves particularly well to individual instruction and small-group study. However, mechanical problems with the projectors and the vulnerability of the film itself discouraged its use.

In the meantime, as sales of 16mm educational films increased, commercial publishers were encouraged to produce film "packages." Along with the individual film for a specific learning objective, companies began to market series of films to be incorporated as major components of various courses. This trend led in the late 1950s to the introduction of complete courses on film. Encyclopaedia Britannica Films, for example, produced a complete course in high school physics, consisting of 162 half-hour films in color.

Television soon became the primary source of most filmed courses used in the instructional setting, and with the rise of videotape technology, television itself, both educational and commercial, became a major force in the growing use of recorded moving images for instructional purposes.

Mr. Edison's dream of the immediate and overwhelming impact of film on education may have been a little fuzzy around the edges—as dreams sometimes are—but it was not, after all, so far off the mark. It took a quarter century longer than the Wizard of Menlo Park had anticipated for film to become an important factor in education and another quarter century for it to reach a state of instructional prominence. His dream did come true, in its own time and in a more realistic way, as dreams sometimes do.

▲

Production of a World War II training film for the U.S. Army.

FIGURE 7.4

In slow motion, a fast event is expanded into a longer screen time by shooting at a speed greater than 24 frames per second.

Animation

Time and space can also be manipulated by **animation.** This is a technique in which the producer gives motion to otherwise inanimate objects. There are various and more or less sophisticated techniques for achieving animation, but basically animation is made up of a series of photographs of small displacements of objects or images. If such an object is photographed, then moved a very short distance and photographed on one frame of film, moved again, then photographed again, and so on, the object when projected will look as though it has been continuously moving through space.

With the continuing evolution of computer programs that can manipulate visual images adroitly, we are experiencing a rediscovery of the art of animation through the video display format (Figure 7.5). Computer-generated animation sequences are being used

FIGURE 7.5

Animation in video is easy to produce with the aid of computer-generated images.

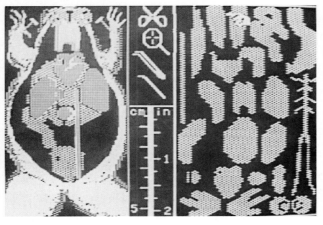

more and more in instructional video programs to depict complex or rapid processes in simplified form.

Understanding Motion Media Conventions

The devices and techniques used in motion media to manipulate time and space are for most of us readily accepted conventions. We understand that the athlete whose jump is stopped in midair is not actually frozen in space, that the flashback is not an actual reversal of our normal time continuum, that the light bulb does not really disintegrate slowly enough for us to see that it implodes rather than explodes. Teachers, however, must keep in mind that the ability to make sense out of motion media conventions is an acquired skill. When do children learn to handle flashbacks, dissolves, jump cuts, and so on? Unfortunately, we know very little about when and how children learn to make sense of manipulation of reality, and much research on the matter remains to be done.

Motion media are not alone in their reliance on accepted conventions for interpretation and apprecia-

▼ **MEDIA FILE**

The City of Gold
Film/Video

Winner of many awards and an Oscar nominee, this film classic (now available in video) tells the story of Dawson City, in the Klondike, scene of the greatest gold rush in history. The film begins with footage of present-day Dawson City, then moves to a fascinating series of still photos taken during the gold rush, and returns to the present. Provocative narration describes life in the gold camp and raises questions about what was sought by those who rushed to the Klondike. The music adds greatly to the atmosphere of the film.

Source: National Film Board of Canada.

tion. Flashback techniques are regularly used in literature and usually accepted by readers. The theatrical convention of the aside is readily accepted by playgoers. The following anecdote about Picasso illustrates how a new artistic convention may seem to the uninitiated as merely a distortion of reality rather than, as intended, a particular and valid view of reality. It also illustrates how a convention (in this case a convention of photography) can become so readily accepted and commonplace that we are amusingly surprised at being reminded it exists.

Picasso showed an American soldier through his villa one day, and on completion of the tour the young man felt compelled to confess that he didn't dig Picasso's weird way of painting, because nothing on the canvas looked the way it really is. Picasso turned the conversation to more acceptable matters by asking the soldier if he had a girl back in the States. The boy proudly pulled out a wallet photograph. As Picasso handed it back, he said: "She's an attractive girl, but isn't she awfully small?"[2]

Advantages

- *Motion.* Moving images have an obvious advantage over still visuals in portraying concepts in which motion is essential to mastery (such as tying knots or operating a potter's wheel).
- *Processes.* Operations, such as assembly line steps or science experiments, in which sequential movement is critical can be shown more effectively by means of motion media.
- *Risk-free observation.* Visual recordings allow learners to observe phenomena that might be dangerous to view directly, such as an eclipse of the sun, a volcanic eruption, or warfare.
- *Dramatization.* Dramatic recreations can bring historical events and personalities to life. They allow us to observe and analyze human interactions.
- *Skill learning.* Research indicates that mastery of physical skills requires repeated observation and practice. Through recorded media, a performance can be viewed over and over again for emulation.
- *Affective learning.* Because of their great potential for emotional impact, video and films can be useful in shaping personal and social attitudes. Documentary and propaganda video and films have often been found to have a measurable impact on audience attitudes.
- *Problem solving.* Open-ended dramatizations are frequently used to present unresolved confrontations, leaving it to the viewers to discuss various ways of dealing with the problem.

- *Cultural understanding.* We can develop a gut-level appreciation for other cultures by seeing film and video depictions of everyday life in other societies. The whole genre of ethnographic films can serve this purpose. Examples of feature-length ethnographic films include *The Hunters, The Tribe That Hides from Man, The Nuer,* and *River of Sand.*
- *Establishing commonality.* By viewing video programs or films together, a disparate group of people can build up a common base of experience to discuss an issue effectively.

Limitations

- *Fixed pace.* Although videos and films can be stopped for discussion, this is not usually done in group showings. And even though the videocassette player has more flexibility than the film projector, one is tempted to let the video play uninterrupted. Because the program runs at a fixed pace, some viewers may fall behind while others are waiting impatiently for the next point. Not everyone's mind runs at 24 (or 30) frames per second.
- *Still phenomena.* Although film and video are advantageous for concepts that involve motion, they may be unsuitable for other topics where detailed study of a single visual is involved (e.g., a map, a wiring diagram, or an organization chart).
- *Misinterpretation.* Documentaries and dramatizations often present a complex or sophisticated treatment of an issue. A scene intended as satire might be taken literally by a young or naive viewer. The thoughts of a main character may be interpreted as the attitudes and values of the producer. For example, the film *Phoebe* uses a stream-of-consciousness approach as Phoebe fantasizes about what the reactions of her parents and her boyfriend will be to her announcement that she is pregnant. Some students (and parents) have misinterpreted the speculations of a troubled mind as being the attitude of the filmmaker toward all the characters in the story.
- *Cost.* Film has become an expensive medium, both the software (films themselves) and the hardware (film projectors). The video version of a title is generally a fraction of the cost of the film version, and the combination of a video player and video monitor costs less than a film projector. These are major reasons why institutions are willing to write off their considerable capital investment in films and projectors and adopt videocassettes as the format of choice for moving images.
- *Logistics.* Because of the cost per unit, videos and films are often acquired, stored, and distributed by central agencies in school districts, regional centers, universities, training centers, and public libraries. Collections in individual schools are normally very

[2]Joan Rosengren Forsdale and Louis Forsdale, "Film Literacy," *Teachers College Record* (May 1966), p. 609.

small. Training programs usually rent videos and films from a distributor or from corporate headquarters. This means videos and films have to be ordered well in advance of their intended use. Arrangements have to be made so that the correct title arrives at the right place at the right time and that the proper equipment is available and in good condition. The complexity of these arrangements may discourage many instructors.

Applications

Videos and films are available on almost any topic and for all types of learners in all the domains of instruction described in Chapter 2—cognitive, affective, motor skill, and interpersonal. As pointed out under their attributes, video and film can manipulate both time and space. They can take the learner almost anywhere and extend students' interests beyond the walls of the classroom. Objects too large to bring into the classroom can be studied as well as those too small to see with the naked eye. Events too dangerous to observe, such as an eclipse of the sun, can be studied safely. The time and expense of a field trip can be avoided. Many companies and national parks provide video tours to observe assembly lines, services, and the features of nature.

Video and film can be used to provide baseline knowledge for all learners. The packaged media can serve as an alternative to lectures. Students are given a viewing assignment before coming to class. Class time is then used for hands-on experiences, discussion, or applications of knowledge.

In the cognitive domain, learners can observe dramatic recreations of historical events and actual record-ings of more recent events. Color, sound, and motion make personalities come to life. The textbook can be enhanced by showing processes, relationships, and techniques. Students can read books in conjunction with viewing videotapes and films. The books can be read before the showing as an introduction to the topic, or the program can be used to interest students in reading about the topic.

The **documentary** deals with fact, not fiction or fictionalized versions of fact. It attempts to depict essentially true stories about real situations and people. The commercial networks (broadcast and cable) and the Public Broadcasting System regularly produce significant documentaries. Special programs, such as "The Second Russian Revolution," present in-depth analyses of recent events and issues. The miniseries "The Civil War" is an example of a documentary presentation of a critical period in U.S. history. Programs such as "Nova" and the National Geographic specials offer outstanding documentaries in science, culture, and nature. Virtually all television documentaries are available for purchase as videos.

Attitudes can be influenced by role models and dramatic messages on video and film. Because of their great potential for emotional impact, video and film can be useful in shaping personal and social attitudes. Documentary programs have often been found to have a measurable impact on audience attitudes. Cultural understanding can be developed through viewing video and films depicting people from all parts of the globe.

Demonstrations of motor skills can be more easily seen through media than in real life. If you are teaching a step-by-step process, you can show it in real time, sped up to give an overview or slowed down to show specific details. With videodisc you can even stop the

FIGURE 7.6
Documentaries bring real-world experiences into the classroom.

action for careful study or move forward one frame at a time. Recording student performances on videotape can provide practice with feedback. The learner can observe his or her own performance and also receive feedback from colleagues and the instructor.

By viewing a video or film program together, a diverse group of learners can build a common base of experience as a catalyst for discussion. When students are learning interpersonal skills, such as dealing with conflict resolution, counseling, sales techniques, and peer relationships, they can observe others on media for demonstration and analysis. They can then practice their interpersonal skills before a camera, watch themselves, and receive feedback from peers and instructors. Role play vignettes can be analyzed to determine what happened and to ask the learners what they should do next. Open-ended dramatizations can be used to present unresolved confrontations, leaving it to the viewers to discuss various ways of dealing with the problem.

Excerpts from videos and films can be used as a part of oral reports. Students can turn the sound off and use their own narration. Student-produced videotapes and video segments on computers are being used for evaluation. Student portfolios with a multimedia approach are being used instead of word processed term papers. Students can research a topic using books, databases, videotapes, videodiscs, CD-ROMs, and other media. Relevant content can be "captured" on video, edited, and displayed for classmates, parents, and the teacher.

Student-Produced Videos

With video, students and instructors are not limited to off-the-shelf materials but can with reasonable ease prepare custom materials.[3] This feature sets video apart from some of the other media. Do-it-yourself television has become commonplace since the popularization of the battery-operated portable video recording systems.

The development of the camcorder (camera and recorder built into a single book-size unit) has increased the ease and portability of ½-inch recording. It allows video production to be taken into the field, wherever that might be: the science laboratory, the classroom, the counseling office, the athletic field, the factory assembly line, the hospital, the neighborhood, and even the home. Equally important, the simplicity of the system has made it feasible for nonprofessionals, instructors, and students alike to create their own video materials.

Locally produced video can be used for virtually any of the purposes described earlier. Its unique capability is to capture sight and sound for immediate playback. This medium thus works well with activities that are enhanced by immediate feedback: group dynamics sessions, athletic practice, skills training, and interpersonal techniques.

Other applications that emphasize the local aspect of video production include the following:

- Dramatization of student stories, songs, and poems
- Student documentaries of school or neighborhood issues
- Preservation of local folklore
- Demonstrations of science experiments and safety drills
- Replays of field trips for in-class follow-up
- Career information on local businesses

Growing numbers of school library media centers are now adding to their environments a small video studio for student productions. Many students come to school with home experiences in using portable cameras. Student production will increase as equipment continues to become less expensive, more light sensitive, and easier to use. Elementary and secondary students can be involved in scripting, recording, editing, and revising their own video productions.

As with all media production, preproduction planning is necessary. The storyboarding process, described in Chapters 3 and 5, can be used by students of all ages to facilitate planning and production of video. Storyboarding is particularly helpful when a group of students is cooperatively involved in designing a video.

Video production requires a camera and microphone. Most cameras are of the viewfinder type. The viewfinder camera is so named because it has built into it a small TV set that allows the operator to monitor the image being received by the pickup tube. Even small handheld cameras typically contain built-in viewfinders with one-inch screens (see "Close-up: How a Video Camera Works").

Hand-held cameras usually come with a microphone built into the front of the camera. This microphone has an automatic level control, a feature that automatically adjusts the volume to keep the sound at an audible level. The camera "hears" as well as "sees." The problem is that these microphones amplify all sounds within their range, including shuffling feet, coughing, street noises, and equipment noise, along with the sounds that are wanted. You may therefore want to bypass the built-in microphone by plugging in a separate microphone better suited to your particular purpose.

The lavaliere, or neck mike, is a good choice when a single speaker is being recorded. It can be clipped to a tie or dress, hung around the neck, or even hidden under lightweight clothing. A desk stand may be used to hold a microphone for a speaker or several discussants seated at a table. For situations in which there is unwanted background noise or the speaker is moving, a

---

[3]A helpful, well-illustrated guide for the beginning video producer is Mendel Sherman's *Videographing the Pictorial Sequence* (Washington, DC: Association for Educational Communications and Technology, 1991).

highly directional microphone should be used. For practical tips on video production, see "How to . . . Set Up a Single Camera Video Production," page 212.

Editing

Standard video editing equipment is very expensive. However, students and teachers can do their own video editing with two VCRs. The VCRs can be connected by a patch cord or cable to record from one tape to another. It is also possible to record from a videodisc to videotape using a similar setup. In all cases be sure to follow the copyright guidelines in Appendix B.

Recent developments in chip technology make it possible to edit videotape, and even create special effects, by simply installing a special circuit board called a "card" in a personal computer. Some cards, such as Videotoaster for the Amiga computer, allow you to add special effects such as dissolves, wipes, and fades to live or recorded video. The card also makes it possible to superimpose images from different video sources, including its own character generator for titles and captions. Some camcorders have this feature built in. Even color characteristics can be manipulated by the card.

Several cards are available that can rearrange segments of a videotape. With these cards the operator can select specific parts of various tapes, store them, and then rearrange them in the desired sequence. If the new arrangement is not effective, you can just re-edit.

Video cards have revolutionized the production of motion media in education and in corporate settings. It is not an exaggeration to say that the right combination of such cards makes it possible to do studio production without the studio. Student-produced videos are becoming more common and much more sophisticated. Students and teachers are able to produce instructional videos for local curriculum needs such as community study in the primary grades.

ACCEPTANCE OF VIDEO

Video in Education

Today video has far surpassed film as the format of choice for presentation of motion media in educational institutions, primarily because of its ease of use, lower cost per copy, and lower cost of equipment. Furthermore, film is more easily damaged than videotape, and replacement film footage is very expensive. Replacing a damaged videotape in its entirety is frequently cheaper than replacing damaged film footage. For all of these reasons, video has become universally adopted in education.

Video collections are increasing in schools—more than doubling between 1990 and 1994. School library media centers are becoming equipped with computer-controlled media distribution systems. These allow teachers to schedule videocassette and videodisc showings and have them sent to the classroom by cable or fiber optics when activated by controls in the classroom. Equipment and materials do not have to be moved around the school. Because of these distribution systems and the ability to receive and record educational and news cable channels, the classroom of the future will have access to a wide variety of instructional video materials within the school.

Video in Corporations

Video is the most frequently used training medium by businesses. According to *Training* magazine, videotapes are used by 92% of U.S. organizations with 100 or more employees. The amount of videotape use is comparable to that of lectures (used in 87% of these organizations) and substantially greater than that of one-to-one instruction (used in 76% of these organizations).[4]

In addition to the advantages already cited, production of video is much easier to handle in-house. With internal production, all phases of production can be managed internally at fairly low cost. While educational institutions have relatively similar curriculum needs and therefore can rely primarily on commercially produced materials, training and communication needs for the most part are situation specific, making in-house production a necessity.

In addition to the demands of customization, there is the factor of rapid change. Increasing competition and technological change dictate an instructional medium that can turn out updated and modified programs rapidly.

Corporate use of video therefore contrasts sharply with school use in terms of the amount of locally produced material that is used. Most large corporate users maintain professional-quality production studios and equipment for in-the-field location shooting. Of course, many corporate skills are generic in nature—such as supervisory skills, management of meetings, and stress management. These lend themselves to off-the-shelf, or commercially produced, media.

Many organizations use video for the following:

- Orientation of new employees
- Training in job-related skills
- Development of interpersonal abilities for management
- Introduction of new products, policies, or markets
- Customer training
- Standardization of training among dispersed offices.

---

[4]"Who's Learning What?" *Training* 31 (October 1994), p. 53.

CLOSE-UP

HOW A VIDEO CAMERA WORKS

Light enters a video camera through the lens. In a portable camera (camcorder), the light is focused onto a light-sensitive electronic assembly called a **charge-coupled device (CCD)**, which changes the wavelengths into electrical charges. A filter connected to the CCD separates the charges by color. These video signals are amplified and sent to the recording mechanism in the camera. The audio is picked up by a microphone attached to the camera (or by a detached microphone) and recorded on one edge of the videotape.

Before the development of the CCD, the video camera had to house three tubes, one for each primary color. A system of dichroic mirrors sent each color to its respective tube. This made the camera so bulky that the signals had to be sent to a separate videotape recorder. The CCD made it possible to include the recording mechanism in the camera, thus creating the portable units so much in favor for nonstudio videotaping. Because of its superior quality, the dichroic mirror system is still preferred for studio production.

The recorded videotape can be played back through the camera itself or through a videotape player. A video signal is so complex that the videotape speed must be much greater than that for an audio recording. This is achieved by rotating the record/playback head, called the drum, at high speed while the tape moves across it in a helical path. The video signal occupies the greater part of the tape while the edges carry the audio and the signals that frame the image on the screen.

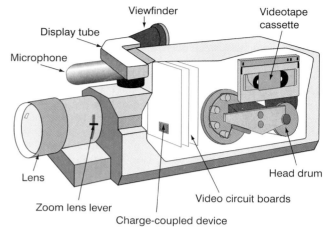

Parts of a video camera.

The magnetic signals on the tape are converted to electrical impulses that are decoded into the primary colors of light: blue, red, and green. These signals are amplified and projected onto the screen by an electronic gun. The screen surface is covered with more than 300,000 phosphor dots arranged in groups of three for the three colors. A metal perforated mask behind the screen keeps each electron beam in line with its own color dots and away from the other colors. The electronic gun scans the picture tube 30 times a second. Persistence of vision converts these scans into a moving image.

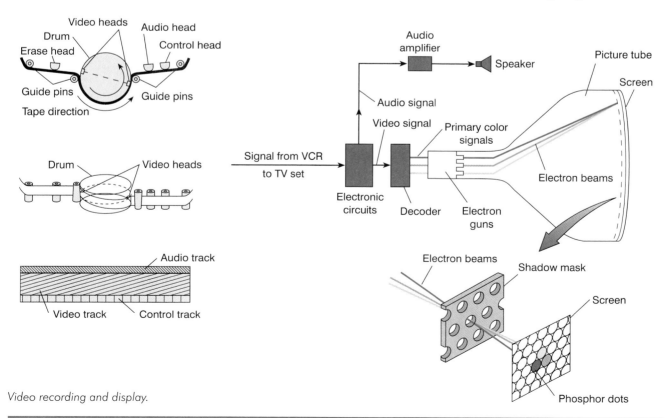

Video recording and display.

Here are some tips for arranging and using equipment for single-camera video recording.

1. The monitor/receiver and recorder are set on a sturdy mobile cart. This allows easy movement of the equipment around the room. The cart can be swiveled around so that the monitor/receiver faces the camera operator (to allow monitoring when a nonviewfinder camera is being used). In most cases it is advisable to turn the monitor/receiver away from on-camera performers to avoid distracting them during recording. It can easily be swiveled back for later instant replay viewing.

2. The camera is mounted on a sturdy, wheeled tripod, maximizing mobility and stable support.

3. The camera is outfitted with a zoom lens, an expensive option but one that adds great flexibility to the system. The zoom lens, having a variable focal length, can be adjusted to provide a wide-angle view, a medium view, or a close-up view with just a twist of the wrist. You should, however, resist the impulse to zoom in and out during a shot unless there is very good reason for doing so.

4. The camera and mobile cart are placed close to the wall. This arrangement helps reduce the likelihood of passersby tripping over the cables that connect the components to each other and to the power source.

5. The camera is aimed away from the window (or other bright-light source). Cameras used in this system usually are equipped with automatic light-level control enabling them to adjust automatically to the brightest light striking the lens. If there is a window in back of your subject, the camera will adjust to that light, thus throwing your subject into shadowy darkness. An important caution when recording outdoors: one of the greatest hazards to the pickup tube in your camera is exposure to direct sunlight. Aiming at the sun can cause its image to be burned into the pickup tube, possibly causing irreparable damage.

6. The subjects are well lighted. If natural light is insufficient, you may supplement it with incandescent or fluorescent lighting in the room. Today's pickup tubes operate well with a normal level of artificial light.

7. The camera is positioned so that the faces of all subjects can be seen. A common mistake in taping a classroom scene is to place the camera at the back of the room. This provides a nice full-face view of the teacher but makes reaction shots of the students nearly impossible to see. Placement of the camera at the side of the classroom is a reasonable compromise when recording classroom interaction.

8. A desk-stand microphone is used. This allows pickup of the voices of all subjects, while reducing the pickup of unwanted background noises.

TROUBLESHOOTING
Problems/Possible Remedies
Recording

- *Videotape is running but there is no picture on the monitor:*
  1. Check that all components are plugged in and turned on. Make sure the lens cap is off the camera and the lens aperture is open.
  2. Check the monitor. Switch it to "TV" and try to tune in a broadcast channel; make sure the brightness and contrast controls are properly set. If you still fail to get a picture, check to see whether there is a circuit breaker on the back of the monitor that needs to be reset. If you get a picture while switched to "TV," you should then check the connection between camera and monitor.
  3. Check the cable connections from camera to recorder and from recorder to monitor.
  4. Check the settings of the switches on the recorder. Is the input selector on "Camera"? Is the "Record" button depressed?

Playback

- *Videotape is running but there is no picture or sound on monitor:*
  1. Make sure the monitor input selector is set at "VTR" and all units are plugged in.
  2. Check connectors between playback unit and monitor (e.g., make sure "Video Out" from playback is connected to "Video In" on monitor). Wiggle the end of the cable to see if there is a loose connection.
  3. Check switches on playback unit.

- *Fuzzy sound or snowy picture:*
  1. Video or audio heads may be dirty. Clean with approved tape or fluid cleaning system.
  2. Brushes under head-drum cover may be dirty or damaged. Have a technician check this possibility.

- *Picture slants horizontally across screen (the audio may also sound off-speed):* If adjustment of the horizontal hold knob does not clear up the situation, you may have a tape or cassette that is incompatible with your playback unit. Obtain a playback machine that matches the format of the tape or cassette.

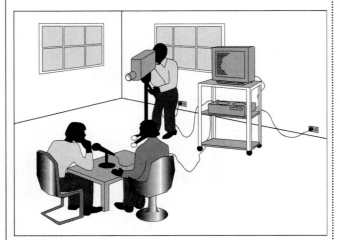

A generalized setup for single-camera recording.

Portability and ease of use are advantages in all these uses of video. For example, a life insurance company can send a video to its sales representatives for them to study at their local office or at home. And each representative can take the video to a potential client's home knowing a VCR will probably be available. In the case of recording product improvements, employees can study product performance immediately rather than having to wait for film processing.

SELECTING MOTION MEDIA

Locating Video Materials

Program guides and directories can help keep you abreast of available materials in your areas of interest and guide you toward selection of materials best suited to your particular teaching needs. Librarians, media specialists, and teachers working as partners should communicate constantly concerning the resources needed for instruction. A basic resource for you, then, is a collection of catalogs of rental agencies you are most likely to use. To be more thorough in your search you will want *The Educational Film/Video Locator,* a comprehensive list of the videotapes and films available in various college and university rental collections. The most comprehensive list of current educational film and video recordings is "A-V Online," which is in CD-ROM format. Other broad listings are *Bowker's Complete Video Directory* and *Video Source Book.* (These and other more specialized catalogs are described in Appendix C.)

Appraising Videos and Films

After you have located some potentially useful videos or films, you will want to preview and appraise them. Some schools and organizations have standard appraisal forms ready to use. Some of these are meticulously detailed, covering every possible factor; others are much more perfunctory. A good appraisal form will be brief enough not to be intimidating but complete enough to help individuals choose materials that may be useful for current and future applications. It should also stand as a public record that can be used to justify the purchase or rental of specific titles. The "Appraisal Checklist: Video and Film" (page 214) includes the most commonly used criteria, particularly those that research indicates really do make a difference. You may wish to use it as is or adapt it to your particular needs.

Sponsored Videos and Films

Private companies, associations, and government agencies sponsor motion media for a variety of reasons. Private companies may make them to promote their products or to enhance their public image. Associations and government agencies sponsor videos and films to promote causes, such as better health habits, conservation of natural resources, and proper use of park and recreation areas. Many of these sponsored videos and films make worthwhile instructional materials. They also have the considerable advantage of being free.

A certain amount of caution, however, is called for in using sponsored programs for instructional purposes. Some privately produced materials may be too flagrantly self-serving. Or they may deal with products not very suitable for certain instructional settings; for example, the manufacturing of alcoholic beverages or cigarettes. Some association and government materials may contain a sizable dose of propaganda or special pleading for pet causes along with their content. You must always preview sponsored materials.

Properly selected, many sponsored materials can be valuable additions to classroom instruction. Modern Talking Picture Service is one of the major distributors of sponsored videos and films. The best single source of information on sponsored films is *Free Videotapes.* Details on this and other sources are given in Appendix C.

UTILIZING MOTION MEDIA

The next step after selecting your materials is to put them into actual use in the classroom.

Preview the Materials

Films and video materials should be previewed for appraisal and selection, but they should also be checked after they arrive in the classroom. Avoid potential embarrassment by making sure the material is what you ordered and that it contains the subject matter and treatment that you expected (Figure 7.7).

Prepare the Materials

You will need to schedule the video or film and the appropriate playback equipment. The equipment should be set up and checked for proper operation before the students arrive.

Decide how you are going to introduce the material and what the follow-up activities will be (discussion, presentation, project, etc.). Adjunct media and materials, such as handouts, charts, and/or visuals, should be assembled or created.

✔ APPRAISAL CHECKLIST

VIDEO AND FILM

KEY WORDS: _____ , _____ , _____

Title _____

Series Title (if applicable) _____

Source _____

Date _____ **Cost** _____ **Length** _____ minutes

Subject Area _____

Intended Audience _____

Brief Description

Objectives

Entry Capabilities Required (e.g., prior knowledge, reading ability, vocabulary level, math ability)

Format
- ❏ **16 mm film**
- ❏ **3/4-inch videocassette**
- ❏ **1/2-inch VHS videocassette**
- ❏ **Videodisc**
- ❏ **Compact disc**

Rating	High	Medium	Low	Comments
Match with curriculum	❏	❏	❏	
Accurate and current	❏	❏	❏	
Clear and concise language	❏	❏	❏	
Arouse motivation/maintain interest	❏	❏	❏	
Learner participation	❏	❏	❏	
Technical quality	❏	❏	❏	
Evidence of effectiveness (e.g., field-test results)	❏	❏	❏	
Free from objectionable bias or advertising	❏	❏	❏	
User guide/documentation	❏	❏	❏	
Pacing appropriate for audience	❏	❏	❏	
Use of cognitive learning aids *(e.g., overviews, cues, summary)*	❏	❏	❏	

Strong Points

Weak Points

Recommended Action _____ **Name** _____ **Date** _____

A computer version of this Checklist is found in "The Classroom Link."

FIGURE 7.7
Previewing the material allows the teacher to properly introduce and follow up the material.

Prepare the Environment

Before students can learn from any media presentation, they first have to be able to see it and hear it! Provide proper lighting, seating, and volume control. These elements are described later in this chapter.

Prepare the Learners

Research in educational psychology as well as the practical experiences of thousands of teachers in all sorts of settings demonstrate that learning is greatly enhanced when learners are prepared for the coming activity (Figure 7.8).

Before the video/film lesson, review previous related study. Help students see how today's lesson fits into the total picture. Create a need to know. Stimulate curiosity by asking questions, and evoke questions the students would like to have answered on the subject.

Clarify the objectives of the lesson. Mention specific things to look for in the presentation. It helps to list such cues on the chalkboard, overhead, or handout so that students can refer to them as the lesson proceeds and during the follow-up activities. If large amounts of new information are being presented, give students some advance organizers, or give them "memory hooks" on which they can hang the new ideas. Be sure to preview any new vocabulary as needed.

FIGURE 7.8
Class discussion can be used before and after viewing material.

FIGURE 7.9
Video materials can be stopped to explain key points.

Provide the Learning Experience

When presenting video and film in the classroom, follow the guidelines in this chapter's "AV Showmanship" (page 217). Be enthusiastic about the material!

Situate yourself so that you can observe learner reactions. Watch for cues indicating difficulties or boredom. (See Figure 7.9.) Note individual reactions for possible use in the follow-up discussion. Deal with individual discipline problems as quickly and unobtrusively as possible.

For troubleshooting techniques, see "How to . . . Operate a 16mm Slotload Projector" on page 218. Operation of video projectors is described in the next section.

REQUIRE LEARNER PARTICIPATION

If active participation was not explicitly built into the video/film program, it is all the more important to stimulate response after the presentation. The ability to generalize new knowledge and transfer it to real-life situations depends on learner practice under a variety of conditions. The possibilities for follow-up activities are virtually limitless. A few common techniques include the following:

- *Discussion*—Question-and-answer sessions, buzz groups, panel discussions, debates
- *Dramatization*—Role playing, skits, oral presentations
- *Projects*—Experiments, reports, exhibits, models, demonstrations, drawings, story writing, bulletin boards, media productions

Learners are quick to detect and act according to your attitude toward the material. Many studies have indicated that the instructor's attitude—often conveyed nonverbally—significantly affects students' learning from media. So if students are expected to be active participants, you should lead by example.

EVALUATE AND REVISE

Assessment of student learning can be carried out informally by observing performance during the follow-up activities. Individual projects can be good indicators of successful learning. In many cases, though, more formal testing serves a valuable purpose. First, tests that are followed by feedback of correct answers can provide an efficient review and summary of the main points of the lesson. Second, objective tests can help pinpoint gaps that need to be followed up in the classroom, and they can identify individuals who need remedial help. In this way, the

The following are some generic tips that apply equally to the enhancement of video or film presentations:

- *Sight lines.* Check lighting, seating, and volume control to be sure that everyone can see and hear the presentation.
- *Mental set.* Get students mentally prepared by briefly reviewing previous related study and evoking questions about the current topic.
- *Advance organizer.* List on the chalkboard the main points to be covered in the presentation.
- *Vocabulary.* Preview any new vocabulary.
- *Role model.* Most important, get involved in the program yourself. Watch attentively and respond when the presenter asks for a response. Highlight major points by adding them to the chalkboard during the lesson.
- *Follow up.* Reinforce the presentation with meaningful follow-up activities.
- *Light control.* When using video projection with videotape or videodisc, dim the light. Turn lights off if dimming is not available. The same light setting should be used for showing films. If you are using a video monitor (TV), you can use normal room lighting. It is recommended you dim the lights above and behind the monitor if possible.

Here are some tips that apply specifically to film showings:

- *Light control.* Many classrooms have a wall-mounted screen at the front of the room. In some classrooms a door with a window in it is near the front of the room. The window allows light from the hallway to fall on the screen, dimming the projected image. Remedy this by covering the window or moving the projector closer to the screen.

Remember, a smaller, brighter image is better than a larger, dimmer one.

- *Preset focus and volume.* Always set the focus and the sound level before the class assembles and note the correct volume setting. Then turn the volume control back down to zero and run the film back to the beginning. The film will then start in focus, and you can smoothly turn the volume up to a comfortable level.
- *Avoid showing leader.* It is poor showmanship to project the film leader (the strip of film with the number countdown on it). The first image the audience should see is the title or opening scene.
- *Smooth startup.* (1) Start the projector, (2) turn on the lamp, (3) turn the volume up to the preset level, and (4) adjust the focus and volume.
- *Restarting.* If you stop the film and then restart it, the viewers may miss a few seconds of dialogue because it takes this long for the sound to stabilize when restarting. Remedy this by (1) reducing the volume, (2) reversing the film a few feet, and (3) going through the startup procedure just mentioned.
- *Smooth ending.* When the film is over, (1) turn the lamp off, (2) reduce the volume, and (3) stop the film. This will give a smooth ending rather than a jarring stop. Run any remaining film through after class.
- *Rewind.* Rewind the film if you are going to show it again or if it belongs to you. If it is borrowed from a rental agency, the agency will probably want to rewind it as part of the film inspection process. So if you used the same size take-up reel that the film came on you can just put it back in the container. Secure the end of the film with a piece of tape.

instructor can complement the media component by catering to individual differences in ways the media cannot.

VIDEO PLAYBACK

Video record/playback machines are highly sophisticated electronic instruments. Maintenance and repair, consequently, should generally be left to the specialist. In addition, videotape recorder/players are far from standardized in their various mechanisms and modes of operation. You should therefore refer to the manufacturer's manual for information about the operating principles and procedures of the particular system you happen to be using. The troubleshooting guide on page 212 is limited to general sorts of problems that occur with virtually any video system and that can be remedied by the nonspecialist.

Video Projectors

Studies have shown that audiences are attentive to images projected onto a large screen. Video images can be projected using video projectors. They connect to any videocassette recorder, videodisc player, live television, or video camera. Some models include a self-contained VHS videocassette player. Other models can also project computer-generated graphs.

Video projectors work well with large audiences (up to several hundred) and for visuals requiring a high degree of detail. Most project an image up to 4 feet by 6 feet. Other features available include built-in speakers and remote control.

The cathode ray tube (CRT) projector uses three "guns," one each to project red, green, and blue light. Video projection equipment may be placed on a cart, mounted to the ceiling, or converted for rear-screen projection.

OPERATION
Set Up

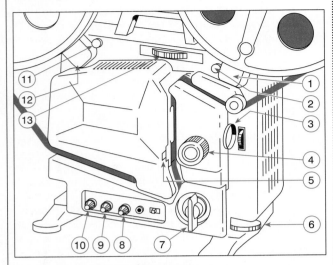

Main parts of the projector

1. Supply arm
2. Supply arm lock button
3. Lens
4. Focus knob
5. Framing lever
6. Elevator knob
7. Function switch
8. Treble control
9. Bass control
10. Amplifier on and off and volume control
11. Take-up arm lock button
12. Take-up arm
13. Still/run knob

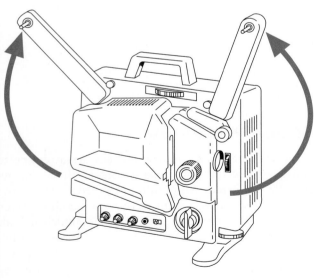

Raise both reel arms until they snap in place

- Place projector on a sturdy projection stand.
- Remove projector cover.
- Extend reel arms and lock in place.
- Place take-up reel on rear arm.
- Place film reel on front arm.
- Make sure motor switch is in off (or stop) position.
- Plug power cord into AC outlet.

Thread Film

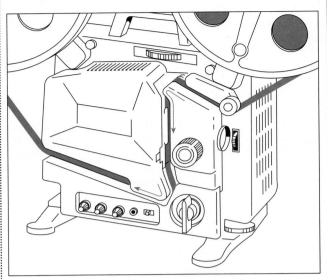

Threading Path

- Be sure Still/Run knob is in "Run" position.
- Hold the film by your fingertips. Beginning at the first guide roller, pull the film along and into the slot, following the direction of the arrows.
- Attach the end of the film to the take-up reel and wind a couple of turns in clockwise direction.
- Check that film is fitted correctly in the film path slot.

Operate

Before the audience arrives:

- Turn on motor and lamp.
- Use the elevator knob to raise or lower the projector as needed.
- If a frame bar is visible, use the framing lever to get one whole frame on the screen.
- Focus image with "Focus" knob.
- Adjust volume and tone control.
- Turn motor switch to "Rewind" position to return to beginning of film.

When ready to show film:

- Turn on motor and lamp.
- Slowly turn up volume to predetermined level.
- Make any final adjustments of focus, framing, and sound.

At end of the film:

- Turn down volume knob.
- Turn off lamp and motor.

Rewind

Film can be rewound in most slotload projectors in two ways: back through the slot path or directly from take-up reel to front wheel. For in-path rewind:

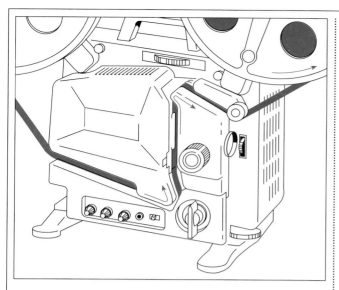

In-Path Rewinding

- Stop the projector before the film is entirely through the projector.
- Turn switch to "Rewind" position (if you show only part of the film, this is the most convenient way to rewind).

For reel-to-reel rewind:

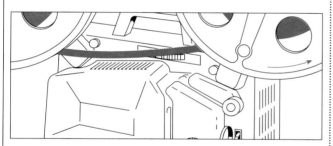

Reel-to-Reel Rewinding

- Let the film run completely through the projector before turning off the motor.
- Bring the loose end of the film from the take-up reel to the front reel, secure it to the reel, and rotate the front reel counterclockwise for a few turns to be sure film is held firmly.

- Turn motor switch to "Rewind" position.
- Turn motor off when film is completely rewound.

Disassemble

- Disconnect power cord from outlet; wrap up and store in well in rear of projector.
- Remove both film reels.
- Unlock both reel arms by depressing release buttons, and move arms down to storage position.
- Turn tilt control knob to completely lower projector.
- Replace cover on projector.

TROUBLESHOOTING
Problems/Possible Remedies

- *Projector completely inoperative:*
  1. Check position of load lever. It should be in "Run" position.
  2. Check that power cord is plugged in.
  3. Be sure electric outlet has power.
- *Film will not thread:*
  1. Be sure motor switch is off.
  2. Check position of load level. It should be in load position.
  3. Rear take-up reel must be in proper position.
  4. Be sure lamp cover and lens cover are closed properly.
- *No sound from speaker:* If exciter lamp lights:
  1. Check threading of film around sound drum.
  2. Be sure volume is turned up.

     If exciter lamp does not light:
  1. Be sure motor switch is in "Projector-Normal" position.
  2. Replace exciter lamp.
- *Sound is soft, fuzzy, or garbled:*
  1. Check volume and tone controls.
  2. Be sure film is tight around sound drum.
  3. Check lower film loop.
  4. See if exciter lamp filament is damaged.
- *No picture:*
  1. Be sure motor switch is in "Project" position.
  2. Check position of load lever. It should be in "Run" position.
  3. Replace projection lamp.

Video projectors vary in weight from about 20 pounds to 150 pounds. Each time the video projector is moved it must be adjusted to ensure a sharp image. Each of the three lenses must be focused and adjusted so that the three images exactly overlay each other (converge). Some newer and more expensive models include a microprocessor that automatically focuses and converges the three images in less than three minutes. The manual process can take up to several hours.

Applications of video projectors include showing videocassettes and videodiscs and other television applications where monitors are currently used. They can also display computer output and demonstrate computer software packages (see p. 150).

OPERATION

Set Up

The video projector will be delivered to you connected to the VCR and audio amplifier as shown in the illustration on the facing page.

- Check all connections.
- Turn on the power to the VCR, amplifier, and projector.
- Insert the videocassette and fast-forward for a few seconds to get into the program.

Operate

Ceiling or floor mount

Portable unit

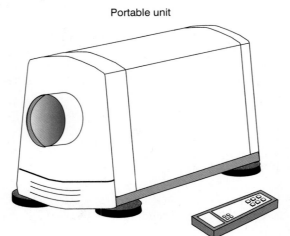

Remote control

- Turn on the projector lamp and wait for it to warm up (about one minute).
- Put VCR on "Play" and adjust the size of the image using the zoom lens ring; then focus the image.

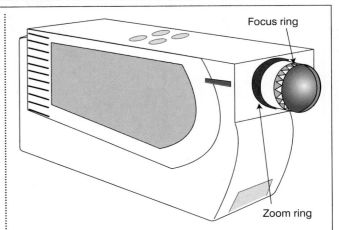

Focus ring

Zoom ring

- Push the "Reset" button. The following image will be super-imposed on the screen:

	+		−
Picture		0	
Brightness		0	
Color		0	
Tint		0	
Sharpness		0	

- Correct the image for each by using the + and - buttons shown in the illustration. The corrections will be evident in the image and will also be shown graphically on the screen.

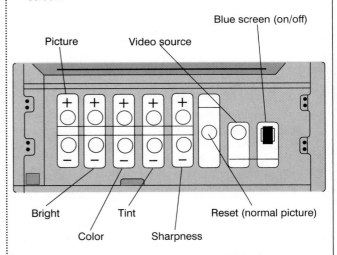

Picture   Video source   Blue screen (on/off)

Bright   Tint   Reset (normal picture)

Color   Sharpness

- Adjust the sound level with the volume control of the amplifier.
- Rewind the tape to the beginning of the program. If the audience will arrive shortly, push the "Blue Screen" button. If you have to wait a while for your audience, turn off the lamp, but remember that it must first cool off before you can turn it on again.

Disassemble

- After presentation of the video, rewind the tape.
- Turn off all power switches.
- Disconnect cord(s) from wall sockets.

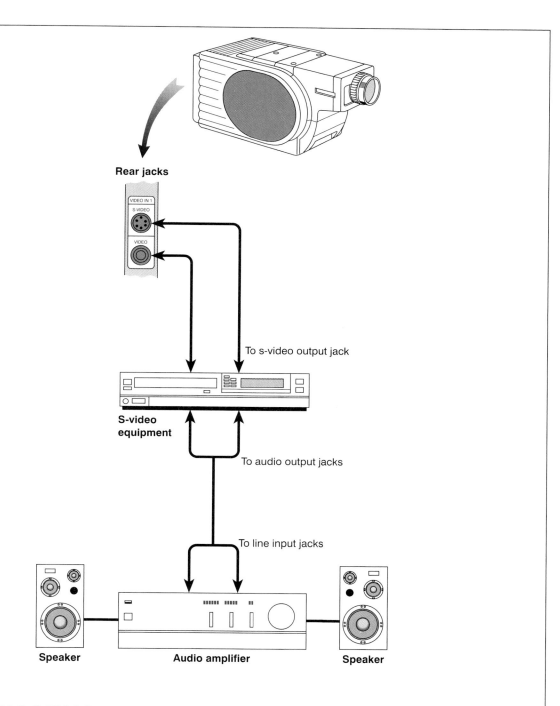

Rear jacks

VIDEO IN 1
S-VIDEO
VIDEO

To s-video output jack

S-video equipment

To audio output jacks

To line input jacks

Speaker   **Audio amplifier**   **Speaker**

TROUBLESHOOTING

Problems/Possible Remedies

- *No picture:*
  1. Ensure that projector and player are plugged into active AC outlet and turn power switches on.
  2. If using remote control, be sure batteries are charged and unit is within effective operating distance.
  3. Check all cords for proper connection.

- *Picture not clear:*
  1. Check focus adjustment.
  2. Adjust picture controls.

- *Picture but no color:* Check settings on video unit.

- *Picture inverted or left–right reversed:* Check settings of horizontal and vertical polarity plugs.
- *Color and picture distorted:*
  1. Check connection of leads between video unit output terminals and projector input terminals.
  2. Confirm that the signal is compatible.
- *No operation from remote control:*
  1. If using wired remote control, check to see if it is plugged into the video unit, and check connection of remote lead between the video unit and the video projector.
  2. If using wireless remote control, confirm that batteries are charged and wireless remote control is within effective operating range.

Elementary School Social Studies

Analyze Learners

General Characteristics

This urban elementary school class is self-contained, with 29 fifth graders (16 girls, 13 boys). The average age is 11 years; the average reading level is fourth grade.

The class has an ethnic and racial mixture typical of an urban setting, with socioeconomic status being lower middle class. Seventeen come from single-parent families. Motivation is usually a challenge with this class.

Entry Competencies

Regarding today's topic, the Panama Canal, awareness is low. In yesterday's discussion of Central America, only Nicaragua and El Salvador were mentioned without prompting. There is an old barge canal on the north side of town, so many students were able to identify canals as human-built waterways but were vague about their purposes.

State Objectives

The fifth-grade social studies students will be able to do the following:

1. Locate the Panama Canal on a wall map of North and South America.
2. Explain the main advantage of the Panama Canal as a shortcut between the Atlantic and Pacific oceans.
3. Visually recognize a canal, distinguishing it from other waterways.
4. Discuss the Panama Canal's historic importance, citing at least its commercial and military advantages and the achievement of overcoming the obstacles to its construction.
5. Demonstrate that they value the cooperative effort represented by the building of the Panama Canal by participating actively in a group project.

Select Methods, Media, and Materials

The teacher decides to begin the class with a large-group discussion, then show a video, and follow up with small-group discussion and projects. The teacher surveys the *Educational Film/Video Locator* under the topic "Panama Canal" and finds four titles that look promising. Two of these are in the school district media library. After previewing both, she selects one because the content and vocabulary come closest to the level of her class. She notes that the political description of Panama is no longer accurate, so she prepares some comments to correct it.

Utilize Media and Materials

Because motivating interest is predictably difficult, she begins to stimulate students' curiosity by rolling down the wall map of North and South America and asking how a traveler in the days before airplanes and automobiles might get from New York to San Francisco. What if you were a merchant who wanted to ship tools and work clothes to the miners of the gold rush in Alaska in 1898? What if you were an admiral needing to move his fleet rapidly from the Atlantic to the Pacific?

Having identified the problem, the teacher states that the video is going to show the solution developed early in the 20th century. She lists several key questions on the overhead projector.

After reviewing the questions by having students take turns reading them, she asks them to look for the answers to these questions while viewing the video. She then shows the video.

Require Learner Participation

After showing the video, the teacher divides the students into groups of three to discuss the questions. Each group elects a recorder who will write the answers agreed to by the group.

After a few minutes of discussion the teacher brings the whole class back together in a large group and calls on two or three recorders to give their answers to question 1, with the whole class reacting to these. This process is repeated for the rest of the questions.

The teacher concludes by going back to question 3, focusing on how the builders of the canal succeeded because of their systematic plan and determination to overcome all obstacles. If we were going to construct a display to tell the story of the Panama Canal, what steps would we have to carry out? What ideas would we put into our display? With questions such as these the teacher builds interest in constructing a display, works out a time line, and organizes the students into groups to carry out the assignment.

Evaluate and Revise

The teacher collects the recorders' written notes and checks to see how accurately the questions were answered. She makes note of test items keyed to the objectives to be included on the written test at the end of this unit. As students work on the display project, she will be able to check the accuracy of the information being put into the display and, regarding the affective objective(s), will circulate among the work groups to assess the enthusiasm exhibited in their work.

A computer template for a Blueprint is found in "The Classroom Link."

REFERENCES

Print References

Adams, Dennis. "Visual Environments: Simple Video Production Techniques." *School Arts* (December 1989): 14–16.

Beasley, Augie E. "The Camcorder Revolution." *School Library Media Activities Monthly* (January 1994): 38–39.

Berg, Bryan, and Turner, Dianne. "MTV Unleashed: Sixth Graders Create Music Videos Based on Works of Art." *Tech Trends* (April–May 1993): 28–31.

Bragg, Richelle Rae, and McWilliams, Micki. "Cultural Exchange: A Video Pen Pal Program." *Journal of Geography* (July–August 1989): 150–151.

Brink, Barbara. "New Frontiers with Science Videodiscs." *Educational Leadership* (May 1993): 42–43.

Brown, Kenneth. "Video Production in the Classroom: Creating Success for Students and Schools." *Tech Trends* (April–May 1993): 32–35.

Cassidy, J. M. "Lights, Camera, Animation!" *School Arts* (February 1984): 36–38.

Choat, Ernest, and Griffin, Harry. "Modular Video with Children Aged 3 to 11." *British Journal of Educational Technology* (May 1988): 123–130.

Cohen, Kathleen. "Can Multimedia Help Social Studies? Or Are Videodiscs Worth the Expense?" *Social Studies Review* (Winter 1993): 35–43.

Compesi, Ronald J. *Small Format Television Production.* Boston: Allyn and Bacon, 1990.

Cravotta, Mary Ellen, and Wilson, Savan. *Media Cookbook for Kids.* Englewood, CO: Libraries Unlimited, 1989.

Curcio, Frances R., and McNeece, J. Lewis. "The Case of Video Viewing, Reading, and Writing in Mathematics Class: Solving the Mystery." *Mathematics Teacher* (November 1993): 682–685.

Davis, Shawn. "The Eyes Have It." *Gallaudet Today 18,* no. 4 (1988): 30–31.

DeLuca, Stuart M. *Instructional Video.* Boston: Focal Press, 1991.

Dewing, Martha. *Beyond TV: Activities for Using Video with Children.* Santa Barbara, CA: ABC-CLIO, 1992.

Elwell, Catherine Callow, et al. "Captioning Instructional Video." *Educational Technology* (August 1992): 45–50.

Gaffney, Maureen, and Laybourne, Gerry Bond. *What to Do When the Lights Go On: A Comprehensive Guide to 16mm Films and Related Activities.* Phoenix, AZ: Oryx Press, 1981.

Griffin, C. W. "Teaching Shakespeare on Video." *English Journal* (November 1989): 40–43.

Higgins, Norm. "Preschool Teacher Uses of Video Technologies." *Journal of Educational Television 19* (1993): 3, 153–166.

Kreamer, Jean Thibodeaux, et al. "Room with a View: Video in Libraries." *Wilson Library Journal* (June 1993): 31–47.

Kyker, Keith, and Curchy, Christopher. *Video Projects for Elementary and Middle Schools.* Englewood, CO: Libraries Unlimited, 1995.

———. *Television Production for Elementary Schools.* Englewood, CO: Libraries Unlimited, 1994.

———. *Television Production: A Classroom Approach.* Englewood, CO: Libraries Unlimited, 1993.

Lankford, Mary D. *Films for Learning, Thinking, and Doing.* Englewood, CO: Libraries Unlimited, 1992.

Marsh, Cynthia. "Some Observations on the Use of Video in the Teaching of Modern Foreign Languages." *British Journal of Language Teaching* (Spring 1989): 13–17.

Pelletier, Raymond J. "Prompting Spontaneity by Means of the Video Camera in the Beginning Foreign Language Class." *Foreign Language Annals* (May 1990): 227–233.

Reeve, Edward M. *Classroom Video Production.* Urbana, IL: Griffon Press, 1992.

Regina, Theresa E. "Composing Skills and Television." *English Journal* (November 1988): 50–52.

Skolnik, Racquel, and Smith, Carl. "Utilizing Video Technology to Serve the Needs of At-Risk Students." *Journal for Vocational Special Needs Education* (Fall 1993): 23–31.

Squires, Nancy, and Inlander, Robin. "A Freireian-Inspired Video Curriculum for At-Risk High School Students." *English Journal* (February 1990): 49–56.

Steinman, Richard C. "Cameras in the Classroom." *Science Teacher* (April 1993): 16–19.

Tibbs, Pat. "Video Creation for Junior High Language Arts." *Journal of Reading* (March 1989): 558–559.

Urban, Marty. "Video Biographies: Reading, Researching, and Recording." *English Journal* (December 1989): 58–59.

Valmont, William J. *Creating Videos for School Use.* Boston: Allyn and Bacon, 1995.

Vandergrift, Kay E., and Hannigan, Jane A. "Reading Images: Videos in the Library and Classroom." *School Library Journal* (January 1993): 20–25.

Vick, Nancy H. "Freedom to View: Coping with Censorship." *Sightlines* (Spring 1981): 5–6.

Voller, Peter, and Widdows, Steven. "Feature Films as Text: A Framework for Classroom Use." *ELT Journal* (October 1993): 342–353.

Watson, Robert. *Film and Television in Education: An Aesthetic Approach to the Moving Image.* New York: Falmer Press, 1990.

Wetzel, C. Douglas. *Instructional Effectiveness of Video Media.* Hillsdale, NJ: Erlbaum, 1994.

Audiovisual References

Basic Film Terms: A Visual Dictionary. Santa Monica, CA: Pyramid Films, 1970. 16mm or videocassette. 15 minutes.

Basic Television Terms: A Video Dictionary. Santa Monica, CA: Pyramid Films, 1977. 16mm or videocassette. 17 minutes.

Basic Video Camera Techniques. State College, PA: Pennsylvania State University. Videocassette.

Camera Techniques for Video. Great Falls, MT: Video International Publishers, 1980. Videocassette. 30 minutes.

Claymation. Santa Monica, CA: Pyramid Films, 1980. 16mm or videocassette. 20 minutes.

The Eye Hears and the Ear Sees. Montreal: National Film Board of Canada, 1970. 16mm or videocassette. 59 minutes.

Forty-Eight Hours: Lights, Camera, War—The Making of the Film "Glory." New York: Carousel Films, 1988. 16mm or videocassette. 43 minutes.

Frame by Frame: The Art of Animation. Santa Monica, CA: Pyramid Films, 1973. 16mm or videocassette. 13 minutes.

Laserdisc in the Classroom: A Teacher's Guide to Getting Started. Chipley, FL: PAEC, 1991. Videodisc.

Learning with Film and Video. Los Angeles, CA: Churchill Films, 1988. 16mm or videocassette. 20 minutes.

Making "Do the Right Thing." New York: Icarus Films, 1989. 16mm or videocassette. 58 minutes.

Professor Bunruckle's Guide to Pixilation. Van Nuys, CA: AIMS Media, 1988. 16mm or videocassette. 16 minutes.

Touch That Dial: Using Video in the Classroom—Broadcast. WGBH, 1993. Videocassette. 10 minutes.

Touch That Dial: Using Video in the Classroom—Satellite. WGBH, 1993. Videocassette. 11 minutes.

Touch That Dial: Using Video in the Classroom—Videocassette. WGBH, 1993. Videocassette. 11 minutes.

Understanding Video: The Basics. Ampex Corporation, 1990. Videocassette. 15 minutes.

Videodisk in the K-12 Curriculum. Upper Saddle River, NJ: Pioneer Communication, 1988. Videocassettes or videodisc. 20 minutes.

Video Encyclopedia of the Twentieth Century. New York: CEL Educational Resources, 1986. 75 videocassettes or 38 videodiscs; index; and four-volume reference set.

Videotape—Disc—Or . . . Columbia, SC: Educational Program Service, 1983. Videocassette. 30 minutes.

Visual Effects: Wizardry on Film. Los Angeles, CA: Churchill Films, 1988. 16mm or videocassette. 29 minutes.

All of the following ½-inch VHS videocassettes are available from Audiovisual Center Marketing, C215 Seashore Hall, University of Iowa, Iowa City, IA 52242.

Operating the Camcorder. 1990. 8 minutes.

Pre-production Planning for Video. 1990. 10 minutes.

Recording the Video Image. 1990. 18 minutes.

Romancing the Eiki: The Story of a Slotloading Projector. 1988. 11 minutes.

Scriptwriting: Filling the Empty Page. 1990. 16 minutes.

Single Camera VCR System. 1983. 7 minutes.

16mm Projector. 1983. 7 minutes.

Videotape Editing. 1990. 8 minutes.

COMPUTERS

Since the advent of the personal computer in the mid-1980s, computers have rapidly become one of the key instructional technologies used in both formal and informal education. The computer can be used by teachers as an aid to managing classroom activities; it has a multitude of roles to play in the curriculum, ranging from tutor to student tool. To make informed choices, you need to be familiar with the various computer applications—games, simulations, tutorials, problem-solving programs, word processing and graphic tools, and integrated learning systems.

It is extremely important to develop critical skills in appraising instructional software because there are so many available programs. The hardware, too, becomes much less intimidating when you know some of the basic terminology. Whether you teach with a single computer in the classroom or a roomful of them, these basic guidelines will help you make optimal use of them.

KNOWLEDGE OBJECTIVES

1. Summarize briefly the development of computer technology and its applications to instruction over the past four decades.
2. Compare the advantages and limitations of computers.
3. Create examples of the use of the computer as an object of instruction and as a tool for instruction.
4. Distinguish between computer-assisted instruction (CAI) and computer-managed instruction (CMI).
5. Compare and contrast the six types of computer-assisted instruction in terms of the role of the computer and the role of the learner, including a specific example of courseware for each.
6. Cite examples of the use of the computer for computer-managed instruction to provide for assessment; to prescribe media, materials, and activities; and to keep records.
7. Describe two applications of local area networks (LANs) for instruction, including the advantages and limitations of such networks.
8. Describe two applications, two advantages, and two limitations of integrated learning systems.
9. Describe how computers can assist in generating instructional materials, in designing instruction, and in locating information in media centers.
10. Outline the process and materials needed for selecting and integrating computer-based programs.
11. Identify five criteria besides cost that are important considerations in purchasing a computer for instructional purposes.

APPLICATION OBJECTIVES

1. Read and summarize an article from a professional journal on the use of computers in education or training.
2. Interview a student or instructor who has used computers for instruction. Report on how the computer was used, including the user's perceptions of its strengths and limitations.
3. Create a list of topics you would include if you were to conduct a one-day computer implementation workshop for teachers or trainers in your content area.
4. Describe how you could use a computer as an object of instruction or as a tool during instruction within your field.
5. Create a situation in which you could use computer-based materials. Include a description of the audience, the objectives, the role of the computer, and the expected outcomes of using the computer.
6. Locate at least five computer programs suitable for your content area using the information sources available to you.
7. Critique an instructional computer program using the "Appraisal Checklist: Computer Software" provided in this chapter.

LEXICON

computer-assisted instruction (CAI)

computer-managed instruction (CMI)

computer literacy

microprocessor

software

database

integrated learning system (ILS)

courseware

hardware

ROM (read only memory)

RAM (random access memory)

byte

bits

megabyte

CD–ROM (compact disc–read only memory)

local area networks (LANs)

wide area networks (WANs)

The computer provides virtually instantaneous response to student input, has extensive capacity to store and manipulate information, and is unmatched in its ability to serve many individual students simultaneously. It is thus widely used in instruction. It has the ability to control and integrate a wide variety of media—still pictures, graphics, and moving images, as well as printed information. The computer can also record, analyze, and react to student responses that are typed on a keyboard or selected with a mouse. (See Figure 8.1.)

There are two major applications of computers in instruction: **computer-assisted instruction (CAI)** and **computer-managed instruction (CMI).** In CAI the student interacts directly with the computer as part of the instructional activity. This may be in the form of material presented by the computer in a controlled sequence, such as a drill-and-practice program, or as a creative activity that is student initiated, like a desktop-published book of student poems. In CMI the computer helps both the instructor and the student in maintaining information about the student and in guiding the instructional process. That is, the computer can be used to store information about each student and about relevant instructional materials that can be retrieved quickly. The learner may take tests on the computer or input information into a personal portfolio. Further, the computer can diagnose the learning needs of students and prescribe optimal sequences of instruction for them.

In addition, the computer can be an object of instruction, as in courses on computer science and com-

FIGURE 8.1
Computers have become pervasive in education and training. Most learners have access to and are influenced by computer-based instruction.

FIGURE 8.2
Innovative computer systems such as the Macintosh have helped popularize the use of micros in business and at home.

puter literacy. It also is a tool that can be used during instruction to do complex calculations, data manipulations, word processing, and presentations.

The term *literacy* once implied exclusively the ability to read and write (i.e., verbal literacy). With the rapid spread of computer use since the mid-1980s came an equally rapid increase in public awareness of the importance of computers in society. Out of this emerged another type of literacy—**computer literacy**—referring to the ability to understand and use computers.

Most computer literacy instruction incorporates three types of objectives—knowledge, skill, and attitude. The knowledge objectives typically include understanding terminology, identifying components, describing applications, and analyzing social and ethical issues concerning the use of computers. Skill objectives typically include keyboarding and the ability to use computers for a variety of applications, such as word processing, searching databases, and retrieving information. Advanced applications include desktop publishing and problem solving. Attitude objectives focus primarily on acceptance of the computer as a valuable tool in the workplace. Further objectives might deal with exploring computers as productivity tools in personal and professional activities.

AN OVERVIEW OF COMPUTERS IN THE LEARNING PROCESS

The possibility of educational applications for computers was mainly conjectural during the 1950s and 1960s,

PLATO: From an Indecisive Committee and a $10 TV Set

In 1960, University of Illinois administrators appointed a committee to suggest ways that the university's mainframe computer could be used for research in education; the military no longer needed the university's computer to solve radar problems. The educators thought the engineers didn't know anything about teaching, and the engineers thought the educators didn't know anything about technology! Consequently, the committee came to the only possible conclusion under the circumstances; they would not agree on any projects worth funding.

One of the researchers in the computer lab who was not a member of the committee said, "That's crazy! Give me two weeks, and I'll come back with a proposal." Within days the researcher prepared a proposal to develop a course in engineering, a subject with which he was familiar, with an eye to educational considerations. The course was to run on the computers already in the lab, which took care of the technical considerations.

The proposal was approved. The researcher hired a technician to build the hardware and a mathematician to help with the programming. Within one month they had developed an interactive video terminal connected to the computer to provide instruction. They developed programs for college-level computer science and high school mathematics. With the help of a friend, they soon added a program to teach French.

The system was built cheaply and hastily, but it worked. The keyboard had only 16 keys. The video display was a cast-off television set that could no longer pick up broadcasts—it cost $10. The system was the first to display slides and computer graphics. The slide-selection process was very primitive. A technician in another room picked them out and displayed them in front of a camera as fast as he could.

The researcher on the team was Donald L. Bitzer. The system was called PLATO—Programmed Logic for Automatic-Teaching Operations. Primitive as it was, the original version had all the elements that were to make PLATO unique: computerized instruction, an authoring system designed to make writing computerized instruction easy, and a learning management system that continually tested the student's understanding of the material and prescribed additional materials if the student needed more help.

Eventually more than 15,000 hours of PLATO courseware covered the span from kindergarten through graduate school in every conceivable subject area, including business and industry training. The course materials were made available at individual terminals throughout the world, connected through telephone lines to a powerful mainframe computer at the University of Illinois. TRO now sells PLATO materials for use on personal computers. The system has come a long way from an indecisive committee and a $10 television set. ▲

Early PLATO terminal.

FIGURE 8.3

The mainframe computer with its massive components was the norm before the advent of the microcomputer.

although important instructional experiments were being conducted. These experiments were spurred by the development of FORTRAN, a computer language easier to learn than its predecessors, and B. F. Skinner's research in programmed instruction. The step-by-step format of linear programmed instruction lent itself well to the logical "mentality" of the computer. The factors of cost, hardware reliability, and the availability of adequate materials remained major barriers to the widespread adoption of computers for instruction.

The advent of the microcomputer in 1975 altered this picture dramatically. The microcomputer was made possible by the invention of the **microprocessor,** a tiny chip of silicon that contained all the information processing ability of those roomfuls of computer circuitry of a few years earlier (Figure 8.4). The development of the silicon chip reduced the cost of computers remark-

FIGURE 8.4

The tiny microprocessor fostered the microcomputer revolution. Chips like this one are used in home appliances, automobiles, toys, and hundreds of other devices, giving each a "brain" of its own.

ably. The microcomputer was on its way to success in the marketplace, especially for use in small businesses and in the home.

ROLES OF COMPUTERS: A CHANGING THEME

The potential uses of computers in educational settings go far beyond direct instruction. One function is administrative—keeping school records, scheduling classes, doing payroll, and managing student assessment data. Another is service oriented, as when guidance programs use computers to deliver career planning assistance. In the domain of instruction there are five broad classes of computer applications:

- As an object of instruction
- As a tool
- As an instructional device
- As a catalyst for school restructuring
- As a means of teaching logical thinking

Within each of these categories, the role of the computer is varied and extensive.

Object of Instruction

The computer itself can be the object of instruction. For example, in computer literacy courses students learn about computers, and in vocational courses students learn to use computers on the job for data processing and analysis purposes. In this role, the computer is treated like any other machine one is learning to use.

When a learner is studying computer programming, the computer and the associated **software** are the objects of instruction. The various programming languages and the techniques for constructing a program using these languages are beyond the scope of this book.

FIGURE 8.5
Some computer software requires learners to interact with one another.

Tool

In its role as a tool, the computer serves as a sophisticated calculator, typewriter, multimedia composer, presentation aid, communication device, and data retrieval source.

Writing.   Computers are being used widely for word processing and desktop publishing. More and more students have access to word processing programs with which they complete term papers and assignments. Some students create multimedia term papers, integrating such media as graphics, sound, and motion for a more complete presentation. Presentation software (discussed in Chapter 5), which incorporates the computer with video projection, can be used for student presentations. Computers also allow students to communicate with others around the world via electronic mail.

Calculating.   The computer can also serve as a tool during instruction. It can be used by the learner to solve complex mathematical calculations, as a pocket calculator is used, but with increased power and speed. Any computer can analyze data, perform repeated calculations, or even gather data when hooked up to laboratory equipment.

Retrieving Information.   Today's students need to learn to manage information; to retrieve, sort, and organize information; and to evaluate their findings. For inquiry and research, students can use **databases,** collections of related information organized for quick access to specific information. Whereas a telephone book is a printed database, databases can also be stored in a computer (e.g., a computer database can include a list of telephone numbers by name or company). A database is a versatile and easy-to-learn computer tool. It can be thought of as an electronic file cabinet (Figure 8.7).

There are two types of databases. Classroom databases are created by students. For example, students can design information sheets and questionnaires, collect data, input relevant facts, and then retrieve data in a variety of ways. The facts selected might include student

FIGURE 8.6
Intense absorption is a common reaction to learning with a computer.

FIGURE 8.7
A database is used to organize information so that it can be easily sorted, ranked, calculated, and stored.

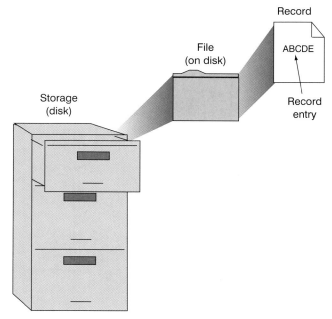

FIGURE 8.8
Icons make it easy to navigate within a database.

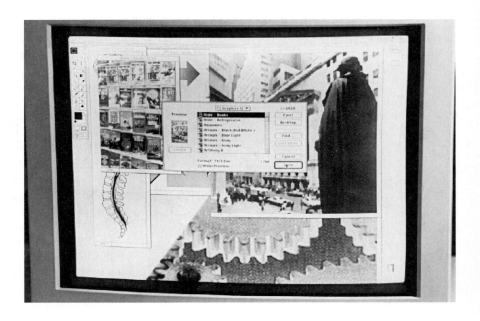

information, book reports, or sample math problems. Having constructed databases as part of their research, students are in a position to engage in higher-level thinking skills as they analyze and interpret the data.

Another type of database is the commercial database. These are either purchased on disks or CDs or accessed via telephone hookup to a computer in another location. For example, *Fifty States,* a database on diskette, contains information such as population, capital, area, major rivers, and state bird, flower, and tree for all the states in the U.S. Several companies have developed database materials for use in the classroom (see "Computer Links" on p. 256). Other larger computer databases are available via telephone and contain medical information, historical data, census figures, and the like.

FIGURE 8.9
"We're getting a new computer in class today. I hope I'm the one it replaces."

Instructional Device

Computer-assisted instruction helps students learn specific skills. For example, the Muncher series from Sunburst Company helps students master facts related to mathematics and language arts. Software is now capable of providing students with complex tasks to engage them in real-world problems. Programs like *National Inspirer* ask students to engage in activities related to geography. Video technologies can easily be incorporated, focusing attention on tangible examples. Word processing, graphics, and a host of computer software help students organize and communicate their ideas.

Summaries of research with students at various levels—elementary, secondary, college, and adult education—show that computer-based instruction generally has positive effects on student achievement. One set of summaries by James Kulik and his colleagues concluded that, on the average, computer-based instruction assisted students in raising their achievement test scores by 10 to 18 percentage points compared with conventional instruction.[1]

Catalyst for School Restructuring

Many education futurists—Perelman[2] being one of the most visible examples—foresee that rapidly burgeoning information technology will force a fundamental

---

[1]See Kulik references at end of chapter.

[2]Lewis J. Perelman, *School's Out: A Radical New Formula for the Revitalization of America's Educational System,* New York: Avon, 1992.

restructuring of the way schooling is organized. Many schools are already experimenting with alternative approaches to education, organizing instruction around technology-rich environments. These environments are typically set up to be problem-oriented, with students working in cooperative groups to grapple with real or simulated problems, employing computer-based tools to gather information, analyze it, discuss it, and eventually reach conclusions. Their project is then documented and reported by means of multimedia software. Examples of this sort of restructured school are provided in "Close-up: A Rural Community Builds Its Future" and in Chapter 11, "Close-Up: Project CHILD—A New Approach to Integrated Learning Systems."

Teaching Logical Thinking

Seymour Papert, in his 1980 book, *Mindstorms,* and again in his 1993 book, *The Children's Machine,* suggests that the computer should be an "object to think with," not a dispenser of information. Using LOGO, a procedural language that was designed for learners, students learn about the complexity of mathematics within their daily lives. Children can build and test theories about mathematics. Beyond the nature of the computer language itself, there is an underlying educational philosophy based on the concept that learners need to manipulate their environment in order to understand the concepts they are exploring. They begin to explore mathematics, seeing relationships between it and other daily activities. Papert suggests that when students have the opportunity to use programs like LOGO, they begin to develop "powerful ideas" and, in doing so, begin to develop a sense of mastery over their learning environment.

Because LOGO is very easy to learn, many believe that it is a children's computer language. Yet it is a very sophisticated computer language, capable of engaging even the expert computer programmer. LOGO is attractive even to younger learners because they find the problem-solving activities to be challenging.

LOGO works in a very logical manner, providing students with experiences that enhance their thinking skills. Because the language is based on building procedures (small sets of commands), students can learn to break a problem into smaller units. Thus, as students engage in LOGO they begin to develop skills in problem solving and logical thinking.

This is not to suggest that other computer programming languages have no place in school. Students learning languages like BASIC, Pascal, C, and others that require them to think logically and systematically can take advantage of the sophisticated thinking skills developed by learning LOGO. Young students with a background in LOGO can begin to explore other computer languages in computer science classes as they mature.

A PREVIEW OF COMPUTERS IN THE 21ST CENTURY

The emergence of computer technology coincided with a heightened awareness among educators of the impor-

CLOSE-UP

A RURAL COMMUNITY BUILDS ITS FUTURE

Teachers in the Traer, Iowa, school district collaborated to provide the students in this rural community with many educational advantages. They carefully examined the school curriculum and looked closely at its articulation. Starting with nothing, they purchased technology and integrated it into the curriculum where appropriate. Together, teachers and students conducted community fund-raisers and attended school board meetings to bring about change and to increase the amount of technology available to students in the school. Today, students have ready access to the school's rich array of resources through a schoolwide network and several computer labs, as well as access to resources outside the school walls through *America Online.* Now students can use these technology-rich resources to enhance their learning by using on-line databases and word processing to complete assignments.

FIGURE 8.10
To ensure good utilization of computers in the curriculum, teachers need continued inservice.

tance of recognizing individual learning patterns among students. Research into new instructional methods consistently indicates that the way a student learns depends in great part on the teaching-learning method employed. There are no panaceas.

In the field of instructional media and technologies for learning there is a great quest for ways of matching individual learners with appropriate instruction. Instruction should be directed at appropriate learning levels and be presented in a compatible medium at the optimal place in the most meaningful sequence. True individualization imposes a tremendous burden of decision making and resource management on the teacher. An instructor might approach an ideal level of individualization with a handful of students, but when dealing with 20, 30, 40, or more students, the logistics of individualization overwhelm any individual teacher's capacity. The computer gives promise of overcoming these and other logistical barriers to the individualization of instruction.

According to diSessa, we are entering the third stage of a computer revolution in education. The first stage "started with the realization that computers could revolutionize the way we think about thinking and the way we deal with learning." The middle stage involves getting computers into the schools. And diSessa suggests that in the third stage we will see computers as tools not only for relieving the burden of mundane activities but also for elevating our concern above that of details (such as symbol manipulation) toward important strategic and problem solving knowledge.[3]

With the current emphasis on restructuring schools, the computer is a viable tool to help educators achieve

their teaching goals in the information age. School reform advocates believe that the structure and the function of education need to keep pace with the needs of students as they enter the workplace. Most advocate the use of the computer to help students develop skills in problem solving and critical thinking. They also believe that students need experience with accessing, organizing, manipulating, and evaluating information. Students should be prepared to be active life-long learners, engaging in authentic tasks and producing realistic projects. The role of the teacher becomes one of facilitator—that is, a guide on their path to learning. Computers and computer-related technologies play a major role in achieving these goals.

FROM TEACHER TOOL TO STUDENT TOOL

Traditional instruction relies on strategies that promote deductive learning. For example, a rule or concept is usually presented to a class with examples and practice activities. Computer-assisted instruction entered the traditional classroom with many types of software that reinforced this approach to education. The software was designed to provide direct instruction to students, often programmed to branch to other segments of the lesson based on student responses. Many of these types of programs are still in use today.

In an effort to recognize the constructive nature of learning, current methods are based on engaging the student in learning in a way that allows students to develop, or construct, their own mental structures (schemata) in a particular area of study. To engage students in this type of learning, the environment must provide them with materials that allow them to explore. Papert's "microworlds"—environments that permit a student to freely experiment, test, and invent—allow students to focus on a problem area and to create solutions that are meaningful to them. Many computer software packages are available that create such learning environments and assist students in constructing their schemata. Programs such as *Inspiration,* a cognitive mapping program, facilitate the construction of concept maps, providing students with the means to relate the information to their lives and to alter those relationships as they continue to explore. Other programs, like *HyperCard* and *Linkway,* permit students to develop files of data that are related in meaningful ways.

Advantages

- *Time savings.* Allowing students to learn at their own pace produces significant time savings over conventional classroom instruction.

[3]A. A. diSessa, "The Third Revolution in Computers and Education," *Journal of Research in Science Teaching 24,* (1987), pp. 343–367.

- *Learner control.* Computer-based instruction allows students some control over the rate and sequence of their learning (individualization).
- *Reinforcement.* High-speed personalized responses to learner actions yield a high rate of reinforcement.
- *Private learning.* The patient, personal manner that can be programmed provides a more positive affective climate, especially for slow learners. Mistakes, which are inevitable, are not exposed to peers and therefore are not embarrassing.
- *Special needs.* Computer-assisted instruction is effective with special learners—at-risk students, students with diverse ethnic backgrounds, and students with disabilities. Their special needs can be accommodated and instruction proceeds at an appropriate pace.
- *Visual appeal.* Color, music, and animated graphics can add realism and appeal to drill exercises, laboratory activities, simulations, and so on.
- *Record keeping.* The record-keeping ability of the computer makes individualized instruction feasible; individual lessons can be prepared for all students (particularly mainstreamed special students), and their progress can be monitored (Figure 8.11).
- *Information management.* Computers can cover a growing knowledge base associated with the information explosion. They can manage all types of information: graphic, text, audio, and video. More information is put easily at the instructor's disposal.
- *Diverse experiences.* Computers provide a broad diversity of learning experiences. These can embody a variety of instructional methods and can be at the level of basic instruction, remediation, or enrichment.

FIGURE 8.11
Computerized gradebooks are an easy and convenient way for teachers to manage student information.

- *Consistency.* The computer supplies reliable and consistent instruction from learner to learner, regardless of the instructor, time of day, or location.
- *Effective and efficient.* Computer-based instruction can improve effectiveness and efficiency. Effectiveness refers to improved learner achievement, whereas efficiency means achieving objectives in less time or at lower cost. Efficiency is very important in business and industrial applications and is becoming increasingly important in educational settings.
- *Communication precision.* One serendipitous effect of working with computers is that they literally force us to communicate with them in an orderly and logical way. The computer user must learn to communicate with explicit, exact instructions and responses.
- *Customized learning.* With the advent of easy-to-use authoring systems, instructors can develop their own customized computer-based learning programs.

Limitations

- *Cost.* Careful consideration must be given to the costs and benefits of computers in education and training. Hardware and maintenance are the major cost factors, especially if equipment is subjected to heavy use.
- *Compatibility.* Compatibility is a problem. Software developed for one computer system may not be compatible with another.
- *Copyright.* The ease with which software can be duplicated without permission has inhibited some commercial publishers and private entrepreneurs from producing and marketing high-quality instructional software.
- *High expectations.* Users, both learners and teachers, may have unrealistic expectations for computer-based instruction. Many view computers as magical and expect learning to happen with little or no effort, but in reality users derive benefits proportional to their investments.
- *Limited range of objectives.* A limited range of objectives is being taught by computers. Most computer-based instruction does not teach effectively in the affective, motor, and interpersonal skills domains. Even in the cognitive domain, current programs tend to teach at the lower levels of knowledge and comprehension.
- *Software development.* Design of software for use with computers can be a laborious task, which often requires a high level of expertise by the developer. Consequently, quality computer-based instruction is expensive.
- *Controlled environment.* Creativity may be stifled in computerized instruction. The computer is slavish in its adherence to its program. Creative or original learner responses will be ignored or even rebuked if

the program's designer has not anticipated such possibilities.

- *Lack of social interaction.* Computer-based instruction often lacks social interaction. Learners tend to work on their own at a computer, and there may be little if any face-to-face interaction with teachers or other learners.

- *Linear programming.* Some learners, especially adults, may resist the linear, lockstep control of the learning process typical of computerized instruction. Adult learners may feel they can skim or read pages of a book faster than the computer presents the information.

- *Novelty effect.* The novelty associated with CAI in its earlier days seems to be decreasing. As learners become more familiar with computers in the home and the workplace, the newness of the computer experience wears off and has less motivational value.

Applications

Implementing Computer Use.

How best to integrate computers into school settings has been an issue since the 1970s. But the issue has been reframed as computers have proliferated in number and their functions have evolved. When initially introduced, most computers were limited to classes in programming, generally in BASIC, an early, simplified programming language. Later, computers assumed some of the mundane instructional functions, such as drill-and-practice exercises and tutorials in basic subject matter. The use of computers in the classroom was limited for a range of reasons. For one, teachers were untrained in the use of this technology. Software selection was limited. And computers were not readily available at all levels. It was not uncommon to see a few computers in the high school, generally located in the mathematics classroom area. In fact, it was most often the math teacher who became the computer expert in the school because generally he or she was interested in learning how to program.

More recently, the abundance of computers in the schools has influenced educators and others to reconsider their use. Many school districts have engaged in efforts to increase the numbers of computers in schools at all levels. Consequently, there has been a continual growth in the number of computers available in schools. In addition, teachers are becoming more familiar and comfortable with using the computer. Computer utilization has become a component of most teacher education programs.

The advances in software have also contributed to the use of computers. No longer is the selection limited to some basic drill-and-practice or tutorial software. Discovery and problem-solving software is readily available. Now the teacher has a range of software that challenges students to think. Further, teachers are also incorporating software into their programs, meaning that students are learning to word process and to use databases as part of their classes. There have been recent trends to involve students in hypermedia projects (see Chapter 9) and to promote electronic mail access, giving individuals opportunities to connect with other students and resources around the world (see Chapter 10). New views of teaching and learning have led educators to give new emphasis to engaging students in active learning projects using the computer as an exploratory tool in the learning process.

Integrating the Computer into the Curriculum.

Advances in computer technology have been influential in the integration of computer technology into the curriculum. Hardware has advanced in capacity, speed, and flexibility. Further, manufacturers have worked to create simple interfaces for users, making it easier to use computers. And software, as it becomes increasingly easier to use, continues to increase in capabilities. It is becoming easier for teachers and students to control the computer, thus making it easier for them to use it.

More emphasis is placed on providing opportunities for problem solving and cooperative learning methods. With increasing ease of use, the computer is becoming a more natural tool to use in these types of learning situations. Software is now available to provide students with experiences in working together to solve complex problems. Often students incorporate several different types of applications to explore a problem situation. For example, when assigned to prepare a report on ecology, a group of students used computer databases to search for resources they could use in their report. They sent electronic mail messages to people in several locations requesting information. They used a database program to store and sort their information. For their report they used a word processor and a hypermedia program to prepare written material and used an LCD projector to display for their classmates the information they had collected about the topic.

The procedure for educating students has shifted from providing students with information to opening doors for students to explore topics and to create meaningful learning experiences for themselves. Computer technology has been avidly incorporated into this process. The implication is that educators are moving away from the idea of school as a place to get knowledge to the view that *school is a place to learn how to learn.* The example of the students working on the ecology report is not new in the school curriculum, but the approach certainly is. The challenge for the teacher is to provide opportunities for all students to use the technology in meaningful ways to accomplish learning tasks. This may mean that the teacher selects specific software

FIGURE 8.12

A spreadsheet is a page of rows and columns that displays word, numeric, and formula entries. A spreadsheet can be used to record, average, and manipulate data.

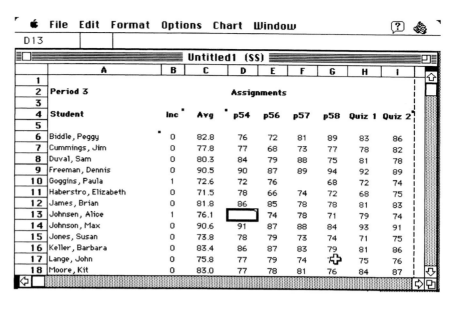

for individual students—for example, to practice specific math skills or to search on-line databases.

The computer also allows the teacher to manage instruction. Computer-managed instruction—using software that helps with, for example, assessments, student records, and scheduling—assists the teacher in managing information about students and their progress.

The One-Computer Classroom.

In many schools access to computers is a problem. Often there is a single computer lab where a teacher can take a whole class of students to work on computers as part of a lesson. However, with an increased interest by teachers in incorporating the computer into their lessons, frequently there are a limited number of times per week that any one teacher can use the computer lab. One solution has been to have a computer placed in each classroom. This single computer is therefore available to the teacher and students to use throughout the day.

It is possible for a teacher to use a single computer with a whole class of students in creative ways. Some software lends itself to being used by single students who need to work on specific tasks; other software is designed for group activities. For example, with *Decisions, Decisions* software, groups of students interact with the program to get specific information before they can proceed with their group activity. The students do not need to work on the computer during the entire lesson; they only work with it at certain intervals as needed. While one group interacts with the computer, the remaining groups are working at their desks.

The one-computer classroom, then, can be viewed as a place where the computer is used in many ways:

- *Large group.* With large-screen projection the teacher can demonstrate to a whole class how to use a particular software program or how to manage a particular set of data.
- *Small group.* A small group of students can work together with the computer. Students can interact with a program in groups, then return to their seats, allowing others to have some time on the computer. Each group has a turn using the software to gather or present data.
- *Lecture tool.* The teacher can prepare a presentation with a presentation program and then use the computer as a large projected blackboard.
- *Learning center.* Individual students or small groups can go to a learning center that has at its core a computer. Integrating a specific software program into the center, the teacher creates another type of interactive learning center.
- *Personal secretary.* Every teacher is responsible for maintaining grades, communicating with parents, and preparing instruction. The computer can assist the teacher with these types of tasks.

Computers in the School Library Media Center.

As instructional activities employ a wider variety of media and printed materials (other than regular textbooks), the task of keeping track of the ever-increasing supply of materials becomes more demanding. Many courses of instruction use booklets and worksheets. The computer can keep a record of the number of such items on hand and signal the teacher when additional copies are necessary. In some cases the text of the booklets and worksheets is stored in the computer and copies can be printed on demand.

Teachers can use the computer to access lists of materials available in their media center. Other databases, including materials available in nearby public and university libraries, can often be accessed through a computer with a modem connection.

With increased concern for efficient allocation of limited funds and other resources, the computer is a handy tool for developing budgets and keeping records of expenditures. Many instructors store in the computer a list of desired materials and equipment for future purchase. As funds become available, a request for these materials, along with necessary purchasing information, can be generated quickly.

INTEGRATION WITH METHODS

Computer systems can deliver instruction directly to students by allowing them to interact with lessons designed especially for the assigned task. As mentioned earlier, this type of teaching tool is referred to as computer-assisted instruction (CAI). The possibilities can be discussed in terms of the various types of available software and the instructional methods used. These types of

software have been changing over time, allowing for more flexibility and complexity while giving the students more freedom to learn.

Concept-Processing Tools

When engaged in thinking, students explore the possible connections between related ideas. Often they employ a technique referred to as concept mapping. Ideas about a topic are linked, forming a complex web of interrelated thoughts. Software packages such as *Inspiration* are designed to facilitate this process (see "Media File"). Students map their ideas in boxes on the computer screen—moving the idea boxes, connecting them, matching them with other ideas, and ultimately creating a graphic representation of their ideas. The program allows the students to weigh the importance of each of the concepts mapped. Further, *Inspiration* will convert the concept map into a formal outline to help students in the writing process.

Drill-and-Practice

Drill-and-practice programs lead the learner through a series of examples to increase dexterity and fluency in a skill. The computer does not display impatience and goes ahead only when mastery is shown. Drill-and-practice is used predominantly for math drills, foreign lan-

---

CLOSE-UP

CLASSROOM USE OF A SINGLE COMPUTER

A high school economics teacher uses a single computer with a class of 24 students. A computer with an LCD panel on top of an overhead projector allows all students to see what is on the monitor.

The teacher uses prepared computer graphics instead of overhead transparencies for key points and illustrative graphs. She can advance from one visual to the next as needed and can also reveal key words from the presentation with the touch of a key.

The biggest advantage of the computer in a large-group instructional situation is its usefulness in presenting "what if" results. For example, while presenting the concepts of supply and demand, the students can discuss the effect of an increase in availability of a product on its cost. Following the discussion the teacher can project the results. The teacher can also put student-suggested values into the computer, and the class can see the results immediately. Economics comes alive in the classroom when years of data can be manipulated within minutes for all to see.

▼ MEDIA FILE

Inspiration
Concept-Processing Program

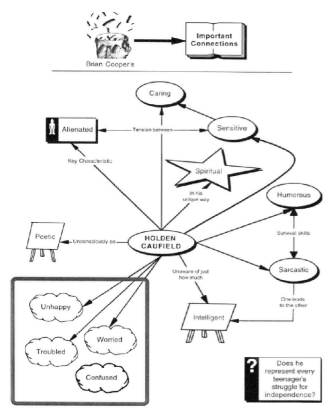

Inspiration is a software package that facilitates brainstorming, concept mapping, and planning. It creates a visual diagram of the ideas generated by an individual or group. Use the program to create overviews, presentation visuals, and flow charts. It is designed to help younger students develop skills in concept mapping. Once their thoughts have been visualized, *Inspiration* easily converts the concept map into a word-processing outline.

Source: Inspiration Software, Inc.

▼ MEDIA FILE

Wordwright
Drill-and-Practice Program

Wordwright is one of a series of courseware packages developed by the Encyclopaedia Britannica Corporation. The package includes a drill-and-practice lesson on word definitions, as well as a range of other word games and tests. The vocabulary drill-and-practice lesson presents a sequence of 10 vocabulary questions. If a student's answer is correct, the machine presents the next question. If a student's answer is incorrect, the machine responds with the correct definition with examples of correct usage. After presenting the 10 questions, the computer gives a summary of all the correct and incorrect words.

Source: Encyclopaedia Britannica Educational Corporation.

---

guage translation, vocabulary building, and the like. For example, the program *Sentences* lets the learners practice sentence construction.

Drill-and-practice programs provide a variety of questions with varied formats. The student is usually allowed several tries before the computer presents the correct answer. Several levels of difficulty can be available within the same drill-and-practice program. The program gives correction, remediation, or encouragement as appropriate.

Tutorial

In the tutorial role, the computer acts as the teacher. All interaction is between the computer and the learner. One example of a tutorial is *Mavis Beacon Teaches Typing*, which guides students to learn touch typing skills (see "Media File").

In this method, the pattern followed is basically that of branching programmed instruction (explained in Chapter 11); that is, information is presented in small units followed by a question. The student's response is analyzed by the computer (compared with responses supplied by the designer), and appropriate feedback is given. A complicated network of pathways, or branches, can be programmed. The more alternatives available to the computer, the more adaptive the tutorial can be to individual differences. The extent to which a skilled, live tutor can be approximated depends on the creativity of the designer.

▼ MEDIA FILE

Mavis Beacon Teaches Typing
Tutorial Program

Mavis Beacon Teaches Typing teaches the learner to keyboard. Included are carefully guided instructions at each level, as well as practice opportunities to improve speed and accuracy. Graphics, charts, and appearances by Mavis herself encourage novice typists to continue to work on their skills. Progress records are maintained for each learner, providing the teacher with information and allowing the learner to resume following an interruption in the instruction.

Source: Software Toolworks: Mindscape.

▼ MEDIA FILE

Language Carnival
Game

**What do you get
when you cross . . .**

Two ducks and a cow?

1. Swimming trunks

2. Quackers and milk

3. A caterpillar

4. A feathered fish

5. A milkshake

Language Carnival uses an amusement park theme to make learning about language fun and exciting. Four separate games are included in each program. Each game is based on a different carnival activity, such as "Dart Throw," "Baseball Toss," and "Muscle Power." When students correctly answer questions, a dart pops a balloon, the strongman rings the bell, or other successful outcomes result. The use of carnival games and humor in *Language Carnival 1* and *2* motivates elementary students to explore, explain, and practice various language and thinking skills.

Source: DLM Teaching Resources.

Games

In Chapter 11 we discuss the distinction between gaming and simulation. A game activity may or may not entail simulation elements. Likewise, a game may or may not be instructional. It depends on whether the skill practiced in the game is an academic one—that is, related to a specific instructional objective or a workplace skill.

Recreational games can serve a useful purpose in building computer literacy in an enjoyable, nonthreatening manner. But the ultimate goal of useful learning must be kept in mind. Instructors experienced in computer utilization recommend rationing purely recreational game use, using it as a reward for completing other assignments. Games range from those with specific learning outcomes, like *Language Carnival* (see "Media File"), to those that emphasize entertainment while teaching problem solving strategies, like *King Arthur's Magic Castle*.

Simulation

The simulation method of instruction is described more fully in Chapter 11. In this method, the learner confronts an approximation of a real-life situation. It allows

▼ MEDIA FILE

Decisions, Decisions
Simulation

Decisions, Decisions is a series of role-playing software packages designed specifically to generate informed discussion and decision making in the classroom using only one computer. The program has a mode for whole-class discussion with the teacher leading the entire group, as in a traditional classroom. In addition, it offers a small-group option for managing a cooperative learning environment. Up to six small groups of students move through the simulation independently directed by the computer.

Source: Tom Snyder Productions.

realistic practice without the expense or risks otherwise involved.

The computer-based simulation *Operation: Frog* allows a student to dissect and reconstruct a frog using the same "instruments" that would be used in a biology laboratory. The student must remove the 23 organs in sequence as in an actual dissection. Help screens and descriptive materials are available at the student's fingertips (see "Blueprint" at the end of this chapter).

In military and industrial settings, training for operation and maintenance of complex equipment—aircraft, weapons systems, nuclear power plants, oil rigs, and the like—is often given on computer-based simulators. As discussed in Chapter 11, these large-scale simulators allow trainees to experience lifelike situations without the danger and expense involved in practice with the actual equipment.

Discovery

Discovery is a general term to describe activities using an inductive approach to learning; that is, presenting prob-

▼ MEDIA FILE

Explorer Series
Discovery Program

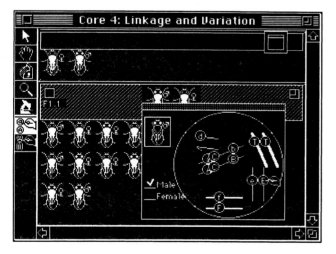

Every classroom is filled with students of varying abilities and learning styles. This innovative series of programs focuses on the everyday experiences students are most likely to have in common and uses them as a springboard for helping them to learn abstract scientific concepts. There are three programs in this series: *Biology Explorer, Chemistry Explorer,* and *Physics Explorer.* Each program includes a series of guided activities that engage learners, incorporating a learning model that leads students from simple to more complex concepts.

Source: LOGAL® Software, Inc.

lems that the student solves through trial and error or systematic approaches. It approximates laboratory learning outside the classroom.

Using the discovery method in CAI, the learner employs an information retrieval strategy to get information from a database. For example, a salesperson interested in learning about competitors' products can select from a set of critical product features, display them on the computer, and draw conclusions about the comparisons of the products. Some discovery lessons analyze large databases of election information, population statistics, or other user-built databases.

Problem Solving

In problem solving, the learner uses previously mastered skills to resolve a challenging problem. The student must examine the data or information presented, clearly define the problem, perhaps state hypotheses, perform experiments, then examine the data and generate a solution. The computer may present the problem, process the data, maintain a database, and provide feedback when appropriate.

One commercially available problem-solving program is *Memory: A First Step in Problem Solving.* It provides students in kindergarten through sixth grade with opportunities to practice the skill and strategies involved in problem solving. The program introduces a generic approach to problem solving across all subject areas as well as in common lifelike situations. The goal is not to present a fixed problem-solving model but to promote the use of an individualized, systematic approach in which the student establishes a model that is appropriate to a specific problem, using strategies from a personal repertoire. The multimedia kit includes a chart showing a problem-solving skill matrix, classroom lessons, software summary sheets, program descriptions for each computer disk, computer disks, and a hand puppet for use with younger students.

Another problem-solving program, *The Factory,* challenges the learner to "manufacture" products according to specifications provided by the computer. There are 72 different combinations from which to select. The sequence in which the three types of machines are used is another critical factor. Of course, there are numerous ways to solve each challenging problem presented by the program (see "Media File").

During problem-solving activities students not only learn about the content under study but also develop higher-level thinking skills. These higher-level cognitive processes include reasoning skills and logical and critical thinking. The primary reason for teaching elementary computer languages, such as LOGO, is not for the students to learn programming itself but to enable them to use the computer for problem solving.

▼ MEDIA FILE

The Factory
Problem-Solving Program

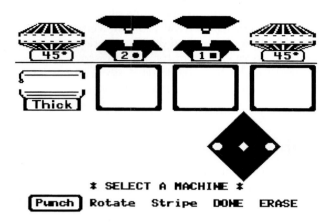

SELECT A MACHINE

Punch Rotate Stripe DONE ERASE

The Factory focuses on several strategies used in problem solving: working backward, analyzing a process, determining a sequence, and applying creativity. The learners are given a square on the computer and three types of machines. The "punch" machine can punch squares or circles with one, two, or three of each. The "rotation" machine can be programmed to rotate the square 45, 90, 135, or 180 degrees. And the "stripe" machine paints a thin, medium, or thick stripe.

The program has three types of activities. The learners can "test a machine" to see what each option does. They can "build a factory" composed of up to eight machines to make a product of their own design. The most difficult task is to assemble and program a variety of machines in the proper sequence to "duplicate a product" shown on the screen.

Source: WINGS for Learning/Sunburst.

Information Tools

As students begin to work with information, they find the computer tools available to them help make the process easier and fun. Using a word processor program for writing makes it easy for students to edit their work. Once they have gathered their ideas into concept maps, they then begin to work those ideas into connected text. The word processor makes it possible for students to work with their ideas and to quickly make changes as they explore various ways their ideas can be presented. Spelling and grammar checking are available to students. A thesaurus makes it easier for them to find the right word for a specific situation. And editing, a process children are not prone to enjoy, suddenly becomes easier. Students are more willing to make changes when the editing process is simplified.

Students enjoy putting their ideas onto the page. They especially enjoy seeing their work in finished copy.

Desktop publishing allows students to not only print a nice copy of their work but also to design layouts that are creative and a pleasure to see. Using a desktop publishing program, students can add graphics to their pages. They can see how their pages will look before they print them. Students of all ages like to produce their writings in formal documents, like small books and newsletters. Class newsletters are very popular with students working together to produce a document that they are proud to share with family and friends.

As students work with large amounts of information, it is essential that they learn how to cluster that information. A database allows students to store large amounts of information in ways that make it easy for them to retrieve it. By learning how to develop databases, students begin to organize their knowledge and understand ways they can group that information.

A database allows students to quickly get the specific information they are seeking. Computer catalogs and on-site/on-line databases allow students to search for information. The amount of information available today is constantly growing. When students understand how information is organized and what the process is for retrieving it, they can gather vast amounts of information quickly and easily.

Graphics Tools

Drawing and creating graphics is a fun activity for students. Computer software such as *KidsPix* can make drawing even more pleasurable. This software allows children to use, for example, a "rubber stamp" that makes noise as it marks on the screen, to erase a picture to find a hidden one behind it, and to use a "drippy"

FIGURE 8.13
Desktop publishing software allows students to produce their own written materials with minimal time and little computer expertise.

TABLE 8.1
Utilization of CAI methods

METHODS	DESCRIPTION	ROLE OF TEACHER	ROLE OF COMPUTER	ROLE OF STUDENT	APPLICATIONS/ EXAMPLES
Drill-and-Practice	Content already taught Reviews basic facts and terminology Variety of questions in varied formats Question-answer drills repeated as necessary	Arranges for prior instruction Selects material Matches drill to student Checks progress	Asks questions "Evaluates" student response Provides immediate feedback Records student progress	Practices content already taught Responds to questions Receives confirmation or correction Chooses content and difficulty level	Conducts trial and error Parts of a microscope Completing balance sheets Vocabulary building Math facts Product knowledge
Tutorial	Presentation of new information Teaches concepts and principles Provides remedial instruction	Selects material Adapts instruction Monitors	Presents information Asks questions Monitors responses Provides remedial feedback Summarizes key points Keeps records	Interacts with computer Sees results Answers questions Asks questions	Clerical training Bank teller training Science Medical procedures Bible study
Gaming	Competitive Drill-and-practice in a motivational format Individual or small group	Sets limits Directs process Monitors results	Acts as competitor, judge, and score-keeper	Learns facts, strategies, skills Evaluates choices Competes with computer	Fraction games Counting games Spelling games Typing (arcade-type) games
Simulation	Approximates real-life situations Based upon realistic models Individual or small group	Introduces subject Presents background Guides "debriefing"	Plays role(s) Delivers results of decisions Maintains the model and its database	Practices decision making Makes choices Receives results of decisions Evaluates decisions	Troubleshooting History Medical diagnosis Simulators (pilot, driver) Business management Laboratory experiments
Discovery	Inquiry into database Inductive approach Trial and error Tests hypotheses	Presents basic problem Monitors student progress	Presents student with source of information Stores data Permits search procedures	Makes hypotheses Tests guesses Develops principles or rules	Social science Science Food-intake analysis Career choices
Problem Solving	Defines problem States hypothesis Examines data Generates solution	Assigns problems Assists students Checks results	Presents problem Manipulates data Maintains database Provides feedback	Defines the problem Sets up the solution Manipulates variables	Business Creativity Troubleshooting Mathematics Computer programming

FIGURE 8.14
Examples of computer clip art.

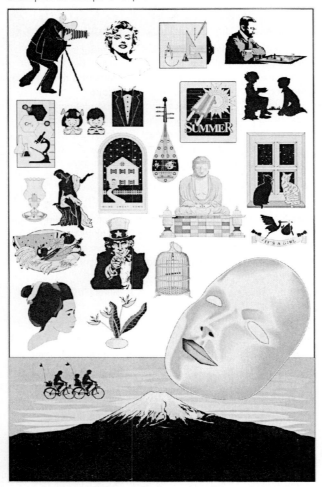

paintbrush. Computer technology thus changes the dynamics of art for children.

As students gain skills in using drawing software, they can expand their skills into more complex drawing and drafting programs. High school students can use computer-aided design (CAD) and graphics programs to prepare complex visuals. Many of the skills associated with these types of software are easy for students to learn. For example, an art program like *Canvas* allows students to develop complex projects using an array of tools, ranging from basic drawing tools for lines and shapes to advanced drawing tools for editing and redesigning. A simple picture can be developed into a very artistic piece with only a few keystrokes.

Further, presentation software has become a very popular format for teachers and students alike. With the computer connected to an LCD panel, it is possible to create colorful and animated overheads. Using a program like Microsoft's *Powerpoint*, sometimes individuals spend more time deciding the color scheme or the font style than they

do actually preparing the content of the presentation. (See Chapter 5 for further discussion of this topic.)

INTEGRATED LEARNING SYSTEMS

In many schools a visible form of computer use is the **integrated learning system (ILS),** referring to a networked set of computer workstations equipped with software that provides a particular set of sequential lessons. Students work through these lessons as prescribed by the built-in management system, which tracks individual student progress. These systems are "integrated" in the sense that each lesson is connected with the next, all lessons are correlated with a set of objectives, and all tests are matched to the lessons and objectives. Further, the software typically is customized to match the content, objectives, and chapter sequence of the textbook used.

An ILS installation might, for example, provide four networked computer workstations in each classroom in a school building. The menu might include hundreds of carefully sequenced lessons throughout several grade levels and several subjects. The teacher can decide which students will use the system for which lessons. Students work individually at the workstations for about 45 minutes per day. When they finish one lesson they are tested and directed to the next appropriate lesson. The management software gathers and stores all information about student progress and supplies reports to the teacher and administrators.

Advantages

- *Self-pacing.* Students can move through the material at their own pace, being tested and branched at frequent intervals.
- *Total package.* A major advantage from the administrative standpoint is having a total integrated package of hardware and software; there is no need to try to piece together your own network or to shop for and evaluate courseware.
- *Validated.* The learning programs can be tested and validated before distribution; with a large base of clients, the vendors can afford to invest in curriculum research and development. The software is revised and updated by vendors on a regular basis. Some vendors even provide "money-back guarantees" of student success.

Limitations

- *Courseware quality.* The quality of the courseware is variable; some of it is low-level, uninspiring drill-and-practice material. The instructional strategies used in computer-assisted programs may be contrary to the teacher's own teaching philosophy. A frequent criticism is overemphasis on low-level knowledge and skills. These criticisms are not necessarily inherent in truly integrated learning systems, but they do apply to many of the commercially sold packages.

- *Evidence of effectiveness.* There is little objective research to indicate the effectiveness of these materials; most of the existing studies have been commissioned by one of the vendors and have been conducted with less than acceptable rigor.
- *Loss of flexibility.* One of the trade-offs made in adopting an integrated computer system is flexibility. Teachers and students are limited to using the same hardware and software in the same way. Some argue that the real potential of computers is achieved when users have control and can take off in their own directions. The standardization imposed by the typical ILS is contrary to the impulses of most teachers to maintain autonomy in terms of content and methods.
- *Reports.* The individual progress reports given to teachers are often hard to interpret.
- *Curricular integration.* Perhaps the most serious risk of the ILS is, ironically, its lack of integration with the curriculum. The components of the computer system are integrated with each other, but the system may not be integrated with the rest of the school curriculum. One of the most frequent criticisms of curricula is that of fractionation—fragments of facts and skills taught in isolation, not coalescing into a whole.

Applications

ILSs are used most commonly for basic mathematics and language arts instruction. Often, low-achieving or special needs students are "pulled out of" their regular classrooms to use the ILS in a cubicle within a computer lab environment. Homebound students can be linked to the network as well. Some systems specialize in software for remediation of basic skills, others offer broad curricula encompassing virtually all the standard school subjects. Some systems use the networking capability to make databases, such as encyclopedias and libraries of video clips, available to all users.

The most attractive applications in the future are likely to be ones like Project CHILD (see "Close-up" in Chapter 11) in which the ILS lessons are one component of an overall school program that combines team teaching, thematic units, student and parent involvement in goal setting, and customization to the prescriptions of the local teaching staff.

SOFTWARE SELECTION CRITERIA

There are several factors associated with selecting software (see "Appraisal Checklist: Computer Software"). Foremost is to examine the software within the context of the learning outcomes. Other factors that should be considered include content, format, ease of operation, design, and completeness of the package.

Accuracy. When looking at software a teacher needs to consider the content of the software in terms of its accuracy. If the software is older, some of the information may be out of date. Also, it is important to consider the sequencing of the information. Information should be presented in a clear and logical manner. Finally, the teacher needs to examine the intent of the lesson and its relation to the intended student goals.

Feedback. It is important that software follow sound educational techniques and principles. In a drill-and-practice program it is important that the students have frequent informative feedback.

Learner Control. Another important criterion is the amount of learner control given to the student. Students should be able to control the pacing and direction of their learning. Software should provide students with opportunities to select topics within areas of study. Also, students need to be able to control how quickly they progress through material. Finally, the information needs to be presented in an interesting manner to maintain student interest and involvement in the tasks.

Prerequisites. Practical examples that relate to the student's own experiences are more valuable within the learning process. Prerequisite skills need to be identified if they are essential for successful use of the software. Information needs to be presented at a level that is appropriate for the student.

Ease of Use. Further, software needs to be easy to use. Software is user-friendly if it makes the computer transparent in the learning process. When a student must focus more on the operation of the software than on developing an understanding of the content, then the computer is interfering with rather than assisting the learning process.

Ease of use is a particularly critical attribute in situations where students are working individually or in small groups on different projects, using different software. If the teacher must continually be interrupted to help students cope with obstacles in using different software, then both teacher and students become frustrated.

Special Features. Sometimes software has special effects or features that may be essential for effec-

✔ APPRAISAL CHECKLIST

COMPUTER SOFTWARE

KEY WORDS: _____ , _____ , _____

Title _____

Series Title (if applicable) _____

Source _____

Date _____ **Cost** _____ **Length** _____ minutes

Subject Area _____

Intended Audience _____

Brief Description

Objectives

Entry Capabilities Required (e.g., prior knowledge, reading ability, vocabulary level, math ability)

Format
- ❑ **Drill and practice**
- ❑ **Tutorial**
- ❑ **Game**
- ❑ **Simulation**
- ❑ **Discovery program**
- ❑ **Problem solving**

Rating	High	Medium	Low	Comments
Match with curriculum	❑	❑	❑	
Accurate and current	❑	❑	❑	
Clear and concise language	❑	❑	❑	
Arouse motivation/maintain interest	❑	❑	❑	
Learner participation	❑	❑	❑	
Technical quality	❑	❑	❑	
Evidence of effectiveness (e.g., field-test results)	❑	❑	❑	
Free from objectionable bias	❑	❑	❑	
User guide/documentation	❑	❑	❑	
Clear directions	❑	❑	❑	
Stimulates creativity	❑	❑	❑	

Strong Points

Weak Points

Recommended Action _____ **Name** _____ **Date** _____
_____

A computer version of this Checklist is found in "The Classroom Link."

tive learning. Often, however, these are only window dressing and add no value to the learning process. In fact, they may interfere with learning. Color, graphics, animation, and sound should be a part of quality software only if they contribute to student learning. As discussed in Chapter 3, text should be presented in a consistent manner, using size, color, and location to reduce the cognitive burden of deciphering meaning. Keystroking and mousing techniques should be intuitive for the student. The manner in which the student interacts with software needs to be transparent, allowing the student to focus on the content.

If the **courseware** is a package of materials that includes software, booklets, or other elements, it should be complete and easy to use. Courseware should be directly relevant to the learning objectives for the course. Multimedia packages need to be complete, so that it is possible to use the materials at once. Certain types of packages require that students work through whole sets of content before moving onto another area. The materials need to be integrated into the curriculum, being flexible enough for the teacher to adapt them as appropriate for specific topics or students. Some packages have management systems built into them, permitting the teacher to vary the order, pacing, or criteria for success. The management system needs to be easy to adapt to the particular needs of the instructional situation.

For learning experiences in which a teacher selects utility software, such as a word processor or database, the teacher needs to appraise the software using similar criteria. It is important to consider ease of use, flexibility, and options that allow students to use the package successfully. It would be inappropriate for a teacher to select a word processing program that is very complex to operate when children are just beginning to learn to use the computer within the writing process. A simple,

easy to manage word processor is better, allowing students the opportunity to understand how the tool can facilitate their writing, rather than frustrating them as they try to write.

COMPUTER HARDWARE

Basic Components

Regardless of the size of the computer or complexity of the system, computers have a number of standard components. The physical equipment that makes up the computer is referred to as the **hardware.** The basic hardware components are diagrammed in Figure 8.15.

Input Device. Input devices transmit information into the computer. The most commonly used input device is a keyboard. Others include mice, track balls, joysticks, and graphics tablets. Graphics tablets can be used by students or teachers to incorporate drawings into their programs. Science laboratory monitoring devices can also be connected directly to a personal computer with the proper interface device.

Central Processing Unit. The central processing unit (CPU) is the core element, or "brain," that carries out all the calculations and controls the total system. In a personal computer the CPU is one of the tiny chips (microprocessors) inside the machine. (See Figure 8.4.)

Memory. Memory stores information for manipulation by the CPU. The memory contains the control function—that is, the programs that are written to tell the CPU what to do in what order. Memory and the CPU are part of the computer and usually are built into the machine.

In computers, control instructions and sets of data are stored in two types of memory:

- **ROM (read only memory).** This consists of the control instructions that have been "wired" permanently into the memory and which the computer will need constantly, such as programming languages and internal monitoring functions.
- **RAM (random access memory).** This is the flexible part of the memory. The particular program or set of data being manipulated by the user is temporarily stored in RAM, then erased to make way for the next program.

A computer's memory size is usually described in terms of how many bytes it can store at one time. A **byte** is the number of **bits** required to represent and store one character (letter or number) of text. A byte is most commonly, but not always, made up of eight bits in various combinations of 0s and 1s (see Figure 8.16).

FIGURE 8.15
Basic elements of a personal computer.

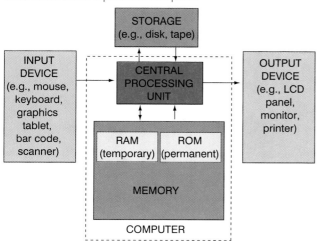

FIGURE 8.16
Representation of the letter A in ASCII (American Standard Code for Information Interchange) code when 8 bits represent 1 byte.

FIGURE 8.16
Representation of the letter A in ASCII (American Standard Code for Information Interchange) code when 8 bits represent 1 byte.

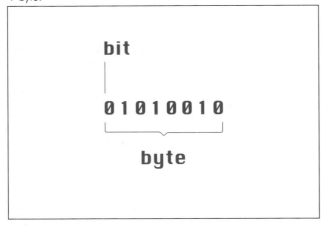

Storage. Computers can process only one program at a time, so you need a place to store the other programs and sets of data for future use. These programs and data are stored outside the computer's CPU.

Part of the storage mechanism includes disk drives, from which information is entered into the computer's memory. The two widely used types of disk drives are floppy disk and hard disk drives. Floppy disk drives are used when storing information outside the computer; hard disk drives are used when storing information inside the computer. These devices allow the computer to read information from and write information onto the disks. Another, newer form of disk drive that is becoming popular for storage is the CD-ROM drive, which allows the user to gain access to a large amount of information stored on a CD-ROM disc. It does not allow the user to change the information on the CD-ROM disc, however.

There are three types of storage disks and several sizes. The basic types are floppy (flexible), hard (rigid), and CD-ROM. A floppy disk (Figure 8.17) is a thin, circular piece of plastic with a magnetic recording surface, enclosed in a plastic or cardboard jacket for protection. The computer reads the information on the disk through an oblong-shaped hole in the jacket. The two standard sizes of disks are 3½ inches and 5¼ inches (see Figure 8.18). They come in both low-density and high-density formats. Because of the larger storage capacity of the high-density floppy disks, these have become the standard format.

Hard disks are made of aluminum and coated with a magnetic recording surface. A large amount of information can be stored on hard disks, and because they operate at very high speeds, the information can be accessed quickly. The size of the hard disk is a consideration

A kilobyte (Kb) refers to approximately 1,000 bytes (1,024, to be exact), and a **megabyte** ("meg" or Mb) indicates 1,000 Kb or approximately a million bytes. A megabyte is the unit used to measure storage capacity of a computer. Thus, if a computer can store 1,024,000 bytes, it is said to have 1 "meg" memory capacity. The more powerful machines are capable of processing more bytes simultaneously, thus increasing their processing capacity.

The memory of the computer can be a limiting factor. You need to be sure that the computer has enough memory to run the software you will be using. If you plan to use more than one application at a time, it is recommended that you have at least four megabytes (4Mb) of RAM. One megabyte of memory can hold approximately 2,000 single-spaced pages of text.

FIGURE 8.17
The floppy disk is a convenient way to transfer information from one computer to another.

FIGURE 8.18
Computer disks: 5¼-inch and 3½-inch.

when selecting hardware. Experienced users tend toward the higher-capacity hard disks, in the 80–100-megabyte range. In general, the larger the hard disk, the smaller the cost per megabyte.

The compact disc (as described in Chapter 6), used for digitally storing and reproducing music and verbal narration, is also used to store and retrieve text and graphics. A **CD-ROM (compact disc-read only memory)** drive connects to a computer, which can read data from a compact disc in much the same way as from a floppy or hard disk. CD-ROM has the advantage of storing more data—approximately 250,000 pages of text or the equivalent of several hundred floppy disks. An entire encyclopedia can be stored on a single CD-ROM with room to spare. A computer can find and list all page references to any topic in that encyclopedia within three seconds.

A disadvantage of current CD-ROM technology is that the user cannot save new information on the disk (the information is "read only"). Some CD-WORM (write once, read many) drives allow users to record data onto a compact disc, but the data can be recorded only once and cannot be altered or updated. Then the disk can be read many times. This is a useful format for anyone with a unique databank that must be read often.

CD-ROM technology has been used to increase the availability of the ERIC (Educational Resources Information Center) database, which contains abstracts of more than 700 journals in education and thousands of unpublished educational documents.

Chapter 9 discusses how compact discs, used as a video source, are combined with computers as interactive video. Newer computers have CD-ROM readers built into them.

Output Device. Output devices display the results of your program. A television-type monitor, referred to as a CRT (cathode-ray tube), is the usual output device of a personal computer. It may be built into the total package, or it may be a separate component.

Computers commonly provide output in the form of data printed on paper sheets (hard copy). Printers are available in a range of prices and quality. As shown in Table 8.3, quality of text and graphics correlates with cost.

COMPUTER LABS AND LANS

The Computer Lab

When a teacher wants each student to be working on a computer during a lesson, it is necessary for the whole class to have access to computers simultaneously. Schools often place 15 to 20 computers together in a single room called a computer lab.

There are advantages to using a computer lab. A group of students can be taught the same lesson simultaneously, which might be more efficient for the teacher. Also, software can be located in one place conveniently. And supervision and security are often easier when all the computers are located in a single room.

The foremost limitation with the computer lab is access. If there are no other computers available to students outside the computer lab, then students may have a problem. If a class is scheduled to use the lab, then students will have to wait until the lab is not scheduled to use the facilities. Also, because of scheduling problems, some classes may not have access to the lab at all.

Labs are often structured to facilitate ease of use by using networks, which make it easy to use the available software. Another solution would be to place computers throughout the school building. Thus, students can access computers in the computer lab, their classrooms, and the media center.

FIGURE 8.19
A printer to use with a computer.

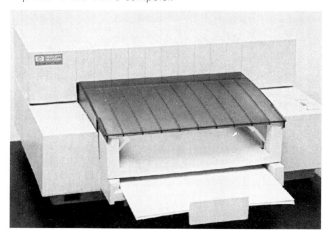

TABLE 8.2
Disk Types

TYPE	SIZE	PHYSICAL CHARACTERISTICS	STORAGE CAPACITY	MACHINES USING
Floppy disks				
	$3^1/_2$ diameter	Thin flexible plastic disk in a stiff plastic case	Double-sided 700 to 800 K Double-sided, high density 1.4 megabytes	Commonly used with Macintosh, Amiga, Atari, ST, IBM PS/2 series, and some PC compatibles
	$5^1/_4$ diameter	Thin flexible plastic disk in a stiff paper case	Double-sided, double-density, 340 to 360K Double-sided, high density, 1 to 2 megabytes	Commonly used with Apple II series, PCs, and PC compatibles
Hard disks				
	Varies— usually $5^1/_4$ in. or $3^1/_2$ in. diameter	Metal or metal-coated platters Internal or external to the computer	80 megabytes most common Up to several gigabytes[1] available for some machines	Available for all personal computers
Compact discs (CD-ROM)				
	$4^3/_4$ in. diameter	Metalicized disc coated with clear plastic	Approximately 550 megabytes	Commonly used with Macs and PCs Also used with special systems like CD-I

[1] A gigabyte is equal to one billion bytes

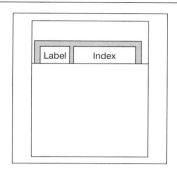

Keep a 5¼-inch disk in its protective envelope when not in use. The 3½-inch disk does not need to be kept in its plastic bag.

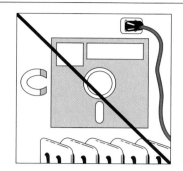

Protect disk from excessive heat and magnetized objects, including power cords which set up their own magnetic fields. Shade disks from direct sunlight.

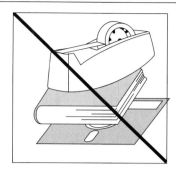

Disks should be stored vertically in their box, not laid flat, especially not with heavy objects set on them.

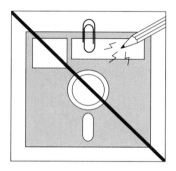

Marking on the disk label should be done only with felt-tip pen, not with a sharp pencil or ballpoint pen. Avoid paper clips, which also could scratch the disk.

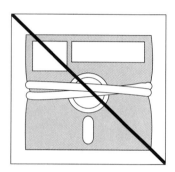

Do not bend, fold, or warp 5¼-inch disks by using rubber bands.

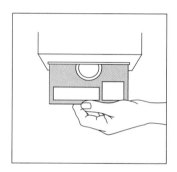

Protect the delicate surface from fingerprints by grasping the disk only by the edge or label area to place it into the disk drive.

Local Area Networks

When computers are connected to each other, they form a network. A **local area network (LAN)** connects computers within a limited area, normally a building or office area (See Figure 8.20). A **wide area network (WAN)** provides connections with computers over a wider range, such as across the city or state or even the country. (We will discuss wide area networks further in Chapter 10.)

A local area network relies on a centralized computer that acts as a "file server." Other computers are connected to this central computer via special wiring. A computer lab is often a LAN because all the computers are connected to a single file server computer, usually tucked away in a closet or other out-of-the-way space. Whole buildings can also be connected to a local area network. A single computer, generally located in the office or media center, can serve an entire school's file server. Thus, all the classrooms would have access to the school's collection of software.

The advantages to having a LAN include ease of communication. A local area network allows people to communicate with each other by leaving messages on the network system. Also, more people have access to

TABLE 8.3

Comparison of the major types of printers

TYPE OF PRINTER	TEXT QUALITY	GRAPHICS QUALITY	COST
Dot Matrix	Low	Low	Low
Letter Quality	Medium	Low	Medium
Ink Jet	High	High	Medium
Laser	High	High	High

FIGURE 8.20
A local area network (LAN) for a computer lab.

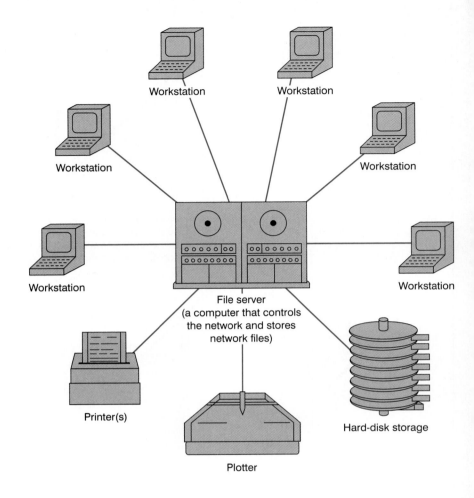

software and information. For example, the media center's catalog of materials can be stored on the file server. Then teachers and students could have easy access to information about what is available on a certain topic.

Limitations to having a LAN include cost. It is expensive to establish a building-wide network. There must be a large-capacity computer to serve as a file server; the entire building must have wiring to connect the computers; and, if the system is to be effective, computers must be located in each room or office to allow everyone access. Some older computers lend themselves to being easily used for connecting to a LAN. Since the file server houses the software and information, the computer connected to the network does not have to be up-to-date.

Another limitation is the need to purchase special network-compatible software. This software generally is more costly, although not as expensive as purchasing separate copies for each station. Finally, a network can be accessed by only a limited number of users. Without extra equipment, some people may have to wait their turn to gain access to the network.

FIGURE 8.21
Networking allows multiple students to use the same software simultaneously.

High School Biology

High school biology students need to study the frog as part of their unit on amphibians. The teacher's intention is to have students incorporate some of their math concepts at the same time.

Analyze Learners

General Characteristics

Robin Meadows's students are primarily sophomores in high school. It is their first biology course; however, they were introduced to biological principles in a general science course the previous year. In general science, the students did not study the frog but did dissect an earthworm. They represent a broad range of socioeconomic backgrounds, grade-point averages, and reading levels. Some students have minor physical handicaps and others have low IQs. Because the school district has a computer literacy program that begins in the elementary schools, all students have keyboarding and computer skills.

Entry Competencies

Approximately 80% of the students are able to do the following:

1. Define or describe simple biological terms: *amphibian, anterior, artery, circulatory system, digestive system, dorsal, posterior, vein, ventral,* and *vertebrate.*
2. Measure an object within two millimeters using a metric ruler.
3. Convert from millimeters to centimeters and reverse the process.

Learning Style

Most students prefer visual learning and manipulation of materials, especially those students with low verbal skills. These students enjoy interacting with their peers, and a majority of them are motivated by using a computer to learn.

State Objectives

The teacher wants the students to learn a frog's anatomy and to practice dissection techniques. The specific objectives are to be able to do the following:

1. Identify by name and function 20 common frog organs and locate these organs on a drawing.
2. Trace the blood flow in the circulatory system of the frog.
3. Describe the nature and function of the female and male urogenital systems of a frog and identify 10 components of each system.
4. Demonstrate proper dissection techniques.

Select Methods, Media, and Materials

The teacher formerly used the standard frog-dissection laboratory to provide hands-on practice in problem solving. A teacher in a neighboring school district mentioned a microcomputer program called *Operation: Frog,* which simulates laboratory dissection of a frog. The teacher previewed the sim-

ulation along with the teacher's handbook. The program features two stages: dissection and reconstruction. In the dissection stage, students use the computer to locate and remove organs and to investigate the frog's body systems close up. In the reconstruction stage, students use the computer to reassemble the dissected frog.

In considering whether to use the simulation, the teacher listed the following strengths: (1) through computer simulation students have an opportunity to see how several organs work in a live frog (which is not possible in an actual dissection); (2) a scoring feature adds an additional level of challenge for some students; (3) the reading level is low; and (4) the cost of enough copies is within the school's budget (computers are already available) and cheaper than obtaining frogs for each student.

The drawbacks include the following: (1) students don't work with all of the frog's body parts, only 23 main organs (no bones and only one sample muscle are included); (2) body organs are unrealistically colored to make them easier to find; and (3) the simulation doesn't provide practice of the manual skills involved in an actual dissection.

Robin considered these trade-offs and decided to remove objective 4 as a goal for this particular lesson and to employ a combination of presentation and simulation methods, using *Operation: Frog* for the hands-on activity.

Utilize Media and Materials

The teacher introduces the lesson by showing a short videotape on the life cycle of frogs. Then the students work in pairs on the computer simulation. While one person in the pair performs the "dissection," the other records information from the screen on laboratory worksheets copied from the teacher's handbook.

The students use the same "instruments" they would use in an actual lab: dissecting scissors, a probe, forceps, and a magnifying lens. Diagrams and text screens offer detailed information about organs and body systems. A special help feature within the program provides prompts and guidance.

Students are instructed to observe the animated blood flow, to remove the common organs, and to explore the urogenital system in detail.

Require Learner Participation

The students are actively involved with both manipulating the dissecting instruments within the simulation and recording data. After the lab they must complete the lab report and then go to the library to research the nature and function of the male and female urogenital systems of frogs.

Evaluate and Revise

Evaluation of student achievement is based on the laboratory report, the research paper on the frog urogenital system, and a paper-and-pencil test covering the common frog organs. The test includes a diagram on which students must identify the common organs. On another diagram they are asked to trace the blood flow within the circulatory system.

A computer template for a Blueprint is found in "The Classroom Link."

REFERENCES

Print References

Adams, Thomas W. "Computer Literacy—The LCD: A Solution to the Classroom Single Monitor Problem?" *Journal of Computers in Mathematics and Science Teaching* (Winter 1988–1989): 11–13.

Alessi, Stephen M., and Trollip, Stanley R. *Computer-Based Instruction: Methods and Development.* 2d ed. Englewood Cliffs, NJ: Prentice Hall, 1991.

Anderson, Marv A. "Technology Integration for Mainstreamed Students." *Computing Teacher* (December–January 1990–1991): 6–8.

Azarmsa, Reza. *Educational Computing: Principles and Applications.* Englewood Cliffs, NJ: Educational Technology, 1991.

Bitter, Gary G., and Camuse, Ruth A. *Using a Microcomputer in the Classroom.* 2d ed. Englewood Cliffs, NJ: Prentice Hall, 1988.

Boston, Jane, et al. "Classroom Technology and Its Global Connections." *Media and Methods* (January–February 1991): 18, 48–49, 54.

Burns, M. Susan, et al. "A Computer in My Room." *Young Children* (January 1990): 62–67.

Cicchelli, T., and Baecher, R. "Microcomputers in the Classroom: Focusing on Teacher Concerns." *Educational Research Quarterly 13* (1989): 37–46.

Cossis, Betty, and Carleer, Gerrit. Technology Enriched Schools. Eugene, OR: *International Society for Technology in Education,* 1992.

Costa, Betty, and Costa, Marie. *A Micro Handbook for Small Libraries and Media Centers.* Lakewood, CO: Libraries Unlimited, 1991.

Costanzo, William V. *Electronic Text: Learning to Write, Read, and Reason with Computers.* Englewood Cliffs, NJ: Educational Technology, 1989.

Crane, Beverly. "Information Technology: Stepping Stone to the Future." *Social Studies Review 32* (1993): 44–49.

Crowley, Mary. "Student Mathematics Portfolio: More Than a Display Case." *Mathematics Teacher 86* (1993): 544–547.

Dockterman, David A. *Great Teaching in the One Computer Classroom.* Cambridge, MA: Tom Snyder Productions, 1990.

Finkel, LeRoy. *Technology Tools in the Information Age Classroom.* Wilsonville, OR: Franklin, Beedle and Associates, 1991.

Flake, Janice L., McClintock, Edwin C., and Turner, Sandra. *Fundamentals of Computer Education.* 2d ed. Belmont, CA: Wadsworth, 1990.

Galbraith, P. L., et al. "Instructional Technology: Wither Its Future?" *Educational Technology* (August 1990): 18–25.

Garrett, Nina. "Technology in the Service of Language Learning: Trends and Issues." *Modern Language Journal* (Spring 1991): 74–101.

Geisert, Paul G., and Futrell, Mynga K. *Teachers, Computers, and Curriculum: Microcomputers in the Classroom.* Boston: Allyn and Bacon, 1990.

Gibbons, Andrew. "The Future of Computer-Managed Instruction (CMI)." *Educational Technology 33* (1993): 7–11.

Gill, Barbara. "A New Model for Evaluating Instructional Software." *Educational Technology 32* (1992): 39–48.

Grandoenett, Neal. "Roles of Computer Technology in the Mathematics Education of the Gifted." *Gifted Child Today* (January–February 1991): 18–23.

Hannafin, Michael J., and Peck, Kyle L. *The Design, Development and Evaluation of Instructional Software.* New York: Macmillan, 1988.

Jonassen, David H. *Hypertext! Hypermedia.* Englewood Cliffs, NJ: Educational Technology, 1989.

Kearsley, G., Hunter, B., and Furlong, M. *We Teach with Technology.* Palo Alto, CA: Dale Deymour Publications, 1994.

Kulik, C.-L. C., and Kulik, J. A. "Effectiveness of Computer-Based Education in Colleges." *AEDS Journal 19* (1986): 81–108.

Kulik, C.-L. C., Kulik, J. A., and Shwalb, B. J. "The Effectiveness of Computer-Based Adult Education: A Meta-Analysis." *Journal of Educational Computing Research 2* (1986): 235–252.

Kulik, James A., Bangert, R. L., and Williams, G. W. "Effects of Computer-Based Teaching on Secondary School Students." *Journal of Educational Psychology 75* (1983): 19–26.

Kulik, James A., Kulik, C.-L. C., and Bangert-Drowns, R. L. "Effectiveness of Computer-Based Education in Elementary Schools." *Computers in Human Behavior 1* (1985): 59–74.

Lockard, James, Abrams, Peter D., and Many, Wesley A. *Microcomputers for Education.* 2d ed. Glenview, IL: Scott Foresman, 1990.

Marcus, Stephen. "Computers in the Language Arts." *Language Arts* (September 1990): 518–524.

Martorella, Peter H. "Harnessing New Technologies to the Social Studies Curriculum." *Social Education* (January 1991): 55–57.

McCoy, Jan D. "Databases on the Social Studies: Not Why but How." *Social Studies and the Young Learner* (November–December 1990): 13–15.

McFarland, Thomas D., and Parker, O. Resse. *Expert Systems in Education and Training.* Englewood Cliffs, NJ: Educational Technology, 1990.

McMahon, Harry. "Collaborating with Computers." *Journal of Computer Assisted Learning* (September 1990): 149–167.

Merrill, Paul F., et al. *Computers in Education.* 2d ed. Boston: Allyn and Bacon, 192.

Milheim, William D. *Artificial Intelligence and Instruction.* Englewood Cliffs, NJ: Educational Technology, 1989.

Muffoletto, Robert, and Knupfer, Nancy N. *Computers in Education: Social, Political and Historical Perspectives.* Cresskill, NJ: Hampton Press, 1993.

Norales, Francisca. "Networking: A Necessary Component in a Computer-Literacy Course." *Collegiate Microcomputer 11* (1993): 259–263.

Novelli, Joan. "There's Never Been a Better Time to Use Technology! What Got Me Hooked." *Instructor 103* (1993): 34–35, 37–40.

Olson, John. *Schoolworlds/Microworlds: Computers and the Culture of the Classroom.* New York: Pergamon Press, 1988.

Oonibene, Richard, and Skeele, Rosemary. "Computers and the Schools: Unused and Misused." *Action in Teacher Education* (Summer 1990): 68–72.

Pitsch, Barry, and Murphy, Vaughn. "Using One Computer for Whole-Class Instruction." *Computing Teacher 19* (1992): 19–21.

Poole, Bernard. *Education for an Information Age: Teaching in the Computerized Classroom.* Madison, WI: Brown & Benchmark, 1995.

Ryba, Ken, and Anderson, Bill. *Learning with Computers: Effective Teaching Strategies.* Eugene, OR: International Society for Technology in Education, 1993.

Schwarz, Baruch, and Bruckheimer, Maxim. "The Function Concept with Microcomputers: Multiple Strategies in Problem Solving." *School Science and Mathematics* (November 1990): 597–614.

Simonson, Michael, and Thompson, Ann. *Educational Computing Foundations.* 2nd ed. New York: Macmillan College Publishing Co, 1994.

Steinberg, Esther R. *Computer-Assisted Instruction: A Synthesis of Theory, Practice and Technology.* Hillsdale, NJ: Lawrence Earlbaum Publishers, 1990.

Trotter, Andrew. "Computer Learning." *American School Board Journal* (July 1990): 12–18.

Warger, Cynthia, ed. *Technology in Today's Schools.* Alexandria, VA: Association for Supervision and Curriculum Development, 1990.

Watson, Bruce. "The Wired Classroom: American Education Goes On-Line." *Phi Delta Kappan* (October 1990): 109–112.

Weiner, Roberta. "Computers for Special Education." *Tech Trends 35* (1990): 18–22.

Wepner, Shelley B. "Holistic Computer Applications in Literature-Based Classrooms." *Reading Teacher* (September 1990): 12–19.

Audiovisual References

Computer Literacy: A New Subject in the Curriculum. Capitol Heights, MD: U.S. National Audiovisual Center, 1983. Videocassette. 30 minutes.

Computer Literacy for Teachers, Parts 1 and 2. Chicago: Encyclopaedia Britannica Educational Corp, n.d. 2 sound filmstrips.

Computers. Calgary, Alberta: Access Network, 1989. Videocassette. 29 minutes.

Counting on Computers. Princeton, NJ: Films for the Humanities and Sciences, n.d. Videocassette. 26 minutes.

Hello PC. Athens, GA: American Association for Vocational Instructional Material, 1990. Videocassette. 70 minutes.

The Information Age. Alexandria, VA: PBS, n.d. Videocassette. 28 minutes.

Microcomputer Application Series. Van Nuys, CA: Aims Media, 1987. Series of 29-minute videocassettes; topics include word processing, computer graphics, and spreadsheets.

Microcomputers for Learners series. Calgary, Alberta: Access Network, 1988. Series of 13 30-minute videocassette programs that investigate the role computers play in classrooms and the potential of the technology.

The New Literacy. Princeton, NJ: Films for the Humanities and Sciences, n.d. Videocassette. 26 minutes.

Technology for the Disabled. Calgary, Alberta: Access Network, 1989. Videocassette. 29 minutes.

Vision: TEST Project. Eugene, OR: International Society for Technology in Education, 1990. Set of 3 videocassettes; Part 1: Video Component; Part 2: For All Our Children; Part 3: The New Media Centers. 20–30 min.

Organizations

Association for the Advancement of Computing Education
P.O. Box 2966
Charlottesville, VA 22902
Publishes:

> *Journal of Artificial Intelligence in Education*
> *Journal of Computers in Mathematics and Science Teaching*
> *Journal of Computing in Childhood Education*
> *Journal of Educational Multimedia and Hypermedia*
> *Journal of Technology and Teacher Education*

CONDUIT
University of Iowa
Oakdale Campus
Iowa City, IA 52244

Evaluates and distributes computer-based instructional materials and publishes a periodical, *Pipeline*.

EPIE (Educational Products Information Exchange Institute)
Box 839
Water Mill, NY 11976

Publishes reviews of microcomputer courseware/hardware and procedures for their evaluation, including the EPIE *Annotated Courseware Provider List*.

International Society for Technology in Education
1787 Agate Street
University of Oregon
Eugene, OR 97403-1923

Collects and distributes information concerning computer applications in K–12 education and publishes *The Computing Teacher.*

Microcomputer Software and Information for Teachers (MicroSIFT)
Northwest Regional Educational Laboratory
1005 W. Main Street, Suite 500
Portland, OR 97204

Clearinghouse for catalogs and review guides; publishes evaluations of courseware, including *Microcomputer Software Catalog List.*

Minnesota Educational Computing Corporation (MECC)
3490 Lexington Avenue North
St. Paul, MN 55126

Develops and disseminates courseware and computer-related materials, especially for elementary and secondary schools.

Selected Periodicals

Learning and Leading with Technology
International Society for Technology in Education
University of Oregon
1787 Agate St.
Eugene, OR 97403-9905

Education and Computing
Elsevier Science Publishers
P.O. Box 211, 1000 AE
Amsterdam, The Netherlands

Education Computing News
951 Pershing Drive
Silver Spring, MD 20910-4464

Electronic Education
Electronic Communications
1311 Executive Center Drive
Suite 220
Tallahassee, FL 32301

Electronic Learning
Scholastic, Inc.
730 Broadway
New York, NY 10003

Journal of Computing in Childhood Education
P.O. Box 2966
Charlottesville, VA 22902

Journal of Computers in Mathematics and Science Teaching
P.O. Box 2966
Charlottesville, VA 22902

LOGO and Educational Computing Journal
Flower Field
St. James, NY 11780

Logo Exchange
International Society for Technology in Education
University of Oregon
1787 Agate Street
Eugene, OR 97403-9905

Teaching and Computers
Scholastic Magazine
P.O. Box 2040
Mahopac, NY 10541-9963

Technology and Learning
2451 E. River Road
Dayton, OH 45439-9907

Computer Links

America Online
8619 Westwood Center Drive
Vienna, VA 22182-2285

Educational resources, services, references, chatrooms, news, current events, forums, entertainment, and a gateway to the Internet.

AT&T EasyLink Services
P.O. Box 4012
Bridgewater, NJ 08807-4012

The AT&T Learning Network offers curriculum materials on a worldwide bulletin board. Support materials available.

CompuServe
P.O. Box 20212
Columbus, OH 43220

Interactive personal computer service. Travel, shopping, finance, encyclopedia, educational games, stories, news, weather, communications, experts. Many optional (extra-cost) services: 1,400 databases, special interest/professional forums, etc.

Kids Network
National Geographic Society
17th and M Streets, N.W.
Washington, DC 20036

Elementary science and geography program.

Prodigy Services Co.
P.O. Box 8667
Gray, TN 37615-8667

Interactive personal computer service. Travel, shopping, finance, encyclopedia, educational games, stories, news, weather, communications, experts. Purchase connection equipment locally.

COMPUTER-BASED MULTIMEDIA

The advocates of computer multimedia see these systems as powerful tools for students to explore microworlds ... and create their own. Like books, these systems allow users to navigate freely through the material. Unlike books, however, they also allow each person to manipulate the information, to change the text, and thus to adapt the material to one's own learning style.

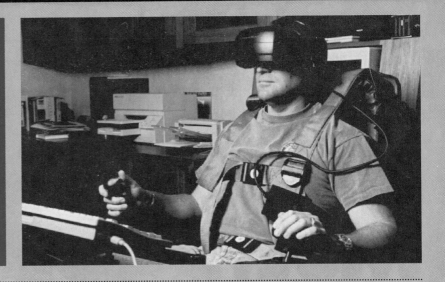

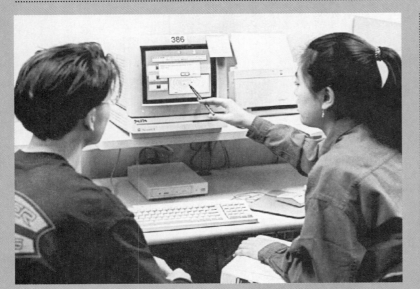

Computers allow you to easily mix text, images, graphics, and data into dazzling multimedia displays. A few years ago these hardware and software combinations were the province of visual designers and computer specialists—today they are accessible to teachers and students. Different configurations have different names: hypermedia, interactive video, CD-ROM, digital video interactive, and virtual reality. Each has advantages and limitations in terms of instruction. Understanding these is the key to making the tools part of your own repertoire.

KNOWLEDGE OBJECTIVES

1. Define *multimedia system*.
2. Describe instructional applications that are especially appropriate for computer multimedia.
3. Describe the purposes of hypermedia and current instructional applications.
4. Describe an instructional situation in which you could use interactive video materials. Your description should include the setting, topic, audience, objectives, content of the interactive video materials, and rationale for using this media format.
5. Diagram and briefly describe the components of an interactive video system.
6. Compare and contrast interactive video as used by small groups and by individuals.
7. Describe instructional applications that are especially appropriate for interactive video.
8. Distinguish computer multimedia from interactive video.
9. Describe an instructional situation in which you might use CD-ROM. Your description should include the setting, topic, audience, objectives, content of the interactive video materials, and rationale for using this media format.
10. Compare and contrast DVI and CDI technologies.
11. Define *virtual reality* and describe how it might be used in education.

APPLICATION OBJECTIVES

1. Plan a lesson in which you use commercial interactive video materials. Use the "Blueprint" template format provided in Chapter 2 or on *The Classroom Link*.
2. Plan a simple hypermedia presentation using the storyboarding techniques suggested in Chapters 3 and 5.
3. Locate and examine several CD-ROM materials that you might use in a classroom. Prepare either a written or an oral report on the possible applications and relative merits of these materials.
4. Locate and examine an interactive video, CDI, or hypermedia program. Prepare either a written or an oral report on the possible applications and relative merits of these materials.
5. Plan a lesson in which you utilize computer multimedia materials. Describe the audience, the objectives, and the materials to be incorporated. Explain the roles of the students and of the instructor using these materials.
6. Plan a lesson in which you have your students prepare their own hypermedia materials. Describe the audience, the objectives, and the materials to be incorporated. Explain how the students will prepare their hypermedia materials.

LEXICON

multimedia
computer multimedia
hypertext
hypermedia
links

hypermediaware
browsing
linking
authoring
scripts

buttons
navigating
interactive video
compact disc read-only memory (CD-ROM)

digital video interactive (DVI)
compact disc interactive (CDI)
virtual reality

Previous chapters have focused on various individual audio and visual media. This chapter discusses computer-managed combinations of these media. The generic term **multimedia** refers to any combination of two or more media formats that are integrated to form an informational or instructional program.

Computer multimedia systems incorporate the computer as a display device, management tool, and/or source of text, pictures, graphics, and sound. More than simply presenting information in multiple formats, they integrate these multiple media into a structured program in which each element complements the others so that the whole is greater than the sum of its parts.

The term *multimedia* was coined in the 1950s and describes early combinations of various still and motion media (even live demonstrations) for heightened educational effect. It reflected a methodology, called the "multimedia approach" or "cross-media approach," that was "based on the principle that a variety of audiovisual media and experiences correlated with other instructional materials to overlap and reinforce the value of each other."[1] The term has been adopted in connection with computers to refer to combinations of sounds and images stored in different devices and amalgamated through computer software into an interactive program.

Since those earlier days of simpler media combinations designers have understood that individual learners respond differently to various information sources and instructional methods, so the chances of reaching an individual are increased when a variety of media is used. Multimedia systems also attempt to simulate more closely the conditions of real-world learning—a world of multisensory, "all-at-once" experiences.

Multimedia systems can provide a structured program of learning experiences to individuals and groups, with a special emphasis on multisensory involvement. As with other instructional systems, several functions must be served: information presentation, student–teacher interaction, and access to learning resources.

---

[1]Donald P. Ely, ed. "Alphabetical Listing of Terminology," *AV Communication Review 11,* Supplement 6 (January 1963), p. 44.

FIGURE 9.1

Hypermedia versus one-way computer-based instruction.

Traditional One-way Computer-Based Instruction

(One-way info transfer)

(Computer)　　　　(Student)

Hypermedia Computer-Based Instruction

(Two-way info transfer)

(Computer)　　　　(Student)

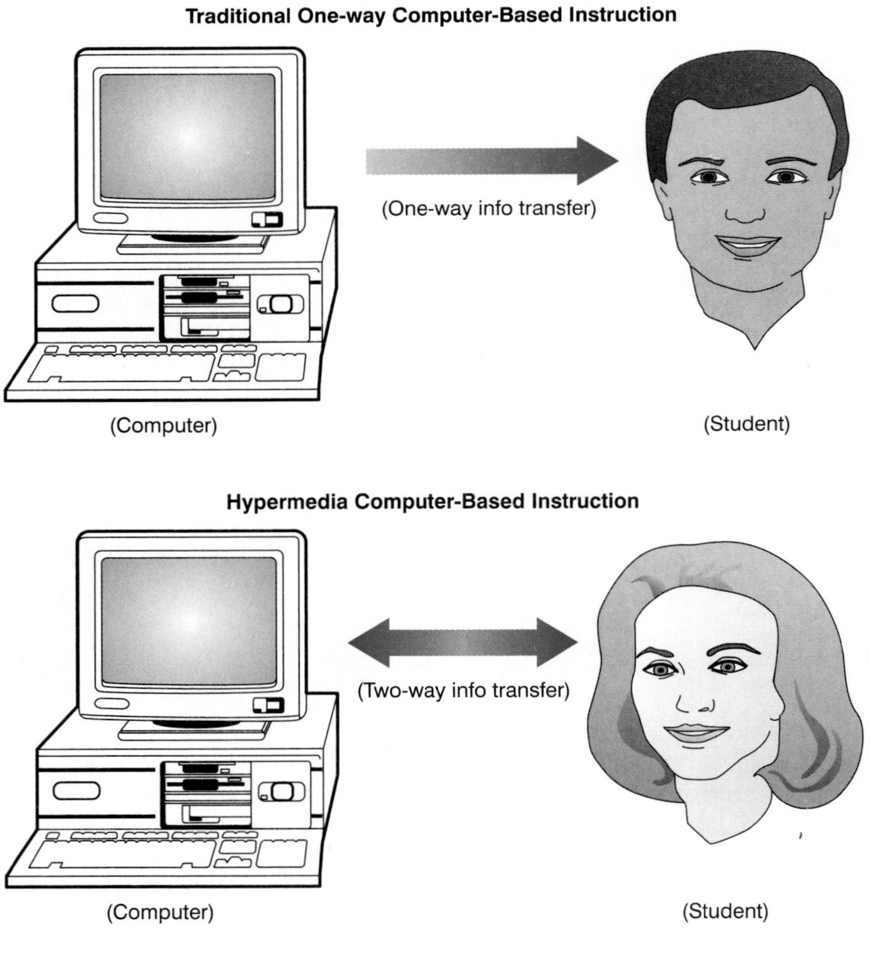

The various multimedia systems differ in the quantity and quality of experiences they offer in each of these areas.

HYPERMEDIA

The term **hypertext** was coined by Nelson in 1974 to describe "nonsequential documents" composed of text, audio, and visual information stored in a computer, with the computer being used to link and annotate related chunks of information (nodes) into larger networks, or webs.[2] The goal of hypertext is to immerse users in a richly textured information environment, one in which words, sounds, and still and motion images can be connected in diverse ways. Enthusiasts feel that the charac-

teristics of hypertext parallel the associative properties of the mind, thereby making the construction of one's own web a creative educational activity.

Hypermedia refers to computer software that uses elements of text, graphics, video, and audio and is connected in such a way that the user can easily move within the information. Each user chooses the pathway that is unique to his or her style of thinking and processing information. According to its very nature, it provides a learning environment that is interactive and exploratory.

Hypermedia is based on cognitive theories of how people structure knowledge and how they learn. It is designed to resemble the way people organize information with concepts and their relationships. These relationships, or **links,** are associations between ideas—for example, when thinking about bicycles, one creates a link between ideas about transportation and recreation. With hypermedia, one can compose and display nonsequential information that may include text, audio, and

---

[2]Theodor H. Nelson, *Computer Lib: You Can and Must Understand Computers Now* (Chicago: Nelson, 1974), and *Dream Machines* (South Bend, IN: The Distributors, 1974).

FIGURE 9.2
Hypermedia organization.

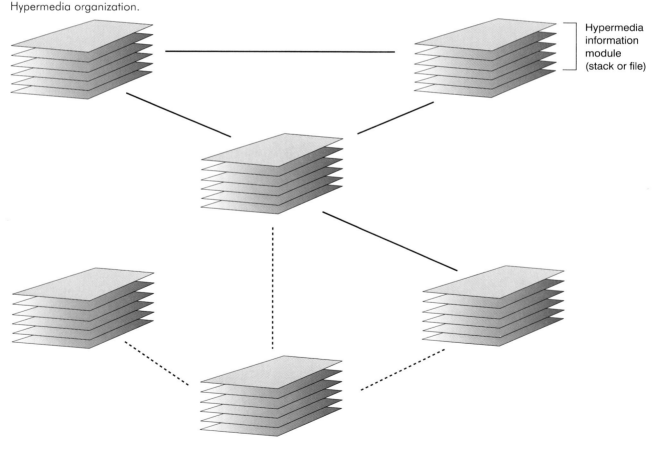

Hypermedia information module (stack or file)

————— Links established by the developer
- - - - - Links established by the user

visual information. There is no continuous flow of text, as in a textbook or novel. Rather, the information is broken into small units that are associated in a variety of ways by the author or user. Using the bicycle example, the learner can connect the word "bicycle" with a photo of a girl riding a bicycle in a field and a video clip of a Hong Kong boy carrying a duck to market on the back of a bicycle.

The intent of **hypermediaware**—software that is based on the utilization of a hypertext environment—is to provide the user with possibilities to move about within a particular set of information without necessarily using a predetermined structure or sequence. The chunks of information are analogous to notes on a collection of cards. Each card contains a bit of information. Subsequent cards or sets of cards may contain extensions of the information from the initial card or other relevant or related information. Hypermedia programs are usually set up so that each computer screen display is equivalent to what is displayed on one of the cards.

Computer hypermedia systems can be used for several different purposes:

- *Browsing.* Users navigate through the information by choosing routes that are of interest. You can explore features in detail as it suits your personal learning style.
- *Linking.* Users can create their own special connections within the information.
- *Authoring.* Users can create their own unique collections of information, adding or linking text, graphics, and audio as they wish. They can use this creation for their own individual use, to share with others, or to prepare a report or presentation.

Hypermedia materials can be created easily (see "How to . . . Create a *HyperCard* Stack, p. 266"). The user can write **scripts** using a special scripting language that is more like spoken language than earlier programming codes (such as those used for BASIC and Pascal). Any

FIGURE 9.3
Sample stack.

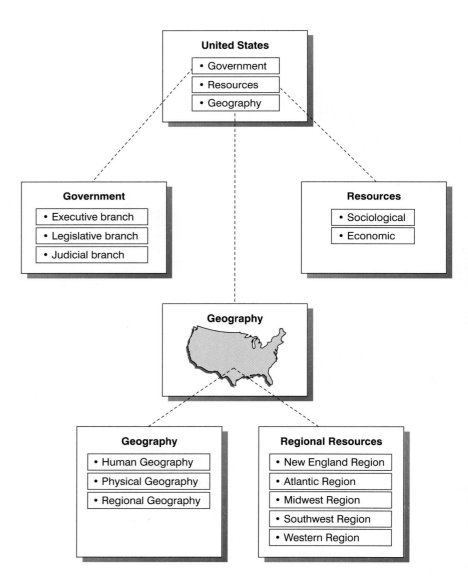

object can become "hyper" through scripting. For example, a word can become "hot," thus allowing the user to connect to a glossary or to other concepts associated with that particular term. Graphics and **buttons** can also be scripted as links to other information. The user, with the aid of a mouse, points to a word or button and clicks the mouse. (A *button* is an icon that might be a picture or graphic or might look like a button one might press on any electric device. The button is used to move around in the hypermedia environment.) In a hypermedia environment, then, the link is activated and the connection is made between pieces of information. The use of the linking interface speeds up the process of **navigating,** or moving about, within a hypermedia environment. The interactive nature of hypermedia is the essence of its advantages. Hypermedia engages the learner to make choices about moving within the material in meaningful ways, thus fulfilling the requirement of learner participation (the *R* of the ASSURE model).

Advantages

- *Engrossing.* The opportunity for deep involvement can capture and hold student interest.
- *Multisensory.* The incorporation of sounds and images along with text expands the channels to the mind.
- *Connections.* By using "hot buttons" students can connect ideas from different media sources; for example, connecting the sound of a foghorn with the word "lighthouse."
- *Individualized.* Web structure allows users to navigate through the information according to their interests

and to build their own unique mental structures based on their exploration.

- *Teacher and student creation.* Software allows teachers and students to easily create their own hypermedia files; student projects can become opportunities for collaborative work.

Limitations

- *Getting lost.* Users can get confused, or "lost in cyberspace," when using hypermedia programs because of limited clues as to where they are in the material.
- *Lack of structure.* Students whose learning style requires more structured guidance may become frustrated. Students may also make poor decisions about how much information they need to explore.
- *Non-interactive.* Programs can be simply one-way presentations of information with no specific opportunities for interactive practice with feedback.
- *Complex.* More advanced programs may be difficult to use, especially for student production because they require the ability to use a scripting language.
- *Time consuming.* Because they are non-linear and invite exploration, hypermedia programs tend to require more time for students to reach prespecified objectives. Because they are more complex than conventional instructional materials, hypermedia systems require time for both teachers and students to learn to use.

Applications

Hypermedia can be developed and used on the same computer systems that are commonly found in schools.

FIGURE 9.4
Components of a hypermedia system. A full range of still, motion, and computer-animated images, high-quality audio, and text are all controlled by the learner through a keyboard and mouse. Some computers have the CD-ROM drive built in.

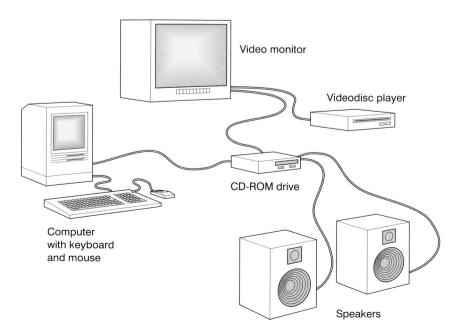

Video monitor

Videodisc player

CD-ROM drive

Computer
with keyboard
and mouse

Speakers

They are applied in all areas of the curriculum, for any learning goals that are suited to individual or small-group exploration of a body of information. Hypermedia programs can be purchased as off-the-shelf courseware; they can be created by teachers to fit unique local needs; or they can be created by students as a way of organizing and synthesizing their research on a topic of interest.

Ready-made hypermedia instructional courseware is becoming available for teachers to use in their classrooms. Many titles have been developed for use in all areas of study. For example, *Handshake* (see "Media File") is designed to help students learn about international geography. *Digestion* (see "Media File") is designed to be used by secondary science students; with complex and accurate diagrams, students can learn about the process of digestion. Both programs are available as complete packages; the teacher does not have to do anything to the software. However, he or she will need to consider how to best introduce the application into the curriculum and what types of follow-up are appropriate.

Teachers can either adapt existing materials or create new materials to fill a need of their own students. Because hypermedia software—for example, *HyperCard* or *Linkway*—provides an easy-to-use authoring lan-

▼ MEDIA FILE

Digestion
Multimedia Program

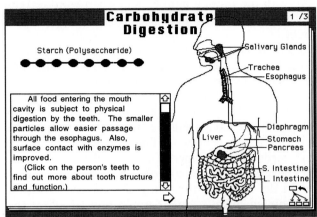

A hypermedia stack designed for high school science students, *Digestion* contains carefully drawn diagrams. The graphics are designed with the complexity necessary to convey the information without being too difficult for the students. In addition, the text is easy to read and the material is presented in a comprehensive manner.

Source: HISC.

▼ MEDIA FILE

Handshake
Multimedia Program

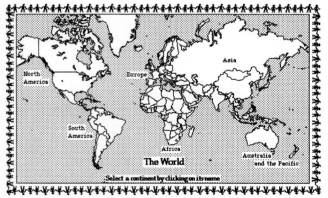

Handshake is a collection of customs, cultures, and facts from other countries which may have influenced us and contributed to the ways we choose to live. It is a hypermedia database about the different countries in the world. It is intended to provide elementary and middle school students with an opportunity to investigate their cultural histories.

Source: HISC.

guage, many teachers have learned to successfully develop their own hypermedia materials. See "How To . . . Create a *HyperCard* Stack" for directions on using one of the most popular authoring systems. One caution: don't think that ability to use the authoring tool automatically bestows expertise either in instructional design or visual design. These skills are usually developed through special study and lots of practice. Some advice on screen design is provided in Chapter 3, "How To . . . Design Computer Screens."

Hypermedia can shift the roles of teacher and learners in the classroom. Because hypermedia materials are so easy to develop, it is feasible for students to create their own programs and thus gain the benefits of creative learning. Given instruction, students can create hypermedia materials that revolve around a particular topic of study. The teacher's role becomes that of resource person for the students. (Read "Close-up: The Westward Movement, Hypermedia Style" to see how one teacher used hypermedia with her third-grade class.)

Digital video can be added to hypermedia files with little effort. Most computer systems have the capabilities of adding digitized "film clips" without any additional software or hardware. For example, *QuickTime* color

CLOSE-UP

THE WESTWARD MOVEMENT, HYPERMEDIA STYLE

Connie Courbat, a third-grade teacher, developed *HyperCard* stacks to use with her students for their study of the Oregon trail and the westward movement. Her academically challenged students used an instructional stack and reported on the information they learned. With her more advanced students, she developed a shell for stacks that her students could use to create their own stacks. These stacks were created to help the rest of the class learn more about the westward movement. All the students had an opportunity to utilize hypermedia in a manner appropriate to their learning levels, and everyone enjoyed their learning experiences.

"movies" can be imported into *HyperCard* stacks with ease. In addition, *QuickTime* "movies" can be added to other types of files, such as word processed documents. At present, *QuickTime* movies are small, using only a quarter of the screen to display them. The only major problem seems to be the amount of memory needed to store and display digitized "movies." This is a problem that will decrease as the memory capacity of computers increases.

It is beyond the scope of this chapter to describe in detail the various techniques for developing hypermedia. Resources on hypermedia development are listed at the end of the chapter.

INTERACTIVE VIDEO

Computer-based **interactive video** creates a multimedia learning environment that capitalizes on the features of both video and computer-assisted instruction. It is an instructional delivery system in which recorded video material is presented under computer control to viewers who not only see and hear the pictures and sounds but also make active responses, with those responses affecting the pace and sequence of the presentation.

The video portion of interactive video is provided through a videocassette, videodisc, or compact disc. The images can be presented in slow motion, fast motion, or frame by frame (as in a slide or filmstrip display). The audio portion of a videodisc may occupy two separate audio channels, making possible two different narrations for each motion sequence.

The interactive aspect of interactive video is provided through computers, which have powerful decision-making abilities. Combining computers and video allows the strengths of each to compensate for the limitations of the other to provide a rich educational environment for the learner. Interactive video is a powerful, practical method for individualizing and personalizing instruction.

Various levels of interactivity are available, ranging from essentially linear video to fully learner-directed sequences of instruction. The goal of most developers of

FIGURE 9.5
Using a multimedia program, *Teaching with Groups*. First, the student places the videodisc into the player. Then, she uses the mouse to press one of the *HyperCard* buttons on the computer screen (on the right) to select a classroom scene to watch on the video player (on the left). While watching and listening to the scene, she can press another button to hear the comments of the teacher shown in the video or other experts.

A simple *HyperCard* stack is the foundation for more complex types of hypermedia materials. By following the steps here, you will be able to create a basic four-card *HyperCard* stack. You will then be able to create more types of hypermedia materials to use with your students. You can also use these steps to get your students started in creating their own hypermedia materials.

1. Start *HyperCard* by double clicking on the Home Card icon to open the Home Stack (do not use the *HyperCard* Player program).

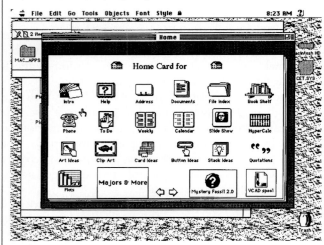

2. Choose *Last* from the Go menu (at the top of the screen). This takes you to the last card in the stack, the USER PREFERENCES card.
3. This screen allows you to change the user level. It should be set at 1-Browsing. You need to change it to 5-Scripting to have full access to all the features of *HyperCard* needed to prepare your own stack. Point the mouse arrow to the 5 and click one time. If you have a version of *HyperCard* that shows you only the Browsing and Typing levels on the screen, then press <⌘> and <M> at the same time. The Message Box will appear at the bottom of the screen. Type "MAGIC" and press

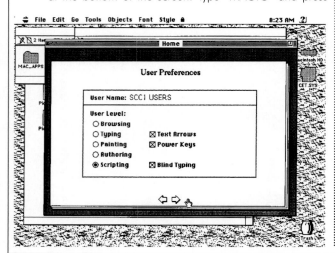

<Return>. You should then see all five user levels appear on the screen.

4. Choose *New Stack* from the File menu at the top of the screen. This will open the *New Stack Dialog Box* on your screen to let you create a new stack. Generally you will want to save your new stack on your own floppy disk; therefore, make certain that the name of your disk appears in the small box at the top left of the dialog box. Make sure there is no "X" in the little box next to *Copy Current Background*. Type in the name of your new stack in the *New Stack Name:* box and click on the

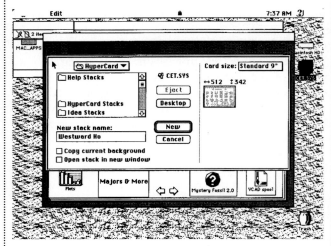

NEW button. It helps to name your stack with a descriptive name.

5. Your first card will appear. This will be the title card for your new stack. Open the Tools menu and select the paintbrush by pointing to it and clicking on it. Draw a "1" in the corner of your card (this will help you later when you try to find your way around your stack). Since this is your title card you will want to type the name of your stack here. Select the "letter tool" from your Tools and click on an area of your card to type.

6. You are now ready to add a card to your stack. Select *New Card* from the Edit menu. A new blank card will appear on your screen. This is your second card in your stack. Use the paintbrush tool to paint a small "2" in the corner of this card. Since this is your second card, let's play with some of the other tools in the Tools menu. Select a rectangle or circle tool. When you move the cursor into the white area of your card, you will see a small "+". Shapes are built on the diagonal in this program, so select the upper left corner of your shape; holding your mouse button down, drag your mouse in a diagonal away from that corner. A rectangle or circle will appear. Make several; design a pretty picture made of shapes.

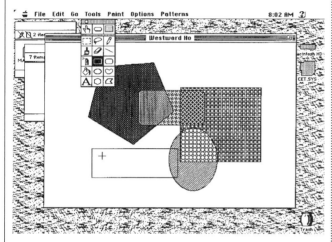

7. Add a third card to your stack by selecting *New Card* from the Edit menu. Another blank card will appear. This is the third card in your stack; mark it with your paintbrush with a "3" in the corner. Let's try using some of the other tools for drawing. Select the spray can or the pencil from Tools and draw a picture on your card. Remember to click and drag with your mouse when you want the image to appear.

8. Now it is time to add buttons to your stack. Select *First* from the Go menu at the top. This will take you to your first card in your stack. Notice the "1" in the corner (you can erase this now, using the eraser in the Tools menu if you want). Select *New Button* from the Objects menu. A new button will appear in the middle of your card. You will recognize it because it says "new button" and will have the "marching ants" around it. You can move your new button by pointing to the middle of it, holding down your mouse button, and dragging it to the location you want. You can resize your button by pointing to a corner, holding down your mouse button, and dragging it to a corner in a diagonal.

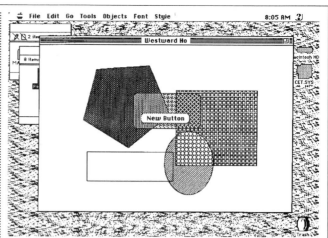

9. Select *Button Info* from the Objects menu. This will open the Button Info Dialog Box. You can give your button a name, like "Go to the Next Card." Make sure there is an "x" in the box next to "Show Name." Also, make sure there is an "x" next to the "Auto Hilite." Select the Script button at the bottom of the dialog box. A window will appear with the words "On Mouseup" and "End Mouseup" at the top. Click on the space between the two phrases and type: "Go Next Card" (without the quotation marks).

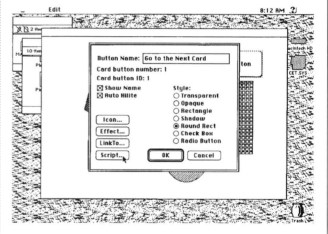

10. Using your mouse, point the pointer arrow at the little white box in the upper left-hand corner (to close the script window). Click one time. You will be asked whether you wish to save the changes to the script; click on the Yes button. You will be back at your card, with the marching ants around the button.

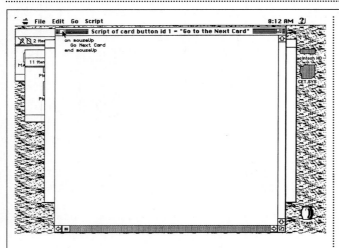

11. Select the *Browsing Tool* from the Tools menu. This is the little hand with the pointing finger. When you move the mouse into the card area, you will see the little hand appear and move with your mouse movements. Put the Browsing Tool on your button and click one time. You will go to your second card.

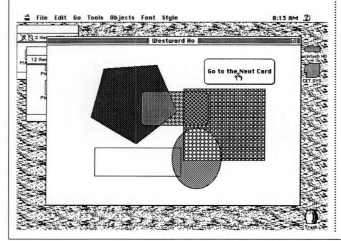

12. Make a button on your second card that will take you to the third one in your stack. Follow the same procedures in steps 8–11.
13. When you are at your third card, you will make a button to link to the first card in your stack. Select *New Button* from the Objects menu to get a button on your card. Select *Button Info* to open the dialog box. After naming your button (perhaps "Go to First Card") and marking "Show Name" and "Auto Hilite," click on the Link To button in the lower left area of the dialog box. A small window will appear with three options: "this card," "this stack," and "cancel." Don't click on any of these options yet.

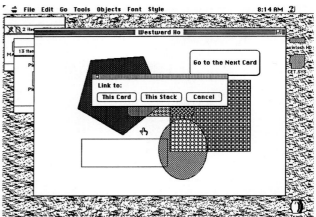

14. Select *First* from the Go menu at the top of your screen. Your first card will appear behind the Link To window. After clicking on the "this card" option one time, you will be back at your third card with the marching ants around your "Go to First Card" button.
15. Select *Browsing Tool* and click on the button. You will go to your first card. Try clicking on each of your buttons. You should now be able to navigate through a simple linear stack that you have scripted and linked. Just imagine all the fun things you and your students can now create!

---

interactive video is to provide fully interactive response-driven instruction featuring embedded questions, response feedback, and branching within a lesson. In addition, student response records can be used to help make instructional decisions.

More recently, with the introduction of hypermedia, it has become easier to prepare teacher-developed and student-developed interactive multimedia. Simple-to-prepare hypermedia stacks are developed that, with specific scripting, can activate the videodisc player. Students are thus discovering an innovative way to activate their learning.

The heart of an interactive video system is the computer, which provides the "intelligence" and interactivity

required. The computer can command the video player to present audio or video information, wait for the learner's response, and branch to the appropriate point in the instructional program from that response.

The learner communicates with the instructional program by responding to audio, visual, or verbal stimuli displayed on the monitor. Input devices provide the means for these responses. These devices include such items as a keyboard, keypad, light pen, bar code reader, touch-sensitive screen, and mouse.

Although the 12-inch laser videodisc is currently the most popular format for video storage, videocassettes are still a viable alternative for some applications. The costs associated with the preparation of a videodisc have

FIGURE 9.6
ABC News InterActive™ is a series of interactive video materials that can be used by the teacher to supplement a unit of study or by students to explore a topic in depth.

		v2.13
ABC News InterActive™ index		
Instant Replay of History	*Understanding Our World*	*Understanding Ourselves*
The '88 Vote	In the Holy Land	AIDS
Martin Luther King Jr.	Communism and the Cold War	Drugs and Substance Abuse
Mission: The Moon	Lessons of War	Teenage Sexuality
	Powers of the Supreme Court	Tobacco
	Powers of the Congress	Alcohol
	Powers of the President	Food & Nutrition

Install

ABC News Index✓ Videodisc settings ? →← ↵
Credits   Sound input settings
Preferences

been decreasing, thus making it more feasible for the classroom teacher to consider preparing a videodisc. (See Chapter 7 for more information about videodisc formats.)

A monitor displays the picture and emits the sound from the video source. It can also display the output from the computer software, which may have text, graphics, or sound effects. In most systems the computer output can be superimposed over the video image.

The interface device provides the link between the computer and the video player, allowing them to communicate. Through this device the computer can control the portions of the video to be shown to the learner.

Advantages

- *Multiple media.* Text, audio, graphics, still pictures, and motion pictures can all be combined in one easy-to-use system.
- *Learner participation.* The *R* of the ASSURE model is achieved with interactive video materials because they require that the learners engage in activities. These materials help to maintain students' attention, and they allow greater participation than does video viewing alone.
- *Individualization.* Individualization is provided for because branching allows instruction on remedial as well as enrichment levels.
- *Flexibility.* The learner may choose what to study from the menu, such as in the ABC News InterActive series (see Figure 9.6).
- *Simulations.* Interactive video may be used to provide simulation experiences in such areas as medicine, machine operations, and especially interpersonal

▼ MEDIA FILE

Columbus: Encounter, Discovery and Beyond
Multimedia Program

This computer-based program with videodisc and CD-ROM components allows learners to explore ideas and events related to Christopher Columbus's encounter with the Americas. Beginning with the "Main Storyteller," the user can branch off onto a wide variety of other subjects, such as deeper historical background, opinions about the cultural impact of European exploration, and music and art of Columbus's time and beyond. These are presented with a combination of live speakers, film footage, still pictures, animated graphics, and sound. Text of narratives, songs, and other material can be displayed on the computer screen below the picture as desired.

This multimedia program also provides a hypermedia experience in that the learner not only navigates through this environment at will but can also store any portions to create new, original presentations. The program won the 1991 Gold Cindy Award for K–12 Education, given by the Association of Visual Communicators.

Source: EduQuest/IBM Corporation.

skills. The development of skills in working with children in a classroom, which otherwise would require role playing or live interactions, can be provided as an individual, self-paced simulation exercise.

Limitations

- *Cost.* The most significant limitation to interactive video is the cost, although the prices of ready-made discs and machines are decreasing.
- *Production expense.* It is expensive to produce videodiscs, making it necessary to rely on commercially prepared discs, which may not meet local needs.
- *Rigidity.* The videodisc cannot be changed once it has been made; therefore, material may become outdated.
- *Search time.* Videotape is relatively inexpensive; however, it is less accurate in the search process than videodisc, and it takes longer for the user to search for specific frames.
- *Less efficient.* Videotape is less efficient in still-frame pause than is videodisc.
- *Less flexible.* Videotape may not have the slow and fast forward/reverse capabilities of videodisc.

Applications

Interactive video is a valuable learning system for tasks that must be shown rather than simply told. Some instruction cannot be adequately presented by printed materials. If the learner needs to interact with the instruction, interactive video is an appropriate choice.

Interactive video systems are currently being used in a variety of instructional applications—from teaching scientific phenomenon to teaching special education students to tell time. The programs can challenge a small group of gifted students or provide remedial instruction for students who might be having difficulty with particular concepts.

Interactive video programs can be used by individuals as well as small groups. There is a growing trend, particularly in elementary education, toward small-group applications, providing opportunities for students to engage in cooperative and collaborative problem-solving activities.

Interactive video may also be used for large-group instruction. However, the relatively high cost associated with the hardware and software may mean a limited number of stations for use at one time. Thus, individual self-paced study may not be possible given these constraints. The instructional program might be used by the teacher only, with large-screen projection or an LCD panel for presentation to the whole class. The teacher can then move through the material in a sequence that will promote learning—stopping where appropriate for discussion, jumping ahead to new material, or reviewing when necessary. The pause-and-discuss method might work well when reviewing a topic.

For example, a teacher might use the ABC News InterActive *In the Holy Land* in a social studies unit. Here students have the opportunity to explore the Middle East from the perspectives of the children who live there. This set includes a videodisc and *HyperCard* stacks that can be used in linear instruction or for creating special presentations. The teacher could use an LCD

CLOSE-UP

SEX, TEENS, AND VIDEOTAPE

Nadine Davidson, a consumer science and family living teacher, has her students prepare formal reports to present in class using the ABC News InterActive series, *Understanding Ourselves.* The students are organized to work in groups, each choosing a particular topic of study. They use the "Teenage Sexuality," "All About AIDS," and "Drugs and Substance Abuse" sets. The students prepare videotapes (although they could use the computer and videodisc player setup) to use within the context of their group presentation to the class.

Nadine has found that not only are her students more excited about doing the group reports, they are more engaged in the learning tasks. They not only use the ABC News InterActive materials, they also rely on information gathered through the school media center and on-line database sources. The students have stated that they find this experience interesting and educational.

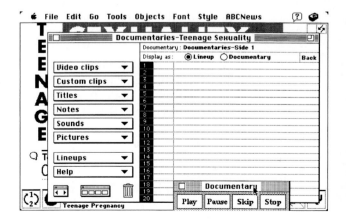

CLOSE-UP

SAFETY TRAINING VIA INTERACTIVE VIDEO

The Clark Equipment Company, manufacturer of forklift trucks in Battle Creek, Michigan, developed an operator safety refresher course using interactive video. The course was designed in response to supervisors expressing concern that they didn't have time to do the refresher training. In addition, the supervisors were concerned about the time they wasted in retraining operators. The operators themselves didn't see the need to be retrained about something they did every day. An interactive videotape system was selected for the safety training.

Training via interactive video was compared with training using conventional videotape. Studies involved Clark employees and operators in other companies that had purchased Clark forklifts. The results indicated that after 24 days the operators using the interactive video system learned and retained at a rate 20% higher than those who didn't use the interactive system. Training time was reduced, as was the time required by the supervisors to provide the training. Consequently, there was a significant reduction in wages the company had to pay and overhead devoted to training.

The training system motivated operators to request other opportunities to learn using interactive video. In addition,

there was no evidence in the interactive group to indicate any effects of age or experience on an operator's score, as there was in the group of operators learning from ordinary videotape.

Source: D. Wooldridge and Thomas Dargan, "Linear vs. Interactive Videotape Training," International Television (August 1983), pp. 56–60.

---

panel for presenting the *HyperCard* material and, if desired, connect the videodisc player to a large monitor for whole-class viewing. One of the options the teacher has is to use the "Documentary Maker" to prepare special lessons for class, thus adapting the materials to meet the needs of the students. The "Documentary Maker" feature of the ABC News InterActive series provides the user with an easy way to create special presentations using the videodisc and *HyperCard* materials in the unit.

Students can utilize interactive video material for preparation of a class presentation. They can use the ABC News InterActive series "Documentary Maker" to prepare their own special presentations as a report to the class. This type of report might take the place of a written paper. It can be saved on disk and submitted to the teacher for evaluation. (See "Close-up: Sex, Teens, and Videotape" for how one teacher uses these materials with her high school family living class.)

Although interactive video is becoming readily available in the schools, it has actually been used in training since the early 1980s by many corporations and the military. The use of packaged programs was more than twice as common as the use of custom-designed programs. Such areas as medicine, auto mechanics, electronic ignition systems, and communication skills were incorporated into interactive videodisc materials.

Interactive video was slow to be adopted in some schools because of the expense and the lack of appropri-

ate materials. Now that the costs of the players have decreased and additional titles are available, more of this type of technology can be found in the schools.

CD-ROM

The **CD-ROM** format was introduced in Chapter 6 as an audio format. CD-ROM has the capacity to handle not only quality sound but also large quantities of text and graphics, as discussed in Chapter 8. CD-ROM is a storage system that utilizes a compact disc that is only 12 centimeters (4.72 inches) in diameter. The discs are rugged and lightweight. They are an optical storage medium that uses a tiny laser beam to retrieve the information on the disc. Because of the technology, they are "read only," which means that the user cannot change or modify the information on the disc.

The storage capacity of a single CD-ROM disc is over 650 megabytes. That is equivalent to several hundred floppy diskettes or the entire text of a 20-volume encyclopedia.

Because CD-ROM discs can store many types of digital information—including text, graphics, photographs, animation, and audio—they are popular in school settings, library media centers, and classrooms of all sorts. Anything that can be stored on a computer disk can be stored on a CD-ROM.

TABLE 9.1

STORAGE DEVICE	CAPACITY	EQUIVALENT
Floppy disk	0.72 Mb	360 pages of text
Hard disk drive	80.00 Mb	40,000 pages of text
CD-ROM	650++ Mb	250,000 pages of text

CD-ROM discs require their own special player; they cannot be played on the audio CD player attached to your stereo system. However, many of the computer CD-ROM players can also play audio CDs. The CD-ROM player must be connected to a computer with an interface cable. Many new computers are being produced with the CD-ROM player already built into the system. A computer monitor is used to display the data once it has been retrieved from the CD-ROM disc. You interact with the information in the same way you would interact with other computer-based multimedia materials.

Advantages

- *Capacity.* Each CD-ROM disc can hold more than 650 megabytes of data, graphics, and/or sound.
- *Size.* CD-ROM discs are small and lightweight, making them ideal for easily transporting data.
- *Durability.* CD-ROM discs are made of very durable plastic and can be handled by even very young children.
- *Decreasing cost.* The cost of players and discs is decreasing, making this an affordable medium in schools.
- *Variety of titles.* Thousands of titles are now available, ranging from resource materials like encyclopedias to graphics libraries that can be incorporated into hypermedia materials and written reports.

Limitations

- *Speed.* When compared with other data retrieval systems, such as computer hard disks, CD-ROM discs are slow.
- *Unchangeable.* CD-ROMs are "read only" and cannot be changed or updated in any way.
- *Inconsistent quality.* There is a lack of consistency and quality among CD-ROM materials.
- *Susceptibility to damage.* If a CD-ROM disc gets scratched or damaged, it might make it difficult to retrieve the data.

Applications

There are many types of applications of CD-ROM technology in schools today. Nearly all school library media centers have at least one station that is designated for database searches. These stations have been equipped with a computer and CD-ROM player with an array of titles available to students. Among the types of materials available are encyclopedias and research databases.

CD-ROM encyclopedias can be complete and unabridged. These appear to be similar to the bound-book format familiar to most students. The advantage of the CD-ROM encyclopedia is that it allows options within the search process. For example, when a student wants to search for information about Queen Elizabeth I, the encyclopedia is a natural place for the student to begin the search. In the traditional bound-book format, the student might choose the "E" volume and look up

▼ MEDIA FILE

Mammals
Multimedia Encyclopedia

Mammals is a CD-ROM disc that serves as a multimedia encyclopedia of this branch of the animal kingdom. It contains entries on more than 200 different animals, 700 full-screen color photographs, 155 animal vocalizations, 150 range maps, essays on every animal, and 45 full-motion film clips from National Geographic specials. *Mammals* has been praised by *Media and Methods* magazine and received an Award of Excellence from *Technology and Learning* magazine.

Source: National Geographic Educational Services.

"Elizabeth, Queen" and that might be the extent of the search. However, with the CD-ROM version of the encyclopedia, when the student types in "Elizabeth," a large menu of choices is displayed on the screen, including "Shakespeare," "Spanish Armada," "Philip II of Spain," and "England's colonial empire." *Kenilworth* might even be shown because of its retelling of the legend of Sir Walter Raleigh. Also, each of these options is linked not only with "Queen Elizabeth I" but also with each other. The student is thus encouraged to explore the interrelationships between people, places, and events.

With other CD-ROM encyclopedias there is the provision for color photographs, animation, and sound. (See Figure 9.7.) Thus, a student who might be searching for information about lions would not only be able to find text-based information but also could view a photograph or short video clip about lions and hear a lion's roar. These encyclopedias tend to be abridged because of the large memory requirements of graphics and video (CD-ROM seems to have limitless capacity, but visuals use a large amount of memory).

In addition to encyclopedias, other types of books are being produced on CD-ROMs. Discis Books was one of the earliest companies to produce such classics as Beatrix Potter's *Peter Rabbit* and Edgar Alan Poe's *The Tell-Tale Heart* on CD-ROM discs. These books not only appear as a text with pictures but are also interactive. The student who is having difficulty with a particular word on a page can point-and-click on that word and get it pronounced or even defined. Further, if the student's reading skills are weak, the whole story can be read by the computer. For many of the stories,

a child's voice is heard by the student; for others, a pleasant adult voice reads the story. In the case of *The Tell-Tale Heart,* the student can experience two different readers' interpretations of the story, thus gaining even further insight into Poe's short story. Background music or other sounds enhance the pleasure of reading. Many of the discs come with two audio tracks—one in English and the other in a designated language, such as French.

These CD-ROM books provide additional help to the teacher. A list can be maintained of all the words that a student identified while reading. The teacher can quickly glance at that list and determine the vocabulary words for which a student might need assistance. Further, comprehension and reading analysis questions are presented to the student for independent study of the story. Along with the questions are suggestions for the types of responses that might be considered. These aids might be used by the teacher to inspire students to explore other answers to those or similar questions.

In the classroom the teacher might find that CD-ROM books are essential to use with students who are having difficulty with the assigned reading. Another possible application might be to provide students with CD-ROM books to supplement their reading and writing experiences. Using a CD-ROM story such as *Just Grandma and Me,* the teacher can have students write their own version of the story. Or, without finishing the story in class, the students could try to write their own endings. Think of the potential vocabulary development and creative writing experiences these might provide for your students.

FIGURE 9.7
Multimedia features a point-and-click approach, allowing the user to move around within an information database such as an encyclopedia.

▼ MEDIA FILE

The Tell-Tale Heart
CD-ROM

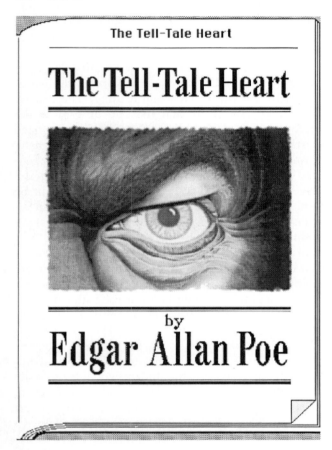

This Edgar Allan Poe classic is a first-person account of a younger man's obsession with an old man's eye. This Discis Book brings this classic to life. Teachers can easily customize the Discis Book experience with a wide range of built-in educational options. Two different oral interpretations of the short story are available, as well as vocabulary help, sound effects, and a Spanish translation. On-line questions are available for further exploration of the text. These questions can be used to stimulate student curiosity and critical thinking and to promote group discussions.

Source: Discis Books.

DVI/CDI

Another compact disc technology is **digital video interactive (DVI)**. DVI consists of a computer with a CD-ROM player. It is capable of compressing and storing up to 72 minutes of video on a compact disc. A special

FIGURE 9.8
"I'm only attending school until it becomes available on CD-ROM."

DVI board or card must be installed in the computer to decompress the video during playback.

A close cousin to DVI is **compact disc interactive (CDI)** technology. Developed by Philips Corporation for home use, CDI relies on a highly intelligent special player that is connected to a standard television set. The compact discs incorporate text, audio, graphics, and animation into the programs. The user interacts with the material using a specialized remote control unit. In addition to the standard remote control types of buttons, this special remote also has a joystick and activation buttons for interacting with the program.

Advantages

- *Ease of use*. Both DVI and CDI technologies are easy to use.
- *Technical quality*. Both technologies have high-quality sound and video.
- *Motion*. DVI has full-motion video that can be viewed on the full screen of the computer monitor.
- *Compatibility*. DVI is compatible with both IBM and Macintosh computer platforms.
- *Storage*. DVI is capable of storing a large amount of video on a single side of the compact disc.
- *Home use*. CDI is easy to connect with the home television set.

- *Cost.* CDI players are relatively inexpensive, costing only a bit more than a high-quality videotape player.

Limitations

- *Limited titles.* Both types of technologies have a limited number of available titles and applications.
- *Cost.* The DVI board may cost as much as a small computer.
- *Information storage.* The CDI player does not have such devices as a keyboard or floppy disk storage to make it possible to save information.
- *Unchangeable.* Both DVI and CDI rely on compact disc technology; thus, the material on the discs cannot be changed.

Applications

Even though only a few titles are available, there are many ways to use DVI and CDI program titles in the classroom. Some CDI titles are specifically designed for the preschool-age child. Because the user interface involves a joystick and some buttons, it is easy for a young child to quickly learn how to operate it.

One favorite of many children is a CDI disc called *Cartoon Jukebox* (see "Media File"). This interactive songbook lets the child select the song and then color the cartoons on the television screen that are associated with it. A child can then play the song, watching the pictures displayed in the colors he or she painted. In addition to the colorful rendition, there are multiple

▼ MEDIA FILE

Cartoon Jukebox
Interactive Songbook

Young children can enjoy hours of interactive play with their favorite tunes, like "Pop Goes the Weasel," "Row, Row, Row Your Boat," and the "Alphabet Song." Children can make the songs come alive when they select the colors and the language in which they want to sing. Each song is illustrated with original animation, and with the CDI controller the figures and characters in each cartoon can be painted with interesting colors. Children can sit back and sing along with their personalized animated renditions of the songs.

Source: Philips

FIGURE 9.9
Virtual reality puts the user "into" a multi-sensory experience.

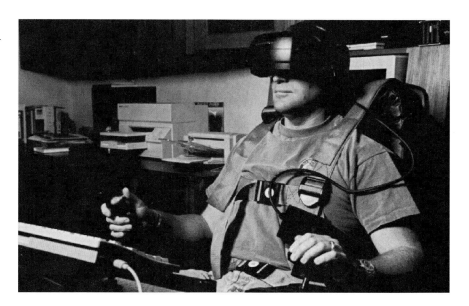

audio tracks, allowing the child to listen to a favorite song in several different languages, including the clucking of a chicken.

Other available applications for the older student include trips to museums, where objects and art pieces can be viewed from several different angles. Thus, a student is able to control the places within the museum that are visited and how he or she might view the particular art objects along the way. In addition, both text and audio are available for information about the particular object being viewed. Again, multiple-language tracks are available with clear and precise audio.

VIRTUAL REALITY

Virtual reality (VR) is one of the newest applications of computer-based technologies. **Virtual reality** is a computer-generated three-dimensional environment where the user can operate as an active participant. The user wears a special headpiece that contains three-dimensional liquid crystal video display and headphones. The user participates within the three-dimensional world by manipulating a joystick or a special glove worn on one hand. The data glove may be used to point, handle, and move objects and to direct the user's movements within the virtual world.

The essence of virtual reality is the expansion of experiences for the user. Because VR places the user into the virtual environment, it provides an opportunity to interact with that environment in a unique way, giving the user the "ultimate" chance to grasp new ideas. For example, students can take a virtual field trip to a city.

Advantages

- *Safety.* Virtual reality creates a realistic world without subjecting viewers to actual or imagined danger or hazards.
- *Expansive.* It provides students with opportunities to explore places not feasible in the real world (e.g., outer space or inside an active volcano).
- *Opportunities to explore.* Virtual reality allows students to experiment with simulated environments.

Limitations

- *Cost.* The equipment is extremely expensive.
- *Complexity.* The technology is very complex and does not lend itself to most classroom uses.
- *Limited titles.* There are limited software "realities" available at this time.

Applications

Several applications of virtual reality have been demonstrated to be highly effective. Architects have found that creating large virtual environments electronically allows them to solve problems before actual construction begins. Clients can "see" a proposed building, and satisfactory changes can be made to the blueprints. Costly mistakes are avoided, and time and money are saved.

Another application has been found in the area of space exploration. Because virtual reality can simulate the outer space environment, the user can practice exploring space safely and efficiently. Without this type of technology, such an experience would be limited.

Virtual reality has shown great promise in the area of medicine. The virtual hospital provides training and updating for medical professionals throughout the country. Given that most hospital staff cannot leave their assigned duties for any length of time, a training climate that simulates the hospital environment while helping staff to upgrade their skills is ideal. The virtual hospital also provides information on new techniques and resources that might prove valuable in particular settings.

More closely aligned with a typical school's budget are pseudovirtual environments that use CD-ROM technology. With a special headset and earphones, a user can be immersed in an environment that is similar to computer-based virtual reality. However, this reality is not fully interactive because the user is unable to change it.

As virtual reality tools improve and their costs decrease, students and teachers will be able to explore ways of using this type of technology in learning. It will become possible for them to create their own unique environments. These types of experiences will add to the dimensions of the classroom in very exciting ways.

COMPUTER MULTIMEDIA

KEY WORDS: _____ , _____ , _____

Title _____

Series Title (if applicable) _____

Source_____

Date_____**Cost** _____**Length** _____minutes

Subject Area_____

Intended Audience _____

Brief Description

Objectives

Entry Capabilities Required (e.g., prior knowledge, reading ability, vocabulary level, math ability)

Format
- ❏ **Hypermedia**
- ❏ **Interactive video**
- ❏ **CD-ROM**
- ❏ **DVI**
- ❏ **CDI**
- ❏ **Virtual reality**

Rating	High	Medium	Low	Comments
Match with curriculum	❏	❏	❏	
Accurate and current	❏	❏	❏	
Clear and concise language	❏	❏	❏	
Arouse motivation/maintain interest	❏	❏	❏	
Learner participation	❏	❏	❏	
Technical quality	❏	❏	❏	
Evidence of effectiveness (e.g., field-test results)	❏	❏	❏	
Free from objectionable bias or advertising	❏	❏	❏	
User guide/documentation	❏	❏	❏	
Clear directions	❏	❏	❏	
Stimulates creativity	❏	❏	❏	

Strong Points

Weak Points

Recommended Action _____ **Name** _____ **Date** _____

World History: The Magna Carta

The 11th-grade world history class has been studying England in the Middle Ages. Their study has focused on the events leading up to the reign of King John and the signing of the Magna Carta. Now they are studying the Magna Carta itself.

Analyze Learners

General Characteristics

These 11th graders are 16–17 years old. They represent a mixed socioeconomic community, as this is the only high school in their midsize city. Their intellectual aptitude is generally average, with some special-needs students mainstreamed into this section. They have demonstrated that they are more engaged in learning when they are more actively involved.

Entry Competencies

The students are near the middle of the course on world history. They have begun to understand how different socioeconomic and political interests compete for power within nations. Unit test scores up to now indicate a range of achievement from below the expected criterion to slightly above it. About a quarter of the students are substantially below their grade-level in reading skills.

State Objectives

Upon completion of the lesson, the students will be able to:

1. Describe the governance of England in the years just prior to 1215.
2. Identify the groups that were vying for political power in England at this period.
3. Paraphrase the main ideas contained in the Magna Carta.
4. Relate the main ideas of the Magna Carta to the interests of the contending groups.
5. Find ideas in today's world parallel to those of the Magna Carta.

Select Method, Media, and Materials

The teacher, Rod Winters, felt that his students did not have a high level of interest in this topic and saw little relevance to their own lives. However, he also knew that they enjoyed working in small groups, especially if they could choose their own teammates and topics. So he decided to approach this topic through the discovery method by forming the students into project groups, each selecting a different question to pursue.

Mr. Winters knew that some of the students were learning to create *HyperCard* stacks in their computer skills class. He felt that they would be excited about using this tool to prepare their reports, so he engaged the computer science teacher, Philip Hibbard, to be a consultant to the students as they developed *HyperCard* reports.

Because a wealth of materials was available he worked with other teachers to make these materials accessible to his students. Mr. Winters worked with the school library media specialist to place some books on reserve in the library, along with some videos, maps, and other materials. He also arranged for one member of each team to have a special account number for the local university's online database service. The media specialist helped him plan a field trip to the museum that included a visit with a historian from the university.

Utilize the Materials

The groups were scheduled to meet with Mr. Winters during the first and second weeks of the project. These meetings were to provide Mr. Winters with information about students' progress on their topic. In addition, he was able to help each group with further ideas about sources of information. The meetings helped to ensure a coordinated effort on the part of each group.

The computer science teacher worked with the students to develop a *HyperCard* stack shell that would be used by all the groups. The students extended their knowledge of *HyperCard* and how to design stacks. They also learned how to help their group members when working with *HyperCard*.

During the third week of study, Mr. Winters and Mr. Hibbard worked together during class time and during other non-scheduled computer lab times to help the groups prepare their stacks.

Require Learner Participation

Each group met with Mr. Winters several times during the two-week period. They presented information about their activities and the ways they were working together as a group. These meetings assured Mr. Winters that each student in the group was participating in the activities.

The groups worked together in the computer lab during class time. Although this made for crowded conditions, the students did not seem to mind. Mr. Hibbard insisted that each member of the group have equal opportunity to work on the *HyperCard* stack.

When all the stacks were ready, the group leaders met and developed a stack that would provide the user with access to the whole set of stacks. This stack included cards for the title, names of the group members, and a menu of choices to access the various stacks.

Evaluate and Revise

The students were delighted with the results of their activities and requested that they share their stack with the eighth-grade social studies class. They had learned that these students were learning about English history and thought that their stacks might be of interest to them. They also asked the eighth graders what they liked about the stacks.

Students were given an opportunity to study the information from the class project in preparation for a written test on the objectives. Mr. Winters prepared a short-answer test that focused on each of the topic areas in the *HyperCard* stacks. For students with reading difficulties, Mr. Winters arranged time to meet with them to discuss each of the topic areas, thus checking their knowledge of the events.

A computer template for a Blueprint is found in "The Classroom Link."

REFERENCES

Print References

Hypermedia

Ambrose, David W. "The Effects of Hypermedia on Learning: A Literature Review." *Educational Technology* (December, 1991): 51–55.

Babbitt, Beatrice C. "Hypermedia: Making the Mathematics Connection." *Intervention in School and Clinic 28* (1993): 294–301.

Babbitt, Beatrice C., and Usnick, Virginia. "Hypermedia: A Vehicle for Connection." *The Arithmetic Teacher 40* (April, 1993): 430–432.

Byrom, Elizabeth. "Hypermedia (Multimedia)." *Teaching Exceptional Children 22* (Summer 1990): 47–48.

Dillner, Martha. "Using Hypermedia to Enhance Content Area Instruction." *Journal of Reading 37* (December–January 1993–1994): 260–270.

Fitzgerald, Gail E., et al. "Authoring CAI Lessons: Teachers as Developers." *Teaching Exceptional Children 24* (Winter 1992): 15–21.

Grabowski, Barbara L., and Curtis, Ruth. "Information, Instruction, and Learning: A Hypermedia Perspective." *Performance Improvement Quarterly 4* (1991): 2–12.

Hasselbring, Ted S., et al. "Making Knowledge Meaningful: Applications of Hypermedia." *Journal of Special Education 10* (Winter 1989): 61–72.

Holzberg, Carol S. "Teacher Tested Ideas: Hypermedia Projects That Really Work." *Technology and Learning 14* (January, 1994): 31–34.

Jonassen, David H., and Mandl, Heinz, eds. *Designing Hypermedia for Learning*. New York: Springer-Verlag, 1990.

Locatis, Craig, et al. "Hypervideo." *Educational Technology Research and Development 39* (Summer 1990): 41–49.

Megarry, Jacquetta. "Hypertext and Compact Discs: The Challenge of Multi-Media Learning." *British Journal of Educational Technology 19* (October 1988): 172–183.

Meyer, Nadean J. "Hypertext and Its Role in Reading." *Journal of Youth Services in Libraries 7* (Winter 1994): 133–139.

Power On! New Tools for Teaching and Learning. Washington, DC: Office of Technology Assessment, U.S. Congress, 1988.

Wilson, Kathleen S. "The Palenque Optical Disc Prototype: The Design of Multimedia Discovery-Based Experience for Children." *Children's Environments Quarterly 5* (1988): 7–13.

Interactive Video, CD-ROM, DVI/CDI, and Virtual Reality

Atkins, M. J. "Evaluating Interactive Technologies for Learning." *Journal of Curriculum Studies 25* (July–August 1993): 333–342.

Barron, Ann E. "Optical Media in Education." *The Computing Teacher 20* (May 1993): 6–8.

Blissett, Gillian, and Atkins, Madeleine. "Are They Thinking? Are They Learning? A Study of the Use of Interactive Video." *Computers and Education 21* (July–September 1993): 31–39.

Boyce, Carol. "Interactive Video." *Gifted Child Today 15* (September–October 1992): 22–23.

Brewer, Sally, et al. "CD-ROMs . . . Millions of Ideas for Millions of Learners." *Educational Media International 30* (March 1993): 14–17.

Cates, Ward Mitchell. "Instructional Technology: New Optical Technologies." *Clearing House 66* (July–August 1993): 324–325.

Chapman, William. "Color Coding and the Interactivity of Multimedia." *Journal of Educational Multimedia and Hypermedia 2* (1993): 3–23.

Cohen, Kathleen. "Can Multimedia Help Social Studies Teachers? Or Are Videodiscs Worth the Expense?" *Social Studies Review 32* (Winter 1993): 35–43.

Dalton, David W. "The Effects of Cooperative Learning Strategies on Achievement and Attitudes During Interactive Video." *Journal of Computer-Based Instruction 17* (Winter 1990): 74–84.

Fabris, Marta E. "Using Multimedia in the Multicultural Classroom." *Journal of Educational Technology Systems 21* (1992–1993): 163–171.

Flanders, Bruce. "Multimedia Programs to Reach an MTV Generation." *American Literature 23* (February 1992): 135–137.

Gates, William. "The Promise of Multimedia." *American School Board Journal 180* (March 1993): 35–37.

Gayeski, Diane M. "Making Sense of Multimedia: Introduction to Special Issue." *Educational Technology 32* (May 1992): 9–13.

Hartigan, John M. "The Marriage Broker for Television and Computers." *CD-ROM Professional 6* (May 1993): 69–71.

Moore, Noel. "How to Create a Low-Cost Virtual Reality Network." *Educational Media International 30* (March 1993): 37–39.

Morris, Sandra. "Digital Video and DVI Multimedia Products." *Instruction Delivery Systems 6* (January–February 1992): 18–20.

Padgett, Helen L. "All You Need to Know About Videodiscs: One Easy Lesson." *Media and Methods 29* (March–April 1993): 22–23.

Pantelidis, Veronica. "Virtual Reality in the Classroom." *Educational Technology 33* (April 1993): 23–27.

Pearson, LaTresa. "Is CD-ROM About to Bloom?" *Training 30* (November 1993): 5–8.

Schwier, Richard. *Interactive Video.* Englewood Cliffs, NJ: Educational Technology Publications, 1988.

Skurzynski, Gloria. "The Best of All (Virtual) Worlds: What Will Become of Today's New Technology?" *School Library Journal 39* (October 1993): 37–40.

Trotter, Andrew. "Planning for Multimedia." *Executive Educator 15* (June 1993): 18–21.

Winn, William, and Bricken, William. "Designing Virtual Worlds for Use in Mathematics Education: The Example of Experimental Algebra." *Educational Technology 32* (December 1992): 12–19.

Yildiz, Rauf, and Atkins, Madeleine. "Evaluating Multimedia Applications." *Computers in Education 21* (July–September 1993): 133–139.

DISTANCE LEARNING

Advances in telecommunications technology have created new possibilities for learning across the boundaries of time and place. All levels of education, both formal and nonformal, are expanding their use of distance learning methods. It has long been possible to broadcast lessons over radio and television, and these remain popular media all around the world. But computers, satellites, and other emerging technologies have allowed the creation of truly interactive communication systems, enabling high-quality, high-speed communication at a lower cost.

Audio and video teleconferencing are growing in prominence. And the coming of the "information superhighway" is making computer conferencing easier. These new systems demand radically different roles for teachers as well as learners. By understanding these possibilities you have more options for your professional future.

KNOWLEDGE OBJECTIVES

1. Define *distance education*.
2. Describe the "information superhighway."
3. Compare and contrast the difference between computer bulletin boards and electronic mail.
4. State a rationale for the educational use of telecommunications at the elementary, secondary, postsecondary, and nonformal education levels.
5. Compare and contrast how audio, computer, and video telecommunication systems facilitate distance learning.
6. Distinguish among the various telecommunications systems.
7. Compare the advantages and limitations of each of the types of telecommunications systems.
8. Distinguish between the delivery systems for one-way and two-way television on the basis of their communication capabilities.
9. Create an example of an educational telecommunication application that incorporates two or more delivery systems.
10. Describe an instructional application that would be especially appropriate for either audio or video teleconferencing in elementary, secondary, postsecondary, or nonformal education.
11. Describe the functions performed by a classroom teacher in distance education.

APPLICATION OBJECTIVES

1. Investigate the use of radio for instructional purposes in a local school or college. Check with a local public radio station to see if it supports any specific instructional activities.
2. Interview a teacher who regularly uses broadcast television programs in the classroom. Prepare a brief written or recorded report addressing the objectives covered, techniques utilized, and problems encountered.
3. Create an instructional activity that utilizes any one or a combination of the various telecommunications systems. An example might be elementary students using Internet to investigate a community issue.
4. Generate a list of interesting uses of audio, audiographic, or computer conferencing telecommunications for a course you are currently enrolled in. Whom might you and your classmates communicate with? For what purposes?
5. Prepare an abstract of a report of a research or demonstration project related to instructional telecommunications (e.g., two schools sharing one teacher by means of interactive instructional television).
6. Observe a class taught at a distance. Describe how the teacher and students interact with each other. Also, describe the types and uses of media within the lesson.

LEXICON

distance education
telecommunications
Star Schools
computer conferencing
modems
information superhighway

networks
wide area network (WAN)
electronic mail (e-mail)
bulletin board system (BBS)

Internet gateway
audio teleconference
audiographic teleconference
instructional television fixed service (ITFS)

closed-circuit television (CCTV)
compressed video
origination classroom
distance site

DISTANCE LEARNING

One of the greatest advantages offered by modern electronic technology is the ability to instruct without the presence of a teacher. That is, we can "time-shift" instruction—experience it at some time after the live lesson—and "place-shift" instruction—experience it at some place away from the live teacher. Of course, the book was the first invention that made it possible to time-shift and place-shift instruction, and it continues in that use today.

For nearly a century people in all parts of the world have been able to participate in guided independent study through correspondence courses via the mail system. Learners receive printed lessons, do written assignments, and get feedback from the remote instructor. But the proliferation of newer electronic technologies now makes it possible to experience place-shifted instruction with a stunning array of additional auditory and visual stimuli, far more rapidly, and with a far richer range of interaction, not only with the instructor but also with other learners.

Distance education has become the popular term to describe learning via telecommunications. In this chapter the term **telecommunications** embraces a wide variety of media configurations, including radio, telephone, television (broadcast, wired, and satellite), and computers. What they all have in common is implied in the Greek root word *tele,* which means "at a distance" or "far off"; that is, they are systems for communicating over a distance.

More formally defined, distance education is a form of education characterized by the following:

- Physical separation of learners from the teacher
- An organized instructional program
- Technological media
- Two-way communication

FIGURE 10.1
The proliferation of telecommunications makes video accessible at more and more locations, such as libraries.

As the examples in this chapter will make clear, the converging of electronic technologies has fostered a rich hybridization of media configurations. We seldom see an instructional telecommunication system that is of one pure type. Typically, programs are distributed by a combination of broadcast, wired, or satellite-relayed transmissions, and students respond through some combination of mail, fax, telephone, microphone, or computer transmissions. Familiarity with these alternative pathways to learning is essential to today's educators:

> Technologies for learning at a distance, while reaching a small but growing number of teachers today, will clearly affect the teaching force of tomorrow. Some will teach on these systems, others will use them to provide additional resources in their classrooms, and many will receive professional education and training over them. Few will be unaffected.[1]

Elementary Education

At the elementary school level, teachers tend to use prerecorded videocassettes more often than live broadcast television programs. Still, several broadcast series are frequently used: at the early elementary level, "Sesame Street" and "Mister Roger's Neighborhood"; at the higher levels, "Reading Rainbow," "3–2–1 Contact," "Voyage of the Mimi," and "Newton's Apple." These programs are used as enrichment rather than as the core of instruction. "Voyage of the Mimi" is frequently used as the main element of a lesson. Teachers who use educational television programming tend to use more than one program (usually two or three), but not a whole series.[2]

Secondary Education

At the secondary level, television is used mainly to expand the curricular offerings of a specific high school. Rural schools are thus able to offer a full core curriculum. In advanced or specialized subjects for which there are not enough students in one school to justify hiring a teacher, television is frequently used to connect several schools, thus creating a large enough "class" to be affordable. For example, the TI-IN network, a satellite network based in Texas, reaches high school students across the United States via satellite. TI-IN offers such courses as foreign languages (Spanish, French, German, Latin, and Japanese), calculus, physics, psychology, and art history. These live, interactive classes, which use telephone talkback, are scheduled throughout the school

[1]U.S. Congress, Office of Technology Assessment, *Linking for Learning: A New Course for Education* (Washington, DC: U.S. Government Printing Office, 1989), p. 20.

[2]*A Study of the Role of Educational Television Programming in Elementary Schools* (New York: Children's Television Workshop, 1990).

FIGURE 10.2
Big Bird, a main character on "Sesame Street," which after more than 25 years is still the most recognized educational series for children.

day on two channels. As opposed to the elementary school pattern, these programs tend to be used in their entirety and provide core instruction.

Distance learning at the K–12 level in the United States gained impetus in the late 1980s from the **Star Schools** program initiated by the U.S. Department of Education. This program provides multimillion-dollar grants for regional consortia to develop instructional networks that reach elementary and secondary students in rural, disadvantaged, and small schools. TI-IN's collaboration with schools throughout the country is an example of the type of network that is providing students with educational opportunities that would be difficult or impossible to obtain. Star School projects also include single statewide networks that link schools within a state.

Projects such as the Iowa Distance Education Alliance (IDEA) have trained teachers, provided courses for students, and expanded the nature of distance education at the state level. For example, students who were studying manned space flight via distance education became engaged in dialogues with James VanAllen, of the University of Iowa, and NASA space scientists. The Iowa project uses a statewide fiber-optic telecommunication system that connects elementary, secondary, and postsecondary educational facilities in all 99 counties.

The opportunities offered through projects like IDEA and TI-IN continue to expand the educational horizons for many students. Whole courses and special events provide students with the means to expand their educational opportunities in rural areas.

Postsecondary Education

At the postsecondary level, telecommunication systems are used extensively for both on-campus and off-campus education. Hundreds of community colleges, technical schools, colleges, and universities in North America use telecommunications as part of their regular instructional programs. The purpose generally is to expand the number of students who can be reached by one instructor in a given course. For example, closed-circuit television is often used to connect classrooms of students in different buildings, or even in different cities, to a professor speaking from a studio or camera-equipped classroom.

The fastest growing application, though, is for reaching off-campus audiences with college or university courses. An early large-scale distance education program in the United States was begun in the mid-1950s with "TV College," an extension of the City Colleges of Chicago, using the broadcasting facilities of WTTW-TV, a public television station.

More recently, government-sponsored distance education programs throughout the world have emulated the idea of the British Open University, which began with an enrollment of 40,000 in 1971 and grew to 200,000 by the mid-1990s. In Canada, Thailand, Indonesia, and dozens of other countries, these types of programs provide access to postsecondary education in situations where conventional universities simply cannot handle the demand for further education. In each case, radio, television, and other telecommunication systems play a significant role in providing part of the instructional program. However, printed materials and various sorts of face-to-face instruction remain a major component of these and most other distance education programs.

Nonformal Education

As pervasive as telecommunications have become in formal education, there is an equally formidable range of applications outside the confines of degree-granting educational institutions. Hospitals, government agencies, businesses, engineering and architectural firms, and corporations of all sorts use telecommunications to fill part of their need for constant training and upgrading of their personnel. Here the rationale is clearly economic—to provide cost-effective training to large numbers of people who may be distributed across numerous sites. In many cases, such as with multinational corporations, it is often vitally important that the training be

CLOSE-UP

THE UNIVERSITY WITHOUT A CAMPUS

In the fast-paced world of high technology, a corporation's knowledge base can become obsolete overnight. How can a nation keep its engineering talent up to date? In the United States, instructional television lessons delivered by satellite are one answer. The National Technological University (NTU) was formed in 1984 through the collaboration of more than a dozen large corporations, two dozen universities, and the federal government. It now operates as a private nonprofit university offering its own master's degrees in computer engineering, manufacturing systems, and other fields.

The students at NTU are engineers employed at cooperating businesses and government agencies. Each organization maintains classrooms and a satellite downlink. The employee students choose from among dozens of courses, which are broadcast 20 hours a day, six days a week, on two channels. Most of these classes are videotaped and broadcast one way via satellite, but about 30% are live and interactive, with two-way audio feedback from the receiving sites.

Through NTU, engineers can stay current in their fields and advance toward a master's degree without leaving their jobs or commuting long distances. Because this school without a

campus involves many of the leading engineering universities in the nation, students have access to the top specialists in their fields of study. NTU demonstrates vividly how technology can be harnessed to promote productivity.

Source: National Technological University, P.O. Box 700, Fort Collins, CO 80522.

---

standardized. For example, the marketing strategy for a line of garden tractors or a new type of insurance policy demands that all the sales representatives emphasize the same points in their sales presentations. A packaged training course based around television can provide the fast, mass-distributed, simultaneous, standardized training needed.

A telecommunications application that combines formal education and on-site corporate training is a program offered by National Technological University (NTU). This graduate degree-granting engineering program serves on-the-job engineers with televised courses, some of which allow audio interaction (see "Close-up: The University Without a Campus").

INSTRUCTIONAL COMMUNICATION FUNCTIONS

Regardless of the technology used, from live teacher to computer conferencing, an instructional telecommunication system must perform certain functions to be effective:

- *Information presentation.* A standard element in any lesson is the presentation of some sort of information to the learner. Common examples include the following:
  - Teacher lecture and demonstration

- Printed text and illustrations (e.g., textbooks, handouts, correspondence study materials)
- Live or recorded voice, music, and other sounds
- Full-motion images (video, CD-ROM)

- *Student–teacher interaction.* We know that most learning takes place when learners are participating actively—mentally processing the material. Teachers attempt to induce activity in various ways, such as the following:
  - Question-and-answer sessions (carried out during or after the lesson)
  - Practice with feedback (carried out as drill and practice or discussion activities during the class or as homework)
  - Testing

- *Student–student interaction.* For many educational objectives, student interaction with other students, in pairs or small groups, can be extremely effective. Some common ways of structuring student interaction are the following:
  - Discussion groups (in or out of class)
  - Structured group activities (e.g., role playing or games)
  - Group projects
  - Peer tutoring

- *Access to learning resources.* Lessons and courses are usually structured with the assumption that learners will spend time outside of class working individually with the material, doing homework, projects, papers, and the like. The external learning resources may take the form of the following:

- Printed materials (e.g., textbooks, supplementary readings, worksheets)
- Audiovisual materials (e.g., audio- or video-cassettes, multimedia systems, CD-ROM)
- Computer databases (e.g., for on-line searches)
- Kits (e.g., for laboratory experiments or to examine specimens of real objects)
- Library materials (e.g., original source documents)

Each of the various telecommunication systems has strengths and limitations in these areas. The characteristics of the systems are summarized in Table 10.1 and discussed at greater length in the following sections of this chapter.

COMPUTER NETWORKS IN DISTANCE LEARNING

As we have seen from the previous chapters, computers have been used for a variety of instructional activities. With improvements in technology, along with improvements in the types of telecommunication systems, it has become possible to use the computer in new and expanded ways. Now, instead of thinking of the computer as a device that stands alone in the classroom, running selected software for students to use, it is possible to use the computer to connect to people and resources outside of the classroom.

Computer conferencing, connecting two or more computers together to conduct information (text or graphics or both) exchange, is not a new technique. In the past, this type of technology was very expensive, so educators were not able to afford it. Now the classroom computer can be connected with people and resources well beyond the limits of the school building.

TABLE 10.1
Telecommunication systems

SYSTEM	PRESENTATION	INTERACTION
Radio, broadcast	Voice, music	Homework, tests by mail
Audio teleconference	Voice, music (live)	Question-and-answer with live feedback Homework, tests by mail
Audiographic teleconference	Voice, music (live) Still pictures, graphics	Question-and-answer with live feedback Still pictures, graphics Homework, tests by mail or fax
Computer conference	Electronic text, data, graphs (time-shifted)	Written (typed) exchange with other students Written (typed) exchange with teacher
Television, one-way video, one-way audio	Voice, music Still pictures, graphics Motion images	
Television, one-way video, two-way audio (video teleconference)	Voice, music (live) Still pictures, graphics Motion images	Vocal question-and-answer with teacher Vocal exchange with other students Homework, tests by mail
Television, two-way video, two-way audio (two-way video teleconference)	Voice, music (live) Still pictures, graphics Motion images	Vocal and visual question-and-answer with teacher Vocal and visual exchange with other students Homework, tests by mail

FIGURE 10.3

A hypothetical instructional telecommunications system. You should be able to trace and name at least a half dozen different pathways a radio, TV, or computer message could follow to reach one of the school buildings. This would make a good self-test after reading the chapter.

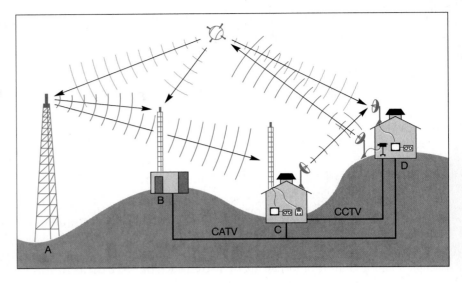

To connect with other computers beyond the walls of their building, students use **modems,** devices that change the computer data into audio signals that can be sent across telephone lines. One must use special communication software to connect the computer to a telecommunication service. Generally these services are thought of as an attendant waiting to help the user make connections, as telephone operators did before the advent of digital technology. In this case, the attendant is a computer that is programmed to help the users make connections to resources or to other services.

The **information superhighway** consists of fiber-optic strands smaller than a human hair that transmit multiple forms of information at the speed of light. The term conjures up an image of a national highway system, connecting major points throughout the country. In fractions of seconds, a single strand of fiber can carry as much information as can a thousand copper wires. The types of information that can simultaneously be transmitted include voice, data, and video. It will take some time for the entire fiber system to be built; however, sections are already in place.

Local area networks (LANs) were introduced in Chapter 8. These **networks** are designed to help connect the computers within a room or building. The term **wide area network (WAN)** describes the types of telecommunications that extend beyond the walls of a room or building. A WAN is a system of connecting with other networks, within an institution and beyond. One example is a "hard-wired" configuration, such as a campuswide network connecting all of the buildings via a cable or fiber system. All the buildings are linked to a centralized computer that serves as the host for all the software used in common in different buildings.

Another example of the use of wide area networking is accessing information via the computer, using a modem and telephone lines, from locations throughout the world. People who access information use an array

of devices, including **electronic mail (e-mail),** bulletin board systems (BBS), and information resources, such as databases and libraries. E-mail can be thought of as private mail sent in electronic form. A **bulletin board system (BBS)** can be viewed as a common pool of information and messages for a particular interest group. Users dial into a bulletin board to review messages and to leave messages for others. The location of the computer is no longer an issue because telephone lines can link any computer to the central computer system that houses the teleconferencing service. The service is available 24 hours a day, every day of the week, at home or at work, making it possible for the user to access information when it is convenient.

Internet and Other Communication Systems

Communications via computer-based systems require that the user have access to a telecommunication service. To gain access, one must use communication software to link to a computer that will then link the user to **Internet.** Internet is a worldwide noncommercial system of computer-based services, connecting more than 3,000 computer networks. It provides the user with four basic types of connection services: electronic mail for person-to-person communication; news, a type of electronic public bulletin board whereby a person connects with a group interested in the same topic; information search capabilities for accessing libraries and databases of information throughout the world; and access to specialized programs, allowing a person to use highly specialized computer programs not readily available to the individual.

Many of the commercial networks that are readily available to business and industry are developing ways to connect to the Internet system. These connections are referred to as **gateways** and are designed to provide access to many different conferencing services; the capabilities of any one service are thus expanded. The attraction of all this connectivity is that the maze of connections is largely "transparent" to the user. Users just "log on" (a way to enter the computer system, often with a special password for privacy) to their computer, connect to their networking service, and begin the information exchange process.

The potential for education using these communication systems is growing. Increasing numbers of schools are gaining access to networking services such as America Online and Internet. Opportunities to gain access to information for students and teachers are expanding. Students and teachers can enhance classroom learning by accessing information from an array of sources (databases, libraries, special interest groups), communicating via computer with other students or with experts in a particular field of study, and exchanging data via computer. Activities such as those conducted using *KidsNet,* a National Geographic learning package, make it possible for students and teachers alike to reap the benefits of connecting into a national network.

Advantages

- *Time savings.* Computer networking allows both place-shifting and time-shifting of instruction. People in various locations can share ideas, just as they do now on the telephone, but without playing the "telephone tag" game so common among busy people. The computer allows the parties to "speak" at different times and to keep records of their exchanges.
- *Cost.* The cost of the hardware, software, telephone charges, and telecommunication service rates are nominal.
- *Information access.* The benefits in terms of accessing information in education are only now emerging. Until recently, educators were limited to the resources in their classrooms or school buildings. Now, with the ability to connect students to resources in the community and throughout the world, new vistas to the teaching and learning process have opened up. Students can access libraries and databases well beyond the limits of their own community; this expands the horizons for smaller and rural schools.
- *Idea exchange.* Students can engage in "conversations" with experts in specific fields of study. Further, they can engage in activities that allow them to exchange ideas with other students, even those living in other countries.

Limitations

- *Access.* All participants must have access to the networks through computers. Whether by means of a hard-wired system or a modem, the user must have a way of connecting to the network.
- *Learning curve.* The telecommunications software needs to be user-friendly so that even young students or first-time users feel comfortable with it.
- *Support.* Good technical support needs to be readily available. Without such support and thoughtful management, a computer network system will die quickly.
- *Lack of immediacy.* Lacking the face-to-face, immediate aspects of everyday conversation can present problems. Computer conferences can easily drift from the intended subject, become dominated by a few participants, or dwindle because of lack of guidance or stimulation.
- *Copyright.* Certain limitations are related to copyright laws and types of information accessed by students. Because information is so easily accessible, it is also very simple to quickly "download" a file and, with a few changes, it can be illegally appropriated by the individual. Thus, a paper that is turned in might not be the student's own work.
- *Age-inappropriate material.* One concern often expressed by teachers is that some of the topics discussed on the Internet are not appropriate for younger students. Students can find their way, innocently enough, into resources for topics that might be too advanced for their understanding or too adult for their viewing. For example, some news topics have sexual overtones and may not be deemed suitable for students.

Applications

Computer-based telecommunications can serve a number of functions:

- *Electronic mail* encourages communication among individuals.
- *Bulletin boards* permit broad communication among groups interested in a certain topic.
- *Information sources* allow the user to subscribe to services such as databases, news services, and electronic catalogs.

Most computer networks involve people who are sharing ideas or are engaged in study of a particular topic. However, computer networks have also been used for coursework, including whole courses or programs of study. One of the largest educational computer conferences involves more than 1,300 students enrolled in information technology courses at the British Open University. More recently, programs at Nova Southeastern University and Mind Extension University in the United States have engaged in computer-based telecommunications to make it possible for students to participate in college.

CLOSE-UP

MODEM PALS

Rick Traw, professor at the University of Northern Iowa, wanted to expand the methods experiences of his elementary education students in the area of language arts. Because of scheduling difficulties, it was impossible for him to have his students go to a nearby school to work on writing skills with a group of elementary children. With the aid of the university's expanded computer network system, it was possible for the students at the local elementary school to be connected to the university students. The elementary students met their university pen pals, and they began to exchange letters. The children had a new and exciting audience for their writing, and the university students had an opportunity to learn about children's writing first-hand. Traw and the classroom teacher provided guidance to the college students in techniques for assisting children with their writing.

A growing use at the K–12 level is to promote writing skills by connecting students with "electronic pen pals." Systems have been set up that allow students from different countries, even those speaking different languages, to learn about each other's cultures through computer-mediated communications. One teacher recently connected her elementary students with students in a language arts methods class at a university across the state. (See "Close-up: Modem Pals") The students exchanged mail, with the university students helping the younger ones with their writing. Both groups benefitted from this experience. The younger students learned ways to improve their writing, and the college students learned how to work with children.

BROADCAST RADIO

When we listen to radio, we hear electronic signals that are *broadcast,* or transmitted through the air, over regular AM or FM radio frequencies. Broadcast radio can be adapted to educational use, as shown in Figure 10.4. Although such radio is basically a format for one-way lectures or dramatic presentations, some degree of interactivity can be added by using printed materials to accompany the programs and requiring listeners to send responses back to the originator. Some programs provide a telephone number for the students to contact the instructor.

FIGURE 10.4

Broadcast radio. A degree of interaction can be added by sending print materials to students through the mail; they can, in turn, send written work back to the teacher for correction and evaluation.

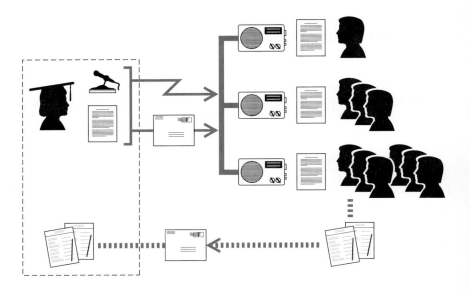

Advantages

- *Cost.* Radio is a less expensive broadcast medium than is television. It is still used in developing countries and in other localities where there are geographic or economic constraints on the technologies they can employ.
- *Range.* Radio programs can reach a large, geographically dispersed population with a single message.
- *Flexibility.* The audio medium is extremely flexible and can have a powerful, dramatic effect, particularly for conveying music, discussion, and storytelling.
- *Imagination stimulator.* Because radio is an audio-only medium, listeners are free to use their imaginations to create the image.

Limitations

- *Schedule.* Broadcast radio is being displaced by prerecorded material. Instructors resist using media that must be used according to a rigid schedule.
- *Operation expense.* It is difficult to justify the expense of operating broadcast facilities when prerecorded materials are readily available.

Applications

Radio was the first telecommunication system adapted to educational purposes in North America. Much of the early technical experimentation with radio broadcasting was carried out at stations operated by colleges and universities.

During that pretelevision period in the United States, many school and college stations linked themselves into networks, usually of statewide scope devoted to providing in-school educational programs at the K–12 level. Ohio started a "School of the Air" in the early 1930s, and others followed in the Midwest, New York, and Texas. Although some of these efforts lasted well into the television era, most languished when television became widely available in their area. In Canada, the Canadian Broadcasting Corporation (CBC) organized educational programming on a national scale.

In developing countries, where large populations still reside in isolated villages, millions of children attend schools where the learning resources begin and end with the teacher and chalkboard. In their search for a low-cost technology that could provide stimulating resources to schools scattered over vast geographic regions, educators have rediscovered broadcast radio (see Figure 10.5). An experimental project in the late 1970s in Nicaragua demonstrated success in providing mathematics lessons over the radio. Lessons were designed with embedded questions and prerecorded feedback to learners' responses. The key to success was the novel format requiring fast-paced responses by the students to questions or other cues given in the broadcast program.

FIGURE 10.5
In Kenya, "interactive" radio has proved to be a cost-effective method for teaching English.

Because of its great success in Nicaragua and in other field trials, "interactive" radio has expanded to other countries, including Honduras, Bolivia, and Kenya. English has become a popular subject for educational radio, with lessons in listening, speaking, reading, and writing. Mathematics, health, agriculture, and economics are also taught by radio.

AUDIO TELECONFERENCE

The **audio teleconference** is an extension of a simple telephone call. Advances in telephone technology now allow individuals or groups of people at two or more locations to hear and be heard clearly and easily.

An audio teleconference—a live, two-way conversation using telephone lines or satellites—connects people at different locations. For example, a class can chat with the author of a book they have recently read. They only need to have a speaker phone connection in their classroom. The author needs only a telephone. For connecting two or more groups, as for a class, a special microphone-amplifier device, preferably voice-activated, is needed at each location. This device assures that the voices are picked up faithfully and amplified clearly at the listening end. In the middle is a "bridge," an electronic system that joins the calls from all participating locations, equalizes the sound levels, filters out extraneous noises, and takes care of disconnections. The bridge may be either supplied by the telephone company or rented for the occasion from a commercial company.

Advantages

- *Cost-effective.* The audio teleconference is often seen as a cost-effective way to hold a meeting or training

FIGURE 10.6
Audio teleconference. Interaction takes place through the telephone system; groups of listeners use amplifiers.

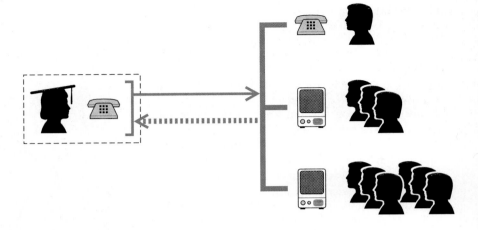

session without the expense of time and money involved in travel. Schools can invite an expert into the classroom to engage in a dialog with the students.

- *Easy to use*. It is the most easily accessible form of telecommunications because it uses telephone service. Commercial phone companies have made it easy to set up audio teleconferences from any touch-tone phone.
- *Interactive*. All participants get the same message—and interactivity. They can talk to the instructor or to the other learners.

Limitations

- *Lack of visual information*. The lack of a visual dimension poses limitations. This can be offset by arranging to have material at the sites in advance.
- *Poor audio*. To have acceptable audio quality, each receiving site needs to have special microphone-amplifier devices.
- *Intimidating*. Lack of experience with this type of communication technology may make some learners less willing to participate.

Applications

This system is frequently used at the secondary and postsecondary levels to connect students at two or more sites with an author to discuss his or her writing or with a public official to discuss current legislation. It has been used heavily in Alaska to bring inservice training to teachers. Audio teleconferencing is popular in corporate and professional education for training—for example, to discuss the features of a new service, to teach sales representatives the latest selling techniques, to update accountants on changes in the tax laws, and so on. It is not unusual to connect 10, 20, or 30 sites for one audio teleconference.

AUDIOGRAPHIC TELECONFERENCE

An **audiographic teleconference** adds still picture transmission to an audio teleconference (Figure 10.7). Several different devices can be used to send pictures and graphics over the same telephone lines as the voice signal: slow-scan (single frame) analog video, facsimile (fax) paper copies, or an electronic graphics tablet. The common denominator in these devices is a method of converting the image to digital form for transmission.

Advantages

- *Visual*. The big advantage of audiographic systems over other audio formats is the addition of the visual element.
- *Cost*. Unless full-motion images are needed, audiographics can provide an audiovisual experience at a fraction of the cost of television.

Limitations

- *Availability*. Hardware and software audiographic technologies are not readily available.
- *Time factor*. It can take nearly a full minute to transmit a still image via fax or slow-scan technologies.

Applications

Many schools and colleges use audiographic teleconferencing to connect students in a number of isolated locales with a teacher. This is especially the case in rural areas where there may not be enough students in one school to justify hiring a teacher for a particular subject, even if it is a required subject. Through audiographics a teacher at any one location can teach students at all the other sites. At Utah State University, for example, graduate classes are made available to sites scattered

FIGURE 10.7
Audiographic teleconference. In addition to hearing each other, participants can see visuals sent to a TV set one frame at a time via a graphics tablet or slow-scan video.

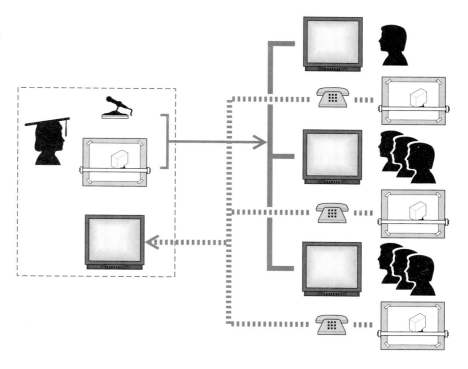

throughout Utah plus sites in Idaho and Wyoming even when there is just one student at a particular site. Corporations in the telephone business, such as AT&T, have been especially aggressive in using audiographics as a major tool for employee training.

TELEVISION IN DISTANCE LEARNING

One-Way Video, One-Way Audio

Of all the uses of television in education, the viewing of prerecorded videocassettes and videodiscs is the most common (this application is discussed in Chapter 7). Here we will consider the next most common form of television use—live viewing of programs without direct feedback to the presenter.

We use the term *one-way television* to refer to all the television delivery systems in which programs are transmitted to students without an interactive connection with the teacher (Figure 10.8). This includes five principal types of delivery systems: broadcast, satellite, microwave, closed-circuit, and cable.

Broadcast Transmission. Broadcasting, the transmission of powerful electromagnetic waves through the air, is the delivery system that made television a popular home entertainment medium. Broadcast

FIGURE 10.8
Television—one-way video, one-way audio. One-way television, such as broadcast, has no provision for feedback to the source.

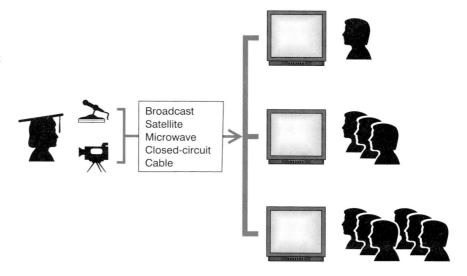

television signals, using the very-high and ultra-high frequencies (VHF and UHF), radiate outward to the horizon from the transmitting antenna (see Figure 10.9). Relay stations carry those signals around obstacles, such as mountains, and to outlying communities beyond the prime coverage area. These signals can be received freely by any standard TV set. Broadcasting is a common format for both commercial and public television programs.

In the United States, most public television stations serve as outlets for the network programming of the Public Broadcasting Service (PBS). Their evening schedules feature PBS offerings and other programs aimed at home viewers in general, while during the daytime hours these stations typically carry instructional programs designed for specific school or college audiences.

FIGURE 10.9
One-way video distribution systems.

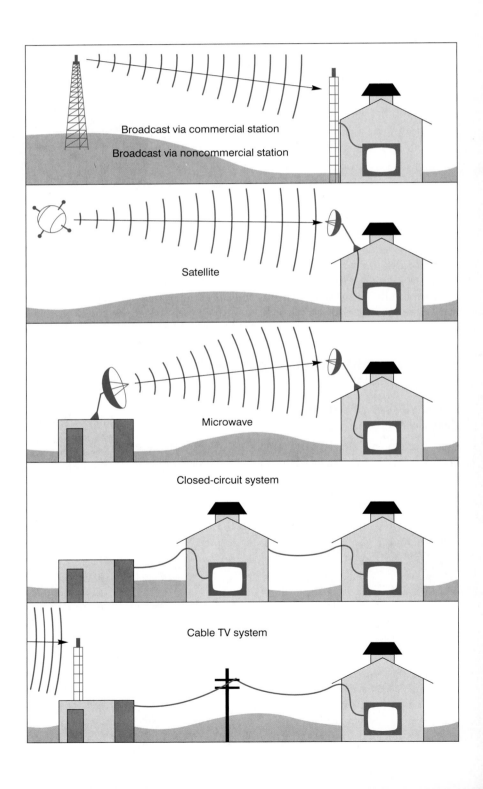

Public television attempts to offer an alternative type of programming for viewers who are not well served by the mass audience programs of commercial broadcasting. In reaching out to selected subgroups, public television programming does not usually attract viewers on a scale comparable to that of the commercial networks. However, well-produced programs such as "Wall Street Week," "Masterpiece Theatre," and "Nova" have won critical acclaim and loyal audiences that in recent years have grown as large as those for many commercial programs.

The types of programs carried on public television—documentaries, dramas, public affairs features, musical performances, science programs, and the like—are often useful as adjuncts to instruction in schools and colleges. Programs for direct classroom use to reach specific curriculum objectives—instructional television (ITV)—are a mainstay of most public television stations' daytime schedules.

ITV programs tend to be about 15 minutes (at the earlier grade levels) to 30 minutes long, and a single program is often repeated at different hours throughout the week to allow for flexibility in classroom scheduling. Contrary to the popular image, broadcast ITV programs usually do not present core instruction in basic subject areas. One leading researcher described ITV's role this way:

- To assist classroom teachers in subjects in which they often have the most difficulty (e.g., art, music, mathematics, science, and health)
- To supplement classroom instruction in subject areas in which limited classroom resources may prevent full examination of historical or international events

- To bring outside stimulation to subject areas, such as literature, where teachers have difficulty exciting and motivating students.[3]

Satellite Transmission. *Satellite communication* refers to an orbiting device in space that receives signals from stations on earth and retransmits them to distant locations (Figure 10.11). Today's satellites are geosynchronous, meaning that their orbits are synchronized with the earth's own rotation so that they appear to be positioned over the same spot on earth, serving, in effect, as a transmitting tower 23,000 miles high. At that altitude, a satellite's coverage area could include nearly half of the earth's surface. This, of course, is a far larger area than for any other transmission method. Satellites now carry most international telephone calls as well as most network television transmissions.

The trend in recent years has been to build larger and more powerful satellites, allowing the ground reception equipment to become smaller and simpler. We now have satellites that allow home reception with dish receivers no more than 18 inches across. There has been a great proliferation of receiving systems for the home, workplace, and school.

Several programming services broadcast to schools directly via satellite, including Channel One and the Discovery Channel. Channel One programs are broadcast at night via satellite and are picked up and recorded at individual schools on timer-activated video recorders (see "Close-up: News for Schools" on p. 298).

---

[3]Saul Rockman, "Instructional Television Is Alive and Well," in *The Future of Public Broadcasting,* Douglass Cater and Michael J. Nyhan, eds. (New York: Praeger, 1976), p. 79.

FIGURE 10.10
Although in-classroom playback of videocassettes is the primary delivery system for instructional television, off-air reception from public TV stations is still common.

FIGURE 10.11
Satellite dishes bring satellite signals directly to any setting, no matter how remote.

"Continental Classroom"

All things considered, Sputnik 1 has to get the credit for breathing life into the "Continental Classroom," the NBC-TV series that ran from 1958 to 1963. Sometime after Sputnik spurted aloft on October 4, 1957, NBC's director of public affairs and education, Edward Stanley, was coming back from Europe. He read that New York's commissioner of education, the late James Allen, was planning a refresher course for science teachers in the state. Probable cost: $600,000. Stanley thought that "for not a great deal more than that you could reach every science teacher in the country." And, he thought further, "we could do the whole damn thing."

Although Sputnik may have catalyzed "Continental Classroom," two people, more than any others, made it work. Ed Stanley had the institutional punch and the moxie to argue and lead at a level essential for a venture of this scope. And Dorothy Culbertson, executive producer of the public affairs department, brought intelligence and persuasiveness to both the critical fund-raising and direct management of the project.

Assembling the series amounted to a kind of benevolent brokerage by Stanley and Culbertson. At his suggestion, she talked to the Fund for the Advancement of Education about using the NBC-TV network for college credit courses. They were "excited." At almost the same time, the American Association of Colleges for Teacher Education (AACTE) approached NBC tentatively. Would it put up $25,000 to study how TV could be used to improve teacher training? "I thought it was a helluva good idea," recalls Stanley. But his vision was broader: Would they be interested in something considerably bigger? Indeed they would, they said. This became vital in the funding arrangements that were to follow.

It seemed apparent that NBC alone could not float the concept. And so, after appeals to the Ford Foundation, it finally agreed to put in $500,000, a major share of the first year's expected cost. Then, following beguiling calls from Culbertson, increments of $100,000 apiece came in from a number of large corporations. As a practical matter, the funds all went to AACTE, which paid NBC for its facilities, at cost.

By then, the apt series title had been locked up, as an outgrowth of a conversation between Stanley and noted educator Dr. James Killian, then science advisor to President Eisenhower. "What you'd have here," Stanley explained, "would be a continental classroom." Dr. Killian liked the idea, and the term stuck.

On October 6, 1958, the daily broadcasts began on the NBC network. That first year, the topic was "Atomic Age

Microwave Transmission. Television signals broadcast in the microwave spectrum (above 2,000 MHz) are referred to as microwave transmission. As with other forms of telecommunications, a license is required to transmit with microwave, and in the United States a specific part of the microwave spectrum has been reserved for educational institutions—the 2500–2690 band, called **instructional television fixed service (ITFS)**.

ITFS (and other microwave transmissions) have one major technical limitation: signals broadcast at these high microwave frequencies travel in a line-of-sight pattern. Consequently, the coverage of ITFS is limited to areas in direct sightline of the transmission tower. More than 100 educational licensees operate several hundred channels in the ITFS spectrum. Even though reception is limited to a line-of-sight radius, this is large enough to cover some school districts. Within higher education,

ITFS is used primarily for graduate and professional school distance education—for example, connecting engineering or medical schools with professionals in the field who desire a refresher course.

Closed-Circuit Television. The term **closed-circuit television (CCTV)** refers to a private distribution system connected by wire. This wire may be regular copper wire that carries electrical impulses or thin glass optical fiber that carries impulses in the form of light. CCTV signals cannot be received outside the private network. A major advantage of CCTV is that such systems do not require government licensing and can be set up freely by any institution that desires to do so. Closed circuit is used mainly to connect the buildings on an individual school or college campus and gives a private, multichannel capability within those confines. The cost of distribution rises as the network

Physics," a college-level course 165 lessons long. Says Stanley, "Physics was the subject that was in trouble then. Many people teaching it had received their degrees before atomic energy was invented." The man to teach these lessons was Dr. Harvey White, professor of physics at the University of California at Berkeley. Joining the NBC project, he lined up a veritable "Who's Who" of American scientists as guest lecturers. There's probably never been another national refresher course quite like it.

White and other "Continental Classroom" teachers had to do 130 lectures of their own in a year's time, five per week. They were under fantastic pressure, working from outlines rather than from prepared scripts. NBC tried to let their talent go into the studio when they wanted. Largely, this meant afternoon sessions. A four-hour stretch of studio time allowed for camera blocking, a dress rehearsal, and tape recording.

NBC's audience-research specialists estimated that 400,000 people viewed "Physics," while 600,000 tuned in to "Chemistry," in the second year. But at no time during the five-year span of "Continental Classroom" did more than 5,000 sign up for actual credit in a course. Even so, to Lawrence McKune of Michigan State, that first series on physics was unique:

> For the first time in the history of education, 4,905 students . . . in all parts of the United States, studied precisely the same course with the same teacher at the same hour, using the same outlines and the same texts.

In the second year, NBC repeated physics at 6:00 in the morning, then ran its new chemistry course at 6:30. Physicists began watching chemistry, and the chemists brushed up on their physics, a neat refresher switch.

By 1960, the mathematicians were asking for a course. This time, a new approach was tried. The first half of the year was devoted to algebra; John Kelley of Berkeley taught three days a week, and Julius Hlavaty took Tuesdays and Thursdays. Then, in the second "term," Frederick Mosteller, chairman of statistics at Harvard, carried the main load on lessons in probability and statistics, while Paul Clifford of Montclair State College did the "applications" on Tuesdays and Thursdays. By that term, as many as 320 colleges and universities were granting credit for the course. Stanley notes that "few of them were giving probability in those days."

At that point, the Ford Foundation decided to cut off its financial support. And even though a number of corporate sponsors stuck with the project, Stanley began to feel a budget squeeze (a cutback to two TV cameras instead of the normal three). Regardless, Stanley still managed to come up with a star performer for that fourth year—the late Peter Odegard, then chairman of the political science department at Berkeley and former president of Reed College. Was it successful? Stanley says that Odegard's "American Government: Structure and Function" had an audience of 1.5 million. The League of Women Voters, he recalls, "were convinced we did this especially for them!"

But then "Continental Classroom" folded. Why? "Money," says Stanley. "The company did lose a little, and wasn't willing to take a chance on raising some money the next year." The series budget—it ran between $1.2 million and $1.5 million annually—was "not a helluva lot for a network, not really." But NBC must have thought so. "American Government" was rebroadcast in the fifth year, and "Continental Classroom" ended officially on May 17, 1963.

Excerpted from Robert D. B. Carlisle, College Credit Through TV: Old Idea, New Dimensions (Lincoln, NB: Great Plains National Instructional Television Library, 1974).

▲

---

expands (unlike with broadcast TV), so CCTV is not generally used for reaching a large geographic area. However, several states, such as Indiana and Minnesota, have CCTV networks connecting schools and colleges hundreds of miles apart.

It is difficult to characterize the applications of CCTV because, being unregulated, it has no central information source. Also, CCTV systems can be as simple as a camera connected to a monitor in the same room (e.g., for image magnification of a science demonstration) or as complex as a campuswide wired distributed system (e.g., for distribution of video programs from a central library to any classroom). Because the cost of building a CCTV system increases with larger geographic areas, it is not widely used to interconnect buildings spread out over a school district. However, it is frequently used to connect buildings on a college or university campus.

Cable Television. The cable concept of television program delivery was first applied commercially in the 1950s in an isolated town where, due to interference from a mountain overshadowing the town, people were unable to receive a viewable signal from the nearest TV station. Local businesspeople developed the idea of building a master antenna atop the mountain. There the weak signals were amplified and fed into a coaxial cable that ran down the mountain into the town. By paying an installation charge and a monthly subscription fee, a customer could have his or her home connected to the cable. This idea of having a single tall antenna to serve a whole community gave the process the name *community antenna television*, or *CATV*, now more commonly known as cable television. Many schools and most postsecondary institutions are now connected to commercial cable systems, often without monthly charges. Educational institutions are

CLOSE-UP

NEWS FOR SCHOOLS

Elementary and secondary school students have daily access to a specially produced 15-minute news program through "CNN Newsroom." Each program contains current news presented with scripting and graphics that give students a context for understanding the news they hear.

Participating schools can tape the programs off cable or satellite without charge and can receive free teachers' guides to accompany the programs.

There is evidence that even this brief daily exposure to real-world events can have a beneficial effect on students. In the early days of "CNN Newsroom," one enthusiastic fourth-grade teacher reported that his class scored at the 88th percentile on standardized tests in both science and social studies after a year of watching and discussing "CNN Newsroom."

These scores translate to an equivalent of ninth grade in social studies and seventh grade in science; they were more than 10 points above the average for the rest of the school's fourth graders, who don't have access to the program.[a]

"CNN Newsroom" originated as a rival to Channel One, a secondary school news service of Whittle Communications. Channel One provides a daily 12-minute news program that includes two minutes of commercials. In exchange for promising that students watch the programs (including the commercials), the schools receive video reception, recording, and playback equipment. The inclusion of commercials has made Channel One controversial in many locations.

[a]"CNN Newsroom Improves Science and Social Studies Test Scores," *Advisory Group Briefing. Turner Educational Services, Inc. (December 1991), pp. 4–5.*

---

often invited to use one of the cable channels for their own purposes.

The availability of multiple channels with cable facilitates a number of special services:

- Transmission of several programs simultaneously and repetition of programs at different hours for more flexibility with classroom schedules

- "Narrowcasting," or aiming specialized programs at small subgroups (e.g., those speaking foreign languages or having sight or hearing impairments)
- Retrieval of remotely stored libraries of video materials, allowing teachers or individual students access to materials on demand without the logistic struggle often associated with instructional media use

FIGURE 10.12

Cable television distribution system. Multiple program sources are combined at the "head end" and sent out through trunks, feeders, and drop lines to individual homes, schools, and businesses.

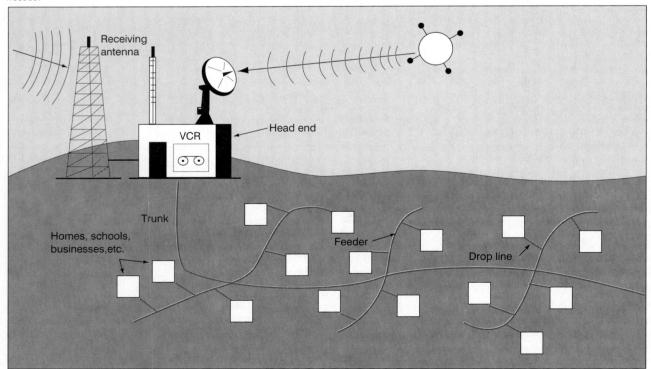

Furthermore, many cable operators provide schools with special programming, teachers' guides, and even special computer services. Many of the program sources available via cable are not retransmitted from broadcasts but are sent out only on cable. A number of these offer high-quality programming suitable for school use. The Discovery Channel, the Learning Channel, Cable News Network, and C-Span are a few examples, all of which offer program guides for teachers. The school library media specialist may already have these available for the teacher or can assist in obtaining them.

One-Way Video, Two-Way Audio.   Virtually all the television modes mentioned so far can be converted into a two-way communication system by using a device for sending audio feedback to the presenter. In the case of broadcast, satellite, and microwave transmissions, the talkback capability is usually added by means of a telephone for calling the originating studio. In the case of closed-circuit and cable systems, the talkback channel may be incorporated in the CCTV or CATV wiring itself. See Figure 10.13.

Two-Way Video, Two-Way Audio

Fully interactive television with two-way communication of both audio and video, or two-way television, is achieved by equipping both the sending and receiving sites with camera and microphone and interconnecting them by some means capable of two-way transmission. This may be fiber optics, cable, microwave, satellite, or a combination of these. A school or other organization may operate its own facilities or lease them as needed for particular occasions.

Most two-way video, two-way audio systems rely on full-motion video pictures. Technically, it is much more difficult and expensive to transmit a full-motion video image than a still picture. The full-motion image requires a signal channel as broad as that used by broadcast TV stations, whereas a still picture uses a narrow signal and can be sent over a telephone line. A recent technological breakthrough called **compressed video** removes redundant information, transmitting only the frames in which there is some motion. In this way the video information can be "squeezed" through a telephone line. This compression is important because it costs only about one-tenth as much to transmit through a phone line as through a broadband channel. There is a perceptible difference in the fluidity of the motion depicted, but participants easily adapt to this. Compressed video is gaining popularity rapidly wherever two-way television is being used. (See "Close-up: School–University Cooperation Through Compressed Video.")

Role of the Student

Students need to know their roles in a distance learning experience. Early attempts at this type of instruction tended to involve a "talking head," with students passively sitting in the distance sites, often not attending to the "head." More recently, with technological advances, interactions among students and between sites is feasible. Students can become more engaged in their learn-

FIGURE 10.13
Television—one-way video, two-way audio. This is probably the most widely used and most economical means of adding interactivity to instructional TV.

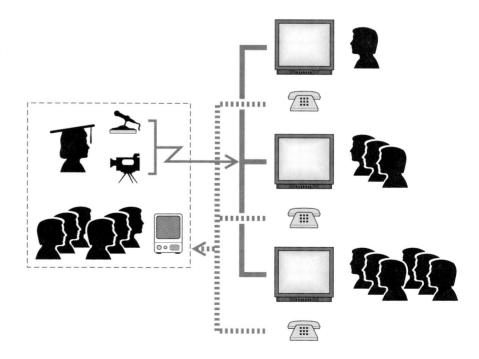

FIGURE 10.14
Video-teleconference participants often view the program on projection TV, giving feedback to the speaker via telephone.

ing. It remains the teacher's responsibility, however, to guide students on how to interact appropriately.

Students need to know how to use the technology to communicate with the teacher and with each other. When students want to ask questions, or want to add to the discussion, they must be able to use the technology to interact. Students not only need to know how to operate the microphone, they also need to understand communication etiquette. A student's "right to interrupt" becomes an important concept when working with multiple sites in a course. If the teacher does not give equal time to all sites, or if the student has a question that needs to be addressed, it may be necessary for the student to interrupt the teacher's instruction.

CLOSE-UP

SATELLITE SERVES RURAL HIGH SCHOOL

Eddyville (Oregon) High School is a small, rural high school serving a logging community located on the Pacific Ocean. It is part of a sparsely populated school district covering 1,800 square miles. The school, like many others in similar situations, has difficulty offering a broad enough curriculum to meet the diverse needs of the students. In this case, the interactive television programs delivered by satellite from TI-IN network in San Antonio, Texas, helped to fill the gaps. In 1988 Eddyville High School was about to eliminate classes in French and Spanish because the teacher of those subjects moved away. By subscribing to TI-IN the school enabled its students to take not only those language courses but also psychology, sociology, and art appreciation.

The video lessons are broadcast on a regular schedule, and the students participate along with students at many other sites around the country. At each site there is a telephone to allow question-and-answer (one-way video, two-way audio) sessions. Students, teachers, and parents appreciate the chance to have an enriched curriculum at a cost even a small school can afford.

Source: Star Student News (December 1988–January 1989). Published by TI-IN Network.

CLOSE-UP

SCHOOL–UNIVERSITY COOPERATION THROUGH COMPRESSED VIDEO

The Wyoming Centers for Teaching and Learning Network (WCTLN) is a cooperative venture among school districts and the School of Education at the University of Wyoming. This network uses compressed video and other technologies to connect schools in nine districts with each other and with the university.

The telecommunication network was set up to deal with the problem of small populations spread over a vast geographic area. Many teachers work in small, isolated schools with limited curriculum offerings. Because of the relatively low cost of building and operating a compressed video system (compared with regular broadband video), it is now possible for students in one locale to participate in live, two-way audio and video exchanges with students and teachers at other schools.

Besides being used to enrich the curricula at K–12 schools, the system is used by teachers and administrators for electronic inservice meetings, saving them from driving hundreds of miles to meet face-to-face. The School of Education uses the system to enable teacher trainees to observe real classrooms. The system also allows student teachers to be observed by their School of Education supervisors while they are working in the field. Considering that some of these school sites are a seven-hour drive from the university, the video system yields tremendous savings in time and effort.

Source: Landra Rezabek and Barbara Hakes, College of Education, University of Wyoming.

Role of the Teacher

When we begin to talk about the teacher in the distance learning classroom, it is necessary to think about the setting in a new light. The classroom is now a series of rooms, connected electronically. The **origination classroom** is the one where the teacher is present. **Distance sites** or remote classrooms are the locations that have been connected by the telecommunications system. At the distance sites, there may be only one or two students, or there may be a full class. Additionally, there may be a distance-site facilitator, an adult whose responsibility it is to work with the teacher. The facilitator may be another teacher or a classroom aide. The duties of the facilitator vary depending on the course content and the origination classroom teacher's needs.

Experience has shown that in K–12 education, student success increases when the teacher and the dis-

FIGURE 10.15
Television—two-way video, two-way audio. Full auditory and visual interactivity requires a camera and microphone at each reception site.

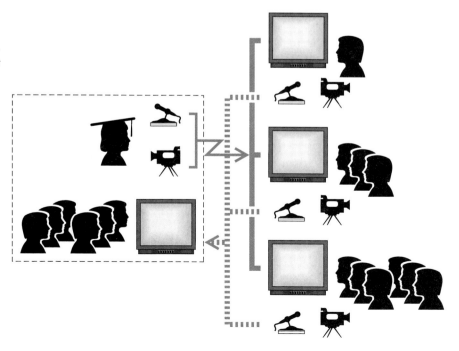

CLOSE-UP

SHARING TEACHERS VIA VIDEOCONFERENCING

How can small rural schools offer advanced courses in mathematics and foreign languages when no single school has a large enough enrollment to justify its own teacher? Four school districts in Carroll County, Illinois, have been experimenting with a simplified two-way videoconferencing system as an answer to this question. Each participating school has set up one classroom as a teleconference room, equipped with cameras, microphones, video recorder, monitors, and a special effects generator/switcher. Classes are taught live at the school in which there is a qualified teacher; students in any of the other three schools may participate.

Students in the receiving schools watch and listen to the class. They can also be heard and seen by activating the camera and microphone in their own classroom. A camera mounted on top of the teacher's desk gives close-up views of visual materials.

Lessons can be videotaped for review by absent students. They can also be videotaped in advance when the instructor must be absent during usual class times.

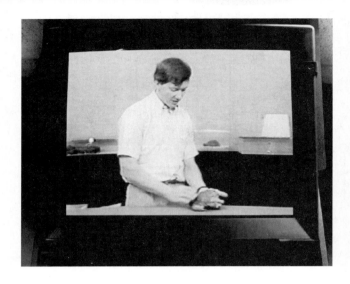

Source: Peter C. West, Rhonda S. Robinson, and Keith Collins, "A Teaching and Telecommunications Partnership," Educational Leadership (March 1986): 54–55.

tance-site facilitator work as a team. In one major project, for example, students learned more in cases where the distance-site facilitator did the following:

• Watched and participated actively in all programs with the students
• Encouraged interaction with the teacher and other students
• Answered questions at that site
• Solved immediate problems

• Provided additional quizzes and worksheets
• Took responsibility for operating and troubleshooting the equipment

To play an active, facilitating role requires advance planning and training. Ideally, the distance teacher and facilitator meet before the classes start to discuss goals for the class and instructional strategies. For example, they may agree to allow students in receiving classrooms to discuss and explain points to each other during class

FIGURE 10.16
Videoconferencing systems can be designed so that the teacher can select the image to be shown by touching the screen.

with talkback microphones off. Such peer cooperation can greatly enhance the learning atmosphere in what might otherwise be a stilted, restrictive environment.

Visualizing Instruction

With technologies for distance learning that rely on television, the teacher may need to change existing teaching materials. The document camera is a valuable teaching tool for showing students visuals and for demonstrating specific tasks. Although teachers may be able to use classroom materials such as overhead transparencies, these materials tend to be in a format that is not easily seen on the monitors. Television has a horizontal, or "landscape," orientation, which means that materials prepared in a vertical orientation will not be as easily seen. It may be necessary to redo materials. One suggestion is to have all classroom materials prepared so they can be used in either a regular or a television classroom setting.

Color, size, and design are important considerations. Television is not a very good medium for quality color transmission. So, for example, a science teacher who is demonstrating a chemical reaction that relies on color change may find that students at the distance sites do not see the desired outcomes. Although it is possible to zoom a document camera in for close-up of a page, definition and quality may be lost. Also, some graphics may be too "busy" for television, creating distractions for students.

Accessing Resources at a Distance

One element often overlooked in a distance learning situation is the access students have to resource materials. If a teacher wishes to have students engage in research or certain types of activities, it is critical that students

FIGURE 10.17

Classroom setup for interactive TV. At the originating classroom, both teacher and students must have camera(s), microphone(s), and monitor(s) to communicate with students in remote classrooms.

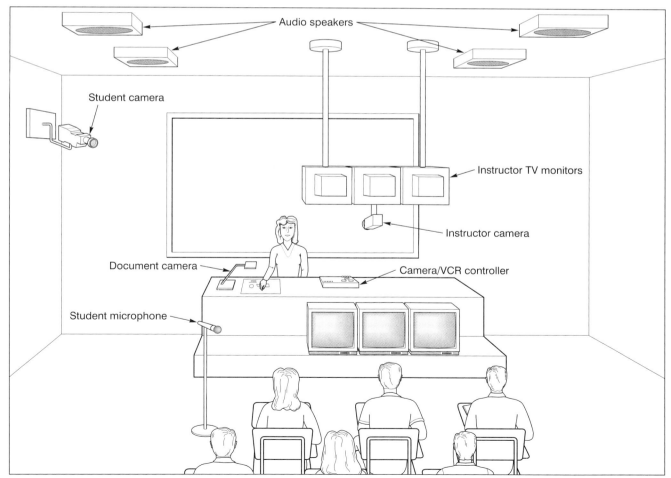

FREE CLEARINGHOUSE ON DISTANCE LEARNING

The National Distance Learning Center (NDLC) is a centralized on-line database containing detailed program listings for distance-learning courses, including credit and noncredit school courses, teleconferences, seminars, and inservice training courses. The listings pertain to all audiences—primary, secondary, and continuing education. NDLC provides program information on courses available in all distance-learning formats, including satellite broadcast, audio- and videocassette, and print.

There is no charge to access the system or to scan the database, and access requires only a computer and modem; communications software for the modem will even be sent without charge if needed.

For more information, contact the National Distance Learning Center, Owensboro Community College, 4800 Hartford Road, Owensboro, KY 42303.

---

have access to related materials. A teacher may need to change particular types of activities or to make special arrangements for materials to be sent to the distance-site classrooms. The student at a distance site should not be at a disadvantage in the learning process because of limited resources. It is the teacher's responsibility, often working closely with the school library media specialist, to ensure that all students have equal access to the materials essential for learning.

Advantages

- *Cost efficiency.* All forms of broadcasting share the attribute of reaching geographically dispersed audiences in a cost-efficient way.
- *Audiovisual capacity.* All television systems allow the transmission of motion images and sound over a distance.
- *Two-way possibilities.* When learners can communicate with the instructor and other students via telephone or two-way video you can approximate a live classroom interaction.

Limitations

- *Cost for two-way.* Adding the capacity for two-way communication may require costly hardware installation, including a bridge if multiple sites are connected at once. If telephones are used there will be toll charges for the calls.
- *Facilities for two-way.* The special setups needed for two-way video require that a classroom be dedicated to this use, thus making it difficult to use the room for other purposes.
- *Isolation.* Learners who participate in broadcast lessons without talkback capabilities can feel like second-class citizens having little rapport with the rest of the group.

Applications

Commercial and noncommercial stations are providing programming for use in educational settings. In fact, one-quarter of the programs used by teachers in schools originate from commercial stations. These include dramas, dance and music performances, documentaries, and news and public affairs programs. Popular television programs can also be used to spark discussions of social issues.

Noncommercial broadcasting is generally thought to be public or "educational" television. Although not all noncommercial networks are publicly owned, they tend to operate along similar lines. Most of these networks are outlets for PBS programming. During the day, programming typically is instructional, designed for specific school audiences. Evening programming tends to be oriented to an audience that does not find the commercial broadcast offerings of interest.

With the advent of two-way communications in television programming, many different types of instructional activities can occur. Courses, either whole or in part, can be offered to students in geographically dispersed locations. For example, in Bergen County, New Jersey, a cluster of urban elementary and secondary schools is interconnected via fiber optics. A class can be offered, resources can be shared, and students can collaborate easily on projects. Kirkwood Community College, in Cedar Rapids, Iowa, has been offering advanced placement classes to local high school students since 1982. Students can participate in the college class, allowing them an enriched learning experience.

FUTURE OF DISTANCE LEARNING

As with many of the technologies that have been introduced into education, there is a lag in widespread acceptance of distance learning. This delay in the use of

Problem Solving: Mystery Buildings

A middle school teacher, Amy Clymer, wanted to highlight higher level thinking skills in her class. She was looking for a motivating way to get her students to use problem solving strategies.

Analyze the Learners
General Characteristics

The 25 seventh graders in this class are 12–13 years old and reside in a town in the middle of a farming region. They are a heterogeneous group, both in terms of socioeconomic background and learning abilities; two have special needs. In general, they prefer hands-on learning activities to more passive methods.

Entry Competencies

The students have studied three problem solving strategies: using patterns, using equations, and logical reasoning. They have demonstrated their ability to use all three with classroom activities, although some students needed special prompting by the teacher in order to be successful in those activities. In addition, the students have worked with the library media specialist to utilize the library's database materials to enhance their study of logical reasoning strategies.

State Objectives

The seventh-grade students will be able to do the following:

1. Using the school's computer facilities, log onto *Gopher* successfully within no more than three attempts.
2. Using the resources of Internet, identify specific "mystery" buildings and their locations; they will receive five clues about each building.
3. In a written log, describe briefly the problem solving strategy they used to identify each mystery building.

Select Methods, Media, and Materials

The teacher decides to use a discovery approach in order to provide practice situated in a more realistic and motivating context. Remembering that the students enjoyed corresponding with other students via electronic mail on Internet, she decides to have them use Gopher as the primary medium for exploring the identity and location of some mystery buildings.

Because some of the students will need prompting in using Internet and because she wants them all to be conscious of the problem solving strategies they are using, she decides to have them work in pairs. They are instructed to talk about and write down their strategies before they log onto the network.

Ms. Clymer used the Internet to select a dozen well-known buildings for her students to identify. She made up sets of clues using index cards. For example, a clue card for the CN Tower in Toronto contained the following:

1. I'm in North America.
2. I'm the world champion in height.
3. I was completed in an Olympics year, the year that Mao Zedong died.
4. My city is located on a great lake.
5. The street at my feet has "front" in its name.

Utilize the Materials

The students were divided into pairs and given instructions on using the computer search facilities and on recording their strategies. Student pairs are scheduled to work in the school library media center in 30-minute blocks; they have two weeks to solve as many of the mysteries as they can. When they are not on the computer they are preparing their strategies and making entries in their logs.

As the students work on the computer, Ms. Clymer or the library media specialist is available to give assistance. They take notes about the students' difficulties and triumphs. As student pairs solve one mystery they are given another to work on.

Require Learner Participation

The active working of each pair is monitored by requiring each group to present its search plan to the teacher before logging onto the computer. Their log must show what resources they accessed and what steps they followed in their search. The teacher and library media specialist also observe how the pairs work together at the computer.

Evaluate and Revise

At the end of the two-week unit, the teacher conducts a whole-class debriefing to compare their findings and discuss their strategies. By listing these strategies on the overhead projector, students are able to compare their strategies, and the teacher gets a record of the discussion that she can refer to in the future. She also collects the logs of each pair and the observation notes she and the library media specialist made.

From these data, she decides that the students were enthusiastic about the challenge and that most groups worked diligently to try to solve as many mysteries as they could. Some groups needed reminding about the logs and some wanted to plunge into the computer search without a plan. It's clear that the first search was the most difficult, and the teams became more efficient with each subsequent search. The teacher and library media specialist made a note to make sure that extra help was available during the first days of the work at the computers.

A computer template for a Blueprint is found in "The Classroom Link."

telecommunications has been related to such issues as funding, teacher training, and available resources. As these barriers are eliminated, greater use of distance learning technologies will be seen.

As the information superhighway is expanded at the national level, it is hoped that funding for hardware, software, and costs associated with connecting to the system will be available for schools. Further, communities and private corporations will begin to recognize that to keep themselves open to the worldwide marketplace, access to information will require more advanced technologies, as well as trained personnel. Partnerships between schools and telecommunications companies will help schools gain access to the advancing technologies at reasonable costs.

It is essential that teachers receive the types of training they need to successfully implement these technologies in their teaching. Teachers need to know not only how to use these technologies, but also how to teach their students to become successful users. Such basic skills as searching for information take on new meaning when the library card catalog suddenly becomes a broad range of databases and libraries throughout the world. Here the classroom teacher and school library media specialist need to work closely together to provide their students with meaningful and enlightening experiences. Teacher training programs, at both the preservice and inservice levels, are engaging their students in various types of activities that require students to use telecommunications. Some offer whole courses, while others provide opportunities for networking among students and faculty. And, as teachers begin to use these technologies, their interest in sharing them with their students will expand.

Finally, the amount of available information resources is expanding at an exponential rate. With the advent of *Gopher,* a simple menu-based system for exploring Internet, and *Netscape,* an interface for the World Wide Web, resources are merely a computer screen away.

REFERENCES

Print References

Barker, Bruce, et al. "Broadening the Definition of Distance Education in Light of the New Telecommunications Technologies." *American Journal of Distance Education 15* (1989): 20–29.

Bearne, Colin. "Teaching with the Dish." *British Journal of Language Teaching 26* (Spring 1988): 54–56.

Bradshaw, Dean H., and Desser, Karen. *Audiographics Distance Learning: A Resource Handbook.* San Francisco: Far West Laboratory for Educational Research and Development, 1990.

Branscomb, Anne W. "Videotext: Global Progress and Comparative Policies." *Journal of Communication 38* (Winter 1988): 50–59.

Buchanan, Peggy. "Project INSITE: Developing Telecommunications Skills for Teachers and Students." *Journal of Computers in Mathematics and Science Teaching, 12* (1993): 245–260.

Chute, Alan G. "Strategies for Implementing Teletraining Systems." *Educational and Training Technology International 27* (August 1990): 264–270.

Clark, G. Christopher. "Distance Learning: A Spectrum of Opportunities." *Media and Methods 26* (September–October 1989): 22, 24–27.

Cyrs, Thomas E., and Smith, Frank A. *Teleclass Teaching: A Resource Guide.* 2d ed. Las Cruces, NM: Center for Educational Development, New Mexico State University, 1990.

Dede, Christopher J. "The Evolution of Distance Learning: Technology-Mediated Interactive Learning." *Journal of Research on Computing in Education 22* (Spring 1990): 247–264.

Descy, Don E. "Two-Way Interactive Television in Minnesota: The KIDS Network." *Tech Trends 36* (1991): 44–48.

England, Richard. *A Survey of State-Level Involvement in Distance Education at the Elementary and Secondary Levels.* ACSDE Research Monograph No. 3. University Park, PA: Pennsylvania State University, 1991.

Farr, Charlotte, and Shaeffer, James. "Matching Media, Methods, and Objectives in Distance Education." *Educational Technology 33* (1993): 52–55.

Garrison, D. R. *Understanding Distance Education.* New York: Routledge, 1989.

Gilbert, John K., Temple, Annette, and Underwood, Craig, eds. *Satellite Technology in Education.* New York: Routledge, 1991.

Giltrow, David. *Distance Education.* Washington DC: Association for Educational Communications and Technology, 1989.

Hanson, Gordon. "Distance Education and Educational Needs: A Model for Assessment." *Media and Methods 27* (September–October 1990): 14, 17–18.

Harris, Judi. *Way of the Ferret: Finding Educational Resources on the Internet.* Eugene, OR: International Society for Technology in Education, 1994.

Holmberg, Borje. *Theory and Practice of Distance Education.* New York: Routledge, 1989.

Hudspeth, Delayne R., and Brey, Ronald G. *Instructional Telecommunications: Principles and Applications.* New York: Praeger, 1986.

Hurley, Paul, Laucht, Matthias, and Hlynka, Denis. *The Videotex and Teletext Handbook.* New York: Harper and Row, 1985.

Interactive Radio Instruction: Confronting a Crisis in Basic Education. Washington, DC: U.S. Agency for International Development and Education Development Center, 1990.

Keegan, Desmond. *Foundations of Distance Education.* 2d ed. New York, Routledge, 1990.

Kitchen, Karen, and Kitchen, Will. *Two-Way Interactive Television for Distance Learning.* Alexandria, VA: National School Boards Association, 1988.

Mason, Robin, and Kaye, Anthony, eds. *Mindweave: Communication, Computers, and Distance Education.* Oxford, Pergamon, 1989.

Massoumian, Bijan. "Successful Teaching via Two-Way Interactive Video." *Tech Trends 34* (March–April 1989): 16–19.

Milheim, William D. "Computers and Satellites: Effective New Technologies for Distance Education." *Journal of Research on Computing in Education 22* (Winter 1989): 151–159.

Miller, Elizabeth. *The Internet Resource Directory for K-12 Teachers and Librarians.* Englewood, CO: Libraries Unlimited, 1994–1995.

Moore, Michael G., and Thompson, Melody M. *The Effects of Distance Learning: A Summary of the Literature.* ACSDE Research Monograph No. 2. University Park, PA: Pennsylvania State University, 1990.

Mugridge, I., and Kaufman, D. *Distance Education in Canada.* London: Croom Helm, 1986.

Naidu, Som. *Computer Conferencing in Distance Education.* ERIC Information Analysis. Syracuse, NY: ERIC Clearinghouse on Information Resources, 1988.

Novelli, Joan. "Rhymes Around the World." *Instructor 103* (1993): 57–60.

Ostendorf, Virginia A. *Teaching Through Interactive Television.* Littleton, CO: Virginia A. Ostendorf, 1989.

———. *What Every Principal, Teacher, and School Board Member Should Know About Distance Education.* Littleton, CO: Virginia A. Ostendorf, 1989.

Pease, Pamela S. "Strategies for Implementing Distance Learning Technologies: Why, When, and How." *School Business Affairs 55* (October 1989): 15–18.

Platt, Carolyn. "Mystery Pen Pals." *Learning 22* (1993): 74.

Robertson, Bill. "Audio Teleconferencing: Low-Cost Technology for External Studies Networking." *Distance Education* (March 1987): 121–130.

Schamber, Linda. *Delivery Systems for Distance Education.* ERIC Digest. Syracuse, NY: ERIC Clearinghouse on Information Resources, 1988.

Telecommunications for Learning. Educational Technology Anthology Series, Vol. 3. Englewood Cliffs, NJ: Educational Technology Publications, 1991.

U.S. Congress, Office of Technology Assessment. *Linking for Learning: A New Course for Education.* Washington DC: U.S. Government Printing Office, 1989.

Verduin, John R., and Clark, Thomas A. *Distance Education: The Foundations of Effective Practice.* San Francisco: Jossey-Bass, 1991.

Waggoner, Michael D., ed. *Empowering Networks: Computer Conferencing in Education.* Englewood Cliffs, NJ: Educational Technology Publications, 1991.

Wall, Milan. "Technological Options for Rural Schools." *Educational Leadership* (March 1986): 50–52.

Wallin, Desna L. "Televised Interactive Education: Creative Technology for Alternative Learning." *Community/Junior College Quarterly of Research and Practice 14* (July–September 1990): 259–266.

Wilson, Virginia S., et al. "Audio Teleconferencing as Teaching Technique." *Social Education* (February 1986): 90–92.

Witherspoon, John, and Kovitz, Roselle. *The History of Public Broadcasting.* Washington, DC: Current, 1987.

Zigerell, James. *The Uses of Television in American Higher Education.* New York: Praeger, 1991.

Audiovisual References

Accessing Data Networks. Washington, DC: Association for Educational and Communication Technology, 1994. Videocassette. ½ inch.

Communication II—Today and Tomorrow. Irwindale, CA: Barr Films, 1990. Videocassette, ¾ or ½ inch.

Cruisin' the Information Highway: Findin' On-ramps and Gettin' up to Speed. Washington, DC: Association for Educational and Communication Technology, 1994. Videocassette, ½ inch.

Gophers, Armadillos, and Other Internet Critters: Getting Started with Internet Tools. Washington, DC: Association for Educational and Communication Technology, 1994. Videocassette, ½ inch.

Journey North. Minneapolis: Journey North (125 North First St., Minneapolis, MN 55401), 1995. Interactive classroom kits.

Linking for Learning: A New Course for Education. Manhasset, NY: S. L. Productions, 1990. Videocassette. ½ inch.

Spinnin' the Web and Beyond: Expanding Your Internet Skills. Washington, DC: Association for Educational and Communication Technology, 1994. Videocassette, ½ inch.

Surfin' the Internet: Practical Ideas for K–12. Washington, DC: Association for Educational and Communication Technology, 1994. Videocassette, ½ inch.

Telecommunications. Calgary, Alberta, Canada: Access Network, 1989. Videocassette, ¾ or ½ inch.

Touch That Dial: Using Video in the Classroom—Broadcast. Boston: WGBH, 1993. Videocassette, ½ inch.

Touch That Dial: Using Video in the Classroom—Satellite. Boston: WGBH, 1993. Videocassette, ½ inch.

Organizations

Action for Children's Television
20 University Road
Cambridge, MA 02138

Agency for Instructional Technology (AIT)
P.O. Box A
Bloomington, IN 47402-0120

Produces television programs and computer courseware as the coordinating agency of a consortium that includes most of the United States and the Canadian provinces. It serves as a national distribution center also. It publishes a newsletter and an annual catalog listing dozens of series incorporating several hundred separate programs. Emphasis is on the elementary and secondary levels.

Association for Educational Communications and Technology (AECT)
1025 Vermont Avenue, NW
Suite 820
Washington, DC 20005

Holds conferences, publishes journals and books related to instructional uses of media (including TV), and represents the educational communication/technology profession. Its Division of Telecommunications addresses the concerns of members who work in instructional TV and radio.

Cable Television Information Center
1700 Shaker Church Rd., NW
Olympia, WA 98502

Children's Television Workshop
1 Lincoln Plaza
New York, NY 10023

Corporation for Public Broadcasting (CPB)
901 E Street, NW
Washington, DC 20004-2006

Nonprofit, private corporation established and funded in part by the federal government. It performs a broad coordinating function for the nation's public radio and television stations and supports the interests of public broadcasting in general. CPB carries out research on the educational applications of television and coordinates the Annenberg Project, aimed at providing programming for higher education.

International Television Association (ITVA)
6311 North O'Connor Road
Suite 230 LB-51
Irving, TX 75039

Organization of nonbroadcast television professionals in 14 countries, primarily in North America. It supports the use of television in the private sector—training, communications, and public relations—and sponsors regional and national conferences and an awards program.

Public Service Satellite Consortium (PSSC)
600 Maryland Ave. SW
Suite 220
Washington DC 20024

PROCESS
TECHNOLOGIES

One of your biggest challenges as a teacher is to get learners actively engaged in the lesson; another is to provide for individual differences. The techniques that we refer to as process technologies can be of great assistance in achieving these goals. Learning centers, integrated learning systems, cooperative groups, games, and simulations are examples of process technologies.

A great advantage of these techniques is that they provide ready-made frameworks around which you can develop lessons. These frameworks revolve around active practice and feedback, so it is no surprise that research shows that process technologies rank among the most powerful instructional methods.

KNOWLEDGE OBJECTIVES

1. Define *process technology*, including four critical attributes and distinguishing between "hard" and "soft" technologies.
2. Relate practice and feedback to process technologies.
3. Describe programmed instruction and distinguish it from other process technologies.
4. Generate five guidelines for using programmed instruction in the classroom.
5. Describe programmed tutoring and distinguish it from other process technologies.
6. Identify two advantages of programmed tutoring that distinguish it from programmed instruction.
7. Describe the Personalized System of Instruction and relate it to other individualized instruction systems.
8. Compare and contrast two different types of cooperative learning technologies.
9. Define *game* and *simulation* and properly classify examples of each.
10. Describe mastery learning, including at least four critical attributes.
11. Describe programmed teaching, including at least four critical attributes.

APPLICATION OBJECTIVES

1. Observe an actual class session (it may be the course you are taking, one taught where you work, or a class in another setting) and critique it in terms of the characteristics of a process technology as defined at the beginning of this chapter.
2. Review some print or computer-based programmed material related to your own teaching interests and prepare an appraisal report using either the "Appraisal Checklist: Programmed Materials" or a form of your own.
3. Generate two ideas for using learning centers in your own teaching.
4. Describe an instructional situation relevant to your own teaching that is appropriate for use of instructional games, simulations, or simulation games.
5. Review a game or simulation related to your own teaching interests and prepare an appraisal report using the "Appraisal Checklist: Simulations and Games" or a form of your own.
6. Prepare a debriefing guide for a lesson utilizing a game or simulation.
7. Describe a real or hypothetical instructional situation in which you believe a process technology (or a combination of more than one) would be appropriate; justify your recommendation.

LEXICON

hard technology
soft technology
process technology
programmed instruction
linear programming
branching programming

programmed tutoring
Personalized System of Instruction (PSI)
learning center
instructional module
cooperative learning

game
frame game
simulation
role play
simulator

simulation game
cooperative game
debriefing
mastery learning
programmed teaching

Throughout the 20th century a certain pattern of organizing instruction in schools has become well established and is easily recognizable as the traditional model of classroom teaching: using the textbook-based curriculum with its grade-level sequencing; dividing the day into periods for teaching different subjects, with each subject subdivided into units and lessons; and teaching with whole-class instructional methods. The standard pattern entails the following:

- Beginning the lesson with review
- Introducing and developing the new content
- Leading the group in practice or application activities
- Assigning seatwork for individual practice (possibly remediation or enrichment)
- Testing to determine achievement

Of course, this whole-class pattern is not limited to schools. It is also the predominant model in higher education and, despite its lack of relevance, is still common in corporate education as well.

This traditional pattern is nobody's concept of the *ideal,* but it has certain enduring strengths and works reasonably well for the mythical average student. Among its shortcomings are that it is teacher dominant, encouraging passive and "inert" learning; it is prone to be boring; and it makes little accommodation for individual differences—providing remediation and enrichment, giving different assignments based on learning style, or selecting content and materials suited to students with widely varying backgrounds.

Many idealistic plans have been proposed as replacements for the traditional model. So far, none of these solutions has succeeded in displacing the traditional model on a massive scale, mainly because of the sheer momentum of the existing system, enshrined as it is in law, custom, and the personal experiences of parents and teachers. In this chapter we propose some alternative methods that address the shortcomings of the traditional model without requiring fundamental changes in the basic whole-class pattern. Most of these alternatives were envisioned by their creators as wholesale replacements for the entire traditional system, but each can also be adapted to fit within the traditional system. All have been used in schools and have been proven in practice.

WHAT ARE PROCESS TECHNOLOGIES?

Thoughtful reflection on the experiences of many generations of practice has led educators to understand that the "magic" of technology—if there is any magic—lies in the instructional design of the software, not in the hardware. A poorly designed instructional video does not deliver better results if it is shown on a fancier monitor or even converted to video disc or CD-ROM. It

produces better results if the pedagogical design is improved or if the using teacher compensates for weaknesses in the program by her skillful utilization techniques.

In Chapter 1 we provided a definition of technology that differentiated between **hard technologies**—*products* such as computers and satellites—and **soft technologies**—*processes* or ways of thinking about problems. This chapter focuses on technology as a process. We also cited Galbraith's definition of technology as "the systematic application of scientific or other organized knowledge to practical tasks." What would *instruction* look like if it were designed according to this definition? We propose that a number of successful efforts have been made to do this. These efforts share certain characteristics necessary to be considered "a systematic application of scientific knowledge."

First, to be a "systematic application," the technique must have a carefully designed framework that provides a *total system* of teaching–learning. Next, to be an "application of scientific knowledge," the technique must embody ideas (theories) that have been tested and found successful, and the application itself should have been validated through testing. Finally, the framework or template must be sufficiently structured so that the teaching-learning pattern can be repeated reliably by other teachers. Validity and reliability are key elements of any scientific application.

Process technologies for learning, therefore, are specific teaching-learning patterns that serve reliably as templates for achieving demonstrably effective learning.

For those familiar with computers, the concept of an operating system (as in Windows, for example) might be a helpful analogy. An operating system consists of a package of rules and procedures that provides a standardized, consistent pattern for using the computer. Once this template is installed, the user doesn't have to rethink and reinvent procedures for processing data. In a similar way, process technologies are packages of tested and proven procedures, ready to be "loaded" with some specific content and to lead learners through a particular kind of learning experience.

An important element of being a "scientific" application is that of being validated by research. Each of the process technologies discussed in this chapter has been subjected to extensive testing, both in the form of formal "method A versus method B" experimental comparisons and in the form of qualitative observations. The specific research will be discussed in conjunction with each of the technologies. What is notable is that the technologies discussed here have demonstrated the most dramatic positive outcomes of any ideas ever studied in educational research. Innovative pedagogical techniques (e.g., text-embedded questions, advance organizers, supplementary media) typically demonstrate an improvement in average student achievement of a few points in percentile rank. But these process technologies typically show an increase of 15, 20, or more points; that is, the average student scores at the 50th percentile in conventional instruction but scores at the 65th percentile in the group taught with process technologies.

Each of these technologies is designed to overcome one or more of the shortcomings of traditional whole-class instruction, as discussed earlier in this chapter. All of them directly address the problem of passivity in that they place the learner in direct, active engagement with the subject matter. The whole point of process technologies is to require learner participation (the *R* in the ASSURE model).

The process technologies combat boredom by providing a change of pace from lecture and seatwork and by adding motivational features that excite learner interest. They also provide a means for individualizing instruction to a greater degree. Some of the technologies discussed in this chapter are specifically designed as independent study methods, allowing individuals to progress at their own pace. Others are designed to be used in small groups; as such, they enlist the energies of students to assist those who need extra explanation, coaching, and practice.

Importance of Practice and Feedback

As mentioned earlier, all these process technologies center on the provision of ample opportunities for practice. Their creators were guided by different theoretical perspectives, so they have different rationales for doing so. The behaviorist perspective proposes that individuals learn what they *do*—that is, learning is a process of trying various behaviors and keeping those that lead to favorable results. If this is so, the instructional designer must find ways to constantly keep the learner *doing* something. Cognitivists propose that learners build up and enrich their mental schemata when their minds are actively engaged in struggling to remember or apply some new concept or principle. The sociopsychological perspective stresses the importance of interpersonal communication as the social basis for knowledge acquisition.

All perspectives also emphasize the importance of *feedback*:

- Behaviorists, because knowledge-of-correct-response serves as a reinforcer of appropriate behaviors
- Cognitivists, because information about results helps to enrich the learner's mental schema
- Social psychologists, because interpersonal feedback provides both corrective information and emotional support

Feedback can come from oneself (e.g., experiencing the "feel" of swinging a golf club), from print sources (e.g., turning to the back of the book to find the correct answer to a practice exercise), from a device (e.g., the computer gives a corrective statement after you choose an answer to a multiple-choice question), or from other people (e.g., another member of your group agrees with your solution to a problem). Research indicates that the most powerful is interpersonal feedback because face-to-face reactions are more vivid than printed or graphic information, such reactions are more personalized (giving specific performance correction), and group discussion can continue as long as necessary.[1]

All the process technologies discussed here emphasize active and continuous practice of relevant knowledge, skills, and attitudes, and all, as part of the total system, provide for rapid, effective feedback. Many of them are driven by the search for ways to build interpersonal feedback into all instruction.

Organization of This Chapter

The rest of this chapter is devoted to an examination of the nature and uses of a number of specific process technologies. These are organized according to their typical application—for individual instruction, for small-group instruction, or for large-group instruction. We begin with process technologies for individual instruction: programmed instruction, programmed tutoring, Personalized System of Instruction, and learning centers. (Related to these is the integrated learning system, discussed in Chapter 8.) Next we look at process technologies typically used with small-group instruction: cooperative learning, games, simulations, and simulation games. Finally, we examine technologies for large-group instruction: mastery learning and programmed teaching. We will emphasize certain of these technologies because they are most accessible to individual teachers—they can be adopted without changing the overall structure of the school or classroom, and they can be used on an occasional basis as a change of routine regardless of the classroom structure (e.g., self-contained, team teaching, individualized).

Virtually all of these process technologies originated and evolved before computers were widely available on the educational scene. So they are not dependent on computers for implementation. However, each can be transformed into a computer-mediated form, and these transformations will be discussed in conjunction with each technology.

---

[1]David W. Johnson and Roger T. Johnson, "Cooperative Learning and Feedback in Technology-Based Instruction," in J. Dempsey and G. Sales (eds.), *Interactive Instruction and Feedback* (Englewood Cliffs, NJ: Educational Technology Publications, 1993).

PROGRAMMED INSTRUCTION

Programmed instruction is notable among pedagogical techniques in that it was developed by a theorist, B. F. Skinner, as an explicit application of principles of learning theory—operant conditioning or reinforcement theory. Since reinforcement theory suggested that people have a tendency to learn behaviors that are followed by reinforcers, Skinner wanted to develop a method of instruction whereby students would spend most of their time performing the skills or displaying the knowledge that was being taught—not just sitting and listening. And each performance must somehow be followed by a reinforcer. Skinner decided that since humans were naturally curious, he could use "knowledge of the correct response" as the reinforcer that would follow the correct performance.

Skinner's initial inventions were elaborate machines that would mechanically present chunks, or "frames," of information; wait for a response to be written or a button to be pressed; then compare the response with the correct answer. If the answer was correct, the machine would display the next frame. Research and practical experience soon indicated, however, that students learned just as well when the sequence—information, question, response, answer—was presented in book form.

The earliest programmed instruction texts arranged the frames across the page in horizontal strips. The correct response for each question could be checked only by turning the page (see Figure 11.1). Later, this method was relaxed, allowing the frames to be arranged vertically, as in conventional printed pages, and became known as **linear programming.** These programmed texts were meant to be read with a piece of paper covering the rest of the page while a frame was being read.

After writing an answer in the blank on the first frame, for example, the user moved the cover down to see the correct answer printed in the box to the left of the second frame. You will have a better idea of how programmed instruction works if you go through the example in Figure 11.2.

The framework of programmed instruction began with the linear format just described. Early research, however, cast doubt on the necessity or desirability of following this rigid format. An early and successful challenge to the linear convention came from Norman Crowder in the form of "intrinsic programming."[2] The basic method of intrinsic programming was to present a large block of information followed by a multiple-choice question requiring application of the facts or principles presented. Each answer choice directed the reader to a different page. Correct choices allowed the reader to go ahead to new material; incorrect choices led to remedial explanations and more questions.

Because the pattern of frames in intrinsic programming resembled the branches of a tree, it became known as **branching programming** (Figure 11.3). The major advantage of the branching format is that learners who catch on quickly can move through the material much more efficiently, following the "prime path."

Although this was largely forgotten later, programmed instruction played a unique pioneering role in the evolution of process technologies. It was Skinner who invented the concept of technologies for learning, and it was programmed instruction that demonstrated in a dramatic way to the general public that students could learn without teachers. Self-instructional materials had been used in North American schools—in some

---

[2]Norman Crowder, "On the Differences Between Linear and Intrinsic Programming," *Phi Delta Kappan* (March 1963), pp. 250–254.

FIGURE 11.1

An early programmed textbook was *The Analysis of Behavior*, by James B. Holland and B. F. Skinner (1961). Each frame required a written response, with the answer revealed on the next page, so the pages were read in "stripes."

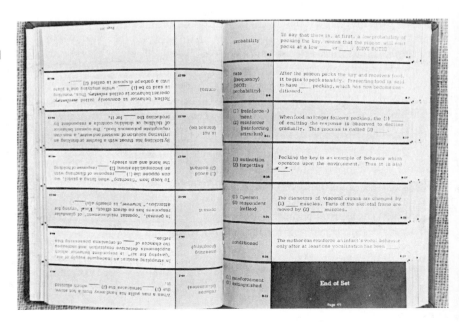

FIGURE 11.2

To use this example of programmed instruction, cover all of the page except the first frame with a piece of paper. Write your answer in the blank in the first frame. To verify your answer, slide the cover down to see the correct answer printed to the left of the second frame.

	1. Psychologists differ in their explanations of what learning is and precisely how it occurs. The series of statements or "frames" presented here deal with one particular explanation of the process of _____.
learning	2. We cannot observe learning directly, but we can infer that is has occurred when a person consistently makes a *response* that he or she previously was unable to make. For example, if a student says "nine" when asked "What is three times three?" she is making a _____ that was probably learned through practice in school.
response	3. If you read "kappa" when asked "What Greek letter is represented by *K*?" you are making a _____ that you learned through some prior experience.
response	4. The word or picture or other sensory stimulation that causes you to make a response is a *stimulus* (plural: *stimuli*). Therefore, if "kappa" is your response, "What Greek letter is represented by *K*?" would be the _____.
stimulus	5. To the stimulus "good," the student of Spanish responds "bueno"; the student of Arabic responds "gayid." To the stimulus "silver," the student of Spanish records "plata"; the student of Arabic responds "fida." They are responding to English words which are serving as _____.
stimuli	6. In these frames the written statements are the stimuli to which you are writing _____ in the blanks.
responses	7. We learn to connect certain verbal responses to certain stimuli through the process of forming *associations*. We say that the student associates "nine" with "three times three"; he learns to associate "kappa" with *K*; and he _____ "plata" with "silver."
associates	8. Much verbal learning seems to be based on the formation of associations between _____ and responses.
stimuli	etc.

schools on a large and prominent scale—since the early 20th century, but those materials had not carried the promise (or threat) of replacing teachers altogether with a method that was far more powerful than anything teachers could do on their own. Of course, programmed instruction has not done that, but it has been the stepping stone for many of the other process technologies discussed in this chapter (see Ellson in the References). For example, computer-based instruction evolved out of the search for electronic rather than mechanical means for monitoring student responses and giving appropriate feedback.

Advantages

- *Self-pacing.* Programmed instruction allows individuals to learn at their own pace at a time and place of their choice.

FIGURE 11.3

Comparison of linear and branching formats of programmed instruction.

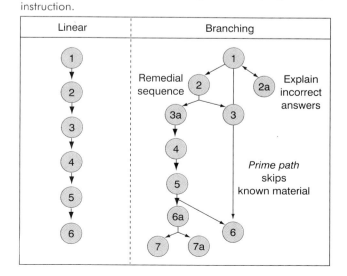

- *Practice and feedback.* It requires the learner to participate actively in the learning process and provides immediate feedback for each practice attempt.
- *Reliable.* This technology provides a reliable form of learning, in that the instructional routine is embodied in print so that it can be mass produced and experienced by many people in exactly the same form.
- *Effective.* Hundreds of research studies compare programmed instruction with conventional instruction. Summaries of these studies indicate slight superiority for programmed instruction. While the student in conventional instruction scores at the 50th percentile, the programmed instruction student scores at the 54th to 60th percentile.[3,4] It is clear that not all programmed materials are created equal. Some are particularly effective and others are not. The same, of course, can be said for lectures, videos, computer-assisted instruction, and so on.

Limitations

- *Program design.* As with many other media and technologies, the quality of the software varies greatly. Some programmed materials are poorly designed and have little value.
- *Tedious.* The repetition of the same cycle and plowing through an endless series of small steps taxes the attention span and patience of many students. For highly motivated learners with the required reading skills and self-discipline, programmed instruction can give them a chance to go off on their own and progress as far and as fast as they like. For others, it can be tedious.
- *Lack of social interaction.* Most programmed materials are meant to be used by one individual at a time. Long periods of independent study are inappropriate for younger children. Even older students and adults prefer more social interaction in their learning. Some kinds of skills and understanding are enhanced by the social exchange of group-based instruction. Affective and interpersonal skills are unlikely candidates for programmed instruction.

Applications

Programmed materials have been used successfully from the elementary school through the adult education level and in almost every subject area. By itself or in conjunction with other strategies, a program can be used to teach an entire course or a segment of a course. Many teachers use short programmed units to teach simple principles and terminology. Programmed instruction is particularly useful as an enrichment activity. It can help provide highly motivated students with additional learning experiences that the teacher might ordinarily be unable to provide because of classroom time pressures.

Programmed materials have also proven to be effective in remedial instruction. The program can function as a "tutor" for slow learners in situations where more personalized attention may be virtually impossible (in overcrowded classrooms, for example). Students can even take this particular tutor with them when they leave the classroom! Another reason for the success of programmed materials in remedial instruction is their "failure-proof" design. Because these materials break learning down into small steps and allow the student to take as much time as needed for each step, and because the materials are tested, evaluated, and revised carefully prior to publication, they are more likely to provide the slow learner with a successful experience.

Like any other instructional material, programmed texts need to be carefully appraised before selection (see "Appraisal Checklist: Programmed Materials"). Also, the success of programmed materials, as with other materials, depends on the skill of the instructor in choosing materials appropriate for the audience and purpose and in integrating them into the instructional program.

PROGRAMMED TUTORING

Programmed tutoring (also referred to as structured tutoring) is a one-to-one method of instruction (Figure 11.4) in which the responses to be made by the tutor are programmed in advance in the form of carefully structured printed instructions. In a typical program the tutor and student go through the lesson material together. The tutor's book has the answers to the exercises; the student's book does not. An excerpt from a typical programmed tutoring tutor's book is shown in Figure 11.5. Note how the tutor's role in the program is set forth, step by step, to conform with learner responses to the materials.

Because the tutor goes to the next step on the basis of the learner's last response, programmed tutoring is a form of branching programming. As such, it shares the basic advantage for which branching was originally developed: the fast learner can skip quickly through the material without tedious and unnecessary repetition.

Programmed tutoring uses what might be called "brightening" as opposed to the "fading" or gradual reduction of prompts used in linear programmed instruction. In brightening, the item is first presented in a rela-

[3] James A. Kulik, Peter A. Cohen, and Barbara J. Ebeling, "The Effectiveness of Programmed Instruction in Higher Education: A Meta-Analysis of Findings," *Educational Evaluation and Policy Analysis* 2:6 (November–December 1980), pp. 51–64.

[4] Chen-Lin C. Kulik, Barbara J. Schwalb, and James A. Kulik, "Programmed Instruction in Secondary Education: A Meta-Analysis of Evaluation Findings," *Journal of Educational Research* 75:3 (January–February 1982), pp. 133–138.

PROGRAMMED MATERIALS

KEY WORDS: _____ , _____ , _____

Title _____

Series Title (if applicable) _____

Source _____

Date _____ **Cost** _____ **Length** _____ minutes

Subject Area _____

Intended Audience _____

Brief Description

Objectives

Entry Capabilities Required (e.g., prior knowledge, reading ability, vocabulary level, math ability)

Rating	High	Medium	Low	Comments
Match with curriculum	☐	☐	☐	
Accurate and current	☐	☐	☐	
Clear and concise language	☐	☐	☐	
Arouse motivation/maintain interest	☐	☐	☐	
Learner participation	☐	☐	☐	
Technical quality	☐	☐	☐	
Evidence of effectiveness (e.g., field-test results)	☐	☐	☐	
Free from objectionable bias or advertising	☐	☐	☐	
User guide/documentation	☐	☐	☐	
Exemplifies principles of programming, e.g., relevant practice	☐	☐	☐	
Test frames are parallel to objectives	☐	☐	☐	
Feedback provides remediation and/or branching	☐	☐	☐	

Strong Points

Weak Points

Recommended Action _____ **Name** _____ **Date** _____

A computer version of this Checklist is found in "The Classroom Link."

FIGURE 11.4
A typical arrangement for a programmed tutoring lesson.

tively difficult form. If the learner responds correctly, he or she is reinforced and goes on to a new item. If the response is incorrect, a series of increasingly clearer prompts or hints is given. For example, in teaching a beginning reader to follow written instructions, the student's book might say, "Point to your teacher." If the learner does not point to the teacher when first shown the instruction, the tutor might follow this sequence of brightening prompts:

1. "Read it again." (Wait for response.)
2. "What does it say?"
3. "What does it tell you to do?"
4. "Do what it tells you to do."

The sequence of prompts would continue until the learner gives an acceptable response. Then reinforcement would be given. The idea is to lead the student toward the solution with brightening hints but to avoid actually giving the correct answer.

Advantages

- *Self-pacing.* Programmed tutoring shares with programmed instruction the characteristic of individualized pacing.
- *Practice and feedback.* Like programmed instruction, programmed tutoring requires constant learner participation. The use of a live tutor as a mediator adds immensely to the flexibility of the feedback system, and it adds another major advantage over printed self-instructional material by employing social reinforcers in the form of praise ("That's great"; "Oh, what a good answer"; "You're really on the ball today") rather than just simple knowledge of results.
- *Reliable.* Like programmed instruction, programmed tutoring provides reliable instruction in that the

teaching-learning pattern is embodied in a set of written instructions for the tutor. Compared with unstructured tutoring, programmed tutoring has higher reliability because there is a predetermined pattern to the tutor's action. With trained and motivated tutors, this has proven to be one of the most powerful technologies for learning. Administered flexibly and creatively by a live guide, this technology can overcome the monotonous pattern that sometimes results with other programmed formats.

- *Effective.* The effectiveness of programmed tutoring has been well established through the evaluation studies carried out by its originator, Douglas Ellson. The evidence from these was persuasive enough that in the early 1980s the U.S. Department of Education recognized programmed tutoring as one of the half dozen most effective compensatory education programs. Summaries of research have also found structured tutoring, variously defined, to be among the most effective and cost-effective innovations, with tutees scoring from the 70th to the 79th percentile compared to the 50th percentile for conventional instruction.[5, 6]

Limitations

- *Labor intensive.* Programmed tutoring depends on the availability of volunteer tutors. In schools, tutoring is usually done by peers, older students, or parents.

[5]Henry Levin, Gene Glass, and Gail Meister, "Cost-Effectiveness of Computer-Assisted Instruction," *Evaluation Review 11* (1987), pp. 50–72.

[6]Peter A. Cohen, James A Kulik, and Chen-Lin C. Kulik, "Educational Outcomes of Tutoring: A Meta-Analysis of Findings," *American Educational Research Journal 19*:2 (Summer 1982), pp. 237–248.

FIGURE 11.5

The directions given in the tutor's guidebook structure the programmed tutoring lesson.

STEP 1	Tell the student that this exercise will help him learn to sound out new words.
STEP 2	Point to the first word and ask the student to *sound* it out.
	a. If the student reads the word correctly, praise him; then go on to the next word.
	b. If the student is unable to read the word or reads it incorrectly, have him make the individual sounds in the word separately and then assist him in blending the sounds.
	Example:
	Word: "THIN"
	Tutor: Place your finger over the last two letters in the word and ask "What sound does the *th* make?" If the student answers correctly, praise him and go to the next sound. If he answers incorrectly or fails to answer, tell him the sound and have him repeat it. Follow the same procedure for each sound in the word, and then show him how to blend the separate sounds.
STEP 3	Follow step 2 for each word on the sheet.
STEP 4	At the end of the session, praise the student.
STEP 5	Fill out your tutor log.

Source: Grant Von Harrison, Beginning Reading 1: A Professional Guide for the Lay Tutor (Provo, UT: Brigham Young University Press, 1972), p. 101.

- *Development cost.* The success of programmed tutoring depends on the design of the tutoring guides; their development requires an investment of time and expertise.

Applications

Reading and mathematics have been by far the most popular subjects for tutoring. Being basic skills and highly structured by nature, these subjects lend themselves well to this approach. Remedial instruction is a typical application of tutoring programs.

In using programmed tutoring, keep in mind that research consistently indicates that tutors also learn from tutoring, sometimes more than their tutees! So give everyone a chance to be a tutor. This can be done effectively with materials that are prestructured to make the tutor's job replicable.

Consider using tutoring to make productive use of high-absence days. Train those who are present to tutor absentees when they return. Tutors will deepen their knowledge; absentees will catch up.

PERSONALIZED SYSTEM OF INSTRUCTION

The **Personalized System of Instruction (PSI),** one of the best-known individualized instruction systems, can be described as a template for managing instruction. It is derived from the same roots as mastery learning, the idea that all students can succeed—achieve basic mastery—but need different amounts of time and practice to get there. (Mastery learning is discussed in greater detail later in this chapter, where it is examined as a process technology in its own right.) A major principle of mastery learning is that students should not be permitted to go on to later units of study until they have demonstrated that they have mastered the prerequisite knowledge and skills.

PSI differs from the whole-class application of mastery learning in that it adheres to the notion of using individual self-study as the main form of learning activity. In many PSI courses there are *no* whole-class learning activities at all; in some cases, however, they are used for course orientation, guest speakers, and review sessions. Students work individually at their own pace using any of a variety of instructional materials—a chapter in a textbook, a computer-based module, a programmed instruction booklet, an interactive videodisc, and so on.

The essential idea of PSI is that the learning materials are arranged in sequential order and the student must demonstrate mastery of each unit before being allowed to move on to the next. Mastery is determined by means of a test taken whenever the student feels ready for it. Study help and testing are handled by proctors, usually more advanced students who volunteer to help others. Proctors are a critical component of PSI, for it is their one-to-one assistance that makes the system personalized. As illustrated in Figure 11.6, after scoring each test the proctor reviews it immediately with the student, asking questions to probe weak points and listening to defenses of alternative answers. Such explanations can depict the learner's understanding of the content better than the test answers alone. If performance is below the mastery level, the student must return at a later time and take another form of the test.

Advantages

- *Self-pacing.* PSI allows students to progress at their own rate and to take full responsibility for determining when, where, and how they study. And, although this is not often done because of constraints of cost and convenience, students with differing learning styles and interests could be given study materials best suited to their needs.

- *Mastery.* The main claim of PSI is that it prevents the "accumulation of ignorance." Students are not

FIGURE 11.6
Guidance given by a proctor during independent study provides personalization in the PSI approach.

allowed to go on to advanced units until they show that they have mastered the prerequisites. One of the most frequent causes of failure in conventional instruction is that students plunge ahead into new material without completely grasping the prerequisite knowledge or skill.

- *Effective.* The effectiveness of PSI has been documented in a large number of studies comparing PSI and conventional versions of courses. In the first decade after PSI's invention in 1968, at least 75 studies of its effectiveness had been published. A review of those studies reported this conclusion: "In a typical published comparison, PSI and lecture means are separated by about two-thirds of a standard deviation. How large a difference is this? Let us take an average student, Mary Smith, who may take her introductory physics course, for example, by either a conventional method or by PSI. If she takes a typical lecture course, her achievement in physics will put her at the 50th percentile on a standardized test. . . . If she takes the same course in PSI format, she will achieve at the 75th percentile. . . . In our judgment, this is the most impressive record achieved by a teaching method in higher education."[7] A later review of PSI research reported that student preferences also strongly favored PSI courses: "Students rate PSI classes as more enjoyable, more demanding,

and higher in overall quality and contribution to student learning than conventional classes."[8]

Limitations

- *Development cost.* PSI demands a great deal of time in planning and developing materials, since it is essentially an organizational framework and does not come with a given set of materials. Each course requires its own set of self-study materials. Even though lecture time is reduced or eliminated, instructors must be prepared to spend about half again as many hours conducting a PSI course as conducting a conventional course. The additional time is consumed in developing materials, training and supervising proctors, and meeting with individual students.
- *Behaviorist commitment.* The instructor adopting PSI must also be willing to adopt its behaviorist structure, including specification of precise performance objectives, derivation of tests from these objectives, and selection or design of material that leads learners efficiently to those objectives. The mastery perspective also requires abandonment of norm-referenced testing and grading ("grading on the curve") in favor of criterion-referenced grading, expecting and demanding that all students persist until they reach the A or B level.
- *Self-discipline.* Dealing with the freedom of PSI can be a problem for students, especially younger learners who may need practice in the required self-discipline. Procrastination is allowed in PSI and students must learn to avoid it or suffer the consequences.

Applications

Fred S. Keller developed the first PSI course at the University of Brasilia in the mid-1960s (hence PSI's alternate name, the Keller Plan). Since then, this technology for learning has been applied most frequently to postsecondary education, particularly at the community college level. At that level it has been most successful in mathematics, engineering, and psychology and slightly less successful in the life sciences and social sciences. It has also been applied in elementary and secondary education, military training, and corporate education. More recently it has become a popular framework for structuring some computer-based courses and distance education courses.

Specific guidelines for setting up and conducting PSI courses can be found in the references at the end of this chapter.

[7]James A. Kulik, Chen-Lin C. Kulik, and Beverly B. Smith, "Research on the Personalized System of Instruction," *Programmed Learning and Educational Technology* (Spring 1976), pp. 13, 23–30.

[8]James A. Kulik, Chen-Lin C. Kulik, and Peter A. Cohen, "A Meta-Analysis of Outcome Studies of Keller's Personalized System of Instruction," *American Psychologist* 34:4 (April 1979), pp. 307–318.

LEARNING CENTERS

Among the legacies of the open-education movement of the 1960s and 1970s were a more flexible notion of the physical arrangement of learning spaces and a heightened acceptance of student-controlled learning. These trends combine in the **learning center,** a self-contained environment designed to promote individual or small-group learning around a specific task. A learning center may be as simple as a table and some chairs around which students discuss, or it may be as sophisticated as several networked computers used by a group for collaborative research and problem solving.

An individual teacher may use one learning center within one classroom as a way of breaking the class into small groups to perform hands-on activities (e.g., in a science class with a laboratory-type learning center). Or a whole school may be organized to incorporate learning centers into the daily mix of activities, as in the Project CHILD schools, see "Close-up" on p. 324.

Learning centers may be set up in any suitable and available classroom space. Or they may be set up outside the classroom—in a laboratory, for example, or even in a school corridor. They are also commonly found in school library media centers. Learning centers with many stations are found in business, industry, medical facilities, and the armed forces.

Learning center materials may include practically any or all of the media and multimedia formats mentioned in this text. Center materials and software may be purchased from commercial producers or may be teacher-made.

Although simple learning center activities might be carried out at a student's desk or some other open space, it is advisable that learning centers be confined to a clearly identifiable area and that they be at least partially enclosed to reduce distractions. Learning *carrels,* or booths, which may be purchased from commercial sources or made locally, provide a clearly defined enclosure. Carrels may be made by placing simple cardboard dividers on classroom tables.

Carrels are often referred to as being either "dry" or "wet." A dry carrel provides private space for study or other learning activities but contains no electrical equipment. The typical library carrel is a dry carrel. A wet carrel, on the other hand, is equipped with outlets for audiovisual devices such as cassette recorders, projection screens, television monitors, or computer terminals (see Figure 11.7). An extensive exploration of the possibilities of computer-based learning centers is found in Riedl (1995).

Advantages

- *Self-pacing.* Centers encourage students to take responsibility for their own learning and allow them to learn

FIGURE 11.7
A "wet" carrel is equipped with media hardware.

at their own pace, thus minimizing the possibility of failure and maximizing the likelihood of success.
- *Active learning.* Learning centers provide for student participation in the learning experience, for student response, and for immediate feedback to student response.
- *Teacher role.* Learning centers allow the teacher to play more of a coaching role, moving around the classroom and providing individual help to students when they need it.

Limitations

- *Cost.* A great deal of time must be spent in planning and setting up centers and in collecting and arranging for center materials. The equipment and materials used in the center, too, entail costs.
- *Management.* Teachers who manage learning centers must be very good at classroom organization and management.
- *Student responsibility.* Any form of independent study will be successful only insofar as students are able and willing to accept responsibility for their own learning.
- *Student isolation.* Learning centers need not be limited to individual student use; small groups can be assigned to work together. If students do work alone, other provisions must be made to provide for the social dimension of learning.

Applications

Learning centers can be used for a number of specialized purposes. Some of the specialized types are described next.

Skill Centers. These can provide the student with an opportunity to do additional practice, typically

FIGURE 11.8
Learning centers offer opportunities for informal teacher–student interaction.

to reinforce a lesson that has previously been taught through other media or methods. Basic skills that are built up through drill and practice lend themselves to the skill center approach. For example, a skill center might be designed to give practice in using prefixes for students who are learning to write.

Interest Centers.   Interest centers can stimulate new interests and encourage creativity. For example, a get-acquainted center on insect life might be set up in the classroom before actually beginning a unit on specific insects.

Remedial Centers.   Remedial centers can be used to help students who need additional assistance with a particular concept or skill. A student who has dif-

ficulty determining the least common denominator of a group of fractions, for example, could be given the needed help in a remedial learning center.

Enrichment Centers.   Enrichment centers can provide stimulating additional learning experiences for students who have completed other classroom activities. Students who have completed their assigned math activities, for example, might be allowed to go to the center that features computer math games.

COOPERATIVE LEARNING

Cooperative learning has gained momentum in both formal and nonformal education from two converging forces: first, the practical realization that life outside the classroom requires more and more collaborative activity, from the use of teams in the workplace to everyday social life, and second, a growing awareness of the value of social interaction in making learning meaningful.

The notion of students working together in small groups is not new, but assuring that their efforts are truly collaborative has recently become a point of emphasis. For example, in the past five students might have been assigned to a project team to prepare a report on Peru. One researched the pre-Columbian Incas, another gathered pictures of llamas, the third prepared a report on the Peru Current and fishing, and the others gathered clothing and food items to give atmosphere to their final presentation. Note that although their efforts were pooled at the end, most of the work was done independently. Today's notion of cooperative learning entails a deeper level of interaction, based on the principle that articulating and negotiating your ideas with others forces you to process information in a way that

FIGURE 11.9
An example of directions given at a learning center for elementary language arts.

Listening Center

1. Sit down at the table—no more than six people at a time.

2. Pick one of the story cassettes to listen to. Everyone should help decide on the choice. Only one person should operate the cassette player.

3. Put on the headsets and listen to the story.

4. After listening to the story, form teams of two. Each team will write a new ending to the story. Use your imagination!

5. When your new ending is written, put it in the "In" basket at the writing center.

An instructional module is any freestanding, self-contained instructional unit designed for use by a single learner or a small group of learners without a teacher's presence. Since the whole purpose of modules is to facilitate learning without the constant supervision of a teacher, all the elements of a lesson that are usually provided by a teacher have to be built into a set of printed, audiovisual, or computer-based materials (or a combination of all of these). That is, the module has to gain the student's attention, introduce the topic, present new content, provide practice-and-feedback activities, test for mastery, and assign follow-up remediation or enrichment. The main difference between a module and just a simple book, filmstrip, video, or computer lesson is that all of the instructional management procedures have to be built in.

Virtually all the individual and small-group techniques described in this chapter depend on instructional modules as the core of each individual or group activity.

COMPONENTS OF MODULES

There are many different formulas for designing instructional modules, but certain components are essential:

1. *Rationale.* Provide an overview of the content of the module and an explanation of why the learner should study it.
2. *Objective.* State in performance terms what the learner is expected to gain from studying the module.
3. *Entry test.* Determine whether the learner has mastered the prerequisite skills needed to enter the module.
4. *Multimedia materials.* Use a variety of media to involve learners actively and to utilize a number of their senses. Most media formats lend themselves to use in modules.

5. *Learning activities.* All the methods described in Chapter 1 may be incorporated into modules. Having a variety of methods and media increases student interest and meets student needs.
6. *Self-test.* Give students a chance to review and check their own progress.
7. *Posttest.* Assess whether the objectives of the module have been mastered.

MANAGING INSTRUCTION WITH MODULES

A module should include an introduction to the topic, preferably in the form of a question or a problem that will stimulate curiosity. It also must provide instructions or suggestions about how the components of the module are to be used. In most cases, a printed guide serves as the pathfinder through the various activities of the module. Questions and space for answers may also be contained in the printed guide. (See "How to . . . Design Text," p. 109.)

Some teachers prefer to put their "user's guide" on audiotape, which can be helpful for those with reading problems. (See "How to . . . Record Audiocassettes," p. 188.)

When individuals or small groups are using modules on their own, the teacher needs a plan for monitoring their progress. Ideally, after finishing a module, the individual or small group meets with the teacher to discuss the content they were pursuing, their outcomes, and their understandings. They also report any difficulties they might have had in using the module. Such discussions, in addition to or instead of more conventional tests, provide valuable feedback about student progress and the strengths and weaknesses of the module.

CLOSE-UP

INDY 500 LEARNING CENTER

A fifth-grade teacher capitalizes on local enthusiasm for automobile racing by designing a math learning center based on car numbers and speeds. Center material includes a variety of questions, such as "What is the difference in speed between Car 20 and Car 14?" "How many cars have even numbers?" "If a race car gets 1.8 miles per gallon, how many miles can it go on one tank of fuel (40 gallons)?" The center has colorful pictures and souvenir postcards of the cars and drivers. Each student draws, colors, and numbers his or her own race car, which goes in the "victory circle" when the lesson is completed. The students complete worksheets, for which they are awarded "completed laps" rather than numerical points. When they have completed their 500 miles, they have "finished the race" and receive a miniature checkered flag. The center is designed so that all students can eventually master its content and be rewarded by receiving a flag.

PROJECT CHILD—A NEW APPROACH TO INTEGRATED LEARNING SYSTEMS

Several dozen schools in Florida are involved in a research and development project to test and refine a computer-integrated instructional program for kindergarten through grade five.

In Project CHILD (Computers Helping Instruction and Learning Development), classrooms become learning resource rooms for three hours each day, each focused on one of the core subject areas: reading, language arts, mathematics, and science. Children move from classroom to classroom working at a variety of learning centers. A typical classroom has a half dozen computers, a teacher station for small-group activities, and learning centers for hands-on activities and quiet reading and writing.

Students stay with the same team of teachers for three years in the primary cluster (K–2) or intermediate cluster (3–5). Each teacher has special training to use technology and cooperative learning techniques in his or her designated specialty area. Required curriculum content is covered in six-week thematic units, emphasizing whole language, writing, and problem solving across curricular areas.

For example, the Project CHILD reading and language arts curriculum is integrated through literature themes (fantasy, biographies, modern fiction, etc.). Students learn reading strategies in whole-class and small groups. Teachers plan reading lessons to include a wide array of materials, including newspapers, library books, song books, magazines, games,

charts, reference books, and material written by students in the language arts center in the school. They use computers to write and to practice specific language skills. The computer activities are based on a wide range of software from many different sources.

Formal evaluations indicate positive effects on academic achievement, attitude toward school, and self-esteem. Another indicator of success is that parent demand for entry is strong. Parents have moved across county lines and left private schools to get their children into Project CHILD schools.

Source: Sarah M. Butzin, "Integrating Technology into the Classroom: Lessons from the Project CHILD Experience," Phi Delta Kappan, December 1992, pp. 330–333.

---

improves meaningfulness and retention. This new concept of cooperative learning can be defined as the instructional use of small groups so that students work together to maximize their own and each other's learning.

Recent research by Robert Slavin, Spencer Kagan, and David and Roger Johnson has revealed that not only does cooperative learning yield better acquisition and retention of what is taught, but it also promotes better interpersonal and thinking skills. This research has highlighted the importance of *interdependence* as the key to success in cooperative learning. That is, the group members must have a stake in each other's understanding and mastery of the material. If the brightest student is allowed to "carry" the others, dependency is created and the purpose is defeated. The challenge is to devise management schemes that require learners to truly collaborate.

Various specific cooperative learning formats have been devised and validated by researchers. They are discussed here as process technologies because they fit the definition: each provides a specific template, expressed in the form of operating rules, procedures, and materi-

als; these templates are structured enough that they can be implemented successfully by teachers working in different circumstances; and they have been validated through field testing. Two particular formats will be elaborated as examples of cooperative learning technologies: Johnson and Johnson's Learning Together model and Slavin's Team-Assisted Individualization (TAI).

Learning Together Model

Johnson and Johnson have determined that feedback about your performance—knowing what is working well and what is not—is a critical factor in successful learning.[9] Further, their research indicates that the most powerful and effective source of feedback is another person. For this reason, they have developed a specific format for cooperative learning that maximizes interpersonal feedback. Their research indicates that this format

---

[9]David W. Johnson and Roger T. Johnson, "Cooperative Learning and Feedback in Technology-Based Instruction," in J. Dempsey and G. Sales (eds.), *Interactive Instruction and Feedback* (Englewood Cliffs, NJ: Educational Technology Publications, 1993).

of instruction works most effectively when the operating rules require that group members are *inter*dependent—that is, each is dependent on the others for achieving their goal.

Johnson and Johnson's interdependent learning group, also known as the Learning Together model, requires four basic elements:

1. Positive interdependence. Students must recognize that all the members of the group are dependent on each other to reach success: "We are going to sink or swim together." First, the teacher creates positive *goal* interdependence by requiring teammates to agree on objectives. Second, the teacher structures *role* interdependence by assigning each student a role: for example, in a math lesson the "reader" reads the problem aloud to the group; the "checker" monitors to make sure that each group member can explain how to solve the problem; and the "encourager" prompts all members to participate. *Reward* interdependence is established by giving each group five points if all members score above 90% on the end-of-unit test.

2. Face-to-face helping interaction. After silently working on the problem on scratch paper, the learners teach each other and discuss any confusion or misconceptions.

3. Individual accountability. Students know that they will be tested individually, with the results given back to the individual and the group. One way to reinforce individual accountability is to randomly select one student's test to represent the whole group.

4. Teaching interpersonal and small-group skills. Students cannot just be thrown together and told to cooperate. To function effectively as a group, they must be taught the skills of communication, leadership, and conflict management and must learn to monitor the processes in their group, making corrections if there are shortcomings.

Team-Assisted Individualization (TAI)

Robert Slavin and his colleagues have developed a different format for cooperative learning, Team-Assisted Individualization (TAI), which was developed for mathematics instruction in grades three to six.[10] TAI was specifically intended to avoid some of the problems encountered with individualized programmed instruction. It incorporates features that allow students to proceed more efficiently and effectively on their own with fewer demands on the teacher for individual checking

and motivating. The format includes direct instruction to small groups, individual follow-up practice using programmed materials, and team study techniques (Figure 11.10). TAI has achieved impressive results in field tests. Not only do the TAI students score higher on computation and application skills, they also show better social relations with handicapped students and with students of other races.

TAI follows this pattern:

1. Teaching groups. The teacher gives short lessons to small homogeneous groups—learners who are at about the same point in the curriculum. These lessons prepare students for major concepts in upcoming units.

2. Team formation. Every eight weeks, students are assigned to four-member teams that are as heterogeneous as possible in terms of achievement levels, gender, and ethnic background.

3. Self-instructional materials. Students work independently using self-instructional materials, which include step-by-step procedures for solving problems, a set of problems, self-test items, and a summative test.

4. Team study. Students work in pairs within their assigned team, working on problems and having their solutions checked by their partner. When they have four correct in a row they take a quiz. If they succeed on the quiz they go to a monitor on another team to take a final test. Remedial instruction and practice continue if needed until the student passes the final test.

5. Team scores and team recognition. Team scores are computed at the end of each week; certificates are given to those who greatly exceed the criterion level.

FIGURE 11.10
Team-Assisted Individualization encourages students to help each other learn.

[10]Robert E. Slavin, "Team-Assisted Individualization," in M. Wang and H. Walberg (eds.), *Adapting Instruction to Individual Differences* (Berkeley, CA: McCutchan, 1985).

Computer-Assisted Cooperative Learning

Computer assistance can alleviate some of the logistical obstacles to using cooperative learning methods, particularly the tasks of managing information, allocating different individual responsibilities, presenting and monitoring instructional material, analyzing learner responses, administering tests, and scoring and providing remediation for those tests.

Mentioned earlier was the critical problem of assuring that learners recognize their interdependence. Some software programs parcel out different information to different individuals so that they have to constantly check with each other and pool their information to make good decisions. Other programs provide information or give feedback only in displays that are flashed for a limited period of time. Group members are forced to delegate responsibility for watching for certain kinds of messages if they are to succeed. Each member has something different and essential to contribute to the group deliberations.

Group-oriented programs of this sort can also deal with the logistical problems of assisting a number of groups simultaneously, as is necessary in the single-computer classroom. The software manages a rotation of the teams so that there is little time lost waiting in line.

GAMES

The terms *game, simulation,* and *simulation game* are often used interchangeably. But because these terms have different meanings, they will be discussed separately here. A **game** is an activity in which participants follow prescribed rules that differ from those of real life as they strive to attain a challenging goal.

The distinction between play and reality is what makes games entertaining. Most people seem to enjoy setting aside the logical rules of everyday life occasionally and entering an artificial environment with different dynamics. For example, in chess the markers each have arbitrarily different movement patterns based roughly on the military potentials of certain societal roles in some ancient time. Players capture each other's markers by observing elaborate rules of play rather than simply reaching across the board to grab the marker.

Attaining the goal usually entails competition—individual against individual, as in chess; group against group, as in basketball; or individual against a standard, as in golf (with "par" as the standard). With video games, players typically are competing against their own previous scores and ultimately against the designer of the game as they approach mastery.

To be challenging, goals should have a probability of achievement of approximately 50%. A goal that is always or never attained presents no real challenge; the outcome is too predictable. People exhibit the most interest and motivation when the challenge is in the intermediate range.

On the other hand, striving to attain a challenging goal does not necessarily have to involve competition. Communication games, fantasy games, and encounter games exemplify a whole array of activities in which participants agree to suspend the normal rules of interpersonal communication to pursue such goals as self-awareness, empathy, sensitivity, and leadership development. These activities are considered games but do not entail competition. There is a movement today toward developing cooperative games designed to foster cre-

FIGURE 11.11
Increasingly, computer-mediated instruction is treated as a cooperative learning activity.

FIGURE 11.12

Game, simulation, and *instruction* are separate concepts. However, they do overlap, so a particular activity could be an instructional simulation (IS), an instructional game (IG), a simulation game (SG), or even an instructional simulation game (ISG).

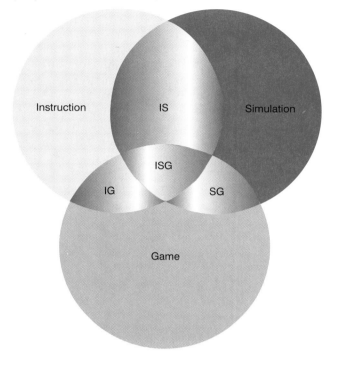

tional games. Individual-versus-individual competition can be a highly motivating device as long as the contenders are fairly matched and the conflict does not overshadow the educational objective. Group-versus-group competition entails the same cautions, but it has the added attraction of providing practice in cooperation and teamwork. When competitions are carefully organized to ensure fair matches, highly successful and highly personalized learning can be fostered.

For instructional purposes, competition involving the individual or team against a given standard is often the safest approach. It allows individualization because different standards can be set for different players. In fact, one of the most effective standards can be the student's own past performance, the goal being to raise the level of aspiration continually.

In any event, in cases in which competition is an element, the scoring system provides a clue as to what type of competition is being fostered. Is one individual or team declared the winner? Or is it possible for all players to attain equally high scores, making everyone a winner? Some instructional games are designed to encourage players to decide among themselves what criteria to apply in determining success.

Advantages

- *Attractive.* Games provide attractive frameworks for learning activities. They are attractive because they are fun! Children and adults alike tend to react positively to an invitation to play.
- *Novel.* As a departure from normal classroom routine, games arouse interest because of their novelty.
- *Atmosphere.* The pleasant, relaxed atmosphere fostered by games can be especially helpful for those (such as low achievers) who avoid other types of structured learning activities.

ativity and collaborative decision making. These games specifically avoid provoking competition between players. Examples of cooperative simulation games are discussed on p. 333.

Because individuals react differently to competitive environments, the element of competition must be handled very thoughtfully in choosing and using instruc-

FIGURE 11.13

Game playing appeals to young and old alike.

- *Time on task.* Games can keep learners interested in repetitious tasks, such as memorizing multiplication tables. What would otherwise be tedious drills become fun.

Limitations

- *Competition.* Competitive activities can be counterproductive for students who are less adept at competing or who are weak in the content or skill being practiced.
- *Distraction.* Without careful management and debriefing, students can get caught up in the excitement of play and fail to focus on the real objectives.
- *Poor design.* To be instructionally meaningful the game activity must provide actual practice of the intended academic skill. A fatal shortcoming of poorly designed games is that players spend a large portion of their time waiting for their turn, throwing dice, moving markers around a board, and performing similar trivial actions.

Applications

Instructional games are particularly well suited to the following:

- Attainment of cognitive objectives, particularly those involving recognition, discrimination, or memorization, such as grammar, phonics, spelling, arithmetic skills, formulas (in chemistry, physics, logic), basic science concepts, place names, terminology, and so on
- Adding motivation to topics that ordinarily attract little student interest, such as grammar rules, spelling, and math drills
- Small-group instruction, providing structured activities that students or trainees can conduct by themselves without close instructor supervision
- Basic skills such as sequence, sense of direction, visual perception, number concepts, and following rules, which can be developed by means of card games.[11]

---

[11]Margie Golick, *Deal Me In!* (New York: Jeffrey Norton, 1973).

CLOSE-UP

GAMES IN ELEMENTARY MATHEMATICS

Mathematics Pentathlon is a series of 20 instructional games that motivate the development and practice of mathematics concepts and skills. Designed for grades K–7, the games also promote active problem solving, especially the ability to solve problems that are continually undergoing change.

Classroom use of the program involves students in cooperative communication; in the integration of spatial, logical, and computational reasoning; and in the use of a wide variety of mathematics manipulatives to foster conceptual understanding.

The program also offers tournament competition. Tournaments are organized into four divisions combining two grade levels in each: Division I, K–1; Division II, 2–3; Division III, 4–5; and Division IV, 6–7. Within each division, individuals or teams compete in five different games; hence the name *pentathlon.* This phase of the program involves the entire educational community and offers students the unique opportunity to balance cooperation with constructive competition.

Mathematics Pentathlon relates to a mathematics curriculum and staff development program known as Mathematics Experience-Based Approach (MEBA). MEBA fosters mathematical understanding by building deliberate connections between physical models, pictures, and symbols and associated concepts and procedures. It also helps learners form and use mental images in solving problems.

MEBA and the associated games are designed to give students practice in nonroutine problem solving—that is, using heuristics to solve problems where known, routine procedures don't work. Examples of heuristics exercises include building a model or drawing a picture of the problem, finding a simple problem that is analogous to the one being studied, working backwards, and breaking the problem into its subcomponents.

For further information, contact Mary Gilfeather, Pentathlon Institute, Inc., P.O. Box 20590, Indianapolis, IN 46220.

- Vocabulary building. Various commercial games, such as Boggle, Fluster, Scrabble, and Probe, have been used successfully by teachers to expand spelling and vocabulary skills, although they were designed and are marketed primarily for recreational purposes.

Frame Games

Although most teachers do not design new instructional games from scratch, they often adapt existing games by changing the subject matter while retaining the game's structure. The original game is referred to as a **frame game** because its framework lends itself to multiple adaptations. When one is modifying a frame game, the underlying structure of a familiar game provides the basic procedure of play, or the dynamics of the process. The designer loads the desired content onto a convenient frame.[12]

Familiar games such as tic-tac-toe, rummy, concentration, and bingo, which were intended for recreation rather than instruction, can also serve as potential frameworks for your own instructional content. Some television game shows have been modeled after such parlor games; they can suggest additional frameworks. Here are some sample adaptations:

- *Safety tic-tac-toe.* A three-by-three grid is used; each row represents a place where safety rules pertain to home, school, and street; each column represents the level of question difficulty. Teams take turns selecting and trying to answer safety-related questions, attempting to fill in three squares in a row.
- *Spelling rummy.* Using alphabet cards instead of regular playing cards, players attempt to spell short words following the general rules of rummy.
- *Reading concentration.* This game uses about a dozen matched picture–word pairs of flash cards. Cards are placed face down. On each turn the player turns over two cards, seeking to match a pair. Both reading ability and memorizing are exercised.
- *Word bingo.* Each player's card has a five-by-five grid with a vocabulary word (perhaps in a foreign language) in each square. The leader randomly selects words; players then seek the words on their boards, and if they are found, the square is marked. The winner is the first player with five correctly marked squares in a row.

SIMULATIONS

A **simulation** is an abstraction or simplification of some real-life situation or process. In simulations, participants usually play a role that involves them in interactions with other people or with elements of the simulated environment. A business management simulation, for example, might put participants into the role of production manager of a mythical corporation, provide them with statistics about business conditions, and direct them to negotiate a new labor contract with the union bargaining team.

Simulations can vary greatly in the extent to which they fully reflect the realities of the situation they are intended to model. A simulation that incorporates too many details of a complex situation might be too complicated and time-consuming for the intended audience. On the other hand, if the model is oversimplified, it may fail completely to communicate its intended point. A well-designed simulation provides a faithful model of elements that are most salient to the immediate objective, and it informs the instructor and participants about elements that have been simplified or eliminated completely.

Simulation and Discovery Learning

One particular value of simulation is that it implements the discovery method as directly and clearly as possible. In discovery learning, the learner is led toward understanding principles through grappling with a problem situation. Most simulations attempt to immerse participants in a problem.

Through simulations, we can offer learners a laboratory in areas such as the social sciences and human relations as well as in areas related to the physical sciences, where laboratories have long been taken for granted. It tends to be more time-consuming than the straightforward lecture approach, but the payoff is a higher level of comprehension that is likely to be long-lasting.

The great advantage of this sort of firsthand immersion in a topic is that students are more likely to be able to apply to real life what they have practiced in simulated circumstances. This raises the issue of the degree of realism captured by a simulation. A common defect in poorly designed simulations is an overemphasis on chance factors in determining outcomes. Much of the reality is spoiled if chance-element cards cause players to gain or lose great quantities of points or other resources regardless of their strategic decisions. An overemphasis on chance or an overly simplified representation of real relationships might end up teaching lessons quite contrary to what was intended.

Role Plays

Role play refers to a type of simulation in which the dominant feature is relatively open-ended interaction

[12]Harold D. Stolovitch and Sivasailam Thiagarajan, *Frame Games* (Englewood Cliffs, NJ: Educational Technology Publications, 1980).

CLOSE-UP

GAMES FOR TEACHING READING

Reading is generally the most emphasized skill at the elementary school level. It is also a subject in which a great deal of practice and a high degree of individualization are necessary. For these reasons, reading teachers find game playing to be an especially valued method.

Featured here are several games involving decoding and comprehension skills. They have been reviewed and recommended by Dixie Lee Spiegel, instructional resources reviewer for *The Reading Teacher.*

Decoding

Road Race (Curriculum Associates) is a board game for two to six players. Players move markers around a track based on the number of words they have made and read. Players roll 10 dice with word parts on them (e.g., *-ight, -ake, -en*) and made words by matching the dice with the letters, digraphs, or blends written on the game board. Players who are waiting their turn can challenge words made by others.

Word Trek (DLM) is a board game for two to four players. In this game, players are dealt eight empty pockets for holding word-family cards. They draw cards containing blends and digraphs and try to form words; if not challenged, they place the words in the pocket until someone completes eight of them. The opportunity to challenge keeps other players involved.

Comprehension

Context Clues (Learning Well) provides practice in determining the meaning of a difficult word encountered in sentence context. The game comes in basic and intermediate versions.

Cause and Effect (Opportunities for Learning, Inc.) provides challenging practice in differentiating between causes and effects. The player reads a paragraph and chooses a cause for a given effect, or vice versa. The game comes in two levels: basic and intermediate.

Spiegel cautions that with many games of this type the teacher must anticipate modifying the materials to make them more instructionally effective. In *Cause and Effect,* players are not required to read at every turn. Because many of the squares on the game board are blank, players can advance without reading. Spiegel simply changed the rules of play so that every square required reading, and the originally designated reading squares were given double value.

Source: Dixie Lee Spiegel, "Instructional Resources: Decoding and Comprehension Games and Manipulatives," The Reading Teacher 44:3 (November 1990), pp. 258–261.

---

among people. In essence, a role play asks someone to imagine that he or she is another person or is in a particular situation; the person then behaves as the other person would or in the way the situation seems to demand. The purpose is to learn something about another kind of person or about the dynamics of an unfamiliar situation. The role descriptions may be very general, leaving great latitude for the participant. The purpose in many cases is to allow the person's own traits to emerge so that they can be discussed and possibly modified. In other simulations, such as historical recreations, highly detailed roles are described to project the realities of life in that period.

The role-play simulation has proven to be a motivating and effective method of developing social skills, especially empathy (putting oneself in someone else's shoes). Our day-to-day social behavior tends to be governed by our assumptions about who we are, who our peers are, and why they act the way they do. A potent way of challenging, and thereby changing, these assumptions is to experience a slice of life from someone else's perspective.

The sorts of tasks that lend themselves especially well to role playing are counseling, interviewing, sales and customer services, supervision, and management (Figure 11.14). The settings most often simulated are com-

▼ **MEDIA FILE**

Starpower
Instructional Simulation

Content areas: Social studies, government

Age level: High school and above

Starpower centers on the trading of tokens that have been distributed randomly at the start of the exercise. During each round, participants try to increase their wealth and move upward in the three-tiered class structure that evolves. Later in play, the rich players make the rules.

Source: Simulation Training Systems.

mittee meetings, negotiation sessions, public meetings, work teams, and one-to-one interviews.

Simulators

Competencies in the motor skill domain require practice under conditions of high feedback, which gives the learner the feel of the action. Although it might be ideal to practice such skills under real-life conditions, some (e.g., piloting an airplane or driving a car) can be practiced much more safely and conveniently by means of simulated conditions. The devices employed to represent physical systems in a scaled-down form are referred to as **simulators.** (See Figure 11.15.)

One familiar example of a simulator is the flight trainer, a mock-up of the interior of the cockpit complete with controls and gauges. Today the flight crews of most major airlines receive a large portion of their training in flight simulators, which are controlled by computers and offer highly realistic audiovisual effects. Besides eliminating the possibility of loss of life and aircraft, these simulators allow significant savings of energy, in millions of gallons of fuel annually, and other costs. One recent study estimated that in-air training costs about $4,000 per hour, compared with only $400 per hour on the flight simulator, with no loss in effectiveness.

Simpler simulators are in widespread use in applications such as training workers in a broad range of manual skills from chiseling to welding. A full discussion of such devices, including a number of examples, can be found in Romiszowski.[13]

---

[13]A. J. Romiszowski, *The Selection and Use of Instructional Media,* 2d ed. (New York: Nichols, 1988).

FIGURE 11.14
Role-playing is an effective method for developing interpersonal skills.

FIGURE 11.15
Doron's driver training simulator simulates the sights and sounds of hazardous road conditions without the real-life risks.

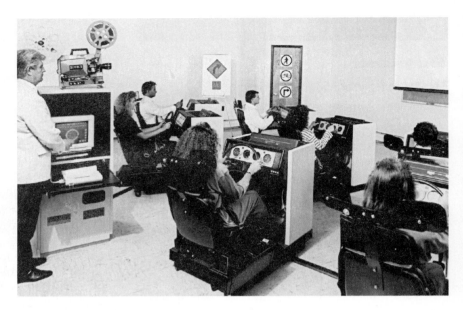

Advantages

- *Realistic.* The prime advantage of simulations is that they allow practice of real-world skills under conditions similar to those in real life.
- *Safe.* Learners can practice risky activities—for example, cardiopulmonary resuscitation—without risking injury to themselves or others.
- *Simplified.* Simulations are intended to capture the essential features of a situation without dwelling on details that might be distracting or too complex for the learner's current level of understanding.

Limitations

- *Time-consuming.* Simulations are often used with discovery or problem-solving methods, allowing learners to immerse themselves in a problematic situation and to experiment with different approaches. Such trial-and-error learning typically requires more time than more expositive methods.
- *Oversimplification.* Constructivists argue that learning should take place in fully realistic situations, with all the complexity of real life. They would be concerned that a simulation might give students a false understanding of the real-life situation.

Applications

Instructional simulations, including role plays, are particularly well suited for the following:

- Training in motor skills, including athletic and mechanical skills, and complex skills that might otherwise be too hazardous or expensive in real-life settings

- Instruction in social interaction and human relations, where displaying empathy and coping with the reactions of other people are major goals
- Development of decision-making skills (e.g., microteaching in teacher education, mock court in law school, management simulations in business administration)

SIMULATION GAMES

A **simulation game** combines the attributes of a simulation (role playing, a model of reality) with the attributes of a game (striving toward a goal, specific rules). Like a simulation, it may be relatively high or low in its modeling of reality. Like a game, it may or may not entail competition.

Because they combine the characteristics of both simulations and games, instructional simulation games have advantages, limitations, and applications in common with both formats. In this regard one of the major reasons for using simulation and gaming methods is that they provide conditions for *holistic learning*. That is, through the modeling of reality and through the players' interactions as they strive to succeed, learners *encounter a whole and dynamic view of the process being studied*. Conventional instruction tends to segment reality into separate packages (e.g., biology, mathematics, psychology), but that is not how the real world is organized. Through participation in simulation games we can see the whole process and its dynamic interrelationships in action. In addition, our emotions come into play along with the thinking process. Participants commonly experience excitement, elation, disappointment, even anger, as they struggle to succeed (Figure 11.16). This, of course, is how learning takes place in the world outside the classroom.

▼ MEDIA FILE

The Green Revolution Game
Instructional Simulation Game

Content areas: Community development, social studies

Age level: College and adult

The setting of this game is a village in contemporary India. Players attempt to manage their limited resources to provide for their families. Pests, drought, crop failures, shortage of cash and credit, and deaths of family members are among the realistic variables with which each player must contend.

Source: Marginal Context Ltd.

Applications

Instructional simulation games are found in curriculum applications that require both the repetitive skill practice associated with games and the reality context associated with simulations. Societal processes (e.g., Ghetto, Democracy), cultural conflicts (e.g., Bafa Bafa), historical eras (e.g., Empire, Manchester), and ecological systems (e.g., Extinction) are popular topics.

In general, instructional simulation games are frequently used to provide an overview of a large, dynamic process. The excitement of play stimulates interest in the subject matter, and the holistic treatment of the game gives students a feel for the total process before they approach parts of it in a more linear way.

FIGURE 11.16
A well-designed simulation game stirs emotions comparable to the reality being modeled.

▼ MEDIA FILE

Where in the World Is Carmen Sandiego?
Computer-based Simulation Game

Content areas: History, geography

Age level: Grades 6 through 10

Learners play the role of detective as they follow a trail of clues to track down and apprehend one of the members of Carmen Sandiego's notorious band of thieves. The detective utilizes resource materials, problem-solving skills, planning methods, and organizational skills to catch the thief. Other variations are available, for example, *Where in the USA . . . , Where in Europe . . . ,* and *Where in Time. . . .* Each employs different resource materials. As the detective catches more thieves, the chase becomes more difficult.

Source: Broderbund.

Cooperative Simulation Games

Traditionally, games—both athletic contests and tabletop board games—have emphasized competition between adversaries. In recent years, sports psychologists and educational psychologists have developed new theories questioning the value and necessity of competition in human development. They contend that if children are nurtured on cooperation, acceptance, and success in a fun-oriented atmosphere they develop strong, positive self-concepts. Out of this new awareness has come the "new games" movement, generating hundreds of **cooperative games** that challenge the body and imagination but that depend on cooperation for success.[14]

---

[14]Alfie Kohn, *No Contest: The Case Against Competition* (Boston: Houghton-Mifflin, 1986).

▼ MEDIA FILE

Save the Whales
Cooperative Simulation Game

Content areas: Ecology, social development

Age level: Grade 3 through adult

Players learn to act cooperatively as they face oil spills, radioactive waste, and whaling ships in trying to save eight types of whales from extinction. Players earn "survival points" and make group decisions on protecting the whales. This is one of a family of cooperative games distributed by Animal Town Game Company. All aim to encourage cooperation rather than competition.

Source: Animal Town Game Company.

Instructional simulation games have been developed that pursue a similar philosophy. *Save the Whales* (see "Media File") demonstrates that these endangered species can be preserved only through human cooperation. In *Mountaineering*, players work as a team to ascend and descend the mountain depicted on the game board, complete with crevasses, avalanches, and blizzards. In *Sky Travelers*, players learn about the earth as they explore it as stranded aliens from outer space; only through teamwork and strategic decision making can they reunite with their mother craft.

The computer has opened up even wider possibilities for simulating problem situations elaborately. A number of development groups have made computer-based simulations that challenge participants to work together to unlock a mystery. One particularly successful collection of cooperative computer simulations has been developed by Groupware of Ontario, Canada (see "Media File: *Longhouse*"). The unique feature of these simulations is that they require a group of learners to work synchronously and cooperatively to arrive at a successful conclusion.

▼ MEDIA FILE

Longhouse
Computer-based Cooperative Simulation

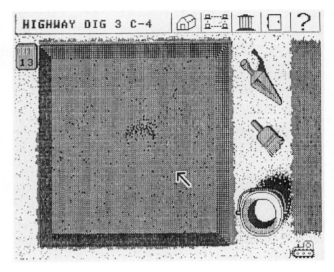

Content areas: History, archeology

Age Level: Grades 4 through 8

Longhouse is a networked discovery-learning simulation based on actual archeological excavations. Students cooperatively learn about several different Native American cultures, within the Iroquois and Algonquian groups, by working in teams to dig up buried artifacts. They attempt to discover, piece together, and identify their finds. By means of a window they can communicate with teammates at different workstations as they explore different dig sites. Artifacts can be compared with authentic items in an electronic museum. The simulation was developed in Ontario, Canada, for the Unisys Icon system. The cooperative simulations developed by Groupware have consistently won awards for excellence from the Association for Media and Technology in Education of Canada (AMTEC).

Source: Groupware Corporation.

MASTERY LEARNING

One of the persistent problems of traditional large-group instruction is that of dealing with individual differences in student learning ability and learning style. The **mastery learning** approach grows out of the theory that students differ in the amount of time needed to master each objective, not in their inherent ability to learn the subject matter. The traditional curriculum allocates a fixed amount of time and a single set of instructional materials for teaching particular content and accepts the outcome that students will vary in their level of mastery at the end of that time. The mastery learning

SIMULATIONS AND GAMES

KEY WORDS: _____ , _____ , _____

❑ **Game Features**
❑ **Simulation Features**

Title _____

Series Title (if applicable) _____

Source _____

Date _____ **Cost** _____ **Length** _____ minutes

Subject Area _____

Intended Audience _____

Brief Description

Objectives

Entry Capabilities Required (e.g., prior knowledge, reading ability, vocabulary level, math ability).

Rating	High	Medium	Low	Comments
Match with curriculum	❑	❑	❑	
Accurate and current	❑	❑	❑	
Clear and concise language	❑	❑	❑	
Arouse motivation/maintain interest	❑	❑	❑	
Learner participation	❑	❑	❑	
Technical quality	❑	❑	❑	
Evidence of effectiveness (e.g., field-test results)	❑	❑	❑	
Free from objectionable bias or advertising	❑	❑	❑	
User guide/documentation	❑	❑	❑	
Provides practice of relevant skills	❑	❑	❑	
Game: Winning dependent on player actions rather than chance	❑	❑	❑	
Simulation: Validity of game model; realistic, accurate depiction of reality	❑	❑	❑	
Clear directions for play and debriefing	❑	❑	❑	

Strong Points

Weak Points

Recommended Action _____ **Name** _____ **Date** _____

A computer version of this Checklist is found in "The Classroom Link."

GROUP DEBRIEFING

It is usually preferable to conduct a **debriefing** as a group discussion if time and conditions permit. As an aid in planning for this stage, follow the "Four Ds of Debriefing":

1. Decompressing
2. Describing
3. Drawing comparisons
4. Deriving lessons

Step 1: Decompressing (feelings)

You will want to relieve any tensions that may have built up during the simulation or game. Some situations may engender conflict and anger. Also, players who feel they did not do very well in the game may be experiencing anxiety and feelings of inadequacy. In any event, participants are not likely to be focusing on *your* questions and concerns until these pent-up feelings simmer down to a manageable level.

Start with some "safety valve" questions. In games, players will have attained some sort of score, so you can start simply by asking for and recording the scores. Jot down scores on a chalkboard or flip chart. Also note comments. These bits of information form a database you can refer to in later stages of debriefing.

After tabulating these scores you will be able to declare the winner(s) in cases of competitive games. Let the winner(s) show off a little bit by asking them to explain their strategy. Low scorers should also have a chance to tell what went wrong for them, if they wish.

At this point be sure to explain any hidden agendas or "tricks" the designer may have inserted to make a certain point. Explain how these may have affected the scores. Also, point out the role that chance can play in the scoring, as it does in real life.

To deal further with any emotional residue, ask several participants how they felt while playing. Did anyone else feel that way too? Let those who want to chime in freely.

Step 2: Describing (facts)

The nature and purpose of the activity will usually have been explained before the beginning of play. But some students may not have fully appreciated the meaning or significance of the activity. Others may have lost track of it in the heat of play. For example, players of Triangle Trade might need to be

reminded that it simulates the experiences of 17th-century British colonists. Ask basic questions such as "What real-life situation was represented in this activity?" or "What was [x] intended to symbolize?"

Step 3: Drawing Comparisons (transfer)

Help the participants transfer the game experiences to reality. Encourage them to compare and contrast the game with reality by asking such questions as "How does the scoring system compare with real-life rewards?" "What elements of reality were missing from or downplayed in the simulation?" "Would these solutions work in real life?"

Step 4: Deriving Lessons (application)

Get the participants to verbalize exactly what they have learned from the activity. Verbalization will bring to conscious awareness what has been learned. Ask questions such as "What conclusions can you draw from the experience?" "What did you learn about specific real-life problems?" "Did the activity change any of your previous attitudes or opinions?" "What do you plan to do differently tomorrow as a result of this activity?"

INDIVIDUAL DEBRIEFING

In situations where participants finish simulation or game activities at different times or the schedule prevents immediate group discussion, a form of individual debriefing may be used.

One method developed to help participants reflect on their feelings immediately after play uses a simple sentence-completion form to be filled out individually. Each participant writes a completion to each of the following sentences:

1. I was _____. [the role you played in the game]
2. I did _____. [actions you performed]
3. I felt _____. [emotions you felt during play]
4. I wish _____. [open response]

The reactions captured on this form can either substitute for group discussion or can supplement the later discussion, with participants referring back to their sheets to remind themselves of their reactions.

---

model establishes a minimum mastery level and gives different amounts of time and a variety of instructional materials for each student to arrive at that outcome. Initially, mastery learning took the form of self-instruction and individualized tutoring. Later, it was adapted by Block and others for implementation in traditional large-group-based elementary and secondary schools.[15] They have developed a specific tech-

nology, known as Learning for Mastery (LFM), that incorporates specific procedures to implement mastery learning.

The heart of LFM is the teach–test–reteach–retest cycle. It begins by informing students of the objectives and giving instruction needed to achieve those objectives. Following this instruction and follow-up practice activities, students are tested for mastery (typically defined as passing 80% of the items). Those who demonstrate mastery may move on to the next unit. Meanwhile, those who do not demonstrate mastery

---

[15]James H. Block, Helen E. Efthim, and Robert B. Burns, *Building Effective Mastery Learning Schools* (New York: Longman, 1989).

receive additional instruction—usually incorporating different methods, media, or materials—and additional practice activities and then are tested again. Theoretically, this cycle could be continued until all demonstrate mastery, but typically the class moves on to the next unit after one test–retest cycle. Thus, in practice, large-group-based mastery learning programs are a compromise between the traditional curriculum that gives little or no extra time to slower learners and an ideal mastery learning curriculum that allows slower learners as much time as they need.

Many studies compare achievement in mastery learning classes with achievement in traditional classes. Overall, mastery learning approaches seem to work quite well in almost all cases. Student achievement is often dramatically superior. Various meta-analyses of these studies have shown that the average student would score at about the 76th percentile in a mastery learning classroom, compared with the 50th percentile in a traditional classroom.

For an individual teacher implementing mastery learning in a single classroom, this technology is basically a systematic approach in which time and effort is invested outside of class planning and preparing for in-class contingencies. The mastery learning teacher begins by determining expected outcomes, then constructs a test of performance exercise that will assess mastery of those outcomes. Mastery level is usually set at a standard indicative of good-quality work. The entire course is then broken down into units of two to three weeks containing a number of skills, concepts, and attitudes. These units are sequenced so that the material in one unit prepares students for the next one.

For each unit, the teacher designs the unit's *original instruction,* building on existing lesson plans. A short, ungraded diagnostic test is needed for each unit and two sets of *alternative instructional materials* are keyed to each item on the test. One set is called *correctives;* it reteaches the pertinent material and is assigned to those who miss that item. The other set is called *enrichments*—activities for those who exceed mastery; these encourage participants to go deeper into the material or apply it more broadly.

Several efforts have been made to transform the mastery learning approach into a specific package containing all the elements needed for a teacher to implement it. The best-known program of this type is Chicago Mastery Learning Reading (CMLR), developed in the mid-1980s to teach reading in the Chicago schools. It follows the teach–test–reteach–retest pattern and provides all the curriculum materials needed for original teaching and alternative instructional materials—correctives and enrichments—as well as all diagnostic and final tests. It has subsequently been adopted in more than 200 school districts.

PROGRAMMED TEACHING

Programmed teaching, also known as Direct Instruction, is an attempt to apply the principles of programmed instruction in a large-group setting. In this approach, a whole class is broken into smaller groups of 5–10 students. These smaller groups are led through a lesson by a teacher, paraprofessional, or student peer following a highly prescriptive lesson plan. The critical features of these lessons include *unison responding* by learners to prompts (or cues) given by the instructor, *rapid pacing,* and procedures for *reinforcement* or *correction.*

The scripted lesson plans are developed by instructional designers and tested and revised before full-scale use. The scripting affords quality control, assists instructors who are weak in instructional design skills, and allows the substitution of paraprofessionals, advanced students, or even student peers for teachers. The cost-efficiency and educational effectiveness of programmed

FIGURE 11.17
With programmed teaching, older students can guide the work of younger ones.

Electrical Circuits

The setting is a middle school, a self-contained seventh-grade classroom in a crowded residential district of a large city.

Analyze Learners
General Characteristics

These seventh graders are 12 and 13 years old. They come from a poor, declining urban area. More than half are non-white, and about one-quarter are recent immigrants, several of whom barely speak or read English. Their reading levels range from 2nd grade to 12th grade, averaging around 5th grade.

Because of the wide range of abilities and deficiencies of this class, the teacher can seldom rely on group-based "chalk and talk" instruction. This is particularly true in science, where many of the children have very low confidence and interest.

Entry Competencies

Regarding the topic of electric circuits, most of the students have at least a verbal understanding of basic terms such as *source, output device, connection, switch, series,* and *parallel* because they have just completed a hands-on activity with a simple circuit in which they connected lamps with batteries. They have learned the basic principle that an open switch stops the current and that bulbs will light only if the circuit is complete.

In arithmetic the class has been working on fractions, proportions, and decimal-to-fraction conversions. With a few exceptions, students have sufficient mastery of the basic concepts in these areas to go on to study electrical circuits.

State Objectives

The teacher wants the students to have usable, applied skills, not just inert verbal knowledge. He decides to give them practice to reinforce and extend their understanding of electrical circuits. After this lesson, they will be able to do the following:

1. Distinguish closed from open circuits, given a symbolic circuit diagram.
2. Construct series and parallel circuits, arranging batteries, bulbs, and switches so that they function correctly.
3. Explain the consequences of opening a switch in a circuit.
4. Explain the consequences of disconnecting one battery in a series circuit and in a parallel circuit.

Select Methods, Media, and Materials

The teacher has found that these seventh graders respond best to active, hands-on learning situations. He is determined to find an activity that will employ the discovery method. It should also be suitable for small-group work because he knows that some of the students will need help from others. He cannot provide by himself all the remedial assistance the students will need.

The bulb and battery equipment he used last week is not sophisticated enough to provide different kinds of circuits, and there is not enough money to buy more actual lab equipment. He starts thinking along the lines of a simulated lab activity (no computers, of course).

At an in-service science workshop, another teacher told him about Circuitron, a game developed in Scotland that she had used with good results. He was able to borrow the game

---

teaching has led some economists to recommend it as a way of improving education in situations in which cost reduction is a strong consideration.

Programmed teaching is seen by its proponents as a total system for organizing classroom instruction. However, in North America it has been adapted for use as one component of a whole-group classroom setting. It is particularly advocated for basic-skills acquisition at early grade levels, especially in reading and mathematics. It has been tested most in the teaching of disadvantaged and handicapped children. Although programmed teaching has yielded impressive achievement gains in its own right, it has proven to be especially beneficial when combined with other methods to carry students toward higher-level skills such as problem solving.

Programmed teaching lessons are designed to generate high rates of responding by all students. To avoid inattention or mere imitation of other students' responses, all are required to respond vocally at the same time, at a hand signal by the instructor. When the teacher detects an error, he or she follows the procedures specified in the protocol to correct and remediate the error.

Programmed teaching can be regarded as a technology for learning in that it has a definite pattern: teacher cue, unison vocal response, and reinforcement or correction. Because this pattern is incorporated into the scripted lesson plan, a certain amount of quality control and reliability can be expected.

A wealth of research evidence supports programmed teaching in more than a dozen English-speaking countries.[16] One large-scale study compared 20 different instructional models; among them, programmed teaching was the most effective in building basic skills, cognitive skills, and self-concept.[17] Programmed teaching has been used successfully in numerous experimental programs in North America and many other parts of the world, including the Philippines, Indonesia, and Liberia in the primary grades.[18]

[16]Carl Binder and Cathy L. Watkins, "Precision Teaching and Direct Instruction: Measurably Superior Instructional Technology in Schools," *Performance Improvement Quarterly* 3:4 (1990), pp. 74–96.

[17]Cathy L. Watkins, "Project Follow Through: A Story of the Identification and Neglect of Effective Instruction," *Youth Policy 10*:7 (1988), pp. 7–11.

[18]Sivasailam Thiagarajan and Aida L. Pasigna, *Literature Review on the Soft Technologies of Learning* (Cambridge, MA: Harvard University, 1988).

materials from her. After examining the game, the teacher decided to use one of the five games included in the set.

Utilize Media and Materials

The teacher consults with the math teacher, and they agree to devote two double periods to the game. The math teacher will help monitor the game and offer remedial help as needed.

The class is grouped into pairs in which the children with deficient English and conceptual skills are paired with more able ones. Two pairs work at each table with a game set.

The teacher briefly explains the objectives of the lesson and outlines the procedures and basic rules of Circuitron. He circulates among the tables during play to monitor and troubleshoot.

The components of circuits—bulbs, batteries, switches, and so on—are represented by cardboard pieces that can be fitted into large boards with slots. Players take a handful of pieces and try to form them into a circuit, with teammates helping each other to correct mistakes and rearrange the elements to score more points. Then the competing pair at their table check the circuit and try to score more points by using pieces from their own hands. The scoring system reflects the complexity of the circuits, with no points awarded for circuits that would not actually work in real life.

Require Learner Participation

By its very nature, the game requires active learner participation. The teachers circulate to make sure, as much as possible, that both members of each team are actively engaged in their task.

Evaluate and Revise

While play is going on, the teachers jot down notes for the debriefing, recording incidents or comments that could be used and preparing questions to be asked.

After an hour and a half the lead teacher calls time-out and gets everyone to stop playing. He elicits a preliminary tally of the scores, and he offers to the struggling teams some remedial help after class. The next day he restarts the game; after about 45 minutes he calls time-out. He starts the debriefing by asking teams to report their scores. He asks the higher scorers to tell how they managed to do so well. Then he prompts several of the others to say a few words about how they felt during the game. He is able to jog their memories by citing some specific incidents or statements that he observed during play.

Next, he focuses on the main objectives of the exercise, asking, "What is the difference between an open and closed circuit?" and "What would happen if you disconnected one battery in a parallel circuit?" During the discussion he makes note of those who still do not seem to have a firm grasp of the objectives. During the next day's follow-up projects he has them play the game again along with a few of the average and superior performers, as a remedial exercise. Immediately after the debriefing he takes two minutes to jot down his impressions of what worked and what problems arose. He files these notes along with his lesson materials to try to improve the smoothness of the activity next time.

Source: Jaquetta Megarry, "Simulation and Gaming," in International Encyclopedia of Educational Technology, Michael Eraut (ed.). Oxford: Pergamon, 1989.

A computer template for a Blueprint is found in "The Classroom Link."

REFERENCES

Print References

Addams, Dennis, Carlson, Helen, and Hamm, Mary. *Cooperative Learning and Educational Media.* Englewood Cliffs, NJ: Educational Technology Publications, 1990.

Bell, Irene Wood. "Student Growth Through Gaming in the Library Media Center." *School Library Media Activities Monthly* (February 1986): 36–39.

Bullock, Donald H. *Programmed Instruction.* Instructional Design Library, Vol. 8. Englewood Cliffs, NJ: Educational Technology Publications, 1978.

Butler, J. Thomas. "Games and Simulations: Creative Educational Alternatives." *Tech Trends 33* (September 1988): 20–23.

Coldeway, Annabel E., and Coldeway, Dan O. "An Extension of PSI Through the Application of Instructional Systems Design Technology." *Canadian Journal of Educational Communications* (Fall 1987): 279–293.

Cregger, Ronald, and Metzler, Michael. "PSI for a College Physical Education Basic Instructional Program." *Educational Technology* (August 1992): 51–56.

Deutsch, William. "Teaching Machines, Programming, Computers, and Instructional Technology: The Roots of Performance Technology." *Performance and Instruction 31* (February 1992): 14–20.

Ehly, S. W., and Larsen, S. C. *Peer Tutoring for Individualized Instruction.* Boston: Allyn and Bacon, 1980.

Ellson, Douglas G. *Improving the Productivity of Teaching: 125 Exhibits.* Bloomington, IN: Phi Delta Kappan, 1986.

Heitzmann, William Ray. *Educational Games and Simulations.* Rev. ed. Washington, DC: National Education Association, 1987.

Johnson, David W., Johnson, Roger T., Holubec, E. J., and Roy, P. *Circles of Learning: Cooperation in the Classroom.* Alexandria, VA: Association for Supervision and Curriculum Development, 1984.

Jones, Ken. *Simulations: A Handbook for Teachers.* 2d ed. New York: Nichols, 1987.

LeFevre, Dale N. *New Games for the Whole Family.* New York: Putnam/Perigee Books, 1988.

Orlick, Terry. *The Second Cooperative Sports and Games Book.* New York: Pantheon, 1982.

Pear, Joseph J., and Kinsner, W. "Computer-Aided Personalized System of Instruction: An Effective and

Economical Method for Short- and Long-Distance Education." *Machine-Mediated Learning 2* (1988): 213–237.

Pearson, Margot, and Smith, David. "Debriefing in Experience-Based Learning." *Simulation/Games for Learning* (December 1986): 155–172.

Powers, Richard B. "The Commons Game: Teaching Students About Social Dilemmas." *Journal of Environmental Education* (Winter 1985–1986): 4–10.

"Purchasing and Managing an ILS." *Media and Methods 29* (January–February 1993): 12–13.

Riedl, Joan. The Integrated Technology Classroom. Des Moines, IA: Longwood/Allyn & Bacon, 1995.

Rixon, Shelagh. "Language Teaching Games." *ELT Journal* (January 1986): 62–67.

Scannell, Edward E., and Newstrom, John W. *Still More Games Trainers Play: Experiential Learning Exercises.* New York: McGraw-Hill, 1991.

Sherman, J. Gilmour, Ruskin, Robert S., and Semb, George B., eds. *The Personalized System of Instruction: 48 Seminal Papers.* Lawrence, KS: TRI Publications, 1982.

Shockley, H. Allan. "Turnkey or Turkey? Integrating an Integrated Learning System." *Educational Technology 32* (September 1992): 22–25.

Slavin, Robert E. *Using Student Team Learning.* 3d ed. Baltimore: Center for Research on Elementary and Middle Schools, Johns Hopkins University, 1986.

———. *Cooperative Learning: Theory, Research and Practice.* Englewood Cliffs, NJ: Prentice Hall, 1990.

Sobel, Jeffrey. *Everybody Wins: Non Competitive Games for Young Children.* New York: Walker, 1983.

Stolovitch, Harold D. "D-FITGA: A Debriefing Model." *Performance and Instruction* (August 1990): 18–19.

van Ments, Morry. *The Effective Use of Role-Play: A Handbook for Teachers and Trainers.* Rev. ed. New York: Nichols, 1989.

West, R. P., Young, R., and Spooner, F. "Precision Teaching: An Introduction." *Teaching Exceptional Children 22* (1990): 4–9.

Audiovisual References

Belief Systems and Instructional Improvement: A Lesson in Mastery Learning. Dayton, OH: Institute for the Development of Educational Activities, 1986. VHS videocassette.

Mastery Learning Systems. Novato, CA: Alan Cohen Associates, n.d. Audiocassette.

Outcome-Based Education: Success for All. Redwood City, CA: Spady Consulting Group, 1986. VHS videocassette, 50 minutes.

Taking the First Steps [in Outcome-Based Education]. Redwood City, CA: Spady Consulting Group, 1986. VHS videocassette.

LOOKING AHEAD

You are now prepared to move into the exciting future of instructional media and technologies for learning. The trends you will be involved with include multimedia systems and instant access to information and people around the globe.

As we continue to learn more about learning, your students might well be using new psychological technologies, such as those discussed in this chapter.

The school of the future will be different as well. Futurists predict that the structure of the classroom and the organization itself will change. The role of the teacher and the use of instructional media and technologies must change if schools are to improve.

The nature of workers and the workplace will also continue to change. Consequently, education must prepare workers for the 21st century—much training will take place at the workstation itself. The levels of knowledge will continue to accelerate, and students will learn how to access specific knowledge when needed.

This is an exciting and challenging time for professionals in education and training. Learn to use media and technology to ASSURE learning.

KNOWLEDGE OBJECTIVES

1. Discuss the trends in *hard technologies* (media and telecommunications hardware) that you feel will have the greatest future impact on teaching and learning.
2. Discuss the trends in *soft technologies* (psychological and organizational processes) that you feel will have the greatest future impact on teaching and learning.
3. Describe several applications of expert systems to educational problems.
4. Critique the conventional self-contained classroom as an organizational setting for incorporating technology.
5. Critique the "craft approach" of public education in terms of the environment it provides for the use of technology.
6. Discuss the ways in which the roles of teachers or media/technology specialists are changing due to the impact of technology.
7. Discuss changes in the workplace, indicating how media and technologies for learning will relate to these changes.
8. Relate the privatization of schools movement to the use of media and technologies for learning.
9. Relate the accountability movement in public education to the use of media and technologies for learning.
10. Describe the various types of career opportunities available in educational technology.

APPLICATION OBJECTIVES

1. Interview two or more professionals working in educational technology. Compare and contrast their duties in a two- to three-page written report or five-minute cassette recording.
2. Survey the content of several different educational technology journals and write a one- to two-page report summarizing the types of articles and information covered in each.
3. Predict the potential impact of one of the future technologies for learning (write a two- to three-page report or tape a five-minute recording).
4. For a week, collect reports of new developments in electronic media from newspapers, news magazines, and other popular media sources. Write a two- to three-page report describing the potential impact on learning of these new developments.
5. If you work in a school or other instructional setting, analyze the structure or organizational factors that either impede or facilitate your full use of new media and technologies for learning.
6. Prepare an oral or a written report discussing the potential advantages, limitations, and applications of the information superhighway.
7. Explore the privatization of public schools and prepare a two- to three-page report or a five-minute recording about the pros and cons.
8. Acquire a recent "Technology for Education Plan" from a local school district or state office of education. Assess how all areas of the school's curriculum are touched by technology.
9. Read a book or chapter on the future of formal education, such as *School's Out* or *The Learning Revolution,* and critique the ideas presented.

LEXICON

accelerated learning	division of labor	craft approach	accountability
expert system	low-cost learning	performance support	biochip
hyperlearning	technology	system	

The previous chapters of this book have focused on the various media and technologies for learning, including their advantages, limitations, and potential applications to improving learning. In this final chapter we attempt to give a broad perspective on how media and technology fit into the overall scheme of education and training. The emphasis is on change: trends that have brought us to where we are now, new developments that hold promise for improving learning, impediments that limit the implementation of these developments, and potential avenues for getting around these impediments.

TRENDS IN MEDIA AND TECHNOLOGY

Merging of Media

A major trend in media and technology is that of merging. In the 1950s, the common media were separate entities sometimes used in combination and called "multimedia," such as books with phonograph records and multimedia kits with real objects, photographs, and explanatory manuals. (Figure 12.1 represents the common media of the 1950s.)

In the 1980s, the computer began to combine some of these distinct media, as shown in Figure 12.2. The combination of the computer and video led to interactive video. Audio media began to evolve from audiocassettes to audio CDs. And virtual reality began to emerge. The digitization of print, images, and sound made many of these combinations possible.

FIGURE 12.2

During the 1980s the computer fostered the convergence of the previously distinct media.

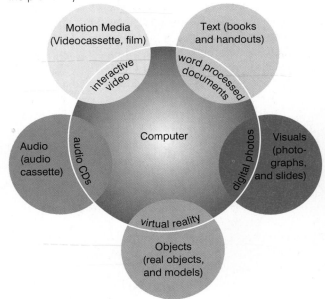

Digitization has led inevitably to the development of a number of systems for storage, retrieval, and transmission of information. It has also led to the convergence of media formats, with the potential for making older formats obsolete. For example, if still and motion images can be combined on the disc, and the same piece of equipment can display both, why have filmstrip and 16mm projectors around? If laser discs are damage resistant and can store still and motion images, why maintain an inventory of fragile filmstrips and films?

By the 21st century all of these media might exist individually but also will be available in a single format that will center on the computer. It will be more difficult to separate text, audio, visuals, and motion media (see Figure 12.3).

Convergence of Telecommunications Technologies

High-speed networks and digitization are reshaping the world's telephone, broadcasting, entertainment, and publishing industries. Driving these changes and media convergence is the computer's ability to reduce all conventional information forms into a common form—streams of digital bits. Represented in this "stew" may be complex combinations of text, numbers, sound, motion images, simulations, integrated learning systems, and job aids. All these will be combined into interactive programs that will be cross-indexed and stored in databases for instant retrieval and use.

FIGURE 12.1

In the 1950s the various types of media were distinct.

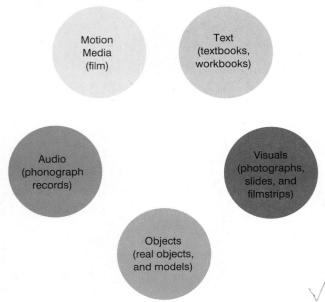

FIGURE 12.3

web-based ✓

By the 21st century it will be difficult to distinguish among the various types of media.

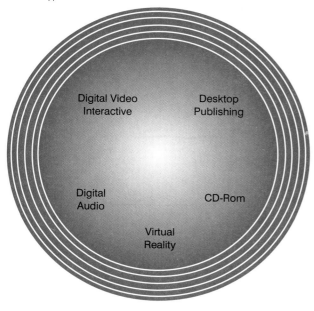

Digital Video Interactive

Desktop Publishing

Digital Audio

CD-Rom

Virtual Reality

Based on recent experience, future hardware developments can be predicted with some confidence. The rule of thumb that is widely accepted is known as Moore's Law (named after Gordon Moore, chairman of Intel Corporation): At any given price level, microchips will double in performance every 18 months.

As communication capacities grow and networking technologies develop, the individual computer will become a node in a massive global network.

peer to peer networking

Converging and Disappearing Computers

Computers are becoming ubiquitous. Yet the computer itself, as we know it today, is likely to converge onto one platform and eventually disappear.

Historically, IBM-type computers and Macintosh computers have been unable to run each other's software. In 1994 Apple released the PowerMac PC computer line, which used the PowerPC chip (microprocessor). The PowerPC chip may become a common computer hardware standard. If so, there could be a single hardware platform to run all types of software.

We are seeing trends in the nature of computers themselves and the way they are used. In the future there will be so many specialized computers that we may not even be aware we are using one. In the computer's place will be computing resources embedded unobtrusively into other tools—into pens, notebooks, chalkboards, books, and desktops, for example.

The user interface—the devices we use to interact with computers—has come a long way since the time of punch cards and alphanumeric terminals. Today we use pull-down menus, windows, and mice. Even mice have evolved (see Figure 12.5). Alternative input devices include pens, the data glove (see Chapter 9), even the human voice. The pen interface allows the user to input data directly onto a computer screen with a stylus. A new generation of hand-held computers will bring the pen interface into widespread use. Even young students will be able to enter and edit text with a pen.

Voice recognition allows you to talk to your computer and it will talk back. The voice interface is especially useful for pocket-size computers whose screens limit the amount of information they can display.

Computers will continue to get smaller, faster, and cheaper. We are already seeing some trends in the use of computers in today's schools. The computer was once the object of instruction; it is fast becoming a tool for learning. It is moving out of the computer lab and into the classroom. As discussed in Chapter 10, all computers within a school or school district will soon be part of a worldwide network.

Whereas in the past we envisioned students working alone at computers, we now see groups of students engaged in cooperative learning around the computer.

FIGURE 12.4

Microprocessor chips such as those shown here are common components in today's computers.

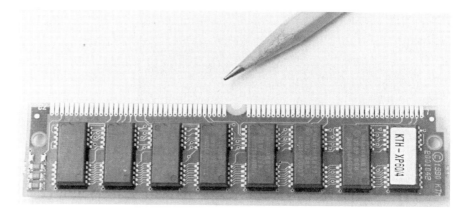

FIGURE 12.5
This Interlink Electronics ad cleverly depicts the evolution of the mouse.

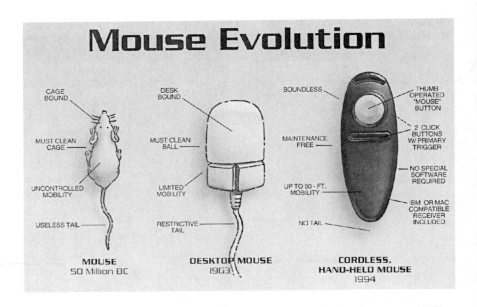

The applications of the computer are moving from drill-and-practice to higher-level skills. The computer has become a discovery tool.

Telecommunication Systems

Satellite dishes and fiber optics are two fascinating and contrasting examples of trends in telecommunications systems. One satellite can transmit the same number of programs as hundreds of microwave relay stations or multiple cables on the ocean floor. A satellite positioned over the Atlantic Ocean can handle 30,000 phone calls simultaneously. Satellite dishes are currently as small as eighteen inches in diameter.

Optical fibers, on the other hand, retain the physical link of phone lines but are only a fraction of the diameter of wire (see Figure 12.6). All homes, schools, libraries, and offices in a city can be interconnected and tied into state, national, and international networks. An optical fiber carries digital—rather than analog—signals as pulses of light generated by a laser device no bigger than a grain of salt. The millions of pulses per second emitted by the laser make it possible to carry many more messages than copper wires or coaxial cables. For example, two optical fibers can handle 6,000 telephone conversations at one time, a task that would take 250 copper wires. The use of fiber optics also helps to save scarce resources. Silicon, used to make the optical fibers, is the second most abundant element on the earth, whereas copper reserves are dwindling.

The digital code can transmit print, audio, and images either separately or simultaneously. The digital signal is also devoid of background noise and is much less vulnerable to distortion caused by external sources such as magnetic fields and electrical storms.

Education networks have become prime users of the technology of fiber optics. New facilities are using optical fibers in place of cable, and older facilities are replacing cables with space-saving optical fibers. Hooking up computers with cables or over phone wires is the most common type of network today. However, such setups limit what can be transferred from one computer to another. They are too slow to handle multimedia applications, such as video, sound, and animation. Wireless networks are now in development and promise to provide easier and better transmission of multimedia materials. Schools will find it practical to build a network combining wireless and fiber-optic cable technologies. The emergence of wireless and high-speed networking will augment the usefulness of collaborative software packages and make them less expensive, as well as more accessible to students.

FIGURE 12.6
A single optical fiber can transmit as many messages as more than one hundred copper wires.

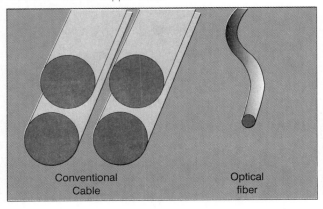

Information Superhighway

Educational institutions and individuals will be "stops" on the information superhighway. This emerging network of cable and telephone lines will deliver vast amounts of information directly to individuals at school, work, and home. The National Information Infrastructure (NII), proposed in the United States, will be a combination of media, computers, cables, telephones, cellular networks, satellites, and microwave transmissions. Through computer on-line systems, you and your students will have access to information now housed in multiple, distant, and inaccessible libraries around the world.

In the future, individuals will be able to communicate instantly with text, picture, voice, data, and two-way video. The resulting interactions will change the roles of students and teachers. Teachers can be separated geographically from their students and students can learn from other students. Along the information superhighway individuals will each have an electronic mailbox—an address where messages can be stored and then accessed from anywhere else on the highway.

Alan Kay predicted that "ten years from now [1991], computers will become as ubiquitous as television and will be connected to interlinked networks that span the globe more comprehensively than telephones do today."[1] Computers will have the ability to supply any and all media, including books, movies, and recordings of voice and music. Finally, the computer will become a boundless library. Resources once beyond the dreams of the most affluent will be potentially accessible to anyone. For schools, the benefits include student access to many perspectives, not just that of the textbook, and the possibility of interaction with others far beyond the walls of the school building.

---

[1]Alan Kay, "Computers, Networks, and Education," *Scientific American 265*:3 (September 1991), p. 146.

FIGURE 12.7

"I'm trying to locate the information superhighway, but I can't seem to find the on-ramp."

Telecommunication Networks

The technology is now available to store information and make it available instantly in different forms to almost anyone in the world. Time will tell when this will become widespread. Schools, homes, and businesses eventually will be interconnected—students, families, and businesspeople will be able to communicate with anyone else in the world and to access any information instantly.

Just as teenagers cruise the streets of their hometowns, students and teachers can cruise the Internet (described in Chapter 10). Internet provides access to information sources and allows users to communicate with each other around the world.

In the future, students and teachers can be like Spiderman and maneuver around the World Wide Web—also referred to as WWW, the Web, or W3. The Web will represent a major advance in making information retrieval quick and efficient. The system will create connections between sources of information that will allow you to easily find related information.

As shown by analogy in Figure 12.8, the Web leads you to information from around the world stored on countless different computers and from multiple databases without your being aware that you are moving from one to another. It will automatically contact the appropriate computer to get the information you need. It will become an ever-expanding multimedia or hypermedia system, giving you and your students access to text, data, sound, visuals, and video.

FIGURE 12.8
The World Wide Web encircles the globe like a spiderweb.

Telecommunication networks will alter the institutional structures that have been put in place by prior means of communication and transportation. We used to operate on the assumption that the learner had to go to the "territory" of the teacher. By relying on the school bus and the private car, we consolidated schools and built large public school complexes.

Advances in technology have made it administratively and economically feasible to educate smaller groups of students in a larger number of instructional settings. Proponents of decentralization as a step toward greater public participation in the control of public education may well have an unexpected and powerful ally in technological advances such as electronic systems for the distribution of instruction.

In addition, parents are concerned about the sometimes excessively long bus rides their children take, as well as the high cost of transportation. These factors make it attractive to return to smaller and more numerous "attendance centers." Some futurists maintain that the home will be the ultimate attendance center. Realistically, however, if parents continue to leave the home to go to work, children will continue to spend the larger part of the day in some sort of caregiving center. Thus the opportunity to improve the quality of education is a more compelling reason why educators should find telecommunications attractive. With high-quality education deliverable by telecommunications, the neighborhood school can hold its own programmatically with the larger school.

However, schools also face social and political problems in reverting to smaller units. Competitive sports, particularly football, thrive in larger schools. We may settle on a compromise—in high schools perhaps there will be electronic distribution within a larger than necessary plant; elementary schools will perhaps become smaller but more numerous.

In the future, continuing professional development is likely to be carried out through learning networks rather than on campuses. Telecommunications networks make possible large-scale collaborative efforts between industry and education. The National Technological University (NTU) (see "Close-up" in Chapter 10, p. 286) is an example of how such collaboration can create learning opportunities for practicing professionals beyond the traditional campuses and degree programs. NTU delivers its programs by satellite.

NEW PSYCHOLOGICAL TECHNOLOGIES

Shifting our attention from technology as product to technology as process, we can recognize that new scientific understanding of human learning will contribute to changes in how instruction is carried out in the future. Conventional educational research and development (R & D) have already yielded the sorts of process technologies described in Chapter 11: programmed instruction, programmed tutoring, Personalized System of Instruction, and the like. Looking into the future, though, breakthroughs in improving learning may well be coming from less conventional sources.

Expanding the capabilities of the brain is a goal of several different R & D projects. For example, meditative techniques can have physiological and psychological effects on humans, and these effects can have instructional consequences. Studies have shown that medita-

FIGURE 12.9
Satellites make communications among students in different parts of the world a reality.

tion reduces anxiety, thereby facilitating complex problem solving by groups under stress. Individuals often report that the relaxation and fresh perspective lent by meditation heighten their study abilities. Both relaxation and stimulation similar to motivation are claimed to result from microelectrical impulses sent to selected areas of the brain.

A number of new and emerging psychological technologies are discussed in *The Learning Revolution,*[2] a book offered as a handbook for educators and a do-it-yourself guide for lifelong learning. The authors describe brain-based methods of enhancing learning, such as brainstorming, Mind Mapping, visual memory techniques, lateral thinking, Montessori method, and accelerated learning. Here we will focus on accelerated learning as an example of these brain-based psychological methods, look briefly at the possibilities of parapsychology, and then discuss another major area of psychological exploration—artificial intelligence and expert systems.

Accelerated Learning

One of the best known of the psychological technologies is **accelerated learning,** an approach based on putting oneself into a special state of relaxation in which the brain is most open and receptive to incoming information. This approach grew out of earlier research done by psychologist Georgi Lozanov in Bulgaria. Lozanov found that by inducing a state of conscious relaxation prior to a lesson, and by using special techniques involving music and drama during the lesson, adults could learn foreign languages with unusual ease and high rates of retention. He concluded that individuals each have an optimum learning state, "where heart-beat, breath-rate and brain-waves are smoothly synchronized and the body is relaxed but the mind concentrated and ready to receive new information."[3]

The technique begins with deep breathing. Then music, specifically having 50 to 70 beats per minute, such as baroque music, is used to harmonize the body and brain. The brain wave pattern that is believed to link best with the subconscious mind is the alpha wave, 8 to 12 cycles per second. When a person is in this state of relaxed alertness, it is believed that the brain's logical filters are lowered and new information is taken in and stored more efficiently.

Parapsychological Techniques. Although many claims have been made for the possible uses of

parapsychology, such as mental telepathy, there is still no credible evidence that such phenomena exist, much less that they can aid learning. The most recent large-scale review of scientific studies in this field[4] by the National Research Council found no support for the usefulness of any parapsychological phenomena. Biofeedback techniques did seem to have some potential benefit for individuals but did not seem promising for educational purposes.

Artificial Intelligence and Expert Systems

Almost immediately after computers became a reality, scientists were intrigued by what they saw as parallels between how the human brain works and how the computer processes information. They wondered whether the computer could "learn" as well as retrieve and collate information. Their experiments led to computers playing games such as checkers and chess with human experts—and winning. Then they explored whether the computer could enable an amateur to play on an equal footing with an expert. It certainly could. But, they reasoned, why limit this capability to playing games? Why not see if this "artificial intelligence" could be applied to more useful problems?

This line of experimentation led to the development of so-called **expert systems.** These are software packages that allow the collective wisdom of experts in a given field to be brought to bear on a problem. One of the first such systems to be developed is called MYCIN, a program that helps train doctors to make accurate diagnoses of infectious diseases on the basis of tests and patient information fed into the computer. Expert systems are slowly making their way into education.

---

[4]Daniel Druckman and Robert A. Bjork, eds., *In the Mind's Eye: Enhancing Human Performance* (Washington, DC: National Academy Press, 1991).

FIGURE 12.10

Computers have revolutionized the way information is handled in all professional fields.

---

[2]Gordon Dryden and Jeannette Vos, *The Learning Revolution* (Rolling Hills Estates, CA: Jalmar Press, 1994).

[3]Terry Tyler Webb, with Douglas Webb, *Accelerated Learning With Music: A Trainer's Manual* (Norcross, GA: Accelerated Learning Systems, 1992).

Scholastic Publications has developed a unique program that learns the rules of any game as it plays with its human partner. The student may play the game with self-chosen rules but must identify for the computer the criteria for winning the game. The computer absorbs the rules and eventually wins. Another expert system, The Intelligent Catalog, helps a student learn to use reference tools. Any learning task that requires problem solving (e.g., qualitative analysis in chemistry) lends itself to an expert system. SCHOLAR is an expert system on the geography of South America. It is an example of a "mixed-initiative" system. The student and the system can ask questions of each other, and SCHOLAR can adjust its instructional strategy according to the context of the student's inquiry.

One example that involves individualized learning is an expert system call CLASS LD. Developed at Utah State University, the program classifies learning disabilities by using an elaborate set of rules contributed by experts. In tests, the program has proven to be at least as accurate as informed special education practitioners. The next step is to develop a software package that will design an individualized education program (IEP) for children diagnosed by CLASS LD. Because many children with learning disabilities are in mainstreamed classes, the expert system would make more manageable the classroom teacher's job of providing appropriate instruction. The school benefits from more effective and more efficient decision making.

Further down the road is an expert system that could truly individualize learning. We can imagine an expert system that learns all the important aptitudes and personality traits of an individual. When presented with a large body of material to be mastered, the learner would use the expert system as guide to learning the content in the most effective manner. The program would adjust the content, instructional method, and medium to the learning styles of the student. The learner, not the experts, would be in charge of the program. When this becomes possible, we will really have individualized learning.

A new professional specialty has emerged from the development of expert systems. The term *knowledge engineers* has been coined to describe the people who work with experts in a field to assemble and organize a body of knowledge and then design the software package that makes it possible to train someone to become skilled in the area or to enable anyone to call upon the skills of experts to solve a problem. The work of knowledge engineering is similar to that done by instructional designers in task analysis and module design.

THE SCHOOL OF THE FUTURE

Perelman, in his book *School's Out,* describes a radical "new formula" for the revitalization of America's educa-

tion system. He introduces the concept of **hyperlearning** (HL), which he describes as follows:

> Not a single device or process, but a universe of new technologies that both possess and enhance intelligence. The hyper in hyperlearning refers not merely to the extraordinary speed and scope of new information technology, but to the unprecedented degree of connectedness of knowledge, experience, media, and brains—both human and nonhuman. The learning in HL refers most literally to the transformation of knowledge and behavior through experience—what learning means in this context goes far beyond mere education or training as the space shuttle goes beyond the dugout canoe.[5]

Perelman predicts that school buildings will be replaced by hyperlearning systems. He discusses many of the media and technologies for learning described in this textbook. Some see his ideas as controversial because he is calling for a complete reinvention of the traditional educational system. He sees no need for schools as we know them today, pointing out that learning and expertise are diffused throughout the world. Therefore, people of any age and social status may be engaged in learning any time, thus making the infrastructure of "schooling" irrelevant and even obstructive.

Describing all of Perelman's ideas is beyond the scope of this book, but we recommend that you read his proposals. There is reason to be skeptical of radical propositions such as Perelman's, but there is also good reason to reconsider time-honored assumptions that may no longer be valid.

As we have explored changes in telecommunications and technology, we can envision changes in the role of the teacher in instruction and the way new technologies will affect library media centers. To discuss the future of our schools, however, we must look at the influences that structure has on teaching and learning and the way some organizational impediments stand in the way of change.

Structure of the Classroom

The typical setup of the classroom, almost everywhere in the Western world and at virtually every level, has the fundamental weakness of being organized around a single adult who attempts to orchestrate more or less diverse activities for a generally large group of learners. This one person typically is expected to be responsible for selecting and organizing the content of lessons; designing materials; producing materials; diagnosing individual needs; developing tests; delivering instruction orally to the group or through other media individually or in different groupings; administering, scoring, and interpreting tests; prescribing remedial activities; and

---

[5]Lewis J. Perelman, *School's Out.* (New York: Avon Books, 1992), p. 23.

coordinating the numberless logistical details that hold the whole enterprise together. Other sectors of society have long since recognized that improvements in effectiveness and productivity require **division of labor**, but this concept has not yet been accepted in the world of formal education.

An example of a profession in which division of labor has been accepted is that of medicine. Physicians have tended toward the practice of specializations, enabling each to keep better abreast of innovations in practice. They have adopted differentiated staffing within their offices and clinics so that less critical functions can be delegated to paraprofessionals and technicians, reserving to the physicians the function of diagnosing and treating conditions that merit their attention. Physicians have an incentive to accept this restructuring in societies that have a free marketplace for their services. In this environment, embracing a division of labor increases their profits.

Educators work in a very different environment. Reigeluth feels that there is a fundamental problem with the structure of institutions in public education:

> Just as the one-room schoolhouse, which was so appropriate for an agricultural society, proved to be inadequate for an industrial society, so our present system is proving to be inadequate for an information society. It is the fundamental structure of our educational system that is at the heart of our current problems.[6]

Microcomputers are accelerating the trend toward increased use of nonhuman resources in the education

[6]Charles M. Reigeluth, "Restructuring: The Key to a Better Educational System for an Information Society," IDD&E Working Paper 16 (Syracuse, NY: School of Education, Syracuse University, 1983), p. 1.

FIGURE 12.11
Have we come full circle? Compare the one-room schoolhouse of the late 1930s with the one-room schoolhouse of the late 1990s. There are some notable similarities: both serve children of different ages and different grade levels; each in its own way accommodates large-group presentations as well as small-group and individual study. What differences do you see?

of our children, but the current structure of our educational system cannot adequately accommodate the effective use of these powerful tools. Alternative classroom structures do exist, however, and have been adopted in many places. In Chapter 11 we described programmed tutoring, Personalized System of Instruction (PSI), and cooperative learning, each of which provides a total and radically different pattern for setting up a learning environment.

More recently, a plan that incorporates virtually all the technologies for learning and centers on the notion of division of labor has been field-tested in a number of countries, including Indonesia, Liberia, and the Philippines. The classroom teacher, who may or may not be a fully certified teacher-training institution graduate, uses materials that are centrally designed and rather fully scripted to lead participatory lessons. Parents, volunteers, and student tutors share other teaching and logistical tasks. Thus, there is a division of labor in both the design and the implementation of instruction. The plan takes a somewhat different shape in each locale and is known by a different name in each country, but the generic name and concept is **low-cost learning technology.**[7] It is essentially a systematic method for implementing a variety of managerial and instructional innovations. It focuses on improving student learning outcomes while reducing overall costs, especially labor costs.

Structure of the Organization

The underlying reason why many teachers and trainers teach the way they do, embracing certain methods, however inefficient or ineffective, is that they are following the "rules of the game" that their daily environment reinforces. A useful way of analyzing this situation is to compare teaching as a craft with instruction as a technology.[8] In a **craft approach** the emphasis is on the use of tools by the skilled craftsperson. In a technology approach the emphasis is on the design of tools that produce replicable, reliable results. In a craft, ad hoc decision making is valued, whereas in a technology, value is placed on incorporating decisions into the design of the tools themselves (e.g., the scripted lesson plan used in low-cost learning technology).

The organizational structures that evolve because of craft thinking are fundamentally different from those that evolve from engineering or technological thinking. Because a craft makes a virtue of the use of tools, the

power and the discretion of a craftsperson in any given situation are very high, whereas the power and the discretion of management in the same situation are relatively low. However, in an engineering operation, the power and discretion of the individual operator are low, and the power and discretion of the team designing the required tools are extremely high. It is inadvisable to attempt to place the products developed by an engineering team into the organizational structure of a craft. The craftspeople will have a natural tendency to modify arbitrarily the engineered products.

This is precisely what happens in traditional education and training. The organizational structures are built around a craft approach, which gives considerable discretion to each instructor in the classroom. When engineering products (e.g., fully scripted lesson plans) are placed in this environment, the individual instructor constantly second-guesses decisions that have already been built into the instructional system. The instructor tends to reduce such systematic products to separate bits of material to be used at his or her own discretion.

The craft tradition of education leads to a structure that stops short of developing specific instructional products centrally because it assumes that such specific decisions are made by the person in face-to-face contact with learners. It is expected that any products that are developed may be used or ignored by the instructor in the classroom. In this structure, technological products represent an added cost, serving only to aid the teacher when he or she deems it appropriate. Solutions that increase overall costs and demand special efforts to produce and implement are not likely to flourish.

Technology and Education

Because our society in general is receptive to new technology, we tend to assume that our subcultures are also receptive. This simply isn't so. Education is the classic example of a subculture that has a spotty record at best in using technological developments to change the way instruction is performed. As described earlier, the organization of instruction is basically the same as it was 100 years ago.

New technology carries no imperative. What matters is how it is perceived. If a new development is useful, easy to master, and nonthreatening, the likelihood of acceptance is very good. The problem is that people within the same organization vary in their perceptions of new technology according to how it will affect what they do. For example, the introduction of the overhead projector was accepted and usually welcomed by teachers because it was viewed as a more versatile chalkboard, fit easily into their established practice, and reinforced their status in the classroom. But if a principal joins a satellite network because she wants her school to benefit from the coursework offered, her staff may perceive the

---

[7]Daryl G. Nichols, "Low-Cost Learning Systems: The General Concept and Specific Examples," *NSPI Journal* (September 1982), pp. 4–8.

[8]Robert Heinich, "Instructional Technology and the Structure of Education," *Educational Communication and Technology Journal* (Spring 1985), pp. 9–13.

technologically delivered courses as an affront or a challenge to their professional status. Whole courses delivered technologically could easily be perceived as replacing teachers, thus threatening their job security. If high school students can learn Japanese by means of two-way television, why not geometry or history?

Principals and school boards in areas that are rural and poor are more likely to take the risk of experimenting with distance learning because such schools have little realistic hope of maintaining a faculty large enough and diverse enough to teach all the courses needed in a modern comprehensive curriculum.

Recent experiences with projects such as TI-IN (see Chapter 10) have demonstrated that courses delivered by two-way television can successfully fill gaps in the secondary school curriculum. The demonstrated success of technology-based instruction, then, raises the possibility of expansion beyond just filling gaps. But expanding technology's role in this way would eventually alter the basic organizational structure and power structure of schools. It remains to be seen if the education profession, students, their parents, and other decision makers are willing to make such fundamental changes.

Courses delivered by satellite, via computer networks, or on interactive television programs are more likely to be accepted by rural schools because their staffs cannot support a full curriculum. Technology can expand curriculum offerings. We know that it can fundamentally alter the instructional organization, as well as the curriculum, of public education.

FIGURE 12.12
The modern media center facilitates individualized and cooperative learning.

The Changing Role of the Teacher

As Ely points out in *Trends in Educational Technology*, the teacher's role in the learning process is changing as new technologies are introduced into the classroom.[9] Teachers are not being replaced by technology, but their role has changed from that of presenter of information to that of coordinator of learning resources. In addition, they serve as facilitator, manager, counselor, and motivator. Their new role frees them to work more independently with individuals and small groups while leaving the formal presentations to another medium. Teachers help students find and process information from many sources (media). In some schools, teachers are given major roles in the decision-making process related to instruction; this is sometimes called site-based management.

Impact of New Technologies on School Library Media Centers

Materials for life-long learning will continue to be available through libraries and information centers. These materials, however, will be assessed and searched using new technologies. In many cases, cable television connections will allow learners of all ages to bring such materials into their homes without having to go to the library or resource center.

School library media specialists will need to think not only in terms of shelving and circulation but also in terms of downloading and uploading—electronically receiving, storing, indexing, and distributing information to teachers, students, classrooms, and homes. The interactive technologies will create a new generation of teachers and learners, who will become not only viewers of such materials but users and creators of them.

Learning stations will be specially equipped for those with learning or physical disabilities. Students will be able to control the rate of speech delivery, enlarge information on a computer screen so they can read the results of a database search, use a voice synthesizer to have a printed page read to them, or take notes in class through an electronic storage device that will later print out the document in Braille.

Callison identifies aspects of technology that will support learning now and into the next century.[10] According to this researcher, future technology will perform the following functions:

[9]Donald P. Ely, *Trends in Educational Technology* (Syracuse, NY: Clearinghouse on Information Resources, 1992), p. 29.

[10]Daniel Callison, "The Impact of New Technologies on School Library Media Center Facilities and Instruction," *Journal of Youth Services in Libraries* 6:4 (Summer 1993), pp. 414–419.

- Provide continuous access to information, 24 hours a day, seven days a week
- Allow computers on teachers' desks to act as secretaries, administrative assistants, and record keepers
- Provide for cable and satellite reception in every classroom (Many classrooms today don't even have a telephone!)
- Allow all rooms and offices to be wired so that every computer is networked with instructional programs, records, library collections, and information networks
- Design communications networks that feature e-mail; connections among media centers, classrooms, and offices; and dial-up access to various types of information, including media center catalogs, CD-ROM networks, homework hotlines, writing labs, and student files
- Design media centers that include a communications resource facility to accommodate audio conferencing and distance learning
- Allow students and teachers to access information and courses from sites throughout their region, their nation, and the world via two-way interactive television and satellite dishes
- Meet the needs of students with disabilities and special needs with the aid of computers equipped with adaptive devices
- Provide staff development opportunities throughout the year.

CONSEQUENCES OF WORKPLACE CHANGES

Growth of Workstation Training

One of the fastest growing techniques for improving human performance is the *job* (or *performance*) *aid*, a set of procedures that workers follow to make sure a task is performed properly. The instructions may be verbal (print or audio), visual (still or motion), or a combination of the two. The important distinguishing characteristic of the job aid is that it is used at the workstation, not at a training site. For employees working at a keyboard, the job aid for a particular task can be summoned at the touch of a key. Originally, improving performance was the purpose of job aids, but training directors are broadening their use to include instruction at the workstation.

Performance Support Systems

An educational and training concept borrowed from Japanese manufacturing is *kanban,* or "just-in-time." Rather than teaching people many skills and much knowledge that they *might* use in the future, just-in-time

training would deliver knowledge and expertise when it is needed. At the heart of this type of training is the use of performance support systems on the job.

Performance support systems use a variety of on-line aids both to improve current job performance and to plan further career development. Computer-based systems allow access to specific reference documents when they are needed and may even advise workers if they are having difficulties on the job. The consequence of just-in-time training is that it changes the role of formal education from teaching content to having students learn how to learn. Raybould describes an electronic performance support system that improves worker productivity by providing on-the-job access to integrated information advice and learning experiences.[11]

In the introduction to their book *Future Work,* Winslow and Bramer discuss the emergence of Integrated Performance Support (IPS) systems. They believe that, "above all, Integrated Performance Support anticipates the next phase of the world economy: the movement from an information economy to a knowledge economy. Here, the basic economic resource will not be capital, not labor, nor natural resources, but rather knowledge."[12] IPS systems support worker performance with the knowledge whenever and wherever a worker needs support. It may include advice, tools, reference, and training provided to a worker at his or her work location at the moment of need. Using performance support systems, workers will take a fraction of the time to reach basic proficiency levels. Employees will be able to meet customer expectations because the knowledge they need to respond to a customer's request is right there at the workstation. The result will be more satisfied customers. Future workers, while they are still in school, will need to learn how to effectively and efficiently use performance support systems.

The Changing Work Force

The nature of the North American work force is changing dramatically. For one thing, it is getting older. As a consequence, the educational systems must be able to provide life-long learning. In addition, the makeup of the work force is becoming increasingly multicultural. Education and training will need to be provided in a variety of languages and at various aptitude levels. Also, because society is becoming more mobile, the need for job retraining will continue to increase. The media and technologies for learning described in earlier chapters can help workers cope with many of the changes and open doors to future possibilities.

---

[11]B. Raybould, "Solving Human Performance Problems with Computers," *Performance & Instruction* 4:14 (1990), p. 4

[12]C. D. Winslow and W. L. Bramer, *Future Work.* (New York: Free Press, 1994), p. 4.

FIGURE 12.13
Workstation training will keep workers up to date in the future.

The Changing Nature of Work

About 60% of U.S. workers today hold jobs that entail mainly handling information. Even more are in the "knowledge industry." Knowledge work involves not only crunching and shuffling data but learning in elaborate systems combining human teams and intelligent machines. With the number of hands-on production jobs approaching zero, our schools must teach people to work with their brains.

Professionalization of the Field

The need for professional expertise in the design and development of instruction becomes much more apparent when technology is involved. The International Board of Standards for Training, Performance, and Instruction has put together a set of standards for trainers, instructional designers, and training managers. There has also been a movement by a consortium of companies to codify the skills needed for developing training programs. The American Society for Training and Development has published a comprehensive guide to the skills required for the various levels of training in program development. All these efforts indicate a growing professionalization of the field that is sure to continue into the future.

ON THE HORIZON
Computers in the Classroom

Regular classrooms are becoming the basic setting for the use of digital technologies. Originally, computers were housed in laboratories. Students and even entire classes were scheduled into the computer lab. Teachers had to plan in advance to spend a large block of time in the lab to justify the trip to the computers.

Now, with more and more computers in the regular classroom, teachers, groups of students, and individual learners can use the computer when needed and for the amount of time needed—even if it is just a few minutes.

Media and Technology: From Enrichment to Replacement

Media used to be called "audiovisual aids"—media for enrichment. They were an extension of the teacher. Some teachers used media to "fill time," whereas others tried to integrate the use of media within the curriculum. Media were enrichment tools for improving the quality of teaching.

There is a current trend to use media and technology to replace live, face-to-face instruction. More teachers are expressing themselves and their ideas via a certain medium—a videotape, a computer disk, printed material, or a combination of these—to present instruction.

When rural schools cannot find a teacher to teach a specialized subject, they can turn to one of the distance education technologies to deliver the instruction. Teachers in their traditional roles in front of a class are being replaced by teachers instructing via media and technology.

Growth of Integrated Learning Systems

ILSs offer comprehensive coverage in terms of lesson plans and integration of electronic media. They generally make fewer demands on the teacher than do individual programs that treat small sections of the curriculum.

> ILSs [integrated learning systems, described in Chapter 8] are the fastest growing segment of the educational software industry. . . . They are an "industry" that is among the formidable forces that will shape the future of education.[13]

Privatization of Schools

The recent expansion of the number and variety of privatized schools is likely to continue. In an effort to improve their schools, some school districts are turning the management of their schools over to for-profit corporations. The intent is to maximize resources, to provide preventative maintenance, and to institute a more "businesslike" orientation. Like other vendors that provide services to schools, the corporation provides management services. The local school board retains control and the authority to make final approvals for curriculum and staffing.

In some cases, parents and teachers have opposed the privatization of schools. One of their concerns is that the quality of the student experience may be sacrificed for the sake of the bottom line on the account ledger. Considering the financial plight of many schools, administrators contend that something needs to be done. The next couple of decades could be an exciting time for experimentation with various approaches to privatization of functions that were once thought of as public.

Closing the Technology Gap

Traditionally, the schools have been the avenue to equal access to opportunity. They have tried to even out the disparities in educational opportunities between lower- and upper-income families. Today, this means making sure that all students have full access to information-handling experiences and technology. We know that many children from upper-income families have access to computers at home. The school must make sure that children from low-income families also have access to computer facilities. If they don't, the gap will continue to widen.

Increased Accountability of Education

Historically, public schools, while they have been open to public inspection, have not been subjected to rigor-

FIGURE 12.14
Privatized schools are managed as businesses.

ous scrutiny in terms of the quality of their output. Parents and taxpayers have been left to draw their own conclusions about how successfully students have been learning. Generally, people assume that the schools they know themselves are doing a good or excellent job of educating, but schools elsewhere are somewhat suspect. These assumptions have gone unchallenged because there has not been hard evidence by which to compare success. As public schools continue to lag behind other sectors of society in terms of productivity, more and more voices are calling for stricter measurement of quality. They would like to see objective tests that would allow direct comparison from school to school and district to district. Such data would allow taxpayers to calculate how much growth was taking place at what cost. Such information would allow school boards to hold administrators accountable for decisions.

Increased **accountability**—holding school administrators and teachers responsible for the resources invested in education—is expected to promote the adoption of technology. First, instruction delivered by technology, such as integrated learning systems, is more visible and open to external evaluation than conventional classroom instruction. Second, when materials and devices are substituted for teacher-led instruction, costs can be lowered while results—immediate performance on achievement tests—tend to rise.

State Adoption of Technologically Based Instruction

The practice of state adoption of textbooks has been around for a long time. Until recently, other media formats have been excluded from consideration. Several states are now encouraging publishers to submit "media programs" and "technology tools" for state adoption.

---

[13]M. Sherry, "The Future of Integrated Learning Systems," *Inventing Tomorrow's Schools* 1:1 (November 1991), p. 6.

This is tantamount to admitting technology into the mainstream of curriculum implementation on an equal footing with textbooks.

Course Credit for Technology-Based Courses

In addition to state adoption, increased use of telecommunications and the positive results from programs such as the TI-IN network will promote the notion of giving students full credit for successful completion of courses delivered by technology. As more and more colleges accept such courses for advanced placement and as state education departments get more involved in telecommunications, pressure will be put on the regional accreditation agencies to give full credit to students taking such courses.

School District Development of Accredited Courses

As regional accreditation agencies set the criteria for accreditation of technology-based courses, school districts will develop and deliver courses based on those criteria in the same way that they now hire certified teachers to fulfill accreditation requirements.

Flexibility in Teacher Certification Requirements

The recent trend toward loosening teacher certification requirements, primarily to permit knowledgeable laypersons to teach, will probably be accelerated by the acceptance of courses delivered by technology and the advantages of having a differentiated staff. Certification of educational personnel somewhere between the paraprofessional and the full professional level is likely. Future schools will have a more varied instructional roster than in the past.

Technologically Based Collaborative Learning (Groupware)

In the past, students worked either with the entire class or individually. Employers of graduates, particularly college graduates, began asking for students who could work cooperatively in small groups. On the job, many were not able to function in "quality circles" and "work teams." The computer has made it easier for students to study and work in groups, with the computer providing guidance, direction, and feedback. Dynamic, small-group interaction is difficult, if not impossible, for a single teacher and 30 students. Software that facilitates collaborative learning within small groups is now available;

this software is often called *groupware,* as discussed in Chapters 10 and 11.

Local Technology Plans

As the 21st century unfolds, more and more schools are developing plans for instructional uses of technology across the curriculum. Teachers are involved in developing these "action plans," which often result from in-service workshops with opportunities for discussion and visits to other schools that have successfully implemented technology. These plans often recommend computers in the classrooms, networks within the school, distance education, home delivery of instruction, electronic mail for students and teachers, and in-service technology training for all school staff.

INTO THE NEXT CENTURY

Hardware developments are occurring so rapidly that our sense of expectation increasingly lags behind reality. In previous generations our vision extended beyond our capabilities. Now our vision struggles to keep up with what is available. For example, wireless telephone communication is now commercially available. Only a short time ago, it was the stuff of science fiction.

An emerging new technological approach, still verging on science fiction, involves applying the techniques of genetic engineering, with recombinant DNA, to construct tiny biological microprocessors of protein, or **biochips.** Biochips measuring in the 10–25-nanometer range (a nanometer is one-billionth of a meter) are about a hundred times smaller than the current silicon chips. Protein circuits as small as a single molecule are being envisioned.

Software is developing just as rapidly. The digitization of information discussed earlier in this book represents a new paradigm for software development. Hypermedia and CD-ROM are also opening doors into a new era of software. The new software will make selecting and assembling information from a variety of sources infinitely easier and faster for teachers and students. The greater boon may be for students, who will be able to access and process information much more meaningfully because the systems will lend themselves to individualized learning strategies.

One of the characteristics of new software is that it can be put into the hands of amateurs to do professional work. Desktop publishing is just the start of a long-term trend in what will be a transformation of the knowledge-handling industry. Coupled with this will be just-in-time education and training, in which everyone will be able to access information when they need it. It will no longer be necessary to learn something and put it into "cold storage" and hope you don't forget it before you need it.

YOUR FUTURE IN THE FIELD

You are entering this field at an exciting time as a teacher, trainer, or media professional. This book has been dedicated to helping you become a more effective instructor (or manager of instruction) through application of instructional media and technology. You may, however, wish to specialize in the fascinating and fast-growing field of instructional technology. (A directory of graduate programs in instructional technology is co-published by the Association for Educational Communications and Technology.)[a] If so, what opportunities for professional employment are likely to be open to you? Unlike some education areas, instructional technology is becoming more and more pervasive in formal and nonformal education each year, and, correspondingly, ever larger numbers of people are being employed in this specialty.

Traditionally, the growth of instructional technology has created career opportunities in the various media programs at school, district, regional, and state levels. At all these levels, media professionals are employed to run programs and, depending on the size of the organization, produce materials for use in schools. As school districts and regional media centers have built up their collections of audiovisual materials for distribution, they have employed instructional media professionals to select these materials. Another career area at all education levels is in professional management of media collections, including classification, storage, and distribution.

The fastest growing specialty is school technology coordinator. Regardless of the quality and sophistication of computer hardware and software, the success of technology often depends on the support and encouragement that students and teachers receive. The technology coordinator can assist with planning, selecting software and hardware, consulting on purchases, assisting with implementation, and supervising maintenance and repair.

Instructional product design—the development of validated and reliable instructional materials—has been an important

specialty in the field of instructional technology for some time. Publishers and producers of instructional materials, along with school districts, community colleges, and colleges and universities, employ specialists trained in the skills of product design. Computer-assisted instruction, interactive video, and other emerging forms of individualized instruction constitute an important growth area within the instructional product design field.

Organizations other than schools also require specialists in educational technology. Health care institutions, for example, are heavily involved in instructional technology and have been employing an increasing number of professionals to help develop the instruction used in those programs.

Training programs in business and industry need a variety of professionals. These specialties include the following:

- *Trainer.* Presents information, leads discussions, and manages learning experiences
- *Instructional designer.* Assesses training needs; translates training needs into training programs; determines media to be used; designs course materials
- *Training manager.* Plans and organizes training programs; hires staff; prepares and manages budgets

Most training programs rely heavily on instructional media. Consequently, specialists in instructional technology are in demand in these programs.

---

[a]Donald P. Ely, ed., *Educational Media and Technology Yearbook, 1996* (Englewood, CO: Libraries Unlimited, 1996).

Earlier we mentioned experiments to enhance the capabilities of the brain. The convergence of these experiments with the technology of biochips raises the possibility of interfacing the brain with external electronic devices, either indirectly (by detecting brain waves with external sensors) or directly (by employing implanted electrodes). Just a few years ago we thought it was crazy to think that you could talk to your computer, have it do what you said, and also talk back to you. In the future it will undoubtedly be possible to think something and have your computer do it . . . and maybe communicate back to you via brain waves!!!

All these developments and trends make this an exciting and challenging time for professionals engaged in education and training. Make the most of it!

CLOSE-UP

PROFESSIONAL ORGANIZATIONS IN EDUCATIONAL TECHNOLOGY

Whether your interest in instructional technology is general or whether you intend to specialize in this area of education, you should be familiar with some of the major organizations dedicated to its advancement.

Association for Educational Communications and Technology (AECT)

AECT is the leading international organization representing instructional technology professionals working in schools, colleges and universities, and the corporate, government, and military sectors. Its mission is to provide leadership in educational communications and technology by linking professionals holding a common interest in the use of educational technology and its application to the learning process. AECT has 11 divisions designed around areas of special interest represented within the membership. Divisions encompass members' interests in instructional design, research and theory, media management, distance learning, school media programs, industrial training, media production, computer-based instruction, interactive systems, international interests, and systemic school restructuring.

The association maintains an active publications program, including *TechTrends*, published six times during the academic year; *Educational Technology Research and Development*, a research journal published four times a year; and a large number of books and videotapes. AECT sponsors an annual convention and the InCITE exposition in February each year. The annual convention features over 300 educational sessions and workshops focusing on how new technologies and teaching methods are being used in the classroom; the exposition showcases a broad range of the latest in educational and instructional hardware and software. In addition, the association sponsors an annual professional development seminar and leadership development conference each summer. For more information, contact AECT, 1025 Vermont Avenue NW, Suite 820, Washington, DC 20005.

American Library Association (ALA)

The ALA is the oldest and largest library association in the world. Its 57,000 members represent all types of libraries—public, school, academic, state, and special libraries serving persons in government, commerce, the armed services, hospitals, prisons, and other institutions. The association also has 11 divisions focusing on various types of libraries and services. The American Association of School Librarians, one of the divisions, holds national conferences focusing on the interests of school media specialists. For more information, contact the ALA, 50 Huron Street, Chicago, IL 60611.

American Society for Training and Development (ASTD)

ASTD is composed primarily of professionals engaged in training and human resource development programs in business and industry. It is by far the largest association for people engaged in workplace performance improvement programs in

business, industry, government, and other institutions. The society publishes a monthly magazine, *Training and Development;* sponsors research in the field of workplace performance improvement; and conducts an annual international conference that includes a varied and significant educational program. ASTD publishes a newsletter on instructional technology and organizes conference sessions on the topic. For more information, contact the ASTD, 1640 King Street, Box 1443, Alexandria, VA 22313-2043.

International Interactive Communications Society (IICS)

The IICS is the premier worldwide nonprofit organization for interactive media professionals. Dedicated to the advancement of interactive arts and technologies since 1983, members of the IICS include professionals involved in the rapidly integrating digital "convergence" industries. Currently IICS has close to 5,000 members. Membership benefits include a monthly newsletter, annual membership directory, local chapter activities, and various discounts on publications and services related to the interactive multimedia industry. For more information, contact IICS Executive Office, 14657 SW Teal Blvd., Suite 119, Beaverton, OR 97007.

International Society for Performance Improvement (ISPI)

ISPI is the leading international association dedicated to improving productivity and performance in the workplace. Founded in 1962, ISPI represents over 10,000 members in the U.S., Canada, and 33 other countries. ISPI members work in business, governmental agencies, academic institutions, and other organizations. The ISPI Annual Conference and Expo, several association publications, and more than 60 different chapters provide professional development, services, and information exchange. For more information, contact ISPI, 1300 L Street NW, Suite 1250, Washington, DC 20005.

International Society for Technology in Education (ISTE)

The mission of ISTE is to improve education through the use of technology in learning, teaching, and administration. It is the

CLOSE-UP

(continued from page 359)

largest nonprofit professional organization dedicated to the improvement of education through the use of computer-based technology. ISTE members include teachers, administrators, computer coordinators, information resource managers, and educational technology specialists. The organization maintains regional affiliate memberships to support and be responsive to grassroots efforts to improve the educational use of technology. Their support services and materials for educators include books, courseware, and conferences. ISTE publishes *Learning and Leading with Technology, Journal of Research on Computing in Education, ISTE Update*, books, and courseware packages. For more information, contact the ISTE, 1787 Agate Street, Eugene, OR 97403-1923.

International Television Association (ITVA)

ITVA was formed 27 years ago to enhance the skills and knowledge of video professionals working in corporate and organizational settings. It has since grown to 8,000 members; largely because it continues to evolve in response to the industry's rapid pace of change. The annual conference, held in conjunction with INFOCOMM International, brings together video professionals from all over the country to participate in seminars and workshops given by experienced practitioners. Local chapters provide further opportunities for professional development and networking. In addition to the usual benefits expected from a national association (annual directory, newsletters, etc.), ITVA offers its members special low-cost

phone, hotel, credit card, health insurance, and production insurance services. The association has published several books and pamphlets and was a key participant in the recent establishment of new IRS guidelines governing the classification of workers as employees or independent contractors in the video industry. For more information, contact the ITVA, 6311 N. O'Conner Road, Irving, TX 75039.

International Visual Literacy Association (IVLA)

The IVLA is dedicated to exploring the concept of visual literacy—how we use visuals for communication and how we interpret these visuals. It is particularly concerned with the development of instructional materials designed to foster skills in interpreting visuals. The organization draws membership from a variety of disciplines and professions, including higher education, public schools, business and communication, professional artists, production specialists, and design specialists. For more information, contact the Center for Visual Literacy, Arizona State University, Tempe, AZ 85287.

State Organizations

Several of the national professional organizations have state affiliates (AECT, ALA, ISTE) or local chapters (ISPI, ASTD). By joining one or more of these, you will quickly come in contact with nearby professionals who share your particular concerns.

You, as a teacher or an instructional technology specialist, will want to be active in at least one local or state organization. If you are a full-time student, you can join many organizations at a reduced rate.

REFERENCES

Print References

Adams, Steve, and Bailey, Gerald D. "Education for the Information Age: Is It Time to Trade Vehicles?" *NASSP Bulletin* (May 1993): 57–63.

America 2000: An Education Strategy Sourcebook. Washington, DC: Department of Education, 1991.

Carter, Kim. "Images of Information in a 21st Century High School: How Southegan High's Information Center Supports Its Innovative Approach to Learning." *School Library Journal* (February 1994): 25–29.

Darling-Hammond, Linda. "Reframing the School Reform Agenda: Developing Capacity for School Transformation." *Phi Delta Kappan* (June 1993): 752–761.

Dede, Chris, et al. "Trends and Forecasts." *EDUCOM Review* (November–December 1993): 35–38.

Dixon, R. G. "Future Schools: And How to Get There from Here." *Phi Delta Kappan* (January 1994): 360–365.

Ely, Donald P., and Minor, Barbara B., eds. *Educational Media and Technology Yearbook.* Englewood, CO: Libraries Unlimited, annual.

Farley, Raymond P. "Classrooms of the Future." *American School Board Journal* (March 1993): 32–34.

Gates, William. "The Promise of Multimedia." *American School Board Journal* (March 1993): 35–37.

Heinich, Robert. "Restructuring, Technology, and Instructional Efficiency," in Gary Anglin, ed., *Instructional Technology: Past, Present, and Future.* Englewood, CO: Libraries Unlimited, 1991.

Hicks, David. "Reclaiming the Future: What Every Educator Needs to Know." *Australian Journal of Environmental Education* (September 1993): 71–84.

Hunter, Barbara, et al. "Technology in the Classroom: Preparing Students for the Information Age." *Schools in the Middle* (Summer 1993): 3–6.

Lee, In Sook, and Reigeluth, Charles M. "Empowering Teachers for New Roles in a New Educational System." *Educational Technology* (January 1994): 61–72.

Lester, June. "Education in Response to Change." *Journal of Library Administration* (1993): 39–54.

CLOSE-UP

PROFESSIONAL JOURNALS IN EDUCATIONAL TECHNOLOGY

All of the professional organizations in instructional technology publish journals of interest to their members. Various other periodicals are of special interest to teachers interested in using instructional media. *Media and Methods*, for example, highlights new software and hardware. *Booklist* will keep you current on the availability of new instructional materials. *Learning* gives practical ideas for improving instruction. *Educational Technology* addresses both teachers and educational technologists, providing articles on a broad range of topics, from the theoretical to the practical. For the business or industry setting, *Training* covers new developments in training techniques in a lively, popular style.

School Library Media Quarterly publishes research that pertains to the uses of technology for instructional and informational purposes. Special issues have dealt with such themes as communications and technology and facility design for learning environments that require a great deal of technology.

T.H.E. (Technological Horizons in Education) *Journal* concentrates on technology in higher education. *The Canadian Journal of Educational Communications* gives in-depth coverage of the broad field of educational technology.

The computer area has spawned a large number of journals, such as *Electronic Learning, Journal of Educational Multi-*

media and Hypermedia, Journal of Computing in Childhood Education, Journal of Computers in Math and Science Teaching, Technology and Learning, and New Media.

As you work with instructional media and technology and gain experience in whatever position you find yourself, you may want to explore the possibility of deepening your professional interest in one of the specialties in instructional technology. Through regular reading of one or more of the journals in the field, you can stay informed about developments in instructional technology.

Luna, Gaye. "Change Drivers: Impacting Technology Education in the 1990s." *Technology Teacher* (January 1992): 27–28.

Malfitano, Rocco, and Cincotta, Phil. "Network for a School of the Future." *T.H.E. Journal* (May 1993): 70–74.

Moore, Noel. "How to Create a Low-Cost Virtual Reality Network." *Educational Media International* (March 1993): 37–39.

Piskurich, George M. *The ASTD Handbook of Instructional Technology.* New York: McGraw-Hill, 1993.

Reeves, Thomas C. "Evaluating Schools Infused with Technology." *Education and Urban Society* (August 1992): 519–534.

Reisman, Sorel, ed. *Multimedia Computing: Preparing for the 21st Century.* Harrisburg, PA: Idea Group, 1984.

Ross, Tweed W., and Stewart, G. Kent. "Facility Planning for Technology Implementation." *Educational Facility Planner* (1993): 9–12.

Ruck, Gary. "The Future School: Designing for Student Success." *School Business Affairs* (January 1993): 15–18.

Rudiger, Charles W., and Krinsky, Ira W. "Getting to 2001." *International Journal of Educational Reform* (July 1992): 285–290.

Skurzynski, Gloria. "The Best of All (Virtual) Worlds: What Will Become of Today's New Technology?" *School Library Journal* (October 1993): 37–40.

Solomon, Sylvia R. "Familiar Script, Strange Stage: The Changing Roles of Teachers." *Education Canada* (Summer 1993): 36–41.

Sullivan, Howard J., et al. "Perspectives on the Future of Educational Technology." *Educational Technology, Research and Development* (1993): 97–110.

Taylor, Jay. "The Uses of Technology." *American School Board Journal* (August 1993): 18–19.

Van Dam, Janet M. "Redesigning Schools for the 21st Century Technologies: A Middle School with the Power to Improve." *Technology and Learning* (January 1994): 54–58, 60–61.

Yelland, Richard. "Pulling Together: The Need for International Cooperation in Facility Planning." *Educational Facility Planner* (1992): 18–20.

Audiovisual References

CD-ROM: The New Papyrus. Seattle, WA: Intermedia, 1986. Videocassette. 22 minutes.

High Technology: How It Works. Educational Dimensions Group, 1983. Filmstrips. "Holography," 21½ minutes;

"Television," 20½ minutes; "Fiber Optics," 17½ minutes; "Videodisc," 20 minutes.

Introduction to Communication. Bloomington, IN: Agency for Instructional Technology, 1990. Videocassette. 17 minutes.

Overview of Technology. Bloomington, IN: Agency for Instructional Technology, 1990. Videocassette. 15 minutes.

Power On: New Tools for Teaching and Learning. Manhasset, NY: SI Productions, 1989. Videocassette.

Producing and Transmitting Messages. Bloomington, IN: Agency for Instructional Technology, 1990. Videocassette. 17 minutes.

The Promise of New Educational Technology. Manhasset, NY: SI Productions, 1988. Videocassette.

Tyler, Ralph. *The Development and Use of Technology in Education.* Bloomington, IN: Phi Delta Kappan, 1985. Videocassette. 20 minutes.

Virtual Reality. New Dimension Media, 1993. Videocassette. 13 minutes.

Virtual Reality Playhouse. The Waite Group Press, 1992. Book, diskette, 3-D glasses.

EQUIPMENT AND SETUPS

Most users of technology are not—and do not expect to become—electronic wizards, but they want to be able to use the hardware safely and effectively. The most fundamental elements of effective technology use are simply getting the equipment properly set up, keeping it running, and being ready to cope with snags, which always seem to occur at the most inopportune times.

This appendix provides guidelines for arranging equipment and facilities properly and hints for the safe care and handling of audiovisual equipment and computer hardware.

SAFETY

Safety is the paramount concern whenever teachers and students are using technology. Accidents involving heavy pieces of equipment can be serious, even fatal. The U.S. Consumer Product Safety Commission has noted at least four deaths of children and four serious injuries resulting from top-heavy projection carts that tipped over, dumping a heavy object onto the child. In seven cases the carts had a TV monitor on the top shelf, and the eighth had a film projector there. Particularly hazardous are carts over 50 inches (127 centimeters) high. With the increasing number of TV monitors being used in schools, this hazard is a growing concern.

All educators must be aware of their responsibility—and legal liability—regarding students' exposure to hazardous conditions. The operating rule today is to *NEVER allow children to move carts with heavy equipment on them.*

Adults, too, can sustain injuries from mishandling equipment. Many back injuries occur when people attempt to lift heavy objects by simply bending over, grasping the object, and pulling directly upward. This puts a strain on the lower back. The recommended procedure is to bend at the hips and knees, and lift upward with the *legs* providing upward spring, as shown in Figure A.1.

All educators must recognize that they serve as role models for safe practices when using technology. They thus have a special responsibility to know and practice good safety habits.[1]

CARE AND HANDLING OF AUDIOVISUAL EQUIPMENT

Overhead Projectors

The overhead projector is a simple apparatus with few components requiring special maintenance procedures. Reliable as it is, however, it should not be taken for granted. You should take a few basic precautions to ensure that the projector keeps putting on a bright performance.

Keep the overhead projector as clean as possible. The horizontal stage tends to gather dust, fingerprint smudges, and marking-pen traces. It should be cleaned regularly with window spray or a mild solution of soap and water. The lens in the head assembly should also be kept free of dust and smudges. Clean it periodically with lens tissue and a proper lens-cleansing solution. The fresnel lens under the stage may also need cleaning eventually, but this procedure is better left to the equipment specialist. The lens is a precision optical element requiring special care. In addition, some disassembly of the unit is required to get at the lens.

The best way to prolong the life of the expensive lamp in the overhead projector is to allow it to cool before moving the projector. Move the projector with

---

[1] For a comprehensive guide to safe handling of audiovisual equipment, see Ralph Whiting and Roberta Kuchta, *Safety in the Library Media Program: A Handbook* (Manitowoc, WI: Wisconsin Educational Media Association, 1987).

FIGURE A.2
Many overhead projectors are equipped with a spare lamp, which can be simply slid into place.

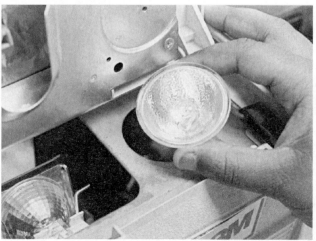

FIGURE A.1
The wrong way (left) and the correct way (right) to pick up heavy equipment.

Loading Projection Carts

- *Prohibit children from moving carts.* Only adults should be allowed to move loaded carts. A safety sticker showing the ICIA warning (shown below) should be placed on all carts.
- *Lock casters.* Be sure to engage caster locks before loading a cart.
- *Unplug cords.* Disconnect all power cords from wall outlets and wrap them around the equipment.
- *Use lower shelves.* Place equipment on the lower shelves before moving. Disconnect VCR from TV monitor before moving units to lower shelves.

Moving Projection Carts

- *Unlock casters.* Disengage all caster locks before moving the cart.
- *Push, don't pull.* Always push the cart, applying force on the narrow dimension, and watch where you're going. Never pull the cart.
- *Elevator angle.* When entering or leaving an elevator, push the cart at an angle so that one caster at a time passes over the gap between building and elevator.

- *Strap for ramp.* If a cart is to be moved up or down a ramp, use a strap to secure equipment to the cart.

Using Equipment

- *Lock casters.* Engage the caster locks as soon as the projection cart is in place.
- *Center on shelf.* Make sure equipment is centered on the cart shelf, with nothing protruding over the edge.
- *Check power cords.* Inspect for frayed cords and loose plugs. When unplugging, pull the plug, *not* the cord.
- *Secure cords.*
    - Keep power and speaker cords out of traffic lanes; leave a lot of slack.
    - Wrap the power cord around the bottom of a leg of the cart so that if someone does trip on the cord, the cart (not the equipment) is pulled.
    - Use duct tape to cover cords that could be a tripping hazard.

Source: Adapted from guidelines provided by the International Communications Industries Association (ICIA). Additional information, including safety warning stickers for carts, is available from ICIA, 3150 Spring Street, Fairfax, VA 22031.

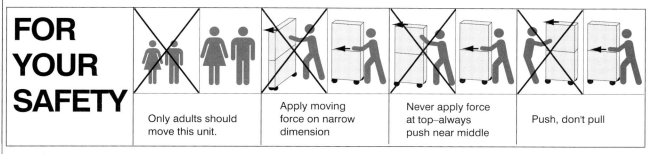

FOR YOUR SAFETY

| Only adults should move this unit. | Apply moving force on narrow dimension | Never apply force at top–always push near middle | Push, don't pull |

This safety sticker, available from the International Communications Industries Association, should be on all carts.

care. Keep it on a cart that can be rolled from one location to another. When hand-carrying the apparatus, hold onto the body of the projector, not the thin arm of the head assembly. The head assembly arm is not intended to be a carrying handle; used as such, it can easily be twisted out of alignment, thus distorting the projector's image.

Slide Projectors

With normal use, slide projectors require little special attention to keep working smoothly. The only regular maintenance required of the user is to clean the front element of the projection lens if it shows finger marks. More likely to cause difficulties are the slides themselves, which should always be stored away from heat and handled only by their mounts. The most frequent cause of foul-ups in slide presentations is a slide that jams because it is warped or dog-eared. Remount slides that could cause jams.

The Kodak Ektagraphic III projector has a number of desirable features not found on earlier models (Figure A.3). For example, the projection lamp can be changed from the rear of the projector without having to turn the projector over. There is a quick release on the elevation stand so the projected image can be raised without having to turn the adjustment knob many times by hand. In addition, the "Select" function allows the carousel tray to be turned when the power is off. Finally, the controls are on the side of the projector, where the operator usually stands.

Even though some current model projectors, such as the Ektagraphic III, do not project a distracting bright white square when there is not a slide in position, it is still recommended that you include a dark slide at the beginning and end of your presentation. Solid plastic slides work best.

The purchase and use of a carrying case for your slide projector is highly recommended if the projector is to

FIGURE A.3

The Kodak slide projectors feature convenient controls.

be moved from location to location, especially from building to building. Slide projectors should be moved only on a projector cart or within a carrying case. The case provides a place to store the projector, tray, remote control unit, a spare lamp, and remote extension cords. The carrying case helps to keep all the accessories together, decreasing the chances for loss, as well as providing protection from damage and dust.

More serious damage can occur if the slide projector falls because it has been propped up precariously on top of a stack of books or on some other unstable base. This happens all too often because the projector's elevation leg seems never to be quite long enough to raise the image up to the top of the screen. It is better to use a higher projection table, raise the whole projection table, or raise the whole projector by placing it on a sturdy box or similar platform.

Film and Film Projectors

Because film projectors and 16mm films are comparatively expensive instruments of instruction, it is particularly important for instructors to prolong the life of these items by taking proper care of them.

The average life of an acetate-based film is approximately 100 showings. The newer mylar-based film has the potential for 1,000 showings. Mishandling, however, can greatly reduce this life span of service. On the other hand, careful threading, inspection after each use, periodic lubrication of the film, and proper storage (at room temperature, 40% humidity) can lengthen the working life of the film.

Proper care of the projector can also help extend the service life of film. It is important to keep the projector's film path clean to prevent undue wear on the film. An aperture brush or other soft-bristled, nonmetallic brush should be used regularly to clean the film path, the film gate, and the area around the sound drum.

The lens of the projector should be kept free of dust and smudges by periodic cleaning with lens tissue and cleaner. The projector's volume- and tone-control mechanisms sometimes develop internal carbon buildup, causing crackling sounds when the knobs are turned to adjust audio. This debris can generally be eliminated simply by spraying around the external extensions of the control knobs with an aerosol tuner cleaner while turning the knobs.

FIGURE A.4

The varied types of equipment carts are suited to different purposes.

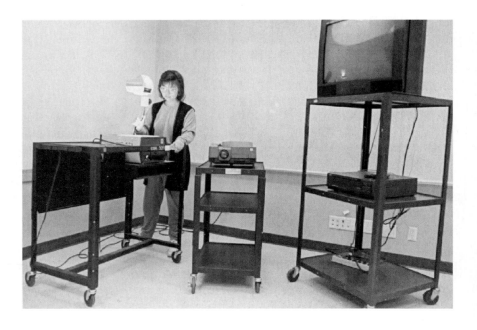

Given the electromechanical complexity of the film projector, you should not go much beyond these routine cleaning procedures to help keep your projector in good working order.

Projection Carts

Wheeled projection carts come in many different sizes and shapes suited to different types of equipment, as shown in Figures A.4 and A.5. Carts are designed both for inside-only use and inside-outside use. You take a great risk in moving equipment out of doors on a cart designed for inside use. The small wheels can catch in cracks in the pavement and cause the cart to tip over. For this reason, even for exclusive indoor use it is wise to purchase carts with 5-inch wheels.

Manufacturers normally offer power outlet cord assemblies for their carts. These are worthwhile investments. You plug your projector into the outlet on the cart and the cord on the cart into the wall outlet. If someone should trip over the power cord, the cart moves but the projector does not crash to the floor. In addition, the cord on the cart is considerably longer than the typical power cord furnished with the projector. The longer cord can be laid on the floor along the wall, thereby reducing the risk that someone will trip over it.

FIGURE A.5
A locking storage compartment can be used to secure special equipment.

The "Appraisal Checklist: Audiovisual Equipment" provides some criteria to consider when appraising new AV equipment. After purchase, there's still one major step before the process is complete—permanent identification. Most schools and other organizations identify their ownership of equipment with large, visible markings including the organization's name, address, and phone number plus an inventory number and even the lamp replacement number. Such information deters theft, simplifies taking inventory, and helps ensure that the correct replacement lamp will be inserted, a great aid for the harried teacher.

AUDIO SETUPS

Built-in Speaker Systems

Most audiovisual equipment intended for use in educational settings comes equipped with a built-in speaker system. This kind of unit is suitable for many but not all instructional purposes. Small speakers built into the chassis of portable recorders, filmstrip projectors, and so on often lack the fidelity necessary for audio clarity for a large audience area.

Portable cassette recorders are particularly troublesome when used for playback in an average-size classroom. Even under the best conditions, the sound quality of portable cassettes is severely limited by their undersized speakers. If such a unit is used to play back material in which audio fidelity is essential (e.g., a musical composition), an auxiliary speaker should be used. A high-efficiency speaker—for instance, one having a 6- or 8-inch diameter—may be plugged into the external speaker jack or earphone jack of the cassette player to provide better fidelity.

Size alone, however, does not guarantee high-quality sound from a speaker. If high-fidelity audio is needed, two-way speakers (bass and treble speaker in one cabinet) or three-way speakers (bass, midrange tweeter, and regular tweeter) are highly desirable. Such speakers may require an auxiliary amplifier when used in conjunction with AV equipment, but they are capable of reproducing the complete frequency range audible to humans.

Another problem with built-in speakers is that they are often built into the side of the machine containing the controls. This is fine when the operator of the tape recorder or the phonograph is also the listener. But if the apparatus is placed on a table or desk and operated by an instructor for the benefit of an audience, the speaker will be aimed away from the audience (see Figures A.6 and A.7). A simple way to remedy this situation is to turn the machine around so that the speaker faces the audience and operates the controls from beside rather than in front of the machine.

☑ APPRAISAL CHECKLIST

AUDIOVISUAL EQUIPMENT

Type _____   **Price** _____

Manufacturer _____   **Model** _____

Audio

Speaker Size _____   Amplifier Output _____

Inputs   Outputs

_____   _____

_____   _____

Sound controls   Tape

_____   Size _____ Tracks _____

_____   Speeds _____

Other Features

Projector

Lamp_____ Wattage_____ Exciter lamp_____

Power controls   Lamp level control

_____   _____

_____   _____

Lens_____

Rating	High	Medium	Low	Comments
Sound quality	☐	☐	☐	
Picture quality	☐	☐	☐	
Ease of operation	☐	☐	☐	
Price range	☐	☐	☐	
Durability	☐	☐	☐	
Ease to maintain	☐	☐	☐	
Ease to repair	☐	☐	☐	

Other Features

Strong Points

Weak Points

Recommended Action _____   **Name** _____   **Date** _____

FIGURE A.6

In this position the built-in speaker is facing the teacher, making the record less audible to the students.

FIGURE A.7

With the built-in speaker facing the students, audibility is much improved.

In the case of film projectors with a built-in speaker, the problem is compounded because film projectors are usually set up near the back of the room. Thus, the speaker will be behind most, if not all, of the audience. The problem may be further aggravated by noise from the projector itself. This is a tolerable situation if you have a small audience. But an auxiliary speaker will be necessary if you have a large audience.

If you are operating in a lecture hall or auditorium that has a built-in public address system, you will want to plug your projector or player into that system. This might require an adapter to match up the output plug and input jack.

Detached Speaker Systems

The detachable speakers that accompany some film projectors and stereo tape recorders are generally large and sensitive enough to provide adequate sound quality throughout the instructional area if, as with other separate speaker systems, you give consideration to their individual placement.

Whenever possible, speakers should face toward the center of your audience. If reverberation is a problem, however, especially in long narrow rooms, the speaker may be aimed diagonally across the audience to help alleviate this situation.

In the case of film projection, it is also important that the speaker be placed as close as possible to the screen. We are conditioned to expect sound to come directly from its source. We are consequently most comfortable with film sound when it appears to be coming directly from the screen image that constitutes its source.

Be sure nothing obstructs the sound waves as they travel from the speaker toward your audience. Classroom furniture (e.g., desks, chairs) and the audience itself may present physical obstructions to sound. To avoid such interference, place the speaker on a table or some other kind of stand so that it is at or above the head level of your seated audience, as in Figure A.8.

In summary, the rules of thumb for speaker placement are as follows:

- Face speaker toward the center of the audience.
- Place speaker near the screen.
- Raise speaker to head level of seated audience.

If you are using a stereophonic system, the speakers should be far enough apart so that the sound is appropriately balanced between the two. As a rule of thumb, the distance between the speakers should equal the distance from each speaker to the middle of the audience. Thus, in the typical 22- by-30-foot classroom, stereo speakers would be placed about 15 feet apart, or nearly in the corners of the room.

FIGURE A.8

For film projectors and cassette players with detachable speakers, this sort of placement gives better audibility.

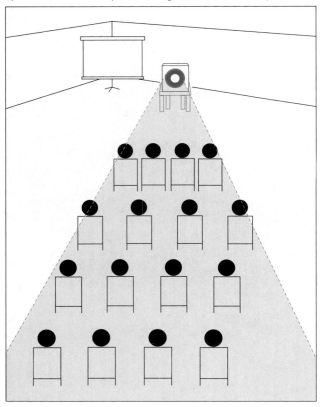

FIGURE A.9

A hand-held microphone should be held at a 45-degree angle and below the mouth.

Microphone Handling and Placement

Microphones should be placed at least 6 inches (15 centimeters) from the presenter's mouth. Placed closer to the mouth, the microphone is likely to pick up "pops" and "hisses" when the presenter says words with plosive or sibilant sounds. As shown in Figures A.9 and A.10, the microphone should be placed below the mouth so that the presenter talks across it rather than into it. The rule of thumb for microphone placement, then, is to place the microphone *below* and at least six inches *away from* the mouth.

Feedback is that annoying squeal that sometimes intrudes when public address systems are being used. The usual cause is simple: the signal coming out of the loudspeaker is fed back into the microphone. The most direct remedy is to make sure that the speakers are set up in front of the microphone, as shown in Figure A.11. If you experience feedback, here are some possible solutions:

- Place the microphone in back of the speaker(s) or move the speaker(s) in front of the microphone.
- If neither step is possible, adjust the volume and tone controls to reduce the interference.

FIGURE A.10

A lavaliere microphone should be clipped to the presenter's clothing below the mouth.

FIGURE A.11

To avoid feedback, keep the microphone in back of the speakers.

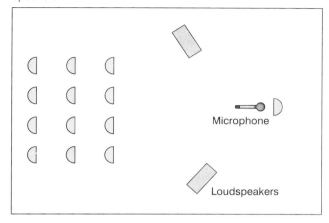

Listening Centers

As discussed in Chapter 11, many classrooms, especially at the elementary level, are arranged in a more open form with flexible furnishings to allow diverse yet simultaneous activities. In such a classroom, learning centers are a common format for learning. One popular type of learning center is a listening center, an area especially set up for audio media. Listening centers can be set up to accommodate either an individual student or a small group, as shown in Figure A.12.

A listening center should be situated away from noisy areas or at least partially enclosed to reduce visual and auditory distractions. If intended for an individual, it will probably be equipped with an audiocassette player or a CD player with a headset. Older types of headsets are designed to close the listener off from all room sounds except those coming from the player. Newer ones, referred to as "hear-through" or dynamic velocity

headsets, allow the listener to hear ambient sounds in the room also.

For a small group, the listening center would typically contain a record player or cassette player and should be equipped with a multiple headset device that allows up to eight headsets to connect to a single source.

PROJECTOR SETUPS

Screen Alignment

The first requirement in projector placement is to align the projection lens perpendicular to the screen (i.e., it must make a 90-degree angle with the screen). Thus, the lens of the projector should be about level with the middle of the screen. If the projector is too high, too low, or off to either side, a distortion of the image will occur, referred to as the *keystone effect* (Figure A.13). The effect takes its name from the typical shape of a key-stoned image—wide at the top, narrower at the bottom, like a keystone. To remedy this situation, move either the projector or the screen to bring the two into a perpendicular relationship (see "How to . . . Eliminate the Keystone Effect," p. 373).

The keystone effect is especially prevalent with the overhead projector because it is ordinarily set up very close to the screen and lower than the center of the screen to allow the instructor to write on its stage. For this reason many screens used for overhead projection are equipped with a "keystone eliminator," a notched bar at the top that allows the screen to be tilted forward (see Figure A.14).

Projector Distance

Once you have properly aligned the projector and screen, consider the distance between them. If the dis-

FIGURE A.12

A quiet corner of a classroom may be set aside as a listening center.

FIGURE A.13

The "keystone effect" describes a projected image that resembles the architectural keystone, the wedge-shaped stone at the top of a rounded arch that locks its parts together.

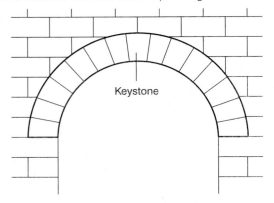

Keystone

tance is too long, the image may spill over the edges of a given screen. If it is too short, the image will not fill the same screen properly. Your goal is to fill the screen as fully as possible with the brightest image possible. The principle to remember here is that the image becomes larger and less brilliant with an increase in distance between the projector and screen. Here are some rules of thumb:

- If the projected image is *too large* for your screen, push the projector *closer.*
- If the image is *too small,* pull the projector *back.*

Positioning a projector at the proper distance from the screen need not be done solely by trial and error. Because classroom-type projectors usually are fitted with certain focal-length lenses, their proper placement can be estimated in advance. Figure A.15 shows the place-

FIGURE A.14

Portable tripod screen with keystone eliminator.

ment of the overhead, slide, and 16mm film projectors when they are equipped with their most typical lenses.

The projection distances described here assume appropriate lighting conditions. Where the room light is so bright that it is washing out the screen image and it cannot be dimmed any further, you must move the projector forward. This will give you a brighter image but also a smaller one. In some cases, however, it may be possible to compensate for this reduction in image size by having your audience move closer to the screen.

Power Cords

It is best to place all projectors, except the overhead and the opaque, behind the audience to minimize the number of people stepping over the power cords. For the same reason, extension cords should be used so that the power cords can run along the wall to the outlet rather than across the center of the room. Any cord that lies where it might be tripped over should do so only temporarily and should be firmly taped down during that time.

All modern audiovisual equipment is made with a grounded plug; you should use a matching extension cord. The outlets in older buildings may not be made for grounded plugs, so you will need to use a three-prong adapter to connect newer equipment. Extension cords are made to serve different purposes—indoor and outdoor, higher and lower power capacity. Whenever using an extension cord, be sure that you are not

FIGURE A.15

Approximate placement of projectors when used with typical lenses and screen.

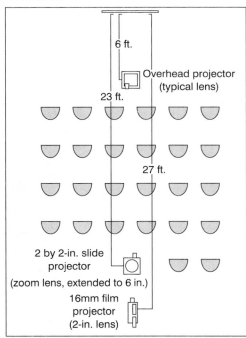

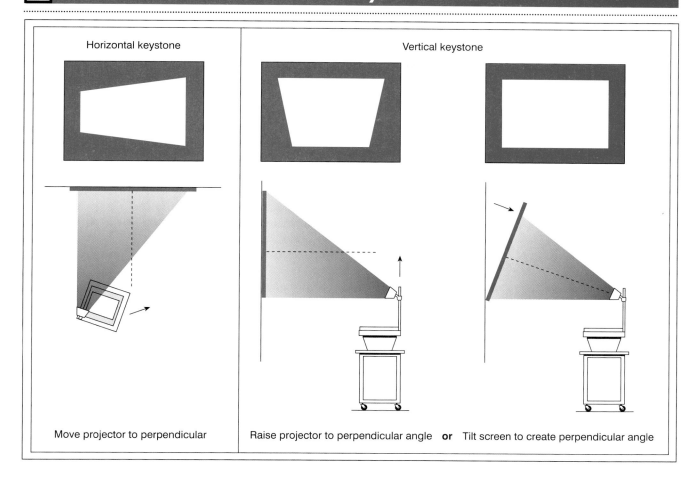

Horizontal keystone | Vertical keystone

Move projector to perpendicular | Raise projector to perpendicular angle **or** Tilt screen to create perpendicular angle

exceeding its power capacity. If in doubt, consult a media specialist.

Lamps

Types. There are three types of projection lamps: incandescent, tungsten halogen, and tungsten halogen with surrounding reflector. The incandescent lamps should be watched because they have a tendency to blister; such blisters can become so big that the lamp cannot be removed from the projector. If the lamp does blister to the extent that it must be broken for removal, an audiovisual technician should be contacted.

The first innovative response to incandescent blistering was the tungsten halogen lamp. These lamps do not blister, but they do require the same high wattage and thus have the associated heat problems and fan noise.

The newest type of lamp is the tungsten halogen lamp with surrounding reflector. These lamps generally operate at one-half the wattage of the incandescent and tungsten halogen lamps.

Coding. Projection lamps are labeled with a three-letter ANSI (American National Standards Institute) code, which is printed on the lamp and on the box. In addition, many projectors now have stickers in the lamp housing of the projectors with the ANSI code stating which lamp should be used in that projector.

Replacement of Lamps. Replacement lamps should have the same ANSI code or an authorized substitute. Substitutes can be found in replacement guides written by the lamp manufacturers; these are available from the manufacturers or from local audiovisual dealers. Do not use higher-wattage lamps than specified—you might burn the materials in the projector!

Handling. When handling a lamp, never touch the clear glass bulb. The oil from your fingers can shorten the life of the lamp. The lamp should always be manipulated by its base. The incandescent lamps and tungsten halogen lamps (without exterior reflector) are supplied with a piece of foam or paper around the lamp. This material or a cloth should be used to hold the lamp when it is inserted into the projector.

When removing a burned-out lamp, wait until the lamp has cooled to prevent burning your fingers. It is wise to always use a cloth when removing a lamp. Even a lamp that burns out when the projector is first turned on will be hot enough to burn you. (Figure A.16.)

FIGURE A.16
Avoid directly touching burned-out lamps (because they are hot) and replacement lamps (because the oil on your fingertips can shorten the life of a lamp).

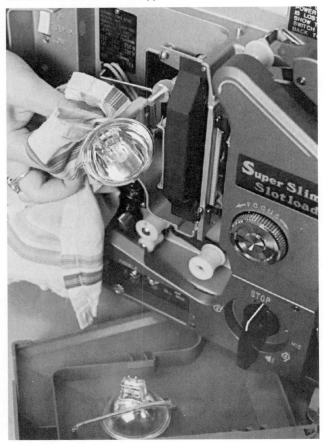

Expense. Lamps for audiovisual equipment are expensive. They usually cost about 20 times the cost of a household light bulb. Because the average lamp life is only 50 hours, projectors should be turned off when not in use. If the projector offers a low lamp setting, use it if possible to increase the life of the lamp. A projector should not be jarred when the lamp is on, as this can cause a premature burnout of the lamp. You should *not* leave the fan on for cooling after use unless the projector is going to be moved immediately, as this also will shorten the life of the bulb.

Lenses

For everyday media use you do not have to pay much attention to technicalities about lenses. Whatever lens your projector is equipped with is usually sufficient. However, understanding some basic ideas about lenses can help you cope with extraordinary situations.

First, lenses vary in focal length (measured in inches in the United States, in millimeters elsewhere). The *focal length* is the distance from the focal point of the lens to

the image plane when the lens is focused on infinity. Remember, the *longer* the focal length, the *smaller* the image at a given distance. Your objective is to project an image that will fill the screen, so the shorter the projection throw, the shorter the lens (in terms of focal length) that will be needed to enlarge the projected image sufficiently. Fortunately, the actual length of most lenses corresponds roughly with their focal length; the longer of two lenses will have the longer focal length. Figure A.17 illustrates the relationship between the lens and the size of its projected image.

One type of lens has a variable focal length—the zoom lens. It can be adjusted to cast a larger or smaller picture without moving the projector or changing its lens. The most commonly encountered zoom lens (found on many slide projectors) has a focal-length range of 4 to 6 inches.

When precise specifications are needed in selecting lenses for particular conditions, media specialists use calculation guides prepared by manufacturers, such as the "Da-Lite Lens-Projection Screen Calculator" or Kodak's "Projection Calculator and Seating Guide."

Screens

Arranging a proper environment for viewing projected visuals involves several variables, including screen size, type of screen surface, and screen placement. In most cases the instructor has to deal with only a couple of these variables. For everyday teaching situations the classroom will often be equipped with a screen of a certain type attached in a fixed position.

There may be times, however, when you will have to make decisions about any or all of these screen variables. For example, let's assume the room you are to use for projecting visuals is 22 feet wide and 30 feet long, a fairly typical size for a classroom. Let's further assume that you must arrange seating for between 30 and 40 viewers, a fairly typical audience size. Figure A.18 illustrates a conventional seating pattern for a group of this

FIGURE A.17
The longer the focal length of the lens, the smaller the image.

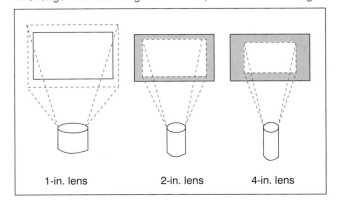

1-in. lens   2-in. lens   4-in. lens

size (in this case, 36 viewers). Note that the seats are arranged across the narrower room dimension. If the seats were turned to face the left or right side of the room and arranged across its 30-foot length, viewers along either end of the rows would have a distorted view of the screen. Note too, that the first row of seats is set back somewhat from the desk area, where the screen is to be set up, so that front-row students will not be too close to the screen for comfortable viewing.

Screen Size.

A rule of thumb for the relationship between screen size and viewer seating is called the *two-by-six rule:* No viewer should be seated closer to the screen than *two* screen widths or farther away than *six* screen widths.

This means that in our hypothetical case, in which the farthest viewer could be 30 feet from the front of the room, a screen about 5 feet wide (60 inches) would be required to ensure that this farthest-away viewer is within six screen widths of the screen ($30 \div 6 = 5$). A square screen is generally preferable because it can be used to show rectangular images (film, slides, filmstrips, etc.) as well as square images (overhead and opaque projections). Thus, in this case a screen measuring 60 by 60 inches is recommended (see Figure A.18).

With a zoom lens on a carousel slide projector or a 16mm projector, you can put the projector at the rear of any normal-size classroom and fill a 70-inch screen.

FIGURE A.18

Appropriate screen size for the typical-size classroom according to the two-by-six rule.

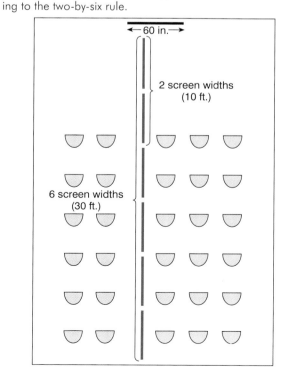

Screen Placement.

In most cases placement of the screen at the center in the front of the room will be satisfactory. In some cases, however, it may not be. Perhaps light from a window that cannot be fully covered will wash out the projected image (sunlight is much brighter than any artificial light), or maybe you wish to use the chalkboard during your presentation and a screen position in the center front will make it difficult or impossible for you to do so. Also, the screen should not be at center stage if it will attract unwanted attention while nonprojection activities are going on. An alternative position is in a front corner of the room. In any case, nowhere is it written in stone that the screen must be placed front and center. Position your screen wherever it will best suit your purpose.

The height of the screen should generally be adjusted so that the bottom of the screen is about level with the heads of the seated viewers. The bottom of the screen should be at least 4 feet above the floor to prevent excessive head interference (see Figure A.19). Other inhibiting factors aside, this arrangement will allow reasonably clear sight lines for the most viewers. In general, the higher the screen, the greater the optimal viewing area. Of course, care must be taken that the screen can be seen without viewers uncomfortably craning their necks.

VIDEO SETUPS

Before students can learn from any material presented on a video monitor, they first have to be able to see and hear it! This means providing proper seating arrangements, placement of the monitor, lighting, and volume control.

Seating

For group showings, an ideal seating arrangement may sometimes be difficult to achieve. In some cases there are simply not enough monitors available to seat all students in the most desirable viewing area. It may be possible to have students move closer together to get more people into the desirable viewing area. Try to stagger the seats to reduce blocked sight lines.

Here are some basic rules of thumb for seating:

- The total number of viewers should be no more than the number of inches of screen size. For example, for a 23-inch monitor, the largest number of viewers would be 23.
- Seat no-one closer than twice the *inches* of screen size. For example, for a 23-inch monitor, the closest viewer would be 46 inches (or about four feet) from the screen.
- Seat no-one farther *in feet* than the size of the screen in inches. For example, for a 23-inch monitor, the

FIGURE A.19
The bottom of the screen should be above head level to avoid obstruction of the view.

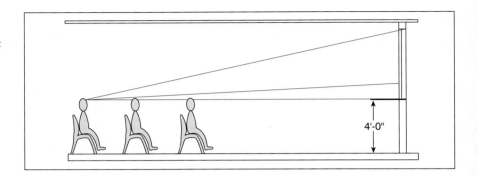

4'-0"

farthest viewer would be 23 feet away. (The maximum viewing distance would be much smaller if the lesson included details that were critical to learning.)

Monitor Placement

In addition to distance from the screen, viewing angles—both up-and-down and side-to-side—must be considered. As shown in Figure A.20, the monitor

placement should require no more than 30 degrees of head tilt. In general, a 54-inch-high monitor provides a good viewing angle for group viewing. In terms of side-to-side angles, no viewer should be located more than 45 degrees from the center line.

Lighting

Video monitors should be viewed in normal or dim light, not darkness. Besides being more comfortable to

FIGURE A.20
Recommended monitor placement and seating distances for TV viewing.

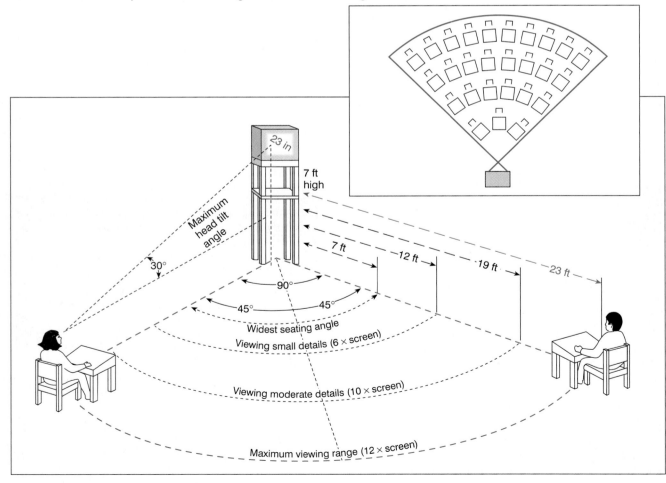

the eye, normal illumination provides necessary light for student participative activities (e.g., for referring to handouts and for note taking).

The television receiver should be located so that harsh light from a window or light fixture does not strike the screen and cause glare. Do not place the receiver in front of an unshaded window that will compete with light from the television screen and make viewing difficult.

The rules of thumb for lighting conditions for video monitors are as follows:

- View in normal or dim light.
- Avoid direct light onto screen, causing glare.
- Avoid sunlight behind monitor.

Volume

For proper hearing, the volume of the receiver should be set loud enough to be heard clearly in the rear of the viewing area but not so loud that it bowls over those in the front. Normally this happy middle ground is not difficult to achieve if your seating arrangement is within acceptable bounds and your receiver's speaker mechanism is functioning properly.

Obviously, volume should be kept low enough so as not to disturb neighboring classes. Unfortunately, open-plan buildings with only movable room dividers as walls provide a poor environment for TV and other audiovisual presentations. Under such conditions, cooperation is critical. Teachers in neighboring areas can agree to lower their sound level to minimize interference (this is better than escalating the problem by trying to drown

each other out!). Sometimes the only alternative is to seek an enclosed room that can be reserved for audiovisual use.

Projected Video

Ordinary video monitors are well suited to individual or small-group viewing but not to large-group situations. Large groups require multiple monitors for adequate viewing, and playing a video recording also requires wires to connect the video player with each of the monitors. A better option in such cases is the video projector, discussed in detail in Chapter 7. In addition to being used for showing television images, they can also be used for showing computer data, text, and graphics.

Small tabletop video projectors can project an image large enough to fill a screen up to 4 by 6 feet. Larger units that may be permanently mounted at ceiling level or placed on low carts are used for larger screens. The smaller units require less setup adjustment and may have a video playback unit built in. (See Figures A.21 and A.22.)

The larger units require color focusing adjustments whenever they are moved. They have three color "guns," and all three images must converge precisely to have a clear image without color fringes.

Other than the special focusing considerations, projected video setups follow the size, seating, and placement rules for other sorts of projection onto a screen.

The rules of thumb for lighting conditions for video projection are as follows:

- View in dim light or darkness.

FIGURE A.21
Setup for using a tabletop video projector.

FIGURE A.22
Rear projection with a ceiling mounted video projector.

- Seat audiences as close as possible to the center of the screen.
- Make sure that all can see the image clearly.

COMPUTER SETUPS

Computers and computer workstations may be arranged in an infinite variety of configurations, depending on how many computers are used in a room and for what purposes they are used. The setups described here are meant to show how to get the most out of each situation. A number of typical situations are illustrated, each showing a different number of computers being used in different ways. (See Figures A.23 through A.28.)

COMPUTER HARDWARE SELECTION

It is becoming increasingly common for instructors to be involved in the selection of instructionally related computer hardware for their institution. This section will give you at least some general guidelines for participating intelligently in such a selection process.

FIGURE A.23

A single-computer classroom with computer projection used for large-group viewing.

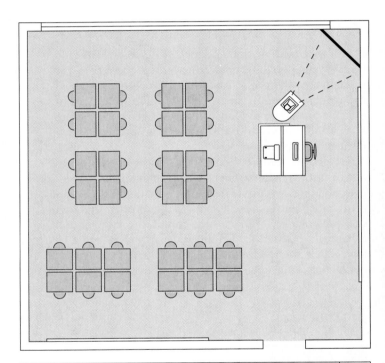

FIGURE A.24

An elementary classroom with four computers (along left wall) used for individual and small-group study. (Plan developed by Interactive Learning Systems, Inc., Cincinnati.)

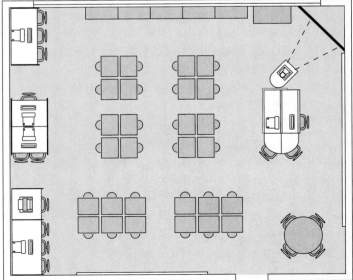

FIGURE A.25

A high school classroom with 12 computers and 2 printers (along both walls) used individually. (Plan developed by Interactive Learning Systems, Inc., Cincinnati.)

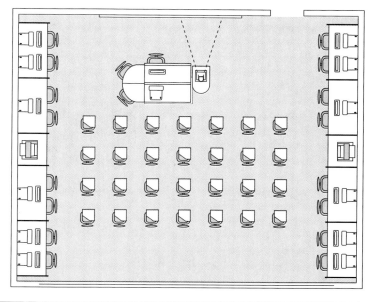

FIGURE A.26

A middle school classroom with four computers arranged in clusters for collaborative learning. (Plan developed by Interactive Learning Systems, Inc., Cincinnati.)

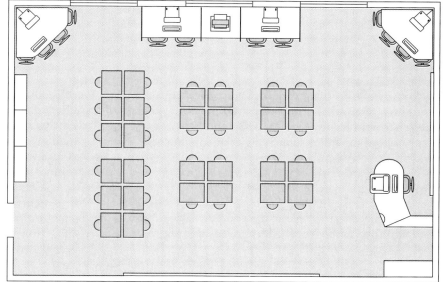

Analyzing Needs

The first step in the evaluation and selection of computer hardware is to identify the need for the hardware. Why are you buying the computer? What software are you planning to use on the system? Without identifying specific needs for the hardware, you may hastily purchase an inadequate system or one more elaborate than you could ever use.

The selection of computer software is the most important first step in the selection of hardware. Computer hardware is no better than the software that drives it. Without software a computer will not function. The computer's utility may be limited by an inadequate quantity or quality of available software. A computer may have great features, but they are of little value if there is no software to take advantage of them.

On the other hand, it is difficult for computer software to overcome limitations of the computer hardware. Since software written for one computer may not run on another computer, make sure software is currently available for the computer you are interested in.

The computer hardware industry is changing so rapidly that hardware selection decisions cannot be based solely on present needs. One must consider future software and hardware needs. By purchasing hardware with significant limitations, one is unlikely to be able to take advantage of new advancements without purchasing new hardware. It is difficult to make selection decisions for the present and an unknown future. To prevent

FIGURE A.27
A computer setup for collaborative learning.

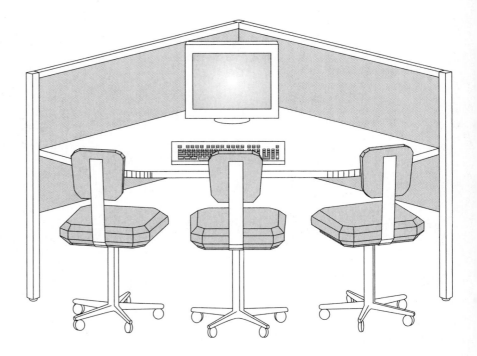

unexpected problems, it is important to look at the past performance of the hardware company from which you intend to purchase. Is the company financially stable? Are other institutions using the same equipment? Is the company committed to supporting their equipment?

Compatibility

The next major factor in selecting computer hardware is compatibility with previously purchased equipment.

However, do not allow yourself to be trapped by equipment that can never meet your needs. If a change is required, it is often better to make it sooner than later. What other computers do you have currently? What operating system do the other computers use? Is there a need for exchanging files and programs among different hardware? If so, mixing several different computers may make it difficult. In addition to being compatible with other systems currently in use, the new hardware components must be compatible with each other. Can a monitor from one manufacturer be used with a particu-

FIGURE A.28
A teaching station that can accommodate individual or small-group use and also large-group presentations.

COMPUTER HARDWARE

Manufacturer _____

Model _____

Monitor _____**Graphics** _____

Sound _____**Memory** _____**Expandable** _____**Hard Drive** _____

Peripherals _____

Rating	High	Medium	Low	Comments
Ease of operation	☐	☐	☐	
Durability/reliability	☐	☐	☐	
Availability of software	☐	☐	☐	
Monitor display quality	☐	☐	☐	
Keyboard layout and touch	☐	☐	☐	
Expandability	☐	☐	☐	
User documentation	☐	☐	☐	
Technical support	☐	☐	☐	
Local service support	☐	☐	☐	
Video display projection capability	☐	☐	☐	
Portability	☐	☐	☐	

Other Features

Strong Points

Weak Points

Recommended Action _____   **Name** _____   **Date** _____

A computer version of this Checklist is found in "The Classroom Link."

lar computer of a different make? Although some feel that it is cheaper to order various components from a catalog, the buyer must beware that not all components are necessarily compatible. Get specific assurance of compatibility from the vendor.

Expandability

Expandability is also an important consideration when purchasing a computer system. You don't want the announcement of a new model shortly after your purchase to render your equipment obsolete. Nor do you want to buy a system that is sufficient for your current needs but unable to be upgraded to accommodate your growing ambitions. To protect yourself, be sure that the system you purchase has the ports and slots to accommodate additional memory, additional disk drives, audio or video enhancement, and the like. (A port is an outlet on a computer where the user can plug in a peripheral. A slot is an area in the computer where the user can add additional electronic boards or cards for specific purposes.)

Documentation

The documentation, or user's manual, must be easy for you to understand. It should have an extensive index and table of contents to allow easy access to the information. Diagrams should be included to show the various parts of your system and how to put them together.

Service

Be sure the hardware company you buy from is committed to supporting and maintaining the equipment you plan to purchase. How long has its service center been established? You may want to talk with others who have used their service. Were they satisfied? Was service prompt? Finding someone to service computers often becomes a difficult and frustrating experience. Sometimes you have to ship hardware to a service location, thus being inconvenienced for a time. If shipping is required, do you have easy access to shipping locations nearby or does the shipping service provide pickup of your packages?

A maintenance contract should be a consideration when purchasing hardware. Such a contract may vary in cost from a few dollars a month for each machine to many times that amount. However, most personal computer systems tend to be reliable. Most failures and problems occur during the warranty period. Once through the warranty period, breakdowns are infrequent as long as you take proper care of your equipment. The actual cost of the repairs may be cheaper than the cost of a maintenance contract.

In comparing models, many different criteria should be considered. The "Appraisal Checklist: Computer Hardware" includes the most important criteria for selecting a computer for instructional uses. The weighting of the criteria may vary depending on the specifics of your particular situation.

REFERENCES
Print References

Anshel, Jeffrey. "Visual Ergonomics in the Workplace: How to Use a Computer and Save your Eyesight." *Performance and Instruction* (May–June 1994): 20–22.

Barron, Ann E., and Orwig, Gary W. *New Technologies for Education: A Beginner's Guide.* Englewood, CO: Libraries Unlimited, 1993.

Bullard, John R., and Mether, Calvin E. *Audiovisual Fundamentals: Basic Equipment Operation, Simple Materials Production.* 3d ed. Dubuque, IA: Wm. C. Brown, 1984.

Casciero, Albert J., and Roney, Raymond G. *Audiovisual Technology Primer.* Englewood, CO: Libraries Unlimited, 1988.

The Directory of Video, Computer, and Audio-Visual Products. Fairfax, VA: International Communications Industries Association, annual.

Hofstetter, Fred T. "Design and Construction of a Multimedia Technology Cart." *Tech Trends 38* (March 1993): 22–24.

Meisel, Susan Lee. "A Hard Look at Audiovisual Equipment." *Media and Methods* (October 1983): 9–11, 48.

Novak, Paul. "How to Use Media Equipment," in G. M. Piskurich (ed.). *The ASTD Handbook of Instructional Technology.* New York: McGraw-Hill, 1993.

Schroeder, Don, and Lare, Gary. *Audiovisual Equipment and Materials: A Basic Repair and Maintenance Manual.* 2d ed. Metuchen, NJ: Scarecrow Press, 1989.

Sherry, Annette C., and Strojny, Allan. "Design for Safety: The Audiovisual Cart Hazard Revisited." *Educational Technology* (December 1993): 2–47.

Teague, Fred A., Rogers, Douglas W., and Tipling, Roger N. *Technology and Media: Instructional Applications.* Dubuque, IA: Kendall/Hunt, 1994.

Audiovisual References

David's Legacy. Fairfax, VA: International Communications Industries Association, 1989. Videocassette. 15 minutes.

A Layman's Guide to Minor VCR Repair. Charlotte, NC: Multi-Video, 1988. Videocassette. 45 minutes.

The following VHS videocassettes are available from Audiovisual Center Marketing, C215 Seashore Hall, University of Iowa, Iowa City, IA 52242.

General Operating Principles for AV Equipment. 1983. 7 minutes.

(Media Fears) Programming the Multislide Show. 1989. 13 minutes.

Operating the Camcorder. 1990. 8 minutes.

Pre-production Planning for Video. 1990. 10 minutes.

Programming Synchronized Slide-Tape Shows. 1988. 11 minutes.

Romancing the Eiki: The Story of a Slotloading Projector. 1988. 11 minutes.

Single Camera VCR System. 1983. 7 minutes.

16mm Projector. 1983. 7 minutes.

Videotape Editing. 1990. 8 minutes.

COPYRIGHT GUIDELINES

BACKGROUND: THE COPYRIGHT LAW

To protect the financial interests of the creators, producers, and distributors of original works of information and art, nations adopt what are referred to as copyright laws. These laws set the conditions under which anyone may copy, in whole or in part, original works transmittable in any medium. Without copyright laws, professionals like writers, artists, and media producers would not "receive the encouragement they need to create the remuneration they fairly deserve for their creations," according to the legislative 1976 Omnibus Copyright Revision Act. The flow of creative work would be reduced to a trickle, and we would all be the losers.

The first copyright law in the United States was passed by Congress in 1790. In 1976 Congress enacted the latest copyright law, taking into consideration technological developments that had occurred since the passage of the Copyright Act of 1909. For example, in 1909, anyone who wanted to make a single copy of a literary work for personal use had to do so by hand. The very process imposed a limitation on the quantity of materials copied. Today, a photocopier can do the work in seconds; the limitation has disappeared. The 1909 law did not provide full protection for films and sound recordings, nor did it anticipate the need to protect radio and television. As a result, violations of the law and abuses of the intent of the law have lessened the financial rewards of authors, artists, and producers. The 1976 Copyright Act has not prevented these abuses fully, but it has clarified the legal rights of the injured parties and given them an avenue for redress.

Since 1976 the act has been amended to include computer software, and guidelines have been adopted for fair use of television broadcasts. These changes have cleared up much of the confusion and conflict that followed in the wake of the 1976 legislation.

The fine points of the law are decided by the courts and by acceptable common practice over time. As these decisions and agreements are made, we modify our behavior accordingly. For now, we need to interpret the law and its guidelines as accurately as we can and to act in a fair, judicious manner.

INTERPRETING THE COPYRIGHT ACT

Although detailed examination of the law is beyond the scope of this text, here we describe the basic framework of the law and present examples of violations and of reasonable interpretation of "fair use" to help guide you in the decision you need to make about copying protected works for class use. The law sets forth in section 107 four basic criteria for determining the principle of fair use:

- The purpose and character of the use, including whether such use is of a commercial nature or is for nonprofit educational purposes
- The nature of the copyrighted work
- The amount and substantiality of the portion used in relation to the copyrighted work as a whole
- The effect of the use on the potential market for or value of the copyrighted work.

The following interpretations are based on several sets of guidelines issued to spell out the criteria in section 107.

For educational use, a teacher may make a single copy of a chapter from a book; an article from a periodical or newspaper; a short story, short essay, or short poem, whether or not from a collective work; an illustration from a book, periodical, or newspaper. The context in which the term *teacher* is used seems to be broad enough to include support personnel working with teachers and trainers.

The guidelines further stipulate the amount of material that may be copied and the special circumstances that permit multiple copies. "Fair use" is defined as one illustration per book or periodical, 250 words from a poem, and 10% of a prose work up to 1,000 words. Multiple copies cannot exceed the number of students in a class, nor can there be more than nine instances of multiple copying for one course during one class term. Not more than two excerpts or one short poem, article, story, or essay may be copied from the same author. These limitations (i.e., nine instances of multiple copying; two excerpts or one short item) do not apply to current news periodicals, newspapers, and current news sections of other periodicals.

However, multiple copies must meet a "spontaneity" test. The copying must be initiated by the individual teacher, not directed or suggested by any other authority. The decision to use the work and the "inspiration" for its use must be close enough to the moment of use to preclude waiting for permission from the copyright holder. This means, of course, that the same "inspiration" cannot occur the same time next term.

The last guideline, concerning market value, means that copying must not substitute for purchasing the original or creating or replacing an anthology or compilation of works protected by copyright. It also prohibits copying works intended to be consumable (e.g., workbooks and standardized tests).

If a work is out of print (i.e., no longer available from the copyright holder), you are not affecting the market value of the work by copying it. The market value guideline can act in favor of the user, as we will see from the following examples.

The term, or period of time, of the copyright has been changed by the new act. For an individual author, the copyright term continues for his or her life and for 50 years after his or her death. If a work is made for hire (i.e., by an employee or by someone commissioned to do the work), the term is 100 years from the year of creation or 75 years from the year of first publication or distribution, whichever comes first. Works copyrighted prior to January 1, 1978, are protected for 28 years and then may have their copyrights renewed. The renewal will protect them for a term of 75 years after their original copyright date.

Computer Software and Copyright

Congress amended the copyright act to clear up questions of fair use of copyrighted computer programs. The changes defined the term *computer program* for copyright purposes and set forth permissible and non-permissible use of copyrighted computer software programs. According to the amended law, with a single copy of a program, you *may* do the following:

- Make one back-up or archival copy of a computer program; also, a "locksmith" program may be used to bypass the copy-prevention code on the original to make the archival copy.
- Adapt a computer program from one language to another if the program is not available in that language.
- Add features to a copyrighted program to make better use of the program.
- Adapt a copyrighted program to meet local needs.

Without the copyright owner's permission, you *may not* do the following with a single copy:

- Make multiple copies of a copyrighted program.
- Make additional copies from an archival or back-up copy.
- Make copies of copyrighted programs to be sold, leased, loaned, transmitted, or given away.
- Sell a locally produced adaptation of a copyrighted program.
- Make multiple copies of an adaptation of a copyrighted program even for use within a school or school district.
- Put a single copy of a program onto a network without permission or a special site license.
- Make any use of the printed copyrighted software documentation unless allowed by the copyrighted program.

These guidelines seem to be reasonable while still protecting the proprietary rights of copyright holders. In fact, the guidelines are more liberal than those affecting the use of audiovisual materials.

Off-Air Videotaping

The Copyright Act of 1976 did not cover educational uses of videotaped copies of copyrighted broadcasts. A negotiating committee composed of representatives from industry, education, and government agreed on a set of guidelines for video recording of broadcasts for educational use. According to these guidelines, you *may* do the following:

- Ask a media center to record the program for you if you cannot do so or if you lack the equipment.
- Retain a videotaped copy of a broadcast (including cable transmission) for a period of 45 calendar days, after which the program must be erased.
- Use the program in class once during the first 10 school days of the 45 calendar days, and a second time if instruction needs to be reinforced.
- Have professional staff view the program several times for evaluation purposes during the full 45-day period.
- Make a limited number of copies to meet legitimate needs, but these copies must be erased when the original videotape is erased.
- Use only a part of the program if instructional needs warrant.
- Enter into a licensing agreement with the copyright holder to continue use of the program.

You (and media centers) *may not* do the following:

- Videotape premium cable services such as HBO without express permission.
- Alter the original content of the program.
- Exclude the copyright notice on the program.
- Record a program in anticipation of a request for use; the request to record must come from an instructor.
- Retain the program, and any copies, after 45 days.

Remember that these guidelines are not part of the copyright act but are rather a "gentleman's agreement" between producers and educators. You should accept them as guidelines in good faith.

Distance Learning Settings

The electronic delivery of instruction has created new concerns related to the copyright law. For the most part, the Fair Use clause (see next section) applies. However, certain specific considerations have been recognized in distance learning:

- Tapes for nonprofit educational institutions are to be retained no more than 45 days.
- Off-air recordings may not be altered from their original content. This includes combining or merging, physically or electronically, to constitute teaching anthologies or compilations.

Broadcasting of copyrighted materials is allowed if the following terms are met:

- The broadcast is part of a systematic, ongoing instructional activity.
- It is directly related and of material assistance to the teaching content.
- Transmission is received in classrooms only, or similar settings normally devoted to instruction.
- The broadcast is aimed at regularly enrolled students and conducted by a recognized educational institution.
- If the class is being recorded, it is a definite copyright infringement if prior approval for material presentation is not obtained.

Media and Fair Use

Until the courts decide otherwise, teachers (and media professionals) can use the fair use criteria to decide when to copy materials that would otherwise be protected. Some examples follow.

Example 1. If the school media center subscribes to a journal or magazine to which you refer students and you make slides of several graphics or photos to help students understand an article, this would be fair use based on the following criteria:

- The nature of the work is general, and its audience (and market) is not predominantly the educational community.
- The character of use is nonprofit.
- The amount copied is minimal.
- There is no intent to replace the original, only to make it more useful in a class in conjunction with the copyrighted words.

Example 2. If you subscribe to a journal and include several pictures from it in a presentation in class, it would seem reasonable to do so for the same reasons as identified in Example 1.

Example 3. Suppose a film or video you frequently use drops out of the distributor's catalog; it is now "out of print." To protect the print you now have, it would seem reasonable, after unsuccessful attempts to reach the copyright owner to get permission, to copy the film or video and use the copy in class. If, at a later date, the title is put back on the market by the same or another distributor, you must go back to using your original print. This is not uncommon. For example, *Pacific 231,* an effective film to demonstrate editing, was originally distributed by Young America Films. After Young America Films was purchased by another company, *Pacific 231* was dropped from the catalog. It was not available for almost 20 years. Then, Pyramid Films secured the distribution rights, and it is now available for purchase. During the period of unavailability, it would have been reasonable to use a videotape copy.

Example 4. From experience you know that recordings of literary works put out by major record labels may disappear from their catalogs in a few years. For example, RCA Victor once made available a recording of Shakespeare's *Midsummer Night's Dream* with Mendelssohn's incidental music inserted at the appropriate place. It is no longer available. If you had taped the records, put the tapes on the shelf as a contingency, and used the records in class, you would at least have the tape available if your records were damaged. You would not have intended to deprive anyone of income; you would simply have used the technology to guarantee availability to yourself.

Example 5. You have rented a film for a specific date, but circumstances beyond your control prevent you from using it before it is due back. It would seem reasonable, after requesting permission (a telephone call could clear it), to videotape this film, use the videotape, and then erase the tape after use. Again, you have not deprived anyone of income. (This should never be done if you have the film on a preview basis.)

With the cited exceptions of broadcast programs and computer software, there are no guidelines for fair use of nonprint materials. Until the courts decide otherwise, it would seem reasonable to extend the print guidelines to nonprint materials in a judicious fashion.

We are not advocating deliberate violation of the law. On the contrary, we support the intent of the copyright law to protect the financial interests of copyright holders. What we are saying is that the proper balance in the application of the guidelines eventually has to be decided by the courts and accepted common practice. In the meantime, reasonable interpretations of fair use may permit you to do copying that might seem on the face of it to be prohibited.

EDUCATORS AND THE COPYRIGHT LAW

What happens if an educator knowingly and deliberately violates the copyright law? The 1976 act contains both criminal and civil sanctions. The criminal penalty can be a fine up to $1,000 and a year in jail. Copyright owners may recover up to $50,000 in civil court for loss of royalties due to infringement. Furthermore, in any infringement lawsuit, the employing institution can be held liable along with the educator. In 1990, Congress amended the copyright law to strip public institutions and agencies of "sovereign immunity," a principle rooted in English law that exempts the "sovereign" from being sued without its consent.

In 1982 a home economics teacher in San Diego was found guilty of copying and distributing substantially more than 10% of a copyrighted book. In a highly publicized case, Kinko's, a copy shop, was found guilty in 1990 of violating the copyright law by mass-producing collections of protected materials for professors. Since that ruling, Kinko's and other photocopying stores have tightened up compliance with copyright regulations before putting together collections of articles for class use.

A Board of Cooperative Education Services was found guilty of distributing videotapes of copyrighted material. The media personnel in this case flagrantly violated the law. You may become a media professional in charge of a media center. Before copying material at the request of a teacher, make sure you are not violating the law, or you may find yourself in court.

Many teachers rely on media centers to produce multimedia presentations for them. If the presentations are for class use, the fair use guidelines apply. But if the presentations are for a conference or other public event, permission for use of copyrighted material must be obtained. Normally this is no problem if the public event is educational in nature and no fee is paid to the presenter.

We must remember, punitive damages aside, that in professions devoted to promoting ethical behavior, deliberate violation of the copyright law is unacceptable. A particularly thorough and up-to-date guide for educators and librarians is found in Bruwelheide (see References).

Seeking Permission for Use of Copyrighted Materials

Aside from staying within the guidelines that limit but recognize our legal right to free use of copyrighted materials, what else can we do to assure our students access to these materials? We can, obviously, seek permission from copyright owners and, if requested, pay a fee for their use. Certain requests will ordinarily be granted without payment of fee—transcripts for the blind, for example, or material to be tried out once in an experimental program. Permission is not needed for use of materials in the public domain—materials on which copyright protection has run out, for instance, or materials produced by federal government employees in the course of their regular work.

In seeking permission to use copyrighted materials, it is generally best to contact the distributor or publisher of the material rather than its creator. Whether or not the creator is the holder of the copyright, the distributor or publisher generally handles permission requests and sets fees. The address of the producer (if not given on the material) can be obtained from various reference sources, including *Literary Market Place,* *Audio-Visual Market Place,* and *Ulrich's International Periodical Directory.*

Be as specific as possible in your request for permission. Give the page numbers and exact amount of print material you wish to copy. (If possible, send along a photocopy of the material.) Describe nonprint material fully. State how you intend to use the material, where you intend to use the material, and the number of copies you wish to make.

Remember that fees for reproduction of copyrighted materials are sometimes negotiable. If the fee seems to be too high or otherwise beyond your budget, do not hesitate to ask whether it can be lowered.

If for any reason you decide not to use the requested material, make this fact known to the publisher or producer. Without this formal notice it is likely to be assumed that you have in fact used it as requested and you may be charged for a fee you do not in fact owe.

Keep copies of all your correspondence and records of all other contacts that you made relevant to seeking permission for use of copyrighted instructional materials.

Primacy of First Sale

Have you ever wondered why public libraries, book rental businesses, and video rental clubs are not in violation of the copyright law when they do not pay royalties to copyright owners on the items they circulate or rent? They come under the protection of what is referred to as the "primacy of first sale." This means that the purchaser of a copyrighted work may loan or rent the work without having to pay a second royalty. Great pressure is being put on Congress to amend the law to require anyone who rents a copyrighted work to pay a royalty to the copyright owner. As you might expect, the television and motion picture industries are putting on the pressure, and video rental agencies are resisting the change.

Although it is not likely that the free circulation of materials from public libraries and regional media centers will be affected by a change such as this, college and university rental of films and videotapes certainly will be. Educators need to be aware of possible changes in the first-sale doctrine that could adversely affect access to materials.

SUMMARY

We have concentrated here on the problem of copyrighted materials for educational purposes and on the guidelines set up under the 1976 act to help ensure that such duplication does not violate the law or otherwise infringe on copyright ownership. The act itself contains hundreds of these provisions, covering all aspects of copyright law and ownership. Some of these provisions are of particular interest to educators—provisions covering copying by libraries, for example, or use of copyrighted materials for instruction of the visually handicapped or the hearing impaired. Other provisions may be of interest to those who have authored or plan someday to author or produce instructional materials. In any case, it behooves each of us to be familiar at least with those aspects of the law likely to affect our own special activities and interests.

REFERENCES

Print References

AIME. *Copyright Information Packet.* Elkader, IA: Association for Information Media and Equipment, 1993.

Bruwelheide, Janis. *The Copyright Primer for Librarians and Educators.* 2d ed. Chicago: American Library Association, 1995.

"Copyright Law and the Classroom." *Journal of Law and Education* (Spring 1986): 229–236.

Cyrs, T., and Smith, F. *Teleclass Teaching.* Las Cruces, NM: Center for Educational Development, 1990.

Fischer, L., Schimmel, D., and Kelly, C. *Teachers and the Law.* White Plains, NY: Longman, 1991.

Helm, Virginia M. *What Educators Should Know About Copyright.* Bloomington, IN: Phi Delta Kappan, 1986.

Hoadley, D., and Hoadley, M. *Copyright: Rights and Liabilities of Authors and Users of Multimedia Presentations.* STATE Technology and Teacher Education Annual, 1993.

Jensen, M. "CD-ROM Licenses: What's in the Fine or Nonexistent Print May Surprise You." *CD-ROM Professional* (March 1991): 13–16.

KIDSNET. *Copyright: Staying Within the Law—A Resource Guide for Educators.* Alexandria, VA: PBS Elementary/Secondary Service, 1988.

Miller, J. K. *Using Copyrighted Videocassettes in Classrooms, Libraries, and Training Centers.* 2d ed. Friday Harbor, WA: Copyright Information Services, 1990.

National Education Association. *The New Copyright Law: Questions Teachers and Librarians Ask.* Washington, DC: National Education Association, 1977.

Reed, M. H. "Computer Software: Copyright and Licensing Considerations for Schools and Libraries." *ERIC Digest* (ED308856). Syracuse, NY: ERIC Clearinghouse on Information Resources, 1989.

Sinofsky, E. *A Copyright Primer for Educational and Industrial Media Producers.* 2d ed. Washington, DC: Association for Educational Communications and Technology, 1994.

Soloman, K. "Copyright Issues and Distance Learning." *Teleconference* (1993): 18–21.

Talab, R. S. *Copyright and Instructional Technologies: A Guide to Fair Use and Permissions Procedures.* 2d ed. Washington, DC: Association for Educational Communications and Technology, 1989.

The Visual Artist's Guide to the New Copyright Law. New York: Graphic Artists Guild, 1978.

Vlcek, C. W. "Writing Your Own School Copyright Policy." *Media and Methods* (March–April, 1988): 27.

Audiovisual References

Computer/Copyright Seminar, 1987. Friday Harbor, WA: Copyright Information Services, 1987. Audiocassettes and documents.

Copyright Law. Lincoln, NB: Great Plains National Instructional Television Library, 1986. Videocassette. 20 minutes. Produced by the Office of Instructional Technology, South Carolina Department of Education and South Carolina ETV Network.

Copyright Law: What Every School, College, and Public Library Should Know. Skokie, IL: Association for Information Media and Equipment, 1987. Videotape.

Don't Copy That Floppy. Washington, DC: Software Publishers Association, 1992. Videotape.

Video/Copyright Seminar, 1987. Friday Harbor, WA: Copyright Information Services, 1987. Audiocassette and documents.

INFORMATION SOURCES

nstructors ordinarily begin their search for needed instructional media in the media collection at their own facility. School personnel then turn to the catalogs of media collections housed at the school district or regional educational service center. But where can you turn beyond your own organization? And where can your organization obtain the materials that you need? This appendix will help you to gain access to the wealth of audiovisual resources available for rental or purchase from commercial and noncommercial sources.

COMPREHENSIVE INFORMATION SOURCES

Assuming that you have identified an instructional need for which audiovisual materials are not available within your organization, where might you begin searching for another supplier? The most comprehensive information sources are listed on CD-ROM and in a set of four printed directories compiled by the National Information Center for Educational Media (NICEM).

The online and CD-ROM product is "A-V Online." Here is a brief description of what it offers:

> Distributional sources for educational media on videotape, film, audiocassette, and other formats. Incorporates records from the Library of Congress, publishers' catalogs, and library collections. Materials from 1900 to present. Over 350,000 descriptions of videotapes, 16mm films, audio-tapes, filmstrips, slide sets, transparencies and film cartridges of educational, documentary, or informational nature.[1]

NICEM produces four print directories:

- *Audiocassette and Compact Disc Finder: A Subject Guide to Educational and Literary Materials on Audiocassettes and Compact Discs*
- *Film and Video Finder*
- *Filmstrip and Slide Set Finder*
- *Index to AV Producers and Distributors*

These directories are published by:

Plexus Publishing
143 Old Marlton Pike
Medford, NJ 08055

For more information, contact:

NICEM
Access Innovations, Inc.
P.O. Box 40130
Albuquerque, NM 87196

The Multimedia and Videodisc Compendium is an index devoted exclusively to videodiscs and multimedia. It lists them by subject category for laserdiscs, CDs, and multimedia software. Also included are prices and phone numbers for producers. It is published by:

Emerging Technology Consultants
P.O. Box 12444
St. Paul, MN 55112

Other reference works covering a broad range of media and content areas include the following:

Donavin, Denise Perry, ed. *American Library Association Best of the Best for Children: Books, Software, Magazines, Videos, Audio, Toys, Travel.* New York: Random House, 1992.

Lee, Lauren K., ed. *The Elementary School Library Collection: A Guide to Books and other Media, Phases 1-2-3.* 19th ed. Williamsport, PA: Brodart, 1994.

It would be impractical to list here all the thousands of suppliers of free and inexpensive materials, much less to offer up-to-date addresses. Instead we recommend that you consult one of the many books, catalogs, and magazines devoted specifically to free and inexpensive materials. They are updated regularly and contain current addresses and cost information.

The most comprehensive information source of free and inexpensive materials is the series of guides published by:

Educators Progress Service
214 Center Street
Randolph, WI 53956

There is a cost for the guides themselves; the materials listed in the guides are either free or inexpensive. Revised annually, the titles in this series include:

- *Free Curriculum Materials* (printed materials)
- *Free Films*
- *Free Filmstrips and Slides*
- *Free Guidance Materials* (mixed media)
- *Free Health, Physical Education, and Recreational Materials* (mixed media)
- *Free Home Economics and Consumer Education Materials* (mixed media)
- *Free Science Materials* (mixed media)
- *Free Social Studies Materials* (mixed media)
- *Free Videotapes*
- *Guide to Free Computer Materials* (mixed media)
- *Grade Guide to Free Teaching Aids* (printed materials)
- *Index of Free Materials* (printed materials)

The following books and magazines also list sources of free and inexpensive materials:

Bowman, Linda. *Freebies for Kids and Parents Too!* Chicago, IL: Probus, 1991.

Freebies editors. *Freebies for Teachers.* Los Angeles: Lowell House, 1994.

---

[1] From the Introduction to "A-V Online" database. "A-V Online" is available on DIALOG (File 46), via Compuserve, or on CD-ROM from SilverPlatter.

Langston, Diane Jones, and Smith, Adeline M. *Free Magazines for Libraries*. 4th ed. Jefferson: NC, 1994.

Freebies: The Magazine with Something for Nothing (published five times per year); P.O. Box 5025; Carpinteria, CA 93014-5025

The following national service offers free loan of videotapes and films:

Modern Talking Pictures Service
5000 Park Street N.
St. Petersburg, FL 33709

This agency provides sponsored videos and films for free loan from its offices in major cities throughout the United States and Canada.

The U. S. government offers free and inexpensive materials, such as *Selected U.S. Government Publications*, through the following agencies:

Superintendent of Documents
U.S. Government Printing Office
Washington, DC 20402

National Audiovisual Center
National Archives and Records Administration
8700 Edgeworth Drive
Capitol Heights, MD 20743-3701

SPECIALIZED INFORMATION SOURCES

Audio

Schwann Record and Tape Guide. Monthly. Boston: ABC Schwann Publications. (Available from many record and tape stores.)

Voegelin-Carter, Ardis. *Words on Tape: A Guide to the Audio Cassette Market*. Westport, CT: Mecrier, 1991.

Video and Film

Blenz-Clucas, Beth, and Gribble, Gloria, eds. *Recommended Videos for Schools*. Santa Barbara, CA: ABC-CLIO, 1991.

Bowker's Complete Video Directory. Annual. New York: R.R. Bowker.

Stevens, Gregory I., ed. *Videos for Understanding Diversity: A Core Selection and Evaluative Guide*. Chicago: American Library Association, 1993.

Video Source Book. Annual. Syosset, NY: National Video Clearinghouse.

Simulations and Games

Gredler, Margaret E. *Designing and Evaluating Games and Simulations: A Process Approach*. Houston, TX; London: Gulf Publishing Co., 1994.

Computer Courseware, Multimedia

Amazing Computing. 12 issues per year.
AC's Guide. Annual.

Both software programs are available for the Amiga. For more information, contact:

Amiga
P.O. Box 869
Fall River, MA 02722-0869

A catalog of shareware programs for IBM PCs and compatibles is available free from:

Reasonable Solutions
2101 West Main Street
Medford, OR 97501

Microcomputer Index. Annual. Santa Clara, CA: Microcomputer Information Services.

Neill, Shirley Boes, and Neill, George W. *Only the Best: Annual Guide to Highest-Rated Education Software/ ΔMultimedia for Preschool–Grade 12*.
Education News Service
P.O. Box 1789
Carmichael, CA 95609.

Parent's Guide to Highly Rated Educational Software
EPIE Institute
103 West Montauk Highway
Hampton Bays, NY 11946

Pride, Bill, and Pride, Mary. *Prides' Guide to Educational Software*. Wheaton, IL: Crossway Books, 1992.

Software Encyclopedia includes Mac shareware. For more information, contact:

EDUCORP Computer Services
7434 Trade Street
San Diego, CA 92121-2410

What's What in Educational Shareware for IBM-Compatible Computers
Computer Stewards
P.O. Box 8266
Colorado Springs, CO 80933-8266

CD-ROM

CD-ROMs in Print
Meckler Publishing
11 Ferry Lane West
Westport, CT 06880

Shelton, James, ed. *CD-ROM Finder*. 5th ed. Medford, NJ: Learned Information, 1993.

Sorrow, Barbara Head, and Betty S. Lumpkin. *CD-ROM for Librarians and Educators: A Resource Guide to Over 300 Instructional Programs*. Jefferson, NC: McFarland, 1993.

Equipment

The Directory of Video, Computer, and Audio-Visual Products. Annual. Fairfax, VA: International Communications Industries Association.

COMMERCIAL INFORMATION SOURCES

Commercial producers and distributors of audiovisual materials publish promotional catalogs of their wares. Companies often assemble a special school and library catalog, arranged by subject or medium, to display their offerings more effectively. When you use these catalogs, keep in mind the bias of the seller. The descriptions given and the claims made do not pretend to be objective. Any purchases should be guided by objective evidence such as field-test results, published reviews, and local appraisals based on previews.

A sampling of major audiovisual producers and distributors follows. The alphabetical lists of companies are grouped roughly according to the media format(s) with which they are identified.

Nonprojected Visuals

Educational Insights
19560 Rancho Way
Dominguez Hills, CA 90220

Encyclopaedia Britannica Educational Corp.
310 S. Michigan Avenue
Chicago, IL 60604-9839

Society for Visual Education, Inc. (SVE)
55 East Monroe, 34th floor
Chicago, IL 60603-5803

Overhead Transparencies

Denoyer-Geppert Science Co.
5215 N. Ravenswood Avenue
Chicago, IL 60640

Encyclopaedia Britannica Educational Corp.
310 S. Michigan Avenue
Chicago, IL 60604-9839

Rand McNally
8255 Central Park Avenue
Skokie, IL 60076

3M Company
Visual Systems Division
Building A146 5N-01
6801 River Place Boulevard
Austin, TX 78726

Filmstrips

Ambrose Video Publishing Co.
381 Park Avenue South
New York, NY 10016

Argus Communications
One DLM Park
P.O. Box 7000
Allen, TX 75002

Coronet/MTI Film and Video
108 Wilmot Road, 5th floor
Deerfield, IL 60015

Denoyer-Geppert Science Co.
5215 N. Ravenswood Avenue
Chicago, IL 60640

Educational Images, Ltd.
P.O. Box 3456, West Side
Elmira, NY 14905

EMC Publishing
300 York Avenue
St. Paul, MN 55101

Encyclopaedia Britannica Educational Corp.
310 S. Michigan Avenue
Chicago, IL 60604-9839

Hawkhill Associates, Inc.
125 E. Gilman St.
Madison, WI 53701-1029

International Film Bureau
332 S. Michigan Avenue
Chicago, IL 60604

January Productions
210 Sixth Avenue
P.O. Box 66
Hawthorne, NJ 07507

Knowledge Unlimited
P.O. Box 52
Madison, WI 53701-0052

National Film Board of Canada (NFBC)
1251 Avenue of the Americas, 16th floor
New York, NY 10020

Society for Visual Education, Inc. (SVE)
55 East Monroe, 34th floor
Chicago, IL 60603-5803

Weston Woods Studios
389 Newton Turnpike
Weston, CT 06883

Slides

American Museum of Natural History
Central Park West at 79th Street
New York, NY 10024

The Center for Humanities, Inc.
Box 1000, Communications Park
Mt. Kisco, NY 10549

Harcourt Brace Jovanovich
6277 Sea Harbor Drive
Orlando, FL 32887

Metropolitan Museum of Art
Educational Marketing
6 East 82nd Street
New York, NY 10028

National Audubon Society
700 Broadway
New York, NY 10003

National Geographic Society
Education Services Division
1145 17th Street NW
Washington, DC 20036

Society for Visual Education, Inc. (SVE)
55 East Monroe, 34th floor
Chicago, IL 60603-5803

Ward's Natural Science Establishment, Inc.
P.O. Box 92912
Rochester, NY 14692-9012

Audio Materials

Achievement, Inc.
485 S. Broadway, Suite 12
Hicksville, NY 11801

Alacazam!
P.O. Box 429
Waterbury, VT 05676

American Audio Prose Library
910 E. Broadway
P.O. Box 842
Columbia, MO 65205

American Management Association
135 West 50th Street
New York, NY 10020

Books on Tape
P.O. Box 7900
Newport Beach, CA 92658

CareerTrack Publications
P.O. Box 18778
Boulder, CO 80308-1778

Columbia Records
550 Madison Avenue
New York, NY 10022

Coronet/MTI Film and Video
108 Wilmot Road, 5th floor
Deerfield, IL 60015

Educational Activities, Inc.
1937 Grand Avenue
Baldwin, NY 11510

Educational Corp. of America/Rand McNally
8255 Central Park Avenue
Skokie, IL 60076

G.K. Hall Audio Publishers
70 Lincoln Street
Boston, MA 02111

Grolier Electronic Publishing
Sherman Turnpike
Danbury, CT 06816

January Productions
210 Sixth Avenue
P.O. Box 66
Hawthorne, NJ 07507

Listening Library, Inc.
1 Park Avenue
Old Greenwich, CT 06870

Mish Mash Music
P.O. Box 3477
Ashland, OR 97520

National Public Radio
2025 M Street NW
Washington, DC 20036

nView
860 Omni Blvd.
Newport News, VA 23606

Pacifica Foundation
P.O. Box 892
Dept. A
Universal City, CA 91608

Poet's Audio Center
P.O. Box 50145
6925 Willow Street NW
Washington, DC 20091

Recorded Books, Inc.
270 Skipjack Road
Prince Frederick, MD 20678

Scholastic Records
740 Broadway
New York, NY 10003

Science Research Associates (SRA)
155 N. Wacker Drive
Chicago, IL 60606

Society for Visual Education, Inc. (SVE)
55 East Monroe, 34th floor
Chicago, IL 60603-5803

3M Company
3M Center
St. Paul, MN 55144

Video, Film, Videodisc

Agency for Instructional Technology
P.O. Box A
Bloomington, IN 47402-0120

AIMS Media
9710 De Soto Avenue
Chatsworth, CA 91311-4409

Ambrose Video Publishing Co.
381 Park Avenue South
New York, NY 10016

American Management Association
135 West 50th Street
New York, NY 10020

American Media, Inc.
4900 University Avenue
West Des Moines, IA 50265

artsAmerica Inc.
12 Havemeyer Place
Greenwich, CT 06830

Barr Films
12801 Schabarum Avenue
Irwindale, CA 91706-7878

Benchmark Films
145 Scarborough Road
Briarcliff Manor, NY 10510

BFA Educational Media
468 Park Avenue South
New York, NY 10016

Blanchard Training and Development
185 State Street
Escondido, CA 92025

British Broadcasting Corporation TV
630 Fifth Avenue
New York, NY 10020

Bullfrog Films
P.O. Box 149
Oley, PA 19547-0149

Catticus Corp.
2600 10th Street
Berkeley, CA 94710

CBS/Fox Video
1330 Avenue of the Americas
5th Floor
New York, NY 10019

CEL Educational Resources
655 Third Avenue
New York, NY 10017

Center for Southern Folklore
Box 226
152 Beale Street   •
Memphis, TN 38101

Churchill Media
12210 Nebraska Avenue
Los Angeles, CA 90025-3600

Cinema Guild
1697 Broadway
New York, NY 10019

Close-up Foundation
44 Canal Center Plaza
Alexandria, VA 22314

Coast District Telecourses
11460 Warner Avenue
Fountain Valley, CA 92708-2597

Coronet/MTI Film and Video
108 Wilmot Road, 5th floor
Deerfield, IL 60015

Corporation for Public Broadcasting
P.O. Box 2345
South Burlington, VT 05407-2345

CRM Films
2233 Faraday Avenue, Suite F
Carlsbad, CA 92008

Direct Cinema Limited
P.O. Box 10003
Santa Monica, CA 90410

Disney Educational Productions
500 Buena Vista Street
Burbank, CA 91521

Eastern Educational Television Network
120 Boylston Street
Boston, MA 02116

Electronic Arts Intermix
536 Broadway, 9th floor
New York, NY 10012

Encyclopaedia Britannica Educational Corp.
310 S. Michigan Avenue
Chicago, IL 60604-9839

Ergo Media, Inc.
668 Front Street
P.O. Box 2037
Teaneck, NJ 07666

Evergreen Video
228 West Houston Street
New York, NY 10014

FASE Productions
4801 Wilshire Blvd.
Los Angeles, CA 90010

Film Australia
P.O. Box 46
Lindfield, New South Wales 2070
Australia

Filmmakers Library
133 E. 58th Street
New York, NY 10022

Films for the Humanities and Sciences
P.O. Box 2053
Princeton, NJ 08543-2053

Films, Incorporated
5547 Ravenswood Avenue
Chicago, IL 60640-1199

Great Plains National Instructional
   Television Library (GPN)
Box 80669
Lincoln, NE 68501-0669

Hawkhill Associates, Inc.
125 E. Gilman St.
Madison, WI 53701-1029

Icarus Films
153 Waverly Place, 6th floor
New York, NY 10014

Indiana University
Field Services
Center for Media and Teaching Resources
Bloomington, IN 47405

International Film Bureau
332 S. Michigan Avenue
Chicago, IL 60604

International Historic Films
P.O. Box 29035
3533 South Archer
Chicago, IL 60629

Janus Classic Collection/Film Inc.
745 Fifth Ave.
New York, NY 10022

The Kentucky Network (KET)
431 South Broadway
Lexington, KY 40508

Kidvidz, Inc.
618 Centre Street
Newton, MA 02158

Knowledge Unlimited
P.O. Box 52
Madison, WI 53701-0052

Kultur Video
121 Highway 36
West Long Branch, NJ 07764

Lee Canter
1553 Euclid Street
Santa Monica, CA 90404

Maryland Center for Public Broadcasting
11767 Bonita Avenue
Owings Mills, MD 21117

MCA Home Video
11312 Penrose Street
Sun Valley, CA 91352

Meridian Education Corporation
236 E. Front St.
Bloomington, IL 61701

Minnesota American Indian AIDS Task Force
1433 East Franklin Avenue
Minneapolis, MN 55404

National Asian-American Telecommunications Associa-
   tion/Cross Current Media
346 9th Street, 2nd floor
San Francisco, CA 94103

National Audiovisual Center
National Archives and Records Administration
8700 Edgeworth Drive
Capitol Heights, MD 20743-3701

National Film Board of Canada (NFBC)
1251 Avenue of the Americas, 16th floor
New York, NY 11020

National Geographic Society
Educational Services Division
1145 17th Street NW
Washington, DC 20036

Native American Public Broadcasting Consortium
P.O. Box 83111
Lincoln, NE 68501

New Day Films
121 West 27th Street
Suite 902
New York, NY 10001

Nuvo, Ltd.
157 Theresa Way
Chula Vista, CA 91911

PBS Video (Public Broadcasting Service)
1320 Braddock Place
Alexandria, VA 22314-1698

Pennsylvania State University
Audio Visual Services
University Park, PA 16802

Pioneer New Media Technologies, Inc.
2265 East 220th Street
Long Beach, CA 90810

Pyramid Film and Video
P.O. Box 1048
Santa Monica, CA 90406

Rainbow Educational Video
170 Keyland Court
Bohemia, NY 11716

Scholastic
730 Broadway
New York, NY 10003

Sharp Electronics Corp.
Sharp Plaza
Mahwah, NJ 07430-2135

Shenandoah Film Productions
538 G Street
Arcata, CA 95521

Silver Burdett & Ginn
160 Gould Street
Needham Heights, MA 02194

Smithsonian Institution
Office of Museum Programs
2235 Arts and Industries Bldg.
Washington, DC 20560

Sony Electronics, Inc.
3 Paragon Drive
Montvale, NJ 07645

Southern Educational Communications Association (SECA)
939 South Stadium Road
P.O. Box 5966
Columbia, SC 29250

Sunburst/WINGS for Learning
101 Castleton Street
Pleasantville, NY 10570

TV Ontario
Video Division
143 West Franklin Street
Chapel Hill, NC 27516

United Learning, Inc.
6633 West Howard
P.O. Box 48718
Niles, IL 60714

University of California-Berkeley
Extension Media Center
2223 Fulton Street
Berkeley, CA 94720

University of Washington
Instructional Media Services
Kane Hall DG-10
Seattle, WA 98195

Video Data Bank
The Art Institute of Chicago
Columbus Drive and Jackson Blvd.
Chicago, IL 60603

Videodiscovery
1700 Westlake Avenue N., #600
Seattle, WA 98109-3012

VideoLabs, Inc.
5270 West 84th Street
Minneapolis, MN 55437

Voyager Company
1351 Pacific Coast Highway
Santa Monica, CA 90401

WETA-TV
3620 27th Street
Washington, DC 20013

Women Make Movies, Inc.
225 Lafayette Street, Suite 206
New York, NY 10012

World Video
P.O. Box 30469
Knoxville, TN 37930-0469

Ztek Co.
P.O. Box 1055
Louisville, KY 40201-1055

Broadcast and Cable Television

Arts and Entertainment
235 E. 45th Street
New York, NY 10017

Cable in the Classroom
Connell Communications
86 Elm St.
Peterborough, NH 03458-9971

Children's Television Workshop
One Lincoln Center
New York, NY 10023

CNN (Cable News Network)
Turner Educational Services
1 CNN Center
Atlanta, GA 30348-5366

C-Span
400 N. Capitol Street NW
Suite 650
Washington, DC 20001

The Discovery Channel
7700 Wisconsin Avenue
Bethesda, MD 20814-3522

KIDSNET
6856 Eastern Avenue NW
Suite 208
Washington, DC 20012

The Learning Channel
7700 Wisconsin Avenue
Bethesda, MD 20814-3522

PBS Elementary/Secondary Service
1320 Braddock Place
Alexandria, VA 22314-1698

TI-IN Network
A Division of Westcott Communications, Inc.
1303 Marsh Lane
Carrollton, TX 75006

Multimedia Programs

ABC News InterActive
P. O. Box 543
Blacklick, OH 43004

Agency for Instructional Technology
Box A
Bloomington, IN 47402-0120

AIMS Media
9710 De Soto Avenue
Chatsworth, CA 91311-4409

Britannica Learning Materials
Britannica Place, Box 2249
Cambridge, Ontario N3C 3N4

Computer Curriculum Corp.
1287 Lawrence Station Road
Sunnyvale, CA 94089

David C. Cook Publishing Co.
850 N. Grove Avenue
Elgin, IL 60120

The Discovery Channel
Interactive Multimedia Division
7700 Wisconsin Road, Suite 900
Bethesda, MD 20814-3522

Emerging Technology Consultants
P.O. Box 120444
St. Paul, MN 55112

Encyclopaedia Britannica Educational Corp.
310 S. Michigan Avenue
Chicago, IL 60604-9839

Facts on File
460 Park Avenue South
New York, NY 10016

IBM Corp.
EduQuest Division
P.O. Box 2150
Atlanta, GA 30055

InFocus Systems, Inc.
7770 SW Mohawk Street
Tualatin, OR 97062

Intellimation
130 Cremona Drive
Santa Barbara, CA 93117

Laser Learning Technologies, Inc.
120 Lakeside Avenue
Suite 3240
Seattle, WA 98122-6552

Logo Computer Systems, Inc.
3300 Côte Vertu Road, #201
Montreal, Quebec
Canada H4R 2B7

Magic Quest
125 University Avenue
Palo Alto, CA 94301

MECC
6160 Summit Drive North
Minneapolis, MN 55430

MPI Multimedia
5525 West 159th Street
Oak Forest, IL 60452

National Geographic Society
Educational Services Canada
211 Watline Avenue
Suite 210
Mississauga, Ontario L4C 1P3

National Geographic Society
Education Services Division
1145 17th Street NW
Washington, DC 20036

Optical Data Corp.
30 Technology Drive
Warren, NJ 07059

Q/Media Software Corp.
312 East 5th Avenue
Vancouver, British Columbia
Canada V5T 1H4

Synapse Technologies
3400 Wilshire Blvd., Bungalow H
Los Angeles, CA 90010

Texas Learning Technology Group (TLTG)
7703 North Lamar Blvd.
Austin, TX 78752

Turner Educational Services, Inc.
1 CNN Center
Box 105336
Atlanta, GA 30348-5366

Videodiscovery, Inc.
1700 Westlake Avenue N., #600
Seattle, WA 98109-3012

The Voyager Company
1351 Pacific Coast Highway
Santa Monica, CA 90401

Ztek Co.
P.O. Box 1055
Louisville, KY 40201-1055

Simulations and Games

Animal Town Game Co.
P.O. Box 485
Healdsburg, CA 95448

Aristoplay, Ltd.
P.O. Box 7028
Ann Arbor, MI 48107

Avalon Hill Microcomputer Games
4517 Harford Road
Baltimore, MD 21214

Brøderbund Software Inc.
500 Redwood Blvd.
Novato, CA 94948-6121

Denoyer-Geppert Science Co.
5215 N. Ravenswood Avenue
Chicago, IL 60640

Didactic Systems, Inc.
P.O. Box 457
Cranford, NJ 07016

Doron Precision Systems Inc.
P.O. Box 400
Binghamton, NY 13902

Education Research
370 Lexington Avenue, 27th floor
New York, NY 10017

Groupware Corporation
78 Glenburnie Crescent
London, Ontario N5X 2A3

Houghton Mifflin Co.
Software Division
One Wayside Road
Burlington, MA 08103-9842

Interact Company
P.O. Box 997-Y92
Lakeside, CA 92040

John Wiley and Sons, Inc.
605 Third Avenue
New York, NY 10158

Pentathlon Institute
P.O. Box 20590
Indianapolis, IN 46220-0590

Wff'N Proof
1490-TZ South Boulevard
Ann Arbor, MI 48104

Computer Courseware/CD-ROM

Access Innovations, Inc.
P.O. Box 40130
4320 Mesa Grande, SE
Albuquerque, NM 87196

Apple Computer, Inc.
20525 Mariani Avenue
Cupertino, CA 95014

Avalon Hill Microcomputer Games
4517 Harford Road
Baltimore, MD 21214

Beagle Bros.
6215 Ferris Square, #100
San Diego, CA 92121

Brøderbund Software Inc.
500 Redwood Blvd.
P.O. Box 6121
Novato, CA 94948-6121

CDiscovery
Computerworks of Northport
260 Main Street
Northport, NY 11768

Chariot Software Group
3659 India Street
San Diego, CA 92103

Compton's NewMedia
722 Genevieve, Suite M
Solano Beach, CA 92075

Compu Teach
14924-21st Dr. SE
Mill Creek, WA 98012

CONDUIT
The University of Iowa
100 Oakdale Campus
Iowa City, IA 55242

Davidson & Associates, Inc.
19840 Pioneer Avenue
Torrance, CA 90503

Didatech Software, Ltd.
720 Olive Way, Suite 930
Seattle, WA 98101-7874

Dymaxion Research, Ltd.
5515 Cogswell Street
Halifax, Nova Scotia
Canada B3J 1R2

EBSCO Publishing
P.O. Box 2250
Peabody, MA 01960-7250

Edmark Corp.
6727 185th Avenue NE
P.O. Box 3218
Redmond, WA 98073-3218

Education Systems Corp.
6170 Cornerstone Court East, Suite 300
San Diego, CA 92121-3170

Educorp USA
531 Stephens Avenue, Suite B
Solana Beach, CA 92075

EduQuest Resource Center
Dept. 135, P.O. Box 1000
Plymouth, MI 48170-9989

The Electronic Bookshelf, Inc.
5276 South County Road 700 W
Frankfort, IN 46041

Electronic Courseware Systems
1210 Lancaster Drive
Champaign, IL 61821

Electronic Learning Systems, Inc.
2622 NW 43rd Street, Suite B4
Gainesville, FL 32606

EME-Educational Materials and Equipment Corp.
P.O. Box 2805
Danbury, CT 06813

Franklin Electronic Publishers, Inc.
122 Burrs Road
Mt. Holly, NJ 08060

Gamco Education Materials
P.O. Box 1911
Big Spring, TX 79721-1911

Harcourt Brace Publishing Media Solutions
301 Commerce Street
Suite 3700
Fort Worth, TX 76102

Hartley
3001 Coolidge Road
Suite 400
East Lansing, MI 48823

Houghton Mifflin Co.
222 Berkeley Street
Boston, MA 02116-3764

IBM Corp.
EduQuest Division
P.O. Box 2150
Atlanta, GA 30055

January Productions
210 Sixth Avenue
P.O. Box 66
Hawthorne, NJ 07507

John Wiley and Sons, Inc.
605 Third Avenue
New York, NY 10158

Jostens Learning
5521 Norman Center Drive
Minneapolis, MN 55431

K-12 MicroMedia
6 Arrow Road
Ramsey, NJ 07446

Lawrence Productions
1800 South 34th
Gatesburg, MI 49053

Leeson Howe Associates, Inc.
1275 Summer Street
Stamford, CT 06905

Micrograms
1404 North Main Street
Rockford, IL 61103

Milliken Publishing Company
1100 Research Boulevard
P.O. Box 21579
St. Louis, MO 63132

Mindplay
3130 North Dodge Blvd.
Tucson, AZ 85716

Minnesota Educational Computing Corporation
   (MECC)
6160 Summit Drive North
Minneapolis, MN 55430

Multilis
505 Rene Levesque Blvd. W
Montreal, Quebec
Canada H2Z 1Y7

Optical Data Corp.
20 Technology Drive
Warren, NJ 07059

Scholastic, Inc.
2931 East McCarty Street
Jefferson City, MO 65102

Skills Bank Corp.
15 Governors Court
Baltimore, MD 21244-2791

Society for Visual Education, Inc. (SVE)
55 East Monroe, 34th floor
Chicago, IL 60603-5803

Sunburst/WINGS for Learning
101 Castleton Street
Pleasantville, NY 10570

Symantec/Edutech
P.O. Box 51755
Pacific Grove, CA 93950

Teacher Support Software
1035 N.W. 57th Street
Gainesville, FL 32605

Tom Snyder Productions, Inc.
80 Coolidge Hill Road
Watertown, MA 02172-2817

Ventura Educational Systems
910 Ramona Avenue, Suite E
Grover City, CA 93433

Waterford Institute
1590 East 9400 South
Sandy, UT 84093

Worldview Software
76 North Broadway, #4009
Hicksville, NY 11801

Integrated Learning Systems

Computer Curriculum Corp.
1287 Lawrence Station Road
Sunnyvale, CA 94089

Crestron
101 Broadway
Cresskill, NJ 07626

Galaxy Institute for Education
200 North Sepulveda Blvd.
El Segundo, CA 90245

Harcourt Brace
301 Commerce Street
Suite 3700
Fort Worth, TX 76102

Jostens Learning
5521 Norman Center Drive
Minneapolis, MN 55431

Minnesota Educational Computing Corporation
 (MECC)
6160 Summit Drive North
Minneapolis, MN 55430

Tom Snyder Productions, Inc.
80 Coolidge Hill Road
Watertown, MA 02172-2817

REVIEW SOURCES

AFVA Evaluations
American Film and Video Association
P.O. Box 48659
Niles, IL 60648

Booklist
American Library Association
50 East Huron Street
Chicago, IL 60611

Curriculum Review
Curriculum Advisory Service
212 West Superior Street, Suite 200
Chicago, IL 60610-3533

EPIE Reports
Educational Products Information Exchange Institute
P.O. Box 839
Water Mill, NY 11976

Library Journal
Cahners Publishing Co.
249 West 17th Street
New York, NY 10011

Media and Methods
American Society of Educators
1429 Walnut Street
Philadelphia, PA 19102

School Library Journal
Cahners Publishing Co.
249 West 17th Street
New York, NY 10011

School Library Media Quarterly
American Association of School Librarians
American Library Association
50 East Huron Street
Chicago, IL 60611

Science Books and Films
American Association for the Advancement of Science
1776 Massachusetts Avenue NW
Washington, DC 20036

Sightlines
American Film and Video Association (AFVA)
P.O. Box 48659
Niles, IL 60648

Video Rating Guide for Libraries
ABC-CLIO, Inc.
130 Cremona Drive
Santa Barbara, CA 93117

Courseware, CD-ROM, Multimedia

CD-ROM Databases
Worldwide Videotex
Box 138
Babson Park
Boston, MA 02157

CD-ROM Librarian
Meckler Publishing
11 Ferry Lane West
Westport, CT 06880

CD-ROM Professional
Pemberton Press, Inc.
11 Tannery Lane
Weston, CT 06883

Curriculum Product News
992 High Ridge Road
Stamford, CT 06905

Digest of Software Reviews: Education
School & Home Courseware, Inc.
3999 N. Chestnut Diagonal, Suite 333
Fresno, CA 93726-4797

The Educational Software Selector (TESS)
Educational Product Information Exchange Institute
P.O. Box 839
Water Mill, NY 11976

InCider/A+
P.O. Box 50358
Boulder, CO 80321-0358

InfoWorld
InfoWorld Publishing
155 Bovet Road, Suite 800
San Mateo, CA 94402

MicroSIFT
Northwest Regional Educational Lab
300 S.W. 6th Street
Portland, OR 97204

Multimedia Monitor
P.O. Box 26
Falls Church, VA 22040

Multimedia World
501 Second Street, Suite 600
San Francisco, CA 94107

New Media
901 Mariner's Island Blvd., Suite 365
San Mateo, CA 94404

Software Digest Ratings Report
National Software Testing Laboratories
Plymouth Corporate Center, Box 100
Plymouth Meeting, PA 19462

Software Review
Meckler Publishing
520 Riverside Avenue
Westport, CT 06880

Teaching and Computers
Scholastic, Inc.
P.O. Box 2040
Mahopac, NY 10541-9963

OTHER REFERENCE TOOLS

For more extensive, annotated guides to media reviews or descriptions or other audiovisual information sources, consult the following:

Media Review Digest. Annual. Ann Arbor, MI: Pierian Press.

Educational Media and Technology Yearbook. Annual. Englewood, CO: Libraries Unlimited.

Accommodation The cognitive process of modifying a schema or creating new schemata.

Accountability The idea that a person or agency should be able to demonstrate publicly the worth of the activities carried out.

Acetate A transparent plastic sheet associated with overhead projection.

Ad hoc network An electronic distribution system that is rented by the user and set up for one-time use (e.g., for a teleconference).

Advance organizer An outline, preview, or other such preinstructional cue used to promote retention of verbal material, as proposed by David Ausubel. Also referred to as preinstructional strategies.

Affective domain The domain of human learning that involves changes in interests, attitudes, and values and the development of appreciation.

Animation A film technique in which the artist gives motion to still images by creating and juxtaposing a series of pictures with small, incremental changes from one to the next.

Aperture The lens opening that determines the amount of light that enters a camera. Also, the opening through which light travels from the lamp to the lens in a projector.

Arrangement The pattern or shape into which the elements of a visual display are organized.

Articulation The highest level of motor skill learning. The learner who has reached this level is performing unconsciously, efficiently, and harmoniously, incorporating coordination of skills. See also *motor skill domain*.

ASCII American Standard Code for Information Interchange; pronounced "ask-ee." A binary code used in computers; the universal code for English letters and characters.

Aspect ratio Length/width proportions or format of an audiovisual material, such as 3 by 4 for a filmstrip or motion picture frame.

Assimilation The cognitive process by which a learner integrates new information into an existing schema.

Audio card reader A device for recording and reproducing sound on a card with a magnetic strip. The card may contain verbal and/or pictorial information. Separate tracks may provide for a protected master and erasable student responses.

Audioconference A teleconference involving transmission of voices only. The voices are amplified at each end by a speaker system.

Audiographic conference A teleconference involving voice plus graphic display. The graphics may be transmitted by a fax machine or electronically by means of slow-scan video or a graphics tablet.

Audio head A magnetic element in a tape recorder that records or plays back sound.

Audio-tutorial system Technology for managing instruction that employs a study carrel equipped with specially designed audiotapes that direct students to various learning activities. This component is known as an independent study session. Large-group and small-group assemblies are also major components of this system.

Auditory fatigue The process by which attention to a sound gradually decreases because of the monotony of the sound.

Authoring system A computer programming tool designed to simplify the programming process by automating the generation of code; allows users who are not programming experts to develop CAI courseware.

Automatic level control (ALC) On audio recorders, a circuit used to control the volume or level of the recorded signal automatically to provide uniform level without distortion due to overloading. Sometimes called automatic gain control (AGC) or automatic volume control (AVC).

Automatic programmer See *programmer*.

Balance The sense of equilibrium that is achieved when the elements of visual display are arranged in such a way that the "weight" is distributed relatively equally.

Bandwidth The range of frequencies an electronic communications channel can support without excessive deterioration.

405

Bar graph   A type of graph in which the height of the bar is the measure of the quantity being represented.

Bass   See *frequency*.

Baud   The switching speed, or number of transitions (voltage or frequency changes) made per second; the speed at which modems transfer data. At low speeds, one baud is roughly equivalent to one bit per second.

BBS   See *bulletin board service*.

Behaviorism   A theory that equates learning with changes in observable behavior; with this theory, there is no speculating about mental events that may mediate learning.

Beta (video)   A ½-inch videocassette format not compatible with the VHS format, which is also ½ inch but differs electronically.

Bidirectional   A microphone that picks up sound in front of and behind itself and rejects sound from the sides.

Biochip   A (hypothetical) miniature microprocessor constructed of organic matter, such as a protein molecule.

Bit   An acronym for *binary digit;* the smallest unit of digital information. The bit can be thought of as a 1 or a 0 representing a circuit on or off, respectively.

Bit map (or bitmap)   In computer graphics, an area in memory that represents the video image. Each pixel on a video screen is controlled by bits that set color and intensity.

Branching programming   A format of programmed instruction in which the sequence of presentation of the frames depends on the responses selected by the learner.

Brightening   A pedagogical technique used in programmed tutoring in which the desired response is gradually revealed to the learner in the form of hints or partial prompts.

Broadband   Telecommunications channels that are capable of carrying a wide range of frequencies (e.g., broadcast television, cable television, and satellite transmission). These systems carry a large amount of information in a short amount of time but are more expensive than those that require less bandwidth (such as telephone systems).

Broadcasting   Transmission of signals to many receivers simultaneously via electromagnetic waves.

Bullet   In text, a circle, star, or other symbol used for emphasis at the beginning of a line of type.

Bulletin board service (BBS)   Computer system used as an information source and message posting system for a particular interest group.

Byte   The number of bits required to store or represent one character of text (a letter or number); most commonly, but not always, made up of eight bits in various combinations of 0s and 1s.

Cable television   A television distribution system consisting of a closed-circuit, usually wired, network for transmitting signals from an origination point (see *head end*) to members of the network. Typically, the origination point receives and retransmits broadcast programs, adding recorded programs and/or some live originations.

Camcorder   A video camera and videotape recorder combined into one unit.

Capstan   A rotating shaft or spindle that moves tape at a constant speed during recording or playback in tape recorders.

Cardioid microphone   A microphone that picks up sound primarily in the direction it is pointed, rejecting sounds from behind it; a unidirectional microphone.

Carrel   A partially enclosed booth that serves as a clearly identifiable enclosure for learning-center activities.

Cassette   A self-contained reel-to-reel magnetic tape system with the two reels permanently installed in a rugged plastic case.

Cathode-ray tube (CRT)   The video display tube used in video monitors and receivers, radar displays, and computer terminals.

CCD   See *charge-coupled device*.

CCTV   See *closed-circuit television*.

CDI   See *compact disc-interactive*.

CD-ROM   Compact disc–read only memory. Digitally encoded information permanently recorded on a compact disc. Information can be accessed very quickly.

CD-WORM   Compact disc–write once, read many. A compact disc on which the user may record information digitally one time and then access it many times.

Characterization   The highest level of affective learning. The learner who has reached this level will demonstrate an internally consistent value system. See also *affective domain*.

Charge-coupled device (CCD)   A device that changes a pattern of different wavelengths into corresponding electrical charges.

Cinema verité   A filmmaking technique in which the camera becomes either an intimate observer of or a direct participant in the events being documented.

Circle graph   A graphic form in which a circle or "pie" is divided into segments, each representing a part or percentage of the whole.

Closed-circuit television (CCTV)   Any system of television that transmits signals through self-contained pathways (such as cable) rather than via broadcasting.

Close-up   In motion or still photography, a shot in which the camera concentrates on the subject or a part of it, excluding everything else from view; a close-up of a person shows at most the head and shoulders.

Cognitive domain   The domain of human learning involving intellectual skills, such as assimilation of information or knowledge.

Cognitive psychology   A branch of psychology devoted to the study of how individuals acquire, process, and use information.

Cognitivism   A theory according to which mental processes mediate learning and learning entails the construction or reshaping of mental schemata.

Communication model   A mathematical or verbal representation of the key elements in the communication process.

Compact disc (CD)   A 4.72-inch disc on which a laser has recorded digital information.

Compact disc interactive (CDI)   A compact disc system that incorporates a computer program as well as graphics, audio, and print information.

Composition   The creative process of manipulating a camera to frame a picture to suit some contemplated purpose.

Comprehension   The level of cognitive learning that refers to the intellectual skill of understanding: this includes translating, interpreting, paraphrasing, and summarizing. See also *cognitive domain*.

Compressed video   Video images that have been processed to remove redundant information, thereby reducing the amount of bandwidth required to transmit them. Because only changes in the image are transmitted, movements appear jerky compared with full-motion video.

Computer-assisted instruction (CAI)   Instruction delivered directly to learners by allowing them to interact with lessons programmed into the computer system.

Computer conference   An arrangement in which two or more participants exchange messages using personal computers that are connected to a central computer via telephone lines.

Computer hypermedia system   A computer hardware and software system that allows the composition and display of nonsequential documents that may include text, audio, and visual information and in which related information may be linked into webs by author or user.

Computer literacy   The ability to understand and use computers, paralleling reading and writing in verbal literacy. Actual computer literacy exists along a continuum from general awareness to the ability to create computer programs.

Computer-managed instruction (CMI)   The use of a computer system to manage information about learner performance and learning resources and to then prescribe and control individual lessons.

Computer multimedia system   A computer hardware and software system for the composition and display of presentations that incorporate text, audio, and still and motion images.

Computer network   An electronic connecting system that allows physically dispersed computers to share software, data, and peripheral devices.

Concrete–abstract continuum   The arrangement of various teaching methods in a hierarchy of greater and greater abstraction, beginning with *the total situation* and culminating with *word* at the top of the hierarchy.

Condenser lens   Lens between the projection lamp and slide or film aperture that concentrates light in the film and lens apertures.

Condenser microphone   A microphone, also referred to as an electrostatic or capacitor microphone, with a conductive diaphragm that varies a high-voltage electric field to generate a signal. It may be of any pattern (uni-, bi-, or omnidirectional).

Consequence   In psychology, the result of a particular behavior. Learning may be facilitated by arranging positive consequences to follow desired behaviors.

Contrast   The difference in brightness between the white and black areas or among the colored areas of an image (as in a photo or video screen) or combination of images (as in a bulletin board display).

Cooperative game   A game in which the attainment of the goal requires cooperation rather than competition among the players.

Cooperative learning   An instructional configuration involving small groups of learners working together on learning tasks rather than competing as individuals.

Copy board   A device that makes a paper copy of what is written on a type of electronic whiteboard.

Copy stand   A vertical or horizontal stand for accurately positioning a camera when photographing flat materials.

Courseware   Lessons delivered via computer, consisting of content conveyed according to an instructional design controlled by programmed software.

Covert response   A learner response that is not outwardly observable. See also *overt response*.

Craft approach   An approach to problem solving in which the emphasis is on the use of tools by a skilled craftsman. Such ad hoc decision making contrasts with the technology approach.

Criterion   As part of a performance objective, the standard by which acceptable performance is judged; may include a time limit, accuracy tolerance, proportion of correct responses required, and/or qualitative standards.

CRT   See *cathode-ray tube*.

DAT See *digital audiotape*.

Database A collection of related information organized for quick access to specific items of information.

Debriefing Discussion conducted among simulation or game participants after play to elucidate what has been learned.

Decoder In electronics, the device in a synchronizer or programmer that reads the encoded signal or pulse and turns it into some form of control. In human communications, the element that translates any signal into a form decipherable by the receiver.

Dedicated system An electronic distribution system (e.g., for teleconferencing) that is owned and operated by the user.

Deductive learning See *expository learning*.

Definition The sharpness or resolution of an image.

Degausser See *head demagnetizer*.

Depth of field In photography, the region of acceptably sharp focus around the subject position, extending toward the camera and away from it. Varies with the distance of the camera from the subject, the focal length of the lens, and the f/stop.

Desktop publishing Computer applications that allow a personal computer to generate typeset-quality text and graphics.

Desktop video Video production using a personal computer and low-cost video equipment.

Dichroic mirror A mirror coated so that only one color of the spectrum is reflected. In a video camera, three dichroic mirrors direct the three primary colors to three respective video tubes.

Digital Representation or storage of information by combinations of numbers (a series of 0s and 1s).

Digital audiotape (DAT) Audio recording technology that stores sounds as strings of binary numbers.

Digital recording Advanced method of recording that involves a sequence of pulses or on–off signals rather than a continuously variable or analog signal.

Digital video Video recording technology that stores video images as strings of binary numbers.

Digital video interactive (DVI) A system similar to compact disc interactive but with the addition of moving images. The DVI format can accommodate 72 minutes of digitized audio and video.

Digitize To convert an auditory or visual signal from its analog form into strings of binary numbers.

Diorama A static display employing a flat background and three-dimensional foreground to achieve a lifelike effect.

Direct Instruction See *programmed teaching*.

Discovery method A teaching strategy that proceeds as follows: immersion in a real or contrived problem situation, development of hypotheses, testing of hypotheses, and arrival at conclusion (the main point).

Dissolve An optical effect in film and video involving a change from one scene to another in which the outgoing and incoming visual images are superimposed or blended together for a discernible period of time as one scene fades out while the other fades in; also applicable to sequential slides.

Dissolve unit A device that controls the illumination from one, two, or more projectors in such a manner that the images fade from one into another at either a fixed or variable rate.

Distance education Any instructional situation in which the learner is separated in time or space from the point of origination, characterized by limited access to the teacher and other learners.

Division of labor In economics, the reorganization of a job so that some tasks are performed by one person or system and other tasks are performed by others for purposes of increased efficiency or effectiveness.

Documentary A film or video program that deals with fact, not fiction or fictionalized versions of fact.

Dolly The movement of a camera toward or away from the subject while shooting.

DOS Disk operating system. Computer software that translates the user's commands and allows application programs to interact with the computer's hardware.

Downlink The reception end of a satellite transmission; entails a satellite dish with a decoder and a display screen.

Download To transfer programs and/or data files from a computer to another device or computer; to retrieve something from a network.

Drill-and-practice game A game format that provides repetitive drill exercises in an interactive mode and has game-type motivational elements.

Drill-and-practice method A method of learning that presents a lengthy series of items to be rehearsed; employed with skills that require repetitive practice for mastery.

Dry mounting A method of mounting visuals on cardboard or similar sheet materials in which a special tissue impregnated with a heat-sensitive adhesive is placed between the visual and mount board and is softened by the heat of a dry-mounting press to effect the bond.

DVI See *digital video interactive*.

Economy of scale In economics, the principle that certain functions decline in cost as they are expanded to encompass a larger population.

EIAJ standards   Electronic equipment standards, notably involving videotape recorders, promoted by the Electronic Industry Association of Japan. They allow for the compatibility of the equipment of all affected manufacturers.

Electronic blackboard   A system in which images drawn on a special surface are transmitted over telephone lines and reproduced on a video screen at the reception end.

Electronic mail (e-mail)   Transmission of private messages over a computer network; users can send mail to a single recipient or broadcast it to multiple users on the system.

Electronic viewfinder   A small picture tube built into a video camera to enable the operator to see what is being scanned by the camera.

Electrostatic copying   A method of making overhead transparencies; also called xerography. Similar to the thermal process, this process requires specially treated film that is electrically charged and light sensitive.

Encoder   In electronics, a device used with a tape recorder or other information-storage device to produce the synchronized signals or pulses that are decoded to operate combinations of devices (projectors) at one time. In human communication, the element that converts the thoughts of the source into visible or audible messages.

Exciter lamp   The small lamp that projects its single-coil illumination through the optical sound track on 16mm film. The varying light intensity is read by the projector's photoelectric cell, which converts the light impulses into electronic signals amplified and made audible by a loudspeaker (or earphones).

Exhibit   A display incorporating various media formats (e.g., realia, still pictures, models, graphics) into an integral whole intended for instructional purposes.

Expert system   A computer program, assembled by a team of content experts and programmers, that teaches a learner how to solve complex tasks by applying the appropriate knowledge from the content area.

Expository learning   The typical classroom teaching approach that proceeds as follows: presentation of information (the main point), reference to particular examples, and application of the knowledge to the students' experiences.

Fade in/out   In motion pictures and video, an optical effect in which a scene gradually appears out of blackness or disappears into blackness.

Fax   A facsimile transmission system in which images of printed text, diagrams, or hand lettering are sent via telephone lines to another site where the images are mechanically reproduced on paper.

Feedback   In electronics, the regeneration of sound caused by a system's microphonic pickup of output from its own speakers, causing a ringing sound or squeal. In communication, signals sent from the destination back to the source that provide information about the reception of the original message.

Fiber optics   A transmission medium using spun silicon shaped into threads as thin as human hairs. It transmits more signals with higher quality than can metal cables.

File server   In local area networks, a station dedicated to providing file and mass data storage services to the other stations on the network.

Film, motion picture   Photographic images stored on celluloid. When projected at 24 frames per second, the still images give the illusion of motion.

Filmstrip   A roll of 35mm film containing a series of related still pictures intended for showing one at a time in sequence.

Flip chart   A pad of large paper fastened together at the top and mounted on an easel.

F/number   See *lens speed.*

Focal length   Loosely, the focal distance when a projector lens is focused on infinity; more accurately, the distance from the focal point of the lens to the image plane when the lens is focused on infinity.

Format   The physical form in which a medium is incorporated and displayed. For example, motion pictures are available in 35mm, 16mm, and 8mm formats.

Frame   (1) An individual picture in a filmstrip or motion picture. (2) The useful area and shape of a film image. (3) A complete television picture of 525 horizontal lines. (4) In programmed instruction, one unit in a series of prompt–response–reinforcement units; a block of verbal/visual information.

Frame game   Any game that lends its structure to a variety of subject matter.

Freeze frame   A film technique in which a filmmaker selects an image in a motion sequence and prints that image over and over again so that one moment is held frozen on the screen.

Freeze-frame video   A single, still image held on a video screen.

Frequency   The rate of repetition in cycles per second (Hertz) of musical pitch or electrical signals. Low frequencies are bass; high frequencies are treble.

Fresnel lens   A flat glass or acrylic lens in which the curvature of a normal lens surface is collapsed into an almost flat plane, resulting in concentric circle forms impressed or engraved on the lens surface. Because of its low cost, light weight, and compactness, it is often used for the condenser lens in overhead projectors and in studio lights.

Front-screen projection An image projected on the audience side of a light-reflecting screen.

F/stop Numerical description of the relative size of the aperture that determines the amount of light entering a camera.

Full-motion video A normal, moving video image. The familiar illusion of normal motion is achieved by projecting 30 frames, each slightly different, every second.

Game An activity in which participants follow prescribed rules that differ from those of reality as they strive to attain a challenging goal.

Gateway A computer that interconnects and makes translations between two different types of networks.

Geosynchronous satellite A communications satellite traveling at such a speed that it appears to hover steadily over the same spot on the earth.

Gestalt learning A theory of learning based on analysis of the unified whole, suggesting that the understanding of an entire process is better than the study of individual parts or sequences of the whole.

Goal A desired instructional outcome that is broad in scope and general with regard to criteria and performance indicators.

Gopher On electronic networks, a menued program that takes a request for information and connects to the network.

Gothic lettering A style of lettering with even width of strokes and without serifs (the tiny cross strokes on the ends of letters).

Graphical user interface (GUI) An interface made up of pictures to which the user points rather than typing characters to give commands to a computer.

Graphics Two-dimensional, nonphotographic materials designed to communicate a specific message to the viewer.

Hard copy Computer output printed on paper.

Hard disk Metal disk covered with a magnetic recording material; the permanent storage device for a computer.

Hardware The mechanical and electronic components that make up a computer; the physical equipment that makes up a computer system, and, by extension, the term that refers to any audiovisual equipment.

Head demagnetizer A device that provides an alternating magnetic field used during routine maintenance to remove the residual magnetism from recording or playback heads.

Head end The origination point of a cable television system.

Headphone A device consisting of one or two electro-acoustic receivers attached to a headband for private listening to audio sources; sometimes called *earphone*.

Hearing A physiological process in which sound waves entering the outer ear are transmitted to the eardrum, converted into mechanical vibrations in the middle ear, and changed in the inner ear to nerve impulses that travel to the brain.

Hertz (Hz) The frequency of an alternating signal; formerly called *cycles per second* (*cps*).

High-definition television (HDTV) A system for high-resolution color television.

Holistic learning An approach to learning in which learners encounter a whole and dynamic view of the process being studied. Emotions are involved along with the thinking process.

Hollywood syndrome In video or teleconferencing, the tendency to adopt the highly polished techniques of commercial television at the expense of instructional values; for example, the use of fast-paced visuals for eye-catching effect rather than substance.

Hybrid system Any arrangement that combines two or more communications technologies.

Hypermedia See *computer hypermedia system*.

Hypertext A computer program that enables the user to access continually a large information base whenever additional information on a subject is needed.

Iconic Pertaining to an image that resembles a real object.

Inductive learning See *discovery method*.

Information superhighway Popular name given to the concept of an international information network of extremely high carrying capacity. Also refers specifically to the fiber-optic network being constructed in North America.

Input Information or a stimulus that enters a system.

Instruction Deliberate arrangement of experience(s) to help a learner achieve a desirable change in performance; the management of learning, which in education and training is primarily the function of the instructor.

Instructional development The process of analyzing needs, determining what content must be mastered, establishing educational goals, designing materials to help reach the objectives, and trying out and revising the program according to learner achievement.

Instructional module A freestanding instructional unit, usually used for independent study. Typical components are rationale, objective, pretest, learning activities, self-test, and posttest.

Instructional technology "A complex integrated process involving people, procedures, ideas, devices, and organization, for analyzing problems and devising, implementing, evaluating, and managing solutions to those problems in situations in which learning is purposive and controlled."[1]

Instructional television Any planned use of video programs to meet specific instructional goals regardless of the source of the programs (including commercial broadcasts) or the setting in which they are used (including business and industry training).

Integrated learning system (ILS) A set of interrelated computer-based lessons organized to match the curriculum of a school or training agency.

Interactive media Media formats that allow or require some level of physical activity from the user, which in some ways alters the sequence of presentation.

Interactive video Computer-controlled video playback incorporating some method for users to control the sequence of presentation, typically by responding to multiple-choice questions.

Interface A shared boundary; the point at which two subsystems come in contact. The connection between two devices.

Internalization The degree to which an attitude or value has become part of an individual. The affective domain is organized according to the degree of internalization. See also *affective domain*.

Internet A worldwide system for linking smaller computer networks together, based on a packet system of information transfer and using a common set of communication standards.

Interpersonal skills domain The domain of learning that involves interaction among people and the ability to relate effectively with others.

IPS Inches per second; more properly written in/s. Standard for measuring the speed of tape movement.

ITFS Instructional Television Fixed Service. A portion of the microwave frequency spectrum (2500–2690 MHz) reserved by law in the United States for educational use.

ITV See *instructional television*.

Jack Receptacle for a plug connector for the input or output circuits of an audio or video device. There are several common sizes and formats of plugs, including:

Standard phone:　0.25" or 6.35mm diam.

Small phone:　0.206" or 5.23mm diam.

Mini:　0.140" or 3.6mm diam.

Micro:　0.097" or 2.5mm diam.

Keystone effect The distortion (usually creating a wide top and narrow bottom) of a projected image caused when the projector is not aligned at right angles to the screen.

Kilobyte (K or Kb) Approximately 1,000 bytes; more precisely, 1,024 bytes.

Lamination A technique for preserving visuals that provides them with protection from wear and tear by covering them with clear plastic or similar substances.

Landscape A horizontal arrangement of a visual image or printed page in which the width is greater than the height; the opposite of *portrait*.

Lavalier mike A small microphone worn around the neck.

LCD See *liquid crystal display*.

Learning A general term for a relatively lasting change in capability caused by experience; also, the process by which such change is brought about. See also *behaviorism* and *cognitivism* for different interpretations of learning.

Learning center A self-contained environment designed to promote individual or small-group learning around a specific task.

Learning style A cluster of psychological traits that determine how a person perceives, interacts with, and responds emotionally to learning environments.

Lens speed Refers to the ability of a lens to pass light, expressed as a ratio: the focal length of the lens divided by the (effective) diameter. A fast lens (which passes more light) might be rated f/1.1 or f/1.2; a much slower lens (which passes less light) might be designated f/3.5 (f/number = focal length/aperture).

Linear programming A format of programmed instruction in which the frames are arranged in a fixed, linear sequence.

Line graph The most precise and complex of graphs based on two scales at right angles. Each point has a value on the vertical scale and on the horizontal scale. Lines (or curves) are drawn to connect the points.

Line of sight A transmission path between two points that is uninhibited by any physical barriers such as hills or tall buildings.

Liquid crystal display (LCD) A data display using a liquid crystal material encased between two transparent sheets. Liquid crystals have the properties of a liquid and a solid; a network of electrodes and polarizing filter creates a grid of pixels that open and close to pass or block light.

---

[1]Association for Educational Communications and Technology, *The Definition of Educational Technology* (Washington, DC: AECT, 1977).

Listening   A psychological process that begins with someone's awareness of and attention to sounds or speech patterns, proceeds through identification and recognition of specific auditory signals, and ends in comprehension.

Local area network (LAN)   A local system (typically within a building) connecting computers and peripheral devices into a network; may give access to external networks.

Low-cost learning technology   An approach to formal education featuring systematic selection and implementation of a variety of managerial, instructional, motivational, and resource-utilization strategies to increase student learning outcomes while decreasing or maintaining recurrent educational costs.

Mainframe computer   A high-speed, multiple-purpose computer intended primarily for business and scientific computing; designed for processing huge amounts of numerical data.

Material   An item in a particular medium or format; in the plural, a collection of items in various media or formats.

Mb   See *megabyte*.

Mediagraphy   An alphabetical listing (like a bibliography) of audiovisual materials.

Medium   A means of communication. Derived from the Latin *medium* ("between"), the term refers to anything that carries information between a source and a receiver. Plural: *media*.

Megabyte (Mb or M)   Basic unit of measurement of mass storage, equal to 1,048,576 bytes, or 1,024 kilobytes.

Megahertz (MHz)   One million cycles per second.

Message   Any information to be communicated.

Meta-analysis   A statistical technique that allows researchers to combine and summarize data from many different research studies to report overall quantitative findings.

Method   A procedure of instruction selected to help learners achieve their objective or to internalize a message.

MHz   See *megahertz*.

Microcomputer   A term coined in the mid-1980s to differentiate the small desktop computer (using a microprocessor as its processing element) from the larger minicomputer and mainframe computers.

Microfiche   A sheet of microfilm (usually 4 by 6 inches) containing multiple micro-images in a grid pattern. It usually contains a title that can be read without magnification.

Microfilm   A film in which each frame is a miniaturized image of a printed page or photograph; may be 16, 35, 70, or 105mm.

Microform   Any materials—film or paper, printed or photographic, containing micro-images that are units of information, such as a page of text or drawing—too small to be read without magnification.

Micro/minicassette   One of several audiocassettes much smaller than the compact cassette; used principally for note taking and dictation.

Microphone   A device that converts sound into electrical signals usable by other pieces of audio equipment. Microphones vary in sound quality, generating system used, directional patterns, and impedance.

Microprocessor   The brain of the microcomputer; the electronic chip (circuit) that does all the calculation and control of data. In larger machines, it is called the central processing unit (CPU).

Microprocessor game   Inexpensive, limited-purpose calculator-type toy, such as Dataman, Little Professor, Speak & Spell, and Teach & Tell. Marketed primarily to the mass home market for arithmetic, spelling, or discrimination practice.

Microwave transmission   A television distribution system using the ultra-high and super-high frequency ranges (2,000–13,000 MHz); includes ITFS in the United States (2,500–2,690 MHz).

Model   A three-dimensional representation of a real object; it may be larger, smaller, or the same size as the thing represented.

Modem   Acronym for *mo*dulator/*dem*odulator. An electronic device that translates digital information for transmission over telephone lines. It also translates analog information to digital.

Module   A freestanding, self-contained component.

Monitor   A TV set without broadcast-receiving circuitry that is used primarily to display video signals.

Motion media   General term for audiovisual systems in which a rapid sequence of still images creates the illusion of motion; may refer to film, video, or computer display.

Motion media convention   A widely used and accepted device or technique for producing a special effect in motion media, such as time lapse, slow motion, or animation.

Motor skill domain   The category of human learning that involves athletic, manual, and other physical action skills.

Multi-image   The use of two or more separate images, usually projected simultaneously in a presentation. Multiple images are often projected on adjacent multiple screens.

Multimedia Sequential or simultaneous use of a variety of media formats in a given presentation or self-study program. See also *computer multimedia system.*

Multimedia kit A collection of teaching-learning materials involving more than one type of medium and organized around a single topic.

Multimedia system A combination of audio and visual media integrated into a structured, systematic presentation. See also *computer multimedia system.*

Multipurpose board A board with a smooth white plastic surface used with special marking pens rather than chalk. Sometimes called *visual aid panels,* the boards usually have a steel backing and can be used as a magnetic board for display of visuals; may also be used as a screen for projected visuals.

Multiscreen The use of more than one screen in a single presentation. Multiple images are often projected on adjacent multiple screens.

Narrowband A telecommunications channel that carries lower frequency signals; includes telephone frequencies of about 3,000 Hz and radio subcarrier signals of about 15,000 Hz.

Network A communication system linking two or more computers.

Networking The interconnecting of multiple sites via electronic means to send and receive signals between locations.

Newsgroup On computer networks, a discussion group created by allowing users to post messages and read messages among themselves.

Node A point at which two or more functional units interconnect transmission lines; more generally, a point of intersection.

Noise (1) In audio systems, electric interference or any unwanted sound. (2) In video, random spurts of electrical energy or interference; in some cases it will produce a salt-and-pepper pattern over the televised picture. (3) In communication, any distortion of the signal as it passes through the channel.

Nonformal education Purposeful learning that takes place outside the boundaries of formal education institutions.

Objective A statement of the new capability that is intended to result from instruction.

Offline Not connected to or not installed in a computer.

Omnidirectional A microphone that picks up sound from all directions.

Online Connected to or installed in a computer.

Opaque projection A method for projecting opaque (nontransparent) visuals by reflecting light off the material rather than transmitting light through it.

Open reel Audio- or videotape or film mounted on a reel that is not enclosed in a cartridge or cassette.

Optical disc A type of disc storage device that records and reproduces digital information using a laser beam, e.g., videodisc and CD.

Optical sound Sound that is recorded by photographic means on motion picture film. The sound is reproduced by projecting a narrow beam of light from an exciter lamp through the sound track into a photoelectric cell, which converts it to electrical impulses for amplification.

Oral history Historical documentation of a time, place, or event by means of recording the spoken recollections of participants in those events.

Output In electronics, the signal delivered from any audio or video device; also a jack, connector, or circuit that feeds the signal to another piece of equipment such as a speaker or headphones. In communication, information or a stimulus leaving a system.

Overhead projection Projection by means of a device that produces an image on a screen by transmitting light through transparent acetate or a similar medium on the stage of the projector. The lens and mirror arrangement in an elevated housing creates a bright projected image over the head or shoulder of the operator.

Overlay One or more additional transparent sheets with lettering or other information that can be placed over a base transparency.

Overt response A learner response that is outwardly observable (e.g., writing or speaking). See also *covert response.*

Password A unique series of letters or characters used to log on to a computer system to verify the authenticity of the user.

Patch cord An electrical wire used to connect two pieces of sound equipment (e.g., a tape recorder and record player) so that electrical impulses can be transferred between the two units to make a recording.

Performance objective A statement of the new capability the learner should possess at the completion of instruction. A well-stated objective names the intended audience, then specifies: (1) the performance or capability to be learned, (2) the conditions under which the performance is to be demonstrated, and (3) the criterion or standard of acceptable performance.

Peripheral A device—such as a printer, mass storage unit, or keyboard—that is an accessory to a microprocessor and transfers information to and from the microprocessor.

Persistence of vision The psychophysiological phenomenon that occurs when an image falls on the retina of the eye and is conveyed to the brain via the optic nerve. The brain continues to "see" the image for a fraction of a second after the image is cut off.

Personalized System of Instruction (PSI) A process technology for managing instruction that puts reinforcement theory into action as the overall framework for a whole course. Students work individually at their own pace using a variety of instructional materials. The materials are arranged in sequential order, and the student must show mastery of each unit before moving on to the next.

Pictorial graph An alternate form of the bar graph, in which a series of simple drawings is used to represent the quantitative values.

Pixel A single dot; the smallest picture element on a computer data display. The resolution of a screen is often expressed in pixels per inch.

Playback A device to reproduce a previously recorded program for hearing or viewing.

Portrait A vertical arrangement of a visual image or printed page in which the height is greater than the width; the opposite of *landscape*.

Process technology In general, technology as a way of thinking. Applied to instruction, a specific teaching-learning pattern that serves reliably as a template for delivering demonstrably effective instruction.

Programmed instruction A method of presenting instructional material printed in small bits or frames, each of which includes an item of information (prompt), a sentence to be completed or a question to be answered (response), and the correct answer (reinforcement).

Programmed teaching A process technology for learning involving scripted presentations, small-group instruction, unison responding by learners, cues given by the teacher, rapid pacing, and reinforcement and correction procedures.

Programmed tutoring A one-to-one process technology in which the decisions to be made by the tutor are "programmed" in advance by means of carefully structured printed instructions.

Programmer A multichannel, multifunction device used with a tape recorder or microprocessor to perform certain predetermined functions when called upon to do so by the synchronizer. In addition to synchronizing projectors and controlling dissolves, it can be arranged to perform other functions (often via interfaces), such as operating a motorized screen or adjusting room lights.

Projected visual Media formats in which still images are projected onto a screen.

Projection lens A convex lens or system of lenses that creates an enlarged image of the transparency, object, or film on a screen.

Prompt Information about the desired response, in the form of hints or explicit instruction, that is given to the learner prior to asking for a response.

RAM See *random access memory.*

Random access The ability to retrieve in any sequence slides, filmstrip frames, or information on audio- or videotapes or videodiscs regardless of original sequence.

Random access memory (RAM) The flexible part of computer memory. The particular program or set of data being manipulated by the user is temporarily stored in RAM, then erased to make way for the next program.

Range-finder camera A camera featuring a built-in, optical range-finder, usually incorporated into the viewfinder and linked mechanically with the focusing mount of the lens so that bringing the range-finder images into coincidence also focuses the lens.

Rate-controlled audio playback An audiotape system that can play back recorded speech at either a faster or a slower rate than the rate at which it was recorded, without loss of intelligibility. See also *speech compression and expansion.*

Read only memory (ROM) Control instructions that have been "wired" permanently into the memory of a computer. Usually stores instructions that the computer will need constantly, such as the programming language(s) and internal monitoring functions.

Real object Not a model or simulation but an example of an actual object used in instruction.

Rear screen A translucent screen of glass or acrylic with a specially formulated coating on which the image is transmitted though the screen for individual or group viewing. The screen is between the projector and the viewer.

Receiver In communication theory, the element of the system that detects and gathers the signal. In electronics, a device for collecting broadcast transmissions and decoding them for output on an audio or video player.

Redundancy The repetitious elements in messages transmitted through any communication channel.

Reel-to-reel Film or tape transport in which separate supply and take-up reels are used; they may be open or enclosed.

Referent That which is referred to.

Reinforcement The process of providing reinforcers (consequences that increase the likelihood of the preceding behavior) following desired behaviors.

Reinforcement theory A body of psychological theory centering on the role of reinforcement in learning—that is, the consequences that follow responses.

Reliability The quality of being dependable and consistent in yielding results in different situations.

Resolution The quality of a video image in terms of sharpness of detail.

Responder A device used with some audiovisual equipment to allow a student to respond to the program (e.g., by answering multiple-choice questions).

Role play A simulation in which the dominant feature is relatively open-ended interaction among people.

ROM See *read only memory.*

Roman lettering A style of lettering resembling ancient Roman stone-carved lettering. Vertical strokes are broad and horizontal strokes are narrower; curved strokes become narrower as they turn toward the horizontal.

Rule of thirds A principle of photographic and graphic composition in which an area is divided into thirds both vertically and horizontally and the centers of interest are located near the intersections of the lines.

Saturation The strength or purity of a color.

Scanner A computer device that converts an image on a piece of paper into an electronic form that can be stored in a computer file.

Scenario Literally, a written description of the plot of a play. In simulation and game design, it refers to a description of the setting and events to be represented in a simulation.

Schema A mental structure by which the individual organizes his or her perceptions of the environment. Plural: *schemata.*

Self-instruction A learning situation designed for individual, self-paced study guided by structured materials.

Sequencing Arranging ideas in logical order.

Shareware Computer software that is available at no cost.

Shot The basic element of which motion pictures are made; each separate length of motion picture footage is exposed in one "take."

Showmanship Techniques that an instructor can use to direct and hold attention during presentations.

Shutter The part of a camera (or projector) that controls the amount of light that can pass through the lens.

Simulation An abstraction or simplification of some real-life situation or process.

Simulation game An instructional format that combines the attributes of simulation (role playing, model

of reality) with the attributes of a game (striving toward a goal, specific rules).

Simulator A device that represents a real physical system in a scaled-down form; it allows the user to experience the salient aspects of the real-life process.

Single-lens reflex (SLR) camera A camera in which the viewfinder image is formed by the camera lens and reflected to a top-mounted viewing screen by a hinged mirror normally inclined behind the camera lens. During exposure of the film, the mirror flips up, allowing light to pass through onto the film.

Slide A small-format (e.g., 35mm) photographic transparency individually mounted for one-at-a-time projection.

Slow motion A film technique that expands time by photographing rapid events at high speeds (many exposures per second) and then projecting the film at normal speed.

Slow-scan video A device that transmits or receives still video pictures over a narrowband telecommunications channel; usually refers specifically to a still-frame video unit that accepts an image from a camera one line at a time, requiring several seconds to capture one full frame.

Soft technology Techniques and methods that form psychological and social frameworks for learning, as opposed to the hardware used to deliver instruction; an example is Keller's Personalized System of Instruction.

Software Computer program control instructions and accompanying documentation; stored on disks or tapes when not being used in the computer. By extension, the term refers to any audiovisual materials.

Speech compression and expansion A method of maintaining the intelligibility of normally recorded speech when it is played back at speeds greater than normal (compression) or less than normal (expansion); the effect is attained by electronically correcting the pitch to approximate the pitch of normal speech. Variable speeds of playback may be set, from 50% to 250% of normal speed.

Spirit duplicating An inexpensive duplicating and printing process using master sheets that release color through type indentations when a colorless alcohol fluid is applied; images can be imprinted on paper, card stock, or acetate.

Sponsored film or video Media produced by a private corporation, an association, or a government agency usually with the purpose of presenting a message of interest to the sponsor for general public consumption.

Spreadsheet Computer software that allows the user to manipulate data and generate reports and charts.

Star Schools A program initiated in the United States by the Department of Education to promote instructional networks providing distance education for elementary and secondary schools.

Storyboarding An audiovisual production and planning technique in which sketches of the proposed visuals and verbal messages are put on individual cards or into a computer program; the items are then arranged into the desired sequence on a display surface.

Study print A photographic enlargement printed in a durable form for individual or group examination.

Stylus The needle assembly of a phonograph cartridge.

Suggestive-accelerative learning and teaching (SALT) A U.S. adaptation of "suggestopedy" as proposed by Lozanov; major features are conscious relaxation, visual imagery, positive suggestion, multisensory input, and presentation of information to be learned in meaningful units, often to musical accompaniment.

Synchronizer A single-function device that, together with a tape recorder or other type of playback device, operates other equipment (e.g., for signaling slide changes).

Tacking iron A small thermostatically controlled heating tool used to tack or attach dry-mounting tissue to the back of a print or to the mount board to hold it in place while the print is trimmed and heated in the dry-mount press.

Take-up reel The reel that accumulates the tape or film as it is recorded or played.

Team-Assisted Individualization (TAI) A process technology developed by Robert Slavin that combines the use of self-paced instructional modules with discussion and remediation in small groups that are competing with other groups for higher scores on unit tests.

Technology (1) A process of devising reliable and repeatable solutions to tasks. (2) The hardware and software (i.e., the product) that result from the application of technological processes. (3) A mix of process and product, used in instances where the context refers to the combination of technological processes and resultant products or where the process is inseparable from the product.

Technology for learning An application of technology to aid the learning process; may refer to either "hard" technologies (communications media) or "soft" technologies (processes or procedures that follow a technological approach).

Telecommunication system A means for communicating over a distance; specifically, any arrangement for transmitting voice and data in the form of coded signals through an electronic medium.

Teleconference A communications configuration using electronic transmission technologies (audio and/or video) to hold live meetings among geographically dispersed people.

Teleconference, audio A live, two-way voice conversation among groups at different locations via telephone lines or satellites.

Teleconference, video A live, two-way communications arrangement connecting groups at different locations via telephone lines or satellites; voice is transmitted both ways, and video distribution may be either one-way or two-way.

Telelecture An instructional technique in which an individual, typically a content specialist or well-known authority, addresses a group listening by means of a telephone amplifier. The listeners may ask questions of the resource person, with the entire group able to hear the response.

Teletext Print information transmitted on a broadcast television signal using the "vertical blanking interval," a portion of the signal not used to carry visual or auditory information.

Teletraining The process of using teleconferences for instructional purposes.

Television The system of transmitting moving picture and sound electronically, either through the air or through wires, and displaying it on a cathode-ray tube.

Template A pattern used as a guide in making accurate replications of something. In computers, a ready-to-use permanent document set up with a basic layout, commands, and formulas.

Thermal film Specially treated acetate used to make overhead transparencies. In this process, infrared light passes through the film onto a prepared master underneath. An image is "burned" into the film wherever it contacts carbonaceous markings.

Threading Inserting or directing a film or tape through a projector or recorder mechanism.

Tilt The swiveling of a motion picture or video camera upward or downward.

Time-lapse A film technique that compresses the time that it takes for an event to occur. A long process is photographed frame by frame, at long intervals, and then projected at normal speed.

Transaction In simulation and game design, the specific actions and interactions carried out by the players as they engage in the activity.

Transparency The large-format (typically 8 by 10 inches) film used with the overhead projector.

Treble See *frequency*.

Two-by-six rule A general rule of thumb for determining screen size: no viewer should be seated closer to the screen than two screen widths or farther away than six screen widths.

UHF (ultra-high frequency)   Television transmission on channels 14 through 83 (300–3,000 MHz).

Ultraviolet (UV)   Rays just beyond (i.e., shorter than) the visible spectrum; ordinarily filtered or blocked to prevent eye damaging and dye fading.

U-matic   A particular videocassette system offered by several manufacturers in which ¾-inch tape moves at 7½ ips between two enclosed hubs.

Unidirectional microphone   See *cardioid microphone.*

Uplink   A ground station that transmits a signal to a satellite for retransmission to other ground stations.

Upload   To send a file from a computer system to a network.

User-friendly   A subjective measure of how easy an item of hardware or software is to use.

VCR   See *videocassette recorder.*

VHF (very high frequency)   Television transmission on channels 2 through 13 (30–300 MHz).

VHS   Video home system. A ½-inch videocassette format; not compatible with the Beta format, which is also ½ inch but differs electronically.

Video   The storage of visuals and their display on a television-type screen.

Videocassette   Videotape that has been enclosed in a plastic case. Available in one ¾-inch format (U-matic) and two ½-inch formats, Beta and VHS (video home system).

Videocassette recorder   A device that records and plays back video images and sound on magnetic tape stored in a cassette.

Videoconference   A teleconference involving a television-type picture as well as voice transmission. The video image may be freeze-frame or full-motion video.

Videodisc   A video recording and storage system in which audiovisual signals are recorded on plastic discs rather than on magnetic tape.

Videotex   Two-way, interactive transmission of text and graphics linking the user to a computer database.

Viewfinder   The part of a camera (usually some type of lens) that allows the user to frame the subject being photographed.

Virtual reality   Highly realistic computer simulations that give the impression of being inside a three-dimensional space.

Visual literacy   The learned ability to interpret visual messages accurately and to create such messages.

Volume unit meter (VU-meter)   A device that indicates the relative levels of the various sounds being recorded or played. Usually calibrated to show a point of maximum recording level to avoid tape saturation and limit distortion.

Web   See *World Wide Web.*

Wide-angle lens   A camera lens that permits a wider view of a subject and its surroundings than would be obtained by a normal lens from the same position.

Wide area network (WAN)   A communications network that covers a large geographic area, such as a state or country.

World Wide Web   A graphical environment on computer networks that allows you to access, view, and maintain documents that can include text, data, sound, and video.

Zoom lens   A lens with a continuously variable focal length.

REFERENCES

Deluca, Stuart M. *Instructional Video.* Boston: Focal Press, 1991.

Freedman, Alan. *The Computer Glossary.* 6th ed. New York: AMACOM, American Management Association, 1993.

Reynolds, Angus, and Anderson, Ronald H. *Selecting and Developing Media for Instruction.* 3d ed. New York: Van Nostrand Reinhold, 1992.

Rosenberg, Kenyon C., and Elsbee, John J. *Dictionary of Library and Educational Technology.* 3d ed. Englewood, CO: Libraries Unlimited, 1989.

CREDITS

Fig. 1.19: Martha Campbell. Reprinted by permission.

Fig. 3.4: Copyright SafeAir. Reprinted by permission.

Fig. 4.17: Tom Darcy of Newsday newspaper. Used by permission of Times Mirror Corp.

Fig. 7.1: Martha Campbell. Reprinted by permission.

Fig. 8.9: Martha Campbell. Reprinted by permission.

Fig. 8.14: Used by permission of C.A.R., Inc., 7009 Kingsbury, St. Louis, MO 63130. These illustrations taken from the Clipables® EPS Graphics Library. Clipables is a registered trademark of C.A.R., Inc. All rights reserved.

Fig. 9.8: Martha Campbell. Reprinted by permission.

Fig. 12.5: RemotePoint Cordless Hand-Held Mouse, Interlink Electronics. Used by permission.

Fig. 12.7: Copyright 1994 by Bill Keene, Inc. Distributed by Cowles Syndicate, Inc. Reprinted with permission.

PHOTO CREDITS

All photographs not listed below are by Scott Cunningham/Merrill/Prentice Hall. Photographs are copyrighted by the individuals or companies listed.

(t) = top; (c) = center; (b) = bottom; (l) = left; (r) = right

Title page and chapter opener background photo by Tom Watson/Merrill/Prentice Hall. Photo essay: Brad Feinknopf/Merrill/Prentice Hall: p. 2 (3); Andy McGuire: p. 3 (5, 8).

Chapter 1 Darrell Fremont: p. 6(tl); Anne Vega/Merrill/Prentice Hall: p. 14; Brad Feinknopf/Merrill/Prentice Hall: p. 18; Michael Neff: p. 19; Xerox Imaging Systems, Inc: p. 22(b); Missouri Historical Society: p. 25; David Derkacy: p. 27.

Chapter 2 Courtesy of Robert F. Mager: p. 44; Andy McGuire: p. 46; Anne Vega/Merrill/Prentice Hall: p. 57(r).

Chapter 3 Brad Feinknopf/Merrill/Prentice Hall: p. 69(rc); Thomas Cecere/Indiana University Audio-Visual Center: pp. 72, 73; Superstock: p. 70(t); Dennis Pett: p. 94(tl, tr).

Chapter 4 Barbara Schwartz/Merrill/Prentice Hall: p. 103(t); David Derkacy: pp. 103(b), 105, 121 (both), 127, 128; Courtesy of Varitronic Systems, Inc.: p. 119(b); Andy McGuire: p. 125 (both).

Chapter 5 David Derkacy: pp. 145, 151(l), 153, 157; Proxima: p. 149; Institute of Texan Culture: p. 151(r); Andy McGuire: p. 163 (both), 166; Canapress Photo Service: p. 164(t); Dukane Corporation: p. 164(b).

Chapter 6 SounDocumentaries: p. 179; David Derkacy: p. 181(t); Manny Greenhill: p. 181(b); Mitzi Trumbo: p. 182; The Library of Congress: p. 184; CareerTrack: p. 186.

Chapter 7 Superstock: p. 196(tl, tr); Barbara Stimpert: p. 196(c); CRM Films: p. 200(b); Bullfrog Films, Inc.: p. 203(b); The Bettmann Archive: pp. 204(b), 205; Andy McGuire: p. 206(bl); National Film Board of Canada: p. 206(br).

Chapter 8 Courtesy of Apple Computer, Inc.: p. 228(t); Computer-Based Education Research Laboratory, University of Illinois: p. 229; Anne Vega/Merrill/Prentice Hall: p. 231(t), 234; Todd Yarrington/Merrill/Prentice Hall: p. 231(b), 233; In Focus Systems: p. 238.

Chapter 9 Los Angeles Times Photo: pp. 258(t), 275(b); Darrell Fremont: p. 258(b); David Derkacy: pp. 265 (both), 273; EduQuest/IBM Corporation: p. 269(b); National Geographic Educational Services: p. 272; Philips: p. 275(t); Discis Books: p. 274.

Chapter 10 The Children's Television Network: p. 285; Academy for Educational Development: p. 291; NBC/Globe: p. 296; Milt Hamburger, Instructional Television Service, Indiana University: p. 300(t); TI-IN Network: p. 300(b); Jeff Martin/University of Northern Iowa, Office of Public Relations, p. 302(b).

Chapter 11 Pentathlon Institute: p. 310(t); Barbara Schwartz/Merrill/Prentice Hall: p. 310(lc), 325; David Derkacy: pp. 321, 330, 333(b); Anne Vega/Merrill/Prentice Hall: p. 324; Ken Wonnacott, Metro Detroit MPT: p. 328; Simulation Training Systems: p. 331(t); Doron Precision Systems, Inc.: p. 332; Michael Molenda: p. 334(l); World Vision: p. 337.

Chapter 12 J. S. Cangelosi: p. 342(cl); David Derkacy: pp. 342(cr), 351(b), 353, 358; Honda of America, Inc.: p. 342(b); The Bettmann Archive: p. 351(t); Todd Yarrington/Merrill/Prentice Hall: p. 356; AECT Candid Photo: p. 359.

Appendix A David Derkacy: All photos.

Classroom Link

Contents

Introduction

Learning the ropes of the teaching profession can sometimes be a confusing process. Trying to determine what type of lesson plan to use, or deciding which media format to use to accompany that lesson, can detract from the lesson's main point. The extra time spent on deciding which lesson plan or media format to use may divert attention from the most important aspect of teaching: the needs of the students.

Classroom Link is designed to make this process easier. It is an interactive computer program to be used in accordance with *Instructional Media and Technologies for Learning* (5th edition). The modules in the program correspond to the subject matter outlined in the textbook, making the concepts more easily accessible.

System requirements

Computer hardware and software requirements depend on whether you're installing Classroom Link for Microsoft Windows or the Macintosh. Refer to the appropriate section below. All instructions assume that you have a basic understanding of how your computer and its operating system software work.

Windows

Operating system	DOS 3.1 or later, plus Microsoft Windows 3.1 or later, or Windows for Workgroups 3.1 or later
Processor	80386 or higher
RAM memory	4 Mb minimum
Configuration	386 enhanced mode with at least a 2 Mb permanent swap file
Hard disk space	5 Mb minimum
Disk drive	One 3.5-inch high-density drive
Display	VGA (640 x 480 pixel resolution) recommended
Pointing device	Mouse or trackball

Macintosh

Operating system	System 7.0 or later
Processor	68030 or higher
RAM memory	4 Mb minimum
Hard disk space	5 Mb minimum
Disk drive	One 3.5-inch (1.4 Mb) drive
Display	Any 12-inch or larger Macintosh-compatible monitor with at least 640 x 400 pixel resolution

Where to Find Classroom Link

Classroom Link can be found on the Prentice-Hall main World Wide Web site. The Internet address is:

(URL=) http:\\www.prenhall.com

The Classroom Link program can be downloaded from the Web site and installed on your computer by following the instructions below. **NOTE: there are two separate versions of Classroom Link (Macintosh and Windows). Be sure that you download the right version for your computer.** If you are not sure how to access the World Wide Web and download files, please see your instructor for additional help.

Creating Classroom Link installation disks

After Classroom Link is downloaded to your computer, you must prepare the files for installation. Classroom Link requires two 1.44Mb high density diskettes for this procedure.

1. Format the first of the disks and label it DISK 1. Next, format the second disk and label it DISK 2. NOTE: If the disks are not properly labeled, Classroom Link will fail to install.
2. The program is downloaded in compressed state for easier file transfer. In order to create the installation disks, you must first decompress the downloaded files.

Macintosh:

3. The files were compressed using Stuffit, and you will need to decompress the files using the same program. NOTE: There will be two files when decompressed, INSTALL.1 and INSTALL.2.
4. When you have decompressed the download file, you should have two files, one called INSTALL.1 and the other INSTALL.2. Copy INSTALL.1 to the disk labeled DISK 1 and INSTALL.2 to the disk labeled DISK 2. The installation disks are now completed. Please refer to the "Installing Classroom Link" section of this manual for further instructions on program installation.

Windows:

3. The files were compressed using PKZIP, and you will need to decompress the files using the same program. NOTE: There will be more then 200 files when decompressed. The files will reside in two separate directories called DSK1 and DSK2. To avoid unzipping the files into a single directory you must use the -d option of PKUNZIP.
4. When you have decompressed the download file, you should have over 200 files in the two directories called DSK1 and DSK2. Copy all of the files in the directory DSK1 to the disk labeled DISK 1. Copy the files in the directory called DSK2 to the disk called DISK 2. The installation disks are now completed. Please refer to the "Installing Classroom Link" section of this manual for further instructions on program installation.

Installing Classroom Link

Installation transfers the Classroom Link files to your hard disk and decompresses them so they can be used. Follow the instructions below for the type of computer you are using. Other important information, including changes since this manual was printed, can be found in the README.TXT file on the installation disks.

Before installing, make sure you have at least 10 Mb of free space on your hard disk. The installation process requires at least 5 Mb of space on your hard disk in addition to the space used for the program files. This space is only required during the installation.

Installing in Windows

1. Start Windows and close all open applications. Disable any virus-checking software before installing.
2. Place Classroom Link Disk 1 in drive A or B.
3. In the Windows Program Manager, choose Run from the File menu.
4. In the Command Line box, type the letter of the drive containing Disk 1 (A or B), followed by a colon and

the word **SETUP**. For example, if you placed Disk 1 in drive A, type **A:SETUP**, then click OK.

5.   A window appears, asking you to choose a folder where you would like to store the Classroom Link files, and a name for the program group that will contain the Classroom Link icon. When you are satisfied with the entries, click Continue. Click Cancel Setup to stop the installation.
6.   When prompted, remove Disk 1 from the drive and insert Disk 2. Click OK to continue the installation.
7.   When you see a message that Setup has completed the installation, click OK to return to Program Manager.
8.   You must restart Windows before you use Classroom Link.

Installing on the Macintosh

1.   Start the Macintosh and close all open applications. Disable any virus-checking software before installing.
2.   Place Classroom Link DISK 1 in the Macintosh disk drive.
3.   Open the disk labeled DISK 1. Its window will appear on your desktop.
4.   Double-click the icon labeled INSTALL.1.
5.   A window appears. Under the heading "Install Location" select the drive where you would like the Classroom Link files to be stored. You do not need to select a folder as the install program will create one for you. When you are satisfied with the entries, click Install. Click Quit to stop the installation.
6.   A second dialog window appears notifying you that your computer must be restarted after installation. To continue installation click continue. If you have other applications open, click Cancel, close those applications, and then begin the Classroom Link installation again.
7.   When prompted, insert the Classroom Link Disk 2 into the drive to continue installation.
8.   When installation is complete, a dialog window appears to notify you that the application has been successfully installed and that the computer must be restarted. Click Continue to restart the computer.

Reinstalling Classroom Link

In the unlikely event one of the Classroom Link program files is accidentally erased or becomes corrupted, you can reinstall Classroom Link by repeating the procedures above. If you have already created lesson plans, be sure to make a backup of your data beforehand. Reinstalling will erase any lesson plans or media evaluations you might have created. After you have finished reinstalling, you can restore your data from the backup. The Utilities menu commands section beginning on page 5 explains how to back up and restore data.

Menu Command Reference

This section describes each pull-down menu command. Many commands have keyboard shortcuts that are listed beside the command name on the pull-down menu. These are two (or sometimes three) keys that, when pressed simultaneously, carry out the same function as the menu command. For example, pressing CTRL plus X (Windows) or COMMAND plus X (Macintosh) has the same function as choosing Cut from the Edit menu.

File menu commands

```
┌──────┐
│ File │
├──────┴──────────────┐
│ Exit Program        │
│ Return to the Main Menu │
└─────────────────────┘
```

Exit Program   Quits Classroom Link and returns you to Windows or the Macintosh Desktop. The message "Do you wish to quit Classroom Link" appears; click Yes to quit or No to continue working with Classroom Link. Classroom Link automatically saves your work when you quit.

Return to the Main Menu   Saves your work and returns you to the Main Menu. This command is available only while using a media evaluation window.

Edit menu commands

```
Edit
Cut        Ctrl+X
Copy       Ctrl+C
Paste      Ctrl+V
Clear

Select All  Ctrl+A

Preferences
```

Cut	Removes selected information from your lesson plan or media evaluation and places it in the Clipboard. The Clipboard can hold only one selection at a time, so any information already in the Clipboard will be replaced.
Copy	Duplicates the selected information and places that copy in the Clipboard. Any information already in the Clipboard will be replaced.
Paste	Places a copy of the Clipboard contents into your lesson plan or media evaluation at the location of the insertion point. Before choosing Paste, be sure to click where you want the selection to go.
Clear	Permanently removes the selected information. The selection is not placed in the Clipboard, nor are the contents of the clipboard changed. The DELETE and BACKSPACE keys have the same function. Be careful when using this command; it can't be undone.
Select All	Selects everything in the field, or text entry area, where the insertion point is located. This command is useful when a field contains more text than can be displayed at one time.
Preferences	Displays the Calculator Preferences window when the Calculator tool is active. This window lets you set the operation of the NUMLOCK key (the CLEAR key on Macintosh keyboards), as well as the number of decimal places the calculator will display.

Tools menu commands

The Tools menu is available only when you are creating or modifying a lesson plan or media evaluation.

```
Tools
Calculator
Calendar/Diary
Puzzle
```

Calculator	Displays a standard mathematical calculator. Make entries by clicking keys with the mouse or typing entries on your keyboard's numeric keypad. You can copy and paste amounts between the calculator display and your lesson plan or media evaluation.
Calendar/Diary	Displays a calendar with the current month and date highlighted. You can enter short memos, reminders, or schedules for each day in the diary area to the right of the calendar. Click a different day on the calendar to make new entries, or to display existing diary entries for that day. Use the buttons at the bottom of the Calendar/Diary window to display other months or years, or return to the today's date. You can enlarge the Calendar/Diary window to the full screen width to gain more space for diary entries.

The Text and Diary menus appear on the menu bar when Calendar/Diary is active. Commands on the Text menu allow you to change the appearance of your diary entries. (The Enlarge Font, Reduce Font, and Spelling commands are not active in the |

current release of Classroom Link.) Commands on the Diary menu duplicate the functions of the buttons at the bottom of the Calendar/Diary window. They also allow you to move the highlight between the diary and calendar portions of the window, and to delete outdated diary entries.

Puzzle Displays a game when you're ready to take a break from planning lessons. Double-click a tile to move it into the adjacent empty space. Click Shuffle to begin a new game.

About menu commands

About Displays a copyright message. The message disappears when you click the mouse or press any key.

Utilities menu commands

The Utilities menu is available only when the Main Menu is displayed.

Backup Databases Makes a copy, or backup, of the Classroom Link data files on another disk for safekeeping. It's a good idea to make frequent backups of your work. If the data ever becomes corrupted, you can use Restore Databases to copy data files from your most recent backup to the hard disk, minimizing the amount of lost work.

When you choose Backup Databases, the Backup Databases dialog box appears, asking you to specify a destination for the backup files.

Backup Databases dialog box

If you are backing up to a floppy disk, make sure the disk is formatted and inserted in the appropriate drive. Click the "Select folder to place backup" button; the Select Directory dialog box appears.

Select Directory dialog box

Choose a disk drive from the drop-down list at the bottom of the dialog box, then highlight a folder in the scrolling window directly above it.

Warning: If the location you choose contains an earlier Classroom Link backup, your new backup will replace the earlier backup.

When you are satisfied with your choices, click the Select button. The Backup Databases dialog box reappears with your destination drive and folder displayed. Click Cancel if you want to stop the backup, or click Backup to begin copying data files. A message will notify you when the backup is complete. Click the mouse or press any key to return to the Main Menu.

Restore Databases

If any of the Classroom Link files become corrupted, you can restore a set of undamaged files from the disk that contains your most recent backup. The restore process copies the full set of Classroom Link data files from the backup disk to your hard disk. Any changes you made to the original data files after the last backup will have to be reentered.

Restoring is nearly identical to the process of backing up, which is described on the previous page. Instead of choosing a destination disk and folder, you'll be asked to specify the source of the files to restore. If you are restoring files from a floppy disk, make sure the disk is inserted in the appropriate drive.

Append Database(s)

Choosing this command lets you append, or add, specific Classroom Link data files to a set of files on another disk. It is especially useful if you want to share lesson plans and media evaluations with colleagues or students, because you can add new or changed information to their files, and vice-versa, without replacing any information that either of you might have already accumulated.

Note: Appending is not the same as making a backup. Appending adds new information to selected data files on another disk. It does not disturb any lesson plan or media evaluation data that might already exist on that disk. In comparison, the backup process copies the entire set of Classroom Link data files to another disk, and replaces all existing lesson plan and media evaluation data on that disk.

Choosing this command displays the Append Database(s) dialog box.

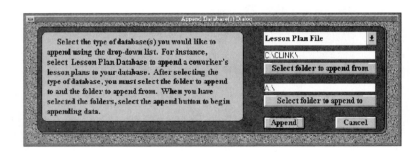

Append Databases dialog box

First, choose the type of database file to append from the drop-down list. Note that all your lesson plans are stored in one file, while each type of media evaluation is stored in a separate file. Choose All Database Files if you wish to append all files simultaneously.

Click the appropriate buttons to select source and destination folders. In the file dialog box that appears, choose a drive from the drop-down list at the bottom of the dialog box, then highlight a folder in the scrolling window directly above it. If you are appending to or from a floppy disk drive, make sure the disk is properly formatted and inserted in the appropriate drive before you choose it, or an error message will appear. When you are satisfied with your choices, click the Select button.

When you have chosen the source and destination drives and folders, you'll see them displayed in the Append Databases dialog box. Click Cancel if you want to stop the process, or Append if you're ready to begin appending data. A message will prompt you when the process is complete. Click the mouse or press any key to return to the Main Menu window.

Creating a lesson plan

This section describes how to start Classroom Link, create a new lesson plan, navigate through the lesson plan windows, print the lesson plan, and make changes to your work. These are the most common activities you'll perform.

Getting started

Start Classroom Link   Double-click the Classroom Link icon in the Windows Program Manager or Macintosh Desktop. The Main Menu window appears.

Create a new lesson plan   In the Main Menu window, click the Lesson Plans button. The Create or Modify a Lesson Plan window appears; click Create. The Input Lesson Plan Name window appears. Type the name of the lesson plan in the box that appears at the top of the window.

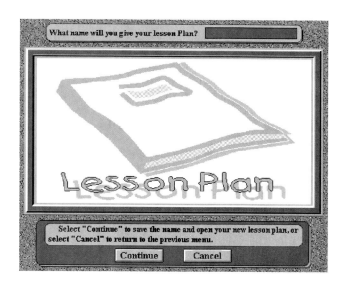

Input lesson plan name window

When you are satisfied with the name, click Continue or press ENTER twice. The Analyze Learners window appears, and you can begin entering information.

The lesson plan window

The lesson plans you create are based on the ASSURE model described elsewhere in this text. Each step in the ASSURE model corresponds to a separate data entry window. Together, they make up a complete lesson plan.

Each window is divided into two parts. The *entry area* at the top contains *fields* where you enter information about the lesson and the type of learners you're targeting. The *control area* at the bottom displays the name of the current lesson plan and contains buttons to help you navigate to other windows and manage the information you accumulate.

Using the entry area

The *entry area* consists of two to six *fields*. Most fields allow you to enter text, although some only serve to remind you of activities you need to perform. The names of the fields and the type of information you'll enter vary from window to window. The illustration on the following page shows a typical entry area.

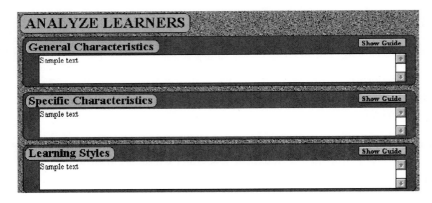

Entry area

Entering and editing text

To enter text in an empty field, click anywhere in the field. A blinking vertical bar, or *cursor,* will appear in the top left corner of the field. As you type, notice that the cursor moves, always indicating where the next letter will appear. If you make a mistake, simply backspace and retype. As you get to the end of a line, the text will automatically *wrap* to the next line – there's no need to press RETURN unless you want to start a new paragraph. If you fill up the entire field, the text will begin to *scroll*, allowing you to enter as much text as you like. You can use the up and down scroll arrows at the right edge of the field to view all parts of your entry.

If you'd like to insert a word or sentence, move the mouse pointer to the place where you want to insertion to appear, then click. Notice that the pointer changes to an I-beam shape when it's over a text field, to help you choose a position more easily. When you click, the cursor moves to the new position. If you now type a word, any text to the right of the cursor will move to make room for the new entry. (If it doesn't, press the INS key to change from overstrike to insert typing mode; "Ins" will appear on the status bar at the bottom of the screen.)

To move a word or sentence to a new position, click at the beginning, hold the mouse button down, *drag* to the end, then release the mouse button. Your *selection* will appear highlighted. If you selected the wrong text, just try again. Choose Cut from the Edit menu; the selection will be removed. Click where you want to move the selection to, then choose Paste from the Edit menu. The text will reappear at the new position. Refer to the Edit menu commands section for more information on cutting, copying, pasting, and clearing text.

Getting help

Each field has its own *online help*, which describes what sort of information you should enter. To display online help for a particular field, click its Show Guide button. The view will expand to show your entry (where applicable) at the top of the window and the guidelines directly below. Click Return to hide the guidelines.

In addition, the Analyze Learners window has a Show Details button that displays brief descriptions of the types of entries recommended for each field. The State the Objective window has a drop-down list of The Helpful Hundred action verbs. When you select a word from the list, it will be copied to the Clipboard. To add the word to your lesson plan, position the insertion point in the appropriate text field and choose Paste from the Edit menu.

Using the control area

The *control area* at the bottom of the lesson plan entry window displays the name of the current lesson plan and contains buttons to help you navigate to other windows, save or delete your work, and print the information you accumulate. A typical control area is shown below.

Control area

The following buttons appear in the control area of all lesson plan entry windows.

ASSURE buttons   Click a letter to display a window where you can enter information corresponding to the respective step in the ASSURE model. For example, clicking U displays the Utilize Materials window. You can display lesson plan entry windows in any order.

Delete Lesson Plan   Deletes the current lesson plan. Clicking this button displays a dialog box with the message, "Permanently delete the current Lesson Plan?" Click No to keep the current lesson plan, or click Yes to delete the lesson plan and return to the Create or Modify a Lesson Plan window.

Print Lesson Plan   Prints all entries for the current lesson plan. Clicking this button displays the Printing Options dialog box, pictured below.

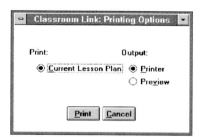

Printing Options dialog box

Click the Printer button if you want to send the lesson plan to the printer that is currently selected in the Windows Control Panel or the Macintosh Chooser. Click the Preview button if you want to display the lesson plan on the screen. When you have chosen a destination, click Print. Click Cancel to return to the current window.

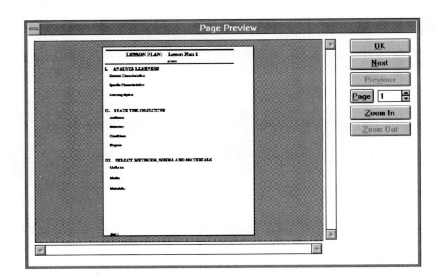

Page Preview window

The Page Preview window displays the lesson plan in full-page view. For a full-size view, click Zoom In, or click on the part of the page that you want to enlarge. Use the scroll arrows to show other parts of the page. Click Zoom Out to return to full-page view. Click Next to display subsequent pages, and Previous to return to previous pages. To go directly to a particular page, click the arrow buttons beside the box displaying the page number until the desired page number appears, then click Page to display that page. If you select a page number that doesn't exist, the Page Preview window will display the last page. Click OK to close the Page Preview window.

Save Lesson Plan Saves the current lesson plan to the hard disk. The message "Saving Lesson Plan..." appears at the top of the screen. The message disappears when you move the mouse.

Save and return... Saves the current lesson plan and returns you to the Main Menu window. When you click this button, a dialog box displays the message, "Save lesson plan and return to the Main Menu?" Click Yes to save your work and return to the Main Menu window, or click No to remain in the current window.

The following buttons also appear in the control area, depending on the lesson plan entry window being used.

Show/Hide Details Available only in the Analyze Learners window, this button displays (or hides) prompts that briefly describe the types of entries recommended for each field.

Media Evaluations Available in the Select Methods, Media, and Materials window and in the Evaluate and Revise window, this button displays the Media Evaluations menu, where you can select a media category to enter, edit or review. When you have completed your work with media evaluations, click Return to Lesson Plan in the Media Evaluations menu to return to the lesson plan entry window you started from.

Print Checklist Available only in the Utilize Materials window, this button prints a two-page checklist to help you prepare for the presentation of your lesson. Clicking this button displays the Printing Options dialog box. Click the Printer button if you want to send the checklist to the printer that's currently selected in the Windows Control Panel or the Macintosh Chooser. Click the Preview button if you want to display the checklist on the screen. When you have chosen a destination, click Print. Click Cancel to return to the current window.

The Page Preview window displays the checklist in full-page view. For a full-size view, click Zoom In, or click on the part of the page that you want to enlarge. Use the scroll arrows to show other parts of the page. Click Zoom Out to return to full-page view. Click Next to display subsequent pages, and Previous to return to previous pages. Click OK to close the Page Preview window and return to the Utilize Materials window.

Modifying a lesson plan

Choose a lesson plan   From the Main Menu, click the Lesson Plans button. The Create or Modify a Lesson Plan window appears; click Modify. The Modify Existing Lesson Plan window appears.

Highlight the name of the Lesson Plan you wish to modify in the pull-down menu, and then select the "Select" button to begin editing your lesson plan, or select "Cancel" to return to the previous menu.

Lesson Plan 1 ↨   Select   Cancel

Modify Existing Lesson Plan window

Display the drop-down list of existing lesson plans. Click a name, then click Select. The Analyze Learners window appears, with the name of the lesson plan you selected displayed in the control area.

Make changes   Add, change or delete information as you desire.

Save your work   Click Save and Return to the Main Menu. The "Save Lesson Plan and Return to Main Menu?" dialog box appears. Click Yes.

Creating a media evaluation

This chapter describes how to start Classroom Link, create a new media evaluation, navigate through the media evaluation windows, print a media evaluation, save your work, and quit.

Getting started

Start Classroom Link   Double-click the Classroom Link icon in the Windows Program Manager or Macintosh Desktop. The Main Menu window appears.

Access media evaluations   In the Main Menu window, click Media Evaluations. The Media Evaluations window appears. Click a button corresponding to the type of media you wish to evaluate. The Appraisal checklist appears and you are ready to begin entering information. The Media Evaluations window is pictured on the following page.

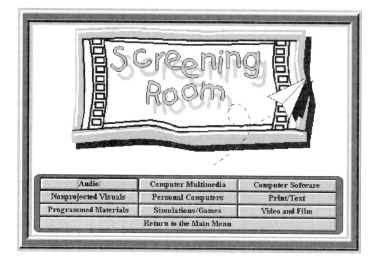

Audio	Computer Multimedia	Computer Software
Nonprojected Visuals	Personal Computers	Print/Text
Programmed Materials	Simulations/Games	Video and Film
Return to the Main Menu		

Media Evaluations window

The media evaluation windows

Like the Lesson Plan window, each Media Evaluation window is divided into an upper *entry area*, where you enter information, and a lower *control area* that helps you manage and navigate through media evaluation information. The entry area of each media evaluation is further divided into two parts, only one of which is visible at a time. *Part #1*, the Appraisal Checklist, allows you to record objective, descriptive information about a media resource, such as an audio tape or computer software package. *Part #2*, the Rating, allows you to record subjective ratings and comments about the resource.

Using the Appraisal Checklist (Part #1)

The Appraisal Checklist consists of several text fields into which you can enter information about the media resource. Where applicable, it also contains buttons you can click to indicate the resource's format. To display the Rating window, click the Go to Part #2 button. The illustration on the following page shows a typical Appraisal Checklist.

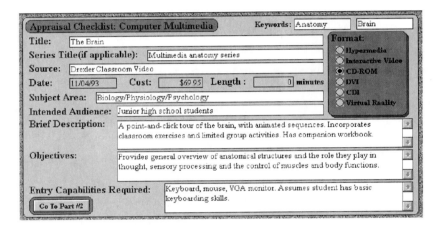

Appraisal Checklist

Using the Rating (Part #2)

The Rating section of a Media Evaluation consists of several *rating criteria,* each of which you can rate High, Medium or Low by clicking the appropriate button. It contains a text field where you can record any comments about the resource, as well as its strong or weak points. Fields are also provided for you to enter the name of the reviewer and the date of the review. To display the Appraisal Checklist window, click the Go to Part #1 button. The illustration below shows a typical Rating window.

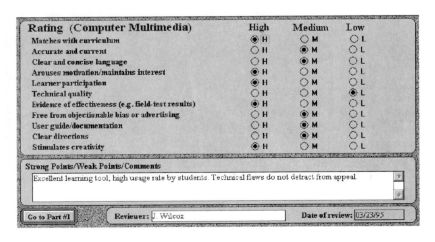

Rating

Making media evaluation entries

To enter text in an empty field or make changes to existing entries, refer to the instructions in the "Entering and editing text" section. To simplify the entry process, you can press the TAB and SHIFT-TAB keys to move from field to field. When a field is highlighted, any keyboard entry will replace the current contents of the field. If a field doesn't apply to the media resource you're evaluating, leave it blank. Most fields are self-explanatory, but a few deserve special mention:

Keywords	Two keyword fields are provided on each Appraisal Checklist. Keyword entries should be short, easily-remembered words that divide media titles into broad categories. You can use Classroom Link's keyword search capability to quickly locate media resources associated with a particular category.
Format	A list of formats is provided where appropriate. Click the button that best describes the format of your media resource. Only one button can be selected at a time. Classroom Link's search capability lets you locate all media titles having a particular format.
Title	In order to save a media evaluation, you must at least enter a title. It's a good idea to keep a record of the media titles you enter. Later, you can use Classroom Link's search capability to locate a specific title.
Brief Description	Descriptive information should be objective, content-related information. You can use Classroom Link's search capability to locate a particular description, but this is practical only if your descriptions are limited to a few words.
Date/Date of review	Enter date information in the MMDDYY format. You do not need to type the separator character (/). For example, June 5, 1995 would be entered 060595.
Cost	Enter an amount up to 999999.99. You should type a decimal point where you want it to be placed, but you do not have to type the dollar sign. To enter an even $50, type 50 followed by a decimal; the 00 to the right of the decimal will be inserted for you.
Minutes	Enter a whole number up to 99999999.
Floppy disk drives	This field applies only to Personal Computers. The drop-down list displays available choices. Choose the best description of the computer's equipment; the list will disappear and the field will display your choice.

Using the control area

The *control area* appears at the bottom of each Media Evaluation window and helps you manage information, navigate, search, and print the information you accumulate. The control area is shown in the illustration below.

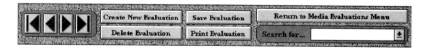

Control area

Browse buttons	The group of arrow-shaped browse buttons at the left end of the control area helps you navigate among all the media appraisals of a particular type that you have entered. For example, if you choose Audio in the Media Evaluations window, the browse buttons let you navigate through all the audio evaluations you have entered.
	Listed from left to right, the buttons' functions are First, Previous, Next and Last. The buttons will be inactive (dimmed) until you have entered more than one evaluation of a particular type.
Create new evaluation	Creates a new media evaluation record. It isn't necessary to choose this button before entering your first media evaluation of a particular type.

When you create a new media evaluation, it will be placed after the last media evaluation of its type that you have previously entered. For example, if you've entered three video evaluations and click Create new evaluation, the new video evaluation will become the fourth video evaluation in your records. Once created, the order that media evaluations are stored in Classroom Link cannot be changed.

Save evaluation   Saves the current media evaluation to the hard disk. The message "Saving Media Evaluation…" appears at the top of the screen. The message disappears when you move the mouse.

Delete evaluation   Deletes the current media evaluation. Clicking this button displays a dialog box with the message "Permanently delete the current Media Evaluation?" Click No to keep the current media evaluation, or click Yes to delete the media evaluation.

Print evaluation   Prints all entries for the current media evaluation. Clicking this button displays the Printing Options dialog box, pictured below.

Printing Options dialog box

Click the Printer button if you want to send the media evaluation to the printer that's currently selected in the Windows Control Panel or the Macintosh Chooser. Click the Preview button if you want to display the media evaluation on the screen. When you have chosen a destination, click Print. Click Cancel to return to the current window.

The Page Preview window displays the media evaluation in full-page view (see illustration of this window on page 10). For a full-size(100%) view, click Zoom In, or click on the part of the page that you want to enlarge. Use the scroll arrows to show other parts of the page. Click Zoom Out to return to full-page view. Click Next to display subsequent pages, and Previous to return to previous pages. To go directly to a particular page, click the arrow buttons beside the box displaying the page number until the desired page number appears, then click Page to display that page. If you select a page number that doesn't exist, the Page Preview window will display the last page. Click OK to close the Page Preview window.

Return to Media…menu   Saves your work and returns you to the Media Evaluations window.

Using the search function

The control area's Search for button provides access to a powerful search function that can help you locate a particular media evaluation, or locate all those meeting specific criteria.

Search for…   Allows you to locate a particular media evaluation by keyword, title, format (where applicable) or brief description. This function is available for all media evaluation types except personal computers.

To set a criterion to search for, display the drop-down list of available choices. Click the search criterion you wish to use; the list will disappear and the Search for field will display your choice. The list is pictured below.

Search for… drop-down list

The Search Dialog window will appear. Enter the text you wish to search for, exactly as it was originally entered, including any punctuation. Capitalization is not important. For example, if you used the keyword "Brain, Human" you could enter "brain, human" but not "brain" or "human". The maximum entry is 40 characters. The search dialog is pictured on the following page.

Search Dialog window

When you are satisfied with your entry, click Search to begin the search or Cancel to return to your media evaluation.

If your entry is not found, the message "No matches for this search. Press any key to continue." will appear. Press a key or click the mouse to return to your media evaluation.

If the search is successful, Classroom Link will display all evaluations that match the search criteria. A modified control area, pictured below, will appear to allow you to browse through the matching evaluations or print the search results.

Search control area

The following buttons appear in the search control area.

Browse buttons If more than one media evaluation matches the search criteria, the browse buttons are activated to allow you to navigate to the first, previous, next or last matching evaluations. The search control area browse buttons operate the same as those in the standard media evaluations control area.

Return to...Evaluation Returns you to the type of media evaluation you were working with before the search.

Print: Search Results In most respects, this button operates the same as the Print Evaluation button in the standard media evaluations control area. However, in the Printing Options dialog box, you can choose to print the current media evaluation or all media evaluations that match the search criteria.

Retrieving, editing, and saving a media evaluation

Choose a media type From the Media Evaluations window, click the button corresponding to the type of media evaluation you wish to retrieve. The first media evaluation of that type appears. Use the browse buttons or the search function to locate a specific media evaluation.

Make changes Add, change or delete information as you desire.

Save your work Click Save Evaluation. The message "Saving media evaluation..." appears.

Quit Click the Return to Media Evaluations Menu button.

Quitting Classroom Link

From a lesson plan   Click Save and Return to the Main Menu. The "Save Lesson Plan and Return to Main Menu?" dialog box appears. Click Yes. When the Main Menu window appears, click Exit Program. The "Do you wish to quit Classroom Link?" dialog box appears. Click Yes.

From a media evaluation   Click Return to Media Evaluations Menu. If you accessed Media Evaluations from a lesson plan entry window, click Return to Lesson Plan and follow the directions in the previous paragraph. Otherwise, click Return to Main Menu. When the Main Menu window appears, click Exit Program. The "Do you wish to quit Classroom Link?" dialog box appears. Click Yes.

Classroom Link was developed using Microsoft FoxPro.

Information in this document is subject to change without notice. Companies, names and data used in examples herein are fictitious unless otherwise noted.

Apple is a registered trademark and Macintosh is a trademark of Apple Computer, Inc. Microsoft, MS, MS-DOS and FoxPro are registered trademarks, and Windows is a trademark of Microsoft Corporation. All other product names are copyright and registered trademarks/tradenames of their respective owners.